Date Due

NOV 16			
MAY 13			
MAY 26			
FEB 12			
FEB 27			
MAR 11			
MAR 25			
APR 8			
APR 26			
OCT 20			
MAR 20 '70			

Theodore Lownik Library
ILLINOIS BENEDICTINE COLLEGE

DATE DUE

48319
U. S.

St. Procopius College Library
Lisle, Illinois

The books in the reference section are to be used only in the library.

Books reserved for the use of certain classes are to be used in the library during class hours. By special arrangement they may be used outside the library after class hours.

All other books may be retained for two weeks and renewed once for the same period.

One cent a day is charged for each book kept overdue.

Damage to books beyond reasonable wear and all losses shall be paid for.

No books may be taken from the library without being charged.

Complete regulations may be found in the Library Handbook, which every student is urged to consult for full use of the library.

CONTEMPORARY FOREIGN GOVERNMENTS

Associates in Government
United States Military Academy

COLONEL HERMAN BEUKEMA

LT. COLONEL JOHN D. F. PHILLIPS

LT. COLONEL GORDON H. HOLTERMAN

LT. COLONEL EDWARD C. DUNN

LT. COLONEL LINSCOTT A. HALL

LT. COLONEL EDWARD A. BAILEY

LT. COLONEL JOHN F. RHOADES

LT. COLONEL GILBERT H. WOODWARD

LT. COLONEL CHESTER L. JOHNSON

MAJOR CHARLES A. CANNON, JR.

MAJOR HERBERT M. BOWLBY, JR.

MAJOR SAMUEL H. HAYS

MAJOR JOHN H. CAMP

MAJOR PAUL H. KRAUSS

LT. COMMANDER NEVILLE T. KIRK

CAPTAIN LEON SEMBACH

CONTEMPORARY

FOREIGN

GOVERNMENTS

ASSOCIATES IN GOVERNMENT

DEPARTMENT OF SOCIAL SCIENCES

UNITED STATES MILITARY ACADEMY

Revised Edition

RINEHART & COMPANY · INCORPORATED

Publishers · 1949 · New York

354.4
U58c

First Printing February, 1949
Second Printing February, 1950

Copyright, 1946, by Herman Beukema and William M. Geer
Copyright, 1949, by Herman Beukema
Printed in the United States of America
All Rights Reserved

48319

FOREWORD TO THE 1949 EDITION

THE THREE YEARS WHICH HAVE intervened between the preparation of this edition and its predecessors have witnessed the radical transformation of the world picture. In 1945, in spite of misgivings aroused in some quarters by Soviet Russia's policy of installing Communist regimes in the states on its periphery on the grounds of security, hopes were high that the United Nations might soon provide the way to world peace, world security, and the unhampered establishment of the democratic pattern among peoples who desired that way of life. Today we know that these goals are still far distant. The immediate problem confronting the Western, democratic nations remains the resistance to aggression and infiltration stemming from a dynamic totalitarianism. Recognition of this problem is evidenced on the one hand by the hurried rearmament of the Western nations, accompanied by a pooling of military resources, and, on the other, by an integration of the economies of these countries, a development which is furthered by the operation of the so-called Marshall Plan. These twin efforts must inevitably develop political ties between the separate states which hitherto have been more familiar with political barriers.

The educational problem posed by these developments is spelled out by Dr. J. B. Conant in his *Education in a Divided World*. In his view, the ambitious plans of American educators are doomed unless the fundamental ideals of the Western tradition, among them equality of opportunity and social democracy, can survive the mounting impact of Soviet Russian imperialism. To the extent that our educators can give the student an awareness and understanding of the political world in which he lives, thus fortifying his allegiance to democratic values, the chances of survival of those achievements will improve. Such awareness and understanding acquire substance only when based on a broad and thorough knowledge of essential facts and events, of the men behind the events, and lastly of the complex of conditions motivating human action.

In preparing the current edition, the authors have attempted to present an adequate, though condensed, analysis of all essential elements in the confused political picture of a sick world. The tests of adequacy applied in the revision were relatively simple: first, does the material provide a valid basis for the student's arrival at sound value judgments on those major policies, domestic and foreign, which mark the course of postwar political development? Secondly, is the historical background of the separate political systems and also of the international efforts to achieve security on a world basis set forth in sufficient detail to provide a sound frame of reference for the analysis of the current scene? Such limitations of treatment have necessarily resulted in the elimination of much detail that is not only interesting but valuable for the student who plans to concentrate on the study of a single political system. It is not believed, however, that they interfere with the attainment of the basic objective sought in this survey.

DEPARTMENT OF SOCIAL SCIENCES
UNITED STATES MILITARY ACADEMY

West Point, N. Y.
December, 1948

ACKNOWLEDGMENTS

THE PRESENT WORK IS THE eighth revision of a text which first was produced by this Department in 1938 under the title of *The Governments of the Major Foreign Powers,* and which was revised periodically during the ensuing years. Parts of the chapters in the current edition embody the research performed by the officers who served with the Department during the past decade. These individuals are too numerous to mention by name.

In addition the Department is indebted to many other individuals and activities, in particular agencies of the federal government; for various reasons these individuals and agencies must likewise remain anonymous.

The chapters of the current edition were wholly or largely rewritten by the following officers, all instructors in the Department:

GREAT BRITAIN—Lieutenant Commander Neville T. Kirk, USNR and Major Herbert M. Bowlby, USA

FRANCE—Lieutenant Colonel Edward A. Bailey, USA and Major John H. Camp, USA

ITALY—Lieutenant Colonel Linscott A. Hall, USAF and Major Samuel H. Hays, USA

GERMANY—Lieutenant Colonel Edward C. Dunn, USA and Captain Leon Sembach, USA

USSR—Major Paul H. Krauss, USA and Lieutenant Colonel John F. Rhoades, USA

JAPAN—Lieutenant Colonel Chester L. Johnson, USA and Major Charles A. Cannon, Jr., USA

NATIONAL SECURITY AND INTERNATIONAL ORGANIZATION—Lieutenant Colonel Gordon H. Holterman, USA and Lieutenant Colonel Gilbert H. Woodward, USA

The text was edited by Colonel Herman Beukema, USA and Lieutenant Colonel John D. F. Phillips, USA, Professor and Associate Professor, respectively, of the Department.

ASSOCIATES IN GOVERNMENT
DEPARTMENT OF SOCIAL SCIENCES
UNITED STATES MILITARY ACADEMY

FOREWORD TO THE 1946 EDITION

EARLY IN 1940 SEVEN NATIONS were by common acceptance classed as great powers. Out of the ruins of World War II only three powers—the United States, Soviet Russia, and the British Commonwealth of Nations—have emerged with their great power ratings still valid. A fourth, France, suffered so heavily as to raise doubts about her ability to return at any foreseeable time to the status she once enjoyed in international affairs. As for the former Axis states, it is difficult to visualize either the time or degree of their restoration to a position of major significance in world diplomacy. Execution of the Potsdam and earlier agreements will go further and deeper than the extraction of the Axis states' military claws. The resultant damage to their economic resources and their future economic development should for many years to come hold them to the level of third-rate (or lower) national entities, regardless of the nature and duration of the victors' exercise of active control over the defeated powers' actions.

A second type of casualty chargeable to the war was the League of Nations contribution to political stability and international collaboration. The war, in that sense, dates back to the day in 1931 when Japan's launching of her Manchurian adventure revealed the League's inability to solve a major international crisis. What little political stability has been seen at the international level since 1931 occurred in the war years from 1942 to 1945, when necessity compelled the members of each of the two opposing alliances to pool their respective resources and scrap their separate differences. The termination of the fighting released the powerful disruptive forces which had been held in abeyance, throwing them into conflict with constructive efforts aimed at a world organization for stabilized peace. By the end of 1945 world affairs were once more in a highly fluid state. The same condition prevailed within the separate states, particularly those which had suffered most heavily from the war. The exceptions among foreign governments were the Soviet Union and the British Commonwealth of Nations.

The description of national political institutions under the conditions outlined above runs the danger of being out of date before it can reach the printed page. It is likewise open to criticism on the grounds that the accurate appraisal of facts and the sound analysis of trends is impossible at so short a range in time. On the other hand, once due allowance has been made for such shortcomings, the survey of the immediate and recent political picture serves a sound purpose in bringing the student face to face with problems only less grave than those which would have resulted from an Axis victory. If, in addition, he can examine the pattern of development which brought each national political picture to its present status, the student is left in fair case to evaluate both the long- and short-range trends. Moreover, such study is not only desirable but a prerequisite for a proper examination of the confused international scene as a whole, and in particular the effort to achieve lasting peace and security through global collaboration.

This text represents an effort to present in condensed form a survey of the political institutions of those foreign powers which until recently were classed as major powers. For obvious reasons, the title of the previous edition has been changed from *Governments of the Major Foreign Powers* to the present one, *Contemporary Foreign Governments*. Scope and coverage have been limited to the time made available to the cadets of the United States Military Academy by their curriculum. The relative emphasis given to recent and current political developments is necessitated by the fact that the graduates of the Military Academy must anticipate going on foreign service soon after they have been commissioned. The nature of their service is likewise responsible for the attention given to the power factor in politics, one which has too long been ignored in standard texts in the field of foreign government.

DEPARTMENT OF ECONOMICS,
GOVERNMENT, AND HISTORY
UNITED STATES MILITARY ACADEMY

West Point, N. Y.
November 23, 1945

CONTENTS

men. The Privy Council. The Imperial Conference. The
Premier. The Cabinet. Ministry of Greater East,Asia Affairs.
Ministry of Munitions. Other Cabinet Agencies. The Civil
Service.

LIST OF ILLUSTRATIONS

LIST OF DOCUMENTS

CONTEMPORARY FOREIGN GOVERNMENTS

THE GOVERNMENT OF

GREAT BRITAIN

◇◇

Background and Structure of the British Government

THE EVOLUTION OF THE BRITISH GOVERNMENT.—The government of Great Britain is not the product of any single, logical plan. It is the end result of centuries of evolution during which the British people have generally displayed their native antipathy for sudden change and their regard for the political traditions of the past. Therefore, a constitutional basis of democratic government under a limited monarchy grew out of customary political procedures, traditional institutions, and changes in governmental structure which answered the needs of succeeding generations. It was not—to repeat—the product of deliberate invention, resulting from a theory. In their ability to adopt working compromises without violence and to adapt old forms and institutions to new needs, the British people have demonstrated their particular genius for self-government. Most of the basic principles of government have grown from compromises or political expedients which met a timely need in the past. The principle of government by a "responsible ministry," for example, arose in part from the historical accident that kings of the House of Hanover were for two generations little interested in English government. For decades while these kings were inarticulate or unable to maintain their royal prerogatives, the king's ministers gradually became responsible to the representative legislature, called the "Parliament," and hence to the electorate, as the Parliament became more representative of the people. This evolution of a responsible Ministry is typical of the form and functioning of a government which was not planned but grew, and which consequently lacks that clear definition to be found in countries where written constitutions rather than custom, precedent, and legislation have been the major forces in molding the governing structure.

TERMS DESCRIPTIVE OF THE BRITISH GOVERNMENT.—The United Kingdom of Great Britain and Northern Ireland is a nation comprising the territories commonly known as England, Scotland, Wales, and Northern Ireland. It is the heart of the British Empire-Commonwealth, which in turn is a conglomeration of separate geographical and political units linked to the mother country by relationships varying from rigid bonds of control by military governors to those mere intangibles of common history, race, and interests, which form the chief links with the self-governing dominions. Normally the following distinctions in terms are made: Great Britain refers to England, Scotland, and Wales; the United Kingdom refers to Great Britain and Northern Ireland; the British Empire refers to the colonies, protectorates, and other possessions under the governance of the United Kingdom; and the British Commonwealth of Nations refers to the United Kingdom and the self-governing British dominions. Nevertheless, there is a looseness in the use of these terms and their derivatives. The expression "British Empire" is often used to include the dominions as well as the colonies. A more exact term which also has this inclusive meaning is the expression "British Empire-Commonwealth." The single word "Britain" normally refers to Great Britain, but often it implies Great Britain supported—as it usually is—by the whole British Empire-Commonwealth.

ORGANIZATION OF THE BRITISH GOVERNMENT.—The United Kingdom of Great Britain and Northern Ireland is a unitary, parliamentary democracy with the form of a limited monarchy. Its principal organs of government are a central legislature, an executive responsible to that legislature, a judiciary, and popularly elected local authorities in town and county areas. Parliament, the national legislature, consists of two houses: the House of Commons, a body elected by universal adult suffrage, and the House of Lords, a nonelective body of very limited powers. The House of Commons is without question the more important body.

The titular head of the state is the king, who is the representative of his dynasty. The actual executive head of the government is a prime minister controlling a cabinet of ministers who administer the principal departments and an additional number of ministers who supervise less important departments. The prime minister, the Cabinet, and the remaining ministers are known collectively as the Ministry. The ministers are constitutionally required to be members of Parliament. The Ministry is collectively responsible through the House of Commons to the sovereign electorate for its policies and the administration of the government. The British courts, whose judges are appointed by the executive for life, administer justice under the law but lack any power of judicial review of statutes enacted by Parliament.

The British Constitution

NATURE OF THE CONSTITUTION.—Even though there is no single document which can be called a British constitution, a constitutional basis of government does exist, and it is strictly adhered to in practice. What is called "the British Constitution" is a series of charters, petitions, and laws which have been formulated in England during the past thousand years, plus principles of governing, judicial decisions, customary methods of administration, political practices, traditional prejudices, and all of the accepted usages of British government which have come into being. The various enactments of the king and of Parliament which have not been repealed are a part of this constitution. Some of their measures of particular importance, such as the Magna Charta of 1215, the Petition of Right of 1628, the Bill of Rights of 1689, and the Parliament Act of 1911, are fundamental laws and therefore have come to be considered prominent parts of the constitution. Some of the rules of British government are to be found in the more ordinary enactments of Parliament, some have been established by decisions of the courts, while others do not have the force of law at all but are simply usages which are always followed. Yet, all of these things contribute to the constitutional practices of the nation. It may be said of them that they are like individual stones which, when pieced together, form a constitutional mosaic.

Most modern national states have created unified codes of constitutional law, such as the Constitution of the United States, for example. Usually such codes are considered superior to other legislative enactments. Yet, in Britain, no serious attempt has been made since the seventeenth century to correlate and consolidate the country's fundamental laws and procedures into a single document.

CONSTITUTIONAL LAW AND CONVENTIONS.—In pursuing the question of the nature of the British constitution one step further, the constitution can be arbitrarily divided into two elements: (1) the law of the constitution and (2) its conventions or customs. The law of the constitution consists of those acts and other instruments which the courts will recognize and enforce; the conventions of the constitution are those traditional usages which are not enforceable in the courts but about which no such question is likely to arise. Most of the law of the constitution is written, but not all of it. The law includes four principal elements: (1) There are certain historic documents, like the Magna Charta, which have been agreed to in times of crisis. (2) There are parliamentary statutes defining the powers of the crown, regulating suffrage, guaranteeing civil rights, and creating governmental machinery, such as the Act of Settlement of 1701, the Habeas Corpus Act of 1679, and the Municipal Corporations Act of 1835. (3) Judicial decisions fixing the meaning of charters and statutes are enforceable by the courts and hence a part of the law of the constitution. As mentioned previously, British courts in making decisions do not review and invalidate statutes. They merely define and apply them. (4) The principles of English common or cus-

THE MAGNA CHARTA (1215)

John, by the grace of God king of England, lord of Ireland, duke of Normandy and of Aquitaine, and count of Anjou, to his archbishops, bishops, abbots, earls, barons, justiciars, foresters, sheriffs, reeves, ministers, and all his bailiffs and faithful men, greeting. Know that . . .

1. We have in the first place granted to God and by this our present charter have confirmed, for us and our heirs forever, that the English Church shall be free and shall have its rights entire and its liberties inviolate. . . . We have also granted to all freemen of our kingdom, for us and our heirs forever, all the liberties hereinunder written, to be had and held by them and their heirs of us and our heirs.

9. Neither we nor our bailiffs will seize any land or revenue for any debt, so long as the chattels of the debtors are sufficient to repay the debt. . . .

13. And the city of London shall have all its ancient liberties and free customs, both by land and by water. Besides we will and grant that all other cities, boroughs, towns, and ports shall have all their liberties and free customs.

28. No constable or other bailiff of ours shall take grain or other chattels of any one without immediate payment therefor in money, unless by the will of the seller he may secure postponement of that [payment].

30. No sheriff or bailiff of ours, nor any other person, shall take the horses or carts of any freeman for carrying service, except by the will of that freeman.

38. No bailiff shall henceforth put any one to his law by merely bringing suit [against him] without trustworthy witnesses presented for this purpose.

39. No freeman shall be captured or imprisoned or disseised or outlawed or exiled or in any way destroyed, nor will we go against him or send against him, except by the lawful judgment of his peers or by the law of the land.

40. To no one will we sell, to no one will we delay or deny right of justice.

42. Every one shall henceforth be permitted, saving our fealty, to leave our kingdom and to return in safety and security, by land or by water, except in the common interest of the realm for a brief period during wartime, and excepting men imprisoned or outlawed according to the law of the kingdom. . . .

45. We will appoint as justiciars, constables, sheriffs, or bailiffs only such men as know the law of the kingdom and well desire to observe it.

52. If anyone, without the lawful judgment of his peers, has been disseised or deprived by us of his lands, castles, liberties, or rights, we will at once restore them to him. . . .

60. Now all these aforesaid customs and liberties, which we have granted, insofar as concerns us, to be observed in our kingdom toward our men, all men of our kingdom, both clergy and laity, shall, insofar as concerns them, observe toward their men.

63. . . . By the witness of the aforesaid men and of many others. Given by our hand in the meadow that is called Runnymede between Windsor and Staines, June 15, in the seventeenth year of our reign.

tomary law are also a part of the law of the constitution. This body of law is based on usage and has never been enacted by Parliament. Nevertheless, it is fully accepted and enforced as law. It includes the right to trial by jury in criminal cases and the right of freedom of speech. Common law is not statutory law, and it appears in writing only when it is embodied in decisions, reports, commentaries, and legal opinions.

The conventions of the constitution relate to matters of utmost importance even though they cannot be enforced in courts. If they were enforceable, they would become law, not conventions. Consisting of understandings, habits, or practices which are based upon political morality rather than law, they are decisive influences on every level of governmental functioning. Without being written into law they are generally known and taken for granted. It is only by convention, for example, that Parliament is convoked at least once a year, that the speaker of the House of Commons takes no part in partisan politics, or that only the "law members" attend when the House of Lords is sitting as a court. These and many other usages are a part of the very fabric of the government. They have originated because they were found at some time in the past to have been useful. They have become customary as their usefulness has continued. They have become inviolable and constitutional because they are now a part of British political morality.

AMENDING THE BRITISH CONSTITUTION.—The basic rule of the British constitution can be said to be that there is no legal limit to the power of the British Parliament. This practice means that any act which is passed by both Houses of Parliament and assented to by the king is absolutely binding upon the courts. No act of Parliament can be held by the courts to be unconstitutional.

Thus it follows that the constitution can be changed as easily as, say, the laws of inheritance. A simple majority in both Houses can change the entire constitution. Because of this and also because of the nature of the British constitution, any parliamentary enactment automatically becomes a part of the law of the constitution. If the Parliament sets aside or revises earlier enactments, the constitution is amended to that extent.

This procedure does not mean that since such things as the kingship, jury trial, and private property are at the mercy of the Parliament, they are in danger of being swept away. Members of Parliament, with few exceptions, are respected members of a well-ordered society. They live under the restraint of powerful traditions. Just as conscious of their limitations in effecting changes as though those limitations were written into law, they make a constitutional change only when practical circumstances require it. Nevertheless, almost every Parliament makes some constitutional change. More often than not, however, the statute merely puts into law what has long existed in fact. For example, the Cabinet has existed and functioned in British government since the late seventeenth century even though it was not recognized in law until the Ministers of the Crown Act of 1937 gave it a legal definition.

Because of the long evolutionary development of conventions of the constitution, they are rarely changed. Born of the need of the moment, they mature and achieve relative permanence or wither and die, though slowly, according to the measure of their proved usefulness.

CONSTITUTIONAL THEORY AND PRACTICE.—Subtle distinctions occur between British constitutional theory and constitutional practice. The best example of these exists in the basic structure of the government. In theory the power of the British government is in the hands of the king. The law is the king's law, the ministers are the king's ministers, the Navy is the Royal Navy, and so on throughout the government. In practice, however, this is sheer legal theory, for the king has no personal control of these elements of government. The people of Great Britain through their representatives in Parliament enact new laws, control ministers, regulate the Navy, and govern Great Britain.

The difference in constitutional theory and practice in the above and in other instances comes from the peculiar way in which the British constitution evolves. Deferences to tradition in Great Britain is so habitual that even when the constitution is changed the change is gradual. Normally a modification in a convention precedes a formal change of the basic law on the subject. Even then the change often takes place within the framework of traditional governmental forms. The evolution of British monarchy provides an example of this process. Seven centuries ago, England was an absolute monarchy. During the time which has passed since then, the king has been divested of his powers bit by bit until few of them remain. The forms of the old monarchy have been preserved, however, in this gradual evolution, even though the government has become democratic and representative in practice.

PRINCIPLES OF BRITISH GOVERNMENT.—In the first place, the government of the United Kingdom of Great Britain and Northern Ireland is unitary, or nonfederal, in form. All power is concentrated in a single government. Local subdivisions of government receive their authority from and are regulated by the central government in London, although they are permitted local discretion.

A second British principle is the ultimate supremacy and legal omnipotence of the Parliament. Parliament can alter any law, change any institution, dismiss any official, or invalidate any judicial decision. True, an appearance of the separation of executive, legislative, and judicial branches of government does exist. Furthermore, in practice there is an effective separation of powers. In its purely administrative capacity the crown is less subject to legislative control than the American executive. As we have noted, there is no legal limitation upon the authority of Parliament. The courts are surrounded by ample guarantees of independence. But, unlike the United States, where the principle of separation was written into the constitution, in Britain the separation of powers exists because Parliament is willing to delegate executive and judicial powers to the other branches of government.

A third principle of British democracy is the guarantee of civil rights. Protection of these individual rights is maintained in two ways, by statute and by common or customary law. Such rights as that of bearing arms, the writ of habeas corpus, immunity from excessive bail, and protection from cruel and unusual punishments are provided for in various great statutes. Other rights, such as freedom of speech and assembly, rest on common-law principles.

A fourth principle of British democracy is the "rule of law." This principle means that law rather than arbitrary action is the basis of English policy. Under the rule of law the state can ordinarily take no action except in accordance with law administered by competent authorities. Thus under modern conditions the British government is a monarchy only in form. The king exercises almost no real political powers himself. The government is conducted in his name by representatives of the British people.

Exceptions to all these principles exist in British constitutional history, since the government of Great Britain is based on a balance of tradition and expediency. However, the fact that these and other British constitutional principles have usually guided British policy is more important than the fact that exceptions occasionally occur.

Executive Organization

THE KING.—The British people, while adopting wholeheartedly the principles and institutions of democracy, have at the same time carefully preserved the ancient political institution of a monarchy. Although the king has been shorn of his former executive powers, he has not been made into a museum piece but remains a very useful and integral part of the government. First, he embodies the unity of the nation, and in that capacity performs a wide range of social and ceremonial functions. Secondly, he plays an essential part in the practical working of the constitution, as will be presently explained. Lastly, he symbolizes the cohesion of the various parts of the British Empire.

The present King of England is George VI, who succeeded to his office on the abdication of his brother, Edward VIII, on December 10, 1936. The king holds his office as head of the state under the Act of

Settlement of 1701, which sets forth the rules of succession to the kingship. These rules of succession are substantially the same as the common-law practices concerning the inheritance of land. The Act of Settlement also provides that the king shall be a "faithful Protestant."

The royal family supplies the element of personality in government. This element has a particular appeal for the average individual, who usually feels no great personal regard for elected officials and is often incapable of comprehending the abstraction known as "the state," to which he is supposed to give his allegiance and for which, on occasions, he is supposed to risk his life. The great value of the monarchy to Great Britain lies not in the few remaining political functions of the monarch, but rather in his activities as the ceremonial head of the government. The king is a national institution serving as a tangible symbol of country and empire, commanding a sentiment and patriotic attachment which can be approximately compared to the feeling of the American people for their flag. In serving as a national symbol, which is always a most powerful force in commanding the emotions and allegiance of a people, the king receives the highest loyalties of the British people and personifies the unity of the British Empire.

Although the king exercises no real governing powers today, he has a large number of state functions to perform. He has to give his consent to and have his seal placed upon every measure passed by Parliament before it can become an act, but this consent is automatic. The king's most important constitutional function is to name a prime minister, but the person called on is almost always the leader of the party which wins a majority in the elections. Thus the choice is settled by the electorate. If a prime minister resigns or dies in office, the king chooses his successor. Even here he makes his choice in accordance with the advice of the leaders of the majority party. Occasionally, in a complex political situation, no automatic choice is available, and the king's personal judgment may have to be exercised. But as long as the two-party system works in British politics, the decision of the king in "choosing" a prime minister remains wholly formal. When serious crises, like those precipitated by both World Wars, demand the temporary suspension of political differences in order to create a common front, a coalition government is called on to conduct the nation's affairs. The selection of a prime minister under such conditions demands the assurance of full support by all important political groups represented in Parliament.

The king is also the head of the Army, the Navy, and the Air Force, but here again his office is purely titular. He himself would never issue an order. The king is likewise titular head of the Church of England. Queen Victoria is said on occasion to have expressed strong views on religious matters, but her successors seem to have taken a less active part in problems of the church.

Although the king has a considerable private fortune, Parliament makes him an annual grant called the Civil List. It has been said that the duties of the king are not light and that he more than earns his salary.

Because his office has a life tenure, the king may have a long reign, spanning the terms of office of several prime ministers. In such instances the king may come to have the role of elder statesman and participate in directing public affairs. Although he cannot direct the prime minister to do or not to do anything, he may offer him advice. In many instances such influence on the part of the king has changed the course of events.

The people of the self-governing dominions (except Eire) continue to give their allegiance to the king, who in theory rules each dominion as a separate entity. The unity of the dominions and Great Britain is based largely on sentiment and common interests, save for their mutual allegiance to the king, which serves to strengthen these intangible ties. The British Commonwealth of Nations is welded together by an idea, personified in the king.

THE CROWN.—The king, as a person and as the purely ceremonial head of the state, must be distinguished from his office, which possesses the real executive power of the British government. Whereas the king originally reigned and ruled, today he merely reigns. His powers have been removed from his person. Nevertheless, constitutionally, the king's powers still exist; they are exercised in his name. What has happened is this: the king's real powers have been transferred from his person to his office, which is called the crown.

The transfer came about by a process of gradual development over a period of several centuries, the history of which includes two revolutions, a series of conflicts between king and Parliament, and a gradual growth of constitutional conventions which can be summarized in the present constitutional principle that the king has no real power. In order to comprehend the British system of government, one must clearly understand this vital distinction between the king as a person and the crown which is now the repository of all executive power and is sometimes referred to as an artificial person. The government is still conducted in the name of the king, but the prerogatives and functions of his office and the executive power of the government are exercised partly by the Parliament, but mainly by the ministers, and particularly by the Cabinet. The king, who legally possesses all authority, is not actually the personal king, but the institutional king. To make this distinction somewhat clearer, the institutional king is called the crown.

The crown, therefore, has become the supreme executive authority of the state. Its powers also include some legislative and judicial functions. The crown supervises the enforcement of national laws, the collection of national revenues, and the expenditure of national funds. It manages foreign relations and appoints foreign representatives. It possesses treaty-making powers, usually, however, subjecting international agreements to parliamentary approval. In the field of executive control of the British Empire-Commonwealth, the crown appoints governors-general for the dominions, and administrative agents for colonies.

Technically, all legislative power in Great Britain is vested in the "King in Parliament," which means historically the king acting in conjunction with the Parliament. Every statute declares itself to have been enacted "by the King's Most Excellent Majesty, by and with the advice and consent of the Lords Spiritual and Temporal, and the Commons," even though the king personally has no legislative function except to have his seal placed upon laws. Some lawmaking powers, therefore, belong to the crown. The crown, that is, the king acting on the advice of the Cabinet, has power to summon Parliament, dissolve it, and order new elections to the House of Commons. The crown recommends legislation at the opening of each parliamentary session.

Executive laws called "orders in council" are issued under parliamentary authority by the king-in-council. The expression "king-in-council" means a session of the Privy Council at which the king presides. It has become customary, and therefore constitutional, for the members of the Cabinet to act as privy councilors in this instance and to issue collectively orders-in-council in the name of the king—which is to say, the crown.

The crown's judicial powers are limited to pardons and, in exceptional cases, the removal of judges. The crown confers honors and titles. It has large powers of control over the Church of England, and some power over the Presbyterian Church of Scotland. The crown administers the armed forces. In time of emergency or war there is practically no limit to the authority which the crown may be allowed to exercise.

Some of the powers of the crown are exercised formally by the king in person, but only on the advice of the prime minister or the Parliament. The crown, through the person of the king, delivers a message to Parliament on the first day of each parliamentary session, proposing legislation and policies. The message is written by the Cabinet, which directs most of the actions of the crown. In certain instances the courts or administrative agencies exercise a few powers of the crown.

THE PRIME MINISTER.—The prime minister is the head of the Cabinet and the real head of the British government. He occupies a key position as the coordinating factor in the government and as the sole link maintaining official relations between the Cabinet (which is the real executive exercising most of the powers of the crown) and the king. The British adhere rigidly to the fiction that the entire government functions by act of the king on the advice of the Cabinet, even though in reality the conventions of the constitution require the king to act on decisions which the Cabinet and the prime minister make. In addition to his position within the government, the prime minister is an outstanding political figure and is usually the leader of the largest party or coalition of parties in the House of Commons.

An examination of the prime minister's position and functions furnishes a valuable insight into the way in which the British government actually works. The prime minister, having received the king's formal request to form a new Ministry or government, selects some sixty ministers to administer various departments of the government. From his ministers he selects a smaller group of about twenty who constitute his Cabinet. Thereafter, he may terminate his government at any time by tendering his personal resignation to the king, and he may dismiss ministers or dissolve Parliament and cause a general election by so advising the king. Prime ministers do not allow this last power to go unused. On various occasions when major issues have arisen they have dissolved Parliament and taken the issue directly to the people by calling for the election of a new Parliament in order to obtain a clear mandate and to avoid prolonged legislative bickering and procrastination detrimental to the interests of the country.

It is a basic convention of the constitution that the whole Ministry must resign whenever the opposition party obtains a majority at an election and consequent control of the House of Commons. Likewise, the Ministry must either resign or dissolve Parliament and appeal to the electorate when the House of Commons defeats or radically amends one of its major measures, or when the House of Commons passes a vote of censure on, or of "no confidence" in, the prime minister and his government. However, a defeat of the government on a measure of little importance may by custom be ignored by the Ministry unless that body chooses to make an issue of the matter.

The prime minister exercises considerable control over patronage, appointing the superior judges and the occupants of the higher positions in the Church of England, always, of course, through the device of "advising" the king. He makes recommendations to the king for the grants of peerages, other titles, and honors which are made both on New Year's Day and on the king's birthday.

The prime minister has a considerable number of duties and prerogatives aside from his general functions as head of the government. He often holds an administrative position as head of one of the governmental departments. It is typical of the British way in government that the office of prime minister had no legal status and no pay until a few years ago.[1] It has now received legal recognition through the grant by Parliament of a salary of approximately forty thousand dollars a year. In

---

[1] The prime minister did, in fact, receive a salary, but not because he was prime minister. The salary belonged to the office of First Lord of the Treasury, and usually the prime minister was also First Lord of the Treasury.

addition, the residences at 10 Downing Street and at Chequers are per-
quisites of his office.

THE MINISTRY.—As previously stated, the prime minister, on taking
office, appoints a new Ministry by selecting men to fill the vacancies
created by the resignation of the former Ministry. Constitutional precedent requires that all ministers must be members of the House of Commons or the House of Lords or that they must soon become members.
Most of the important ministers are members of the Commons, but a
few are selected from the House of Lords so as to represent the government in that House. If a minister is appointed who is not a member of
either House, he must become one at the earliest opportunity. This is
accomplished either by the minister's entering the House of Lords as
a newly created peer or by his standing for election to the House of
Commons from the first constituency having a vacant seat. This vacant
seat may be provided by the resignation of some loyal, self-effacing member of Parliament whose constituency is "safe" for the party in power.

Each great administrative department is headed by a minister who,
in the case of the main departments, has at least one subordinate minister for his assistant. There are several ministerial positions which entail few or no duties and are usually given to men whose advice and
support are desired but who are unwilling or unable to undertake heavy
administrative responsibilities. Similar positions go to those party leaders
whose primary function is to control the proceedings of the House of
Commons and to keep the majority party together. It is true that the
ministers are selected as much for their political influence as for their
administrative ability. In general, however, the Englishman in public life
possesses a sense of responsibility which prevents him from interfering
with the career civil servants in his department unless he actually possesses knowledge sufficient to warrant such interference.

All the heads of administrative departments and a few other officials
are members of the Ministry, which is an inclusive committee. However,
all sixty-odd ministers are not of the same rank. Twenty or twenty-five of
the ministers are of higher rank and are designated as Cabinet ministers.
In peacetime they form the closely knit executive body within the Ministry which is called the Cabinet. During World War II the normal Cabinet was replaced by a "War Cabinet" of an even smaller number of the
highest ranking ministers. The size of the War Cabinet varied from five
to nine members, each of whom was selected by the prime minister to
assist him in conducting major war functions and in reaching major decisions. Thus, during the war, there were within the Ministry three grades
of ministers: the War Cabinet ministers who controlled all high policy,
the Cabinet ministers who headed the more important departments, and

the ordinary ministers who acted as heads of minor departments and as undersecretaries.

THE PRIVY COUNCIL AND THE CABINET.—The Cabinet is an outgrowth of the system of government of many centuries ago when the king exercised the powers of his office on the advice of his Privy Council, a group of selected advisers. By a process of political evolution the Privy Council as a whole lost its advisory power. This power came to be exercised by a small committee of its members, called the Cabinet because the king's most trusted ministers customarily met in his private room or "cabinet." With the growth of responsible ministerial government the British have preserved the fiction of government by advice of the Privy Council through the expedient of making all cabinet ministers privy councilors.

All privy councilors are appointed by the king on the prime minister's advice. The Privy Council consists of about three hundred and fifty members including all cabinet ministers, ex-cabinet ministers, high church dignitaries, certain judges, and various persons on whom membership has been conferred as a mark of distinction for meritorious services to the nation. It meets rarely and then only on such ceremonial occasions as coronations. It has certain committees, aside from the Cabinet, which exercise governmental functions. The most important of these is its Judicial Committee, which will be discussed later.

THE CABINET.—The prime minister, as has been stated, normally selects from twenty to twenty-five of his ministers to form the executive committee of the crown known as the Cabinet. Ministers are chosen to be cabinet members for one or more of the following reasons: political influence, proven experience and ability, and the importance of the administrative departments which they head. Thus, certain offices, such as those of the Chancellor of the Exchequer,[2] Lord President of the Council, Lord Privy Seal, Lord Chancellor, and the Secretaries of State for Foreign Affairs, Defense, the Home Department, the Dominions, the Colonies, and Scotland, are usually recognized as carrying cabinet rank, while the Postmaster General, the Solicitor General, the Ministers of Works, Transport, National Insurance, Pensions, and the various undersecretaries do not become members of the Cabinet. It sometimes happens, as in the present Cabinet, that certain ministers have cabinet rank but are not members of the Cabinet. They are members of the Ministry who enjoy the prestige of cabinet rank by reason of their position, but who do not sit in cabinet meetings.

The Cabinet governs Great Britain and those parts of the British

[2] This official is the finance minister of the kingdom, even though he is technically Second Lord of the Treasury. The prime minister usually holds the post of First Lord of the Treasury.

Empire which do not enjoy self-government. It has two major kinds of duties. First, it controls and coordinates executive policy. The Cabinet is collectively responsible to the Parliament, especially to the House of Commons, for the policies of the national administration. Generally speaking, if the action of the entire Cabinet or of a single one of its members is repudiated in Parliament, the whole Cabinet must resign. As a result, all important policy questions are considered by the Cabinet as a whole, and speeches made by one minister are regarded as enunciating the policy of the Cabinet.

The second major duty of the Cabinet is to propose and prepare legislation. In peacetime, 90 per cent, and in wartime, 100 per cent of all legislation is proposed by the Cabinet. In the normal process the Cabinet frames a bill, which is then introduced into Parliament by the appropriate minister. This practice relieves the committees of Parliament of a great deal of the labor of framing and revising new bills. It also makes for consistency in legislative enactments—both between different bills and between proposed legislation and executive policy.

The Cabinet's interest in and responsibility for legislative policy and legislation enable it to exercise strong political leadership in the Parliament, for actually the Cabinet is a legislative as well as an executive institution. It is the central agency around which parliamentary forces revolve. It is the directing committee for regulating parliamentary procedure and performance. Since the Parliament is the supreme body in the British government, and since the Cabinet has the position of central influence within it, the Cabinet becomes the key political agency of the nation.

In view of this dominant position, it is argued that the Cabinet possesses an unwarranted power over the majority party as a whole since a revolt in the House of Commons on even one important measure may entail the prime minister's advising the king to dissolve Parliament and to present the issue to the electorate. Since party support in the election might be withdrawn from the recalcitrant members, and since, in any case, election expenses are a considerable item, the Cabinet may well be able to force a measure through Parliament which would not succeed under a different constitutional organization or under a less completely dominant executive. However, this situation does eliminate the possibility of a political stalemate, such as often occurs between the President of the United States and the Congress. It has the further advantage of making the party in power responsible as a unit to the electorate for both executive and legislative action.

In carrying out its functions, the Cabinet usually meets once a week except in times of grave emergency. Its work is kept to a minimum by direct consultations between ministers heading different departments, by the Cabinet's committee system of dealing with specific categories of cabinet business, and by the Cabinet Secretariat, which circulates memorandums and other documents useful to the business of the Cabinet and its committees.

EXECUTIVE WAR POWERS.—When the likelihood of war became apparent in August, 1939, Parliament passed the Emergency Powers (Defense) Act which provided authority for the executive branch of the government to govern Great Britain by administrative order and even permitted the detention of persons at the discretion of the Secretary of State for the Home Department. Further legislation in 1940 instituted compulsory military service for all men between the ages of eighteen and forty-one, and empowered the executive to take control of any person or property in the public interest, thus making possible the conscription of men and women for work in industry. Power was also given to the crown to establish special courts for the trial of civilians, and the death penalty was authorized for acts of espionage and sabotage. Under these laws the power of the crown to legislate by administrative order was limited only by its inability to acquire the ownership of land, to borrow money, or to levy taxes. Many of these emergency powers have remained in operation since the end of World War II and may continue for several years to come because of the need felt by the Labor ministers for extensive government control of trade, industry, and agriculture. The requirement that all administrative orders be laid before Parliament gives that body an ultimate veto over executive action, but no administrative orders have received the formal disapproval of Parliament.

THE WAR CABINET.—The outbreak of World War II was followed by an immediate reorganization of the executive branch of the British government. Ministries of Home Security, Food, Economic Warfare, Shipping, and Information (including censorship) were added to the existing departments.[3] The Ministry of Labor was reorganized as the Ministry of Labor and National Service. On September 3, 1939, Neville Chamberlain, the prime minister, announced the creation of a War Cabinet of nine members, entirely displacing the former Cabinet of larger size. Under the War Cabinet various committees were set up, each dealing with a specific area of policy.

National dissatisfaction with the progress of the war led to a bitter debate in Parliament and the resignation of Chamberlain on May 9, 1940. He was replaced as prime minister by Winston Churchill, who had been First Lord of the Admiralty in the War Cabinet and (before the outbreak of the war) the outstanding parliamentary Conservative leader in the opposition to the policy of appeasement.[4] The Labor and

---

[3] The Ministry of Home Security was later merged with the Home Department which was given very extensive new powers.

[4] See page 63.

Liberal parties, which had refused to join forces with Chamberlain, agreed to form a coalition Ministry under Churchill's leadership.[5]

Relatively minor changes were made in the size, the organization, and the personnel of the War Cabinet from time to time as the needs of the general war effort or specific governmental crises prompted such reorganizations. The size of the War Cabinet was further reduced by Churchill, who himself became Minister of Defense. Under this arrangement the heads of the service departments (War, Admiralty, and Air) were no longer included but met separately in their own committee to plan the execution of the policies decided on by the War Cabinet. Perhaps the best description of the manner in which the business of government was conducted during the war was given in a speech delivered by Prime Minister Churchill in the House of Commons in 1941, in which he said:

"The War Cabinet consists of eight members, five of whom have no regular departments, and three of whom represent the main organisms of the state, to wit: Foreign Affairs, Finance, and Labor, which in their different ways come into every great question that has to be settled. That is the body which gives its broad sanction to the main policy and conduct of the war. Under their authority the Chiefs of Staff of the three services sit each day together, and I, as prime minister and Minister of Defense, convene them and preside over them while I think it necessary, inviting, when business requires it, the three service ministers. All large issues of military policy are brought before the Defense Committee, which has for several months consisted of the three Chiefs of Staff, the three service ministers, and four members of the War Cabinet, namely, myself, the Lord Privy Seal, who has no department, the Foreign Secretary, and Lord Beaverbrook. This is the body, this is the machine; it works easily and flexibly at the present time."

The War Cabinet went out of existence following the surrender of Germany and the subsequent call for a British general election late in 1945 by the Labor party. The coalition which had supported the war cabinet organization was dissolved in May, 1945, when the Conservative party moved to meet the Labor challenge by calling a general election in July. Following this dissolution of the political coalition of parties, the reorganized Churchill Cabinet functioned on the basis of peacetime Cabinet organization.

CIVIL SERVICE.—The administration of the numerous departments is conducted by the permanent civil service, an organization which numbered over 700,000 in March, 1947. This vast structure is not the product of a constitutional provision or specific legislation granting administra-

---

[5] In the wartime government the party representation consisted of forty-seven Conservatives, eighteen Laborites, eight Liberals, and seven Independents. This coalition remained in office until after the defeat of Germany in the spring of 1945.

tive power such as existed in France under the Third Republic, but might be viewed as a huge random edifice built over a period of years under countless authorities granted by king or Parliament. Less than one hundred years ago the service was characterized by inefficiency, favoritism, and patronage. Since then numerous reforms have transformed it from what John Bright called the "outdoor relief department of the aristocracy" to an organization capable of performing the role it plays today.

The structure of the civil service resembles a military formation. At the base of the pyramid is the sub-clerical class. Above this group is the clerical class, a large number of men and women recruited between the ages of sixteen and seventeen who perform the ordinary clerical work. Next in the hierarchy is the executive class, a smaller category whose duties cover a wide field requiring judgment and initiative. At the top of the pyramid is the administrative class, a group of about 1500 officers who occupy the key positions of the civil service. The duties of this class include the formulation of policy, coordination of government machinery, and administration and control of the departments. It is this class that furnishes the heads and deputy heads of the departments of state and hence provides the element of continuity in administration despite changes in political heads. Actually, the administrative class controls the civil service subject to the approval of the ministers and Parliament. At the head of the civil service is the Permanent Secretary of the Treasury.

The Civil Service Commission has the task of recruiting the required personnel. Its method of selection is by open competitive examination with, in certain grades, a supplementary oral examination. Having entered the service, personnel are subject to Treasury control. The establishments division of the Treasury provides central direction and coordination for this vast hierarchy; it makes regulations for controlling the civil service and for the classification, remuneration, and other conditions of service for all public servants. Through the medium of Whitley Councils,[6] a series of joint employer-employee councils, the position of the civil servant approaches that of a junior partner in the business of running the government. In addition, since 1946 the various civil service unions may be affiliated with the Trades Union Congress.

How is it that, despite the demand prevailing in the United States for efficiency and specialization, the British civil service has enjoyed a reputation far surpassing that of our own public servants? There are two principal reasons: (1) the tradition of the British governing classes and, (2) the liaison between the universities and the civil service. In

---

[6] In 1916 wartime industry was threatened by unrest among the workers. A committee under J. H. Whitley devised a scheme whereby industrial disputes would be adjusted by a system of works, district, and national councils composed of equal numbers of representatives of labor and capital.

the past the government service was one of the few fields into which younger sons of the upper classes could enter without losing caste. Furthermore, the public schools and great universities have traditionally impressed upon the students their responsibilities to the state. The parallelism that exists between the gradations of the nation's educational system and the ranks in the civil service, coupled with the relatively low age limits, has encouraged the promising young man to become a candidate for the service before looking further afield; the examinations appear as a normal culmination to his education. Though the pay scales are lower than those found in comparable fields outside the public service, the pension system and relative security offered serve to attract many of the better students. While the system in Britain is less democratic than that of the United States, the former has succeeded in attracting to the ranks of the civil service a younger, more able group of recruits—raw material capable of being developed into public servants well qualified to occupy positions of importance. The difference in the examinations offered by the two nations illustrates what the respective services expect of the candidate. In the United States the recruit is examined for his qualifications to perform the duties of the office he is expected to fill. Usually he can meet this basic requirement but only too often is not qualified to advance much higher in the structure. In Great Britain the candidate is given a general examination to test his over-all mental capacities, as much with the idea of testing his expected worth to the service ten years later as with examining his qualifications for the task on which he is to enter at the outset.

Stability of administration is one of the great advantages of the British system. With the tremendous increase in governmental functions and services it is impossible for a newly appointed minister, who frequently knows little or nothing about his duties, to enter a department and seize the reins firmly. He is dependent necessarily on the permanent staff. Though the true leader will soon play a major role in policy-making decisions, he relies on the self-effacing administrators for the preparation of bills, the writing of speeches, and for data for the question period (see p. 25). Despite accusations that an aristocratic civil service would attempt to sabotage the programs of a Labor government, this eventuality has not occurred in the past nor need it be expected in the future. Though the civil servant might disagree with the views of his minister, he remains strictly nonpolitical in the performance of his duties and, once a policy has been formulated, proceeds to carry them out impartially.

In respect of future developments, the Labor government may be expected to continue the trend toward a democratization of the service. But the nature of that government's program forces it to rely as much as have governments in the past on the permanent members of the staffs.

During the war years there arose an undercurrent of criticism against the civil service. Critics maintained that its leaders lacked vision and aggressiveness, preferring a cautious policy of "Safety First." Others have felt that a system which places young men without business or executive experience in the civil service tends to develop an unrealistic attitude. And long before World War II, writers criticized the increasing importance of the "bureaucracy," pointing out the dangers inherent in the heavy dependence of ministers of departments on the professional expert. Changes resulting from this criticism and from the upheaval brought by World War II may yet occur. However, sweeping reforms or alterations in structure are less likely in the British civil service than in the services of other European countries.

Legislative Organization

RELATIONSHIP BETWEEN THE EXECUTIVE AND THE LEGISLATURE.—In a governing system in which the members of the principal executive committee are also traditionally members of the principal legislative body there are many points where executive and legislative policies coincide. In Britain the integration of the Cabinet and the Parliament is so close as to tend to negate the separation of these two branches of government. On the other hand, the two branches maintain a separation from each other in many types of procedure and action. Thus it is that the Cabinet and Parliament are at the same time interdependent and separate institutions.

The outstanding unwritten conventions of the British Constitution which pertain to the relationship between the executive and legislative branches are as follows: (1) All the ministers of a Cabinet must be members of Parliament. This rule guarantees a close relationship between the executive and legislative, enabling the Cabinet to keep Parliament continually informed of its policies and activities. Conversely, in the House of Commons a portion of each day is set aside for the members of Parliament to address questions to ministers. (2) While each minister is responsible for his own department, all ministers are considered to be pursuing a collective policy and to stand or fall together. This does not mean, however, that the whole Cabinet always finds it advisable to accept collective responsibility for the seemingly poor judgment or inefficiency of a particular minister. (3) The Cabinet and entire Ministry resign office at once when the opposition receives a majority at a general election or upon a vote of the House of Commons indicating a loss of confidence.

An interesting intergovernmental relationship exists in the Lord Chancellorship where important functions of all three branches of

GOVERNMENT OF GREAT BRITAIN

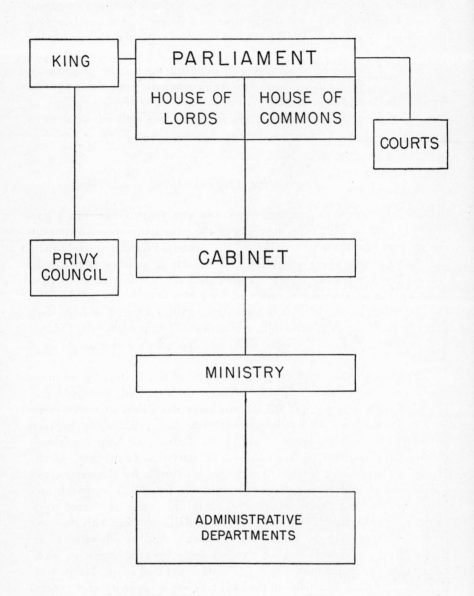

government are combined. The Lord Chancellor is an important member of the Cabinet, he is the presiding officer of the House of Lords, and as the supreme figure in the nation's judiciary he heads the highest court of appeal.

THE HOUSE OF LORDS.—The House of Lords has approximately seven hundred and fifty members who, with some exceptions, hold their positions through hereditary titles. The exceptions are seven "law lords" [7] appointed for life, twenty-six bishops elected by seniority, sixteen Scottish peers elected by their fellow peers for the duration of a single Parliament, and twenty-eight Irish peers elected by their fellows for life. It is assumed that the Irish peers will gradually cease to sit in the Lords because vacancies in their representation have not been filled since the establishment of the Irish Free State in 1921. The members of the House of Lords draw no salary.

Two important restrictions limit the power of the House of Lords. First, all peerages are created by the king, and there is no limit to their number. If necessary, therefore, the prime minister may advise the king to flood the Lords with newly made peers who will vote with the majority of the House of Commons. This threat has been used twice in British history: in 1832 to pass the Reform Bill and in 1911 to pass the Parliament Act. In each instance the House of Lords capitulated to the wishes of the House of Commons. The latter act imposed a second limitation to the Lords' legislative power. Under it the Lords can delay a financial bill for one month only, and other legislation for not longer than two years. After these periods have elapsed, the bill can be passed over their veto.

The House of Lords has been the subject of acute controversy in the past. A legislative body constructed largely on a hereditary basis is clearly not in accord with modern democratic ideals, and, moreover, the House of Lords at present has a huge and permanent Conservative party majority. While it is generally agreed that some reform is necessary, disagreement persists as to how a substitute chamber should be organized.

In October, 1947, the speech from the throne indicated the intention of the government to modify the Parliament Act of 1911 by reducing the period from two years to one year during which the House of Lords may delay legislation. Political considerations were generally conceded to have governed the timing of the government's proposal; in particular its desire to ensure the enactment of measures nationalizing the iron and steel industry before the next general election.[8] Critics of the bill objected

---

[7] See page 44.

[8] Under its existing powers the House of Lords could prevent the nationalization of iron and steel before the next general election; the proposed modification of the Parliament Act of 1911 would enable the government to accomplish its avowed purpose before 1950 even if the Lords refuse to pass the bill.

to its introduction of radical governmental reorganization in a period of economic crisis, and the Conservative opposition called for a thoroughgoing measure of second chamber reform to be taken after full preliminary investigation.

It must be remembered, in any consideration of the House of Lords, that the hereditary peers, who owe their titles simply to birth, play a negligible role, the major part being played by distinguished public servants, legal figures, former colonial governors or administrators, former members of Parliament, and others who have been raised to the peerage as a result of their own achievements. The House of Lords thus embodies a great deal of practical experience, and its debates are frequently on a very high level. In general, it may be said that the Lords do valuable work in improving the caliber of legislation and, being very sensitive about the slogan "Peers versus the People," hesitate to obstruct legislation except when they feel that the majority of the House of Commons no longer represents the people.

The House of Lords also serves as the highest British court of judicial appeal for England, Wales, Scotland, and Northern Ireland, a function exercised by the "law lords."

THE HOUSE OF COMMONS.—Despite the fact that the House of Commons is historically the "lower house" of the British Parliament, it has long been the dominant branch of that legislative body. Indeed, the House of Commons has come to be the constitutional center of the whole British government. British administrations come into office because they can command a majority in the Commons; an administration which loses its majority must resign. All executive agencies are subject to the control of the House of Commons, which is the body through which the sovereign British people express their collective will and control their government.

Before the general election of July, 1945, the House of Commons consisted of 615 members. All except twelve of these were elected by electoral districts in the United Kingdom, there being 485 members from English constituencies, thirty-five from Wales and Monmouth, seventy-one from Scotland and twelve from Northern Ireland. By an odd provision, the remaining twelve members were elected by the graduates of universities, Oxford and Cambridge having two members each. The last revision of constituencies was made in 1918, when seats in the House of Commons were distributed on the basis of one member to every seventy thousand population. Since 1918 very large and permanent shifts of population have taken place, to which must be added the large wartime movement. A recently passed act established permanent machinery for the review of constituencies, consisting of four separate boundary commissions for England, Scotland, Wales and Monmouth, and Northern Ireland. Each of these bodies will undertake regular reviews of the representation of its area, beginning in 1946 and thereafter at intervals of between three and seven years. But as an interim measure, twenty over-sized constituencies with more than 100,000 registered voters were divided into forty-five, on the basis of one to every fifty thousand registered voters. This was done before the general election of July, 1945, so that the present House of Commons has 640 members.

In general, the organization and functioning of the House of Commons is similar to that of the American House of Representatives. There are, however, two major differences arising from the basic principles of the cabinet system. The Cabinet is in office because it commands a majority in the Commons, and one of its major jobs is to draft legislation for the Commons and to push its passage. For this purpose the Cabinet, like the executive departments of the American government, has well-developed facilities for drafting and studying bills. Unlike American practice, however, important bills introduced by the British Cabinet in the House of Commons are not ordinarily referred to a committee of that body until the matter has first been discussed fully by the House itself. For this purpose the House constitutes itself a "committee of the whole" at the time of the bill's second reading. Such a procedure is employed much less frequently in American practice. A second important variation from American usage is the "question hour." A limited time is set aside each day for the members to address oral and written inquiries to ministers on pertinent matters. The ministers may decline to answer on the ground that the matter is confidential, but this expedient is used only when warranted, since the Ministry desires to retain the good will of the Commons. Such questions often precipitate informative and embarrassing discussion on the floor of the Commons and in the press.

The speaker of the House of Commons is elected for each Parliament by vote of the whole House, and he generally carries over from Parliament to Parliament. He is nonpartisan in his conduct of proceedings.

Since the British constitutional theory holds that criticism is an essential element in a democratic political system, it is perfectly consistent that the strongest political party in opposition to the majority party of the House of Commons should be given official recognition. This leading minority party is known as "His Majesty's Loyal Opposition." [9]

One of the primary functions of Parliament is to approve, to disapprove, and to criticize the policies of the Ministry. The criticism is designed not only to make the Ministry modify its policy but also to promote efficiency in administration and to educate public opinion. It

---

[9] Its chief spokesman in the House of Commons is paid a salary of approximately $8,000 a year. Ordinary MP's receive about $4,000 a year.

is true that the Ministry is composed of the leaders of the majority of the House of Commons and can generally rely on the loyalty of that majority. But that majority is very sensitive to the opinion of the public, to which it must account at the next election. When members of the majority feel that they are losing popular support, they may cease to follow the Ministry and become obstreperous. The Ministry must then change its course under pain of losing the confidence of the House.

THE LAWMAKING PROCESS.—As has been pointed out, Parliament may enact laws on any matter and in furtherance of any policy which a majority of the members approve. It is fettered only by the dictates of its own political experience, practical judgment, and the pressure of public opinion. Otherwise it is free to legislate on any subject. In British parliamentary practice, proposed legislation is divided into several categories. The most important distinction is the one made between bills which affect national interests, called public bills, and those which are of only local or individual interest, called private bills. Public bills are further classified according to the manner in which they are introduced. Most of them are introduced by some member of the Ministry. If this is the case, the public bill is called a government bill. The few public bills which are introduced by a member of Parliament who is not also a minister are called private members' bills. Private bills, on the other hand, are always introduced as petitions. Bills of this type are handled by small committees of the house in which they are introduced. Such committees operate in a quasi-judicial manner and conduct hearings in which interests affected by the proposed legislation may have an opportunity to be heard.

Bills may be introduced in either house of Parliament, except that money bills are introduced in the House of Commons and judicial bills in the House of Lords. Since most legislation is introduced by the Ministry and since the lower house has real control of legislation, most bills are introduced in the House of Commons.

The procedure of the House of Commons is, in many ways, similar to that of the House of Representatives of the United States Congress. A bill entered in the Commons passes through five stages before being transmitted to the House of Lords: (1) the first reading, which is merely the formal submission; (2) the second reading, which involves a vote and a debate, either killing the bill or referring it to a committee; (3) consideration in detail by a committee; (4) the report of the bill to the whole House for consideration; (5) the third reading after which, if the bill is passed, it is transmitted to the House of Lords, where it goes through similar stages. If passed there, it goes forward for the royal assent and is placed on the statute books as an Act of Parliament. If amended by the Lords, it is returned to the Commons. If the Commons refuse to accept the Lords' amendments and the Lords persist, the Commons must pass the bill in each of three consecutive sessions over a period of two years before it becomes law. There is no provision for joint committees such as exist in the Congress of the United States.

ELECTION TO THE HOUSE OF COMMONS.—Elections do not take place in Great Britain at fixed intervals as they do in the United States. According to law a general election must be held at least every five years. In such an election the entire membership of the House of Commons must stand for office. But a House of Commons generally does not stay in office for the full five years. A new election is held when Parliament is dissolved by the king—and the king, of course, acts upon the advice of the Cabinet. Therefore, British general elections occur at irregular intervals of usually less than five years.

Through the device of advising the king to dissolve Parliament, the Cabinet can fix the time of the election so as to gain the best advantage for its party. After about four years in power, it may feel that its chances of success would be better in an immediate election than a year later. Again, a general election may be brought about in order to resolve a political deadlock in Parliament. The Cabinet can cause a dissolution and an election so as to take the issue directly to the voters. A third common circumstance in which an election is held before the end of the statutory five years might occur when the Cabinet loses its majority in the House of Commons. The Commons can always dismiss a government by passing a resolution that it has no confidence in that government, and in those circumstances a general election almost always follows. The fact that an election may be held at any time tends to make members of Parliament very sensitive to public opinion.

There have been exceptions to these practices in wartime. The Parliament elected in 1935 prolonged its life during the European phase of World War II and was finally dissolved in May, 1945. When in May, 1940, a heavy adverse vote was registered in the House of Commons against the Chamberlain administration, Chamberlain resigned and Churchill succeeded him as prime minister without a general election.

If a member dies or resigns, what is called a by-election is held in his constituency to fill the seat. These elections may be important in showing the trend of public opinion, but they are not always safe guides. Local issues often determine the result; moreover, the voters show less interest than in the general elections.

The qualifications for membership in the House are remarkably broad. With a few exceptions any British subject who is twenty-one years of age may be elected. Peers of the United Kingdom, clergymen of the Church of England and of the Church of Scotland, Roman Catholic priests, judges, and civil servants are ineligible.

The British method of electing members of the national legislative body differs from the American in the important point that in Britain there is no residential qualification. A constituency may elect a man who resides in an entirely different part of the country, and this is a common practice. Thus a Londoner may be the member for a Scottish constituency and a Scotsman may represent a London area. The British method of national representation has at least two advantages. It gives the candidate for Parliament the opportunity of being elected to the House of Commons even though he may have been defeated in the constituency where he resides. The voters may have a wider choice of candidates than they would have if they were restricted to their own locality. They are more likely to choose someone of national, rather than local, reputation.

The nominating process is very simple. The candidate merely files a nomination paper signed by at least ten qualified voters of the constituency. In addition he makes a deposit of the sum of approximately six hundred dollars. If he fails to receive at least one eighth of the total vote on election day, his deposit is forfeited and turned into the national treasury. This provision in the law assists materially in winnowing the frivolous candidates from those whose candidacies are legitimate.

SUFFRAGE.—In parliamentary elections the franchise is extended to every citizen over twenty-one years of age. Formerly three months' residence in a particular constituency was mandatory, but this requirement was removed for the 1945 election. The local government franchise was previously limited to owners or tenants of property but has now been assimilated to the parliamentary franchise. There are provisions for absent voters' ballots for the Army and Navy. Aliens, felons, and lunatics may not vote. Since peers exert their political influence directly in the House of Lords, they cannot vote for members of the Commons.[10]

Parties and Politics

THE RELATIONSHIP OF PARTIES TO THE GOVERNMENT.—One of the characteristics of British democracy is that there are usually two major divisions of public opinion which find expression in organized political parties. The constitutional structure of executive, legislature, and judiciary is given substance, moved and guided by these extralegal groups. Their

---

[10] Formerly each British citizen could vote in the constituency in which he lived or where he occupied business premises having a yearly rental of not less than ten pounds. The possessor of a university degree could vote for the representative of his university. Under these qualifications an elector could exercise two votes, but only two: one for his residence and one for his place of business or university, provided the votes were cast in different constituencies. Plural voting was abolished by the Representation of the People Act, 1948.

leaders, the politicians, handle the business of nominating candidates to elective office, of staffing the executive departments and agencies, Parliament and local government councils, and the judiciary, high and low. In sum, by giving expression to the interests of clients and supporters, the politicians formulate the policies of government. These political labors, whether the uninspiring leg work of the ward worker going his rounds soliciting signatures for nomination petitions, or cabinet deliberations on matters of high policy, together constitute a service function indispensable to the operation of democratic government.

PARTY ORGANIZATION.—British parties serve to canalize the vote of nearly thirty-three million electors and, in common with political organizations in other democratic nations, they define election issues, "educate" the voters, supply elective candidates, coordinate the activities of government, and, when "out of office" and in minority status, provide continuous critical analysis of public policies. Certain additional characteristics of the British party system have caused it in recent years to come under close study by foreign observers: the two-party alignment, electoral practices both efficient and free from corruption, and party organizations operated by professional staffs.

Although the spoils system is virtually nonexistent in Great Britain, political parties nonetheless derive financial support from persons and organizations whose interests are advanced directly or indirectly by their party's electoral success. This method of raising political funds possesses the undoubted advantage of freeing the taxpayer of opposite political faith from contributing involuntarily to support the party in power. Its effect on civic attitudes has been to create a realistic recognition of the necessary role of money in politics. Thus, the fact that the present-day Conservative party's war chest is maintained largely by industry, business, and the propertied classes while Labor's funds are contributed principally by trade-unions is held by the ordinary Briton to be inevitable, logical, and nowise blameworthy. As another consequence of support by private contribution, parties, like business organizations, are obliged to have regard to the efficiency of employees. These last comprise the clerical, research, and publicity staffs and the body of "parliamentary agents": specially trained organizers and election managers who normally direct party work in the constituencies. All are employed on full-time basis, remunerated from party funds, and wholly divorced from the public pay roll. In short, party leaders are unable because of the nonpolitical character of the civil service to place their workers in government jobs which would afford compensation, nominally for public services performed perfunctorily, actually for labors in behalf of the party "after hours." British democracy, therefore, enjoys the advantages of competent professional management in politics as in government.

Because a general election may constitutionally occur at any time, party organization must be maintained intact continuously at all levels, defining issues, canvassing voters, and—when out of power—keeping "prospective" candidates in the public eye. A voluminous literature issues steadily from the research, publications, and press departments of the major-party headquarters. In the form of periodicals, pamphlets, flyers, "pocket" books, and press releases, this output is addressed to citizens of all ages and economic levels. The Conservative and Labor parties find valuable auxiliaries among major publishing houses whose proprietors or directors hold prominent positions in party council or in Parliament. Of greater importance is the influence of the press. British reading habits have been profoundly affected by modern technology; notably in the substitution, all over the nation, of the large London daily for the older independent local newspaper. In political terms this development has resulted in tremendous gain to Conservative publicity, for the four major "chains" favor that party editorially and in news selection.[11] The Labor voter may read news and views which do no violence to his taste in his party's semiofficial organ, the *Daily Herald*.

In all the techniques that pertain to political campaigns the most significant variation between British and American practice occurs in the field of radio broadcasting. Methods of campaign broadcasting are controlled by two prime factors: the relatively short length of time—ten to twenty days—during which the election campaigns are in progress, and the radio monopoly exercised by the publicly owned British Broadcasting Corporation. In effect, British political party treasuries are relieved of extra strain for purchasing time on the air; few of the candidates have opportunity to amplify their views before the microphone. Campaign speeches are broadcast during general elections only, and the number of "talks" allotted without charge by BBC to the parties has been equitable but limited.

Summer schools are conducted for young people and adults by the Labor, Conservative, and Liberal parties. One- or two-week courses are repeated from June to September, and are attended by party workers and by the more politically minded of the faithful. Government and party officers, from the Cabinet to the local ward club, visit the schools —which are usually held at university towns or holiday resorts—to lecture or to teach courses on party organization, local government, home policy, or international relations. The Conservative party maintains, in addition, a year-round curriculum at its Bonar Law College. More specialized instruction in party organization and elections is given by the major parties to candidates for employment in the permanent staffs. The

---

[11] The *Times*, despite its chain affiliation, retains a fair degree of political independence; the famed *Manchester Guardian* has survived the near disappearance of its party and still presents the Liberal viewpoint.

"graduates" are duly certificated and, when employed as parliamentary agents, maintain their own trade-unions (within the respective party organizations) and professional journals.

HISTORICAL BACKGROUND OF BRITISH PARTY POLITICS.—At all stages in their development British parties have been deeply rooted in the economic bases of politics. Thus the conflict between Whigs and Tories[12] which followed the establishment of parliamentary authority over the royal power, and which constituted the beginning of the British political party system, was essentially a maneuver of the two leading economic interests, the mercantile and the landed. That British politics continued to be conducted within the framework of a two-party system despite a vast multiplication of economic interests and activities is due in large part to the nation's persistent good fortune in avoiding crushing military defeat and to the enduring qualities induced in the original parties by long-continued control of public patronage.[13] Throughout the eighteenth century, parliamentary leaders rewarded their supporters with government contracts, places, and pensions.

The entry into politics, after the Reform Bill of 1832, of factory owners and related mercantile interests, whose influence was furthered by the Industrial Revolution, profoundly affected the development of parties to the close of the century. Demanding repeal of tariffs, especially on grains, increased governmental economy, extended suffrage, and peace, these men soon formed a compact Radical bloc. With the breakup of the old Tory party following the repeal of the Corn Laws in 1846, the two-party system was overshadowed by the emergence of groups having special interests[14] which held the balance of power in Parliament. Rumps of the two older parties, however, still constituted poles of political energy, emerging about 1860 as Conservatives and Liberals.

NINETEENTH-CENTURY POLITICS: CONSERVATIVE VS. LIBERAL PARTIES.— The Reform Act of 1867, by creating a million new voters and doubling the electorate, compelled political leaders to provide centralized direction for the activities of the local associations which had hitherto com-

---

[12] The names "Petitioners" and, shortly afterward, "Whigs" were applied to the supporters of the Exclusion Bills of 1679–1681, which were framed to exclude from the throne James, Duke of York, heir presumptive and a Roman Catholic. Opponents of the measures were called Abhorrers, later Tories.

[13] The Patronage Secretary of the Treasury, precursor of the present chief whip, was expected to produce majorities as cheaply as possible, and on occasion he bought votes. According to tradition, he had a pay window opening on the lobby of the old House of Commons. British victories on land and sea during this period of political corruption may be attributed in part to the fact that the public affairs of opponents on the Continent were even more grossly mismanaged under the prevailing regimes of absolute monarchy.

[14] In succession the Peelites, Radicals, Irish Nationalists, Laborites, and, latterly, the Liberals.

prised the main elements of party organization. In this period, too, the influence of the Victorian businessman became apparent in basic reform measures which made the merit system nearly universal in the civil service. Because of the drastic reduction of political patronage which resulted from civil service reform and from the Corrupt Practices Act of 1883, British public life achieved a purification perhaps unparalleled in the history of politics.

Strongly supporting the landed interests, the Church of England, tariffs, imperial expansion, and, in recent years, the concept of private enterprise as opposed to public enterprise, the Conservative party attracted industrialists, the larger economic interests, and the managerial and clerical forces connected therewith. The Liberal party strength was concentrated in the "Nonconformist" areas of the Midlands, the north of England, Scotland, and Wales, and its financial support was largely derived from businessmen and manufacturers in those regions. Adopting the Radicals' historic platform of "Retrenchment and Reform," Liberal spokesmen advocated the minimum of government control and untrammeled expansion of private enterprise. The doctrinal heirs of Adam Smith, they made free trade central to their policy and worked steadily for international peace and disarmament. In the second half of the nineteenth century, when factory owners were largely self-made men and the expansion of British trade created unprecedented economic opportunity at home, industrial labor voted for its Radical and Liberal employers. Representatives of the latter, John Bright, Jesse Collings, and Joseph Chamberlain, while opposing trade-unionism as inimical to labor's true interests as well as to business enterprise, became the principal champions of universal male suffrage and free education.

The Conservatives, as the party of the landed interests, claimed a freedom from domination by industrialists sufficient to constitute them the logical guardians of labor against abuses of the factory system. In an effort to win workers' votes, discerning Conservative leaders, Disraeli, Lord Randolph Churchill, and others, moved the party to sponsor some milestones of social reform: the Local Government Act, 1875, which laid the foundation of the modern structure of public health agencies; and the Cross Act, 1873, under the provisions of which public housing was first undertaken in Great Britain.

BEGINNING OF THE LABOR PARTY.—The rapid growth of industrial society after 1800 created formidable problems: slums, undesirable working conditions, unemployment, for which neither Whigs nor Tories, Liberals nor Conservatives, were able to offer effective solutions. Following the failure of political action in an abortive working-class movement[15] of the 1840's, labor leaders concentrated on trade-unionism "pure

---

[15] Known as Chartism, this political agitation became strongest in 1848, the year of revolutions on the Continent, and centered on the Charter, a program of six re-

and simple." After a half century of trial, this course of action failed to satisfy labor, and elements of the trade-union movement re-entered the field of politics, eventually forming the Labor party in 1906. With inroads on their working-class vote threatened, the Liberals, who had elected to Parliament an occasional labor leader, now embarked on a policy of social legislation patterned on Bismarck's program of the 1880's and on contemporary French measures. The Liberal party's impressive victory at the polls in 1906 not only paved the way for the legislation of the "New Liberalism," but served to check the growth of the Labor party for the time being.[16]

Defensive sentiment promoted by judicial decisions considered inimical to trade-union interests was a prime factor in bringing about the eventual solidarity of organized British labor in politics. This feeling, while particularly strong in the years preceding World War I, was not sufficient to overcome differences on policy that saw the trade-union elements giving vigorous support to the war effort while many prominent party leaders, including Ramsay MacDonald, opposed the war as brought about by blundering diplomacy and "imperialism" and called for a "negotiated peace."

By 1915 the demands of World War I necessitated the subordination of internal differences and the development of a united front in order to achieve a maximum war effort. Accordingly, a coalition government headed by Lloyd George, and including personnel from the Liberal, Conservative, and Labor parties, was formed for the duration of hostilities.

POLITICAL PARTIES BETWEEN TWO WORLD WARS.—A fundamental fact affecting the course of British party politics between the two World Wars was the decline and virtual disappearance as a parliamentary force of the Liberals, lineal descendants of the seventeenth-century Whigs and the heirs of Marlborough, Pitt the Elder, and Gladstone. This event was due to a great extent to the party's inability to meet postwar economic problems with measures which appeared realistic to the electorate. Having achieved their historic objectives of free trade, free education, and electoral reform, the divided Liberals were unable to divorce their thinking from the bondage of those dated shibboleths. In an age of intensifying economic nationalism their majority groups resolutely adhered to free-trade principles. As the shadow of militaristic fascism lengthened

---

forms, of which the most important were universal manhood suffrage, abolition of property qualifications for members of Parliament, and payment for their services.

[16] Under the driving leadership of Chancellor of the Exchequer Lloyd George who subsequently became prime minister of the World War I coalition government, the Liberal majority enacted old-age and sickness benefits and legislation limiting the financial responsibility of unions for damages incurred in labor disputes. Finally, in 1911, the Liberals succeeded in curbing the legislative powers of the House of Lords which had opposed the foregoing measures.

over Europe, they reiterated their historic opposition to conscription and rearmament. In the same period the Conservatives, staking economic recovery on imperial preference tariffs as well as on the freedom of private enterprise, won a plurality in every general election: 1922, 1923, 1924, 1929, 1931, and 1935.

In 1918, leaders of the fragmented Labor party, foreseeing the decline of the Liberals, seized the opportunity to create a national party capable of opposing the Conservatives as a major rival. Hitherto the Labor party had had no consistent program other than attempting in general to promote working-class interests. Now, however, a policy of evolutionary socialism was embodied in the manifesto *Labour and the New Social Order*.[17] In addition, a nation-wide drive was undertaken to increase the party's membership, which had previously been restricted to members of trade-unions and affiliated organizations. As the Liberal party's strength diminished, the bulk of Liberal electors shifted allegiance in directions which gave the greatest promise of "making their votes count."

Liberals of the business and professional classes as well as the better paid "white-collar workers" swung to Conservatism, as did the Scottish landowners. Labor benefited from defections by industrial workers and received a substantial accretion of strength from ex-Liberal middle-class groups of teachers, professional workers, and "intellectuals," these latter forming an important element in the constituency Labor parties. In this period, too, the Liberal party was the most conspicuous victim of the well-known peculiarity of single-member district electoral systems: the disproportionate advantage accruing to the party receiving the largest number of votes.[18]

With the support of the Liberals, Ramsay MacDonald was able to form the first Labor government in 1924 and the second in 1929, his party in each case having but a minority of seats in the House of Commons. After an eight-month tenure the first coalition broke up over the question of giving diplomatic recognition to the Soviet Union. The second Labor government survived until the economic crisis of 1931 presented the Cabinet with the alternative of reducing unemployment benefit payments or forfeiting the customary financial services afforded the government by private financial institutions. The unity of coalition and Labor party alike was shattered, and a general election resulted in a new coalition of "National" Laborites, Conservatives, and "National" Lib-

---

[17] The principal author, Sydney Webb (later Lord Passfield), in 1884 helped found the Fabian Society, a group of writers concerned with questions of social reform. By providing intellectual leadership for the Labor party during its formative years, the Fabians were largely responsible for shaping its policy of "evolutionary" socialism.

[18] In the general election of 1945 the Liberals cast 2,213,191 votes and elected 11 members of Parliament, contrasted with Labor's 11,991,661 votes and 394 seats won. The Liberal party is, accordingly, the leading advocate of proportional representation in parliamentary elections.

erals. This "National government" which soon became Conservative in all but name continued after the election of 1935 and until the outbreak of World War II.

THE PARTY TRUCE IN WARTIME.—The last prewar general election was held in November, 1935, so that another was due not later than November, 1940. But when war broke out in September, 1939, the three major parties—Conservative, Liberal, and Labor—made an agreement designed to avoid wartime elections. This followed the precedent of World War I. It was felt that the holding of a general election would split the nation into opposing political groups at a time when national unity was most needed. Each year from 1940 to 1944 Parliament passed a short act extending its own life by one year. The parties agreed that when a vacancy occurred in the House of Commons the candidate of the party which in 1939 represented the constituency would not be opposed by the other two parties.

As the defeat of Germany approached, leaders of all parties began to consider the need for a general election as soon as possible after the termination of the war in Europe, or certainly after the end of the war with Japan. The actual breaking of the party truce while Great Britain was still at war with Japan was due to restiveness of the rank and file of the Labor party rather than to any desire on the part of Winston Churchill and the Conservatives to return to party government. When this feeling prompted the Labor Party Congress meeting at Blackpool in May to favor an election in late 1945, notwithstanding the continuance of the Far Eastern war at that time, the Conservatives decided that it would be good political strategy to order general elections immediately. As a result, the Labor members of the coalition War Cabinet and Ministry resigned their posts, forcing the end of the party coalition which had existed since May, 1940. This action of the Labor leaders was prompted principally by the belief of the Laborites that the socialist measures they advocated should be an integral part of the national reconversion program. In other words, the end of the party truce was due almost entirely to the difference of the two major parties on domestic issues and not to any fundamental divergence in matters of foreign policy.

THE GENERAL ELECTION OF 1945.—From the Conservative point of view, the moment chosen was tactically correct, for a government which had led the nation to military victory might reasonably expect a decisive gratitude vote. Such had been the case at the "khaki" elections following the Boer War and World War I. In consideration of the dislocation caused in major party organizations by six years of war as well as by the novelty of a general election for the first time in a whole decade, Prime Minister Churchill caused the campaign period, lasting from the day of nominations to election day, to be extended from the usual ten days to twenty-one.

Ultimate objectives of the major parties were couched in generally similar terms: creation of a British social order in which each citizen would be permitted to develop his latent capacities. The points at issue lay in the respective methods by which the requisite avenues of opportunity were to be kept widely open. Conservatives relied on private enterprise with resort to government aid as required by necessity. Existing social services were to be retained but administered with greater efficiency and expanded with caution. Monopoly capitalism, however, was to be subject to government regulation in all cases. Laborites were agreed that the bulk of economic activity could continue only through the established structure of private enterprise. But industries dominated by great concentrations of capital were to be socialized on the general principle that government encroachment in spheres hitherto reserved to private investment constituted no inherent evil in democracies. Labor spokesmen estimated that nationalization would be confined to approximately 20 per cent of the economy.

Despite a public-opinion survey which predicted the vote within a small fraction of error, most British and practically all foreign observers were wholly taken aback by the decisive victory of the Labor party.[19] For the first time in its history, that party was put into office with a working majority of ample proportions and a complete freedom from dependence on any third-party group.

On examination the election results reveal a shift of political allegiance less far-reaching than the number of transferred seats would suggest. The Conservative vote did not differ greatly from the 1935 figure of 10,496,300, but Labor gained 3,676,169 over its previous showing. The statistics made it plain, however, that a new generation of voters had grown up during the decade since the previous general election. More attracted to the novel program of social reconstruction advanced by the Labor party than to the rather less challenging and somewhat more vague platform of Prime Minister Churchill's "caretakers," they influenced the results decisively.

THE LABOR GOVERNMENT, 1945.—The election, held on July 5, 1945, produced no immediate effect on the continuity of British policy, for the

---

[19] The votes were distributed as follows:

	Votes	Seats won
Labor	11,991,660	394
Conservative and National	9,893,906	216
Liberal	2,213,191	11
Independent	520,436	2
Communist	102,780	2
Independent Labor party	46,679	3
Common Wealth	110,634	1

government of Winston Churchill continued in office during the month required to complete the count of ballots received from members of the armed forces in various parts of the world. Despite the large number of officials concerned with the electoral count, the nature of the returns did not become apparent to the public until the formal announcement of results in August. Winston Churchill thereupon resigned and the king sent for Clement R. Attlee, leader of the Labor party, to form a new government.

The new administration included party veterans of considerable administrative experience together with a leavening of younger men of promise. Prime Minister Attlee, a barrister, had held the wartime office of deputy prime minister, and had served as Undersecretary for War and Postmaster General in the first and second Labor governments, respectively. Herbert S. Morrison, deputy leader of the new House of Commons, was made Lord President of the Council, a post of cabinet rank which entailed no departmental responsibilities and permitted the holder to function as a sort of "Minister of Thought" by affording him time to reflect on the broad problems of policy. Morrison had gained experience in national administration as wartime Minister of Home Affairs and Security and as Minister of Transport in the second MacDonald government.[20] To head the Foreign Office, Attlee selected Ernest Bevin, wartime Minister of Labor and National Service. The combination of pugnacity and perspective which had helped Bevin bring his Transport Workers Union to leadership in British labor affairs was deemed by Prime Minister Attlee to be appropriate to a foreign minister faced with the problem of maintaining Britain's traditional weight in international councils despite her weakened economic position. Of greatest potentiality in the new Cabinet was the controversial figure, Sir Stafford Cripps. One of Britain's most successful barristers and a former Solicitor General, he had been expelled from the Labor party in 1935 for urging a "popular front" of all leftist groups and parties. Readmitted to Labor's ranks four years later, Cripps was named to the wartime coalition Cabinet and proved to be an able and energetic Minister of Aircraft Production. After the Labor election victory, as President of the Board of Trade, he continued to influence the government's economic policies. These became crucial early in 1947 as catastrophic winter weather coincided with war weariness, chronic housing shortages, and an inflationary spiral in the United States which reduced by 40 per cent the purchasing power of the 1946 American loan for reconstruction. Confronted with Britain's gravest peacetime economic crisis, Attlee employed his powers under the Ministers of the Crown (Transfer of Functions) Act, 1946, to set up a

---

[20] As leader of the majority Labor party in the London County Council during the thirties he headed a governmental organization second in size only to the national government.

Ministry for Economic Affairs with Cripps at its head. The new minister became responsible to the Cabinet for planning and coordinating the nation's economic activities under the system of over-all public control which was carried over from the war. As national production "targets" were established to help bring exports into balance with imports over a period of three years, Cripps publicized the concept of "austerity" as a necessity if not a virtue, and urged it on his countrymen with a fervor reminiscent of his wartime chief. In a short time Britain's production showed the sharpest gain since 1945. When Chancellor of the Exchequer Hugh Dalton resigned late in 1947 (in consequence of the protests raised by his disclosures of budgetary information to the press prior to the annual budget speech), Cripps replaced him as head of the Treasury. Cripps also continued to exercise the duties of Minister for Economic Affairs, though the post and title had lapsed.

Among the Labor party's "rising young men" two are conspicuous for their rapid advancement to posts of the highest level. Hector McNeil, economist and journalist, became Undersecretary of Foreign Affairs in 1945 at the age of thirty-five, and next year was promoted to Minister of State, a post of ministerial rank without departmental responsibilities. J. Harold Wilson, formerly of the Oxford University Economics faculty, succeeded Sir Stafford Cripps in the Board of Trade and became, at thirty, the youngest member of the Cabinet. Prime Minister Attlee continued the precedent set by the second MacDonald government and appointed a woman to the Cabinet.[21]

The Conservatives have been handicapped by failure to evolve a program which provides a convincing or challenging alternative to their opponents' regime of controls and austerity. As a parliamentary opposition they have been comparatively ineffective, a condition stemming in no small measure from the heavy election mortality which befell their promising young men in 1945. Winston Churchill heads the party and, as leader of the opposition, directs its parliamentary delegation. Next in importance is former Foreign Minister Anthony Eden, who is generally acknowledged to be Churchill's successor to the party leadership.

Government and the Economy

THE LABOR GOVERNMENT'S POLICY.—Speaking at the Labor Party Conference in May, 1947, Prime Minister Attlee declared that his government was effecting two transitions, the first being "from war to peace economy" and the second "from a capitalism based on private enterprise and pri-

---

[21] The appointee, Miss Ellen Wilkinson, Minister of Education, who died early in 1947, was the second of her sex to enter the Cabinet. The administration now has one woman of ministerial rank, Dr. Edith Summerskill, Parliamentary Secretary to the Ministry of Food.

vate property to a socialist economy based on the control and direction of the wealth and resources of the country." For the accomplishment of these aims certain governmental powers lay ready at hand as an aftermath of Britain's war economy; others were brought into being as the Labor party legislated a far-reaching program of economic controls.

Integration in the effort of total war over a period of six years forced on British industry so great a degree of specialization that conversion to a peacetime basis posed the fundamental problem facing the Attlee government on its accession to office. Replacement and reorganization were required on a scale which amounted to national reconstruction. The coming of peace, however, found the British economy unable, without substantial credits from the United States and Canada, either to supply accumulated domestic needs or to re-establish the pattern of foreign trade necessary to national solvency.

Loss of gold, disinvestment and sale of assets abroad, increased debt, all had combined to worsen the United Kingdom's prewar capital position by nearly $30,000,000,000, including United States and Canadian loans for postwar rehabilitation. Additional losses resulting from reduced returns from foreign investments, lowered net shipping income, and reduction of the export trade to less than 50 per cent of prewar volume threatened to cripple the nation's recuperative powers. Income from exports at the war's end was sufficient to pay for only one quarter of the prewar volume of imports.

PUBLIC PLANNING.—Appreciating the gravity of the situation, the Attlee government undertook extensive economic planning to ensure "the use of national resources in the best interests of the nation as a whole." A series of measures speedily passed through Parliament and became law, nationalizing, with compensation to stockholders, the Bank of England (March, 1946), the coal industry (July, 1946), civil aviation (August, 1946), telecommunications (January, 1947), electricity supply and inland transport (August, 1947). The socialized industries were expected to exert an important influence on the whole economy. Other controls were already available to the government in its effort to meet one of the United Kingdom's prime needs: a rapid expansion of the export trade in order to buy the products and raw materials required from abroad.

Having established new agencies of control and coordinated the old, the Attlee government set about to produce "economic budgets." Though they had some bearing on the Chancellor of the Exchequer's yearly budget, the "economic budgets" differed in respect of measurement units; man-years of work and quantities of goods replaced monetary values. Like the financial budget, however, they strove to attain balance, and recognized the impossibility of consuming more than is produced.

Prepared for the period of the following calendar year by a central staff working with the representatives of the government departments concerned, the economic budgets set out resources and requirements in terms of man power, national income and expenditure, foreign exchange, investment (capital equipment and maintenance), and the strategic materials: power, steel, lumber, and the like. The first economic budgets appeared in the form of a White Paper called *Economic Survey for 1947*.[22] This report fixed a long-term target for exports at 175 per cent of the 1938 volume and arrived at four conclusions with reference to the year 1947:

1. The export target of 140 per cent of 1938 volume by the end of the year is of prime importance;

2. Exports to the Western Hemisphere (and some European countries with which we have deficits, viz., Sweden, Switzerland, Portugal), are of particular importance, for they earn dollars or the equivalent and pay for our essential imports from those countries;

3. Close import control must be maintained, particularly of products which come predominantly from the Western Hemisphere;

4. Home production must be increased along lines which contribute to these policies; agriculture and shipping are of major importance for this.

Taking cognizance of two wartime controls which no longer existed —power to direct distribution of labor, and government purchase of a large part of the national production—the *Economic Survey* laid down the principle that any further general increases in wages and profits must be accompanied by a corresponding increase in production, and added:

> Indeed, the task of directing by democratic methods an economic system as large and complex as ours is far beyond the power of any governmental machine working by itself, no matter how efficient it may be. Events can be directed in the way that is desired in the national interest only if the government, both sides of industry and the people accept the objectives and then work together to achieve the end. . . . The government must lay down the economic tasks for the nation; it must say which things are the most important and what the objectives of policy should be, and should give as much information as possible to guide the nation's economic activity; it must use its powers of economic control to influence the course of development in the desired direction. When the working pattern has thus been set, it is only by the combined effort of the whole people that the nation can move towards its objective of carrying out the first things first, and so make the best use of its economic resources.

---

[22] *Command Paper 7046 (1946)*. Prior to submitting legislation or embarking on a policy of importance, the Cabinet may publish a White Paper surveying the relevant facts and containing a discussion of the legislation or policy.

Law and Courts

DIVERSITY OF COURT ORGANIZATION.—Like other features of British government which have undergone a long evolution, the British courts have considerable diversity of structure. No single form of court organization exists throughout the United Kingdom or in the British Empire. There is one scheme of courts for England and Wales, another for Scotland, and a third for Northern Ireland. Each of the dominions and many of the colonies have varying types of courts. Except in the case of the two high courts of appeal, the discussion here will be limited to the courts of England and Wales.

ENGLISH LAW.—Although most of the legal systems in continental Europe are based upon Roman law, the law of England is a native development. From English origins English law has spread to Ireland, Canada (except the province of Quebec), Australia, New Zealand, various lesser British dependencies, and the United States (except Louisiana and Puerto Rico). Not all of English law is written, but all of it is enforceable in courts. English law may be considered as divided into three parts: common law, equity (or chancery), and statute law.

Common law is customary law which becomes established by judicial decisions rather than by parliamentary enactments. It began in the earliest legal usages and forms which gained acceptance in Saxon England by custom. These usages were the basis for decisions which the king's judges made. Since law, by definition, consists of whatever principles the courts will enforce, customary ideas of justice come to have the force of law even though the greater part of them have never been enacted into statutes. A portion of it exists in written judicial decisions in particular types of cases. Repeatedly, in the last few centuries the common law has been defined and commented upon by great English jurists, notably by Sir William Blackstone in the eighteenth century. It hardly need be said that legal opinions emanating from such sources are usually determinative in the settlement of cases brought into court.

Equity is a supplement to the common law, separate from both common and statutory law. Its purpose is to give justice in cases where common law does not provide adequate remedy for a sound complaint. Most frequently cases in equity involve such matters as inheritances and injunctions. This body of law developed gradually from decisions made by the Lord Chancellor and his assistants in what came to be a regular Court of Chancery, established for the purpose of hearing appeals from the regular courts. Decisions in the Courts of Chancery were made on the basis of justice or equity and in time they came to form a sort of appendix to the common law. Equity has been limited to civil cases, as opposed to criminal ones.

COURTS OF ENGLAND AND WALES

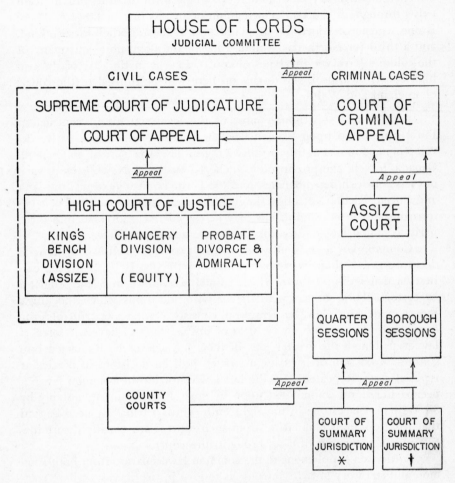

* Conducted by a Justice of the Peace
† Conducted by a Stipendiary Magistrate

Statutory law is the body of law which has been enacted by the Parliament in the six centuries of its existence. It is constantly modifying, codifying, and repealing common law and equity, since it takes precedence over both of them. Yet the greater part of English law today is common law rather than statutory law.

JUDGES.—The crown possesses the power of appointment of all judges and also the power to remove justices of the peace and magistrates. The judges of the Supreme Court of Judicature cannot be removed except by a vote of both Houses of Parliament.

COURT PROCEDURE.—Under the Judicature Act of 1873 the rules of judicial procedure are fixed by a committee which is composed of the Lord Chancellor, seven judges, and four practicing lawyers. New and revised rules must be approved by Parliament before adoption.

In English courts the public is permitted to attend all trials. Both litigants in a proceeding have a right to be represented by counsel and to have their respective sides heard by judge and jury. In almost every type of case the burden of proof rests on the accuser. Guilt or innocence is decided only on the basis of standing law. In serious criminal cases the accused must be tried by a jury. Judgments and the reasons for them are given by judges in open court. Judges have considerable discretion in controlling trials. In every type of case appeal is possible to at least one other court than the one of original jurisdiction. Taken all together, these rules of procedure give the Englishman a reasonable guarantee that he will receive just treatment in court.

CIVIL CASES.—Cases coming before British courts are divided into two general classifications, civil and criminal. Civil cases are those usually brought by a private citizen against another person for redress of some wrong, such as slander, trespass, or breach of contract. Civil court actions involving small sums of money are first introduced in county courts. The county court has jurisdiction in a judicial area which has no relation to any other unit of local government. The county court has one judge. If either party to a suit demands it, a jury trial is held. A member of the King's Bench holds an assize court in the historic counties.[23] Important civil cases are originally heard in this court.

Claims for damages involving larger sums must be taken to the appropriate branch of the High Court of Justice—that is, to the Chancery division, to the King's Bench division, or assize courts, or to the Probate, Divorce, and Admiralty division. Appeals may be taken from these divisions to the Court of Appeal, and then to the House of Lords (on a question of law).

---

[23] For the historic counties see p. 45.

CRIMINAL CASES.—Cases in which a person is tried by state prosecutors after arrest by an officer or on complaint of a private individual for such crimes as murder, theft, or forgery are tried in criminal courts. Petty criminal cases are tried before justices of the peace or, in cities, before stipendiary magistrates. The normal area of jurisdiction for a justice of the peace is a historic county. These officials have considerable prestige, but they serve without pay. The magistrates are paid salaries.

Cases of a slightly graver nature are investigated by a justice of the peace, who may dismiss the charges or send the case to a court of quarter sessions, consisting of as many justices of the peace within a historic county as care to attend. The next higher criminal court is the assize court, which is conducted by a member of the King's Bench of the High Court of Justice (see below) who goes on circuit four times a year into each historic county. The accused appearing before this court is always entitled to jury trial.

Above the local criminal court organization stands the Court of Criminal Appeal. It consists of three or more members of the King's Bench. On points of law, cases may be taken first to this court and then to the House of Lords.

THE SUPREME COURT OF JUDICATURE.—This court is in effect a panel of judges under the direction of the Lord Chancellor. It has original and appellate jurisdiction in civil and criminal cases. It is subdivided into several branches, and its judges never meet as a single body to try cases. The main divisions of the Supreme Court of Judicature are a Court of Appeal and a High Court of Justice. The latter is divided into three elements: (1) Chancery (equity), (2) the King's Bench, and (3) Probate, Divorce, and Admiralty.

THE HOUSE OF LORDS.—The House of Lords serves as the highest court in England and Wales. When it acts as a court only the Lord Chancellor, the seven law lords, and members who have held high judicial office attend. This group or any three members of it may hear cases and pronounce judgments at any time, regardless of whether Parliament is in session.[24]

The House of Lords hears cases only on appeal from a lower court. Its judgments are final. Criminal cases from Scotland are not adjudicated by the House of Lords.

JUDICIAL COMMITTEE OF THE PRIVY COUNCIL.—The Judicial Committee of the Privy Council is, to a degree, the highest court of the British Commonwealth of Nations. It hears appeals from the dominions and the colonies, as well as from the ecclesiastical and prize courts of Great

---

[24] In 1948 the Lords voted away the ancient privilege of the right to trial in criminal proceedings by peers of their own or higher rank.

Britain. These appeals are in practice subject to many restrictions. Under most circumstances a case cannot be brought before the Judicial Committee without the Committee's permission. Moreover, any dominion can prevent an appeal if it so desires, and now New Zealand is the only member of the British Commonwealth which allows cases to go forward freely. The composition of the Judicial Committee is practically the same as that of the House of Lords sitting as a court of law, since the law lords are always made members of the Privy Council and appointed as members of the Judicial Committee.

Local Government

CENTRAL CONTROL OF LOCAL GOVERNMENT.—Within the last century the units of local government in England experienced little regulation or control from the central government. This situation is no longer true. Although a certain control of local affairs remains in the hands of locally elected officials and councils, local government has been drawn into intimate relation with the national government at salient points. The local units are no mere subdivisions of the national government, as they are in France or Japan; nevertheless the local and national structures have been integrated into a single system.

The centralization of English local government has come about gradually, in accordance with no fixed theory or plan. The process has run counter to strong traditions of local independence, and has been accepted grudgingly. The national control has come to be exerted in several ways: Parliament enacts laws which prescribe local areas, their government, and their activities. The crown grants charters, regulates local functions, and controls national administrative activity in the localities. The Ministries of Health, Education, Transportation, and the Home Office regulate such local matters as water supply, schools, roads, and police. This type of control is largely exercised through national subsidies to local agencies on the condition that national supervision of the agencies be permitted.

HISTORIC COUNTIES.—The elements of English local government are deeply rooted in the past. Until the reforms of 1888 the principal units of local government were the fifty-two historic counties of England, such as Essex, Norfolk, and Lancashire. At that time these counties ceased to be administrative units. They are still heard of in connection with parliamentary elections since the county constituencies, which are based on population, are geographical subdivisions of the historic counties.

ADMINISTRATIVE COUNTIES.—Local administration is now carried on through sixty-two administrative counties and a larger number of county boroughs. The latter are the large urban areas throughout the country. One of the sixty-two administrative counties is the county of London, having a special administrative organization and containing nearly one eighth of the population of England. The governing organ of the ordinary administrative county is a council, partly elected and partly chosen by the elected councilors, which deals with such matters as public health, housing, poor relief, police, education, and roads. Within the administrative county are urban districts, rural districts, and municipal boroughs. The rural districts are further divided into parishes for the handling of minor affairs and the distribution of relief. Each parish and each district have an elected council. The district councils handle matters pertaining principally to sanitation, water supply, and public health. The municipal boroughs are small cities which are governed by borough councils, partly elected by the voters and partly selected by the elected councilors. These councils act as a combined executive and legislative authority, supervising the administration of the municipal departments as well as adopting the ordinances, determining the tax rate and budget, and appointing the city officials.

COUNTY BOROUGHS.—When a municipal borough attains a population of over seventy-five thousand it may be taken out of the administrative county by an act of Parliament and it then becomes a chartered county borough, completely independent of the administrative county and possessing the same powers. The form of its government remains the same, but its powers are expanded. This procedure eliminates undesirable duplication of county and municipal government.

Civil Rights

INDIVIDUAL RIGHTS.—English law does not include any legal guarantees of civil liberty comparable to the provisions of the first amendments to the United States Constitution. This condition exists because Parliament may legislate in any way it pleases without any limitation whatever, and no act it passes, however unfair, can be ruled unconstitutional by the courts. But ideas of civil liberties are accepted as being essential to free government, and public opinion will allow Parliament to limit them only in the most extreme circumstances. Even during 1940-1941, when the British Isles were in imminent danger of invasion, civil liberties were little disturbed. All through World War II freedom of speech and of the press remained, and anyone could complain about or quarrel with the policy of the government—or even advocate the ending of the war—so long as there was no evidence of a practical desire to interfere with the British war effort and help the enemy.

LOCAL GOVERNMENT IN GREAT BRITAIN

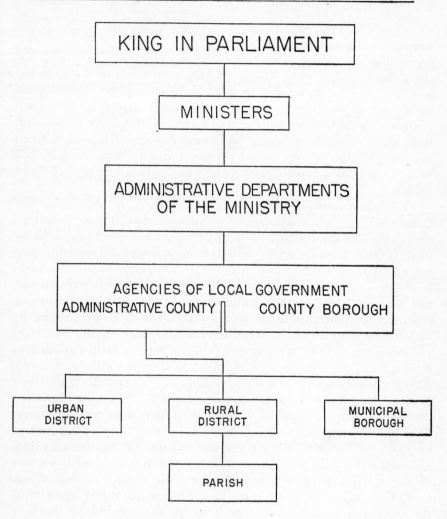

KING IN PARLIAMENT

MINISTERS

ADMINISTRATIVE DEPARTMENTS
OF THE MINISTRY

AGENCIES OF LOCAL GOVERNMENT
ADMINISTRATIVE COUNTY | COUNTY BOROUGH

URBAN
DISTRICT

RURAL
DISTRICT

MUNICIPAL
BOROUGH

PARISH

In the field of radio, it is interesting to note that the only important broadcasting facilities are controlled by the government through its British Broadcasting Corporation. The microphones of this public corporation are used for political discussions within certain mild limitations.

The British Empire-Commonwealth

IMPERIAL RELATIONSHIPS.—Since this chapter deals principally with the government of the United Kingdom of Great Britain and Northern Ireland, only brief attention can be paid to the vast system of British imperial and colonial governments. Despite recent changes in the status of India and Burma and still further changes which may be anticipated, large regions continue to bear some form of political allegiance to Great Britain. This vast aggregation of territories vitally affects the economic welfare, national defense, foreign policy, and national prestige of Great Britain.

Like the government of the United Kingdom, the British Empire-Commonwealth is a product of evolutionary development. Through the centuries it has grown piecemeal without adherence to any definite plan. It grew as a product of British strategic interests, especially those of an economic, naval, and military nature. Leading British statesmen have often regarded this territorial accretion as undesirable and costly, and only toward the end of the nineteenth century was the political control of imperial territories accepted as of benefit to Great Britain. By that time certain territories were beginning to receive large powers of self-government. The end result of this process of erratic evolutionary development has been the creation of political units which have a wide diversity of political forms and a varying degree of dependence on Great Britain. Certain governing principles underlie the whole structure, but the specific territories fall into various categories of relationship to Great Britain's authority. There are at least nine general types: local governments of the United Kingdom of Great Britain and Northern Ireland, Eire, self-governing dominions, colonies, protectorates, colonies and protectorates, trust territories, mandated territories, and condominiums.

These various types of imperial territories are linked together by their relationship to the British government, and especially in the common allegiance to the king which all of them (except Eire) acknowledge. The king is the titular head of every unit of the British Empire, whether that unit is self-governing or not. Two members of the Cabinet act as the channel of communication between the British government and the units of the Empire-Commonwealth. The Secretary of State for Dominion Affairs coordinates policies relating to the dominions, and the Secretary of State for Colonies controls all of the colonies and dependencies. Under these officials there is a large permanent bureaucracy which governs the dependencies and regulates relationships between Great Britain and the Empire-Commonwealth. The king appoints governors-general and governors for colonies, and on the advice of the dominion ministry for the dominions. In recent instances, notably in New Zealand and South Africa, the governors-general have been natives of the dominion to whose highest imperial office they were appointed, rather than residents of the United Kingdom. To facilitate imperial coordination, the self-governing dominions maintain high commissioners in London, and some of the protectorates maintain agents-general there. These officials attend to a variety of official matters in which their governments are interested. By way of reciprocation, the British government now maintains high commissioners in all the dominions. These officials have taken over the actual functions of representing the British government, while the governors-general continue to act as ceremonial representatives of Britain.

Aside from ties of political allegiance and the existence of governmental agencies for the coordination of imperial interests, the British Empire-Commonwealth is held together by intangible ties of a common ancestry for many of its people, similarity of governing principles and governing institutions, and a tradition of cooperation. Economic ties have also proved profitable. London is a large and useful banking center, and imperial trade preferences have encouraged a large exchange of goods within the British Empire-Commonwealth.

THE UNITED KINGDOM OF GREAT BRITAIN AND NORTHERN IRELAND.—The United Kingdom consists of England, Wales, Scotland, Northern Ireland, and the islands near these areas, including the Channel Islands. The government of Wales is an integral part of that of England, except that the Church of England is disestablished there. Scotland has had no separate parliament since the union of 1707 with England; there are Scottish representatives in both houses of the British Parliament and a Secretary of State for Scotland in the Ministry. Scotland, however, has separate law codes, its own court system, and an established church of its own—the Presbyterian. The six counties of Northern Ireland send thirteen members to the British House of Commons, but they also possess a parliament and government of their own for local affairs. The Channel Islands and the Isle of Man have legislatures for local purposes. With these exceptions the government of the United Kingdom is unitary and is centralized by the administrative agencies of the London government.

EIRE.—After long Irish agitation for "home rule" the British government agreed in 1921 to a treaty with Irish republican leaders which established an Irish Free State with a self-governing status in all matters except foreign relations, defense, and judicial appeals. In the 1930's the republican-minded Irish Parliament amended the constitution which had been framed under the treaty so as to abrogate the oath of allegiance to the British king, to abolish the right of the British Governor-General of the Irish Free State to withhold his assent to legislation, and to terminate appeals from the Irish courts to the Judicial Committee of the Privy Council. The British government held that the Irish Free State could legally enact these measures. In 1937 a new Irish constitution was put into effect which declared a new state of Eire, "a sovereign, independent, democratic state."

There is no mention of a British connection in this document. In 1938 Great Britain agreed by a treaty to remove all naval and military forces from Eire. Throughout World War II Eire maintained a studied neutrality, refusing to permit the use of her territory by the British armed forces and accepting the diplomatic representatives of the Axis powers in her cities. In July, 1945, Eire was declared to be a republic by her prime minister, Eamon de Valera.[25] With the passage by the Dail Eireann of the Republic of Ireland Bill 1948 the last official connection with Britain was severed, to become effective in 1949. However, the British government recognizes "factual ties" with Eire and does not consider her citizens foreigners.

SELF-GOVERNING DOMINIONS.—In the late nineteenth century representatives of the British and certain colonial governments began to meet periodically to discuss common problems. After 1907 such meetings had resulted in the formation of a permanent consultative organization composed of the political leaders of the dominions and known as the Imperial Conference. It met every four years. At the Imperial War Conferences in 1918 and during the Versailles Conference it was agreed that the contributions of the self-governing colonies in World War I gave them the right to be coequal in status, but of course not in stature, with the mother country in foreign affairs. At the 1926 Imperial Conference the Balfour Report was adopted in which the self-governing British dominions and the United Kingdom were described as "autonomous communities within the British Empire, equal in status· in no way subordinate one to another in any respect of their domestic or external affairs, though united by a common allegiance to the crown, and freely associated as members of the British Commonwealth of Nations." This statement confirmed the conception of "dominion status," which is an approximation of sovereignty, for Canada, Australia, New Zealand, the

---

[25] In the general election of 1948 de Valera's party, the Fianna Fail, was unsuccessful in achieving a majority, although it received a plurality. Accordingly, James A. Costello, a Dublin lawyer and former Attorney General, became prime minister. His coalition government, including five parties, ranges from his own Conservative Finn Gael to the left-of-center Labor party.

Union of South Africa, Newfoundland, and the Irish Free State. In 1931 the Parliament passed the Statute of Westminster, which confirmed the Balfour Report.

Under the Statute of Westminster the British king and crown are the only common elements in the governments of all of the dominions. Beyond this legal fact there is the intangible feeling for the king which the peoples of the dominions share. Through this identification of themselves with the person of the king and the institution of the crown a British unity of great psychological and political importance is created. This is further developed by the common status or common citizenship which flows from the royal allegiance. In law, however, the fealty to the king which the dominions accept is the only link of governing authority —and that largely symbolic—between the dominions. Since the kingship has this status, the Statute of Westminster declares that no alteration in the British laws of succession to the throne can be made without the approval of the parliaments of all the dominions, as well as of the British Parliament. The Statute of Westminster also declares that no law of a dominion parliament may be held invalid on the ground that it conflicts with the laws of the United Kingdom and that no law of the British Parliament can apply to any dominion unless the dominion parliament requests and consents to such legislation.

Facing bankruptcy in 1934, the dominion of Newfoundland reverted to a colonial status with a British governor and a royal commission in charge. In 1947 that former dominion sought admission to the Canadian confederation. Under the terms of the offer made by the government in Ottawa, Newfoundland would have to adjust its system of public finance to that of a province and would send six members to the Canadian Senate and seven to the House of Commons. The Canadian offer was subject to debate by the Newfoundland national convention and to a public referendum in 1948 in which the voters indicated their desire to become the tenth province of Canada.

The inhabitants of Canada, Australia, South Africa, and New Zealand have long had experience with Anglo-Saxon institutions and have been self-governing since the passage of the British North America Act of 1867, the South Africa Act of 1909, and similar acts passed in 1900 and 1907 for Australia and New Zealand, respectively. The most visible link with the British government is found in the office of governor-general—an appointee and representative of the British king. In exercising political authority the governor-general bears exactly the same relation to a dominion government as the king does to the government of the United Kingdom. As we have seen, the British high commissioner for each dominion conducts the bulk of imperial business. Each dominion has a constitution which it can amend, a parliament, and a responsible cabinet.[26] Each dominion determines whether or not appeals may be taken from its high courts to the Judicial Committee of the Privy Council. Although the dominions have, in the past, depended upon Great Britain for their defense, each has its own naval, military, and air forces. Each dominion likewise has its own representatives in foreign countries and is free to make its own treaties.

COLONIES AND DEPENDENCIES.—Most of the older dependencies are known as colonies and are directly governed under a system called "crown colony government," which is capable of development to complete self-government. Other dependencies fall in the category of protectorates or protected states. In these types central government operates through indirect rule; it governs by means of native administrations which may be developed to permit native peoples to acquire increasing responsibility. Gibraltar and British Guiana are examples of crown colonies; Northern Rhodesia and Somaliland are examples of protectorates.[27] Frequently the original trading settlement became a colony while the rest of the territory remained a protectorate; thus Nigeria is a colony and protectorate.

In some cases the appointed governor rules unassisted; in others he may be assisted by an executive council or executive council and an elected legislative council. In those regions which have achieved responsible government, a legislative assembly, elected on the same general principle as the British House of Commons, and a nominated legislative council, which constitutes an upper house, may enact the laws. The governor possesses the power of veto. Finally there are those dependencies, only one step below dominion status, which have achieved responsible government. The executive council is transformed into a cabinet representing the majority of parliament and directly answerable to the people.

At the close of World War I Britain and some of the dominions assumed responsibility for certain territories under mandate from the League of Nations. This step resulted in the trusteeship under which Great Britain held Palestine, Tanganyika, Togoland, Cameroons, Transjordan, and Iraq.[28] In like manner the Union of South Africa assumed the mandate of German Southwest Africa; New Zealand, that of the former German portion of the Samoan Islands; and Australia, that of German New Guinea. Transjordan and Iraq later achieved independence; and Tanganyika, Togoland, and Cameroons were designated trust

---

[26] Canada and Australia must have the approval of the British government to change their federal and state relationships.

[27] Egypt, a former protectorate, was declared independent in 1922.

[28] The German colonies of Cameroons (Kamerun) and Togoland were designated as British and French mandates following World War I, the larger portion of each coming under French administration.

territories in accordance with the United Nations Charter and the decision in December, 1946, of the General Assembly of the United Nations. In May, 1948, Britain terminated its mandate over Palestine, having been unable to devise a solution acceptable to both Arabs and Jews. Within the British Empire-Commonwealth there are several territories, called "condominiums," in which British authority is joint with that of some other nation. Examples of such arrangements are the New Hebrides, which are under British and French authority, Canton Island and Enderbury Island in the Pacific, which are administered as an Anglo-American condominium, and Anglo-Egyptian Sudan.

BURMA AND CEYLON.—In accordance with the decision of a constituent assembly elected by the Burmese people, Britain granted independence to the sovereign republic of Burma in January, 1948. While the British regretted that Burma did not elect to remain in the Commonwealth, they retained certain commercial interests. In addition, a British military mission was authorized to train the Burmese Army, and British troops were to be allowed to re-enter Burma in the event of any serious military threat.

In February, 1948, Ceylon became a dominion within the Commonwealth.

INDIA.—Profound changes have been made recently in the status of India. For almost two hundred years this huge subcontinent, inhabited by one fifth of the world's population, had been Britain's richest possession. The plan announced in London in June, 1947, for partition, commonwealth status, and self-rule represented the final step in a series of actions designed to make India ready to take its place among the nations of the world. With the future resting in their own hands, the Indians were given an opportunity to demonstrate their fitness to rule themselves. Has British tutelage gone far enough in preparing them for this task? Great differences of opinion exist as to whether this gradual promotion has been too rapid. It may be too soon for us to draw a sound conclusion. However, the fighting between India and Pakistan over Kashmir, a predominantly Moslem state joined by its Hindu ruler to India, is not an omen of peaceful cooperation. A further blow to the cause of peace in India was the tragic death of Mahatma Gandhi early in 1948, at the very moment when his leadership was needed most.

Progress toward self-government in India was greatly accelerated by the two World Wars. In 1919 the Government of India Act provided for increased measures of responsibility: all affairs of the provinces of British India, except finance, law, and order, were placed in the hands of Indian ministers appointed by and answerable to elected legislatures. The Act of 1935 embraced more far-reaching reforms in the creation of an all-India Federation and of provincial autonomy for the eleven provinces of British India. The coming of World War II precluded the solution of the problem of how to fit the Indian states, some five hundred in number, into the larger pattern of all India under the provision of this act. The opposition of the Congress party, representing Indian nationalist sentiment, and the interruption of the negotiations with the Indian states following the outbreak of the war, rendered the act inoperative. Shortly after the commencement of hostilities in 1939, the Congress party announced its refusal to cooperate in the prosecution of the war unless the British government declared India to be an independent nation and free to draw up her own constitution. As a result, in several of the provinces the form of government reverted to administration by the provincial governor. Continuous efforts to break the political deadlock were made throughout the period of hostilities by the viceroy; all were fruitless.

Following the end of the war, bitterness and animosity mounted swiftly between the Hindu-dominated Congress party and the Moslem League. The latter organization feared for the security of the ninety-four million Mohammedans living within the borders of the country should power fall to the Congress party. This hostility prevented the adoption of a plan for self-government proposed in May, 1946, by a British Cabinet mission. Nevertheless, the British government announced in February, 1947, its intention of transferring power in British India to Indian hands by the following June.[29] Since no apparent hope existed for any alternative plan, the British government decided upon partition of the country into the two new dominions of India and Pakistan with the latter state embracing the bulk of the Mohammedans. Consequently, the two new dominions began, in mid-1947, the tremendous job of absorbing the Indian states, dividing the armed forces, exchanging populations, while at the same time attempting to organize working governments in their respective areas. Neither India nor Pakistan have indicated their intentions with regard to remaining in the Commonwealth.

Armed Forces

IMPERIAL DEFENSE.—The real beginning of a central British defense organization occurred in 1904 with the establishment of the Committee of Imperial Defense. Although this advisory committee prepared well-laid plans prior to World War I for the transition from peace to war, it did not solve the problem of executive control in war or the need for inter-

---

[29] The Indian states were to decide their own fate; most of them have joined one of the two dominions. Only Kashmir and Hyderabad attempted to maintain their independence. In September, 1948, after persuasion had failed, the Indian government invaded Hyderabad to force that state to sign an instrument of accession; little resistance was offered by the government of the Nizam of Hyderabad.

service planning. A solution to the former requirement, however, was achieved in both wars by the establishment of a War Cabinet. In addition, during World War II Winston Churchill functioned as Minister of Defense as well as prime minister. He operated primarily through two committees with flexible membership—a Defense Committee (Operations) and a Defense Committee (Supply). A solution for the problem of interservice planning was begun in 1924 with the organization of the Chiefs of Staff Committee. During World War II the ministers of the armed services continued to be associated with the operational conduct of the war through their membership on the Defense Committee (Operations), but the Chiefs of Staff became the authority which issued unified operational instructions, and strategical guidance in the conduct of the war.

In 1946, the government issued a White Paper embodying a plan to consolidate and improve the advances toward centralized control made since 1904. The prime minister was to retain supreme responsibility for defense and to preside over the Defense Committee, which replaced the old Committee of Imperial Defense; the new committee was also made responsible to the Cabinet for the review of current strategy, as well as for coordinating departmental action in preparation for war. Members of the Committee, of which the Minister of Defense is deputy chairman, are the Lord President of the Council, the Foreign Secretary, the Chancellor of the Exchequer, the service ministers, the Minister of Labor, the Minister of Supply, and the Chiefs of Staff. The Minister of Defense was to represent the three service ministers in the Cabinet and to submit to the Cabinet and the Defense Committee proposals embracing forces and equipment in properly balanced proportions. In addition he was to present to Parliament the Cabinet's decisions on these defense proposals and to decide questions arising among the services. Responsibility for preparing strategic appreciations and military plans was to remain with the Chiefs of Staff Committee, which was to submit them to the Defense Committee.

COMMONWEALTH AND COLONIAL DEFENSE.—At present there is no dominion representation in the formulation of British defense policy, even in the advisory capacity which obtained in the old Committee of Imperial Defense. This lack of complete unity in security matters emphasizes long-standing opposition on the part of the dominions to the establishment of a central Commonwealth authority in London to review defense questions. However, despite the tendency of each dominion to regard problems from its own point of view, close and continuous Commonwealth cooperation exists in certain aspects of the security problem. Information is regularly exchanged between the members of the Commonwealth, and frequent consultations are held.

The British government is directly responsible for the defense of the Colonial Empire, and to this end an Overseas Defense Committee functions as a subcommittee of the Defense Committee. Its mission is two-fold: (1) the security of the colonies from external attack, and (2) the development of the full resources of the colonies in the event of war.

BRITISH ARMY.—Control of the land forces is in the hands of an Army Council. The president of the council is the Secretary of State for War, and its members include the Chief of the Imperial General Staff, the Adjutant General, and the Quartermaster. The Permanent Under-Secretary of State for War, a civil servant, acts as secretary of the Army Council.

During World War II the Territorial Army, a force roughly comparable to the United States National Guard, was absorbed by the Regular Army, and reserves of all types were called to active duty. After June, 1945, when the Army reached its peak strength of 2,931,000, demobilization progressed steadily.[30] However, the orderly transition from wartime to peacetime organization was hindered by two conflicting factors: (1) the necessity for large numbers of troops to fulfill continuing strategic and political commitments; (2) the demand for man power in British industry and for economy in government. In July, 1948, the armed forces totaled 846,400, of which about half were in the Army. The permanent peacetime Army was planned to be somewhat smaller, with approximately equal numbers of voluntarily enlisted regulars and conscripts. The Territorial Army was to be reconstituted, and the reserve system was to be designed to ensure speedier expansion in case of an emergency. Compared to its prewar status, the British Army of the future was expected to be larger, better trained and equipped, and much better prepared for rapid mobilization and immediate operational commitment.

BRITISH NAVY.—The Royal Navy is under the command of the Board of Admiralty, headed by the First Lord of the Admiralty. Naval, civil, and political members compose the board. After World War II the size of the Navy was slashed drastically, with the Home Fleet reduced to one cruiser and four destroyers.[31] Personnel was to be reduced to 139,500. This departure from Britain's traditional role as mistress of the seas is a reflection of the current trends to stress air strength as the basis of power at the expense of sea power. However, no reduction was announced in the Royal Navy's submarine flotillas. In an era of atomic warfare, submarines have achieved a new importance.

---

[30] Plans for continued demobilization were changed in the summer of 1948 because of the worsening international situation and the need for troops in areas of unrest, such as Malaya where Communist-inspired disorders took place.

[31] In 1939 the Home Fleet was composed of five battleships, two battle cruisers, two fleet aircraft carriers, six cruisers, twenty-eight destroyers, and twenty other craft.

BRITISH AIR FORCE.—The Royal Air Force is under the control of the Secretary of State for Air and an Air Council, similar to the Army Council. Although the strength of the Air Force was reduced from 760,000 in 1946–1947 to 237,500 in July, 1948, the "Junior Service" enjoys new prestige and occupies the position of Britain's second line of defense.[32] Experimental training with new types of planes is continuous. Despite slashes in strength, the Royal Air Force remains the most formidable air force in Europe.

Foreign Policy

PRIOR TO WORLD WAR I.—Geography and the expert seamanship of Britain's sailors, a logical corollary of Britain's island position, combined to chart the major lines of her foreign policy in the day of sail. The destruction of the Spanish Armada in 1588 gave Britain the opportunity to capitalize fully on the great advantages of her location at the gates of Europe. From then on she could be of the Continent, without being in the Continent. As carrier, processor, and merchant, she could profit handsomely from Europe's growing overseas trade, always provided that extreme commitments to any single power or group of powers were avoided. In politics, as in trade, hers was to be the role of middleman.

The growth of Britain and her Empire down through the nineteenth century is a fair commentary on the success with which she pursued those early half-seen, slowly crystallizing policies which in time became the credo of every British elector and schoolboy. On the Continent, Britain avoided entanglements beyond those necessary to prevent dominance of Europe by any single power. Spain and France, first under the Bourbons and later in Napoleon's day, were humbled in their drives for hegemony. Other would-be aspirants to dominance were blocked off by timely diplomacy.

At the same time British sailors were discovering and opening up backward areas the world over. Where the sailor had planted the nation's flag, the trader, missionary, and colonist soon followed until one could say that "the sun never sets on the British Empire." Rival seagoing imperialist powers, notably Spain, Holland, and France, were met in battle and defeated.

Hand in hand with her development as merchant and sea dog, Britain was perfecting another talent. Her scientists, inventors, and enterprisers pushed British home production to first place in the world, as they combined to launch the Industrial Revolution. For more than a century Britain stood unrivaled among the world's producing nations,

---

[32] Atomic weapons and guided missiles constitute the first line of defense; research in these fields is costing the nation $400,000,000 at present.

securing a lead which helped to bridge a difficult gap when steam replaced sail and her great fleets of merchantmen and war vessels became obsolete. A second temporary checkmate, the loss of her thirteen colonies which emerged as the United States of America, was likewise turned into an asset: first, in the formulation of wiser policies in the handling of the colonies which eventually became dominions of the British Commonwealth; secondly, in transforming early hostility toward, and rivalry with, the United States into a broad community of interest. That mollifying process, it should be noted, worked from both directions.

Britain was thus enabled to embark on her golden age in the century which separates the Congress of Vienna from the assassination at Sarajevo. Her foreign policy during that period, largely the outgrowth or repetition of earlier policy, rested on five pillars. They are worth discussing at this point.

Toward Europe they consisted of a combination of the principle of (1) "Splendid isolation" with her own particular variation of (2) the balance-of-power system. Through this two-pronged policy Britain was able to hold herself aloof from entangling alliances while shifting her weight now and then in the balance of forces on the Continent to assure against any one nation's acquiring dominance on the Continent and also to assure an adequate stability guarding Britain's overseas interests. Overseas, Britain likewise maintained a two-pronged policy. Her long head start in the Industrial Revolution permitted an expansionism which in later years came to be called "imperialism." The two overseas pillars of foreign policy might be called (3) foreign trade and investment and (4) imperialism. The nineteenth century was the century of emigration. Loyal British subjects flowed into territories under the British flag the world around. In this abbreviated oversimplified exposition of British foreign policy between the "world war" with Napoleon and World War I it is essential to cite a fifth pillar of policy. This was the preservation of *peace*. Britain stood to lose trade and resources by any major war, even though she might not be directly involved. The detailed aspects of this ninety-nine year period of British policy, such as the continuous maneuver against Russia to maintain a line of buffer states between that nation and British interests in contiguous areas, all stem in great part from the five basic objectives listed above.

The over-all strength of British policy deteriorated as other countries gained on Britain in the competition generated by the spreading Industrial Revolution. Difficulties increased as other European states strove to emulate Britain in "painting the map red" in Africa and Asia, thereby perhaps causing Britain to annex some areas just to pre-empt them from rivals. The outstanding challenge to Britain's pre-eminence in the closing decades of the nineteenth century and the opening years of the twentieth came from Germany. The latter's swift rise increasingly reduced Britain's capability to control the balance-of-power system in Europe. Germany built a powerful and modern Navy. The German-led Triple Alliance came to feel that perhaps it was strong enough on the Continent to work its will in the critical battle days if war came, even though the British threw themselves into the opposite scale. Besides there was a question, even as prior to World War II a quarter century later, as to whether Britain would fight. The pacifist, merchant influence in Britain was strong.

However, Britain was not alone in this crisis as she faced the powers of central Europe. A vague kind of alliance joined her to France, an alliance so loose that it was not much more than a scrap of paper up to the moment of the final decision. But France was bound to Russia by a pact arising naturally from France's defeat at German hands in 1870. And Russia in turn had appointed herself guardian of the infant Balkan States, particularly in any situation where they might be threatened by Teutonic expansionism. Lastly, Britain was concerned over the possibility that the North Sea ports might fall into the hands of a strong rival, a concern which naturally made her a guarantor of Belgian independence.

All these circumstances, adding up to clear community of interest, served swiftly to knit understandings, hazy pacts, and shadowy agreements into an anti-Teutonic military alliance, headed by the so-called Triple Entente—Britain, France, and Russia. Moreover, British control of the seas included the whip hand over Italy's very existence. This consideration was enough to compel the Italians to forgo their commitments to their Teutonic neighbors and ultimately to come into the war as partners of the Triple Entente.

The surge of the German armies into neutral Belgium destroyed more than the liberty of that nation. It shattered two pillars of British policy—the balance of power on the Continent, and "splendid isolation." It ended *Pax Britannica,* the balance wheel of stability which had given the modern world its greatest period of human advance to that time. And it marked the opening of a new era in world affairs, a period of destruction and bloodshed, of challenges to democratic institutions, of the emergence of political and social philosophies stemming from the darkest period of the Middle Ages. Seen in retrospect, these fateful days of 1914 raise the inevitable question as to whether a stronger British policy in the years after 1900 might have prevented the outbreak of war. One fact is clear, namely that serious doubts of military victory in Berlin would have had to be roused to stay the German decision on war. That decision was based on certain vital premises, among them Berlin's conclusion that the bonds which linked her opponents were weak; also that British pacifism might readily keep her out of war. Both of those premises could have been knocked out by more forthright, realistic British policy before it was too late. Whether it would have prevented German aggression is a matter of conjecture. It is no conjecture that the lack of such a policy helped to pave the way to war.

BRITAIN AFTER VERSAILLES.—After the signing of the Versailles Treaty in 1919 Englishmen believed that security for Great Britain and her Empire had been obtained for many years to come. The British Isles had suffered terribly both in loss of life, especially in the rising genera- tion, and in disruption of industry and commerce. From 1919 to 1938 the overwhelming majority of the British people were pacifist, in the sense that another world war seemed to them the worst catastrophe that could occur. Britain could look forward to the revival of her overseas trade and the cessation of unemployment only through years of peace and international recovery.

Yet Britain did not consider the peace treaty of 1919 as a final settlement to be maintained at all hazards. She was willing after a time to revise its terms, to reduce Germany's reparations payments, to allow Germany to regain her lost military power, and to redress other griev- ances of which Germany complained. The reasons for this generous atti- tude are not to be found solely in British altruism, but also in the fact that the revision of some parts of the Versailles Treaty fitted British na- tional interests. The British found, for example, that German deliveries of coal and merchant vessels under the Versailles agreement reduced British markets for these things and created unemployment in British mines and shipyards. The economic prostration of postwar Germany added to the problems of dwindling British markets because prewar Ger- many had been one of Britain's best customers. The British therefore had a vital stake in German economic recovery and could not share the apprehension and distrust with which France regarded any relaxation of the terms imposed on Germany in 1919.

Another factor which influenced British foreign policy was the fear and distrust of Soviet Russia, which existed not only in the minds of conservative Englishmen but throughout the Western democracies. England and the United States were actually at war with the Soviet gov- ernment in 1920, and even after all British and American troops were withdrawn from Siberia and European Russia, the British and American governments were unwilling to recognize the Communist regime at Mos- cow, partly because of their belief that it had refused to honor Russia's international obligations, and partly through fear of the spread of Com- munism in other parts of the world. A trade treaty between England and Russia was signed in 1921, however, as soon as it was evident that the Soviets were firmly established in power; and in 1924 formal recognition of the Soviet Union was granted by England's first Labor government, led by Ramsay MacDonald. This was almost ten years before recognition was conceded by the United States. Throughout these years the influence of Russia in Germany and in the Far East was a cause of real alarm in Britain and increased the desire of a limited number of British leaders to strengthen the conservative and capitalistic elements in the German state so that they might resist the impact of Communist propaganda. At the same time the unwillingness of the British democracy to face the consequences which a determined stand against Japanese aggression in the Far East might have involved led to a tacit acceptance of the early Japanese attacks upon China.

BRITAIN AND COLLECTIVE SECURITY.—Despite the fact that many influential Englishmen favored the maintenance of the traditional British policies which placed the interests of the Empire ahead of other considerations, and aimed at the maintenance of a balance of power on the continent of Europe, the majority of British voters favored full participation in the collective efforts of the League of Nations to foster peace and disarmament. After 1919 successive British Cabinets worked through the League Council and Assembly in international affairs and strove continuously to promote the rule of law in the community of nations. The British people were probably not sufficiently aware of how necessary a threat of force was as an instrument in building up the authority of the League, but they were sincere in their desire to uphold that authority by all peaceful means.

Unfortunately the British definition of "collective security" did not agree with that of her late ally France. It was the firm belief of the French that the policy of "collective security" should be aimed principally at maintaining the treaty restrictions on Germany. The British refused repeatedly to commit themselves to various French proposals and policies which had this aim in view. When the United States failed to sign the projected triple alliance under which Britain and the United States would have guaranteed the territorial integrity of France, Britain also declined to sign. When France occupied the Ruhr Valley in 1923 to punish Germany for defaulting on her reparations payments, the British government openly disapproved of the French policy. And, in 1924, Britain and her dominions refused to sign the Geneva Protocol, under which members of the League agreed to punish as an aggressor any nation which refused to submit its quarrels with other nations to arbitration. The basis for this refusal was that such an agreement might have committed them to the defense of territories where no vital British interests were involved. Not only did Britain disapprove of French policy when its aim was to prevent the recovery of Germany, but she disapproved also of French commitments to the small nations of central Europe. France had welded these nations together into the so-called "Little Entente" as a safeguard against German aggression. The British saw more clearly than the French that alliances with the small nations of Europe meant the assumption of the liabilities of those nations. In 1925 the British thought they had found the solution for their difficulties with the French when they signed the Locarno treaties, in which they gave the same guarantees to Germany and to France against aggression by the other party. But even the Locarno treaties were allowed to lapse when Hitler moved his armies into the Rhineland in 1936. Englishmen had so accustomed themselves to believe that Germany must be allowed to recover her full status in the family of nations that not even Hitler's flagrant disregard of important international agreements to which he had himself subscribed aroused them fully to a realization of the new danger to the peace of Europe.

During this same period the British government supported the general program of the League of Nations and signed such agreements as the Washington naval agreements of 1922. From 1919 to 1934 Great Britain was the leading nation advocating disarmament. Only after Germany left the Geneva Disarmament Conference of 1933 when France refused to agree to equality of German armament with her own did Britain admit the failure of her disarmament efforts and prepare to strengthen her air forces. With the Japanese invasion of Manchuria in 1931 the League of Nations was subjected to the first of a series of crises. In this instance cooperation between Great Britain and the United States was lacking and, in the absence of a British-American front, the League was impotent. Again, in the Ethiopian crisis of 1935 Britain and France were unwilling to bring the full force of sanctions to bear against Italy. On this occasion fear of Germany and of breaking the Stresa front by driving Italy into Germany's arms resulted in the adoption of halfway measures by the League. This disastrous policy brought defeat for Ethiopia, for the League of Nations, and for British prestige. The limited sanctions that were imposed drove Italy into alliance with Germany and caused Britain to seek safety in rearmament rather than in collective security.

THE FAILURE OF BRITISH POSTWAR POLICIES.—By 1938 it had become apparent that British postwar foreign policies of peaceful rehabilitation, disarmament, and collective security had failed and that Britain must reverse them if she were to survive. Not only had Germany made great progress in rearming her land and naval forces, but her air strength had become a threat to Britain. Italy, after the Italo-Ethiopian War, had allied herself with Germany in the Rome-Berlin Axis agreement of 1936. In the same year Germany and Italy had intervened in the Spanish Civil War, while Britain and France were maneuvered into a position of nonintervention in that conflict. In the meantime Japan had denounced the restrictions upon her naval strength which she had agreed to in the Washington and London Naval Conferences. Shortly afterward Japan obviously began to challenge British interests and sea power in the Pacific. In 1936 Japan joined the growing fascist coalition by signing the Anti-Comintern Pact with Germany.

In the face of these threats to her position in Europe, the Mediterranean, and the Pacific, Britain pursued several new courses concurrently. The desire of the British people for peace resulted in a continued effort to appease the growing demands of Germany. Britain at the same time began to strengthen her armed forces. She abandoned collective security in favor of a series of bilateral treaties with friendly nations and with potential enemy nations which were designed to strengthen the British position. In 1935 Britain independently agreed to German repudiation of the naval restrictions of the Versailles Treaty in return for a pledge that the German Navy would not exceed 35 per cent of the British. In the spring of 1938 the British government negotiated a series of treaties which were designed to appease Italy. Under these agreements Italian troops were to be withdrawn from Spain, Britain recognized the Italian conquest of Ethiopia, and a naval understanding for the Mediterranean Sea and the Suez Canal was reached. At the same time Britain and France had begun to reconcile their differences, reaching an understanding based upon the obvious Axis threat to both their interests when they entered into a military alliance in April, 1938.

APPEASEMENT.—The last great effort of the British government to maintain the peace of Europe has come to be identified with the Ministry of Neville Chamberlain (1937-1940) and is known as the policy of appeasement. It had the dual purpose of maintaining peace at the cost of considerable concessions to the Axis nations and of gaining time in which to increase the armed strength of Britain. The French government was so weakened by internal dissidence and so fearful of its security that it very willingly accepted and followed the British lead in this policy. The underlying desire of the appeasement policy was that a workable understanding, between Britain and France on the one side and the fascist powers on the other, could be reached.

The appeasement policy faced its greatest test in the Munich Conference of September, 1938, when Neville Chamberlain and Edouard Daladier, the responsible heads of the British and French governments, met Adolf Hitler and Benito Mussolini, the dictators of Germany and Italy, and agreed to German demands that the Sudetenland of France's ally Czechoslovakia be annexed to Germany. Prime Minister Chamberlain returned from Munich believing that he had maintained, as he said, ". . . peace in our time." His belief was generally accepted in Britain— although Anthony Eden had resigned as Chamberlain's Secretary of State for Foreign Affairs earlier in 1938 in protest against the appeasement policy. Winston Churchill led Conservative opposition to the policy. At the same time, both the Labor and the Liberal parties disagreed with it.

WORLD WAR II.—The efficacy of the appeasement policy in deterring aggressive German moves was disproved when Hitler, who had said at Munich that Germany had no further territorial demands in Europe, sent German troops to seize the remainder of Czechoslovakia in March, 1939. With this act of aggression the British and French governments abandoned appeasement, continued to strengthen their armed forces, and agreed to stop German expansion at the cost of war if necessary. In the face of German demands upon Poland for possession of the Polish Corridor and upon Danzig for annexation to Germany, the British and French governments announced on March 31, 1939, that they would guarantee Polish independence. A week later they did the same thing for Greece and Rumania.

Germany continued to press demands upon Poland and to prepare for war. On May 22, 1939, she signed a ten-year military alliance with Italy and on August 23 she concluded a nonaggression pact with Russia. On August 29 Germany demanded that Great Britain arrange to have a Polish delegate with full powers to negotiate the Polish-German disputes reach Berlin on the next day. The British government replied that the procedure was unreasonable and the time limit impracticable. On August 31 the German government presented to the British Ambassador to Germany a sixteen-point demand for settlement of the Polish controversy. Before the Polish government could reply and without a declaration of war, German armies moved into Poland on September 1. Great Britain made a final effort to stop the German aggression by presenting an ultimatum to the German government, demanding the immediate withdrawal of German armies from Poland. When the British ultimatum was ignored, the British and French governments announced on September 3, 1939, that they were at war with Germany.

THE COURSE OF THE WAR.—Obviously, no lengthy account of Great Britain's part in World War II can be given in this outline of British foreign policy. Only the salient events and the main British alliances can be noted. All of the dominions of the British Commonwealth of Nations, except Eire, voted to join the British war effort at the very beginning of hostilities. In 1940 Italy declared war against Britain and France and helped defeat the latter in the Axis campaign against France. Italy, in turn, was defeated and compelled to surrender to the British and American forces which invaded the Italian peninsula in 1943. Japan declared war on the United States and Great Britain on December 8, 1941, the day after the attack on the Hawaiian Islands. The Japanese attack automatically brought the United States into the world-wide conflict on the side of Great Britain. Russia was invaded by Germany in 1941 and in May, 1942, entered into a twenty-year military alliance with Great Britain. American interest in the British war effort was shown by official and unofficial aid to Britain before actual American entry into the war. As early as 1940 Great Britain and the United States began their military cooperation with the exchange of fifty American destroyers for the right to establish American bases in certain British dependencies in the western Atlantic. On January 29, 1941, the first American units arrived in Newfoundland. Later in the same year American forces established bases in Bermuda, Trinidad, British Guiana, St. Lucia, Australia, and Jamaica. A major step toward making the United States the arsenal of democracy was taken in March, 1941, when Congress enacted the Lend-Lease Act which authorized the President to "sell, transfer title to, exchange, lease, lend, or otherwise dispose of . . . any defense article" to any nation whose defense be found vital to the defense of the United States. Immediately $7,000,000,000 was appropriated for aid to countries resisting Axis aggression. The identity of American and British major aims was revealed on August 14, 1941, when Prime Minister Winston Churchill, and President Roosevelt issued the Atlantic Charter. In this statement the heads of the two governments expressed the common principles contained in their respective policies: principles of peace, nonaggression, national self-determination, free access to raw materials, economic security, freedom of the seas, and disarmament.

Entry of the United States into the hostilities led shortly to close collaboration of the Allied Nations in their joint operations. On January 1, 1942, the United States and Great Britain led a large group of nations in the formation of the United Nations in opposition to Germany and her Axis partners. Later in the same year the first American units landed in the British Isles and in Egypt to cooperate with British forces. Subsequently British and American forces participated in joint offensives all over the world—in India, the southwest Pacific, north Africa, Sicily, and Italy, and in the air war over Germany. The climax of this joint offensive war came in June, 1944, with the successful invasion of western Europe by way of Normandy, followed later by landings at other places on the Continent. Under the command of General Dwight D. Eisenhower, the Allied armies broke through the coastal defenses, liberated Paris by the end of August, reconquered Belgium and a part of the Netherlands, and at the beginning of the year 1945 were hammering at the western defenses of Germany itself. After a Russian offensive across Poland to the Oder River in the early spring and British and American drives across the Rhine to the Elbe and Danube, a little later, the end of the European phase of World War II came on May 7, 1945, with the unconditional surrender of the German High Command to the Allied army commanders.

On September 2, 1945, Great Britain joined the United States and their allies in accepting the surrender of Japan. Although the major campaigns in the Pacific had been fought by the armed forces of the United States and China, the contributions of the British and Australian naval and land forces had sped the ultimate victory.

Problems Confronting Britain and the Empire

The Briton of today has a bitter pill to swallow. Having survived a war in which for a considerable period he alone confronted unflinchingly the fury of Nazi Germany, he finds that victory for him means prolonged austerity at home and a diminishing role on the international stage. After four years in the trenches of World War I, his father expected to see England transformed, in the words of Lloyd George, to "a land fit for heroes." The promise failed to materialize. Following World War II, the present Briton discarded capitalism with its inherent vice of "the unequal sharing of blessings." To date, however, the Labor government has been unable to offer more than "an equal sharing of miseries" and it is difficult to visualize how a Conservative government could offer a better prospect.

ECONOMIC PROBLEMS.—The sudden end of the war in the Far East was soon followed by President Truman's announcement of the cessation of lend-lease exchanges on a wartime basis. Although the action of the United States was implicit in the Lend-Lease Law as enacted by the Congress, the termination of such aid was publicly lamented in Parliament, both by Prime Minister Attlee and by Winston Churchill. They pointed out that Britain must import food and many other necessities in order to live, that on the basis of her agreement with the United States she had ceased to manufacture for export, converting all her production to the war effort, and that she needed time to reconvert to her normal production for export. In order to assist Britain during the period of reconversion for peace, a loan of $3,750,000,000 was granted by the United States. In the meantime as we have noted before, Britain embarked on a program that had as its goal the raising of exports to 75 per cent more goods by volume than those of 1938 in order to redress the balance of trade.

Britain had become a debtor nation. One of the political parties issued a pamphlet which set forth the nation's financial straits in terms easily understandable to all. "Before 1914 the people of this country were owed by the rest of the world a debt equal to £100 each. Today each one

of us in Britain owes the rest of the world £100." [33] Overseas investments, the heritage of the nineteenth century when Britain was the workshop of the world and London its financial center, have been largely
liquidated by the staggering burden of two great wars. It was this income that made up the difference between the value of her imports and
her exports which for years have not been great enough to pay for the
food and raw materials imported by Britain.

Many factors combine to complicate Britain's attainment of her export goal. Inflation in the United States has had the effect of reducing
the value of the American loan by 40 per cent. Acts of nature, such as
the blizzard of 1947, followed by floods and drought, have upset the economic timetable. The British people are war weary. The stamina and
courage exhibited during the darkest war years are still present, but the
nation is tired and not yet psychologically prepared for a struggle that
will be waged in an atmosphere of grim austerity. In recent decades
there has been a progressive ossification of business enterprise, one of
the evidences being widespread cartel agreements with foreign producers.
Overconservatism and the lack of vigorous leadership on the part of
business permitted British methods of production to lag behind those of
the United States. As a result, much of the industrial machine was already obsolescent when it was subjected to the exacting strain of World
War II production. While Britain is able to sell all the goods she can
produce today, the return of a buyer's market may find her in a poor
position to compete with rivals whose production methods are modern
and efficient. Higher wages and increased governmental benefits, unless
accompanied by rising productivity, inevitably result in higher unit cost
and hence act as an obstacle in competing for the international market.
This fact draws attention to one of the greatest problems confronting
the British government today: as yet, the working class does not appreciate the real gravity of Britain's position. For many years the workers,
united in their support of the Labor party, were taught that "the bosses"
were their enemy, that votes for Labor meant shorter hours, greater pay,
increased privileges. These victories have been won; it is not too much
to say that the workers are now a privileged class and that the hardships
of the middle class have increased. The goal of increasing exports over
the 1938 average can be achieved only by higher production per man-
hour and the removal of restrictive practices that have grown up over

---

[33] It has been estimated that World War II cost Britain about one third of her
national wealth or nearly $30 billion:

War damage at home	$ 6	billion
Depreciation and obsolescence at home	$ 3½	billion
Shipping losses	$ 3	billion
Capital assets sold abroad	$ 4½	billion
Liabilities incurred abroad	$11½	billion

the years. Yet the memory of years of "ca' canny," similar to the American practice of "feather-bedding," cannot be forgotten overnight. Talk of increasing the production per man-hour sounds to the worker like the words to be expected from a capitalist employer but not from a socialist government. In short, he is learning that there is no form of society or government that demands more from the individual than socialism. Furthermore, he does not see about him the evidences of crisis. Jobs are plentiful. What food he can buy is relatively cheap because of price stabilization. There is no inducement for working long hours because he could buy nothing with the extra pay and, under the existing income tax laws, much of the overtime pay would be taken by the government. Consequently, broad plans of social insurance and standard wage rates not closely related to effort on the part of the individual or his standard of productivity appear to have weakened the will to work. A shortage of man power and an unwillingness of the workers to enter certain industries, such as the mines, have further hampered efforts to increase production.

Though the early economic future promises little beyond hard work and doing without, such obstacles may be exaggerated. British management has shaken off its complacency and realizes what must be done. A vigorous campaign is under way to impress upon each citizen the gravity of the situation and his part in determining the future of the nation. Finally, there has been no evidence that Britain, still and always priding itself on losing every battle except the last one, is prepared to go down without a struggle.

COLONIAL PROBLEMS.—World War II brought with it an upsurge of nationalism among the colonial peoples the world over, and particularly in those regions where Japanese military action had forced evacuation by the white colonial powers. This trend, augmented by the traditional anti-imperialist policy of the Labor party, has accelerated the movement of the British colonies toward ultimate self-government within or without the Commonwealth.

In 1940 Parliament passed the Colonial Development and Welfare Act, appropriating approximately $200,000,000 to be spent over a period of ten years "for any purpose likely to promote the development of the resources of any colony or the welfare of its people." Five years later, a second act added five years to the plan and raised the money allocation to $480,000,000. A Colonial Economic and Development Council advises the Colonial Office in framing plans for Empire economic and social development. These acts represent a considerable effort toward the economic development and social improvement of the 60,000,000 people who compose the Colonial Empire, and hence stand as a major step in the direction of eventual self-government.

INTERNATIONAL PROBLEMS.—As World War II closed, the stage was set for continuing friendship and cooperation between Great Britain and the Soviet Union. The British, who had suffered so much during six long years, felt a genuine sympathy for the Russians, from whom victory had exacted an even heavier toll. The United Nations, which the British government had supported enthusiastically from the first, was hopefully regarded as a proper agency for settling international problems. The hope soon died. The year 1946 found the Soviet Union rejecting Britain's cooperation and launching a verbal attack directed at breaking up Anglo-American partnership by striking at the weaker of the two. During this period Britain performed, in a smaller way, the same service for the Western World that she had performed during the periods 1914-1917 and 1939-1941. She faced Soviet Russia, the potential aggressor, while the American public was waking up to the hard realities of the postwar world. The effort did little more than reveal Britain's strategic weakness. Leadership of the Western powers has passed into the hands of the United States. With the deterioration of relations between the Soviet Union and the United States, many in Britain have shown that they would like to follow a middle course and endeavor to construct a bridge between East and West. In general, however, votes in the United Nations and in the meetings of the foreign ministers of the United States, Great Britain, France, and the Soviet Union have found Britain, the United States, and (in later meetings) France in substantial agreement. The ability of the three powers to reach working settlements for points of difference is in direct contrast with the customary Soviet intransigeance.

In January, 1948, Foreign Secretary Bevin announced a historic change in British foreign policy by proposing a "Western Union" of European countries. Such a bloc had long been supported by Winston Churchill, but many British Socialists were extremely reluctant to break with Soviet Russia. The Russian attitude toward the European Recovery Program forced Britain to come to that decision. It is too early to observe the full effects of Britain's abandonment of the balance-of-power concept. Understandably first reactions to the proposal were not enthusiastic. The natural reluctance of the powers concerned to abandon the prejudices and barriers that have existed for centuries is being offset by a realization of the choice they must make. Faced by a hostile union of powers east of the Iron Curtain and unable to depend on the workings of the United Nations to guarantee their security, they have demonstrated a growing appreciation of the need for cooperation and united action. Undoubtedly the problem of their security, like their economic problem, will depend in the immediate future on the amount of aid and support they can expect from the United States.

Previous efforts by Whitehall to bring the East and West together were a direct reflection of the strategic position and strategic predicament of Britain. The geographic conditions which formerly operated to give her security now operate to her disadvantage. No longer is the English Channel an effective obstacle to enemy attack. As a small, densely populated country, Britain is most vulnerable to attack from the air. Completely dependent on imports of food in order to feed her people, she is insecure in an age when the Royal Navy can no longer guarantee safe passage for her merchant ships. Current activity in the Middle East and Africa indicates how new strategic concepts and means of warfare have compelled radical alterations and even reversals of traditional British foreign policy. For almost one hundred years the maintenance of the life line through the Mediterranean Sea was regarded as of primary importance. Yet the withdrawal of British troops from Palestine, with the termination of her mandate, as well as from Egypt, serves to make defense of the Suez Canal and control of the Mediterranean difficult problems in an air age. The contemplated establishment of her Middle East headquarters in Kenya, an area from which an air route across Equatorial Africa could be controlled, as well as the longer ocean route around the Cape of Good Hope may point to the eventual abandonment of the Mediterranean route as unfeasible in the event of war.

Great Britain is a prime example of the impoverishment and dislocation brought by modern war equally to the victor and vanquished. Her search for world peace through the medium of the United Nations is conducted in the light of her experience of the interwar years that any international security organization must be backed by adequate national power (military and economic, for example) and that those nations which have the power must accept major responsibility for maintaining the peace. To that end Britain is stretching the slender means available for her armed forces to the maximum, concentrating those forces in areas of prime importance.

Counting Britain out as a great power is nothing new among the seers and prophets. German and Italian experts of the crystal globe were notably outspoken on that point a few years back, and more recently have been succeeded by the Russians. The admitted weakness of her position, and her poor chances of survival as a world power can, however, be readily exaggerated, as in the past. True, the British government has come to accept the necessity for reducing commitments of man power in overseas regions rather than attempt to cling to military power beyond the capacity of the nation's economic resources to support it. On the other hand, the volume of Britain's trade is still the second largest in the world. Every index of production shows important, if sporadic, gains in her postwar production. World demand for her output is not only well in excess of current productive capacity, but the margin of difference is rising. Such facts provide some silver lining to the cloud of her postwar status, and offer some hope that her income may improve substantially so that it can balance outgo. Britain, in brief, is a convalescent nation rather than a sick one.

The prophets of doom have invariably included in their predictions the disintegration of the British Commonwealth. They point out that these adolescents, now grown to maturity, are speaking up in Commonwealth affairs as independent nations, and they deduce from that fact the conclusion that Britain should no longer look to the dominions to support her foreign policy. Such analysis is both hasty and incomplete. It assumes that the unfailing support which Britain has had from her overseas offspring (except Eire) in every past major crisis will not again be forthcoming. And it takes too little note of the growing strength of these units, or of the further growth open to them. Canada, Australia, and South Africa, in particular, boast natural resources which can support in comfort populations several times the present figures. The flight from austerity in Britain is moving at least a part of the human surplus from the homeland to the dominions as fast as shipping becomes available. A similar surplus exists in almost all parts of the troubled Continent. Such unbalance between the regions of relative glut and sparseness of population, particularly where the sparseness goes hand in hand with abundance of resources, cannot fail to make itself felt. To the extent that the dominions absorb and digest the overflow from Britain and the Continent, their human resources will add to the strength of each favored unit of the Commonwealth.

All these swelling resources, human and material, are of value only if they stand available to the group of nations, the Commonwealth, when needed. It is hardly necessary to add that in the modern world great population units, particularly those separated by vast distances, cannot be effectively bound together by force or by any machinery of governmental structure. The only effective bond is a community of interest. The British Commonwealth of today is cemented by the same tangible items of common interests as existed prior to World War II. They include language, law, culture, ancestry, tradition, history, and economic ties. In addition, the postwar split between East and West has added a powerful intangible to the older bonds of unity. It lies in a common sense of insecurity, combined with the realization that peace has become indivisible. In such a world, the mutual trust and confidence of the members of the Commonwealth in each other beget cooperative action for the common good. The net effect of all these forces makes the British Commonwealth the strongest voluntary regional arrangement in the world today. Moreover, the strong tie of Canada, foremost among Britain's off-spring, to the United States through the Canadian-United States Permanent Joint Defense Board, to mention but one ingredient of the cement, serves to strengthen both the Commonwealth and Britain.

THE GOVERNMENT OF

FRANCE

◇◇

Introduction

FRANCE IN TRANSITION.—Twice in less than five years the French people
have been buffeted by the storms of extreme political transition. The
first crisis came in 1940 at the close of the most disastrous war in France's
history as a national state. It terminated briefly with the division of the
country into two regions, one occupied and ruled by the victorious
Wehrmacht; the other, unoccupied, under the nominal rule of Marshal
Henri Philippe Pétain. Even this poorly disguised semblance of French
autonomy vanished abruptly when, in November, 1942, the Anglo-
American forces under General Eisenhower made good their landing in
French Morocco and Algeria.

The reversal of the military tide which, in 1944, swept France clear
of the invaders brought on the second storm. As the Allied armies advanced, the liberated areas were successively restored to French direction.
Into the gap moved the authority of the Provisional Government of the
French Republic, which had evolved from the Free French Movement,
initiated in London by General Charles de Gaulle soon after France's
surrender in 1940.

Four years of German rule, added to the destructive effect of the
campaigns of 1940 and 1944, had accomplished the economic ruin of
France to a degree where outside relief alone could provide the people
with bare subsistence. Devastated industrial centers, with their half-
starved populations, disrupted communications, and an empty treasury,
provided a poor basis for the rebuilding of a national political organization. No less discouraging was the moral debris which had separated
the French people into those who had wholeheartedly opposed the Germans and those who were deemed tainted by various degrees of collaboration with the enemy.

On such a foundation was it necessary to build a new, healthy,
and vigorous political structure if France was to be restored to its traditional place in the family of nations. Before turning to an examina-

tion of the contemporary Fourth French Republic, a survey of the rise of modern political institutions in France with a brief scrutiny of their development in the Third Republic should make that examination more valuable to the student.

Contrast between British and French Political Institutions

AGE AND CONDITIONS OF DEVELOPMENT.—The first difference which stands out between British and French political institutions is the variance in their ages and conditions of development. As we have seen in the preceding chapter, the British constitution and the governmental apparatus which has grown with that constitution are of ancient origin. Moreover, this progress is noted for having been achieved less by the bloody agony of revolution than by slow, pragmatic evolution. French parliamentary experience, on the other hand, covers a span of scarcely more than a century and a half. Moreover, the political practices and machinery of modern France are the aftermath of a catastrophic revolution whose tremors even yet agitate the body politic; of *coups d'état;* of minor revolts; and of Robespierrean and Napoleonic demagoguery.

GOVERNMENTAL STABILITY.—In view of the evolutionary nature of the development of the government of Great Britain, one is not surprised that the British government has proved itself far more stable than that of France. Britain has had one constitution—in large part unwritten—slowly adapted through the centuries to fit a society evolving within the law that bound all classes. The tradition of government of law has prevented bitter cleavages of British society. From this basic unity of society and avoidance of radical change has ensued a natural reluctance to replace the element in control of government. In a free society, however, there must be a means of expressing the differences of opinion which are inevitable in any society. Thus there must be some means of changing the element in control of the government when that element no longer reflects the considered opinions of a majority of the people. The British people generally adhere to two parties as being the minimum number which can preserve their freedom and the desirable number to ensure stable, efficient government.

Not so the French. Their many bloody political struggles and changes of government by force rather than by general consent have left a legacy of bitter divisions in French society and a feeling of insecurity in the various factions relative to their lawful rights. Consequently, each group gaining control of the government has sought to perpetuate a program by means of a written constitution. The cadavers of these constitutions litter French political history since 1789. A further manifestation of the factionalism of French society is the kaleidoscope of political parties. This multiplicity of parties has usually prevented any one party from securing the support of a majority of the electorate. In order for a cabinet to be formed and the government to function, there must then be a coalition of parties. Such a system permits each party within and without the government to undermine the ministry while enabling each party to disclaim responsibility for any faults of the administration. Likewise, a mere handful of men may be able to dictate what policies shall be or to paralyze the government and force the cabinet to resign. It is little wonder, then, that whereas the average life of a British ministry is measured in years, that of French ministries is reckoned in months.

POLITICAL PHILOSOPHIES.—A third major difference between Britain and France politically is that British political philosophies have tended to follow rather than to anticipate events, whereas the French theorists have tended toward elaborate philosophies sometimes a millennium removed from existing conditions. This dissimilarity may also be said to be in large part a natural consequence of the diverse ages and conditions of development in the two countries. As British political practices have kept pace—however tardily and approximately at times—with the ideas and needs of the politically conscious portions of the populace, there has been little incentive to construct elaborate political castles in the air and to defend them with fanatical fervor. With French political development retarded for so long and with the government failing to keep pace with the ideas and needs of the people, there inevitably resulted a flood of proposed remedies for existing evils. Under conditions such as existed in *l'ancien régime,* men are prone to overlook the thorny paths and pitfalls concealed by a new political philosophy and to think only of the evils the philosophy proposes to eliminate. Could the theories of the French reformers have been put to the test bit by bit, their good points and shortcomings could, perhaps, have been revealed in an atmosphere permitting compromise and conciliation. Royal repression followed by the bloodshed and lawless terror of revolution, however, gave to French political philosophies a dogmatic quality conspicuously lacking across the Channel.

Development of l'Ancien Régime

HISTORICAL BACKGROUND.—To understand why France was torn by revolution, we must—even in this brief survey—glance at the background of that upheaval. While French political institutions are young, French political thought is a part of the streams of Western culture that go back to ancient Rome, Greece, and beyond. We can, however, confine our attention to more immediate times.

TRIUMPH OF DIVINE-RIGHT ABSOLUTISM.—Thus skipping over considerably more than a thousand years of cultural development in what is now France, we arrive at the emergence of the first French kings, the House of Capet, in the tenth century. With them started the long, bloody, bitter struggle to assert the supremacy of the monarchy. Opposed to the establishment of a sovereign French nation under an all-powerful monarch were: the feudal nobility, the church, and at times the *communes*[1] (medieval cities). The objectives of the monarchy were substantially realized in the fifteenth century, but the struggle extended well into the seventeenth century. Finally, absolutism triumphed over all: pope, feudal noble, heretic, townsman, and peasant. Only two institutions—the estates-general and the *parlements*—existed which could have developed into constitutional means of representative government, but these were kept subordinate to royal will.[2] Increasingly, all political power rested in the person of the king.

FRANCE DISUNITED AND INEFFICIENTLY GOVERNED.—The triumph of royal despotism reached its zenith under Louis XIV (1643–1715). However, his political practice of superimposing irresponsible royal authority on relics of feudal and medieval institutions was incompatible with his encouragement of the growth of commerce and industry in the economic field. Thus the outmoded fundamental divisions of French society and the inefficiency of the government became increasingly apparent. The economic center of gravity had shifted from the feudal nobility with their relatively inelastic base of agriculture to the middle class of the towns with their ever-expanding base of commerce and industry. But the political power had shifted from the nobility to the king. The triumph of monarchy had been so complete that no recognized channel existed through which public opinion could be expressed. With the king increasingly insulated from the problems of his realm, the growing dissatisfactions of the people in the eighteenth century could evoke no effective response.

CRITICS OF L'ANCIEN RÉGIME.—While French political development marked time, British evolution continued. In Britain the bloodless revolution of 1688 confirmed the supremacy of government of law over government of men. The apologist after the fact was John Locke (1632–1704). He is important to France as one of the first men to present clearly the idea of the sovereignty of the people and of man possessing inalienable rights. Locke exerted a powerful influence on French writers

---

[1] Each of these was at various times an ally of the monarchy. Thus the *communes* fought on the side of the king against the feudal nobility.

[2] In fact, the estates-general, which should have evolved into a parliament, was of no importance after 1369, and in 1469 the Estates confirmed their impotence by asking the king to rule without them.

who gave voice to the discontent of sections of the population. Among the earliest to be so influenced by Locke was the Baron de Montesquieu (1689–1755), first of the *philosophes*. After Montesquieu (in point of political writing) came such men as Voltaire (1694–1778),[3] Diderot, and Turgot, who attacked tyranny, injustice, intolerance, and superstition. The early *philosophes* were, on the whole, men drawing upon both reason and sober experience in support of their views. About 1760, however, responsible Lockeian thought was all but obscured in the fog of unbalanced thought and perverted history flowing from the school of Rousseau (1712-1778). By blending ideas from such diverse sources as Plato, Machiavelli, and Locke with his own disordered, conflicting thoughts and emotions, Rousseau ran the full gamut from a mythical era of virtuous and noble savagery, through a society embracing the sovereignty and natural rights of the people, on to a final totalitarian state permitting no right of dissent. Across the ocean, the ideas of Locke flowered in the minds of such men as Jefferson and thus transformed traveled to France with American diplomats and with the French officers and soldiers who had participated in the American war of independence.

Given the continued failure of absolutism to cope successfully with either the internal or the external problems of France, we may safely say that revolution was inevitable without benefit of the *philosophes*. However, one may credit them with crystallizing opinion against the evils and abuses of *l'ancien régime:* confusion and incompetence in administration, injustice in taxation, favoritism before the law, outmoded regulation of industry and commerce, and exploitation of the peasantry. We may also credit in large measure the Rousseau school with some of the extreme aspects of the revolution. His was the one clear call to bloody revolt, to the surrender of all individual rights, to the elimination of any right to dissent.

Governmental Progress, 1789–1870

COMPLEX FACTORS.—With almost the entire edifice of *l'ancien régime* swept away in 1789, the French people began a quest for an adequate substitute. To describe the ensuing experiences in terms of a class struggle is only partially correct; the complete story is not so simple. Among the factors involved were: the traditional loyalty of the French people to their ancient monarchy; the continued failure of the monarchy to produce great men; the bitter factionalism engendered by the violence of the Revolution; the political ignorance of the French; their enmity toward England, their best model for reform; the existence of diverse dynasties competing for the throne; the lack of unanimity in any social class; ex-

---

[3] More a popularizer of others' ideas than a speculative philosopher.

istence of radical minorities attempting by force to institute reforms (to complete "the unfinished Revolution") not desired by the majority; ignorance of the economic and social forces of the Industrial Revolution; development of the art of demagoguery; and continued disasters in French foreign policy.

TWO CHARACTERISTICS.—These complex factors gave two principal characteristics to the period of transition from absolute monarchy in 1789 to enduring republic in 1871. First there was the struggle to arrive at a stable division of powers between the executive and legislative branches of the government. The radicals of the Left in reaction against royal authority naturally favored government by sovereign assembly. The conservatives of the Right in reaction against bloodshed and chaos believed in a strong executive which could prevent domination of the legislature by mobs. As both forms of rule in practice developed into dictatorships, the tendency was to evolve a compromise in the form of government responsible to a parliamentary majority. After earlier experiments had proved to lack lasting stability, parliamentary government was definitively adopted by the Third Republic. However, as we shall see later in the chapter, the question of the proper division of powers between the executive and the legislature continues to be a part of French politics.

The second attribute of the transition period was that with monarchical absolutism definitely abolished each government after 1789 tended to retain a major part of the structure existing in the previous regime. For example, the revolutionary governments, after attempting local self-government with unhappy results, found themselves forced to retain the idea of centralization of power that had developed with the monarchy. Succeeding governments added to the structure of a uniform system of government for all France started by the revolutionaries. Upon his coming to power Napoleon I, in a display of civil genius equal to his prowess on the battlefield, further improved upon the governmental edifice. The system, both of law codes and of centralized administration, which he perfected has continued fundamentally unchanged through all the subsequent regimes. Thus, later struggles have generally been to determine which elements of the French nation would control the machinery of government rather than to rebuild the machine.

Background of the Third French Republic

THE SUCCESSION OF MODERN FRENCH GOVERNMENTS.—We have noted that from the French Revolution of 1789 to the present day, various groups and individuals have created and destroyed a series of governments in their struggles for political control of France. The French revolutionaries themselves abolished the centuries-old absolute monarchy of the Bourbon kings and substituted for it the First French Republic in 1792. After several years of experimentation with republican forms this government was converted into an empire by Napoleon Bonaparte in 1804. When Napoleon's government collapsed from the military defeats it had suffered, the Bourbon kings were restored for the short period from 1814 to 1830. The revolution of the latter year elevated Louis Philippe of the Bourbon-Orleans branch of the French royal house to the French kingship until the revolution of 1848 created a Second French Republic. Four years later this government in turn became the Second Napoleonic Empire through the *coup d'état* of the Prince-President Louis Napoleon, a nephew of Napoleon Bonaparte. In 1870 the Second Napoleonic Empire came to an end as a result of French defeat in the Franco-Prussian War.

THE ESTABLISHMENT OF A THIRD REPUBLIC.—A National Assembly was elected in 1871 with power to create a new government. Although the royalist faction in this body was large in total numbers, it was so hopelessly divided as to candidates for the throne that it could not establish a government. Republicans were able to enact a series of three constitutional laws, passed by the National Assembly in 1875, under which a republican form of government was established. Many groups in France in 1875 did not consider that the republican form of government had been irrevocably adopted, and discussion of the propriety of other forms was an important element in the politics of the nation. Nevertheless, this government came to be known as the Third Republic and existed until the defeat of France by Germany in 1940.

The "Constitution" of 1875

THE NATURE OF THE CONSTITUTION.—Despite the frequent changes of governmental form during France's modern history, there has been considerable continuity in French constitutional law. The foundation of the constitutional system was the Declaration of the Rights of Man, which changing forms of government have never wholly displaced.

Taken together, the three constitutional acts of the National Assembly in 1875 became the fundamental legal basis of the Third Republic. That basis, however, is more fragmentary than comprehensive, covering only the method of selecting the members of the national legislature, the executive power, and the organization of the Senate. The constitutional acts provided for their own amendment by vote of a National Assembly, which will be discussed below.

THE CONSTITUTIONAL STRUCTURE OF GOVERNMENT.—In spite of the inadequacies of the "constitution" of 1875, the structural organization of the Third French Republic which emerged from it—supplemented by constitutional amendments, statutory law, and republican usages—was thought to be a satisfactory governing system. Under it France became a democratic republic with parliamentary government preserving the unitary form which had been perfected by the first Napoleon. As in British practice, there was a balance of power between the branches of government. The titular head of the state was the President of the Republic, while the actual head of the government was the premier, who was aided by a Council of Ministers or Cabinet of his own choice. These ministers were the administrative heads of the several governmental departments. The legislative branch of the government was the source of sovereign power and was made up of a parliament of two houses, the indirectly elected Senate and the popularly elected Chamber of Deputies. The French courts, whose judges were appointed by the President of the Republic on the advice of the Minister of Justice, administered justice under the law but, like the British and unlike the American courts, lacked any power of judicial veto over the acts of the legislature.

Executive Organization

PRESIDENT OF THE REPUBLIC.—The President was the chief of state and titular executive head of all the departments and activities of the nation. He was chosen for a seven-year term of office by a majority of the National Assembly.

Constitutionally and in theory the President enjoyed full executive power. In actual fact, his powers were of no real significance, since his official decrees had to be countersigned by a responsible minister. His suspensive veto over legislation was allowed to fall into complete disuse. His most important governmental function was the selection of a new premier when a ministry fell. Because of the multiparty system, the exercise of this apparently simple power demanded a highly sensitive finger on the nation's political pulse. He sat as chairman of the Council of Ministers, in which he had no vote, but he did have an opportunity to express an opinion.

In fairness it must be noted that the President occasionally had an opportunity to render the Republic great service. He was one element of continuity in the government. Primarily a national leader above and beyond the storms of partisan politics, the President, if he was a forceful individual, could sometimes rally the nation in the face of a crisis. Un-

NATIONAL GOVERNMENT OF FRANCE — THIRD REPUBLIC

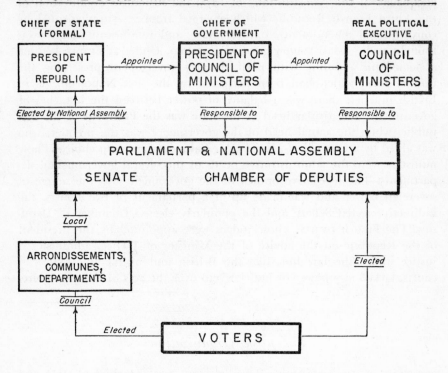

CHIEF OF STATE (FORMAL)
CHIEF OF GOVERNMENT
REAL POLITICAL EXECUTIVE

PRESIDENT OF REPUBLIC — *Appointed* → PRESIDENT OF COUNCIL OF MINISTERS — *Appointed* → COUNCIL OF MINISTERS

Elected by National Assembly
Responsible to
Responsible to

PARLIAMENT & NATIONAL ASSEMBLY

SENATE | CHAMBER OF DEPUTIES

Local

ARRONDISSEMENTS, COMMUNES, DEPARTMENTS

Elected

Council

Elected → VOTERS

STRUCTURE OF GOVERNMENT

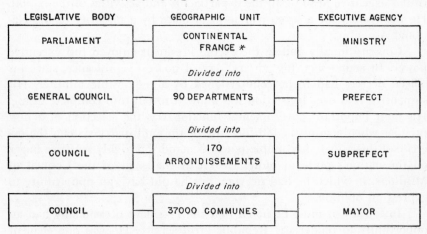

LEGISLATIVE BODY	GEOGRAPHIC UNIT	EXECUTIVE AGENCY
PARLIAMENT	CONTINENTAL FRANCE *	MINISTRY
	Divided into	
GENERAL COUNCIL	90 DEPARTMENTS	PREFECT
	Divided into	
COUNCIL	170 ARRONDISSEMENTS	SUBPREFECT
	Divided into	
COUNCIL	37000 COMMUNES	MAYOR

✻ In addition, various overseas areas constituted departments.

fortunately, few of France's twelve presidents since 1875 were strong leaders.[4]

THE COUNCIL OF MINISTERS OR CABINET.[5]—The President of the Republic selected the President of the Council of Ministers, spoken of usually as the premier. Nominally a neutral in partisan politics, the President usually sought the advice of the President of the Senate and the President of the Chamber of Deputies and other important political leaders in making his selection. The premier usually came from the lower house.

The premier selected the members of his Council of Ministers, or Cabinet. Although ministers usually were members of Parliament, such membership was not necessary. The ministers headed the several administrative departments. Premiers habitually kept for themselves the portfolio of either the Ministry of the Interior, which carried the greatest patronage, or the Ministry of Foreign Affairs, which carried the greatest prestige. In selecting his colleagues, the premier was guided not by his own desires so much as by political expediency. In order to command a majority in Parliament, he had to placate many divergent groups by giving them representation in his Cabinet. The ministers did not render the premier any particular respect or loyalty; hence there was a lack of Cabinet solidarity. Each Cabinet varied in size, an average one having about twenty members.

THE RESPONSIBILITY OF THE CABINET.—The constitutional laws of 1875 provided that the ministers were collectively responsible to the Parliament for the general policy of the government, and individually for their personal acts. Usage in time modified this rule to mean responsibility to the Chamber of Deputies, although the Senate did occasionally force a Cabinet to resign. The existing Cabinet would resign whenever it was given an adverse vote of confidence by either house and a new Cabinet would be formed. This did not mean that an entirely new set of ministers would appear; in general, many of the previous ministers

---

[4] Casimir-Périer (1894–1895) became disgusted with the futility of his role and resigned. Raymond Poincaré (1913–1920) rendered sterling service to the Republic during the difficult World War I days. Alexander Millerand (1920–1924) interfered too sharply in political matters and was forced to resign. Albert Lebrun, originally elected in 1932, was re-elected for a second seven-year term in May, 1939.

[5] When the ministers met under the chairmanship of the President of the Republic, they were known as the Council of Ministers. In other cases, when the premier presided over a meeting of the ministers the same body was called the Cabinet Council. The President of the Republic did not vote when he presided. Most decisions were made in the informal Cabinet Council or Cabinet and were ratified formally when its members met as the Council of Ministers, since the latter body was the only one of the two which was recognized in constitutional law. At the same time, business relating to appointments, decrees, foreign policy, and national defense was discussed in the Council of Ministers.

would be found in the new Cabinet, whose policies would differ little from those of its predecessor. Oddly enough, a repeater frequently headed a different administrative department in the new government.

Although they occupied the positions which wielded the greatest power, the premier and the ministers did not enjoy an altogether enviable status. Their tenure of office was precarious in the extreme; at any moment they might be voted out of power. Unfortunately for all concerned, there were always individuals and groups who were working for the downfall of the existing government. The two especially effective parliamentary practices available to such groups were the "questions" and the "interpellations," addressed to one of the ministers on the floor of Parliament. Unless there were reasons of state that made it inadvisable to answer publicly, the minister was compelled to do so. These questions were often constructive, but the privilege was greatly abused in that many questions obviously were asked with the single purpose of embarrassing the Cabinet.

Legislative Organization

THE SENATE.—The Senate consisted of 314 members, each department (*département*) having from one to five senators, depending upon its population. All were elected for nine-year terms, one third retiring after every three years. Any French citizen over forty years of age was eligible to be elected to the Senate, provided that he was not a member of any royal or imperial family that had ever ruled France. Senators were elected indirectly, that is by an electoral college which was convoked in the departments every three years. These electoral colleges were made up of four elements: (1) the members of the Chamber of Deputies who represented the department; (2) the members of the general council of the department; (3) the members of the various *arrondissement* councils within the department; and (4) delegates chosen by the municipal councils of all the townships (communes) within the department. The delegates from the townships far outnumbered the others.

The Senate, to which most members of the Chamber of Deputies aspired, enjoyed great prestige. Senators were generally men of considerable experience in public life and were inclined to be of the conservative "elder statesman" type. The tendency toward conservatism made the Senate a stabilizing influence in the government. However, because of the long term of office, the Senate was usually years behind changes in public opinion. Under no circumstances could the Senate be dissolved. The President of the Senate ranked next to the President among state officials.

THE CHAMBER OF DEPUTIES.—Little was said in the Constitutional Acts concerning the Chamber of Deputies beyond providing for its election and requiring it to remain in session for at least five months each year. It was considered advantageous to retain a maximum of flexibility regarding the size, organization, and tenure of office. These details were left to be established and altered by statute as conditions would require. In 1940 there were 612 deputies in the Chamber.

Members of the Chamber were elected from the divisions of local government which were called *arrondissements* (subdivisions of the ninety *départements* into which France was divided for administrative purposes). Theoretically, representation was on the basis of equal population, but in practice the size of the constituencies varied greatly, favoring the rural districts at the expense of the urban areas. The term of office was four years, and the entire membership had to submit to reelection or retirement at the end of the term. The prerogative of the President of the Republic to dissolve a chamber before the end of the term, with the consent of the Senate, and to order new elections (exercised only once) fell into discard. Thus the French executive was deprived of a potentially valuable check upon the national legislature. Male French citizens twenty-five years of age were eligible for election. There were no primaries. Each candidate merely filed an intention to offer himself for the office. To be elected, a candidate had to receive a clear majority of the votes cast in his single-member district and at least one quarter of the votes of the total number of registered voters in the district. If no candidate received a majority of the votes cast, a supplementary election was held one week later with all of the original candidates having the right to participate. Usually all except the two strongest candidates withdrew. A plurality of the votes cast was sufficient for election.

NATIONAL ASSEMBLY.—The Senate and the Chamber of Deputies sitting in joint session were designated as the National Assembly and, as such, expressed the sovereign will of the French people. The National Assembly met only for the purpose of electing the President of the Republic and in order to amend the constitution. Twelve presidents were elected to fourteen terms and three amendments were effected during the sixty-five-year life of the Constitution of 1875.

THE PARLIAMENT.—When the Senate and the Chamber of Deputies sat separately, they were known as the Parliament and exercised complete lawmaking power. In addition, they exercised control over the executive branch of the government and its administration of public business. All acts which passed both houses of the Parliament by a majority vote and were signed by the President of the Republic became law. The lawmaking powers of the Parliament were not limited by judicial review.

Members of both legislative houses received an annual salary of approximately $1,700 in 1940. They were exempt from prosecution for opinions voiced or votes cast in the exercise of their functions.

Both legislative houses elected their own officers and determined their own rules of procedure. The Presidents of the Chamber of Deputies and of the Senate conducted all proceedings in a nonpartisan manner. The task of maintaining order in the large and frequently disorderly Chamber was a difficult one. A system of penalties, usually involving suspension for a certain number of days, had to be established for unruly members.

Although intended by the founders of the Third Republic to enjoy powers almost equal to those of the lower house, in practice the Senate occupied a markedly secondary position with respect to the Chamber. Not only did the latter have primary control in making and unmaking ministries,[6] but all financial bills, and nearly all other important measures originated in the Chamber. The Senate provided a check on over-hasty action by the Chamber and, as we have seen, combined with it to form the National Assembly—wherein it was outnumbered by the lower body. In addition, the Senate served as a high court of justice where an official of the government was charged with improper conduct in office[7] or where any individual was accused of an "assault against the security of the state."

Each house had power to question the ministers who headed executive departments concerning matters of public business. More frequently ministers were interrogated in the Chamber of Deputies, but the privilege was also possessed by senators. Three types of interrogation were employed: (1) A "question" was a dialogue between the member asking the question and the minister replying (or possibly an exchange of notes in the official journal). It did not give rise to debate or any sort of vote. (2) An "interpellation" opened a general debate which was followed by a motion to continue the ordinary work of the house. This motion might be a simple one expressing no opinion on the preceding debate, or it might express the confidence or lack of confidence of the members. A minister against whom a vote of no confidence had been passed often had to resign. The frequency with which an interpellation led to the downfall of a minister or a Cabinet amounted to an abuse of the device. (3) "Investigation," which was rarely used, was the examination of a particu-

---

[6] In 1937 the Senate caused the overthrow of the first Blum "Popular Front" government by refusing to agree with the Chamber of Deputies in granting Premier Blum special powers to deal with the financial crisis which gripped France at that time.

[7] The President of the Republic was liable to trial by the Senate only on the charge of treason.

lar act or policy by a committee of one of the houses. The committee might hear witnesses and would present its findings for discussion on the floor. The effectiveness of such measures of control was discussed in connection with the executive branch of the government.

THE ENACTMENT OF LAW.—Two types of bills could come before either house of the Parliament. One was a government measure (*projet de loi*) introduced by a member of the Cabinet. Most bills were of this type. However, any member of either house had the right to introduce legislation in the form of a private member's bill (*proposition de loi*).

Both houses had permanent and special committees to handle legislation according to its subject matter. All bills were referred to the appropriate committee upon introduction. There they were considered by committee members in private sessions. When the bill was ready for consideration on the floor, a private member, known as the "reporter," was named by the committee to report the bill and to pilot it through the house which had it under consideration. It was the "reporters'" function to defend the bill, and in the event of a government measure, to collaborate with the minister responsible.

On the floor the initial debate was on the general provisions of the bill; the details were not considered at all. Then followed a vote on proceeding to the discussion of specific articles. If this vote was unfavorable, the measure was defeated at once; if favorable, the bill was then taken up section by section. Amendment and debate were then in order. In the Chamber of Deputies strict closure rules were observed to prevent lengthy debate by its large membership. Unlike British and American practice, nonmembers of the French Parliament might be introduced on the floor to defend the bill, to clarify it, or to suggest changes in it. These might be ministers having seats in the other house, undersecretaries, or any expert or authority whose views were considered valuable. When the time came to take a recorded vote, an urn was passed from seat to seat and each member dropped into it a ballot bearing his name. France was one of the few countries which permitted its legislators to vote by proxy. An absent deputy could arrange to have a colleague drop his ballot for him. This privilege in time became subject to considerable abuse. For a more exact count, a group of deputies might demand a ballot "at the tribune." No proxy vote was permitted when the vote was taken in this fashion. The vote might also be taken by a show of hands or by a standing vote. The show of hands was the most common method.

SUFFRAGE.—Suffrage was extended to every mentally sound male citizen who was over twenty-one years of age and who was duly enrolled on the voters' list of any locality. Woman suffrage did not exist. No educational tests or taxpaying requirements were provided for. There was no plural voting as in England, and no absentee voting as in America. Persons in the military or naval service were denied the right to vote unless they were present on leave in the commune where they were regularly registered.

Political Parties and Groups

EXISTENCE OF NUMEROUS POLITICAL GROUPS.—Americans and Britons are accustomed to the existence of two or three major political parties, coherently organized and in Britain firmly disciplined. In France, however, the situation has always been markedly different. Under the Third Republic a political "party" often existed only outside the Parliament. Within the Parliament the senators and the deputies were organized into "groups." Sometimes a parliamentary group included most of the senators or deputies from a particular party and was known as the "group of a party." However, there were parties to which no groups corresponded, and vice versa. More confusing still, the "groups" in the Senate did not always correspond to the "groups" of the Chamber of Deputies in name or principles. The party and group labels used in France at large complicated matters still more. They were almost invariably inaccurate, usually outmoded, and frequently meaningless. The moderate Radical-Socialist party was a classic example, for it was neither socialistic nor radical. When one considers the foregoing and the conflicting political programs discussed below, it is not surprising that the Third Republic went down in defeat when it was confronted by superior armaments from without and the cancerous ideologies of Nazism and Communism from within.

ABSENCE OF PARTY DISCIPLINE.—With the exception of the Socialists and Communists, France did not have large or well-disciplined parties. It was by no means exceptional for some representatives of a party to refuse to join the rest of the party's parliamentary group in the support of a particular Cabinet. Conversely, a member of a parliamentary group was sometimes so individualistic that he had no party affiliation at all.

In general, the French deputy or senator was alone responsible for his election or re-election. Consequently he was in no way bound to align himself with any particular group or to maintain allegiance to any group that he might join. Nor did any stigma attach to the deputy who changed his group. A French politician was much more likely to be faithful to a particular leader than to any particular party or group.

POLITICAL COALITIONS.—No single political party or group normally hoped to command a majority in either house. This being the case, in order to get a working majority it was necessary for a certain number of these groups, collectively known as a "bloc," to join forces. This grouping of groups, naturally enough, was at best only a temporary working arrangement, and the disruptive forces of group and party factionalism were constantly at work. The result was that French Cabinets, which had to possess a working majority in Parliament, went in and out of power with amazing rapidity. The Third Republic lasted less than seventy years, and yet during that time more than one hundred different Cabinets were formed, their average life being somewhat less than nine months. Obviously such a system would have been unworkable had there not been a stable bureaucratic structure within the government.

FRENCH POLITICAL PARTIES.—Traditionally, French groups or parties divided on significant issues into what were called parties of the Right and parties of the Left. Broadly speaking, those of the Right were usually clerical, oligarchical, and authoritarian in their views. Some of them represented big business and the large landowners. One was royalist. The most important of these groups was the Republican Federation (URD), a party aggressively opposed to trade-unions, social legislation, anticlericalism, the taxation of wealth, and state intervention in industry. Parties of the Left were heirs of the democratic tradition of the French Revolution. The Radical-Socialists, largest of these parties and nearest to the Center, championed the interests of the great mass of French farmers, merchants, and middle-class people. They were anticlerical, and they advocated moderate social reforms, labor legislation, taxes on wealth, and democratic reforms. The Socialists and Communists formed the extreme Left. In the Center were parties whose views were Rightist on some issues and Leftist on others. The Democratic Alliance, which was an organization coordinating the activities of several parties, was the dominant Center group. By 1940 the Center had largely become aligned with the Right. Yet the Popular Democratic or Social Catholic party was a Center party which tended toward the Left. This strongly antifascist party emphasized Christian social principles. On the other hand, the moderate Radical-Socialists increasingly came to be considered as a Center party.

POLITICAL ORGANIZATIONS.—In addition to political parties, a multitude of organizations such as employers' associations, labor unions, youth movements, and leagues representing various interests contributed in varying degrees to French political life in a fashion not unlike the Congressional lobbies in the American capital.

Foreign Policy

SECURITY QUEST AFTER WORLD WAR I.—After World War I, "security" was the guiding slogan of French foreign ministers. Since the political, territorial, and military clauses of the Versailles Treaty would, if enforced, afford a large measure of security from a German threat, the French government insisted on maintaining the treaty intact. Likewise, France demanded the full execution of German economic and financial commitments under the treaty. Thus, when Germany defaulted on her reparations payments in 1922, France attempted to enforce her demands with an abortive occupation of the Ruhr in 1923.[8] In the diplomatic field, when the diplomatic alliance with the United States and Great Britain failed of acceptance by the United States Senate, France began to construct a series of defensive alliances with the nations neighboring Germany. The resulting cordon consisted of Belgium, Poland, and the Little Entente—Czechoslovakia, Yugoslavia, and Rumania. In addition, France erected new fortifications on her eastern frontier and unsuccessfully attempted to maintain relatively large armed forces at a World War I level of technical efficiency.

After 1924 the new, peaceful trends appearing in the German government—symbolized by Gustav Stresemann's foreign policy—caused in France a relaxation of her intensive efforts to build bulwarks against her Teutonic neighbor. In that year France accepted the Dawes plan for reducing the amount of reparations to be obtained from Germany and agreed to evacuate the Ruhr Valley. In a friendly interlude the next year, both nations agreed at Locarno to guarantee their mutual frontier as it stood. In 1926 Germany entered the League of Nations. In 1930, five years before the specified time, French troops evacuated the Rhineland. Although some objection was expressed to this more conciliatory policy, French leaders never tempted the opposition to full nationalistic fury by permitting any suggestion of equality of armaments or frontier revision to enter their proposals.

PRELUDE TO WORLD WAR II.—Upon the accession of Adolf Hitler to power in 1933, the conciliatory trends of German policy were reversed. With his double policy of preventing further application of the Versailles Treaty and re-creating German armed might, Hitler seriously threatened French security. But as German truculence and military power grew, French willingness to meet force with force to maintain the *status quo* diminished. France had lost her last political "strong man" with the retirement of Raymond Poincaré in 1929. Thereafter a dizzy succession of ministries high-lighted the parliamentary confusion which attended the maneuvers of a multitude of political parties. The nation rocked with demonstrations by extremist groups demanding authoritarian government and with the almost insurrectionary agitation

---

[8] Because of passive resistance offered by the German workers, backed by the German government, net result of the occupation was a financial loss for France. France's former allies were likewise opposed to the occupation.

of labor organizations seeking sweeping social reform. To meet the mounting crisis an odd combination called the "Popular Front" was formed by the Radical-Socialist, Socialist, and Communist parties. Although this coalition in a succession of ministries (1936–1938), with Socialists and Radical Socialists holding office, did succeed in spreading a variety of social laws on the statute books, it did not give France a firm, resolute government or solve her fundamental problems. Such conditions rendered difficult the development of any strong and consistent French policy. Soon it was obvious that the new issue was no longer one of keeping a weak Germany in subjection but rather of preserving the remnants of security and checkmating a strong, rearmed, defiant Reich. The French nation moved blindly with faltering steps and uncertain guidance to meet its new problems.

France's policy of retreat and appeasement is partly traceable to the steadily increasing withdrawal of Britain from European affairs. France, thrown back on her own resources and fearful of finding herself standing alone in a major crisis, failed to exercise the political and military pressure necessary to check the resurgence of German power after 1935.

In 1934 fear drove Poland to sign a nonaggression pact with Germany and thereby evidence doubt concerning her French alliance. France was, however, able to reaffirm that alliance in 1936, and had been able to conclude a mutual-assistance pact with the USSR the year before. France had also constructed the Maginot Line in the years 1930–1934.

Nevertheless, concession born of weakness became the spirit of the times. France along with England stood aside while Germany continued to rearm. Furthermore, in order to placate Italy, France acquiesced in Italian designs upon Ethiopia and thus helped to undermine the League of Nations' effort to maintain a collective security program. When Hitler remilitarized the Rhineland in 1936, the French General Staff demanded counter occupation of the same area, as was permitted by the Versailles Treaty. The leaders of the government reasoned that mobilization would be expensive and would threaten war. It was decided, therefore, merely to dispatch a formal note of protest—as Hitler had hoped.

The internal struggle between factions of the Right and Left made impossible the achievement of any unity on the problem posed by renascent Germany. France's desire to preserve peace was rewarded with rapid loss of prestige and ever bolder Axis moves threatening her security. The Little Entente was weakened by the rapidly shifting balance of forces in Europe. The growth of German influence in the Balkans was reflected by Yugoslavia's renunciation of her alliance with France. Belgium likewise sought safety in renouncing her military alliance with France and proclaimed her neutrality. Italy, from leaning toward Britain and France from fear that Hitler would seize Austria, shifted her position as a result of German cooperation in the Ethiopian war and arrived at a closer understanding with Germany. The Rome-Berlin Axis was formed in 1936 and openly aided the Franco revolt in Spain. Thus the Axis was instrumental in establishing an unfriendly Fascist government on France's southern frontier. In March, 1938, Germany, which had previously been forbidden to form even a customs union with Austria, absorbed that nation and thereby further weakened France's ally Czechoslovakia. In September of the same year, Nazi diplomacy and threats resulted in the Munich Conference in which Germany was "appeased" and "peace" was maintained by Czechoslovakia's being forced to surrender the Sudetenland to Hitler. Thus encouraged, Hungary and Poland also helped themselves to Czech territory. In March, 1939, Germany occupied what was left of that country. Italy, meanwhile, had begun to clamor for the French territories of Savoy, Nice, Corsica, and Tunisia. At the same time, Japan, associated with the Axis powers, threatened to seize French Indo-China.

The traditional cooperation between France and Russia against Germany had been destroyed by the Russian withdrawal from World War I and by the Communist program of world revolution. The Franco-Russian alliance of 1935 failed to restore a feeling of mutual trust and confidence. Steady growth of anticommunism expressed in French governmental action, and increasingly manifest French weakness, caused Stalin, after Munich, to disregard completely his alliance with France.

The only grain of comfort left for France in 1939 was that she had signed a strong military alliance with Great Britain in 1938. Even this consolation was somewhat weakened by the knowledge that in 1938 Britain could with difficulty muster an expeditionary force of three divisions and an air force of proportionate strength.

End of the Third Republic

DEFEAT OF FRANCE.—As the results showed, France defeated herself before the first German soldier crossed her border. Her preparations for downfall were well aided and abetted by the highly efficient work of Germany's fifth columnists who for ten years previously had fomented internal discord and otherwise undermined France's ability to defend herself. And just as they had helped the Nazis to destroy the Weimar Republic in Germany, so too did the Communists help the Nazis destroy the Third Republic. Not without reason were thirty-five of the seventy-two Communist deputies in the Parliament sentenced to prison terms upon the outbreak of war. The Communists had missed no opportunity to paralyze the French industrial machine and to circulate defeatist and pacifist "anti-imperialist" propaganda.

Too late, the Parliament which was unable to act gave Premier

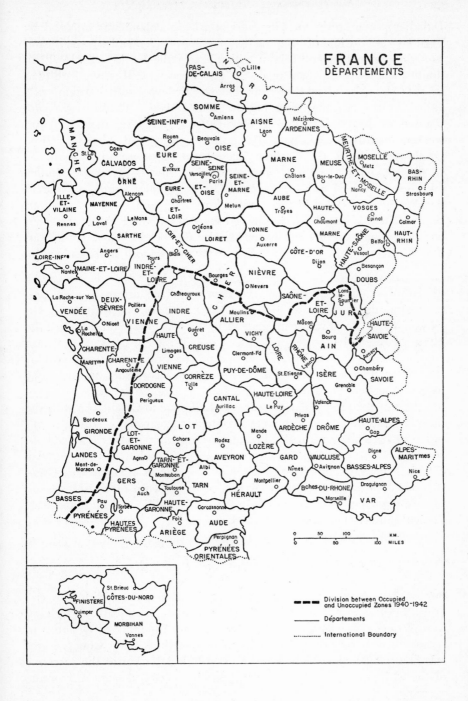

FRANCE
DÈPARTEMENTS

Division between Occupied
and Unoccupied Zones 1940-1942

Départements

International Boundary

Daladier power to do so. The Nazi attack on Poland was followed by France's declaration of war against Germany (September, 1939) and brought momentary enthusiasm and relief to the French people. Then doubts, apathy, and defeatism set in. There was no real sense of unity as in 1914. In spite of pressing war dangers, little political harmony prevailed in the national government. The Daladier Cabinet was supplanted by the Cabinet of Paul Reynaud on March 19, 1940. Reynaud worked mightily but in vain for political unity and effective action. On May 10, 1940, the German juggernaut began to roll toward the Channel. On June 10, the Germans moved southward across the Somme, and Italy declared war on France. The Reynaud Cabinet, unable to decide whether it should move to north Africa and continue the war, resolved its dilemma by resigning. At Bordeaux, where the government had fled, a new cabinet was formed under the World War I hero, Marshal Pétain, who had been recalled from the Spanish ambassadorship.

DESTRUCTION OF THE THIRD REPUBLIC.—On June 22, a French peace delegation from the Pétain government signed an armistice with Germany and three days later signed a similar agreement with Italy. On July 2, 1940, the government moved to Vichy. There, on July 10, the National Assembly granted full powers of government to Marshal Pétain and authorized him to promulgate a new constitution to be ratified by the nation. Instead, a series of constitutional acts—issued in the name of Pétain and never ratified—made Pétain a virtual dictator. A group of members of the French Parliament who had gone to Casablanca with the idea of continuing the war were arrested in compliance with Pétain's orders. In a similar vein, the Pétain government sentenced to death *in absentia* General de Gaulle, who had gone to London and organized a French National Committee to carry on the war in alliance with Great Britain.[9] The political history of France presents no more uninspiring picture than the death throes of the Third Republic and the months of French subservience which followed.

The Establishment of the Vichy Regime

THE CONSTITUTIONAL ACTS.—The constitutional acts, in addition to creating the new title of Chief of the French State for Pétain and giving him plenary powers, adjourned the Senate and Chamber of Deputies to reconvene only on call of the Chief of State (which never came). Later acts first named Pierre Laval and then Admiral Darlan as the successor of the Chief of State in the event of his incapacity, created a Supreme

---

[9] Britain had earlier made a final effort to persuade France to continue the war by proposing an "indissoluble union" of the British and French empires, with a joint constitution, a single cabinet, a combined parliament, and a common citizenship.

Court, defined the responsibilities of governmental officials, and compelled the members of the government to swear fidelity to the Chief of State. The eleventh constitutional act of April, 1942, created the office of Chief of Government and conferred upon its holder "actual direction of the internal and foreign policy of France." The twelfth and final act, November 18, 1942, gave the Chief of Government power to make laws and issue them on his signature alone. It also repealed the act naming Admiral Darlan as the successor to Pétain and provided that the Cabinet should name the successor in the event of the permanent incapacity of the Chief of State.

ZONE OF CONTROL.—Until November, 1942, when American and British forces landed in North Africa, the German Army restricted its official occupation of France to the northwestern territory of France assigned to German control by the armistice. Local French who were willing to collaborate were utilized in governing the zone. The Vichy government was permitted to control southeastern France under such restrictions as the German government laid down. Both because of the inclination of the Vichy leaders and because of German pressure, the Pétain government collaborated with the Nazis. In return, Vichy was given a free hand in local and many state matters. After the Anglo-American invasion of North Africa, the German Army occupied all France. Germany continued to let the Vichy collaborationists administer civil government, but the German authorities dominated the French police and French economic life. With the growing possibility of Allied invasion of France, the authority of Vichy was reduced to a minimum. In addition, by 1943 the Vichy government had lost all control over the former French Empire.

CHANGES IN VICHY LEADERSHIP.—The establishment of the Vichy government under Marshal Pétain gave rise to the vain hope in some quarters that he would become the dominant figure whose prestige would render his position unassailable. However, Pétain's senility, German pressure, and the intrigues of French defeatists and pro-Nazis brought about the emergence of Vice-Premier Pierre Laval to the position of chief importance. As a leading adherent to the collaborationist principle, his disproportionate influence in the regime continued until he was dismissed by Pétain and supplanted by Darlan in December, 1940. In the spring of 1942, when German demands forced Pétain into an obvious figurehead position, his executive powers devolved upon the newly created office of Chief of Government, to which he appointed Pierre Laval.

REPRESSIVE MEASURES.—In order to repress possible centers of unrest and in response to German pressure, the Vichy government severely restricted the civil rights which were guaranteed French citizens under the

Third Republic. The freedoms of speech, press, and association were completely abolished. Newspapers and the radio were made instruments of official propaganda and subjected to rigid censorship. Listeners to United Nations' broadcasts were severely punished when caught. The Vichy government took specific measures against certain categories of French citizens, especially Jews and Freemasons and, after June, 1941, Communists. The Vichy French courts enforced German decrees and regulations as well as French law.

End of the Vichy Regime

FLIGHT OF THE VICHY GOVERNMENT.—After the United Nations' invasion of France, June 6, 1944, the Vichy government adopted a policy of "neutrality." Laval's plan was to form a French government which could maintain itself during the transition of France from German control to liberation and which would promise to keep liberated France neutral. When Edouard Herriot, who had been President of the Chamber of Deputies in the Third Republic, refused to participate in such a scheme, Laval fled to Germany. He was soon followed by the remainder of the Vichy government. Plotting to the last to force de Gaulle's Provisional Government of the French Republic to make concessions in their favor, the Vichyites' government-in-exile failed completely and evaporated with the defeat of Germany.

EVALUATION OF THE VICHY GOVERNMENT.—It is doubtful that the Vichy government is of unique significance. Its initial basis was the desperate hope of many that Marshal Pétain could somehow protect France from the assaults of the Nazis and from the internal cynicism personified by men such as Pierre Laval and Maurice Thorez, extreme reactionaries of the Right and Left, respectively. Other sources of support came from sincere though cowardly defeatists, from those seeking to protect themselves at any cost to others, and from the extremist fringe of the Left and the Right. These groups are present and rise to the surface the world over under conditions similar to those which faced France from 1940 to 1944.

Origin of the Fourth French Republic, 1943

THE FRENCH RESISTANCE MOVEMENT, JUNE 18, 1940–JUNE 3, 1943.—The Fourth Republic originated in the resistance movements of World War II and developed steadily through the Provisional Government stage, culminating in the adoption of a new constitution in 1946.

General Charles de Gaulle, leader of resistance forces, had long and unsuccessfully opposed the French Army's defensive strategy. An advocate of mechanized warfare and blitzkrieg tactics, he was named Undersecretary of War on June 6, 1940, by Premier Paul Reynaud. Refusing to admit defeat when the French government capitulated, he escaped to England. His London broadcast, "France has lost a battle! But France has not lost the war!" rallied about him large numbers of exiled Frenchmen to form the "Free French," later the "Fighting French," movement.

THE FRENCH NATIONAL COMMITTEE.—On September 24, 1941, de Gaulle organized the French National Committee in London with himself as President, to manage the movement's public affairs. FNC's objectives were announced as follows: (1) to free France and her overseas territories from the German, Italian, and Japanese invaders; and (2) to restore to the French people the full exercise of the liberty and sovereignty of which the Axis powers and the Vichy regime had deprived them. To this Committee adhered those parts of the French Empire and those Frenchmen not under Vichy or Axis control.

A new stage of development of FNC began in November, 1942, following the Allied invasion of North Africa. The invasion itself had been made without the knowledge of the French National Committee for reasons of military strategy and security, only a bare minimum of interested agencies having foreknowledge of the operation. Moreover, in order to gain time, to avoid embittering the French troops and authorities in North Africa, and to prevent unnecessary casualties, General Eisenhower's staff negotiated prior to the invasion with various French military and civil leaders in North Africa, for the prompt cessation of French resistance to the Allied Forces. General Giraud, who had escaped from a German prison and was in Vichy France, participated in the negotiations. The success of these negotiations required the exclusion of the FNC, since it was bitterly opposed to the Vichy North Africa administration.

The negotiations were only partly successful and some of the Allied landings were stubbornly resisted by individual French units. Hence it became necessary to enter into relations with Admiral Darlan, supreme commander of all Vichy armed forces, who was in Algiers. At his order, all resistance ceased. He also assumed the headship of the French Government of North Africa and was recognized as such by the Allies. General Giraud, who had been intended for this post, was given command of the French forces in North Africa. Darlan continued as head of the government until his assassination in December, 1942, when the Allies replaced him with General Giraud. The overlap and incompatibility of the FNC and the North African High Commissioner's regime was obvious. General de Gaulle felt that his agency had been snubbed by the Allied High Command by being excluded from the negotiations. Therefore he maintained that the North African administration was under the influence of collaborationists. The Allies made great efforts to reconcile the two French agencies; some success was achieved by inviting Generals Giraud and de Gaulle to the Casablanca conference between Roosevelt and Churchill in January, 1943.

THE FRENCH COMMITTEE OF NATIONAL LIBERATION (FCNL) JUNE 3, 1943 –JUNE 2, 1944.—Following the Casablanca conference the French Committee of National Liberation was established combining de Gaulle's French National Committee with Giraud's North African Government, thus incorporating all free Frenchmen under one agency. As a result, unified control of French internal resistance was facilitated. The FCNL was at first composed of Generals de Gaulle and Giraud as co-Presidents and thirteen commissioners. Subsequently General de Gaulle became sole President, and the membership of the Committee was repeatedly increased. Representatives of all factions of Free French political opinion were included in FCNL, which was hailed as a great strengthening influence for unity. The commissioners functioned as cabinet ministers.

During the course of expanding the membership of FCNL, General de Gaulle resorted to a political expedient which, although it seemed desirable and necessary at the time, later proved to be a grave error. Although he sought unanimous recognition of the FCNL as the legitimate government of France by the Allies, the United States and Great Britain granted only "limited recognition" in 1943. On the other hand, Soviet Russia recognized the FCNL as the *de facto* government of France. Moreover, now that Soviet Russia was fighting against rather than collaborating with Hitler, the French branch of the Communist party was basking in reflected glory and actively seeking to dominate the French underground resistance movements. In view of their expert training and past experience in subversive activities, it was only natural that the Communists should achieve considerable success. This success is even more understandable when one recalls the tendency in the United States during the war years to minimize blemishes on the Communist record. In April, 1944, therefore, de Gaulle, having released French Communists from prison in North Africa and having given the Communists much freedom in the resistance movement, admitted two Communist commissioners into the FCNL. Hence, partly as a result of de Gaulle's policy of expediency, the treasonable activities of the Communists in France which had contributed to the debacle of 1940 faded into the background. By the time France was liberated the Communists dominated the resistance movement and were firmly entrenched in French politics.

The FCNL directed the French war effort and exercised sovereignty over all French territories outside Axis control. It organized armed forces and special courts and appointed governing officials for those French colonies, protectorates, and mandates under its authority. The stated objectives of FCNL were the restoration of "all the French liberties, the laws of the Republic, and the republican regime," and the complete destruction of the Vichy government.

Some of the political aims were accomplished by the FCNL, though others were postponed until the government had assumed a new form in its development. The FCNL participated in the armistice negotiations between the United Nations and Italy. Along with Russia, Great Britain, and the United States, it secured a place on the Italian Advisory Council which handled domestic political questions. The FCNL was also represented on the Allied Commission which applied the Italian armistice.

The recognition question became important in early 1944 when the prospect of Allied invasion of France raised the problem of governing the liberated territory. Even at this time, however, the United States and Great Britain did not unreservedly recognize the FCNL. The United States' policy was that the FCNL would be free to re-establish law and order *under the supervision of the Allied Commander in Chief*. A principal factor in the formulation of this policy was the desire of the United States that the French people be free to select a government which would reflect their views on domestic issues. Obviously with France occupied by the Germans, there was no sure way of knowing how well the FCNL conformed to this requirement.

THE PROVISIONAL CONSULTATIVE ASSEMBLY.—In September, 1943, the FCNL erected a Provisional Consultative Assembly. This body was composed of approximately one hundred members, representing internal and external French resistance movements, former political parties or groups, and those French territories which were loyal to the FCNL. It functioned not as a legislative organization but as a policy-reviewing and an advisory board. For the purpose of uniting within the new bodies in Algiers representatives of all French anti-Axis elements, both the FCNL and the Provisional Consultative Assembly were constantly increased and changed in membership.

THE PROVISIONAL GOVERNMENT OF THE FRENCH REPUBLIC (GPRF).—On June 2, 1944, the FCNL on the recommendation of the resistance groups in France and of the Provisional Consultative Assembly assumed the name of Provisional Government of the French Republic (GPRF). Despite immediate recognition by Belgium, Czechoslovakia, Poland, and other countries, the de Gaulle government continued to be known officially to the United States and Great Britain as the FCNL which, it will be remembered, was not recognized as the official French government. After the Allied invasion of France (June 6, 1944), it was apparent that the invading armies were receiving considerable assistance from French resistance groups. Particularly helpful was a combat organization known as the French Forces of the Interior. Soon, therefore, the United

States recognized the FCNL as the *de facto* government of France. This meant simply that the United States acknowledged the authority of the FCNL though the legal basis of that authority was not mentioned.

Following the capture of Paris in August, 1944, by the Allied forces (which included French troops) the GPRF was transferred to that city from Algiers. By October the GPRF had demonstrated its ability to administer the liberated areas of France. It was as representative of the people as could be expected, and it seemed to have the peoples' support. Consequently, in October, 1944, the United States, Great Britain, Russia, and Canada extended *de jure* or full recognition to the FCNL as the Provisional Government of the French Republic.

GOVERNMENTAL SERVICES OF THE GPRF DURING THE TRANSITIONAL PERIOD.—The Provisional Government of the French Republic performed two primary services during the transitional period from its creation until the adoption of the Constitution of 1946. The first of these services, that of bringing order out of the chaotic internal conditions created in France by war and foreign occupation, involved the liquidation of the Vichy regime. Most of the constitutional acts and laws of the Pétain government were repealed, its militia and all Vichy-sponsored political groups were dissolved, and the development of democratic political parties was encouraged. Although the Third Republic was generally acknowledged to be dead and a new constitution was required, using the political machinery of the pre-Vichy regime was in keeping with the French tradition of retaining important institutions and practices from previous governments. The executive branch of the GPRF differed somewhat from that of the Third Republic in that the President, General de Gaulle, exercised the executive powers, and the President with his Cabinet had the power—with approval of the legislative branch—to rule by decree. The transitional judicial system was substantially the same as that prior to the war except for certain additional courts created to carry out the purge of collaborationists.

The second essential service rendered by the GPRF was the draft of a new constitution. In October, 1945, national election replaced the Provisional Consultative Assembly with a new body, the National Constituent Assembly with transitional legislative functions, but with the primary task of preparing the new constitution. This election was important in French political history. Not only was the first representative assembly elected by the French nation since 1936, but women voted for the first time in French history. Moreover the effects of war, occupation, the resistance movement, and the Communist renaissance all found expression at the polls. Immediately after the 1945 election, the GPRF officials, including General de Gaulle, wisely surrendered their powers to the Constituent Assembly. Within a few days of his resignation, de Gaulle was unanimously elected by the Assembly to the Presidency of the GPRF.

The Provisional Government had a definitely Rightist tone from the French point of view. It has already been noted that the President was the Chief Executive, and although the Cabinet was responsible to the Constituent Assembly, an absolute majority vote[10] of the Assembly was required to upset a cabinet on a no-confidence issue. Simple refusal by the Assembly to grant a cabinet request was insufficient indication of lack of confidence. At first there was little parliamentary strife in the Constituent Assembly, a circumstance that may be explained by the fact that the Assembly was chiefly occupied in drafting the new constitution. It will be seen that the first draft, developed between November, 1945, and April, 1946, represented a shift far to the Left in the GPRF and precipitated a severe struggle within the government.

The Constitution of 1946

THE NATIONAL CONSTITUENT ASSEMBLY.—The Provisional Government had the task of learning the people's desire concerning the form of the permanent French government. In a referendum in October, 1945, only 670,292 out of some twenty-four million registered voters favored a return to the Constitution of 1875. Thus, no doubt existed that the vast majority held the old Constitution responsible for the internal bickering, the foreign appeasement, the completely inadequate leadership of the years immediately preceding World War II. A further charge laid against the old Constitution was that a bare thirty of the total membership of the Senate had opposed the adoption of the Vichy government. A new Constitution was regarded as the symbol of a necessary clean break with the past and of the birth of a new future.

The popular desire for a fresh start had resulted in the post-liberation liquidation of all Vichy-tainted political leaders (chiefly Conservative) from the parties which we have noted. This purge of leaders together with the new party discipline and the proportional representation-election law[11] of August, 1945, resulted in a National Constituent Assembly whose center of gravity was certainly left of center, whose ability may be described as mediocre, and whose spirit of compromise was disrupted by a new rigidity of party lines.

---

[10] Vote equal to one half the authorized strength of the Assembly plus one.

[11] Under this law, the individual voter was restricted to casting his ballot for the list of candidates of a single political party. Seats were apportioned among the parties in proportion to the number of votes cast for their respective lists.

NATURE OF THE CONSTITUTION.—The version of the Constitution finally adopted by France in October, 1946, represents an unequal compromise between two general political objectives. The first objective was that of strengthening the executive. The Third Republic had failed to produce proper coordination and leadership principally because its Ministries were helpless before the faction-torn Assembly. Deadlock between Ministry and Assembly in nearly every case had resulted in formation of a new government—not in dissolution of the Assembly and appeal to the electorate. This outcome meant that either the deadlock remained or the new Ministry bowed to the Assembly. The second political objective was one which became the dominant characteristic of the 1946 Constitution: the government-by-assembly principle. Involved in the strong assembly-weak executive issue were a traditional French fear of dictatorship and an equally traditional distrust of an upper legislative house. The Third Republic Senates had been notably Conservative during the years before World War II.

As we have previously noted, the political complexion of the Constituent Assembly in 1945–1946 was well to the left of Center; consequently, the first draft of the new Constitution, completed in April, 1946, reflected the Assembly's characteristics. This draft provided for a National Assembly which could be dissolved by the Ministry only in case two ministerial crises occurred during the course of an annual session and then only during the last half of the five-year legislative term. Moreover, the draft specified that before the Assembly could be dissolved the President of the Council of Ministers would have to consult the President of the National Assembly. In addition to the coercion permitted the Assembly the first draft provided for an ineffectual President of the Republic and no Senate or substitute for one.

The economic features of the first draft reflect Communist-Socialist agreement. Provision was made for nationalization of "economic monopolies"; for "participation of workers . . . in the management of enterprises"; and for the right of every man to acquire property by work and saving.

In a referendum in May, 1946, the French people rejected the first draft. Obviously, here was an opportunity for compromise: an opportunity for the MRP, supported by de Gaulle who advocated the strong executive, to make their wishes felt.

Very little real compromise resulted, however, as to the conflicting objectives. Although the second draft achieved ratification in a referendum in October, 1946, the vote reflected the growth of general apathy on the part of the electorate. The vote was approximately nine million to eight million with eight million abstaining. The approved version of the Constitution made some concession to a stronger Ministry. The dissolution power was altered by extending to eighteen months the period

THE 1946 CONSTITUTION OF THE FRENCH REPUBLIC

On the morrow of the victory of the free peoples over the regimes that attempted to enslave and degrade the human person, the French people proclaims once more that every human being, without distinction of race, religion or belief, possesses inalienable and sacred rights. It solemnly reaffirms the rights and freedoms of man and of the citizen consecrated by the Declaration of Rights of 1789 and the fundamental principles recognized by the laws of the Republic.

It further proclaims as most vital in our time the following political, economic and social principles:

The law guarantees to women equal rights with men in all domains.

Anyone persecuted because of his activities in the cause of freedom has the right of asylum within the territories of the Republic.

Everyone has the duty to work and the right to obtain employment. . . .

Everyone may defend his rights and interests by trade-union action and may join the union of his choice.

The right to strike may be exercised within the framework of the laws that govern it.

Every worker through his delegates may participate in collective bargaining to determine working conditions, as well as in the management of business.

All property and all enterprises that now have or subsequently shall have the character of a national public service or a monopoly in fact must become the property of the community.

The nation ensures to the individual and the family the conditions necessary to their development.

It guarantees to all, and notably to the child, the mother and the aged worker, protection of health, material security, rest and leisure. . . .

The nation proclaims the solidarity and equality of all Frenchmen with regard to the burdens resulting from national disasters.

The nation guarantees equal access of children and adults to education, professional training and culture. The establishment of free, secular, public education on all levels is a duty of the State.

The French Republic, faithful to its traditions, abides by the rules of international public law. . . .

On condition of reciprocity, France accepts the limitations of sovereignty necessary to the organization and defense of peace.

France forms with the people of its overseas territories a Union based upon equality of rights and duties without distinction of race or religion.

The French Union is composed of nations and peoples who wish to place in common or coordinate their resources and their efforts in order to develop their civilization, increase their well-being and ensure their security.

Faithful to her traditional mission, France proposes to guide the peoples for whom she has assumed responsibility toward freedom to govern themselves and democratically to manage their own affairs; putting aside any system of colonization based upon arbitrary power, she guarantees to all equal access to public office and the individual or collective exercise of the rights and liberties proclaimed or confirmed above.

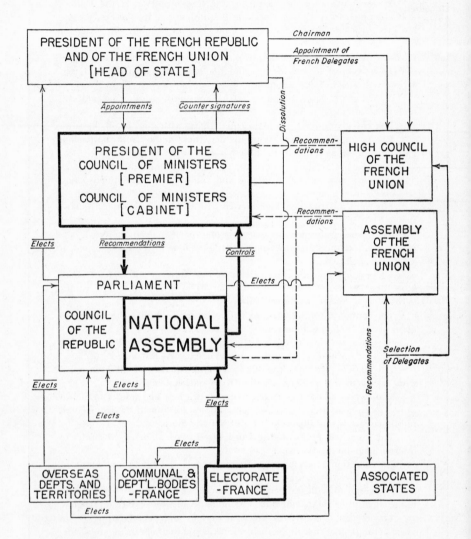

N.B. For simplicity the following institutions have been omitted from this chart: Council of State, Superior Council of the Judiciary, Constitutional Committee, High Court of Justice, and Economic Council. The roles of these institutions are discussed in the text.

in which two ministerial crises[12] may cause dissolution, and permitting considerations of crises after only eighteen months of the legislative term have elapsed rather than one half of the term as in the previous draft. However, to effect a dissolution, the President of the Assembly must now, in addition to concurring, become the new President of the Council of Ministers, and appoint a new Minister of Interior (who controls election machinery) with the approval of the Assembly secretariat. Thus, the Constitution provides essentially for rule by assembly. Other minor concessions incorporated in the second draft are the promotion of the President of France to a position similar to that which he held in the Third Republic and the creation of a second house, the Council of the Republic, with powers essentially deliberative and advisory. Finally, the socialistic reforms were transferred from the body of the constitution to an impressive preamble in the second draft. Except for two innovations, the Constitution of 1946 showed marked similarity to the government under the Third Republic. The first new institution was the French Union, a federation which included metropolitan France and all members of the old Empire. The federation was provided with two representative bodies, both of which are related to the government of France in an advisory capacity. The apparent purpose of the French Union was to unify the empire by focusing the various spirits of nationalism into a common allegiance. The other new institution built into the 1946 Constitution was the Economic Council which is also consultative. Members of the Economic Council are nominated by representatives of labor, management, agriculture, artisans, family associations, cooperatives, and overseas territories. The Council examines bills and proposals of an economic and social character, excluding the budget; may initiate economic and social studies and submit resultant recommendations to the government; and may be called upon to arbitrate economic and social conflicts. The Council must be consulted concerning the establishment of a national economic plan for full employment and best use of resources.

THE EXECUTIVE ORGANIZATION.—The nature of the Presidency of the Republic was changed little by the Constitution of 1946. We have noted that in the Third Republic the requirements that every act of the President be countersigned by a minister and that the ministers were individually and collectively responsible to Parliament prevented all but the strongest of Presidents from personally exercising any of the powers conferred on the office. In addition we have seen that there was little likelihood of a strong man's being elected to the Presidency. In 1946, however, Charles de Gaulle, who had displayed both great strength of will and

---

[12] A crisis can occur only following the withholding of a vote of confidence or the passage of a motion of censure by the National Assembly. A question of confidence may now be put only by the premier and after consultation with his cabinet. A motion of censure originates in the National Assembly.

individual initiative, was not only President of the Provisional Government but also the actual chief executive of the nation. Moreover, he openly sought to strengthen the executive branch of the government. In view of these circumstances and of the fact that socialists and other radicals had in the past advocated the abolition of the Presidency, it is not surprising that the factions in favor of government-by-assembly should have sought to erect further safeguards against the possibility of a President's being able to exercise effective power. However, such barriers as were raised in the new Constitution are more theoretical than real.

For example, the old Constitution had provided no limitation on re-election of a President. The new Constitution, on the other hand, denies to any President more than two terms. The import of this provision is lessened by the fact that no President had ever been re-elected more than once and there existed a strong tradition against more than one term. Likewise, the new requirement that every act of the President must be countersigned by the premier as well as by a minister does not add an appreciable restriction in view of the fact that ministers had been and continue to be both individually and collectively responsible. Similarly, the provisions that the President must normally promulgate a law within ten days rather than thirty days, as was formerly true, and that the President of the National Assembly must proclaim the law if the President of the Republic fails to do so are of little practical importance. The old thirty-day suspensive veto had never been employed and no President had failed to promulgate a law. Even the constitutional transfer of certain fundamental powers to the premier and his cabinet[13] does not change the customary manner of exercising these powers. The premier rather than the President is now charged with ensuring the execution of the laws, with the appointment of subordinate civil and military officials, and with the direction of the armed forces and the coordination of all measures of national defense. These provisions merely recognize officially some of the political facts of life in the Third Republic.

The role which the President should play continues to be a subject of discussion in French politics. An appreciable number of people believe that the Presidency should be strengthened. However, in order for the President to exercise any real power, a corresponding amount of power would have to be withdrawn from the ministers. Consequently either the ministers would be put in the impossible position of trying to serve two masters—the National Assembly and the President—or the political system of France would have to be transformed into a presidential type in which the executive would be responsible to the nation as a whole rather than to the legislature. The de Gaullists in particular advocate this change.

---

[13] Acts of the premier in the exercise of the transferred powers must be countersigned by the ministers concerned.

As in the Third Republic, the actual executive body is the Council of Ministers (the Cabinet) and the true executive head is the President of the Council of Ministers (the premier). The role of the premier and his cabinet remains much as it was in the Third Republic. The pertinent constitutional laws of 1875 and the parliamentary practices of the Third Republic were written into the 1946 Constitution with minor changes, some of which we have already considered.

Such changes as were made appear to have been intended principally to accomplish the sometimes conflicting objectives of augmenting the power of the Assembly and increasing ministerial stability. For example, due to the enhanced position of the second house, the Constitution states that the ministers are *not* responsible to the Council of the Republic. This provision is also intended to remove the possibility of the new "upper" house from precipitating ministerial crises as did the old Senate on occasion. Another attempt to ensure added control of the executive by the Assembly and to increase ministerial stability as well is the requirement that before a new premier and his cabinet may be formally appointed, the program of the premier must be approved by vote of an absolute majority of the Assembly. A third change, however, appears to be intended solely to strengthen ministries by placing a slight check on the capricious putting of questions of confidence by ministries or the putting of motions of censure by the Assembly. The procedures for these measures are now formally laid down in the Constitution. One-day delays are required before either a question of confidence or a motion of censure may be voted upon by the National Assembly. A roll-call vote and an absolute majority is required in either case in order to force the resignation of the Cabinet.

This constitutional definition of ministerial crises is also rendered desirable by the fact that such crises may, as we have already seen, serve as a basis for dissolution of the National Assembly. The dissolution power of the executive appears capable of becoming an effective device for resolving parliamentary stalemates by appealing the issues at stake to the nation in a general election. We should bear in mind, however, that to many Frenchmen the dissolution of the legislature would appear as an attempt at either a *coup d'état* or a dissolution of the nation rather than merely a means of determining the predominant sentiment of the electorate. Moreover, apparently many French politicians are content with a portion of the national political loaf rather than risk having one party crystallize the issues and achieve control of both the Ministry and the legislature as is normally the case in parliamentary democracies such as Great Britain. Thus in general the ever-shifting coalition governments secure their personnel from the same pool of names. If local elections reveal a strong shift in national political sentiment, the controlling parliamentary coalition may easily avoid having to dissolve the Assembly. The

Ministry may merely resign without having received technically either a vote of no confidence or a vote of censure.

This technique is the method which the "Third Force"—a somewhat nebulous coalition of parties such as the Socialists, Radical Socialists, and Popular Republicans—adopted in 1948 after the coalition became stalemated but increasingly doubtful of receiving a majority in a general election. The municipal elections of October, 1947, had indicated a reversal of the post-liberation leftward trend and a shift toward the Right as represented by de Gaulle. Subsequently the Third Force ministries became increasingly ineffective in solving the economic problems confronting France and demands for a general election mounted. Correspondingly, the parties of the Third Force became increasingly fearful of exposing their parliamentary representatives to the mercy of the ballot box. Consequently, when the Ministry of Robert Schuman finally bogged down in July, 1948, it resigned without forcing a vote of no confidence or a motion of censure. The short-lived government of André Marie which then assumed office and the second Schuman government likewise technically avoided ministerial crises. The Assembly could have effectively resolved the situation by passing a law declaring the legislative term at an end [14] and calling for the election of a new Assembly. But much the same reasons which made the ministries seek to continue in office prevented the Assembly from taking action.

LEGISLATIVE ORGANIZATION.—The 1946 Constitution provided for a Parliament consisting of two houses, the National Assembly and the Council of the Republic. They meet as a single body only for the purpose of electing the President of the French Republic.

THE NATIONAL ASSEMBLY.—This body corresponds closely to the Chamber of Deputies of the Third Republic but by virtue of the new Constitution achieved a position almost tantamount to that of a unicameral parliament. Through substitution of the impotent Council of the Republic for the old Senate no question remains as to which house predominates. Not only does the Assembly alone adopt the laws but it also elects one sixth of the membership of the Council. Definite constitutional limitations of the Assembly's authority are confined to narrow, specific activities; there are no effective, sweeping checks. For example, the concurrence of the Council of the Republic is required on a vote to declare war. In addition, the Constitutional Committee and the constitutional amendment procedure, both of which we shall discuss below, may serve to delay legislation somewhat.

Clearly the Assembly is the supreme body of the government. We should remember, though, that such a large legislative body with a mul-

---

[14] The term of the National Assembly is fixed by simple statute.

tiplicity of parties and overlapping factions is inherently incapable of actually governing in the sense of providing effective leadership, especially in time of crisis. The fact that the Assembly possesses complete political power in legal theory does not mean that the Assembly can as a practical matter use this power to formulate and direct the execution of decisive governmental policies. Thus in the summer of 1948 the National Assembly could not decide the basic issue of socialization versus free enterprise even though this decision was vital to the economic recovery of France. As we have seen, the British Parliament also possesses tremendous power, but this power is given practical effect by a two-hundred-year tradition of the prime minister and his cabinet serving in dual roles as leaders of the majority political party in the House of Commons and as ministers of the crown.

In 1947 there were 618 deputies in the Assembly. The 544 members from metropolitan France were selected from the departments by means of universal, direct suffrage and proportional representation; in general there was one deputy for each 50,000 electors or fraction thereof. The remaining deputies represented the overseas departments and territories.

THE COUNCIL OF THE REPUBLIC.—This body was the concession of the Constituent Assembly to those Frenchmen who for various reasons demanded a bicameral legislature. The Council's duties are principally deliberative and advisory; its powers are virtually nonexistent. While the Constitution allows it to speak, the Council is not permitted to act in opposition to the National Assembly. There is little likelihood, however, of serious conflict arising in view of the fact that the electoral system is designed to ensure that the Council shall reflect the party alignment in the National Assembly. In addition, the term of the councilors is fixed by a simple law which presumably may be changed at will by the Assembly.

The Constitution prescribed that the Council of the Republic be elected by "universal, indirect suffrage," the departmental and communal councils being the actual electors. As the terms of these councils do not necessarily coincide with that of the National Assembly, possibly the majority of the councils could elect to the Council of the Republic men out of sympathy with the major factions in the National Assembly. This rather remote possibility is offset by the constitutional provision that the National Assembly may elect by proportional representation one sixth of the total membership of the Council.

As gestures toward the intended deliberative and advisory character of the Council, the Constitution required that the membership be renewed one half at a time and that its total be not less than 250 nor more than 320. This last restriction has the added feature of ensuring that the Council will not be able to dominate Parliament in electing a President.

Although the sole power of passing legislation rests with the Assembly, the councilors have a small measure of influence in legislative and constitutional matters. They may introduce bills which must, however, go directly to the Assembly. The Council is not permitted to propose expenditures and may not study the national accounts. Bills passed by the Assembly go to the Council for study and opinion. The Council is afforded two months (less, in certain cases of urgency) for this purpose. If no opinion is offered in that time, the bill is sent to the President for promulgation. The Assembly must consider any amendments which the Council may offer but need not accept them. The part played by the Council in amending the Constitution is discussed below. Otherwise our picture of this vestigial upper house is complete with the observation that the Council need not suffer any change in status through a constitutional amendment unless the amendment is approved either by it or by a national referendum.

CONSTITUTIONAL AMENDMENT PROCEDURE.—A constitution is supposedly a safeguard against the power of any parliament, but the efficacy of this check depends largely upon the manner in which the spirit and the letter of the constitution are observed. As French laws are not subject to judicial review, the 1946 Constitution created a Constitutional Committee to determine in certain instances the constitutionality of legislation or, as the Constitution states, to "determine whether the laws passed by the National Assembly imply amendment of the Constitution." The Committee is presided over by the President of the Republic. Its membership comprises the Presidents of the National Assembly and the Council of the Republic, seven members elected by the Assembly, and three members elected by the Council.[15] The ten elected members must be chosen by proportional representation of the parties in the two houses. Thus the Committee is more likely to be a partisan organization of active politicians than an impartial body of jurists. Moreover, the fact that eight of the members are chosen by the National Assembly probably assures a committee with the same political bias as the Assembly.

Even so, the Committee is apparently not to be trusted to exercise any initiative, for a specific article of the Constitution defines the conditions under which the Committee will act. First the Council of the Republic must decide by an absolute majority vote that a law passed by the Assembly implies amendment of the Constitution. Then the Presidents of the Republic and of the Council must make a joint request of the Committee that it examine the law. Even after these steps, which must take place in the period allowed for promulgation of the law, the

---

[15] The committeemen selected by the National Assembly and the Council of the Republic respectively may not be members of these two bodies and are elected at the beginning of each annual session.

Committee is not free to proceed alone. It must attempt to bring about an agreement between the Assembly and the Council. Failing in this, the Committee either approves the law for promulgation or returns the law to the Assembly for reconsideration. In any event, the Committee must complete its work within five days (two in an emergency) after receipt of the joint request.

Should the Assembly reconsider the law and adhere to the original vote, the law may not be promulgated until the Constitution has been formally amended. Such an amendment initially takes the form of a resolution by the Assembly which sets forth the purpose of the amendment. If an absolute majority supports the resolution, it is referred to the Council which has a maximum period of three months in which to deliberate. Should the Council fail to agree to the resolution by an absolute majority, the measure is returned to the Assembly for a second reading. The Assembly, if it again votes in favor of the resolution, must then draft the actual amendment. This amendment, unless it is adopted in each house by a three-fifths majority or passes the Assembly on second reading by a two-thirds majority, is submitted to a referendum.

In the final analysis, then, the amendment procedure, as a check against arbitrary action by the Assembly, merely forces a three-months delay and requires a two-thirds instead of a simple majority for the passage of laws of doubtful constitutionality. If this whole procedure were called into play, it would possibly be more restrictive than appears at first glance. For thus far French political opinion has been so mercurial that a coalition has been required for even simple majority control, and these coalitions have been singularly short-lived. On the other hand we should remember that fundamental constitutional changes in France are normally the product of revolution, *coup d'état,* or military disaster or the threat thereof, rather than drawn-out parliamentary processes.

Political Parties and Groups of the Fourth Republic

CHANGES FROM THIRD REPUBLIC.—The political parties which appeared in France under the GPRF all had had the common experience of a rebirth in the resistance movement during the German occupation. Resistance activity was a prerequisite for later survival as a party because many former political organizations bore the stigma of collaboration with the Vichy government. A party's entry into the resistance movement had been a gradual process, completed only when the existing resistance groups developed sufficient confidence in the party to accept it. The Communist party played a dominant role in the resistance, but other prominent organizations were the Socialists, Radical Socialists, Popular

Democrats or Social Catholic party, the Democratic Alliance, and the Republican Federation. When the Provisional Consultative Assembly was created under the FCNL, delgates from the resistance groups formed the largest bloc in that body.

In sharp contrast with the welter of political groups and parties under the Third Republic, the October elections in 1945 showed the emergence of three dominant parties under the provisional government. These parties were the Communist, Socialist, and MRP (*Mouvement Républicain Populaire*) which led in the popular vote in that order. Together they controlled 434 out of 486 seats in the National Constituent Assembly, with the Communists having 153 seats, the Socialists 143, and the MRP 138. The supremacy of the Communists and Socialists in one sense confirmed the leftward trend of postwar Europe, but in a larger sense the Communist strength was the result of General de Gaulle's expedient in 1943 and 1944 of cultivating the Communists. The old-line semiconservative Radical Socialist party, which had often dominated French politics before World War II won only twenty-five seats in the Assembly. Parties in the extreme Right had even fewer seats. Part of the shift of the parliamentary center of gravity to the left may be ascribed to a traditional French fear of dictatorship and to the general European postwar trend, but much was the result of the intensive electioneering work of the Communist party. It should be noted, however, that by 1947 Communism had created its own reaction to this leftward movement.

In addition to the leftward shift, the menace of the Communists tended to cause a definite structural change in the parties of the provisional government. The traditional French political party was, as we have noted, a loosely knit, poorly disciplined organization. The militant, highly controlled, and tightly knit Communist party, whose key leaders had been trained in Moscow, forced the other political parties to adopt similar measures in order to survive. Such discipline tended to create rigid party lines which prevented smooth compromise on constitutional issues.

THE COMMUNIST PARTY.—The French Communist party, in common with all Communist parties, has as its chief mission the implementation of Soviet policy. Prior to Russia's entry into World War II, the French Communists were, as we have seen, so violently opposed to war with Germany that the slowdown policy they adopted with respect to warplant production caused their exclusion from the labor organization, the CGT (*Confédération Générale du Travail*), and the imprisonment of some of their leaders. After Russia entered the war, however, the French Communists played an outstanding role in resisting the German occupation and the Vichy government. This activity, together with the recognition and toleration accorded the Communists by General de Gaulle, had so built the party's power that it was able to poll 26 per cent of the seats in the National Constituent Assembly in 1945, though the party had only approximately one million members.

By that time de Gaulle's policy had changed, for he refused to grant the cabinet portfolios of War, Interior, or Foreign Affairs to the Communists in September, 1945. The change in policy came too late, however, to prevent Communist infiltration into France's controlling labor organization, the CGT. This infiltration was aided by the Communists' prestige from Resistance leadership, by the general apathy of the French people, and above all by the excellent organization and discipline of the party itself. During the postwar period, when other political parties were casting about for political aims and platforms, the Communists merely followed an old pattern: they obtained firm control of labor and prepared to take advantage of any other opportunities which might present themselves.

From 1945 to 1947 the French Communists pursued a policy of collaboration with other parties. For a time a coalition with the Socialists was attempted. Parliamentary, rather than revolutionary methods were used to gain power, and the steady infiltration of the CGT was maintained. During the drafting of the 1946 Constitution, the Communists were able to exert definite influence on its content. Since at this stage they could be more effective by having their power concealed, they favored the strong-assembly weak-executive principle in the proposed government, opposed any system of checks and balances between governmental branches, and advocated broad state control of economic life. In foreign affairs, the Communists favored alliance with Soviet Russia and opposed any policy which might draw France close to the United States and Great Britain.

In accordance with its collaboration policy, the Communist party supported France's "all-out production" program until 1947. During that year the Soviet Union reactivated the Third International at a time when the European Recovery Program, the so-called Marshall Plan, was being considered by the United States. The purpose of the ERP was to revive production and trade, and thus promote the economic stability of the war-torn European countries. Since economic well-being was considered incompatible with the spread of Communism, the French Communist party instituted a vigorous propaganda campaign against the ERP and employed the subversive weapons which it had so energetically sharpened during the preceding two years. The Communist party fomented widespread civil disturbances and strikes. Through their control of the CGT the Communists were able to employ the general strike with considerable effectiveness. Thus by 1947 the French Communist party had supplemented its parliamentary tactics with those of a direct-action character.

THE SOCIALIST PARTY.—The Socialist party in France, as elsewhere in Europe, derives its greatest strength from the laboring classes and from the lower middle class. Since the Communist party also draws its main support from part of the same social bracket, a loss of strength for one party is likely to mean a gain for the other.

In general, there is a similarity, though certainly not an identity, between the political aims of the Communist and Socialist parties. This is perhaps a partial explanation for the Communist collaboration with the Socialist government of 1946. During the drafting of the 1946 Constitution the Socialists favored a single-chamber parliament plus a consultative chamber of experts from trade-unions, business organizations, and agricultural interests. In the event of parliamentary lack of confidence in a government, the Socialists favored the dissolution of Parliament and the calling of new elections on the British pattern. As for the executive branch, the Socialists' traditional desire for parliamentary predominance has been tempered somewhat by fear that without some outside checks a party of the Right or Left hostile to the Socialists would be able to seize control of Parliament. A few Socialists have gone so far as to advocate an executive-legislative relationship on the American or Swiss model. The Socialists have traditionally favored government ownership of key industries but have wanted to maintain a large sector of productivity for free enterprise. In foreign affairs the Socialist party advocates democratization of all nations. It supported the Anglo-French Alliance which was formed in 1947.

THE MOUVEMENT RÉPUBLICAIN POPULAIRE (MRP).—The nucleus of the MRP is the prewar Popular Democratic or Social Catholic party which was composed of communicants of the Catholic Church who had Socialist leanings. However, MRP membership is open to non-Catholics, and numerous Protestants and agnostics are members. The rapid accretion of strength of the MRP up to October, 1947, is attributable to its leaders' work in the resistance movement, to the postwar revival of religious interest, and to the appeal of the organization to Communist-fearing conservatives. The MRP may be considered a center party.

The social-economic program and constitutional aims of the MRP were conditioned by a vague religious background but were otherwise similar to those of the Socialist party. Unlike the Socialists, however, the MRP favored a two-chamber parliament during the formulation of the 1946 Constitution, as a check on overhasty legislative action.

The MRP enjoyed the support of General de Gaulle and strove to strengthen the extremely weak executive power offered by the first draft of the 1946 Constitution. Nevertheless, the second draft reflected only minor changes in the executive and when the MRP accepted the compromise, General de Gaulle's support of the party was withdrawn. By autumn, 1947, the Communist threat, in the form of strikes and civil disturbances, had become so great that a new party, led by de Gaulle, completely upset the October, 1947, municipal elections.

THE RASSEMBLEMENT DU PEUPLE FRANÇAIS (RPF).—The RPF may be described as an emergency party appealing to all who desired a change of political orientation in France. In brief, the party's policy was: strengthening of the executive branch of the government, return to free enterprise, a deflationary monetary policy, support of the American ERP (Marshall Plan), and a strong pro-American, anti-Soviet foreign policy. In the October, 1947, municipal elections this shift toward the Right drew a popular vote of approximately six million. In the same election the Communists drew some 4,700,000 votes, a loss of over a million popular votes from the previous national election. The loss of the MRP was more striking, however, approximately two thirds of its total support going over to the RPF. The October elections, being municipal, had no effect upon the seating in the National Assembly, but they offered a reasonably accurate forecast of future trends.

Armed Forces

ORGANIZATION UNDER THE THIRD REPUBLIC.—From the year 1937, when France was popularly reputed to have the strongest army in the world, to the disastrous defeat by Germany in 1940 was a long drop in prestige, self-respect, and morale for the French armed forces. Contrary to popular opinion, the army was weakened by obsolescent equipment, over-aged leaders who did not understand mechanized warfare, and a home front which lacked the spiritual and material resources necessary to meet the Nazi assault.

France's armed forces during the Third Republic functioned under the control of the premier and the Ministers of War, Marine, and Air. Defense activities were coordinated by a Supreme Council of National Defense consisting of all Cabinet members, the Chiefs of Staff of the Army and Navy, the Undersecretary of Foreign Affairs, and the Inspector of Antiaircraft Defense.

The French Army was divided into the Metropolitan Army, which had active, reserve, and territorial components; and the Colonial Army consisting of voluntarily enlisted white troops and conscripted native troops. The Metropolitan Army's strength was maintained by conscription of all able-bodied Frenchmen at the age of twenty-one for periods of service lasting from one to three years.

The Army as a whole was controlled by the Minister of War; however, appropriations for Colonial troops other than those in Algeria, Tunisia, and Morocco were included in the budget of the Minister for the Colonies. For Army administration, France was divided into the military government of Paris and eighteen corps areas. In 1940 France had only eighty-nine divisions available to meet the German invasion. All were infantry divisions except one armored, three light mechanized, and five mounted cavalry divisions.

The French Navy, under the jurisdiction of the Minister of Marine and his Chief of Staff, had a central administration including directorates of staff, supply, seacoast artillery, construction, finance, submarine defense, air service, and hydrography. Manned partly by conscription and partly by voluntary enlistment, the French Navy was the largest of all continental European navies. France's margin over Italy's naval strength was small, however, and the necessity of splitting the French forces between the Atlantic and the Mediterranean gave a decided superiority to the Italian force in the latter area.

Although it was a separate entity under the Air Ministry, the French Air Force cooperated with both the Army and the Navy. The Air Force was administered through five regional organizations for France plus several colonial headquarters. In 1939 France's three thousand first-line planes and one thousand reserve planes were decidedly inferior to those of Germany in both quality and quantity. Production had been seriously hampered by Communist-inspired labor disaffection in the defense industries.

REORGANIZATION UNDER THE FOURTH REPUBLIC.—From the 1940 nadir of strength and prestige, loyal fragments of France's forces, principally the Army, started the long climb back. General de Gaulle escaped from France with a loyal nucleus, and the Colonial Army in North Africa was added to the Allies after the invasion of North Africa in 1942. From 1940 until 1944 when the Allies invaded France, a dual process of reinforcement functioned continually. Loyal, hopeful Frenchmen made their way from France and Germany to join the French forces in England and in North Africa. Simultaneously, the resistance movement within France was growing and organizing—with Allied help—to the point where the loosely organized underground groups were recognized by the Allies in 1943 as the French Forces of the Interior (FFI). These scattered groups were led principally by former Regular Army officers and, although their operations were necessarily only quasi-military, the groups earned the commendation of the Allied leaders.

Following the Allied invasion of North Africa in 1942 the reorganization of the armed forces began in earnest. The Colonial troops were expanded by voluntary enlistment and conscription in unoccupied

French territory to a force of over three hundred thousand men. These troops were organized as a French Expeditionary Force comprising infantry and armored units armed and equipped by the United States.

At the same time the Navy and Air Force were reorganized. Units of the fleet were assembled from all parts of the world, some ships being modernized in the United States. By January 1, 1945, the French Navy included 305 ships (totaling 300,000 tons of which 180,000 tons were major units) manned by 6,000 officers and 77,000 men. The Navy fought for the duration of the war under the Allied Naval Command. The Air Force had only a squadron, organized in England, fighting the Italians in North Africa as early as 1940, but in 1942 the United States assumed most of the burden of equipping and training the reorganized air arm. By 1944 some twenty-four squadrons were in action under Allied command.

The next great step in the rebuilding of the armed forces followed the Allied invasion of France in 1944. The government being established once more in France, the various Army units which had participated in the invasion were consolidated with the best of the FFI into the French First Army which took over the southern flank of the western front. At the same time plans were laid by the provisional government for expansion of the Army.

There were a number of reasons for this expansion. In 1944 France was still in active war with Germany and consequently needed greater military strength to prosecute the war to a successful conclusion. Moreover, since an army is an instrument for maintaining internal as well as external security, post-liberation France needed a stronger internal security implement than it possessed to cope with the remnants of the Vichy regime and with undisciplined armed resistance groups. Not the least important reason for the planned expansion was prestige. Nazi occupation had dealt a staggering blow to the position of France as a great power. Consequently, General de Gaulle, as we have seen, made foreign recognition one of his major objectives. To gain prestige, to give support to French diplomats at international councils, to occupy an area of Germany, France needed a larger armed establishment.

Expansion, therefore, was started in 1945. For the first six months of that year, military expenses comprised 40 per cent of the national budget. By early 1946 the French Army had a strength of 1,800,000 men. With the cessation of hostilities in 1945, however, economy became a factor in policy making. Consequently, prestige such as could be gained from the military establishment had to be subordinated to economic recovery. By 1947 the military portion of the budget had been reduced to about 29 per cent; approximately five hundred thousand men remained under arms, with further reductions in prospect.

The years of 1946 and 1947 saw additional changes in the armed forces. The economy measures of 1946 were accompanied by plans for greater efficiency. The number of military regions in France was cut to nine (plus one in Algeria). In all services quality rather than quantity was sought. Conscription was continued, but with a new three-year military training program, two years of which were premilitary training supervised by the Ministry of Education. The third year, entirely military, emphasized specialization and physical fitness. In order to foster enthusiastic support of the economy and efficiency measures, many of the conservatives of the Regular Army were retired. Younger officers, many of whom fought in the resistance movement, were chosen to fill the vacancies. However, it should be noted that the influx from the *Résistance* brought no appreciable amount of Communist influence. The Army was still considered one of the most stable elements of the nation.

Along with the 1945 expansion plan, General de Gaulle revised the organization of the high command. He replaced the individual military Ministries with a single Ministry of National Defense. The unification thus obtained was subjected to successive modifications during the following two years. The reasons for the changes were largely political: for example, the National Defense Ministry had been infiltrated by Communists and was abolished in 1947. By that year's end the high command had reverted to an organization very similar to that in 1939. The Superior Council of National Defense was established to discuss Cabinet-level policies. The National Defense Committee, a smaller body of six to ten members including the President, premier, ministers of the three services, a representative of the Secretariat for National Defense, and the head of any other Ministry concerned, was responsible for the formulation and implementation of the actual defense plans. The Secretariat was an advisory agency created earlier in 1947 following the elimination of the National Defense Ministry.

While the organization of the armed forces at the political level with its overlapping high-command agencies was not particularly economical, at the lower level French Armed Forces in 1948 were ruled by the economy principle. Thus, the national defense law submitted to the National Assembly in January, 1948, provided for air, land, and sea forces totaling approximately only 660,000 officers and men. The Army, despite its tactical commitments in Indo-China and Madagascar, and its occupational requirements in Germany and Austria, was limited to 465,000 officers and men. The Navy was restricted to 58,000 officers and men, and the Air Force was allotted only 77,000. Other forces, including the national *gendarmerie,* accounted for the remaining 60,000. Expansion of the Air Force was hampered by the inability of the French aircraft industry to produce sufficient planes. The Navy with some 300,000 tons of vessels (half of its prewar total) could not expect any appreciable expansion in the future.

Although their matériel was largely obsolescent, the French pursued a comprehensive research and development policy aimed at supplying the latest and best equipment whenever its production was feasible. The emphasis was placed on highly mobile, highly trained, compact units.

Taken as a whole, France's armed forces were probably adequate for maintaining the internal security of the French Union as long as no united, coordinated disturbance occurred. Their ultimate effectiveness was directly dependent upon the extent of French economic recovery; by the end of 1948 they were woefully inadequate as an implement of French foreign policy.

Foreign Policy of the Fourth Republic

STRUGGLE FOR RECOGNITION.—When the Fourth Republic first took shape in the form of the French National Committee, the foremost aim of its foreign policy was to obtain recognition by the Allied Powers. To achieve this end General de Gaulle opposed the Allied practice prior to the invasion of North Africa in 1942 of treating with the Vichy government. By granting concessions to the Communists, as we have seen, he purchased Russia's recognition and forced a grudging de facto recognition of the FCNL by the United States and Britain. It was not until the Allied Powers had observed the French people's reception of the FCNL in France in 1944 that the FCNL was accorded de jure recognition as the Provisional Government of France.

RESTORATION OF STATUS AS A MAJOR POWER.—In 1944 the war with Germany presented an immediate problem, but governments must look ahead. For that reason, the Provisional Government of France, once recognized as such, immediately directed its foreign policy toward accomplishing its next objective, the restoration of France to its traditional place as a power among nations. If France's prestige could be re-established, her demands at postwar council tables would have greater weight. Her basic goal, national security, could be obtained more easily. Of the two traditional means of achieving a place among the leading nations, power and diplomacy, her power was pitifully deficient. France chose diplomacy, therefore, to gain her ends.

Unfortunately France's diplomatic machinery was obliged to function under a handicap in the latter months of 1944. In the course of his negotiations in 1943 and early 1944 for recognition of his government, General de Gaulle had exhibited a personality which irritated the leaders of the United States and Great Britain. Since the remaining significant world power was the USSR, and since previous negotiations with Russia had served to win limited recognition from the other Allies, de Gaulle combined security motives with a bid for diplomatic support by concluding a twenty-year mutual assistance treaty with Russia in December, 1944. This treaty provided that neither party would make any international agreement contrary to the interest of the other, that each would continue the war against Germany to final victory, and that both parties would cooperate in preventing or destroying any future German threat.

The treaty with Russia proved to be a step in a direction which France could not follow without sacrificing the support of the Western nations. Apparently realization of this situation caused de Gaulle to withhold recognition of the Russian-dominated government of Poland. It was not surprising, therefore, that this vacillation resulted in the exclusion of France from the Yalta and Potsdam conferences of the Allied Powers in 1945.

While France was not in a position to insist upon acceptance of her demands by the major powers, her interests were accorded important consideration. Thus, as early as 1943 France was given a share in the conduct of Italian affairs after the Allies invaded that country. Further, France was included by the Dumbarton Oaks Conference as one of the five permanent members of the projected Council. A French seat on the European Advisory Commission, the joint United Nations Consultative body in London, membership in the United Nations, with one of the five permanent seats on its Security Council, demonstrate that France was regarded as an important nation by the Allies.

NATIONAL SECURITY.—The two previously discussed aims of French foreign policy, recognition and restoration to status as a major power, were subordinate and incidental to the vital objective, national security. The two primary aspects of security with which the government of France has been concerned are economic and political. So completely interdependent are these factors in an era when a nation's industrial potential determines its defense capabilities that one cannot be discussed to the exclusion of the other.

The problem—with both political and economic aspects—which France considers most vital today is the ultimate status of Germany. The solution to this problem has been at the heart of French foreign policy since long before the end of World War II. The French desire a Germany which never again will be capable of aggression against France. To this end France seeks a loose confederation of autonomous German states with little or no federal defense organization or police force. She further desires international control of the Ruhr industrial area and of the Rhineland. The Saar coal-producing region, an important source of strength to the Third Reich, has voted itself under French control.

Realizing that other powers, principally Great Britain and the United States, are not in complete accord with French ultimate aims con-

cerning Germany, France has attempted to gain as much as possible from
the inevitable compromise. Her government has been an enthusiastic
supporter of the United Nations since it was first created. Should the
French aims for Germany fail to materialize, the French hoped that
the United Nations might develop into a bulwark against aggression.
The UN would also provide a forum in which France could press for
an economic objective, a share of the Ruhr coal production. However,
mindful of the inadequacy of the League of Nations, France sought to
ensure her security in 1944, as we have noted, by concluding a treaty
with Soviet Russia whose government likewise seemed at the time to
desire an emasculated Germany.

Soon after the treaty had been signed with the USSR it became apparent that Russian and French foreign policy had only the German
question in common. The French Communist party was growing steadily
more powerful and at the same time was adhering more openly to the
instructions of Moscow. The Soviet pattern of action was disclosed by the
events in Poland in 1944 and 1945. By refusing to recognize the Soviet-
sponsored Polish government, France started her shift to the camp of
Great Britain and the United States. A pro-Russian policy meant ultimately a complete loss of political security from within, whereas adherence to the Western powers promised a degree of economic security
through the U.S. financial credits. Moreover, some political security
seemed attainable through possible defensive alliances.

Financial credits did come from the United States,[16] but served only
to help keep France alive. They were insufficient to prime the dried-up
industrial pump, and moreover were not a part of a coordinated attack
on the general European economic problem. The country was beset
by inflation, worn-out industrial and mining equipment, labor shortage,
and food shortage. Strikes aggravated the consumer goods shortage which
in turn expanded the black market and led to further inflation. The
lack of consumer goods and the inflation discouraged full-scale agricultural production in France and hampered the food trade with French
overseas territories. By 1947, the economic security of France was in dire
peril. French industry had to be restored to a producing status and a
long-term source of coking coal (for steel production) had to be secured.

By 1947 also, the French had turned completely away from the USSR
and to the United States and Great Britain. The latter powers, together
with those European nations opposing the Russian foreign policy, had
formed the "Western Bloc." However, the United States and Great
Britain, concerned with the problem of the economic rehabilitation of
western Europe as a whole, felt that an economically unified Germany
was essential to the solution of that problem. Although this contingency

---

[16] In the years 1945 through 1947, France received from the United States approximately 2.2 billion dollars in direct and indirect loans.

was contrary to her policy, France was obliged to bow to the situation. She contented herself, therefore, with a fifty-year alliance with Great Britain (the Dunkirk Treaty), signed in March, 1947. This contribution to French political security provided that the two parties would cooperate closely with one another and with the United Nations in preserving peace and resisting aggression. In addition, specific provision for mutual assistance against renewed German aggression was made.

The French vision of Germany as a loose federation of predominantly agricultural states receded further when in the early summer of 1947, General George C. Marshall, the United States Secretary of State, announced that the United States would undertake to supply the minimum needs of the European nations in order to re-establish their economic productivity. France could not afford to ignore this opportunity for internal stabilization, although it meant the revitalization of the Ruhr as an industrial area. She made her bid for the European Recovery Program, as the United States plan was called, at the same time demanding a ceiling on Ruhr steel production at a point lower than that for France. She also renewed her demands for a share of the Ruhr coal production.

Although France's principal concern in her quest for economic and political security has been the German question and the ERP, she is also attempting to solve her colonial problems and is exploring the possibility of further development of the previously mentioned Western bloc. The overseas territories of France are discussed in more detail below. However, from the standpoint of foreign policy it should be noted that postwar conditions have made it necessary to revise French colonial policy. The old overseas empire was renamed the French Union—a term symbolic of the changed relationship between France and her colonies. No longer able to afford the luxury of an empire for its prestige value, France has allowed those elements which were least valuable and most difficult to retain, to secede. Thus, Syria and Lebanon achieved autonomy during the war and were given complete independence in 1946. Other more vital portions are to be consolidated by means of political concessions granted under the 1946 Constitution and, where possible, by force.

The eventual result of France's adherence to the Western bloc of nations remains to be seen. French need for economic security forced her to join the nations subscribing to the ERP. This action, together with the contingent modification of French demands concerning Germany and the realization of Russian aims, resulted, as we have seen, in the Franco-British treaty of 1947. In addition, France joined Italy in the discussion in 1947 of a Franco-Italian customs union. These steps indicate clearly the economic aspects of French foreign policy. The future should reveal whether or not France will become an active member of a Western union of nations bound together by political treaties and openly oriented against Soviet Russia, as was proposed by Great Britain early in 1948. The outcome depends primarily on three factors: the advantages to French security to be gained by such a definite step, the conviction of the French that Germany is a lesser threat than the USSR, and the future trend of internal French politics.

Judicial Organization

HISTORIC BACKGROUND.—As with local government, the fundamental judicial system of France was conceived in the Revolution and during the rule of Napoleon I. These two periods are of especial interest in explaining briefly the two systems of courts and law which exist in France today. The judicial system created during the Revolution in general envisaged only one hierarchy of courts and one system of law. However, the judicial authorities tended to attempt to moderate the radical nature of the revolutionary reforms. In many cases the courts nullified reforms which were being inaugurated by the administrative authorities of the legislative or executive branches of the government. Hence beginning as early as 1789, various laws were enacted providing that judicial and administrative functions would be separate and forbidding the judges to interfere with the operations of administrative bodies. Ultimately, the citizen whose rights suffered at the hands of the administration could not seek any redress from the judiciary. This situation naturally produced a reaction from the abused citizenry. Under Napoleon I, the Council of State and the Prefectoral Councils were established, and out of these developed the present system of administrative courts and administrative law. This system, called the *judicial* administration, safeguards the citizen from injustice at the hands of the *active* administration, that is, the nonjudicial portion of the civil government. Thus, this development which matured over an extended period during the nineteenth century has given France two systems of courts and laws.

The "ordinary" courts handle cases of civil disputes between citizens and of criminal prosecution of a citizen by the state. These courts utilize the "ordinary" civil and criminal codes of law, which are based on the Napoleonic codes, revised and amended but fundamentally unchanged. Unlike Anglo-Saxon common law, the French ordinary codes are written; every law is a statute. In the other of the two judicial systems, "administrative" courts deal in accordance with "administrative law" with the conduct of public officials acting in their official capacities and with the validity of rulings and decisions of the active administration. Administrative law—in contrast with ordinary law—consists of statutes, rulings of the Council of State, and custom.

COURTS UNDER THE THIRD & FOURTH REPUBLICS

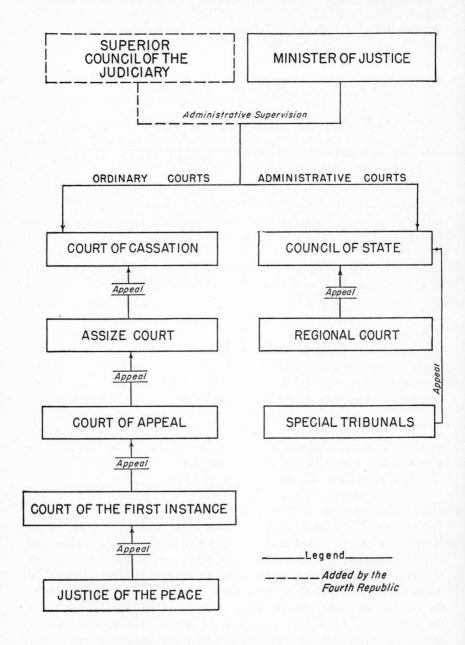

SUPERIOR COUNCIL OF THE JUDICIARY

MINISTER OF JUSTICE

Administrative Supervision

ORDINARY COURTS

ADMINISTRATIVE COURTS

COURT OF CASSATION

COUNCIL OF STATE

Appeal

Appeal

ASSIZE COURT

REGIONAL COURT

Appeal

COURT OF APPEAL

SPECIAL TRIBUNALS

Appeal

Appeal

COURT OF THE FIRST INSTANCE

Appeal

JUSTICE OF THE PEACE

_____Legend_____

_ _ _ _ _ *Added by the Fourth Republic*

THE JUDICIARY OF THE THIRD REPUBLIC.—In the Third Republic, the whole court structure was under the Minister of Justice. The courts were created by ordinary statute, not by the Constitution, and theoretically could be modified or curtailed in the same way. No French court had the power to nullify the acts of Parliament. Judges were recommended for appointment to their position by the Minister of Justice. In most instances their term of office was for life. Students of the law prepared specifically for the career of judge[17] as contrasted with a career as a practicing lawyer and selected their courses of study accordingly. Individuals choosing to become judges sought positions in the service, sometimes without pay, and attempted to work up through the hierarchy of the system.

In the ordinary court system, Justices of the Peace (*Juges de Paix*) handled petty criminal cases and civil cases involving small sums. Courts of the First Instance (*Tribunaux d'Arrondissement*) were organized in the *arrondissements* for similar cases of a slightly graver nature. Courts of Appeal (*Cours d'Appel*) were next in the scale; their jurisdiction was the civil and criminal cases of one to seven departments (*départements*). Each department had an Assize Court (*Cours d'Assise*) to handle misdemeanors in connection with the press and grave criminal cases. This was the only French court which used the jury system. At the summit of the ordinary court system stood the Court of Cassation[18] (*Cours de Cassation*). It heard appeals only. When this court reversed a lower court's decision, it returned the case to a similar lower court for retrial. Cases in all French ordinary courts above the Justice of the Peace level were usually heard by a college of judges. In addition to the ordinary courts which we have noted there were special tribunals such as the Industrial Disputes Councils at the level of the Justices of the Peace and the Commercial Tribunals at the level of the Courts of the First Instance.

The administrative courts consisted in general of three classes. Regional Courts (*Conseils de Préfecture*) handled cases involving the public officials in a group of French departments. The Council of State (*Conseil d'État*), the highest administrative court, heard appeals from the lower administrative courts and had original jurisdiction in certain instances. The third class of administrative courts comprised specialized tribunals such as the Court of Accounts (*Cours des Comptes*), which audited the accounts of the national government, courts which dealt with problems peculiar to the system of military service, and courts which resolved issues pertaining to the state system of education.

---

[17] In France, judges included both the conventional American concept of a judge (*magistrat du siège*) and what we would term a prosecuting attorney (*magistrat du parquet*). The same man could occupy either type of position.

[18] From the verb *casser*—to break.

CHARACTER OF JUDICIARY AND SAFEGUARDING OF CIVIL LIBERTIES.—The French judicial system and court procedure differed from British and American systems and practice in many ways. For example, neither the accused nor anyone else might refuse to testify on the ground that he might incriminate himself. The rules of evidence permitted great latitude in testimony; witnesses were permitted to offer hearsay evidence, or even to voice merely their own personal suspicions. French juries sometimes called the judge to the jury room to ask and be told what the penalty would probably be if a particular verdict were returned. Yet the judicial system appears to have been the logical outgrowth of French historical experience, to have been well adapted to the needs and desires of the people, and to have protected the rights of the individual adequately. The members of the judiciary were usually competent, independent in their decisions, and deeply conscious of their responsibilities. The bench was much respected by the people, and the judges enjoyed high social standing. The principal complaints were that the judiciary was underpaid, promotions were too slow, and some courts did not have enough business to warrant their existence.

THE JUDICIARY UNDER THE FOURTH REPUBLIC.—The historic judicial structure, practices, and law codes were rapidly re-established in liberated France. In general, the only immediate change was the institution of temporary tribunals to try approximately 112,000 cases of suspected collaboration. Both before and after the liberation, however, the systems of justice were subjected to criticisms and demands for reform as were all the other institutions of the fallen Third Republic. Advocates of reform believed that there had not been sufficient check on government by decree during the crises which gripped France between 1926 and 1940. It was felt that even when the legitimate Parliament was paralyzed by enemy occupation of the country, the executive arm of the government should be assisted and where necessary restrained by a council of legal and administrative experts. This belief was given substance in December, 1941, when de Gaulle instituted a judicial committee to examine all proposed decrees and ordinances of the Free French government in order to ensure that they were correctly drawn, in accord with historic French concepts of liberty and justice, and not inadvertently in conflict with existing statutes. This committee was reconstructed at Algiers in 1943 and continued to function until July, 1945, when its duties were transferred by an ordinance to the Council of State. Thus, the Council of State now has the added role of consultant on proposed decrees and legislation. Initiative and final decision rest with the executive and legislature, but custom now appears to require that proposed measures be scrutinized by the Council of State for technical correctness, general soundness, and regard for civil rights. In an emergency, a permanent committee (of the Council) maintained for such occasions examines the proposal. If the Council disapproves the measure, this body is required to submit constructive criticism and advice as to how the desired end, if it is legitimate, may be realized.

A committee for the reform of the ordinary judiciary was established in 1943. Succeeding committees have continued working to the present time. In sum, the reforms proposed are: harmonization of the system of justice with a nation which dislikes equally both conservatism and disorder; elimination of unnecessary courts; substitution of single judges for colleges of judges in most trials; ensurance of the independence of the judiciary; improvement of the quality of the judges; acceleration of the rate of promotion and increase of salaries; and enabling candidates of brilliant intellect but inadequate financial means to obtain an education for the judiciary. There is great disagreement as to the flaws of the existing system and the proper corrective measures. Consequently, the Constitution of 1946, with two notable exceptions, was silent regarding the judiciary. The Assembly has similarly failed to make any great number of changes.

The Constitution created the Superior Council of the Judiciary and charged it with nominating for appointment and ensuring the discipline and independence of judges and with administration of the courts. The only court which the Constitution specifically provided for is the High Court of Justice. However, this court is elected by the National Assembly at the opening of each legislative session. Consequently many French believe it to be too political in nature and a purely temporary institution which will be terminated upon conclusion of the trials of the high Vichy officials for treason. Up to mid-1948, the National Assembly had passed only one major judicial reform bill. This law merely modified somewhat the internal organization and procedure of the Court of Cassation. In view of the fact that the existing judicial structure has survived the rise and fall of empires, monarchies, and republics for over a century, one is inclined to doubt that any drastic changes will be made.

Local Government

CONTINUITY IN LOCAL GOVERNMENT.—From the time of its reorganization during the French revolutionary period, local government in France has had a vitality that has made it virtually immune to the effects of passing political storms. Political upheavals in France have had to do almost entirely with the national government and the city of Paris. While empires, monarchies, and republics came and went, the French system of local government remained substantially the same. Under the Third Republic, its principal changes were in the direction of more democratic procedures.

CENTRALIZATION.—Local government was highly centralized, with most of its officials appointed or otherwise controlled by the national ministries. Geographically, the units of local administration were the departments (*départements*), *arrondissements, cantons,* and *communes.* The chief political official of the department was the prefect (*préfet*). He was the local agent of the Minister of the Interior, and supervised national employees in his area. *Arrondissements* were principally administrative, judicial, and electoral subdivisions of the departments. They were administered by subprefects. Cantons were areas for police control, taxation, elections, and army recruiting. The communes were rural or urban units of township government, headed by mayors elected by the municipal councils. In each of these areas, except the cantons, there were elective councils with limited advisory powers.

PROPOSED DECENTRALIZATION.—The Constitution of the Fourth Republic recognizes only communes and departments (plus overseas territories) as local administrative units.[19] This change, if executed, would be less drastic than one would think, for under previous regimes the canton had no self-government and the assemblies of the *arrondissements* were of minor importance. The important change, if it becomes fully effective, is not in the machinery of local government but in the operation of that machinery. The announced determination of the French—in the words of one of their noted political leaders—is: "We must repudiate equally the centralizing Jacobinism which stifles initiative, the Caesarian authoritarianism which suppresses liberties, and the separatist autonomy which disperses the nation and mutilates the fatherland." Thus the French are endeavoring to achieve a tightly knit nation and at the same time to encourage local initiative and progress. The prefect is to remain charged with supervision of the execution of national laws and decrees, with representing the national interests, with directing and coordinating the civil servants, and with assuring the supremacy of national control over local communities. He is to be somewhat less dependent on Paris than heretofore in making decisions. Moreover, he is to decide many questions which previously the various departmental directors of the state services have been forced to submit to their respective ministries in Paris for decision. In turn, the prefect is to allow the local governments of the departments and communes much more freedom in the direction of their affairs. In effect, this program is to afford to the local governments of the departments a competence and freedom of

---

[19] However in mid-1948 both the *cantons* and the *arrondissements* continued to exist and to fulfill much the same role as under the Third Republic.

action comparable to that long enjoyed by the municipalities. In mid-1948 a program for effecting the desired reforms was under study.

Civil Service

RECRUITMENT.—The Third Republic had no agency corresponding to a Civil Service Commission. Each ministry had one or more agencies concerned with the problem. Any uniformity came only from the tendency to solve similar problems in a similar way and from the action of civil servants' organizations. Nevertheless, entrance to the various branches of the civil service was gained only after rigorous training for and successful passing of competitive examinations. Entrance requirements were geared to the highly coordinated and integrated system of state education. Thus it was necessary to have certificates and diplomas from appropriate educational levels in order even to be eligible to compete for a position with the civil service.

EFFICIENCY AND WORKING CONDITIONS.—The efficiency of the civil service and its amenability to political controls compared favorably with those of other leading nations. Civil servants were protected against discrimination and injustice from the operation of a "spoils" system. On the other hand, there was a tendency to give too much weight to seniority in making promotions, with a resultant loss of individual initiative and drive. Salary scales, rates of promotion, and pension scales were generally considered as unsatisfactory. These faults were offset somewhat by the prestige and certainty of government employment. The working conditions of the civil service were ameliorated to some extent by the activities of the many labor organizations of the employees.

IMPROVEMENT ACTIVITIES.—Under the Fourth Republic, the basic civil service system has been retained, but considerable effort is being made to eliminate possible faults in the system. A Civil Service Administration, attached to the Presidency, is now charged with over-all supervision—in cooperation with the ministries—of the civil service. Within the purview of the administration are such matters as recruitment, classification, pay scales, promotion systems, improvement of general working conditions, and improvement of technical efficiency. Particular emphasis is to be placed on the gradual development of an elite corps of civil servants possessed of a sense of initiative and serving as a constructive force in the nation.

STABILIZING INFLUENCE.—Civil servants gave the Third Republic a stability in its administrative functions which the transient Cabinets could not possibly provide. Senior members of the bureaucracy looked with some condescension upon politicians who were assigned to head executive departments about which they knew little. In practice, the ranking career men in each department usually made all decisions except political ones. The civil service had a tendency, particularly at its top levels, to exercise a strongly conservative influence on national politics.

The preamble of the Constitution of the Fourth Republic emphasizes the right of French workers to strike, to participate in collective bargaining, and to take part in the management of business. Coincidental with the peak of Communist influence in France in 1947, the government was hampered by strike activities of various civil service organizations. Even some units of the National Security Police were disaffected. However, with the waning of Communist influence and with firmer action on the part of the government in dealing with the strikes of civil servants, *les fonctionnaires* will probably continue in the future their tradition of exercising a stabilizing influence on the life of the nation.

French Colonial Empire and French Union

RESIDUE OF EARLIER EMPIRE.—One of the causes of the downfall of absolute monarchy in France was that in pursuing dynastic glory on the continent of Europe, the monarch (notably Louis XIV and Louis XV) let slip from his hands all but a few fragments of a tremendous colonial empire in North America and India. The revolutionary governments and Napoleon I, preoccupied with European expansion and hemmed in by the British Navy, took no effective steps to rebuild the colonial empire. Consequently, until Louis Philippe mounted the throne, France possessed only a few small islands in the Caribbean Sea and the Indian Ocean, French Guiana, and some trading posts in India.

NINETEENTH-CENTURY GROWTH.—Upon the accession of Louis Philippe, France began to build a new colonial empire with the conquest of Algeria. Napoleon III secured New Caledonia and part of Indo-China. Upon this foundation, the Third Republic created within a few years a colonial empire whose extent was second only to that of Great Britain. In 1881, a French expedition from Algeria established a protectorate over Tunis. In 1883–1885, a protectorate was instituted over the remainder of Indo-China—Annam and Tongking. In the same period French Somaliland was acquired. Great Britain and France took joint control of the New Hebrides, and each country claimed other islands of Oceania. Madagascar was subjected to French control. A little later, France added areas along the Congo and Niger rivers to her expanding empire. Then vast stretches of the Sahara and western Sudan were explored and linked up with Algeria and Tunisia on the north and with the Congo, Niger, and Senegal territories in the south and west. In 1892 France acquired the Negro kingdom of Dahomey. The pre-World War I territorial drive of France ended with her making the greater part of Morocco a French protectorate.

ACQUISITIONS FOLLOWING WORLD WAR I.—The division of the German and Ottoman Empires after their defeat in World War I further enriched France territorially. By mandate from the League of Nations, France assumed control over Togoland and Cameroons in Africa and Syria and Lebanon in the Middle East. The mandate of Syria and Lebanon was relinquished following World War II.

IMPORTANCE OF EMPIRE TO FRANCE.—Although one may possibly prove that the governmental expenditures which France has made in acquiring and maintaining her overseas empire have greatly exceeded the direct income which the state has derived from its possessions, the importance of the empire cannot be measured in such simple terms. A complete balance sheet must include economic, political, and strategic columns containing some items which can hardly be reduced to exact monetary figures. In the economic column we must consider the fact that 29 per cent of the French pre-World War II exports went to the Empire and 25 per cent of the imports came from it. These figures are made more impressive by the fact that the economic development of much of the empire has scarcely begun. We must add to this the benefits derived by French merchants from the possession of bases under French sovereignty over a large part of the world. Approximately 95 per cent of the land area and 60 per cent of the population under the French flag lie outside metropolitan France. To give up an appreciable portion of this empire, with attendant danger of the released lands' falling under the domination of hostile economic and political systems, would possibly have profound unfavorable effects on French domestic economy.

Such an economic dislocation would in turn produce political repercussions such as no political party would care to contemplate. In addition to the economic factors involved in the loss of Empire, there is the matter of French pride and prestige. Although the majority of the French now appear to be socialistically inclined and Socialism is theoretically anti-imperialistic, theory and practice often part company in the breast of the average Frenchman when French territorial possessions are involved. It is true that the French do not emigrate in large numbers and that frequently in the past Parliament has been very reluctant to grant the financial means necessary to acquire additional territory. Once the territory has been acquired, however, continued retention involves the sense of honor and patriotism of the average citizen as well as his real or assumed economic well-being.

A third factor is that of the strategic importance of the Empire. In both World Wars, France has looked to her possessions for men, foodstuffs, and materials to bolster the defense of the mother country. In World War II, French Africa played an important role as a base for the regeneration of the French armed forces and the formation of the French Committee of National Liberation. Should there be another world struggle, French overseas possessions could very possibly play an even more important part than in the past. French North Africa, for example, could again serve as a source of reinforcements for the mother country and a guardian of the Mediterranean trade route. In weak or hostile hands, however, French North Africa could be converted into a menace to the security of France. Madagascar is another trade-route guardian that could be either a protector of or a menace to the security of France.

In appraising the regard of the French people for their overseas possessions, one should note that the French branch of the Communist party does not find it advisable to attack openly the retention by France of such areas as Tunisia, Morocco, and Indo-China, even though other agents of the party are actively at work trying to accentuate and control native discontent in these places.

DEMANDS FOR INDEPENDENCE.—France's African and Asiatic dependencies have been affected by nationalistic unrest characteristic of most dependent peoples during the present era. Among the basic factors contributing to this unrest are (1) the economic and social revolution wrought among many of the subject peoples by the impact of Western technological culture; (2) exposure in schools and war propaganda to Western nationalism and ideals of civil liberty; (3) various factors preventing the Western powers from either ruthlessly exploiting and crushing the dependent peoples or carrying out a completely enlightened program of development; and (4) the weaknesses of the Western powers revealed in World War II.

In states such as Indo-China, Madagascar, Tunisia, Algeria, and Morocco, active native minorities have attributed all the ills of their country to the political and economic control exercised by France. Consequently, these minorities demand outright independence or seek to remain only nominally a part of the French Union. As we have already noted, Communists work to accentuate and pervert these movements. Thus far Communists, wearing the mantle of native patriotism, have gained their greatest success in the states of Tonking and Annam (Viet Nam Republic) in French Indo-China. In Africa, the Communists have apparently been unable to exercise dominant leadership in separatist movements. There, agitation for independence appears to look to the Arab League for leadership. Communists do not seem to be able to infiltrate effectively this league of the Middle Eastern Moslem states and the Arabic but predominantly Christian Lebanon.

In each disaffected area there are other native factions which also desire radical improvement of their economic and political lot but within the French Union. Such groups are influenced by the fact that a complete break with France would not necessarily result in appreciable economic or political improvement. None of the states is strong enough to stand alone in an unstable world. Even if they could maintain independence, their progress would be hindered by native hierarchies seeking to resume autocratic powers, by illiterate, impoverished masses accustomed to being ruled from above, and by lack of capital.

Even so, if France is to preserve her Empire intact, she must remove two basic grievances which furnish fuel for the nationalist flames. The low standard of living of the natives is probably the primary grievance. Remedying this requires vast improvements in educational and medical facilities. Urban workers must be granted higher wages and better working conditions. Peasant farmers should be schooled in modern husbandry and enabled to own machine implements and adequate land. The energies of the intelligentsia should be applied to the educational and health programs and the higher civil service positions. An increasing supply of consumer goods must flow to the poorer portions of the native populations. Allied with the necessity for economic reform is the urgent need for governmental reform. Native participation in the government and the form of government must be developed to the point where the native has no justification for feeling that he is being governed principally for the benefit of an alien conqueror—or worse, for the benefit of two sets of masters, the old hierarchy and above that an alien conqueror.

POLICY OF THE FOURTH REPUBLIC.—As we have already noted, under Foreign Affairs above, the firm intention of the Fourth Republic is to preserve her present overseas possessions intact and to rely principally on an "enlightened" policy of development which will federalize and harmonize all elements of the French Union. Unfortunately, the general world situation together with the internal economic and political instability of France has hampered her efforts. Even so appreciable political progress has been made.

COMPOSITION OF THE FRENCH UNION.—In accordance with Title VIII of the Constitution, the French Union has been divided into three political categories. The first category is composed of metropolitan France and the overseas departments of Algeria (divided into three departments), Martinique, Guadeloupe, French Guiana, and Réunion island. The second category, called the Overseas Territories, includes the "former colonies" of French West Africa, French Equatorial Africa, French Somaliland, Madagascar, French Oceania, New Caledonia, New Hebrides, French Settlements in India, St. Pierre, and Miquelon. The former League Mandates of Cameroons and Togoland, now officially trust territories of the United Nations under French administration, are also part of the Overseas Territories. The third category comprises the "former protectorates" of Tunisia, French Morocco, and the Indo-Chinese Federation. These are now called "Associated States."

POLITICAL RELATIONSHIPS WITHIN THE FRENCH UNION.—Title VIII prescribes a variety of political relationships within the French Union and leaves to Parliament wide discretion as to the exact nature of many of the relationships. The President of France is the President of the Union and chairman of the High Council of the Union. The Council is composed of certain members of the Cabinet and "of the representatives that each associated State is permitted to accredit to the President of the Union." The High Council is intended to advise the Cabinet regarding general policies of the Union. In a similar parallel advisory position with respect to the National Assembly is the Assembly of the French Union. This latter Assembly is composed "half of members representing Metropolitan France and half of members representing the overseas departments and territories and the Associated States." The National Assembly of France and the Council of the Republic elect two thirds and one third respectively of the members representing metropolitan France. Regional assemblies elect the representatives of the overseas departments and territories. Each Associated State determines the method of selecting its delegates.

French overseas departments and territories participate further in the government both of the French Republic and of the Union by electing deputies to the National Assembly and the Council of the Republic and by sending representatives to the Economic Council. Moreover, each overseas department and territory elects an assembly which manages local affairs. The composition of the electorate and the powers of the local assembly vary considerably from region to region. In general, the franchise is exercised by French citizens and by a limited number of natives possessing certain qualifications such as the ability to read and write, ownership of property of specified value, or credit for service with French armed forces during the war. Each department in Algeria has a prefect who performs duties similar to those of his counterparts in France proper. Over the three departments and the remainder of Algeria as chief executive is a governor-general appointed by the President of the Republic. Each of the other overseas departments and territories or groups of territories has a chief executive who is likewise appointed by the President. The authority of these representatives of the government varies with the political reliability and development of their respective departments or territories.

The Associated States are theoretically autonomous states each possessing its own constitution and government. In some respects this is true, for each has its native titular sovereign or president. Each possesses an assembly of sorts. There are certain political fields into which the French do not ordinarily intrude. But thus far each state has proved either so politically unreliable or backward or both that final authority rests with a French resident-general or high commissioner. True autonomy remains a goal to be achieved rather than an accomplished fact.

THE GOVERNMENT OF

ITALY

◇◇◇

Italy in Transition

THE IMPORTANCE OF ITALY'S ROLE.—Italy, the ancient preceptor of Western civilization in matters of law and government, once again occupies an important position on the stage of modern governmental and political development. In Italy we have an example of a country in which the struggling growth of political democracy, functioning within the framework of a limited monarchy, was cut short by the meteoric rise of the modern phenomenon of totalitarian dictatorship. Two decades of Fascist rule radically altered the basis of political power, form of government, and basic concepts of the relationship between the citizen and the state. Now, crushed by a military defeat which destroyed dictatorial rule, the Italian people are once again trying to construct a democratic edifice upon the ruins of the earlier state.

The importance of Italy lies not only in her efforts at reconstructing democratic institutions, but also in her position in the forefront of the socioeconomic and political struggle between the conflicting ideals and theories of the liberal, democratic Western tradition and the doctrinaire, militant, class-conscious socialism of Marx and Lenin. The choice of the Italian people between communist dictatorship or democratic government by popular sovereignty and the substance that the Italian people can give to a decision to remain masters in their own house cannot fail to influence materially the course of events in western and central Europe.

The objective evaluation of the present government of Italy begins with an examination of its foundations and the development of the Italian people in the arts of self-government. After all, two decades of dictatorial rule have not wholly obliterated the memory of the earlier democratic experiment.

UNIFICATION OF ITALY.—During the long period from the collapse of the ancient Roman Empire to the latter part of the nineteenth century the Italian peninsula was divided into numerous small states. During the greater part of that time these states either quarreled among themselves for territorial and other advantages or were victims of the covetousness and dynastic rivalries of more powerful European neighbors. From the final downfall of Napoleon Bonaparte in 1815 until 1859, the Italian peninsula was divided into nine states, the most important of which were the Kingdom of Sardinia (Piedmont), Tuscany, the Papal States, and the Kingdom of Naples. Italy, like Germany during the same period, was a geographical area, not a political entity. The ambitions of Italy's powerful neighbors, seeking to make capital out of Italian weakness, and the rivalries of her petty princes combined for a while to frustrate the efforts of those leaders to develop drives for Italian unification. Nevertheless, the *Risorgimento* (Revival), a strongly idealistic and nationalistic movement, gained increasing support in all parts of the peninsula. The *Risorgimento* was dedicated to the re-establishment of a united Italian government, and strongly motivated by its demands for social justice and political democracy. Among its outstanding leaders were Mazzini, Cavour, Garibaldi, and King Victor Emmanuel II of Sardinia.

In the middle of the nineteenth century, Sardinia, under the leadership of its chief minister, Cavour, and the royal house of Savoy, emerged as the state most capable of expelling the Austrian forces from their Italian possessions and of leading the movement for the political independence and unity of Italy. From 1859 to 1861 the major portions of the peninsula were brought under the political sway of the Piedmontese state. Overriding the opposition Republican party headed by Mazzini and Garibaldi, the Sardinian leaders proclaimed a kingdom of Italy in 1861, with Victor Emmanuel II at its head. In 1866 Venetia was acquired as a result of the Seven Weeks' War in which Sardinia allied itself with Prussia against Austria. Finally, Rome was occupied by Italian forces when the French troops, which had upheld papal authority in that city, withdrew during the Franco-Prussian War of 1870. The unity of the entire Italian peninsula in a political sovereignty was thus achieved.

Subsequent Italian history falls into three periods. The first is a period of liberal, parliamentary government under a limited monarchy, lasting until 1922. The second is the period of Fascist dictatorship from 1922 to 1943, in which the monarchy was eclipsed by the will of the dictator who dominated all functions of government.[1] The third period comprises the current efforts to construct a republic and to preserve a democratic form of government against the attacks of Communism.

---

[1] During the final two years of that period the dictator, Mussolini, ruled more in name than in fact. Italy had in effect become a satellite of its ally in arms, Nazi Germany.

Parliamentary Government Under a Limited Monarchy, 1870–1922

BACKGROUND.—Although 1870 marked the achievement of Italian unification, much remained to be done before such a goal could be reached in any other than a politico-geographical sense. Sectional differences were wide and difficult to adjust. Political education was lacking in the people. So great were the forces of disunity that Count Cavour, guiding genius of the new kingdom, turned down the suggestions for local democracy in a framework of regional federalism in order to establish the centralized unitary pattern then prevalent in Savoy. In effect, the governmental system, civil service, army, and political leadership of Savoy expanded their field of action to include all of Italy. This utilization of existing institutions drove underground the popular sentiment for social reform and a democratic republic, which nevertheless persisted in the Italian political conscience. Extremists, as well as proponents of democracy, have obtained from that early defeat ample ammunition for their campaigns down to the present day.

LEGAL BASIS.—The constitution promulgated for the newly united kingdom was the *Satuto Fondamentale del Regno* (Fundamental Statute of the Kingdom), previously granted by King Charles Albert of Savoy and Sardinia to his subjects during the Europe-wide popular upheavals of 1848. It was a brief document, general in its terms. It contained no formal provision for amendment. An Italian school of thought developed which regarded the *Statuto* as a flexible instrument to be changed and expanded by laws and usages, rather than by amendment. Like the British Constitution, the *Statuto* was considered to be ever changing, inasmuch as every act of the Italian Parliament, expressing the will of the people through the voice of their legal representatives, was deemed to be constitutional.

THE EXECUTIVE.—The executive powers of the nation were vested by the *Statuto* in the person of the king. In practice these powers were delegated, as in the British system, to the ministers of the government who administered the realm subject to the will of Parliament. In addition to acting as a symbol of Italian unity and a focus of allegiance for the people, the king exercised direct political influence through his power to select the ministers of the Cabinet, a prerogative in which he enjoyed considerable latitude. Once selected, however, the ministers remained in office only so long as they could command a parliamentary majority. The one outstanding feature of the Italian executive branch was its constitutional power to rule by decree in case the Parliament was not in session or was deadlocked over an important measure. Even though such de-

THE ITALIAN MONARCHIST GOVERNMENT

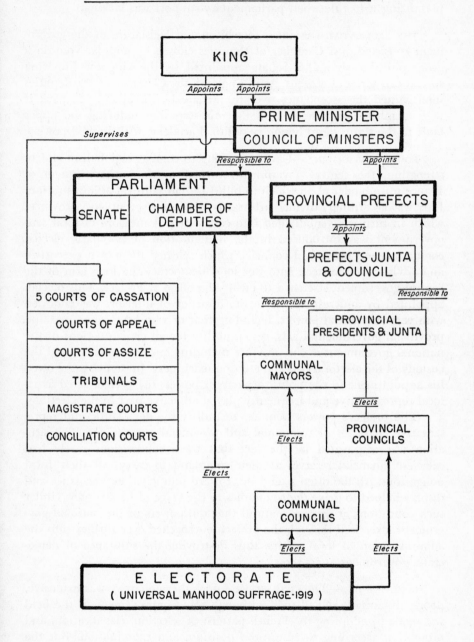

crees were supposed to be subject to eventual approval by the Parliament, this provision gave the government in power a strong political weapon, permitting it to rule when parliamentary support was lacking.

THE LEGISLATIVE BRANCH.—The bicameral legislature of the government consisted of a Chamber of Deputies chosen by popular vote on a geographical basis and a Senate appointed by the king for life from special categories of citizens. As in England, the Chamber of 535 deputies soon gained the ascendancy over the Senate by threatening to pack it with members sympathetic with the ministry, thus reducing the upper body to the status of an honorary political academy with limited powers.

LOCAL GOVERNMENT.—Cavour, seeking to combat regionalism and to strengthen the central government, turned to the unitary system of France for a model upon which to build Italian political administration. Italy was accordingly divided arbitrarily into some seventy-five provinces which in turn were subdivided into communes. A measure of local self-government was introduced in the inauguration of popularly elected communal and provincial councils, which selected their own executives and advisory committees. Into this local democracy the long arm of the central government stretched to create the office of Prefect. This official, appointed by and responsible to the minister of interior, was endowed with very substantial powers, including that of veto over communal and provincial governmental acts, responsibility for all civil functions of the national government in the province including law enforcement, and the custody of the electoral lists and election machinery. Inasmuch as he owed his appointment to the political party in power, the prefect acted as its local representative and frequently played an active part in the elections.

The prefect's powers went far to nullify the democratic and representative character of communal and provincial government. The situation was aggravated by the fact that these subdivisions rarely had sufficient financial reserves at their command to carry out their fiscal obligations. All too often a tendency toward municipal extravagance and display helped to drive the communes to the verge of bankruptcy. Under such conditions, it was but natural that the powers of the national government, exercised through the prefect, encroached ever further into the administration of local affairs, thus destroying the substance of democratic government at its roots.

CIVIL SERVICE.—The civil service under the monarchy was extensive, poorly organized, and ill paid, although some improvement in the field was made by adopting the French pattern of selection, classification, and promotion according to education, position, and examination. But the system in Italy still remained under the control of the individual ministries and hence subject to inevitable political favoritism and corruption.

The number of civil servants was larger than would reasonably be needed for a country the size of Italy, since, in addition to normal gubernatorial responsibilities, the government operated the railroads and insurance businesses as public monopolies. These enterprises, being inefficiently operated, were frequently in debt, thus causing a drain on government expenditures which, in turn, resulted in low salaries for the employees. One consequence of this latter circumstance was the formation by government employees of an Association of Public Employees, which gave them a common voice in requesting pay increases, more favorable pensions, and more uniform promotion procedures.

JUDICIAL BRANCH.—The tendency toward centralization of governmental powers which characterized the union of Italy did not affect the established judiciary. Five Courts of Cassation, each comparable to our federal supreme court as courts of last instance, were located at Turin, Florence, Naples, Palermo, and Rome. Independent within their own districts on all questions of civil and criminal law, these bodies usually considered only errors in the decisions of inferior tribunals. This decentralization caused a certain amount of disparity of legal interpretation among the five districts. Some thirty-four Courts of Appeal, Courts of Assize, Tribunals, Magistrate's Courts and Conciliation Courts functioned at progressively lower levels of the judicial system. In the Courts of Assize and Tribunals the jury system prevailed as in England and the United States. The Italian judiciary was separate from the civil service, its members being appointed by royal decree only after a rigorous examination. A lifetime career with special privileges served to preserve its independence. As in French law, there was a division between the so-called "public" and "private" law. Complaints against the government could be handled only by administrative courts of which the Provincial Junta acted as the court of first instance and the Council of State in Rome acted as the tribunal of last instance.

FOREIGN POLICY.—The leaders of the newborn Italian state were not slow to launch an active and ambitious foreign policy. Substantial areas, wholly or largely Italian in their ethnological make-up, remained to be incorporated into Italian hegemony. The rival ambitions of Italy's great-power neighbors also provided ideal waters for serious fishing. Neither the long-range objective of a great-power status, however, nor the more immediate target, the absorption of Irredentist areas, could be sought until Italy's military arm had won the respect of the older powers. Steps in that direction were taken when the government instituted military conscription on a one-year training basis. A naval construction program was launched at the same time which, in spite of Italy's limited financial means, raised Italy's naval tonnage to seventh place in world ranking by 1914.

The desire to acquire all Italian-speaking regions such as Trentino, Italian Tyrol, Trieste and portions of the Dalmatian coast, as well as Austria's determination to retain sovereignty over those areas, did much to embitter relations between these two powers. Italy's land hunger was at the same time leading her into successive adventures in north and northeast Africa, where substantial areas of relatively worthless terrain remained untouched by Europe's imperial powers. Italy's first war with Ethiopia ended in the disastrous Italian defeat at Adowa in 1896. Tunis, with its modest economic potential, fell to French control in 1881. Its acquisition nevertheless continued to be an Italian objective, so much so that in 1882 Italy became a partner of Germany and Austria in the Triple Alliance. Tripoli fell to Italian arms in 1911, as did the Dodecanese islands, both of them booty of her successful war with Turkey.

Long before the outbreak of World War I, Italian opinion had thoroughly soured on the idea of an alliance with the two Teutonic leaders. After all, Austria remained in possession of valuable parcels inhabited chiefly by Italians. And Germany's raucous militarism and territorial appetite alienated substantial Italian groups which had espoused democratic idealism as a political faith. Moreover, owing to the fact that Italy was extremely vulnerable to any joint Anglo-French military effort, it was only logical that *rapprochement* with Great Britain and France should have prevented her from living up to her commitments in 1914. The same logic led in the following year to the signing of the Treaty of London, bringing Italy into the war on the side of the Western Allies. Italy emerged from the war with the provinces of Bolzano, Trento, Gorizia, Trieste, Pola, and the city of Zara—booty for which she paid some 600,000 war dead, widespread devastation in the war zone, complete economic displacement, and a tremendous national debt. The disillusionment that followed ended the brief period of good feeling in Italy's relations with Britain and France, setting her on a course which ended in 1940 when she became the outright enemy of those powers.

INTERNAL POLITICAL PROBLEMS.—As we have seen, the initial problems of Italian government revolved around the breaking down of the provincialism of Italian political thought, the development of Italian unity, and the political education of the Italian people, unused either to self-government or to the self-discipline necessary to fulfill the duties and obligations of citizenship. While Cavour's attempt to foster unity by the granting of extensive powers to appointed provincial prefects tended to foster national unity, it also seriously retarded the political development of the people by denying them the opportunity to develop initiative and responsibility in solving their local problems. Despite numerous attempts to develop a two-party system of government, strong national political parties pledged to a concerted program failed to develop until too late to have any effect. Italian political groupings degenerated into individual followings which bargained their political support in return for consideration of political patronage. The shifting allegiances, so skillfully managed by politicians like Giolitti, a pre-Fascist premier, precluded the success of any clear-cut program to which a coalition Cabinet might be committed. The system also eliminated the formation of an opposition party on other than temporary, vague, or personal grounds. Political corruption, elections managed by provincial officials, and the use of patronage to gain parliamentary majorities abounded well before the Fascist era. Italy's leaders, in brief, failed to develop either strong democratic leadership or to give her citizens sufficient opportunity for political education to cope with the shortcomings of their government. At the same time, a common distrust for politicians and parliamentary methods left the people vulnerable to the persuasions of any demagogue who could promise them stability, decency, and public order.

PROGRESS OF DEMOCRACY.—Despite such frustrations and the relatively short time, fifty years, in which democratic ideas were allowed to grow, considerable progress should be noted. The franchise, which initially included only a small minority of the population, was successively widened until in 1919 universal manhood suffrage was adopted. After sporadic repression by conservative governments, the practice of certain civil rights, such as freedom of speech and press, was extended to all parts of Italy. The communes were slowly attaining more autonomy in the handling of their local affairs. The rise of a strong labor movement and its resulting pressure on the government brought the enactment of social legislation to ameliorate working conditions and government aid to the cooperative movement. The growth of the Socialist and Populist parties showed some promise of guiding national politics from coalition toward a two-party system. After 1917 governments became more responsive to public opinion with every election, less prone to manipulate the election machinery. On the whole it is fair to say that while liberal democracy in Italy exhibited grievous weaknesses, it had made sufficient strides since its initiation in 1870 to warrant hopes for future progress.

Totalitarian Dictatorship under Fascism, 1922–1943

DEVELOPMENT OF FASCISM.—The opportunity for the continued development of democracy in Italy came to an abrupt end in 1922 with the advent of Mussolini and the Fascist party. The causes for the overthrow of parliamentary government in Italy by this dictatorship stemmed from conditions which had existed prior to World War I. Glaring social inequalities separating the landlord and wealthy industrial classes from the

great masses of impoverished peasants and laborers made Italy fertile soil
for the growth of the socialist dogmas of Marx and Engels as well as for
the more violent revolutionary syndicalism of Michael Bakunin and
Georges Sorel. Agitation for the division of the great estates and for the
development of social legislation spread swiftly throughout the country.
Sometimes this unrest took the form of strikes, often the form of anarchis-
tic attacks against landlords, the monarchy, or the church. Andrea Costa,
Turati, Ferri, and others gave coherence to this growing revolutionary
spirit by founding the Socialist party in 1891. This party, with its platform based on Marxist doctrines, focused a militant hostility toward the
conservative monarchy. Although the party suffered numerous reverses
and was eventually divided between a revolutionary syndicalist left wing
and a moderate reformist right wing, it consistently refused to participate
in the government or to cooperate to any large extent with the other
parties, with the result that the democratic development of a party government was greatly weakened.

As a counterpoise to this revolutionary movement, an equally militant sentiment, nationalistic in character, emerged among the conservative upper middle class elements of the population. It demanded a
stronger central government, one less responsive to mass opinion and
which would go even further toward protecting the vested interests. It
tried to put an end to regional particularism, to weld the provinces into
a more integrated nation, one which would achieve greater international
prestige through an aggressive policy of imperialistic expansion.

As we have seen, the Treaty of Paris, in 1919, frustrated the hopes
of the expansionists and democratic idealists alike. As a result the nationalist position was greatly strengthened, expressing itself in popular
sympathy for the dramatic seizure of Fiume by D'Annunzio. Moreover,
in 1919 Italy faced severely critical economic and social conditions which
tended to intensify her growing domestic political problems. Her industry and agriculture were disrupted by the dislocation and devastation of
the war. Demobilized soldiers returning as victors were embittered to
find that industry was unable to give them work and that the social and
political reforms promised in 1917 had not materialized. Maturing youths,
too young for war, and roused by a nationalistic fervor, were eager for
any type of adventure. Men who had grown up in the violence of the
war found adjustment to peace difficult if not impossible. The Conservatives in business and government grew increasingly afraid of the growing social unrest. Thus, the postwar situation in Italy provided a climate
favorable to revolutionary action.

While the example of successful Communist revolution in Russia
inspired the more radical Socialists, it served likewise as a dire warning
of impending danger to the Nationalists and Conservatives. The return
to the devious political parliamentary juggling of Giolitti was anathema

to both factions and evoked in both a desire for immediate action. On one hand the Socialists, operating through the labor unions, embarked on a series of strikes, including the seizure and attempted operation of the large factories in the north. The Nationalists, on the other, combined with anarchist renegades from the Socialist party like Mussolini, dissatisfied ex-officers, and youth of the middle class to form action squads (*fasci di combatimento*) for the forcible achievement of their program. These *fascisti* were initially aided in secret by a government which feared the growing power of the socialist movement. Officials therefore either looked the other way or openly sided with the *fascisti* when the latter used violence to break up strikes or to overthrow locally elected socialist governments. Conservative landlords and industrialists looked upon the Fascists as a weapon for curbing the strikes and riots of the dangerously dissatisfied working classes which seemed to threaten a repetition of the Russian revolution and the coming rule of the proletariat.

RISE TO POWER.—In 1919 Benito Mussolini, a political opportunist and ex-radical socialist, called upon these Fascist bands to unite their forces in forming the Fascist party. By March of that year the party was organized with Mussolini as its national leader. For the next three years Italy was subjected to incessant strife between militant bands of Socialists and Fascists. Demonstrating a complete lack of scruple, the Fascists were able to take over one by one the prefectural, police, and post offices, together with the railway stations, until their provincial leaders became almost undisputed masters in north Italy.

By 1922 the improvement in economic conditions, the collapse of a Socialist general strike, and the wide split in the Socialist party between the conservative reformists, the Maximalists, and the radical Communists, precluded the danger of any successful proletarian revolution or prolonged economic depression. Despite the improved conditions, however, civic unrest continued with sporadic outbursts of communal violence and anarchy, largely instigated and directed by the Fascists themselves. The skillful use of propaganda made it appear that political and economic disintegration in the nation had reached the point where drastic action had become necessary. The Fascists were aided by a seemingly insoluble parliamentary deadlock in the selection of a ministry, the lack of effective opposition caused by the split in the Socialist party and their associated labor unions, and by the apparent backing of the army and monarchy. Infiltrating into Rome in October of 1922, the Fascists so overawed the Parliament that many politicians, hoping for an end to the violence, urged the king to have Mussolini form a coalition government. To this invitation he readily acquiesced.

With only 35 of the 530 seats in the Chamber of Deputies and less than half of the cabinet positions in Fascist hands, Mussolini lacked the substance of control over the country. He had, however, driven a wedge into the governmental structure which enabled him to inject his party into all levels of the political machinery. By use of threats, coercion, concentration camps, and murder he extended his control step by step until Italy was completely subordinated to his demands.

CONSOLIDATION OF THE FASCIST CONTROL.—Like other examples of modern totalitarian dictatorship, the Fascist type which evolved between 1922 and 1932 fell into a characteristic pattern. It held out to a troubled populace the promise of stability and order. It advanced to power by conforming in some degree to democratic procedure, exploiting the weaknesses and divisions of the parliamentary machinery. It finally gained and maintained power through the unscrupulous use of brutal force in a militant movement which continually sought out for combat, largely of the polemic variety, an internal minority or an external enemy. Above all, it was based on the leadership principle of personal allegiance to the party leader who was the source of all authority.

Basically, Fascist policy and techniques were opportunistic during the twenty-one years in which Mussolini held power. The sole test applied to any element of doctrine or ideology in order to determine its adoption, modification, or rejection was its actual or anticipated effect on Mussolini's power. In its early stages, startling shifts of attitude occurred as il Duce[2] attempted to resolve situation after situation which demanded quick maneuvering. Originally anticapitalistic, Mussolini as a Fascist grew tolerant of capitalism, and thus drew support from some of its leaders. Once a Republican, he used the kingship as a symbol of the national unity which Fascism demanded. Similarly, he shifted from the principles of antimilitarism, anticlericalism, internationalism, popular sovereignty, free speech, and limited executive powers, to a belief in force, compulsory religious instruction, rabid nationalism, repression of democratic procedures, controlled propaganda, and dictatorial executive powers.

In spite of these pragmatic changes on the part of the leading exponent of Fascist doctrine, Italian Fascism over a period of years developed certain concepts:

THE SUPREMACY OF THE STATE.—Above all else Fascism stood for the totalitarian idea of the state as the supreme institution of human affairs. The slogan of the Fascists was "All in the state, nothing outside the state, nothing against the state." Under this concept, the state was the great spiritual entity which carried on from generation to generation the heritage of a people.

---

[2] The leader—supreme head of the party.

THE LEADERSHIP PRINCIPLE.—The glorified state was identified with the government headed by the party's leader, il Duce. He alone, or with the help of a few other select leaders, was capable of representing the nation. It was, therefore, the right and duty of this leader to govern the rest of the nation, even though his will opposed elements of public opinion. The regime was correspondingly authoritarian.

HIERARCHY.—Inherent in Fascism was the idea that virile and discerning citizens should take their place among the governing groups in order to guide the masses to a greater destiny. Accordingly, each Fascist leader was fitted into the governing hierarchy in an order assigned by the party leader or his aides. Majority rule and popular sovereignty were thus discarded for rule by the elite.

NATIONALISM.—Italian Fascism was frankly and aggressively nationalistic. It opposed all international and cosmopolitan movements, especially Communism. It devoted all of its energy and activity toward building up the glorified Fascist state.

IMPERIALISM.—The Fascists taught that the desire to grow and to possess was an immutable law of life. As applied nationally, this growth might come by diplomatic persuasion, by quiet encroachment, or by armed demonstration. In any event, acquisitiveness was held to be a prime law of national life.

NEGATION OF INDIVIDUALISM.—Fascism had no sympathy for democratic doctrines of human equality and the rights of individuals. It held that all individual interests must be subordinated, that all individual capacities must be regimented in the interest of the state and its welfare. The good of the state must be considered to transcend the welfare of individuals. This theory did not imply, however, that the state would completely disregard the welfare of its people; merely that state interests had precedence. The people were to find their welfare served by self-dedication to the higher good of the state. Fascist philosophy asserted that the welfare of the nation could not be planned on a popular, democratic basis, but only by an inner circle of Fascist hierarchs.

TOTALITARIANISM.—Fascism promoted the establishment of an authoritarian government over a disciplined people. Since it subordinated the interests of the individual to those of the social whole, Fascism favored the intrusion of governmental power into every sphere of individual activity; political, social, intellectual, moral, and economic. For example, all economic activity within the Fascist state had to serve the higher ends of the state. Private economic interests were subordinated, like all else, to the higher needs of the nation.

FORCE.—Fascism called for the use of force as an instrument of political power, both in domestic and foreign affairs. It held that perpetual peace was impossible and that force and warfare were instruments which a strong nation must use to attain its rightful ends. "War," said Mussolini, "puts the stamp of nobility upon the peoples who have the courage to meet it."

AUSTERITY.—Fascism demanded of its followers a stern political discipline, difficult for the Italians to achieve. It theoretically disdained individual comfort and demanded sacrifices in conformity with any order of the party Leader.

CONTROL OF THE MASSES.—The importance of the masses in the structure of the dictatorial state cannot be overemphasized. Fascism appealed to the masses by posing as a revolutionary movement for social, economic, and national betterment. It played on mass psychology by means of symbols, such as the *fasci,* slogans, uniforms, and appeals to the glories of the Roman Empire. Mass meetings were employed to whip up the enthusiasm of the participants. While Fascism appealed to the people on one hand with a grandiose program of public works and social legislation, on the other it maintained close control of public opinion through the supervision of all educational institutions and the rewriting of textbooks in accordance with the party doctrine. The Italian populace were subjected to an unrelenting stream of visual and vocal propaganda expressing the views, opinions, and teachings of the Fascist regime. By complete censorship of the press, radio, cinema, and stage, all recreational and instructional material was given a Fascist slant, tending to promote the ends of the dictatorship. Modern dictatorship has been eager for the support of the masses, but while it has appealed with the old Roman formula of bread and circuses, it has at the same time molded public opinion with propaganda and censorship and whipped it into line with secret police and concentration camps.

INTEGRATION OF PARTY AND STATE.—In the organization of the totalitarian state Mussolini began with his own party, purging it of those elements seeking personal benefit from party elections, and bringing the heretofore semiautonomous provincial leaders under his complete control. Once the Fascist party was set up on a hierarchical basis and completely responsible to the will of il Duce, it was integrated into the government. Its national councils and offices became offices of the state appointive by royal decree. The Fascist organization ceased to be a political party in any sense of the word. All other activities, whether cultural, economic, social, or political, were either integrated into the all-pervading Fascist network and made responsive to its direction or suppressed.

THE ITALIAN FASCIST GOVERNMENT

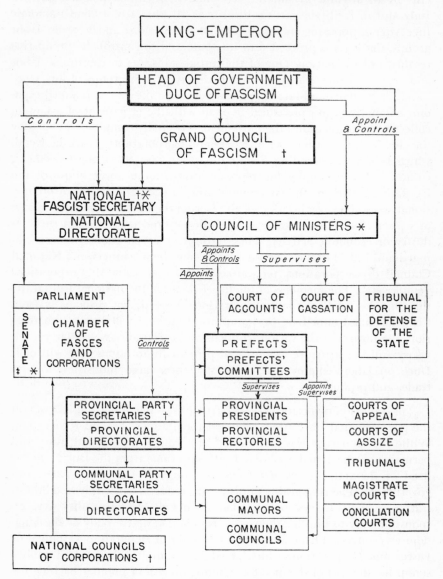

KING-EMPEROR

HEAD OF GOVERNMENT
DUCE OF FASCISM

Controls

Appoint & Controls

GRAND COUNCIL
OF FASCISM †

NATIONAL †✳
FASCIST SECRETARY
NATIONAL
DIRECTORATE

COUNCIL OF MINISTERS ✳

Appoints & Controls

Supervises

Appoints

PARLIAMENT

S E N A T E ‡ ✳ | CHAMBER OF FASCES AND CORPORATIONS

Controls

COURT OF ACCOUNTS | COURT OF CASSATION | TRIBUNAL FOR THE DEFENSE OF THE STATE

PROVINCIAL PARTY SECRETARIES †
PROVINCIAL DIRECTORATES

PREFECTS
PREFECTS' COMMITTEES

Supervises

Appoints Supervises

PROVINCIAL PRESIDENTS
PROVINCIAL RECTORIES

COURTS OF APPEAL
COURTS OF ASSIZE
TRIBUNALS
MAGISTRATE COURTS
CONCILIATION COURTS

COMMUNAL PARTY SECRETARIES
LOCAL DIRECTORATES

COMMUNAL MAYORS
COMMUNAL COUNCILS

NATIONAL COUNCILS OF CORPORATIONS †

✳   Selected members also served in GRAND COUNCIL OF FASCISM .
†   "   "   "   "   "   CHAMBER OF FASCES & CORPORATIONS.
‡   Members nominated by Il Duce for appointment by KING

THE CORPORATE STATE.—The Corporate State was created by the Fascists in an attempt to end the economic strife which plagued postwar Italy and to facilitate party control over all phases of Italian economic life. After suppressing the opposition of the Socialist and Populist labor groups, the Fascists proceeded to integrate and to control the productive resources of the nation. One of the initial steps was to coordinate labor and capital in such a manner that it deprived both groups of any voice in national affairs and forced them to adhere to the Fascist planned economy. Actually begun piecemeal in 1926 with the enactment of a law on collective labor relations, the movement was finally completed in 1939 by the creation of the Chamber of Fasces and Corporations. Thus the trend, which began by extending Fascist discipline into the labor movement, culminated by changing the representation in the lower house of the legislative branch of the government from a geographical to an occupational basis. The organization of the Corporate State was built on a base of separate but parallel groups of employees and employers in each industry or economic activity. These groups or corporations were coordinated and linked to the government through the machinery of a National Council of Corporations (employees) and a Ministry of Corporations (employers). The members of the lower house of the national legislature, the Chamber of Fasces and Corporations, were drawn principally from the National Council of Corporations. Despite its elaborate organization, the powers of the various councils and corporations were largely advisory and the structure was utilized principally to impose the will of il Duce on labor, employment, price structure, large industries, foreign trade, and production.

DESTRUCTION OF DEMOCRATIC INSTITUTIONS.—The impact of Fascism on the governmental institutions changed them almost beyond recognition. While the monarchy was maintained as a symbol of national unity and permanence, the actual executive leadership came from the Duce, who, as head of the state (*Capo del Governo*) presided over both party and government. The responsible ministry was reduced to the role of administrative assistants to, and political lieutenants of, Mussolini; they were responsible only to him for their actions. The legislative body of the kingdom was converted from an elective Chamber of Deputies to a Council of Fasces and Corporations which acted as a sounding board and rubber stamp for the will of the dictator, lending a myth of popular backing for the administration. The civil service and judicial branch were brought under Fascist sway by making political reliability the principal criterion for appointment to office. The support of the Army and Navy was gained by the adoption of an aggressive military policy, supported by large appropriations for the expansion of the armed services. The electoral features of local and provincial government were soon eliminated. Communal and provincial administrators, as well as their advisory councils, were appointed by the government.

FOREIGN POLICY.—The dynamic aspect of Fascism in domestic affairs was paralleled in its foreign policy. The drive for international prestige and territorial acquisitions was given a truculent aggressiveness, marked by demands for a sphere of influence in the Balkans and hegemony in the Mediterranean. While initially Mussolini opposed Nazi Germany's designs on Austria, he readily accepted German support when he launched the Fascist armies in a campaign of pure aggression against the sovereign state of Ethiopia in 1936. Fascist militia intervened in Spain in 1936, together with Nazi "volunteers," to assist the rebel Franco overcome the republican government. Italy and Germany signed the Anti-Comintern Pact in 1936, forming the Rome-Berlin Axis in which Italy gradually became the junior partner. In the spring of 1939 Fascist troops occupied Albania. These aggressive acts roused serious concern among the non-aggressive nations of Europe; however, the indecisiveness of Great Britain and France, which we have noted in preceding chapters, demonstrated to Italy and Germany that the democratic nations were not willing to commit themselves to war in behalf of the democratic cause in Europe. Although Italy's unreadiness for all-out war in 1939 compelled Mussolini to declare Italy neutral during the opening phases of World War II, he could no longer restrain his warlike tendencies when he saw France falling before the victorious Nazi armies in May of 1940. The treacherous "stab in the back" attack on France, on June 10, failed to add to the military glory of Fascism or Italy. Continuing her course of aggression, Italy attacked Greece in October of the same year without a declaration of war, and in 1941 joined Germany in war against Yugoslavia (April 6), Russia (June 22), and the United States (December 11).

In the end, Mussolini's aggressive foreign policy, aimed at "restoring to Italy the glories of Ancient Rome," to quote il Duce, was the direct cause of the downfall of the Fascist regime. Involved in a totalitarian war as a satellite of Germany, its demoralization increased as the war lengthened. Raw materials, including basic foods, became scarce. Inflation could not be controlled. As official corruption and open opposition to the regime increased, new concentration camps had to be opened to confine the swiftly growing numbers of opposition leaders. An even greater threat to Mussolini's rule was the regularity with which his armies were being defeated in the Balkans and in Africa. Despite unlimited propaganda and education, the Italian people had absorbed very little of the disciplined, warlike ruthlessness which Mussolini had tried so hard to inculcate. The defeat of the Axis armies at El Alamein, their retreat from Libya, the victory of the British and American Allies in North Africa followed by their successful invasion of Sicily in July, 1943, and the bombing of some of the largest Italian cities destroyed Italian will to continue the hopeless struggle.

The Anglo-American occupation of Sicily precipitated a startling development in Rome. There the Grand Council of Fascism assembled on July 25, 1943, for the first time since the outbreak of the war. A resolution was introduced by nineteen members, demanding Mussolini's resignation and calling on the king to take over full responsibility for the reorganization of the country. Only seven members of the Council voted against the resolution. Mussolini was forced to hand in his resignation to the king and to submit to protective custody. The king thereupon appointed Marshal Pietro Badoglio, onetime Viceroy of Ethiopia and the victorious commander of Italy's Ethiopian campaign in 1936, to the office of Prime Minister and Head of the Government.

EVALUATION OF FASCIST REGIME.—In surveying the effect of the dictatorship on the Italian nation we may draw certain conclusions. By abdicating their political responsibility and placing all their problems and powers in the hands of a dictator, the Italian people did gain for a brief period a relatively stable political regime which gave the nation the outward appearance of progress and efficiency. Behind the outward façade, however, we find that stability and efficiency were purchased at an exorbitant price. Regimentation of the people resulted in stamping out individual initiative not only in their political and economic life, but in such main springs of human development as education and research. Except for the party fanatics, the people settled back into a cynical attitude of passive observation of the forms and routines for which they had little or no enthusiasm. The continued use of propaganda bred a political hypocrisy which discredited political idealism. The outward show of Fascist efficiency became a cloak for inner corruption which ran rampant through the entire party structure. Power in the hands of the Fascist officials resulted in just as much corruption, although less exposure of cases, as it had in the hands of the parliamentarians. Misleading reports and flattery of superiors reached a point where the true condition of affairs was often hidden even from Mussolini himself. As the regime grew older, its weaknesses became ever more apparent. Dangerous rivalry between lieutenants for the favor of the Duce frequently caused national or international complications.

While on its material side the regime appeared to be working for the general welfare, such projects as the draining of the Pontine Marshes and the reforestation of the denuded hills were completely overshadowed by such extravagant and poorly advised measures as the attempted colonization of Libya. Equally ill-advised were the costly, economically unsound attempts at national self-sufficiency, and the vast expenditures of men, money, and material in military adventures in Africa, Spain, and the Balkans. When the whim of a dictator could become law it was only too easy for sound measures of economic betterment to give way to grandiose schemes directed toward the promised second birth of the ancient Roman Empire.

Having destroyed and discredited democratic institutions and the faith of the people in their own ability to govern themselves, the Fascists tried to replace the vacuum thus created with a new set of loyalties and ideals. Faith in the mission of the Fascist party, its hierarchy, and in the Duce were intended to replace the ideals of popular sovereignty, representative government, and universal toleration. When put to the final test of war, however, this totalitarian edifice which had prided itself on its complete control of all phases of public life, could not command the loyalty nor finally even the grudging support of the Italian people. As the war progressed, the reins of control became progressively looser until the Grand Council of Fascism voted its own abdication. Thus the regime which had arisen amidst a furor of promises, threats, and boasting subsided with scarcely a whimper. It proved itself to be a government of men, not of laws; of men, moreover, chiefly notable for their corruption and personal ambition.

Reconstruction Governments 1943–1948

CREATION OF THE BADOGLIO GOVERNMENT.—On July 26, 1943, a few days after Mussolini's dismissal, Marshal Badoglio formed a cabinet composed largely of officers of the armed forces and experienced civil servants. Only two members of Mussolini's last cabinet were included in the ministry, but many of its members had been closely affiliated with the Fascist regime. The principal qualification for the selection of members of this new governing group was unswerving loyalty to the monarchy.

The overthrow of the Fascist regime was received with great rejoicing and popular enthusiasm throughout the country. This feeling, however, was soon replaced by discouragement when Badoglio announced that the war must go on. The new regime immediately took steps to keep control of the situation. The king assumed command of all of the armed forces, the "defascistization" of the former government officials was instituted, nation-wide martial law was proclaimed, and decrees to prevent disorder and agitation were issued.

"DEFASCISTIZATION" OF THE ITALIAN GOVERNMENT.—Born of the repudiation of Fascism's founder and leader, the Badoglio government had as its first domestic task the dismantling of the Fascist state. In spite of the fact that many of the leading officials of the new government were themselves tainted with former Fascist connections, they assumed their new responsibilities by moving rapidly to exterminate Fascism as a political force, eager to demonstrate that they had broken completely with Mussolini and his principles.

At first, this "defascistization" of the country took the form of altering fundamentally the main characteristics of former Fascist institutions or of destroying them altogether. On the day that the Badoglio cabinet was organized, the Fascist militia was incorporated into the Italian Army in order to subject it to the authority of King Victor Emmanuel and his government. Two days later the cabinet ordered the dissolution of the Fascist party, the suppression of the Chamber of Fasces and Corporations, the Grand Council of Fascism, and the Special Tribunal for the Defense of the State. Matters which had been the responsibility of the latter tribunal were transferred to the regularly constituted military courts. The sweep included orders that emblems and banners of all political parties be barred for the duration of the emergency, that political prisoners be released, that the police be reorganized, and that numerous former Fascists be arrested. Moreover, all Fascist civil officials were called into military service, where they could be more closely observed and efficiently tried. A large-scale reorganization of civil administration followed, involving the displacement of most of the provincial prefects and almost all high state officials. Lastly, the people were promised an election of a new Chamber of Deputies within four months after the cessation of hostilities with the Allied Nations.

In the economic sphere the new government was equally quick to take action and called upon the more revolutionary groups to assist in the reconstruction. To solve the problems of labor relations a committee was appointed for the reorganization of the confederations of workers' syndicates and of professional groups, with the objective of consolidating these organizations into a single national workers' confederation. Meanwhile, in the large industrial zones of northern Italy, shop committees were established in order to maintain relationships between management and labor, to control the stipulations and application of collective contracts of work, and to mediate individual controversies. In addition, a special committee was created for the investigation of the illegal acquisition of property by former Fascist leaders. Confiscation of such property was ordered by the state.

Four anti-Fascist parties which had formerly existed only as underground groups came to light immediately after the new regime was established. These were the Action party, the Communist party, the Liberal Reconstruction party, and the Socialist party. Two additional parties were organized; the Christian Democratic party, a successor to the older Catholic Popular or Centrist party; and the Democratic Labor party.

THE ITALIAN ARMISTICE.—Marshal Badoglio, exercising his authority as prime minister, continued briefly to wage war against the United Nations. Italian military leaders realized the danger of denouncing the German alliance before any agreement on Allied assistance had been reached. Negotiations for an armistice were begun, nevertheless, in mid-August, when General Castellano was sent to Lisbon to make contact with Allied military representatives. The Germans, obviously aware of Badoglio's intentions, scattered troops throughout the country at strategic points in order to prepare for both the inevitable Anglo-American invasion of the peninsula and the Italian capitulation. On September 3, Badoglio's commissioners secretly signed the armistice terms laid down by the Allied Nations. The major item of that instrument called for the unconditional surrender of the Italian armed forces.

On the same day, the British Eighth Army crossed the Straits of Messina and landed on the Italian mainland. Less than a week later and just prior to the combined American-British landing at Salerno, Italy's surrender was officially announced by the Allied Nations. The terms included a clause binding Italy to comply with the political, economic, and financial conditions which might be imposed at the discretion of the British, American, and Russian Allies. The available portions of the Italian fleet and air force were immediately transferred to Allied ports and airfields, and a clause of the armistice agreement gave the Anglo-American forces immediate, free use of all bases and strategic points in Italian territory. The latter provision could be implemented only in southern Italy and in a few of the islands, inasmuch as the German forces in the Italian theater promptly brought all of northern and central Italy under their control.

A Badoglio proclamation to the Italians announced that the armed forces of Italy should abstain from any hostile acts against the Anglo-American forces. In general, Italian troops and patriots attempted to carry out this order and the related directives of the Italian government. At many points in northern Italy they resisted the German forces. The Italian forces garrisoning Corsica offered little or no resistance when some French troops under the command of the French Committee of National Liberation were landed on that island, where they destroyed the German garrison forces.

Anticipating the German occupation of Rome, but taking no determined steps to organize a popular or military defense of that city, the king and Prime Minister Badoglio, along with a few high government officials, fled to Palermo, Sicily. There, on September 11, they established their government under the protection of the British and

American armies. On the same day German paratroops rescued Mussolini from confinement in a villa on the Gran Sasso (the highest peak in
the central Apennines) .[3]

ITALY'S WAR WITH GERMANY.—The Italian armistice and the surrender instrument which supplemented it precipitated numerous and serious problems for Italy in her relations with her former ally and her
conquerors. It was the hope of the Allies that the Italian people would
rally to the legitimate royalist government, and would participate
actively in a war of liberation against the Germans. The anti-Fascist
leaders, however, objected to this government, accusing the king of having supported Mussolini and his war until faced with utter defeat.

On October 13, 1943, the Badoglio government nevertheless formally
declared war on Germany. On the same day a joint statement was issued
by the governments of the United States, Great Britain, and the Soviet
Union accepting "the active cooperation of the Italian nation and armed
forces as cobelligerent in the war against Germany." But because of the
feeling against the king, the tripartite declaration stipulated that the
three nations would later insist upon the untrammeled right of the people of Italy by constitutional means to choose their form of government.

ITALY'S ASSISTANCE TO THE ALLIES.—The war contributions of the now
cobelligerent Italy were both military and economic in nature. Those
ships of the fleet which were able to sail and to escape the new German
rocket bombs joined the Allied fleet at Malta as soon as the armistice
was announced. Thereafter until the end of the war these vessels were
used principally on convoy duty under the direction of the British Mediterranean Naval Command. The contributions of the ground forces were
less effective. In December, 1943, a small select unit, the First Italian
Motorized Group went into action at Monte Lungo a few miles south
of Monte Cassino. Although they attacked with resolution, they were
repulsed. This unit did provide, nevertheless, the nucleus for other combat groups which gave a good account of themselves south of Bologna
more than a year later. Although the Italian air force was of little value,
inasmuch as most of the aircraft were badly in need of repair, it did provide ground crew personnel at various Allied airfields in the rear areas.

The unselfish assistance rendered by individual Italian partisans and
partisan bands operating in rear of the German lines was notable. They
saved the lives of not a few American and British airmen as well as of
other soldiers by hiding them from the Germans and guiding them to

---

[3] A few days later the Fascist Republican Government was proclaimed. For the
next nineteen months, northern Italy continued its war effort under the Fascist
Republican Government, while southern Italy gave its allegiance to the Royal Government. The dividing line between the two regions gradually moved north as the Allied
Armies advanced. The collapse of the northern Fascist regime followed a few days
after Mussolini had been executed by the partisans on April 28, 1945.

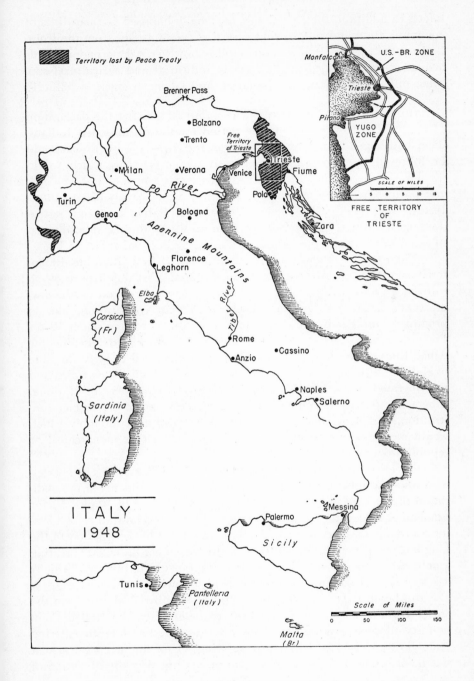

Territory lost by Peace Treaty

Brenner Pass

Bolzano

Trento

Free
Territory
of Trieste

Milan

Verona

Venice

Trieste

Fiume

Turin

Po River

Genoa

Pola

Bologna

Apennine Mountains

Zara

Florence
Leghorn

Elba

Tiber River

Corsica
(Fr)

Rome

Cassino

Anzio

Naples

Salerno

Sardinia
(Italy)

ITALY
1948

Messina

Palermo

Sicily

Tunis

Pantelleria
(Italy)

Scale of Miles

0   50   100   150

Malta
(Br)

U.S.–BR. ZONE

Monfalcone

Trieste

Pirano

YUGO
ZONE

SCALE OF MILES

5   0   5   10   15

FREE TERRITORY
OF
TRIESTE

155

safety. In addition, these partisans continually harassed German lines of communication and supply, thus diverting enemy troops from the front. Perhaps the greatest Italian contributions, however, were economic. This assistance was provided in the form of industrial and agricultural supplies, billets and offices, transportation and labor.

THE ROYALIST GOVERNMENT.—The months following the declaration of war on Germany were a trying period for the disillusioned Italians. They had hoped that a rapid advance of the Allies toward Rome would be followed by the formation of a strong government which would quickly rid the country of Fascist elements and somehow restore peace and prosperity. These sanguine expectations were sharply disappointed. Instead of the swift advance to the north, the Italian campaign settled down to the bitter fighting mile by mile up the peninsula, subordinated in importance to the operations in the West after mid-1944.

When the royal government was transferred from Rome to Italian territory within the Allied lines, Badoglio faced great difficulty in trying to form a cabinet. A series of statements was issued reiterating the government's promise to re-establish the pre-Fascist constitution, but no prominent anti-Fascist political leader was willing to serve under Victor Emmanuel or to accept a simple return to the old *Statuto*. Behind the Allied lines the leaders of the anti-Fascist parties tried to force the king to abdicate in favor of his son or his grandson. In both the occupied and the liberated parts of Italy, the various local Committees of National Liberation (CNL) denounced the idea of returning to the former constitution, and demanded the creation of a constituent assembly which would have power to devise a new constitution, either monarchical or republican.

The crisis came to a head when Count Carlo Sforza, an elder statesman who had returned to Italy from his American exile, urged the abdication of the king in favor of his grandson, the Prince of Naples. Victor Emmanuel vetoed this proposal, thus nullifying the possibility of forming a broadly based cabinet. Badoglio then offered his resignation to the king but was persuaded to withdraw it. In November, instead of creating a political cabinet, Badoglio appointed a "cabinet of technicians," chiefly a group of civil servants without political following.

In March, 1944, following the return of Palmiro Togliatti[4] from the Soviet Union to lead the Communist party in Italy, the Italian Communists adopted a more conciliatory attitude preparatory to entering Badoglio's government. On April 12 King Victor Emmanuel issued a statement promising to withdraw from public life after the liberation of

---

[4] Also known as Ercoli. One of the founders of the Italian CP and a member of the Comintern, fully trained and indoctrinated in communistic principles.

Rome, and to appoint his son, Prince Umberto (Humbert), to exercise the royal powers in his stead.

Badoglio thereupon succeeded in forming a new Cabinet on April 22, 1944. It included representatives of all the six anti-Fascist parties. On the institution of the kingship this ministry made the following statement: "Because they are not timely, many proposals of the utmost importance must be put aside for the time being. Chief of these is the institutional form of the State, which cannot be decided until the country is fully liberated and the war ended. The Italian people shall then be called together in free public meetings and, acting through universal suffrage, shall elect a constituent and legislative assembly."

Rome was captured by the Allies on June 4. The same day Victor Emmanuel named Prince Humbert the Lieutenant General of the Realm. Badoglio resigned for a second time on June 7, and after lengthy negotiations a new cabinet was constituted under Ivanoe Bonomi as President of the Council of Ministers.

ALLIED MILITARY GOVERNMENT.—The confused military, political, and economic situation, which existed in Italy from the hour of the Allied landings in Sicily and continued beyond the German surrender, inevitably posed grave problems on any Italian government. Likewise, these conditions were anything but conducive to the smooth functioning of the Allied Military Government, to an account of which we shall now turn. War's destruction turned the populace of the progressively liberated areas into a dead-weight burden on the occupying forces, quite out of proportion to the help which the Italians were able to give the Allied war effort. Their apathy, the product of defeat and hunger, made most of the natives of little use in restoring the agricultural and other bases of their existence. Politically, they were anti-Fascist for the most part, but beyond that point their ideas sounded all the notes of political difference rather than those of agreement and harmony. These were but a few of the major obstacles to the effective control of Italy which had been foreseen by the Allied leaders. To meet them, plans had long been made and teams of British and American troops had been trained to institute and operate Allied Military Government (AMG) from the hour of the invasion of Sicily. As subsequent events showed, the difficulties which arose often exceeded the estimates of the Allied planners. Moreover, the lack of actual experience with such operations meant that lessons often had to be learned from the beginning. Lastly, the inadequacy of the military government training for Allied combat organizations made for poor understanding and cooperation between AMG personnel and the Allied combat elements.

In several respects military government operations were experimental in nature. In addition, they were progressive—first, with regard to the areas brought under AMG control by the sporadic advances of the Allied Forces; secondly, in that areas left well in the rear of the combat lines by the Axis withdrawal were successively turned over to the Italian government. That policy served the dual purpose of lifting the weight of political responsibility from AMG, while forging the reconstruction of Italy.

The first such transfer, announced early in February, 1944, included Sicily, Sardinia, and that part of the mainland south of the provinces of Salerno, Potenza, and Bari.

In the meanwhile, quite another Italy survived in the German controlled area. There, Mussolini's Fascist Republican government functioned as a German puppet state organized to relieve the German Command of police and administrative functions. (See p. 154.)

ORGANIZATION OF AMG.—AMG operated under the general control of the Allied military commander in Italy and the specific direction of his deputy, the Chief Civil Affairs Officer (CCAO). Its headquarters staff consisted of several divisions or branches, each under the control of a civil affairs officer. The financial division, for example, dealt with such matters as currency, foreign exchange, banks, insurance companies, customs, and similar activities. The public health division directed hospitals, water supply, and disease control. The public safety division handled existing civil police forces, prisons, and public order. Other divisions had charge of legal matters, civilian supply, and Allied and enemy property. In addition to these major administrative divisions, the CCAO included several special activities, among them educational and fine arts sections.

ALLIED COMMISSION.—The Italian armistice provided for the establishment of a commission to regulate and execute the terms of the armistice under the direction of the Supreme Allied Commander. On November 10, 1943, General Dwight D. Eisenhower announced the formation of the Allied Commission for Italy (AC) to assume "the duty of carrying out the terms of the armistice and of aligning Italian economy in complete support of the Allied Nations fight against Germany." The Supreme Allied Commander, Mediterranean Theater, was designated President of the Allied Commission. In practical operation, however, the actual head of the AC was the acting President or Chief Commissioner. In general, the personnel of AC was divided equally among Americans and British, exceptions being a Soviet and a French representative with consultative functions, who were attached to the staff of the chief commissioner. When first organized, the Commission's personnel was entirely military. Before long, however, military personnel was replaced with civilian experts wherever and whenever possible and expedient.

The Allied Commission was divided into four sections headed by the Vice-President of the Commission: political, economic, administrative, regional control and military government. Six independent subcommissions dealt with Navy, Army, Air, war materials, telecommunication, and prisoners of war and displaced persons.

COORDINATION OF AMG/AC.—Consolidation of AMG and AC was accomplished during the early weeks of 1944. The chief commissioner of AC was appointed as Chief Civil Affairs Officer for Allied Military Government. The headquarters and general staffs of the two organizations were made identical and were known as "AMG/AC in Italy." The only distinction between the two branches of the new organization was that AMG generally confined its functions to territory where administration of Allied troops was necessary, while the AC supervised Italian administration in areas returned to Italian control. In those areas returned to Italian control the Allies had envisaged that the Italian government would immediately establish local democratic governments permitting freedom of speech, of religion, of the press, etc.; however this expectation was not realized. The Badoglio government was overwhelmed by the size of the task, and constant criticism by the anti-Fascist groups made it necessary for the AC to take a more active part than originally planned. This guiding hand was particularly obvious in Allied support of Badoglio on the assumption that the retention of monarchy would promote stability; moreover, that the monarchy was desired by the Italians. No further reorganization of AMG/AC occurred prior to the time when Italy became once more the master in her own house.

THE BONOMI GOVERNMENTS.—Ivanoe Bonomi, who organized the cabinet in Rome in June, 1944, had been a pre-Fascist prime minister and one of the leaders of the anti-Nazi and anti-Fascist resistance during the nine months Rome was occupied by the Germans. His pre-Fascist record and his anti-Fascist convictions rendered him a much more generally acceptable candidate for the office than his predecessor, Badoglio. Soon after its formation, the Bonomi cabinet issued a decree which declared: "After the liberation of the national territory the institutional forms will be decided by the Italian people who for that purpose will elect, by universal, direct, and secret suffrage, a Constituent Assembly to devise the new constitution of the State. Methods and procedures will be established by successive provisions." The Bonomi cabinet agreed that, until convocation of the assembly, ministers and undersecretaries were to be bound by an oath to exercise their functions in the supreme interest of the nation. For the same period the cabinet decreed its own power to issue, over the signature of the Lieutenant General, decrees having the force of law.

Much of the difficulty encountered by the first postwar government in Italy may be attributed to the destruction of all effective opposition leadership during the twenty years of Fascism. Opponents of Fascism survived, of course; but they lacked leadership, a program, means of translating policy into action, and money. Bonomi tried to provide that leadership by working closely with the six political parties which had placed him in power, an effort which ended in his satisfying none of them.

The political center of gravity of the combined group of parties lay well to the left of center. After prolonged partisan strife throughout the latter half of 1944, Bonomi's six-party coalition Cabinet fell in late November, because of the current alignment of Communists, Socialists, and, to a limited degree, the Action party on one side, against the Liberals, Christian Democrats, and Democratic Labor party on the other. In a general sense the former group insisted upon a republic, a severe purge of all Fascists, and the institution of strong socialist reforms. The latter group more consistently supported the monarchy and evolutionary reform, while favoring a milder purge program.

Immediately after Bonomi's resignation he was asked by the Lieutenant General of the Realm, Crown Prince Humbert, to form another cabinet more amenable to cooperative action. His first government had represented a coalition of the six parties making up the Committee of National Liberation. The second, which lasted until June, 1945, included only four of those parties. Excluded from participation were the Action and the Socialist parties, primarily because of their opposition to Crown Prince Humbert.

THE PARRI CABINET.—When AMG officials entered the North in the wake of the Allied armies, they found that the Committee of National Liberation of Northern Italy (CLNAI) and the partisans had already established communal and provincial governments, at least in skeletal form. After some friction AMG was able to establish itself. In a great many localities the CLNAI nominees were confirmed as prefects in the provinces or as mayors in the communes.

The Committee of National Liberation of Northern Italy also provoked a conflict with the civil government in Rome when it demanded that the Cabinet be reconstituted and that the "Committee" itself be granted a primary part in organizing the government. This demand precipitated a new cabinet crisis which lasted for more than a month. Bonomi offered to resign, but in accordance with pre-Fascist constitutional custom, he continued in office pending the choice of a successor. When the negotiations reached a deadlock he threatened to retire immediately, leaving the country without any central administration. Such action might have enabled the Lieutenant General to appoint a conservative Cabinet of his own choice; consequently, the parties represented in the CLNAI and the CNL of Rome renewed their efforts to reach agreement. Their choice finally fell on Ferruccio Parri, an outstanding leader of the underground, a member of the Action party, and a man with an unblemished anti-Fascist record, but with comparatively little political experience. The new prime minister himself took the post of Minister of the Interior (with control over the local administration and the police). Pietro Nenni, leader of left-wing Socialists and advocate of unity of action with the Communists, was named Vice Premier and the Minister of the Constituent Assembly. Alcide de Gasperi, leader of Christian Democrats, advocate of mild reforms in industry and agriculture, was given the portfolio of Foreign Affairs.

Despite the complete absence of a parliament, the crisis which developed following the incorporation of the North closely resembled a cabinet crisis of the pre-Fascist era. In like manner the solution to the crisis seemed to follow the old pattern in that the ministerial positions were delicately balanced among various parties, and the ministry was such that it could take effective action only on those matters on which all parties agreed.

The Parri government lasted for nearly six months through a very difficult period. The regions of Lombardy, Emilia, Piedmont, and Liguria, released from Allied control, had to be integrated into the Italian government; there were the tremendous problems of supply and reconstruction at a time when the Allies were redeploying troops from Italy to the United States and the Pacific; there was the difficult ethnic problem of Trieste; and also political riots in Sicily.

The final break occurred in November, 1945, over the Liberal party's demand to broaden the government policies by including some of the older statesmen such as Orlando.[5] The crux of the conflict at this time was the difference between the opportunist outlook of the left-wing groups and the traditional policies of the Liberals.

After two weeks of effort the six leading parties agreed to name Alcide de Gasperi as the candidate for the premiership and early in December he formed a new coalition cabinet. De Gasperi had to reshuffle his cabinet six times prior to the end of 1948, during which period the scope of the problems confronting the nation became clearer. We may, therefore, combine the evaluation of the de Gasperi government with an examination of Italy's current problems.

Current Problems of the Italian Government

SCOPE OF PROBLEMS.—A nation all but broken on the rack of war is in poor condition to re-create or to operate its domestic economic and po-

---

[5] Victor Emmanuel Orlando, eighty-seven, last survivor of Big Four of World War I and member of Italian national assemblies for the last fifty years.

litical machinery. Such was Italy's situation when the war ended. The aid and restraints furnished by the Allied armies of occupation alone prevented complete breakdown into anarchy, while at the same time nurturing Italy's efforts toward self-help and restoration.

After more than five years following her surrender to the Allied Nations, Italy continues to face a critical economic and political situation. Her problems would be difficult to solve in a land of plenty. Under economic conditions where most of the forty-five million Italians are underfed, miserably clothed, and poorly sheltered, Italy's difficulties are numberless. In brief, the Italians are short of everything needful for even the maintenance of bare existence. Moreover, when the last of the American and British troops departed from Italy in mid-December, 1947, in accordance with the terms of the peace treaty (see p. 170), Italy lost an important stabilizing influence.

The difficulties confronting the present Italian government are not new; they existed in fact before the overthrow of Fascism. The important point is that since December, 1945, when Allied Military Government returned all of the northern provinces, except Udine, to the Italians, the full responsibility for the solution of these difficulties has rested upon the shoulders of the Italian government. These problems can be generally grouped as those relating to (1) governmental reconstruction, (2) economic recovery, and (3) international relations and the peace treaty.

RESTORATION OF DEMOCRATIC TRADITIONS.—The Moscow Declaration of November, 1943 gave the Italian people the opportunity freely to determine their new type of government. Although this policy was actively supported by all major parties from the first days of Allied occupation, it soon became obvious that the majority of the Italians would support any party which promised to provide work and food, to remove the stigma of military defeat, and to restore Italy's prestige.

In spite of left-wing pressure for the creation of an interim Parliament pending general elections, it was not until September, 1945, that a Consultative Assembly was appointed to pave the way for national self-government. The Consultative Assembly drafted regulations governing electoral procedures, the powers of the projected Constituent Assembly, and the publication of a decree providing for a popular referendum on the monarchy. In the event that the popular will discarded monarchy in favor of a republic, the Constituent Assembly was to be charged with electing a provisional Head of State to hold office until such time as the details of setting up the new government were completed. The life of the Constituent Assembly was limited to eight months after its first meeting; however, it was given the power to extend that time. In any event the Constituent Assembly was to pass out of existence on the day that the Constitution went into effect. The Constituent Assembly was charged with the drafting of procedures for the election of a national legislature which would function under the projected constitution. Until that legislative body convened, the Cabinet was empowered to rule by decree, subject to retaining the confidence of the Constituent Assembly. The latter body was also authorized to ratify the treaty of peace which would be drawn between Italy and the Allied Nations.

Early in June, 1946, the Italian voters went to the polls on a compulsory basis and, by a margin of some two million votes, declared themselves in favor of the republic. At the same time they elected an Assembly with seats distributed among the parties as follows:

Christian Democrats	206	seats
Socialists	115	"
Communists	105	"
National Democratic Union	40	"
Common Man	30	"
Republican	23	"
Liberty Bloc	17	"
Action	7	"
Others	13	"
Total	556	seats

An early by-product of the voting was the abrupt departure of King Humbert II on June 13, ending a thirty-four-day reign.[6] More important, the vote to establish a republic ended the tension which had prevailed since the election, marked by increasingly serious riots after the Italians had registered their votes. (For a comparison with the 1948 vote, see p. 171.)

PROVISIONS OF THE 1948 CONSTITUTION.—After seven months of work the Statute Committee of the Constituent Assembly reported to that body early in February, 1947, with a draft constitution. Extracts of that report, based on major items of the Constitution, are summarized below:

General

For the first time in history the Italian people have employed democratic processes toward setting up a constitution. In order that it may be understood by all voters, (the Constitution) must be brief, simple, and clear. The political, economic, and social organization of the republic thus constituted is based on democracy and labor.

---

[6] King Victor Emmanuel III formally abdicated on May 10, 1946, in a belated effort to save the monarchy. He died in Egypt December 28, 1947.

Rights and Duties of the Citizen

Inasmuch as many of the fundamental rights were forgotten or destroyed in the last twenty-five years, it is necessary to list all such freedoms and essential inviolabilities. The latter protect the person, domicile, correspondence, freedom of circulation, sojourn, emigration, association, meeting, thought, religion, and press.

All citizens, regardless of sex, race, language, social conditions, political or religious thoughts, are declared equal before the law. All adult citizens, regardless of sex, are electors. Labor is not only the right but also the duty of the citizen. The defense of the country is the sacred duty of the citizen. Military service is compulsory.

The principle of loyalty and obedience to public authorities is balanced by the right to resist when the authorities violate the constitution.

The State and Catholic Church are independent of each other. Relations between them as established by the Lateran Pacts of 1929[7] are confirmed. Furthermore, all other religions are equally free before the law. Their relationships with the state are to be determined by mutual agreement and subsequently fixed by law.

The National Assembly

The National Assembly (the Parliament or Congress) consists of the Chamber of Representatives, whose members are elected by universal and direct suffrage; and the Chamber of Senators, elected on a regional basis, one third by regional councils, two thirds by universal and direct suffrage.

The Head of the State

The Head of the State (the President of the Republic) is elected by the National Assembly for a term of seven years. He is the coordinator of all activities. The President does not govern, although all acts are indorsed and issued by his office under the responsibility of the prime minister. The head of the state appoints the prime minister and revokes such appointments, he can call for a popular referendum, and he may disband the chambers if serious disagreement arises between them. He is also the head of the Armed Forces.

The Prime Minister

The prime minister is the head of the government. He is charged with governing and directing the activities of his ministers. He and his Council of Ministers (the Cabinet) must retain the confidence of the National Assembly or they must resign.

---

[7] The agreement signed by Mussolini and Pope Pius XI.

THE ITALIAN REPUBLICAN GOVERNMENT

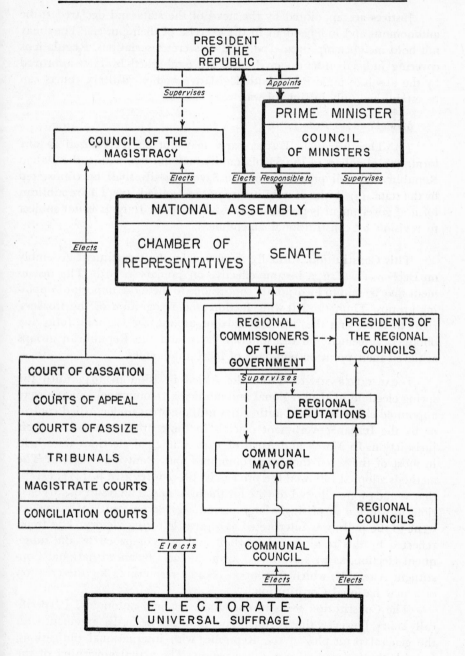

The Magistery or Magistracy

Justices are appointed by the head of the state and declared to be autonomous and independent in the exercise of their powers. They may not hold membership in any political or secret associations. Regulations covering judicial order in civil cases are established by laws approved by the absolute majority of both legislative bodies. Military courts can be established only in time of war.

Miscellaneous Provisions

(1) The disbanded Fascist party may not be reorganized in any form. (2) Members of the Savoia family may not live within the Italian Republic. (3) All properties of the Savoia family shall be confiscated by the state. (4) Titles of nobility are not recognized. (5) The republican form of government is permanently established for Italy. It is not subject to revision by constitutional amendment.

This Constitution, formally approved by the Constituent Assembly on December 22, 1947, became effective on January 1, 1948. The instrument may be said to incorporate concessions to the more important opposing groups. Thus, the left-wing faction won recognition of the workers' right to strike and the freedom of labor unions, the Catholic following obtained agreement on the Lateran Pacts, and the Republican groups achieved their point on emphasis of local autonomies.

LOCAL GOVERNMENT.—From the Allied invasion in 1943 until the spring elections of 1946 regional and municipal (commune) officials were appointed either by Allied authorities in those areas under Allied control or by the Italian government officials in those areas returned to their jurisdiction. In March and April of 1946 municipal elections were held in most of the seven thousand communes and twenty-odd regions. The methods adopted followed the pre-Fascist procedures (see p. 141), except that women were allowed to vote for the first time. The result of this election, in which a surprisingly large percentage (85 per cent) of the voters went to the polls, was interpreted as a great left-wing victory. The trend reflected by this result was important and was confirmed by the subsequent election, as we have noted, of a similarly balanced national Constituent Assembly, which thereupon became responsible for the creation of a new national Constitution.

The Constitution seeks to encourage regional autonomy. It specifically states, however, that regional laws must not be in disagreement with the general principles of the Republic, with international obligations, or with the interests of any other region. The actual governing of the regions and communes is accomplished by locally elected regional councils. These councils were given authority to request national legislation, to select one third of the senators in the national assembly, and to elect the regional head or President. The national government retained some control within the regions through a representative placed in the major city of each region. The duties of this representative are to supervise and coordinate regional administration as related to the government policies. In addition, the national government can by edict disband a regional council for serious violation of national law.

The importance of this local autonomy was indicated in June, 1946, when the Communist-Socialist bloc nearly overthrew the then existing coalition government. This maneuver, which fell just short of its goal, was followed by violent criticism of the government, strikes, and demonstrations designed to show the strength of the Communists and the weakness of the government. All this activity was promoted as an attempt to appeal to the individual voter.

The fact that the well-organized, trained, armed, and well-led Communists outnumber the combined Italian armed forces and *carbinieri* (police) almost ten to one illustrates the danger to liberal government arising from the continued pressure exerted in local elections to swing the trend increasingly to the left.

ECONOMIC RECOVERY.—The improvement in the political atmosphere after King Humbert's flight was not matched by betterment of the economic picture. At the end of 1947, Italy's industrial production was barely 60 per cent of her 1938 figure; her imports and exports were roughly one half and one fourth, respectively, of prewar level. The nation's supply of American dollars was rapidly disappearing, and it was only through periodic American assistance that she was able to purchase sorely needed American products at a rate of approximately forty million dollars a month.

Only the major aspects of Italy's economic problems can be sketched here, noting at the same time how they affect the political situation. In part, her economic ills are of the long-range type, difficult if not impossible to correct. In part, they are the by-product of war and its aftermath, including the grave misfortune of disastrously adverse weather conditions.

The basic, long-range problem, reflected in all difficulties of the recent and current periods, is that of Italy's poverty in raw material resources, particularly the minerals. This lack has stifled Italy's growth and development, increasingly so with each new technological advance made by her rivals. It is hardly necessary to point out that each such advance has widened the economic gap between the nations favored by nature in the matter of mineral resources and those who lack such riches, between the "haves" and the "have-nots." Unlike Japan, modern Italy has been unable to span the gap with a program of thoroughgoing industrialization and full-scale production for export. Like Japan, she is further burdened by overpopulation and a high birth rate. Taken together, these two factors have made for political unrest, particularly on the part of the millions who could never lift themselves above the level of marginal existence.

First among the handicaps left by war is the woeful state of Italy's transport system. Although much has been done to eliminate the bottlenecks created by ruined docks, bridges, tunnels, and railroads, a very serious shortage of rolling stock continues to hamper production and distribution at every stage from the extraction of raw materials to the export of finished goods. Foreign and domestic trade are further restricted by the shortage of working capital, foreign exchange, high production costs—particularly wages—the loss of foreign markets, and the difficulties of opening up trade channels with other nations because of general lack of confidence in the lira.

Italy's postwar ills were multiplied by the extremely adverse weather conditions which prevailed in 1945 and 1946, including late spring frosts and summer droughts. The Communist-inspired farm labor strike of September, 1947, cut further into domestic farm production, in some instances by as much as 40 per cent. Launched as a drive to raise the wages of some 600,000 farm laborers, this strike dovetailed with similar moves of industrial labor. All were clearly aimed at weakening the government, and were in fact part of a cold war campaign of the Communist minority to seize political control.

General starvation and the complete breakdown of the economic system have thus far been averted by stopgap aid from abroad, chiefly the United States. In the early postwar months UNRRA was the principal supplier, dividing its shipments equally between food and basic raw materials. The termination of UNRRA's existence in 1947 further increased the burden to the United States of bolstering Italy. The Italian government vigorously supported the thesis of the Marshall plan (see p. 171) as a possible means of making the nation self-supporting by 1952. Three major provisos were attached by Italy's spokesmen to that hope: (1) unquestioned adherence of the other fifteen participating European nations to the plan as a means toward full revival of Europe's production and purchasing power; (2) sufficient aid to permit the initiation and completion of a five-year reconstruction plan; (3) an over-all grant of $2.5 billion Marshall Plan aid to Italy.[8]

All such plans and actions, including even the direct relief shipments from the United States, are bitterly attacked by Italian Communists and their allies, who charge that the state is being made an "imperial preserve" of the United States. The Communists have proved repeatedly that they can do much to disrupt Italy's rehabilitation. But in so doing

---

[8] Actual allotment to Italy during the first year was 703 million.

they have alienated a considerable proportion of their early supporters, men and women who have come to see that they were being used as tools and expendable pawns for the world Communist drive. Rejecting that sacrificial role, such elements are playing their part in assisting the slow but still progressive improvement in Italy's production.

The economic future is far from clear. Good harvests in 1948, a period of quiet on the labor front, and the successful implementation of the Marshall Plan can do much toward improving a situation which thus far has been largely the reflection of national apathy and despair.

THE ITALIAN PEACE TREATY.—The last of the three great problems facing the de Gasperi government was that of the ratification of the peace treaty. On September 15, 1947, after considerable debate, formal ratifications of the Italian Peace Treaty were deposited at Paris and Moscow, and Italy was officially at peace with her conquerors following a struggle in which 300,000 Italians were listed as killed or missing. Under the terms of the treaty, Italy has lost about three thousand square miles of her homeland, all her African empire, and a number of her Mediterranean islands. She has agreed to pay a reparations debt of 360 million dollars and to limit her army to 185,000 men, her navy and air force to 25,000 each.[9]

Specifically, Italy lost her northeast province, the greater portion of the Istrian peninsula going to Yugoslavia. Cession of this area and the new Free Territory of Trieste cost Italy two ports, more than a million tons annual production of vital coal, as well as some bauxite deposits. Yugoslavia also was awarded a number of Adriatic islands and the city of Zara on her Adriatic coast. The strategically important Dodecanese islands went to Greece. France acquired about fifty square miles of territory in four Alpine districts along the Italian border, when by popular referendum in October, 1947, these areas voted overwhelmingly to join France. These small sectors contained not only strategically located mountain defenses but also a few hydroelectric plants, several winter sports centers and some locally contested grazing grounds. In July, 1948, France demonstrated a conciliatory attitude by consenting to minor rectifications of the treaty line.

Italy also renounced sovereignty over her African possessions of Eritrea, Libya, and Somaliland. The treaty provided that all of these colonies would remain under British administration until September 15, 1948, by which time the Council of Foreign Ministers were to decide upon their final disposition. A belated meeting in Paris on September 14 failed to produce any agreement, and the next day the question of settlement was forwarded to the General Assembly of the United Nations.

---

[9] Her armor to be reduced to two hundred tanks; her airplanes to two hundred fighter and reconnaissance aircraft, and one hundred fifty transports; her ships to two battleships, four cruisers and four destroyers.

Last, but certainly not least, Italy was required to pay to the following countries the amount of reparations indicated:

Albania	$ 5,000,000
Ethiopia	25,000,000
Greece	105,000,000
Yugoslavia	125,000,000
USSR	100,000,000
TOTAL	$360,000,000

These payments were to be made during a period of seven years from September 15, 1947, under definite provisos. Deliveries from current industrial production were not required during the first two years. In addition, the countries entitled to receive reparations from current industrial production were to furnish Italy on commercial terms the materials which are normally imported into Italy and which are needed for the production of these goods.

The provision in the treaty for the removal of Allied troops from Italy within ninety days after the signing of the pact definitely set a precedent for like action in other occupied countries and may have extremely important future political implications. The last United States troops departed from Italy December 14, 1947.

How do these very strict provisions affect Italy and her international status? Italy, in 1939, by possessing strategically located colonies in the Mediterranean area and some along the Red Sea, was in a position to threaten and even to interdict commerce through the Suez. Now her power has been reduced to that of a minor state, her war potential minimized by legal and material restrictions, and the strength of her voice in world affairs all but destroyed. Yet Italy remains a highly important factor in international affairs, first because of her strategic location; secondly, because of the impact on Europe and the entire world of the ideological struggle now occurring in the country. She harbors a powerful, disciplined Communist fifth column led by Palmiro Togliatti. This element could probably go far toward neutralizing what little resistance Italy might be able to offer against a Communist thrust from the East, where Marshal Tito's Yugoslav forces make an effective spearhead for the Communist cause. In several instances Togliatti has in fact given tacit or open support to Tito's demands on Italy, particularly in respect to the controversy over Trieste.

THE NEW REPUBLIC IN ACTION.—Increasing American interest in the Italian spring general elections of 1948 was indicated by the United States' repudiation of her share of Italian war vessels, the passage of ERP, and the donation to Italy of twenty-nine merchant ships. The most widely publicized and acclaimed move in Italian circles was the joint American-British-French proposal in mid-March to revise the Italian treaty so as to restore Trieste to Italy.

These measures, along with vigorous campaigning by members of the Catholic Church, were decisive in maintaining and even increasing the strength of the de Gasperi government and his Christian Democratic party without, however, weakening the absolute position of the Communists. The final outcome of the April elections for the seats in the chamber are compared with the 1946 results of the contest for seats in the Constituent Assembly in the following table:

	1946	1948
Christian Democrats	206	307
Right-Wing Socialists		33
Left-Wing Socialists	115[10]	
Communists	105	182[11]
All Others	130	52
	556	574

Examination of the above table shows that the Communist party lost little, if any of its strength and that the Christian Democrats gained at the expense of the rightist parties. It must not be concluded, therefore, that the results of the 1948 elections in Italy constituted a thoroughgoing defeat of the Communist party.

The new assembly met separately in early May to elect their respective heads. Ivanoe Bonomi, moderate Socialist premier of the early postwar period, was chosen President of the Senate; Giovanni Gronchi, a Christian Democrat, was chosen President of the Chamber. A few days later the legislative bodies met in joint session and chose the popular Luigi Einaudi, a college professor and financial expert, to be the first President of the Italian Republic. An early favorite, Count Carlo Sforza withdrew from the election when he failed to obtain the support of either the strong anti-Communist or the Communist groups.

The first major official act of the new President was to name the new premier—the obvious choice was Alcide de Gasperi. Within a few days Premier de Gasperi announced his sixth Cabinet based on a coalition of Christian Democrats, right-wing Socialists, Republicans, and Liberals. Of the twenty Cabinet posts, including two new ministers to supervise the application of the Marshall Plan, de Gasperi's Christian Democrats strengthened their position and now hold eleven ministries.

Political health and stability await the outcome of events over

---

[10] The Socialist party voted as a unit in 1946.

[11] The left-wing Socialists and the Communists combined into the so-called Popular Front for the 1948 elections.

which Italy has little control. And even a favorable outcome cannot ensure the end of the bitter factionalism and jealous sectionalism which are dividing Italy into several hostile camps. With effective stimulation as a result of the Marshall Plan and the general European economic revival envisaged by that effort, Italy could conceivably look forward to the day when she would again be master in her own political house. Denied such stimulus, she can hardly foresee anything except further and final political disintegration, an outcome which would gravely affect the possibility of survival of democratic institutions in western Europe.

Trieste

HISTORICAL BACKGROUND.—A hard-worn compromise in the Council of Foreign Ministers rejected Italy's demand for the retention of Trieste as well as Yugoslavia's claim to the area. Instead, the Italian peace treaty created the Free Territory of Trieste (see map p. 155) as an independent area under the guardianship of the United Nations' Security Council.

Under Austrian rule, Trieste became the strategic port of central Europe, keystone to Austria's dominance of the Adriatic, and outlet for Danubian trade. Both Italy and the emergent Slav bloc of the Balkans, with Russia in the background, marked on the maps the spot of their future objectives. Treaty settlements after World War I granted Trieste to Italy, whereupon she proceeded to Italianize the area. By 1940 Italians predominated heavily, the Slavs making up the second largest group. Yugoslavia's claim to Trieste after World War II was strongly backed by Soviet Russia. That way, however, lay Slavic control of the Adriatic area, a ready steppingstone to Communist absorption of Italy. Hence the eventual compromise, which left final settlement in the air, at the same time created an atmosphere of dangerous tension within the area.

PRESENT SITUATION.—In theory, Trieste was placed under the supervision of a "neutral" governor appointed by the UN Security Council. Subject to his orders is an occupation force of fifteen thousand men, consisting of equal numbers of United States, British, and Yugoslav troops. They are to remain only so long as the governor deems necessary. A popular assembly and an executive council to be named by that assembly were intended to give the populace a voice in their government. None of these steps could be taken, however, until after the Security Council had appointed a governor. No agreement had been reached on that point by the Western powers and Soviet Russia by March, 1948, when the Western Allies proposed the return of the territory to Italy. In the interim, in accordance with the treaty terms Trieste "shall continue to be administered by the Allied Military commands within their respective zones."

The net result was that two armed forces face each other across the No-Man's Land which followed the boundary line established by the treaty, while a Communist fifth column operated behind the Anglo-American lines to sabotage the life of the area through political strikes and other disorders. This situation made Trieste one of the most critical spots in the postwar world.

THE GOVERNMENT OF

GERMANY

◇◇

Germany in Transition

INTERIM STATUS OF POLITICAL INSTITUTIONS.—Total defeat and unconditional surrender leaves the German nation today without any central government of its own. German territory is being occupied by the armies of the Soviet Union, the United States, Great Britain, and France, each governing a specific zone. Under this system the rectification of chaotic domestic conditions of prolonged war and devastating defeat was begun, with the immediate emphasis on the re-establishment of order, maintenance of the minimum economic base necessary to the people's bare existence, and reconstruction of the institutions of local government. Since 1946, Britain and the United States have sought to expand this minimum level to one ensuring Germany's economic self-sufficiency at a not too distant date as a necessary factor in the convalescence of Europe. France has given some measure of support to such proposals; the USSR has given only its veto.

In a governmental sense a German state does not exist today. On the other hand, a nation of German people with a long national tradition does exist and continues to assert an influence, however indirect, on world affairs. That influence would be felt no less if Germany were left to die of starvation and disease among her ruins. The resultant loss of Germany's productive and consuming power, long a vital factor in Europe's economic life, could not fail to have serious adverse effects on the Continent's convalescence from the ravages of war. World recovery would be retarded in corresponding measure. Equally important are the ultimate decisions and actions of the Allied Nations which will determine whether the future Germany is to function as a single economic unit or as separate areas under varying degrees of outside control. For practical reasons it must be assumed that the eventual political organization of Germany will conform to the prevailing economic pattern. One may assume also that many of the roots of Germany's traditional political system which have persisted through the years of major political changes

from 1870 to 1945 will be found still alive after Germany has again
become master in her own house. For that reason a survey of Germany's
political past is important for any student of affairs concerned with her
future.

Background of German Government

FACTORS AFFECTING THE DEVELOPMENT OF THE GERMAN STATE.—Throughout German history, from the time of Charlemagne down to the present,
geography has exerted a powerful influence on the evolution of government in Germany. To begin with, Germany's location in the center of
Europe placed her peoples at the crossroads between the more highly
civilized populations of western Europe and the less advanced Slavic
peoples of the East. This factor, coupled with a lack of definitive natural
boundaries on both the East and the West, offered at times a threat to the
Germans' security, at other times a temptation for them to expand. Thus
Germany became a traditional battleground on the European Continent.
Furthermore, these same two geographical factors made the Germans'
problem of political unification considerably more difficult than that of
the British, for example, with their island; or that of the French, with
their rather sharply defined boundaries on at least three sides; or even
that of the Italians, with their peninsula. For centuries, constantly shifting boundaries have made it impossible to construct a German *Reich*
which would include only German peoples. The internal topography of
Germany made its contribution to political disunity. The arrangement of
her rivers, mountains, valleys, and plains tended to divide her into com-
partments, and thus to favor the growth of internal disputes, jealousies,
and particularism. The inequitable distribution of Germany's natural
resources, particularly of her forests, fertile soils, and valuable minerals,
further encouraged separatist tendencies among the many German states.
    Ethnic diversity is another centrifugal force which retarded political
unity and sharpened internal disputes. The German people are a mix-
ture of the most varied components of Germanic, Slavic, and pre-Indo-
European peoples. This diversity promoted sectionalism and led to
border fighting and civil wars throughout early German history; it furnished a cause for political struggles during more recent years. Over the
centuries this diversity of racial origin has progressively lost its early
significance as intermarriage mixed the separate blood streams, and
quarrels with non-German neighbors compelled Prussian, Bavarian, and
Saxon to make common cause. Politics and biology thus joined forces to
promote ethnic unity. As a result, the common characteristics of the
people tended to replace their earlier disparate traits as an ethnic factor
influencing national political development. The modern world is familiar

with the methodical, precise, hard-working German, conscientious to the point of perfectionism in his execution; the German who displays the highest sense of duty, sometimes servility, to his superiors, who shows high appreciation of the arts and culture, and, lastly, who has traditionally held to a high sense of personal morality. No less familiar are the traits which have gained deserved condemnation, the sense of superiority among the world's peoples, linking itself with a flair for brutality to give birth to genocide and the "crimes against civilization," so fully disclosed in the Nuremberg trials. The good and the bad in the race merged to make the Germans ideal instruments for the use of flamboyant, unscrupulous fanatics like the Nazi hierarchy. What a military victory in World War II would have done for the German race under such leadership is a matter for conjecture; what defeat has done is becoming clear, chiefly in showing that a sense of individual dignity, integrity, and pride must replace slavishness to superiors and to the state before a German democracy can be born with any hope of survival.

Germany missed almost entirely the civilizing influence of the Roman Empire, and was last of the western and central European countries to become Christianized. Even more important, the Reformation produced a cleavage sharper in Germany than elsewhere. Whereas this great movement created in England a Protestant national church headed by the king, and left Spain, France, and Italy Catholic countries, and the Scandinavian countries predominantly Protestant, it left the German people split between two main religions. When the resultant conflicts culminated in the Thirty Years' War, the end result was extreme territorial decentralization and a strengthening of the powers of the territorial princes against that of the Holy Roman Emperor of Germany.

On the economic side, Germany's comparatively late political unification retarded the development of her agriculture, commerce, and especially her industry. On the other hand, certain economic factors have strongly affected her political development. For example, the limited productivity of the glaciated, sandy plains of Prussia made austerity and parsimony virtues, and undoubtedly contributed to Prussian administrative and military efficiency. Germany's rather limited land area and relative lack of fertile soils helped create the urge to expand, as her population grew. Likewise, her excess of coal and her shortage of iron ore made Germany covet the ores of neighboring nations, even though she was never denied normal commercial access to these ores in times of peace. Even more important, after a late start, the rapidity of her industrialization, with its accompanying urbanization and proletarization, created after 1871 a host of internal social and political problems, and at the same time inevitably led to a search for sources of raw materials and for markets outside Germany. Finally, although Germany under the Weimar Republic made a remarkable recovery from her defeat in World War I, a world-wide economic depression fostered the conditions which eventually led to the overthrow of the German Republic.

Each of these factors: geography, ethnic diversity, national character, religious cleavage, and economic forces, played its part in the evolution of the modern German state. But to understand why there has never been a real democratic revolution within Germany, why internal political changes usually have come from above rather than from below, and why Germany's various governments have been at odds so often with the other governments of Europe and of the rest of the world, we must look further into her background. General agreement among authorities is lacking on the answers to these questions. With this fact in mind, let us now examine briefly the significant aspects of Germany's political development.

THE FIRST REICH: TERRITORIAL ABSOLUTISM.—Germany's political experience extends over many centuries, inasmuch as the Holy Roman Empire of the German Nation, or first *Reich* as it is often called, is one of the oldest of European institutions. However, the First *Reich* was never in fact a strong central government, although it survived in name until 1806. Consequently, the experience of the Germans differed sharply from that of the British or of the French. Through most of the thousand years of the First *Reich*, Germany was a patchwork, a loose federation of many petty states, the rulers of which owed only a shadowy allegiance to the Holy Roman Emperor. For the most part these petty states were under the absolute rule of a secular or ecclesiastical prince. Only in the free cities did any degree of self-government develop. A long line of emperors, preoccupied with interests outside Germany, failed to exploit the potential political strength of the cities, which might have enabled them to break the power of the feudal princes and to form a centralized national state as in France. Thus, the governmental heritage of the great majority of Germans of the First *Reich* was the habit of unquestioning obedience to an autocratic local ruler. While the French Revolution, carried by Napoleon's conquests into Germany, had some over-all liberalizing effect on German political thinking and institutions, the two most important effects of the French conqueror's activities in Germany were (1) a substantial reduction in the number of German states, and (2) an awakening of German nationalism. Out of the era of the Napoleonic Wars emerged a new political structure, the German Confederation, which merits some comment, if only because of its weaknesses.

THE GERMAN CONFEDERATION AND THE BISMARCKIAN WARS (1815-1871).—A product of the concert of European powers, rather than of the German people, the Confederation was, nonetheless, a constitutional step forward for Germany along her traditional path toward federal government. Yet by no standards can the government of Germany under the

Confederation be described as a true federal government. A makeshift, antiliberal alliance of princes, the Confederation was expressly designed by the concert to block further German unification, and to prevent the development of a strong central government in Germany. The very presence within the Confederation of two large states, Prussia and Austria, precluded the participation of the other German states in the government on anything approaching an equitable basis. Furthermore, the historic bitter rivalry between the two great states presaged the eventual domination of Germany by one of them, and the elimination of the other from the German *Reich*. Under the Confederation a degree of economic unity was achieved through the Prussian-sponsored German customs union (*Zollverein*). However, none of the sovereign German states took any real steps toward providing Germany with a politically unified state; they continued instead to bicker among themselves. The only organ of government of the Confederation was the Diet, an assembly of the ambassadors of the sovereign states. There was no executive as such, no federal administrative officers, no federal armed forces, no supreme court, and no means for the federal government to deal directly with the people of the states. The Revolution of 1848, which aimed toward converting the Confederation into a true federal state by correcting these weaknesses and by cutting deep into the sovereignty of the states, failed; it illustrates the relative weakness and political inexperience of the liberal elements within Germany at that time.

The failure of the liberal revolution was followed by a period of reaction, culminating in the unification of Germany by force. Prussia, under the guidance of Chancellor Otto von Bismarck, employed intrigue and war to eliminate Austria from the *Reich* in 1866, thus achieving partial unification. In the course of the successful war against France in 1870–1871, Prussia brought the remainder of the German states into the fold. National unity was implemented at Versailles, France, in 1871, when King William I of Prussia was crowned German emperor (Kaiser), ruler of the Hohenzollern Empire, or Second *Reich*.

THE SECOND REICH (1871-1918) : REACTIONARY MONARCHY.—Under the Hohenzollern Empire the assorted political units were welded into a nation, and Germany achieved the status of a Great Power. Although the Empire was in appearance a federal state with a constitution, it had in reality neither a true federal nor a democratic government. Prussia, which comprised three fifths of its territory and population and which possessed an even larger percentage of its industrial wealth, exercised hegemony over the smaller German states. The Prussian king was the German emperor and the Prussian prime minister was the German chancellor. There was no imperial war office; the Prussian war office performed the imperial functions. The German Army was, in fact, largely

Prussian in its make-up, almost wholly so in its direction. The imperial bureaucracy was Prussia-dominated. Thus Prussia had a far-reaching control over the executive branch of the government. Executive control was complemented by Prussia's domination of the Federal Council (*Bundesrat*). The imperial constitution allotted a definite quota of seats in the Federal Council to each state. Prussia's share was ample to assure reasonably effective control.[1] It should be noted that the Federal Council was not a parliamentary body in the true sense, but merely an assembly of the representatives of the federated states, owing their appointment and allegiance to the heads of those states.

The Hohenzollern Empire also had a second, representative body of limited legislative powers—the *Reichstag*. That body controlled neither foreign nor domestic policy, but it shared with the Federal Council the power to make law. Since it was elected by universal manhood suffrage, its principal service was to focus popular trends upon political issues. At the same time its powers were held in check by the reactionary policies of the Federal Council and by the Hohenzollern dynasty.

The Empire may be classed as a limited monarchy, highly reactionary in motivation and procedures, which made sporadic concessions to social demands in order to bolster national unity. As a system of government it functioned fairly well under the chancellorship of its chief architect, Bismarck. After Bismarck, however, internal dissension mounted, as evidenced by the growth of the Social Democratic party; and under his successors diplomatic blunders helped to plunge Germany into the first World War.

During World War I the actual powers of the government were gradually handed over to the Army. By 1916 Germany was ruled by a virtual military dictatorship of the high command.

THE VERSAILLES TREATY.—The defeat of Germany's armed forces in World War I and the resulting overthrow of the Hohenzollern dynasty ushered in a period of profound political change in Germany. Under the chancellorship of Prince Max of Baden, during the month preceding the armistice of November, 1918, drastic steps were taken toward destroying the military dictatorship of the general headquarters and toward converting the autocratic monarchy into a parliamentary regime. The immediate impetus toward change sprang from the urgent necessity of organizing a type of government with which the Allies would consent to negotiate, rather than from any spontaneous mass movement of the German people toward democracy. Following a national election ordered by a self-constituted provisional government, known as the Council of People's Commissioners, a national constitutional assembly met in the

---

[1] Prussia, holding seventeen of the total of fifty-eight seats, was in a dominating position, since amendments to the Constitution could be blocked by fourteen votes.

city of Weimar to draft a constitution for a German republic and to make a peace with the victorious Allied powers. Representatives of this newly formed Weimar Republic[2] went to Versailles, France, where on June 28, 1919, they accepted Allied peace terms. Under the resulting Versailles Treaty these representatives of Germany accepted for their nation full responsibility for the losses which the Allies had suffered during the war. They agreed to pay for all of the damage done by German armies to the civilian populations of the Allied powers. Although the peace conference was unable to compute the sum of these reparations payments, a commission in 1921 fixed their total at thirty-two billion dollars. Moreover, the Germans agreed to deliver to the Allies large numbers of locomotives, railway cars, automobiles, farm machines, horses, swine, sheep, and cattle. They surrendered the major part of their merchant marine and agreed to construct one million tons of new ships for the Allied nations. They agreed also to make large deliveries of coal, dyestuffs, and chemicals.

Territorially, the Treaty of Versailles reduced Germany in area and population by approximately one tenth. The provinces of Alsace-Lorraine, small districts near Belgium, West Prussia, Posen, Upper Silesia, Schleswig, and the Saar Basin were removed from German control. Germany renounced all rights to her overseas possessions.

To guarantee future peace, surrender of the German Navy and a limitation of its future size were required. The Army was reduced to one hundred thousand men. No submarines or military aircraft were to be maintained, and all fortifications were to be dismantled eastward from the French frontier to a line fifty kilometers east of the Rhine River. The left bank of the Rhine was to be occupied by Allied troops for periods of from five to fifteen years, with the right of later reoccupation reserved to the Allies in case Germany should fail to observe the reparation clauses of the treaty.

Since the Weimar Republic was the government which accepted the peace terms imposed upon Germany by the Allies, it came to bear the onus of having "humiliated" the nation. German nationalists repeatedly accused the Republic of having betrayed Germany by accepting the peace treaty. Thus, at the very outset of its struggle for existence, the Weimar Republic, born of defeat and revolution, was handicapped not only by foreign demands upon its resources, but also by domestic opposition to many of its most important policies. The fact that twentieth-century Germany lacked a tradition of, or experience in, democratic, or even responsible, government was perhaps the greatest obstacle for the Republic to overcome.

---

[2] The Constituent Assembly met in February, 1919, and at once enacted a law establishing the existing regime as the legal government of Germany.

THE WEIMAR CONSTITUTION.—The Constitution which the National Assembly promulgated in August, 1919, created in Germany a democratic republic of federated states. The executive authority was vested in a president, elected by direct universal popular ballot for a term of seven years. The president was given command of the armed forces, the right to issue emergency decrees, and other important powers. However, abuse of these powers was checked by the necessity of obtaining a ministerial countersignature to all acts. The president appointed the chancellor (prime minister), and upon the proposal of the latter he likewise appointed the various national ministers.

Legislative power was given primarily to a popularly elected chamber called the *Reichstag* (National Assembly). The chancellor and the Cabinet were responsible to the *Reichstag*. A second body, the *Reichsrat* (National Council), represented the German states in the formulation of the laws of the *Reich*. This body, like its predecessor, the imperial *Bundesrat*, was composed of delegates appointed by the state governments. The number of seats allotted to each state was based on population, but it was provided that each state, no matter how small, should hold at least one seat, and that no state should be allowed to occupy more than two fifths of the total number of seats. Thus, a curb was placed upon the largest state, Prussia. The *Reichsrat* was not a true upper house, inasmuch as its share in legislation consisted chiefly in assenting to cabinet bills or demanding their presentation before the *Reichstag*, postponing the promulgation of laws, causing the *Reichstag* to reconsider them, or bringing about a popular referendum under certain special conditions.

The *Reich* (central government) exercised exclusive legislative power over foreign affairs, colonial affairs, citizenship, military organization, coinage, customs, and the railway, postal, telephone, and telegraph systems. The *Reich* and the states had concurrent legislative power (with the *Reich* law prevailing in case of conflict) in many fields. These legislative provisions, along with certain others which gave the *Reich* almost complete control over the finances and taxation systems of the states, constituted a definite departure from the federal principle. So little power was left to the states that in actual practice the *Reich* government under the Republic became progressively unitary.

Like the *Reich*, every state had its own constitution. Cabinets were responsible to the popular legislative chamber, the members of which were elected by direct and universal suffrage, employing the secret ballot. In local, state, and national elections the system of proportional representation was used.

The Weimar Constitution gave the president power to take measures for the restoration of public safety and order when such safety and order were seriously disturbed or endangered. Unfortunately for democratic government, at times emergencies were declared which might not be considered to fall within the meaning of the Constitution; thus for some years before Hitler came to power the German people became accustomed to the suspension of their constitutional rights and to government by decree.[3]

An independent judiciary was guaranteed by the Constitution. Extraordinary courts were prohibited; the high court and the regular state courts were authorized to exercise ordinary jurisdiction. Administrative courts were also recognized.

Considerable attention was given to economic matters. Although property rights and freedom of contract were guaranteed, provision was made for the socialization of economic enterprises, subject to compensation. A national Economic Council was established, in which the various occupational groups were represented according to their economic and social importance. This Council had the right to discuss all fundamentally important bills in the field of economic and social policy before such bills were introduced by the Cabinet into the *Reichstag*. It could also prepare bills and have them introduced.

An impressive list of the rights and duties of Germans appears in the Constitution. Equality before the law, freedom of the person, freedom of assembly, and freedom of speech and the press are but a few of the guaranteed rights. In sum they established the framework of a thoroughgoing, modern democracy which, in time, might conceivably have converted Germany into a cooperative partner in the family of Western democratic nations.

Developments under the Weimar Republic

PARTIES AND PLOTS.—The Social Democratic party was numerically the strongest political group in Germany during World War I. Nevertheless, as the war ended and the Weimar Republic was established, this party was unable to exercise strong leadership because it had split into three groups. Its largest wing, the Majority Socialists, led by Friedrich Ebert, the first president of the Weimar Republic, favored a moderate program of progressively socializing industry. Another wing, the Independent Socialists, insisted upon the immediate socialization of industry by con-

---

[3] The president's emergency powers were authorized by Article 48 of the Weimar Constitution. This fatal article allowed the president, in the interests of public safety and order, to suspend most of the fundamental rights of the individual, established elsewhere in the constitution. While the *Reichstag* was given the right to revoke all such measures taken by the president, this check on the executive power proved ineffectual since the president could legally dissolve the *Reichstag*. Thus Article 48, theoretically designed to maintain law and order, and to protect the Constitution in time of danger, became in actual practice an instrument for destroying it.

stitutional means; while the third wing, the radical Spartacists, clamored
for a Communist dictatorship of the proletariat on the Russian model.
After heavy bloodshed, all Spartacist revolts were suppressed by the provisional government by May, 1919. It is worth noting that the leaders of
the government, forced to depend on remnants of the Imperial Army to
crush radical resistance and to stabilize the situation on the eastern border, placed themselves thereby under political obligation to the rightist
leaders of the Army.

At the Weimar Constitutional Assembly in 1919 the Majority
Socialists had the largest number of delegates, but no political party had
a clear majority. Only with the aid of the Democratic party (bourgeois
republicans) and the Catholic Center party were the Majority Socialists,
or Social Democrats, able to assume leadership in framing the Constitution. This same bloc of parties controlled the first Cabinet of the Republic. They formed a center group, with their opposition divided between the Independent Socialists on the left and the Nationalist party
of conservatives and monarchists on the right. Under Majority Socialist
leadership the Weimar Republic attempted a program of reconstruction
and moderate reform. Unfortunately the parties of the ruling coalition
produced few able statesmen or resolute leaders. Suddenly handed the
reins of the government and full responsibility, they lacked the political
experience necessary for a time of crisis. Above all, they lacked realism,
courage, and tenacity—qualities so vitally necessary for leaders in a new
democracy.

Radical groups of both the Left and the Right were dissatisfied with
the moderation of the dominant parties. The Communists incited further
abortive plots against the government. More threatening were the Nationalist demonstrations, led by ex-Army officers who were disgusted
with the rule of Socialists and liberals and who charged that these
groups had "betrayed" Germany by signing an ignominious peace. In
1920 a group of ex-soldiers marched on Berlin but was thwarted in its
rebellious efforts. Three years later General Erich Ludendorff and an obscure propagandist, Adolf Hitler, attempted to overthrow the "inglorious
republic" in a *Putsch* in Munich. They were unsuccessful, and Hitler and
several of his followers were sentenced to prison.

INFLATION.—The Weimar Republic inherited from World War I
a depleted treasury, an inflated currency, and a chaotic economy. The
demobilization of the Army, added to inflation, loss of purchasing power
by the middle classes, and decline of foreign trade, created a vast army
of unemployed. The government, moreover, had to make large reparations payments and meet the expenses of the Allied armies of occupation.
When the financial load proved too heavy to be met by taxation or loans,
the government began to print paper money supported only by its prom-

ise to pay. The added burden of French occupation of the Ruhr, combined with the German policy of passive resistance, caused the German mark to take a precipitate downward plunge. As a result, by 1923 it reached a value of four trillion to one dollar. This uncontrolled inflation, which destroyed the people's savings, insurance, and fixed obligations, such as bonds and debentures, virtually bankrupted the middle class. The government was by no means blameless in the debacle. It is not too much to say that a temporary period of national bankruptcy was welcomed by those in authority as a means of ending reparations payments. Desperate measures of economy, the creation of a new currency, and borrowing from abroad—all these steps had to be taken by the government in order to create a stable financial order. Partial recovery followed these measures, only to vanish in the world depression of 1929-1933. By the latter year seven million Germans were unemployed, and suffering was widespread.

SOCIALIST PROGRAM.—The Republican government extended its control over railroads, banks, mines, public utilities, and other enterprises in the public interest. Railways and air lines were governmentally regulated. Labor unionization was encouraged, arbitration was facilitated in wage disputes, and special labor courts were organized. Women were emancipated—legally, politically, and economically. Essentially, however, the economic system in Germany under the Republic did not differ greatly from that of the Empire. It remained a capitalistic system operated primarily for private profit, with some paternalistic attempts by the government at planned economy. As a result of the financial crisis of 1931, the potential control of the state over industry and banking was enormously increased, thus paving the way for the subsequent Nazi creation of a totalitarian economy. Deprived by the depression of their economic security, practically all classes of the German people were profoundly dissatisfied with the existing system and ready for any change, however radical, which promised better conditions.

THE CIVIL SERVICE.—Upon its accession to power following World War I, the republican government inherited a civil service system manned almost entirely by members of the old imperial bureaucracy. Supported by a tradition dating from the time of Frederick William the Great Elector in the seventeenth century, and strengthened by its close day-to-day connection with the people, the bureaucracy exercised considerable political influence in the government, although it was in theory politically neutral. The Weimar government left this pillar of the German state virtually untouched. The rather idealistic and politically inexperienced Weimar leaders undertook no wholesale housecleaning of the civil service to ensure that only politically reliable citizens, loyal to the new democracy, remained in administrative positions. Instead, the old bu-

reaucracy was retained practically intact, and its members were guaranteed freedom of political opinion and of association. Under the impact of
party politics, the traditional political neutrality of the civil service was
replaced by increasing indifference, then hostility toward the Republic.
That the Nazis' first purge of the civil service in 1933 produced only a
10 per cent turnover is a significant measure of the bureaucracy's lack of
loyalty to the Republican regime. There is little doubt that the failure
of the Weimar government to eradicate the reactionary elements from
the civil service was an important factor in its downfall.

THE ARMED FORCES.—Since no government can stay in power for long
unless it is able to control its military establishment, it is well to examine
the Weimar Republic's handling of this important problem. We have
already noted that the leaders of the new Republic, by depending upon
the remnants of the Imperial Army to stamp out extremist revolts and to
guard the eastern frontier during the first few months of the Republic's
existence, placed themselves under obligation to the generals. This
initial period of uncertainty emphasized the question of security; consequently, the reorganization of the Army became temporarily a rallying
center around which party differences could be reconciled. The National
Assembly at Weimar in March, 1919, enacted legislation which gave legal
status to the hastily reformed remnants of the old Army as the provisional *Reichswehr*, assigning it the mission of maintaining the security
of the frontiers and order within the country. The energetic Gustav
Noske, as the Republic's first war minister, using the machinery of the
old Prussian war office, rapidly built up, trained, and equipped the provisional force from a nucleus of die-hard Prussian officers and men. The
new Army was composed largely of veterans with front-line experience.
By June, 1919, Germany possessed in the provisional *Reichswehr* a battle-
tested, well-disciplined, confident national army of volunteers, 400,000
strong.

It was the intention of the Allies to liquidate this force by implementing the military provisions of the Treaty of Versailles. The German
Army leaders, with the tacit approval of their government, disregarded
the spirit of the treaty, although they complied to the letter of its provisions, at least in the eyes of inefficient outside observers. Keeping the
pick of the existing force, they did cut the strength of the Army to the
prescribed figure of 100,000 but during the ensuing decade, by various
subterfuges, they turned the new professional *Reichswehr* into a training
cadre for officers and noncommissioned officers. The German General
Staff, officially dissolved, appeared under the guise of the "Preparatory
Commission of the Army of Peace," with offices in Berlin. Through their
government the generals obtained from the Allies supplementary delays
in the execution of the disarmament provisions of the treaty, and thus
gained time to conceal a substantial part of their arms.

Germany was, therefore, neither disarmed nor demilitarized after World War I. The fact that most of her territory was left unoccupied by Allied forces, plus the enormity of the task assigned to the inter-Allied commission appointed to disarm the defeated nation, made it possible for Germany to evade a complete liquidation of her military strength.

After 1919 the political influence of the German Army grew in proportion to the nation's desperate feeling of insecurity; for in the eyes of a defeated but proud people, the *Reichswehr* was the one remaining symbol of external security. The reconstituted *Reichswehr* successfully resisted the government's halfhearted efforts to democratize it. Throughout the brief life of the Republic, the monarchist officers in top Army positions remained openly indifferent to the fate of the democratic regime, and when the internal political crisis came, they did nothing to prevent the Nazi rise to power. In a very real sense the Army served as a bridge between the Second *Reich* and the Third.

If the Weimar government may be censured for its failure to indoctrinate the new Army in absolute loyalty to the democratic regime, it is even more open to criticism for permitting the growth of quasi-military armed bands sponsored by political parties, especially the Elite Guard and Storm Trooper detachments of the Nazi party—a wide-open threat to the survival of the existing government.

FOREIGN RELATIONS.—The heritage of hate which World War I left in Germany was expressed in several ways. The German people resented the clause in the Versailles Treaty which declared Germany "guilty" [4] of forcing war upon the world and therefore liable for reparations payments. They denounced the loss of their overseas territories without compensation, and they deplored the humiliating and defenseless position to which the Versailles Treaty had reduced them.

In 1923, after Germany had defaulted on her reparations payments, France seized the Ruhr Valley. In the following year the Dawes plan reduced the size of annual reparations payments, secured for Germany a foreign loan, and led to the French evacuation of the Ruhr Valley. For a few years thereafter Franco-German relations improved greatly. At the Locarno Conference of 1925 both nations agreed to respect their existing frontiers. The next year Germany was given full membership in the League of Nations and a permanent seat on the League Council. During the years 1926-1932 the German Republic made repeated demands that the victor nations of World War I reduce their armaments in

---

[4] Art. 231, Treaty of Versailles reads: "The Allied and Associated Governments affirm and Germany accepts the responsibility of Germany and her allies for causing all the loss and damage to which the Allied and Associated Governments and their nationals have been subjected as a consequence of the war imposed upon them by the aggression of Germany and her allies."

accordance with Article 8 of the League of Nations Covenant in Part I of the Versailles Treaty, and as implied by the preamble to Part V of the treaty. By this means the Germans hoped to secure the effect of a relative increase in their own military strength, a hope that was frustrated when the Allies refused to accede to Germany's demands. When the Kellogg-Briand Peace Pact was proposed in 1928, Germany was one of the first to concur in renouncing war as an instrument of national policy. Shortly after this action, the Young plan reduced German reparations to eight billion dollars. Even that figure proved to be too large a sum for a reluctant debtor to pay in a period of extreme economic depression. The Hoover moratorium of 1931, suspending all reparations payments for a year, was the last act in the fiasco of collecting from Germany. Payments were never resumed. On net balance Germany actually got more in foreign cash and credits (chiefly American) than she paid out as reparations.

In 1930 the last Allied forces of occupation were withdrawn from the Rhineland. Yet even these achievements of the Weimar Republic in diplomacy did not erase the discontent which Germans felt over the remaining military and territorial strictures of the Versailles Treaty.

CAUSES OF THE DOWNFALL OF THE WEIMAR REPUBLIC.—Created under unfavorable circumstances, and repeatedly faced with almost insuperable tasks at home and abroad, the Weimar government failed to produce in Germany a real democratic revolution. The elements which contributed to its collapse were many and complex, but planners of Germany's future may well examine the following factors:

(1) The Weimar Republic had neither effective leaders nor a leading party. The multiple-party system and proportional representation made it impossible for a single political party to secure the support of a majority of the electorate. Since no party could command a majority in the *Reichstag,* the successive cabinets were supported by coalitions, none of which was stable. Thus the government, in the eyes of the German people, with their tradition of unquestioning obedience to authority, appeared weak and vacillating. (2) The government failed to purge its administration of reactionary bureaucrats, and its courts of reactionary judges. (3) It allowed the Army to become an independent power within the state instead of subordinating the military to civil authority. (4) The Republic permitted such complete freedom of expression and action that contempt for its authority led in due time to outright treasonable action. (5) The government failed to publicize and propagandize the very real benefits accruing to the people under a democracy. Instead, it allowed the Nazi movement to acquire a virtual monopoly over the channels of appeal to the masses. (6) The Allied powers mistrusted the Weimar government and failed to give it active support until too late. (7) The

economic crisis of the early 1930's dealt a mortal blow to the confidence of the German masses in the existing government and led a great number of them to welcome dictatorial rule.

The Rise of National Socialism

ORIGINS OF THE MOVEMENT.—National Socialism, like Italian Fascism, grew out of the aftermath of World War I, and drew its leaders and its mass following from dissatisfied groups in Germany paralleling those in Italy. In the long run, because of German thoroughness and because of the longer period of build-up preceding the National Socialist rise to power, the German brand of Fascism created a more truly totalitarian state and secured a far more powerful and relentless grip on its people.

Like the Russian Bolshevist movement, National Socialism had its inner circle of elite, the organizers and revolutionary strategists of the movement. The nucleus of this group was the insignificant German Workers' party, founded in Munich in January, 1919. Its seventh full-fledged member, Adolf Hitler, became the number-one organizer, strategist, and demagogic leader of the new movement, the seeds of which found fertile soil in postwar Germany.

ADOLF HITLER.—Like the dictator of Soviet Russia's totalitarian state, Joseph Stalin, Hitler came originally from the borderland of the nation which he was destined to rule. Born in 1889 of a lower-middle-class family in Braunau, Austria, a small town just outside the German border, he went as a youth to seek his fortune in Vienna. While he had hoped to become a creative artist, actually he was reduced to seeking a meager income as an insignificant odd-job painter, decorator, and draftsman. In the bitterness of his failure he reacted violently against Vienna's cosmopolitan life in which he could find no place. He came to hate the Austrian national state and the urbane Jews whom he found in its capital city. As his bitterness grew he sought solace by embracing the twin ideas of German nationalism and the superiority of the Aryan race.

In 1912 Hitler moved to Munich. During World War I he served in a Bavarian division until he was gassed and hospitalized. When defeat and revolution came to Germany following the war, all that he despised most seemed to him to have triumphed: international socialism, liberal democracy, the Allies, and the Jews. As a result, he entered politics with a consuming passion to resurrect the defeated national power of the German people and to scourge the objects of his hatred.

Soon after joining the German Workers' party in Munich, Hitler became its chief propagandist. In order to benefit from the popularity of nationalism and socialism, he changed its name to National Socialist

German Workers' party (*Nationalsozialistische Deutsche Arbeiterpartei,*
referred to in abbreviated form as the NSDAP or Nazis). As the party
prospered, Hitler secured control of a scandal-mongering weekly newspaper, the *Volkischer Beobachter,* and converted it into a daily. A few
months later he was elected party *Führer* (Leader). Under his guidance
National Socialism, by 1923, had become an important political movement in Germany.

The failure of Hitler's Munich *Putsch* on November 9, 1923, was
but a temporary reverse. Although he and his associates received five-
year jail sentences, and the party was disbanded, Hitler was released from
prison after serving one year of his sentence. Shortly afterward he published his book, *My Battle (Mein Kampf)*, re-established his newspaper,
and rebuilt his party. His second—and successful—drive for power
showed his consummate understanding of the human raw material on
which he was working. For a while he shifted from his earlier emphasis
on the infamy of the Versailles Treaty and turned all the fury of his
oratory against the peril of Communism. These were the days of the
Locarno agreements and a growing German Communist party.

The new strategy brought large contributions to party funds from
wealthy industrialists who, though secretly despising Hitler, thought they
saw in him a convenient tool which they could use to destroy the power
of the Weimar Republic and socialist influences. The Nazi party used its
funds to promote huge mass meetings, finance new propaganda, uniform
its Storm Troopers, break up Communist meetings, terrorize the people,
spread racial hatred, and paint a picture of the Weimar Republic as a
weak government, guilty of accepting a shameful peace. Hamstrung by
its too literal interpretation of the rights of free speech and free assembly, the government allowed the Nazis to say and do things that should
have resulted in the arrest and imprisonment of the Nazi leaders on two
counts—disturbance of public order and open incitement to violence and
revolution.

THE PROGRAM OF THE NATIONAL SOCIALIST PARTY.—The National Socialist party program appealed to the passions aroused in Germany by
the Versailles Treaty and by the acute economic suffering which followed
World War I. The Nazis bade Germans take heart, awaken, unite, and
seek revenge. They charged that Germany had been betrayed by the Republicans who revolted in 1918; they preached that the German Imperial
Armies had not been defeated on the battlefield, but rather scuttled by
defeatism on the home front. Once that point had been established, a
plea for repudiation of the treaty followed in due course.

The Nazi program of twenty-five points, first published in 1920,
called for a union of all Germans in a Greater Germany. It demanded
the abolition of the Versailles Treaty, the acquisition of land for "sur-

plus" German population, the exclusion of non-Germans from Germany, the denial of citizenship to Jews, and their total expulsion from public life. Regarding economic and social matters, the program proclaimed equality of rights and duties for all citizens, made community work a duty, demanded the abolition of unearned incomes, insisted upon the confiscation of all war profits, urged the nationalization of trusts, called for profit sharing in large industries, and favored pensions for the aged. In addition, the program urged protection of middle-class business interests, reform of landownership, and suppression of speculation in business. It denounced Roman law and called for a new German common law. The program demanded national reform in education to fit youth for "the requirements of practical life." In the remaining points, the Nazis demanded a strong army, a controlled press, a "positive Christianity," and a strong central government. In sum, the program was an effective catchall to corral the support of a wide range of political and social groupings. Interestingly enough, this party program contained no mention of the basic Nazi leadership principle. In its ideological substance, however, the program became a blueprint of later action.

Capitalists, nationalists, militarists, war veterans, authoritarians, and, above all, masses of the disillusioned middle classes enthusiastically supported the National Socialist or Nazi program with their votes. As the public distress increased during the depression years after 1929, as unemployment rose, as more people turned to radical groups for solutions to national problems—even larger numbers supported the Nazis. The 800,000 Nazi votes in the 1928 *Reichstag* elections increased to 6,500,000. In the 1932 presidential contest the first election failed to produce a majority for any candidate. In a second, or runoff election held a month later, von Hindenburg, the Republican presidential candidate, polled 19,359,000 votes to 13,418,000 for Hitler and 3,706,000 for the Communist candidate. In the two *Reichstag* elections during the same year, the Nazis won 230 out of a total of 608 *Reichstag* seats in July, but captured only 196 seats in the November election. Von Hindenburg distrusted Hitler as a demagogue; but the president was a very old man who, though he had been a great warrior, had no real understanding of the political and social turmoil which he was expected to reduce to order and stability. His trusted advisers included wealthy *Junker* landowners who agreed with the industrialists in supporting Hitler. Thus von Hindenburg was finally persuaded that Hitler was the best choice he could make for the office of Chancellor.

CREATION OF A TOTALITARIAN STATE.—When Hitler became chancellor in January, 1933, his party lacked a majority in the *Reichstag*. To gain his ends he had to form a coalition Ministry in which most of the Cabinet positions were held by members of the Nationalist party. That this maneuver was merely a steppingstone to direct personal control soon became apparent. At Hitler's instance, a dissolution of the *Reichstag* was promptly decreed by President von Hindenburg and a new election was ordered. Most opportunely for the Nazis, the *Reichstag* building was burned under suspicious circumstances just before the election.[5] On the basis of flimsy evidence the Nazis created the bogey of a nation-wide Communist uprising, which persuaded many Germans to turn blindly toward Hitler as the preserver of law and order.

The incident gave Hitler the pretext for persuading President von Hindenburg to sign a Law for the Protection of the People and the State, under which the personal liberty clauses of the Weimar Constitution were suspended. This law was used ruthlessly to arrest and harry not only Communists but also Democrats and Majority Socialists. The Communist party was suppressed. In the elections which followed, the Nazis polled 44 per cent of the votes, the Nationalists 8 per cent, the Center parties 14 per cent, the Majority Socialists 18 per cent, and the Communists 12 per cent. Thus, with their Nationalist allies, the Nazis controlled 52 per cent of the seats in the *Reichstag,* a bare majority. However, by forcibly barring the Communist representatives from their seats and by intimidating the representatives of the moderate parties, Hitler was able to achieve his immediate ends.

Although the Weimar Constitution was not repealed, Hitler moved rapidly to transform the German Republic into a totalitarian state. Symbolically, he convoked the *Reichstag* at Potsdam in March, 1933, and proclaimed the Third *Reich*—a successor to the Holy Roman Empire and the Hohenzollern Empire. By persuasion and threats he induced the *Reichstag* to pass an enabling act giving his Cabinet full legislative power for four years. This law, later extended from time to time, actually terminated the Weimar Republic and established the Nazi dictatorship. By July, 1933, all political parties other than the Nazi party had been dissolved, and forbidden by decree to reorganize. Germany had become a one-party state. The *Reichstag* was reduced to a body of the Nazi party's own nominees, the civil service was purged of politically unreliable officials, and the courts were rendered subservient to Nazi influence.

In 1933 and 1934 the states were deprived of legislative power and incorporated more closely into the *Reich.* National governors were appointed in all the states except Prussia. The Prussian ministries (except finance) were merged with the corresponding national ministries, and Hitler reserved to himself the nominal position of National Governor of Prussia, delegating the powers of that office to Herman Goering as Prus-

---

[5] Although complete evidence concerning this fire was not produced at the Nuremberg trials, there is good reason to believe that the *Reichstag* building was burned by the Nazis themselves, for propaganda purposes. See *Nuremberg Diary* by G. M. Gilbert, pp. 182-183 and 298 (New York, 1947).

THE GERMAN ENABLING ACT OF MARCH 24, 1933

This so-called Enabling Act, pushed through the Reichstag and the National Council (Reichsrat) following the election of March 7, 1933, and after a threat by Chancellor Hitler that he would act even if the bill were not passed, is the first basic law of the Nazi state. From the moment this law became effective, the Reichstag became a supernumerary body. The National Council (Reichsrat) was abolished in 1934.

The Reichstag has enacted the following law which, with the consent of the Reichsrat and after determination that the requirements for laws changing the constitution have been complied with, is hereby promulgated:

Article 1. National laws can be enacted by the national Cabinet as well as in accordance with the procedure established in the Constitution. This applies also to the laws referred to in article 85, paragraph 2, and in article 87 of the Constitution.

Article 2. The national laws enacted by the national Cabinet may deviate from the Constitution insofar as they do not affect the position of the Reichstag and the Reichsrat. The powers of the President remain undisturbed.

Article 3. The national laws enacted by the national Cabinet are prepared by the Chancellor and published in the *Reichsgesetzblatt*. They come into effect, unless otherwise specified, upon the day following their publication. Articles 68 to 77 of the Constitution do not apply to the laws enacted by the national Cabinet.

Article 4. Treaties of the Reich with foreign states which concern matters of national legislation do not require the consent of the bodies participating in legislation. The national Cabinet is empowered to issue the necessary provisions for the execution of these treaties.

Article 5. This law becomes effective on the day of its publication. It becomes invalid on April 1st, 1937; it further becomes invalid when the present national Cabinet is replaced by another.

Berlin, March 24th, 1933.

The National President
VON HINDENBURG

The National Chancellor
ADOLF HITLER

The National Minister of the Interior
FRICK

The National Minister of Foreign Affairs
FREIHERR VON NEURATH

The National Minister of Finances
COUNT SCHWERIN VON KROSIGK

sian minister-president. The National Council (*Reichsrat*) was abolished in 1934. Following von Hindenburg's death in the same year, an Act concerning the Head of the German *Reich* merged the offices of president and chancellor, and provided that the powers of the former office should be exercised by the *Führer*. The new office also included that of the Supreme Commander of the Armed Forces.

Having achieved full legislative and executive authority, and complete control of the government, national and local, Hitler's general policy took a sharp turn to the right, and in June, 1934, he took drastic action within his own party against an extremist wing which sought to carry the revolution still further. The demands of extremist elements came to a head with an attempt by Storm Trooper leaders to gain control of the *Reichswehr*. Hitler took the side of the Regular Army leaders when the head of the Storm Troopers attempted to take it over, and had sixty officers of his own partisan army executed without trial. Using the Army affair as a pretext, Hitler instituted a widespread blood purge in which approximately one thousand enemies of the regime, including allegedly disloyal party officials and all potential rivals for the number-one position in the dictatorship, were massacred. After this demonstration of the dangers of insubordination, Hitler stood unchallenged in state and party.

National Socialist Doctrine

NATIONAL SOCIALIST IDEOLOGY.—The political and economic principles of National Socialism were diametrically opposed to those underlying British or American democracy, or, indeed, democracy by any acceptable definition. The Nazis considered a highly centralized government of broad scope the ideal political form for the control of human society. They created and directed the totalitarian state, with the political and economic regulation of the individual and of society carried to the point where personal freedom ceased to exist and opposition in any form became a crime against the state.

The theoretical principles of the Nazi state were by no means the product of recent thought. They can be found in the philosophy of many individuals in many ages and countries. In Germany during the last century, principles similar or analogous to Nazi ideas were advocated by many leading thinkers.[6] No philosopher himself, Adolf Hitler cunningly

---

[6] Major contributors to the Nazi stream of thought—to mention only a few— were Johann Gottlieb Fichte, George Friedrich Wilhelm Hegel, Heinrich von Treitschtke, Count Joseph Arthur de Gobineau (a Frenchman), Houston Stewart Chamberlain (an Englishman), Friedrich Nietzsche, and Friedrich Naumann. The original ideas of these thinkers, of course, were somewhat modified and adulterated in the process of being borrowed by the Nazis.

utilized this philosophical background as a basis for creating his political power.

According to Nazi ideology, the National Socialist state rested on three basic concepts: The *Volk* or people, the *Führer,* and the movement or party. Each of these central ideas was developed by corollaries, many of which were left purposely vague and mystical.

THE "FOLK."—The concept of the "folk" was the belief in the people's existence as a self-conscious political community. The "folk" was not necessarily the sum of the inhabitants of a state; it was a product of race, soil, language, religion, and history, and possessed a consciousness of its solidarity and unified will. Thus the German "folk," according to the theory, formed a closed community which recognized no national boundaries. Individuals were important only as they could be identified with the "folk." The state existed in order to aid the "folk" to develop itself more fully. This was the theoretical basis for the authority of the Third *Reich*. The "folk" state was the justification which Hitler used in demanding that Germans and their descendants in foreign countries should identify themselves with the aims of Germany.[7]

RACIAL SUPERIORITY.—A corollary to the concept of the "folk" was the theory of the racial superiority of the Aryan—by Nazi standards, the German, or a person of related blood. According to this view, all the achievements of the Western world were Germanic. It followed from this premise that if Germanic blood were to be diluted, Western culture would suffer. This racial theory provided the basis for discrimination against "non-Aryan" races within the Third *Reich*. Nazi reinterpretation of history, science, music, and other branches of learning and culture sought to prove their racial theories.

THE LEADERSHIP PRINCIPLE.—In Nazi ideology, the *Führer* was supposed in some mystical manner to embody and give expression to the aspirations and wishes of the "folk." His authority was supreme, his decisions were final and always right, and his followers owed him the duty of unquestioning obedience. Whenever he saw fit, the Leader delegated

---

[7] Clear evidence that the Nazi folkish ideas had a long tradition in Germany may be found in a standard college atlas (*Deutscher Kolonial—Atlas* by Paul Langhans) published in 1897. By means of shaded maps in this remarkable textbook, German students were taught, for example, that all of Austria, Luxemburg and the Netherlands, most of Belgium and Switzerland, and much of Denmark and Bohemia were 95 to 100 per cent German-populated. The atlas made more modest but equally astonishing claims for the spread of the German "folk" into the more distant areas of Europe and of the rest of the world. To reconcile the atlas percentages of Germans in the United States with the official statistics published by the United States government would have required the inclusion as Germans of all Dutch, Belgian, Luxemburger, Swiss, Austrian, Hungarian, and Scandinavian immigrants, as well as native-born and second-generation Germans in this country.

responsibilities to a hierarchy of subordinate leaders each of whom owed unconditional allegiance to his immediate superior and at the same time was the absolute leader in his own sphere of jurisdiction. The Nazis declared that the true will of the people could not be expressed through parliamentary votes, but (in its pure and uncorrupted form) only by the Leader. Since the Leader was free from and above all pressure groups, he could accurately transform the feelings of the whole people into a conscious will. Under the theory, plebiscites were not thought of as democratic referendums. Their purpose was not to give the people an opportunity to decide some issues, but rather to express the unity of the people in supporting a decision which the Leader had already made. Dissenters soon came to realize that confinement in a concentration camp was the reward of their independence of thought.

THE PARTY.—Intermediate between the "folk" and the Leader stood the party or the ruling class. The party members owed the closest personal allegiance to the Leader. They represented not only a link between him and the "folk," but also the instrument through which his plans were realized, his intentions carried out. The party was charged with educating the mass of the people into a "politically conscious" or Nazified group. It disseminated Nazi principles, it selected the leaders of the future, and it shaped the "political will of the people" in accordance with the Leader's aims.

Unlike the Communist party in the Soviet Union, the Nazi party did not occupy a position above the state, even though it became the only legal political organization in the Third *Reich*. Nor did the Nazi party identify itself with the state, as did the Fascist party in Italy. In contrast with these two oft-cited parallels, the Nazi party occupied a position alongside and outside the state, and more or less immune to control by the latter. In its final practical application, the party gradually linked together the state and party offices until it had achieved a position of primacy within the *Reich*.

THE TOTALITARIAN STATE.—National Socialism in Germany set as its goal the complete refashioning of economic society, while formally retaining the institutions of private property and capitalism. It sought in some measure to reconcile these institutions with the totalitarian concept which placed all the activities of the people, whether political, economic, or cultural, under the control and guidance of the state. It envisaged a widespread mobilization of all these activities as a normal, rather than an emergency, condition. The government was to be the agency through which all human interests were managed. This totalitarian concept provides a key to the understanding of the changes the Nazi government effected during the period of its ascendancy not only in the domains of industry, labor, trade, agriculture, and finance, but in its extension of control over the church, the press, and even the recreational activities of the people.

IMPERIALISM.—Glorification of racial destiny and strong leadership naturally produced an imperialistic foreign policy. Nazi imperialism expressed itself largely in the desire to gather all persons of German blood into the *Reich* (Pan-Germanism), to secure ample territory (*Lebensraum*) for the development of a greater German state, and the eventual domination of other states in a "New Order."

MILITARISM.—National Socialism included the ideals of disciplined organization and aggressive pursuit of party goals. The former provided the means; the latter, the objectives for Nazi militarism. National Socialism revived the old ideal from which the civilized world was beginning to escape, that war and the use of force are glorious in themselves. In domestic political struggles and in international relations, the followers of Hitler repeatedly demonstrated their belief in the ruthless use of force.

OPPORTUNISM.—It should be pointed out that National Socialism was opportunistic. Like Italian Fascism, it fitted its theoretical conceptions to its momentary purposes. National Socialist theory was used as a means to attain and to maintain political power, rather than as an end in itself. For example, although the Nazis consistently maintained their principle of racial "purity" as a basis for all culture, they officially discovered that the Japanese were Aryans when it became desirable for Germany to make an alliance with Japan.

IRRATIONALITY IN NATIONAL SOCIALISM.—At its core, the Nazi philosophy was irrational; it stood in opposition to the use of human intelligence. It demanded blind, fanatical acceptance of the authority of the Leader. It insisted upon the view that the Leader by intuition, not by reason, could divine the will of the political community. It substituted irrationality for reason in science, force for consent in the regulation of civil society, and conquest for friendly intercourse in the international community.

The Government of the Third Reich

ABSENCE OF CONSTITUTIONAL LAW.—Although never formally abolished, the Weimar Constitution was suspended in 1935 and was not applied after that year. The German government under Hitler—meaning in the last analysis Hitler himself—held all legislative, executive, and administrative power. Its decrees were called law and were enforced as law. In

GOVERNMENT OF THE THIRD REICH

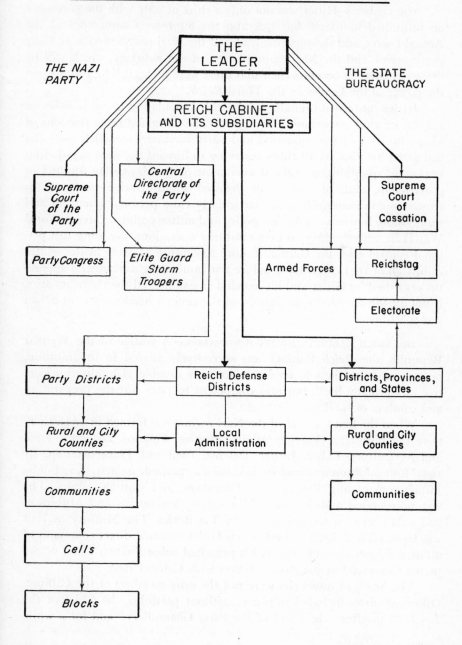

THE LEADER

THE NAZI PARTY

THE STATE BUREAUCRACY

REICH CABINET AND ITS SUBSIDIARIES

Supreme Court of the Party

Central Directorate of the Party

Supreme Court of Cassation

Party Congress

Elite Guard Storm Troopers

Armed Forces

Reichstag

Electorate

Party Districts

Reich Defense Districts

Districts, Provinces, and States

Rural and City Counties

Local Administration

Rural and City Counties

Communities

Communities

Cells

Blocks

other words, the will of the Leader was the supreme law of the land in the Third *Reich*.

THE LEADER.—Hitler was not only a chief of state with the powers of an unlimited monarch, but was also the Supreme Commander of the Armed Forces, and the supreme leader of the Nazi party. In view of these prerogatives, and the Nazi manipulation of the judiciary, which will be discussed later,[8] it becomes clear that there were no legal limitations upon the power of the Leader in the Third *Reich*.

Hitler concerned himself mainly with formulating broad policies on matters of vital importance. Of necessity, he delegated some portions of his authority to a governmental and party hierarchy in which each official acted for him. At all times reserving to himself the final decision on important questions, he turned over most of the day-to-day conduct of government, and, of course, all detailed administrative work, to his trusted subordinates. He gave particularly close personal attention and supervision, however, to foreign policy and military affairs. During World War II he actively directed many military operations, assuming full personal control after the German failure to capture Moscow in the winter campaign of 1941–1942. Long before war came, the governmental apparatus organized by Hitler and his henchmen assumed all the characteristics, if not all the outward appearances, of the general headquarters of a vast war machine.

THE REICH CABINET AND ITS SUBSIDIARIES.—A vestige of the Weimar Republic, the *Reich* Cabinet was successively altered in organization, powers, and functions to render it not only capable of totalitarian control of Germany itself, but also competent to carry out the preparation and conduct of total war.

When the first Cabinet of the Nazi regime was formed in 1933, there were ten ministries: Foreign Affairs, Interior, Finance, Economy, Food and Agriculture, Labor, Justice, Defense, Post, and Transportation. By 1935, four additional ministries had been organized, namely, Air, Public Enlightenment and Propaganda, Education, and Church Affairs. The war necessitated addition of a Ministry of Armaments and Munitions and a Ministry for Occupied Eastern Territories. The Ministry of War was replaced in February, 1938, when Hitler assumed direct command of all armed forces, appointing as his principal subordinate a Chief of Supreme Command of the Armed Forces with Cabinet rank.

The heads of ministries were not the only members of the Cabinet. Other members included ministers without portfolio, the Chief of the *Reich* Chancellery, the Chief of the Party Chancellery,[9] and for a while

---

the Chief of Staff of the SA. The right to participate in cabinet meetings was extended to the heads of various departments of the government such as the *Reich* Forest Master and the Inspector General for Water and Power.

The Cabinet was more than merely an advisory or administrative body. Its collective authority was augmented by the vast legislative powers granted to it in the so-called Enabling Act, passed in March, 1933. Moreover, the Cabinet acquired the powers surrendered by the semi-autonomous state, province, and municipal governments when control of all local government was centralized.

The Cabinet was therefore assigned not only executive and administrative duties, but also broad legislative functions. Since Hitler preferred to consult his ministers singly, meetings of the whole Cabinet became rare. A circulation system was inaugurated, whereby drafts of proposed legislation were sent from the originating office or offices to other Cabinet ministries for written comment. As changes in the domestic and foreign situation necessitated greater concentration of power for increased coordination, certain committees or subsidiaries were formed out of the *Reich* Cabinet.

The first important committee was the *Reich* Defense Council secretly organized in April, 1933. Under the chairmanship of Hitler himself, it included as permanent members the Ministers of War, Air, Foreign Affairs, Interior, Finance, Economy, and Public Enlightenment and Propaganda. Other members included the two respective Chiefs of the Army and Navy Command Staffs, and certain leading industrialists when needed. The *Reich* Defense Council's chief function was to make plans in time of peace for the eventual wartime defense of the *Reich,* surveying and utilizing all resources of the nation. The bulk of legislation which it prepared was kept on file, in readiness for immediate enactment upon the outbreak of hostilities.

In 1938, the need for still greater concentration of power in the *Reich* Defense Council led to its reorganization. A working committee, the *Reich* Defense Committee, was organized within the Council to prepare and supervise the execution of Council decrees, and to secure greater collaboration between the armed forces, the principal *Reich* offices, and the party. An even more important step toward concentration of power was the creation of a "Three-Man College," composed of a Plenipotentiary for Administration, a Plenipotentiary for Economy, and the Chief of the Supreme Command of the Armed Forces. Under each member of this triumvirate certain ministries were grouped for better coordination of their respective roles in war planning. The Plenipotentiary for Econ-

---

tween the *Führer* and all departments of the government. The Chief of the Party Chancellery was both an executive for party affairs and a private secretary for the *Führer*.

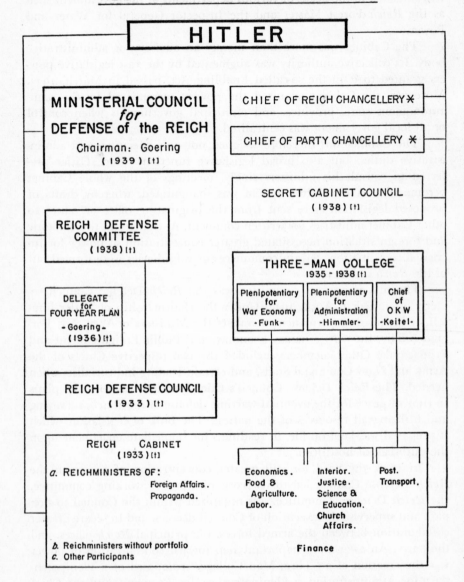

HITLER

MINISTERIAL COUNCIL
for
DEFENSE of the REICH
Chairman: Goering
(1939) [†]

CHIEF OF REICH CHANCELLERY ✳

CHIEF OF PARTY CHANCELLERY ✳

SECRET CABINET COUNCIL
(1938) [†]

REICH DEFENSE COMMITTEE
(1938) [†]

THREE-MAN COLLEGE
1935 - 1938 [†]

| Plenipotentiary for War Economy -Funk- | Plenipotentiary for Administration -Himmler- | Chief of OKW -Keitel- |

DELEGATE
for
FOUR YEAR PLAN
-Goering-
(1936) [†]

REICH DEFENSE COUNCIL
(1933) [†]

REICH CABINET
(1933) [†]

a. REICHMINISTERS OF:

Foreign Affairs.
Propaganda.

Economics.
Food &
Agriculture.
Labor.

Interior.
Justice.
Science &
Education.
Church
Affairs.

Post.
Transport.

Finance

b. Reichministers without portfolio
c. Other Participants

✳ Participated in Cabinet meetings.   [†] Dates above indicate year of activation.

omy headed the group of ministries including Economics, Food and Agriculture, Labor, and to a limited degree the Ministry of Finance and the head of the Reichsbank. Under the Plenipotentiary for the Administration were the ministries of Interior, Justice, Science and Education, Church Affairs, the *Reich* Authority for Spatial Planning, and to a limited degree the ministry of Finance. The Chief of the Supreme Command of the Armed Forces had under his control ministries of Post, Transport, and the General Inspector for German Highways. The Three-Man College was given broad power to issue legislative decrees deviating from existing law and it played a large part in the preparation of total war plans.

It is worth noting that in early 1938 Hitler also created a Secret Cabinet Council to aid him in the conduct of foreign policy. Composed of selected cabinet officials, its powers were advisory only.

With the outbreak of hostilities, the *Führer's* problems were multiplied and intensified especially in the fields of military strategy and foreign policy. Wartime conditions demanded the creation of an additional governmental organ to aid him in the maintenance of uniform leadership. Hence, on August 30, 1939, the eve of the invasion of Poland, out of the *Reich* Defense Council was formed the Ministerial Council for the Defense of the *Reich*, the so-called "War Cabinet." Its composition shows the concentration of power that it effected. Its chairman was Herman Goering, who was not only a high party official and *Reichsminister* for Air, but also head of the Four-Year Plan.[10] The Three-Man College was included. The presence of the *Führer's* Party Deputy (and later the Chief of the Party Chancellery) brought in the entire party machinery. The Chief of the *Reich* Chancellery functioned as a sort of business manager for the Ministerial Council. Other members of the *Reich* Defense Council could be called into the Ministerial Council as special advisers when needed. Most of the regular Cabinet's legislative powers were turned over to the Ministerial Council. Its first task was to issue as decrees the legislation already prepared prior to the war by the *Reich* Defense Council. It continued to legislate by decree throughout the war, except in certain fields, where the Leader deemed it more practical or politic for the *Reichstag* or the ordinary Cabinet to act. The comprehensive jurisdiction of the Ministerial Council for the Defense of the *Reich* gave it a position as the highest and most important permanent governmental organ in wartime Germany. Members of the Ministerial Council made important changes in the national administrative procedures. They or-

---

[10] The Four-Year Plan, announced by Hitler in 1936, was a long-range program designed to render Germany economically self-sufficient. Its main underlying objective was to place the country on a war footing within four years. Goering, as deputy in charge of the plan, was the virtual economic dictator of Germany. The Plenipotentiary for Economy in the Three-Man College named in 1938 was charged with the solution of special short-range economic problems which required action more immediate than that contemplated under the Four-Year Plan.

ganized *Reich* defense districts to correspond to the Nazi party districts (*Gaue*). In these areas they gave each district party leader (*Gauleiter*) the new office of *Reich* Defense Commissioner. These individuals acted as regional executive agents of the Ministerial Council. Their main function was the coordination of civil defense measures, in effecting which they were authorized to give orders to administrative agencies in their respective regions.

In a study of the *Reich* Cabinet and its subsidiaries, one cannot overlook their close relation to the party. The Cabinet and its offshoots furnished the cloak of legality for enacting as law much of the party platform. By January, 1937, all *Reich* ministers had become party members. Rivalries and tensions existed among Hitler's lieutenants, it is true, but from the *Führer* and his deputy on down through the party hierarchy, there was unity of command and unity of purpose between party and Cabinet.

THE MINISTRY OF PROPAGANDA AND PUBLIC ENLIGHTENMENT.—Under the skillful guidance of Paul Joseph Goebbels, the Ministry of Propaganda and Public Enlightenment thoroughly exploited its control of press, radio, theater, moving pictures, universities, schools, and all forms of intellectual activity. All school textbooks were rewritten, and all books available to the general reader were revised in conformity with Nazi ideology.[11] This ministry became one of the most vital governmental institutions. In an extremely blatant but adroit fashion, it instilled Nazi doctrine throughout the length and breadth of Germany and attempted to convert people of other nations to the Nazi ideology. The technique of foreign propaganda of this department has been attacked by many commentators, but its effectiveness within Germany has not been questioned.

THE POLICE.—Because a totalitarian state makes such great demands upon its citizens, it cannot count on their continuing loyalty and enthusiasm. As a result, it must maintain its power largely through coercion. The main instrumentality of that coercion in Nazi Germany was the police.

Heinrich Himmler, who rose to the position of Minister of Interior, was the *Reich* leader of the German police which were divided into two groups, the so-called "Order Police" and the Security Police. While the former group was a uniformed force concerned with ordinary maintenance of law and order, the latter group, organized under the *Reich*

---

[11] All books considered dangerous to Nazi cultural ideas were either destroyed or banned. A manifestation of such preventative measures occurred in early 1933 with the public burning of over twenty thousand books in one huge bonfire in the center of Berlin. Similar scenes spread all over Germany, and several million volumes, foreign and domestic, were destroyed.

Main Security Office, was a secret police whose main mission was to combat the political and ideological enemies of the Nazi regime. The most
important unit of the security police was the notorious Gestapo (*Geheime
Staatspolizei*) or Secret State Police. Organized as a separate police force
in Prussia by Goering in 1933, it was brought under central control by
Himmler in 1934. The Gestapo was a self-contained system of justice
subject only to the orders of Himmler and Hitler. It was empowered to
demand information from, and to give orders to, other agencies of the
government. Actions taken by the Gestapo were beyond normal judicial
or administrative control.

The Gestapo was supported by the *Sicherheitsdienst* (SD) or Security Service unit of the SS (*Schutz-Staffeln*) or Elite Guard, a Nazi
party armed force. The incorporation of the SD into the security police
group and its close coordination with the Gestapo was facilitated by the
fact that Himmler was also the leader of the SS. The SD agents watched
over individuals in every walk of life and were especially assigned the
mission of surveillance of party and state officials. Information of subversive activity was forwarded to the Gestapo for necessary action. Gestapo operators were further aided by the SS operation of concentration
camps and by their policing of occupied territories.

THE REICHSTAG.—We have seen that legislative power passed from
the *Reichstag* to the Cabinet in 1933. From that year on the *Reichstag*
was an assembly of party appointees which rarely met. When meetings
were held, no discussion was expected or permitted. The *Reichstag* lis-
tened to the declarations of the Leader and unanimously ratified by
acclamation any measures which he might care to present to it. Usually
it was called into session to hear a speech by Hitler and was then dismissed. According to National Socialist principles, the *Reichstag* was not
supposed to create any law or make a decision as an expression of the
will of the people. This will was divined or created by the Leader, and
at best the *Reichstag* could merely register popular agreement with it.
Under Hitler's regime the *Reichstag* initially had 813 members, most of
whom held other lucrative offices in the party and the government. In
spite of the inactivity of the body, its members received a monthly stipend
of $240, a not inconsiderable sum in Germany.

ELECTORAL PROCEDURE AND SUFFRAGE.—Notwithstanding its rubber-
stamp character, the *Reichstag* was dissolved by Hitler and re-elected
four times between 1933 and 1939. The Weimar Republic allotment of
one seat for each 60,000 voters was retained in these elections. The voters
were permitted to vote only for candidates on a list drawn up by Nazi
party leaders. As Germany acquired new territories, Hitler provided for
their representation in the *Reichstag* by appointment of additional party
members.

In addition to participation in elections to the *Reichstag,* voters were sometimes asked to express approval of the national policies of the regime through plebiscites. At an election or plebiscite, universal, secret, and direct suffrage was nominally in force but was actually nonexistent. Voters had to be citizens of Germany, of German or related blood. Non-Aryans were excluded from the franchise. Absence from the polls was considered opposition to the regime and was dealt with accordingly. Hence participation approached 100 per cent.

For both elections and plebiscites, occasions were chosen, such as the annexation of Austria in 1938, when national feeling would cause the acquiescence of even those who dissented from the party line. Careful wording of the questions presented was also conducive to the desired results. The National Socialist party had a monopoly of the selection of candidates proposed for election, since the ballot itself failed to afford opportunity to dissent from the regime. When all these methods failed to produce the desired support, the Nazis resorted to breaches of the secrecy of the polls, coercion, and falsification of returns. That the favorable votes should, under these circumstances, have reached 99.57 per cent in the 1938 elections is less surprising than the statistical evidence of any dissent.

CIVIL SERVICE.—As we have already indicated, when the Nazis came to power in 1933 they found it unnecessary to institute an immediate wholesale purge of the civil service. Needless to say, all Jews were excluded from the service at once, but elimination of the remaining "politically unreliable" public servants proceeded gradually. The basic Civil Service Law of 1873 which, with some important changes had been retained by the Weimar regime, was continued in force with some further modifications until the enactment of the National Socialist Civil Service Act of 1937. The new law retained many of the excellent and well-established features of the traditional system. Under the provisions of the law control of the civil service was centralized under the Ministry of the Interior. The service was subdivided into two main categories, namely, the "career service," entered through competitive examination, and the "political service," which required no examination. By far the greater percentage of employees belonged to the career service which, in turn, was subdivided into four grades: lower, intermediate, elevated, and higher.[12] By a rigid system of examinations, candidates could advance through the four grades and, if qualified and politically acceptable, might even leave the career service for a position in the political service. The latter category included such officials as provincial governors and county managers.

---

[12] Candidates for the higher civil service were required to take an oath of personal loyalty to Hitler.

Naturally, the proportion of active National Socialists was larger among the political civil servants, but candidates throughout the civil service were required to obtain at least the stamp of party approval before being appointed to office. Obstructionists to Nazi policy at all levels of government were gradually eliminated through dismissal, retirement, or transfer, and replaced by available Nazis, who might or might not possess adequate qualifications. It should be noted that some civil servants with little or no enthusiasm for party activities were retained because of technical ability. However, it is clear that the Nazis achieved far-reaching control of the entire bureaucracy.

It should also be noted that under the Nazi regime the size of the bureaucracy increased considerably. An enormous expansion in the total number of government officials resulted from the need for detailed supervision of public and private activities, and from the centralization of local government, which made every town and county bureaucrat a *Reich* official, at least indirectly.

Finding its authority in broad Nazi decrees, the civil service made and enforced virtually all administrative rules and regulations. In addition, it operated all governmental services, including the schools, railroads, communications facilities, police and fire departments, and water and power installations. Without the highly disciplined, obedient, and able civil service, the elaborate administrative apparatus of the totalitarian Third *Reich* could scarcely have functioned.

COURTS AND THE LAW.—One of the methods through which the Third *Reich* attained its political ends was the destruction of the rule of law and the weakening of the processes of jurisprudence. The Leader was at once the supreme source of law and the highest judge. Whatever he willed was law, binding on courts and judges alike. Law was no longer an objective concept of justice and impartiality but became subject to the "folkish ordering of life." Such perversion of the principles of justice made impossible any true independence of the judiciary. Hitler had the power to remove judges from office at will and used it repeatedly. In 1933 a decree provided that all judges who had adhered to parties other than the National Socialist party should be removed from office. Although execution of the decree was not complete, all key positions in the judiciary were given to the Nazis, and enthusiastic party members were given all vacancies, including the places of the judges who had retired. The few judges who were not removed and who did not adhere to National Socialism were obliged to keep in line with Nazi policy. After the promulgation of the law of 1935, under which the German courts were reorganized and centralized, all judicial officials were appointed and controlled by the Ministry of Justice.

There was a traditional division of the court system into district courts (*Amtsgerichte*), regional courts (*Landgerichte*), superior regional courts (*Oberlandesgerichte*), and a supreme court of cassation (*Reichsgericht*). These courts handled civil and criminal cases. The administrative courts, intended to give individuals redress against faulty acts of public officials, became less important than formerly, inasmuch as people feared to bring complaints against acts of Nazi officials which might be interpreted as complaints against the regime itself.

The dreaded people's courts (*Volksgerichtshofen*) were summary tribunals permanently established in 1936 under the Ministry of Justice to deal with "treasonable" attacks on the regime. Both professional judges and party members sat on the bench. The people's courts were characterized by severity of punishments, secrecy of proceedings, and failure to allow the accused the rights of an impartial judicial process. Professional groups in Germany were placed under the jurisdiction of special Honor Courts, which tried individuals for violations of professional ethics.

There were relatively few serious complaints about the administration of justice in the civil cases processed during the Nazi period. However, juridical procedure in criminal cases was revolutionized in such a way as to deny even rudimentary justice. Punishments were made severe and revengeful. Persons defined by the Nazi law as "professional criminals" were placed in concentration camps, and many were sterilized. Political offenders and even suspects were placed in permanent "protective custody." Judges were empowered to punish individuals for any act which they deemed to be in conflict with "the healthy sentiment of the people," even though no statute might apply to such an act.

CIVIL RIGHTS.—The foregoing discussion clearly indicates the abolition of civil rights by the Third *Reich*. In fact, a Law for the Protection of the People and the State (February 28, 1933) suspended them; they were never restored by the Hitler government. Individual liberties were not permitted. As we have seen, the press, radio, theater, and all other mediums of public expression operated under the control of the Ministry of Propaganda and Public Enlightenment. Equality before the law applied only to persons defined as "Aryans," and even among them, only to those who were not suspected of opposition to the regime. The interference of the state in religious activities was frequent. The only effective rights which German citizens retained were those of suffrage—in the highly restricted sense already described—and of standing for elective offices.

Local Government

CENTRALIZATION IN LOCAL GOVERNMENT.—For more than a decade prior to 1945 German local government had been in a transitional stage. When the Nazis first came into power they concentrated on gaining control of the central government, while permitting local government to function largely along the lines of the historic divisions and organizations which had formerly existed. However, they did take steps to eliminate political differences within the various states by appointing national governors who, as agents of the central government, promoted political unity and conformity with the *Reich*. In 1934 and subsequently, as we have seen, the Nazis centralized local administration by abolishing the old federal states and the National Council in which they were represented. The Third *Reich* thus became a unitary governing structure; yet the historic areas of the former federal states were still used for some administrative purposes. Efforts toward the reorganization and centralization of local government continued to the end of the Nazi regime.

TOWNS, VILLAGES, AND RURAL COUNTIES.—*Gemeinde* or community (town and village) government was made uniform by the Law on Municipal Order (1935). The executive of each community was a mayor (*Bürgermeister*). In making decisions, the mayor was required to consult the local party boss. Moreover, the mayor was advised by a council which varied in size with the population of the community. Villages, towns, and small cities were grouped together into rural counties (*Landkreise*), which were governed by a national official, called the County Chief. These local governing arrangements provided a basis for the postwar reconstruction of German government.

CITIES AND CITY COUNTIES.—Larger cities formed city counties (*Stadtkreise*), distinct from rural counties. They were governed by a lord mayor (*Oberbürgermeister*), a mayor, city councilors, and city senators. The lord mayor was appointed by the *Reich* Minister of the Interior, and the mayor by the governors of the states (on the recommendation of the Nazi party leader for the county). Hamburg and Bremen, which had never forgotten their history as Hanseatic cities, enjoyed a particular system known as "free city" government. Berlin, as the capital city, had a special and elaborate charter. Following the defeat of Germany, Berlin came in 1945 under the joint control of the four nations occupying Germany, and Bremen became an American occupational enclave in the British zone.

DISTRICTS, PROVINCES, AND STATES.—Above the level of the rural and city counties less uniformity existed in the subdivisions of local government, because historic boundaries were retained along with new government district boundaries. In the former territory of Prussia, for instance, the historic provinces of East Prussia, West Prussia, Pomerania, Brandenburg, Lower Silesia, Upper Silesia, Prussian Saxony, Schleswig-Holstein, Hanover, Hessen-Nassau, Westphalia, and the Prussian Rhineland remained in existence. They were the units through which newer and smaller government administrative districts were administered. Nevertheless, under the Nazis these government administrative districts received all police orders and certain other instructions directly from the *Reich* government. When the former Prussian state government was merged with that of the *Reich*, Adolf Hitler, as *Reich* Governor of Prussia, as we have seen, delegated to Herman Goering, as Prussian minister-president, the exercise of what little authority was left to the once powerful Prussian state. The non-Prussian German state governments were not wholly merged with that of the *Reich*. *Reich* governors, the chief executives of these states, were appointed and removed by the *Reichsführer*.

PARTY DISTRICTS AND REICH DISTRICTS.—The administrative system of the *Reich* resembled a pyramid, with its apex in the *Reich* government and descending through successive strata of provinces or states, government administrative districts, and rural or city counties, to the base in the communities. The structure of the Nazi party was similar. Subdivisions of a few persons, known as blocks and cells, constituted the real base of the Nazi pyramid. The party's local groups coincided with the communities. On the level of the rural and city counties, an ever-increasing similarity between governmental and party boundaries was secured.

In the next stratum differences appeared. Of the regional units of the Nazi party, called districts (*Gaue*), some included only one or a few of the small government administrative districts, while others coincided with the former states or the Prussian provinces. In the Nazi effort to complete the coordination of *Reich* and party organizations many alterations and adjustments were made. Such coordination was apparently intended to place even more government authority in the hands of local party leaders.

When Austria, the Sudetenland, and a part of Poland were annexed to the *Reich* a new local government unit, the *Reich* district (*Reichsgau*), was established in each of the absorbed regions. There the party district and government boundaries and functions corresponded exactly. The party district leaders (*Gauleiter*) were the *Reich* governors of the new subdivisions, and party and state officials were identical in the counties and communities. This arrangement was apparently the type of local governmental organization which the Nazis meant eventually to institute throughout Greater Germany.

The National Socialist Party (NSDAP)

MEMBERSHIP.—The National Socialist German Workers' party, or Nazi party, was an organization which, like the Italian Fascist and the Russian Communist parties, cannot be properly compared with any party in a system of free democratic government. According to Nazi commentators, it was a "people's movement," which, after fifteen years of struggle within the party system of the Weimar Republic, obtained undisputed control of the German nation. Membership in the Nazi party was a definite privilege from both the social and economic standpoints. About two million persons had joined the party prior to January, 1933, when Hitler became chancellor. After 1933, approximately four million more were granted the "privilege" of joining the party. Members of the "old guard" of Nazis in the annexed areas, such as Austria, Sudetenland, and Danzig, were admitted to membership, along with two additional groups: first, members of nationalist and monarchistic organizations, such as the veterans' Steel Helmet organization (Stahlhelm), who could be depended upon to give vigorous support to the Nazi regime; second, persons or professional groups of influence and power, provided they had been nationalists or politically inactive or "unobjectionable" prior to 1933. Thus the Nazi party of Greater Germany comprised a group of some six million persons, superimposed as an elite class upon the German people.

In addition to the active members, the party counted on more than two million "collaborators," most of whom were in Germany. A large proportion of them were candidates for party membership. It is noteworthy that many subordinate officials in party organizations were not members of the party but were merely collaborators.

LEGAL POSITION OF THE PARTY.—The laws which gave Adolf Hitler the power to suspend the Weimar Constitution and to rule by decree placed in the hands of the Nazi party full political power. In July, 1933, a Law Prohibiting the Formation of Political Parties declared that the Nazi party was the only legal political organization in the nation. Penalties were provided for anyone who attempted to form another political party.

THE HIGH COMMAND OF THE PARTY.—Adolf Hitler, as Leader of the party, exercised complete authority over it.[13] Subject to that fact, leadership resided in the hands of the Central Directorate of the party, whose

---

[13] Reports from neutral countries in late 1944 and early 1945 suggested that the exercise of power in the government and the party had been taken from Adolf Hitler by a group of Nazi leaders, especially by Heinrich Himmler. Such reports proved to be unfounded.

members were called *Reich* leaders *(Reichsleiter)*. This relatively small group of sixteen leaders formed a party cabinet which corresponded to the Cabinet of the *Reich* government. Many of the party leaders held important government posts. The Leader of the Party Chancellery was the executive officer for party affairs.

THE PARTY CONGRESS.—Each year in September from 1933 to 1938 a gigantic party rally, called the Party Congress, was held in the city of Nuremberg. It served as a party convention, a state occasion, and particularly as Hitler's sounding board for important speeches.

TERRITORIAL PARTY STRUCTURE.—Territorially the party organization corresponded approximately to the subdivisions of local government, as already indicated. Greater Germany was divided into more than forty party districts *(Gaue)*, which were subdivided in turn into 820 county districts *(Kreise)*, 25,000 community party groups *(Ortsgruppe)*, 100,000 local cells, and 500,000 blocks. Each cell included four or five blocks of forty to sixty members each. The district leaders *(Gauleiter)* were appointed directly by Hitler. Ordinarily they were his personal friends and confidants and often headed the state bureaucracy in their districts. After 1942 they were *Reich* Defense Commissioners, responsible only to the Ministerial Council for Defense of the *Reich* and to Hitler. County leaders were appointed by Hitler at the suggestion of the district chiefs. The latter, in turn, chose the community leaders on the nomination of the county chiefs. Each block was under the control of a block warden who was expected to inform himself fully as to the political, economic, and private life of every resident of his area—whether a party member or not.

FUNCTIONAL PARTY STRUCTURE.—In addition to its territorial organizations, the Nazi party had a number of nation-wide units to perform certain specific functions. These were divided into two general classes: formations and affiliated associations. The principal formations were the Storm Troopers (SA), the Elite Guards (SS), the National Socialist Motor Corps, the Hitler Youth, the National Socialist Students' Association, the National Socialist Women's Organization. The affiliated associations embraced organizations of physicians, lawyers, technicians, teachers, professors, public officials, and, most important of all, the thirty-five million members of the German Labor Front, Nazi successor to the trade-unions. Through these units the National Socialist party exercised a double or triple control over each party member and each German. Some organizations contained only members of the Nazi party, but most were open to nonmembers, thus creating between the people in general and the "elite" party members an intermediate privileged class of persons associated with organizations of the party. Membership in certain organizations, notably those controlling specified professions or trades, was required of all Germans involved, whether members of the Nazi party or not.

THE STORM TROOPERS (SA).—The Storm Troopers (*Sturmabteilungen* or SA) were a semimilitary organization formed in 1921 by the group which later became the core of the National Socialist party. Judged from results, the Storm Troopers' initial function of waging political guerrilla warfare within the Weimar Republic was highly successful. Originally pretending to protect National Socialists from attacks, these armed, brown-shirted SA units marched through the streets, attacked rival groups, and thronged to their own meetings. When the Nazis came to power, the SA organization hoped to merge itself with, and possibly to dominate, the Regular Army. However, in 1934, the bloody elimination of some of its most important members in Hitler's "party purge" led to the downfall of the SA as an organization of military importance.[14]

THE ELITE GUARDS (SS).—The Elite Guards or Shock Troops (*Schutzstaffeln*), unlike the SA, achieved an extraordinary importance. Just as the membership of the Nazi party was supposed to constituted an elite of the German people, so the SS personnel were regarded by National Socialists as the elite of the party, the master members of the master race. The SS was at first a small band of armed men who devoted their lives to the personal safety of the Leader in the days of the struggle for power, but by 1934 it had developed into a formidable military organization, able to execute the will of the Leader in counteracting ambitious moves of the SA as well as of army generals. From 1934 to 1939, the SS grew in importance as shock troops for maintaining public order; its leaders also became more influential in shaping and formulating new ideas and policies. By 1939 it had three hundred thousand members. Since it sought to maintain quality rather than quantity, the SS never became a serious competitor of the large Regular Army (*Reichswehr*) and thus avoided the mistakes which caused the SA's downfall. Instead, it endeavored to secure an influential position in Germany by requiring high standards of efficiency and by obtaining for its leaders key positions in political and economic life. The top man in the SS, Heinrich Himmler, was a prominent Nazi who held the key positions of German Minister

---

[14] The Storm Troopers finally became a group of older and somewhat discouraged party members, used by the party leadership for tasks of minor importance. Largely made up of the human scum which rose to the surface in Germany's hard years after World War I, the SA was an ideal instrument for mob violence against Jews and Communists during Hitler's drive for power. He was shrewd enough to sense that its destructive utility rendered its personnel generally unfit for the constructive tasks of organizing and operating the political and economic machinery which he planned to establish.

of the Interior and Chief of the German Police, including the Gestapo.[15]

Because of the great material and political advantages accruing to a member of the SS, this organization was able to set the most rigorous standards of admission to its ranks. Members were without exception volunteers with high physical qualifications. In the course of World War II, the SS was divided into the General (*Allgemeine*) SS and the Military (*Waffen*) SS. Divisions and corps of the Military SS fought as military formations of the German Army in North Africa, Italy, the Balkans, Russia, and on the western front, achieving on the whole an excellent combat record. Hitler's first desire was to send the military SS units into battle in order to give them a "baptism of fire," and then to withdraw them before casualties mounted. However, in order to maintain their prestige Hitler found it necessary to require more and more front-line service of the SS. Many of the units were decimated in the final disastrous months of the war. As fighters they enjoyed a very high rating, at least until one scans the record of their treatment of prisoners. At that point their rule of neither giving nor taking quarter led to frequent instances of war crimes.

Units of the General SS were used to police the conquered territories. For this duty they worked in close cooperation with the Gestapo. These units of the General SS were organized as highly mobile forces capable of maintaining order wherever necessary. Their attitude and actions, as well as their preferred status, provoked no little hostility on the part of the regular troops, and considerable resentment and fear on the part of the conquered populations.

THE PARTY AND THE ARMY.—A significant step in the nazification of the German Army was taken late in 1944, when a decree ordered all German officers who were members of the Nazi party to "educate their men in the Nazi philosophy" both on duty and off, and "to form a closer link between the armed forces and the party." Previously, members of the German Army had been required to leave the party during their period of armed service. This new decree, however, was part of the Nazi campaign to adapt the German Army to the Nazi pattern of fanatical resistance in order to create a political army that would not give in when militarily defeated. It was also a reaction to the July, 1944, attempt to assassinate Hitler in which certain Army officers had been involved.

HITLER YOUTH.—The youth organizations were devoted to the task of imbuing the young of the nation with the proper Nazi spirit. They were subdivided into various groups, comprising practically all boys and girls between the ages of six and eighteen. In fact, children were really

---

[15] After 1939, the power and size of the SS greatly increased. More and more of the most important positions in private, economic, and political life went to high-ranking SS officers. Consequently, many German leaders in all fields found it advisable to accept appointment as honorary SS leaders. Thus an "elite" of German leaders' was assembled in the upper brackets of the SS.

conscripted into these organizations, known collectively as the Hitler Youth, the membership of which finally reached a total of more than eight million. Since the Hitler Youth movement excluded all rival organizations and rival indoctrination, the influence of the churches among German young people and the authority of the school and the family over them diminished. The success attained in achieving such ends is responsible for one of the gravest postwar problems facing the occupation powers.

PARTY DISCIPLINE.—The National Socialist party possessed within its membership many rival leaders and groups. The most dramatic rivalries were those which arose among the leaders. As we have seen, Hitler once purged the leadership by having oppositionists shot. But other means of maintaining party discipline were practiced also. The Security Service kept party leaders under surveillance. Party leaders were often retired or they simply disappeared. A supreme court of the party was maintained for trying offenses against National Socialism committed by party officials. This court operated swiftly and secretly, and was responsible only to the Leader for its actions.

Armed Forces (Wehrmacht)

HIGH COMMAND.—Adolf Hitler became Supreme Commander of the Armed Forces on the death of Field Marshal von Hindenburg in 1934. Under Hitler the Chief of the Armed Forces High Command was fully responsible for the preparation of national defense in time of peace and for the conduct of operations in war. The three subordinate high commands of the Army, Navy, and Air Force were responsible for the organization, training, and equipment of their respective branches. Considerable interservice friction developed among the subordinate high commands, especially after the tide of battle turned against Germany. The infiltration of Nazi ideology into the armed forces split the officer corps, and there never was a proper balance between the three arms, since Hitler frequently by-passed his Chief of the Armed Forces High Command to issue orders direct to subordinate commands. As the war progressed, his decisions were increasingly influenced by a small, exclusive clique of Army officers headed by a devoted Nazi, General Alfred Jodl.

ARMY (Reichswehr).—Under the Nazi regime the German Army grew from the one hundred thousand men permitted under the Treaty of Versailles to a strength of approximately eight hundred thousand men in 1939. Wartime mobilization brought it to a peak strength of over seven million men and more than three hundred combat divisions in 1943. For the purposes of military administration, training, and replacement, Germany was divided into fifteen corps areas before the war. To this number four more were added from Polish and Czechoslovakian territory during the first three years of World War II.

All physically fit German men were required in peacetime to perform two years of military service; this period usually started when the men were twenty and was preceded by six months of labor service. During the war the usual age of induction was progressively lowered, first to eighteen and then to seventeen in 1942, and finally to sixteen in 1944. In the latter year every able-bodied German boy and man from sixteen to sixty was being called up for the National Militia (*Volkssturm*), which could also recruit women and girls. Some units of this militia did take part in the final operations on both the western and eastern fronts, but were ineffective as fighting units and unable to postpone the final downfall. In the last stages of the war more than one million foreigners were serving under compulsion in the German Army.

In addition to the Army proper, the German ground forces included more than twenty divisions of the Military SS (Elite Guards), as well as a number of field division and parachute units belonging administratively to the Air Force. In its supply and security functions, the Army was aided by many hundreds of thousands of men belonging to various auxiliary organizations such as the German Labor Service, the Nazi Party Motor Transport Corps, and the Todt Organization. The latter was especially active in building highways and fortifications.

The German General Staff Corps was highly developed as a select group of officers who were given a three-year course in military science at the War Academy in Berlin. They occupied all important staff as well as command positions throughout the German Army and were primarily responsible for its traditional efficiency.

NAVY (*Kriegsmarine*).—The program of naval construction which Germany started in 1935 did not produce a large high-seas fleet but did complete a number of powerful and effective vessels. After the outbreak of war, emphasis was laid on construction of submarines, particularly of the smaller types, and of speedboats and other small craft for operations close to the European coasts. A peak strength of between four and five hundred submarines in operation was reached in 1943. The German Navy was also responsible for coast and harbor defense and included many batteries of coast artillery on the shores of the North and Baltic Seas. Under the terms of the surrender all naval vessels and submarines were handed over to the Allies. No organized scuttling of vessels, as in 1918, occurred.

AIR FORCE (*Luftwaffe*).—Under tne leadership of Field Marshal, later Reich Marshal, Hermann Goering, the German Air Force was built up with speed and efficiency between 1935 and 1940. It developed some of the most efficient types of bombers, fighters, and close-support aircraft of modern times. By the outbreak of the war the Air Force had an estimated 3,000 aircraft, and by 1943 it achieved its maximum strength of 5,500 first-line combat aircraft. The Air Force was also responsible for the bulk of German antiaircraft artillery, especially for home defense. Attrition in both quantity and quality of the *Luftwaffe* became apparent in early 1944, and the Allied Air Forces dominated the air over all theaters of ground action after D-Day in Normandy.

DISSOLUTION OF THE GERMAN ARMED FORCES.—On May 1, 1945, Hitler was succeeded as head of the German government and commander of the nation's armed forces by Grand Admiral Carl Doenitz, who proclaimed himself *Führer* with an announcement that Hitler had fallen in battle in Berlin and had designated him (Doenitz) as his successor. On the next day the capitulation of Germany began with the unconditional surrender of the armies in Italy. By May 7 the final surrender of all the German armed forces was effected by authority of the Doenitz government in the Act of Military Surrender. The combat forces involved in the surrender totaled roughly 250 divisions. Many of these, however, were down to a minor fraction of their authorized strength.

Under the terms of surrender the German armed forces were at first disarmed and then progressively disbanded. With the Allied occupation of Germany, they ceased to exist; no provision was made for any eventual re-establishment of even minimum formations.

Foreign Policy

ORIGIN.—The general aims of Hitler's foreign policy were the logical offspring of its forebears, the dynamic policies of Bismarck and Emperor William II. All had their roots in the concept of German racial superiority and divine mission of world leadership—if not dominance. Born in the minds of nineteenth-century intellectual leaders, that concept gained wide acceptance among the leaders of the German people in the twentieth. Obstacles interposed by foreign powers to the attainment of the Germans' grandiose dream only served to stimulate the national ambition and sense of mission. To be sure, the ambitions of the early German dreamers did not begin to encompass anything like the objectives which finally obsessed the Nazis of 1940. Throughout their evolution, from Bismarck's day to Hitler's, these hopes were fed by military victory, fed no less by defeat and military disaster, since failures were analyzed only to the end that errors of strategy and tactics might be corrected before the next opportunity for aggression arrived. That the over-all objectives or the premises on which their ambitions were based could be wrong was a thought that apparently never occurred to more than a handful of Germans.

There were other lessons in the book of German foreign policy which the Nazis might have examined to their great advantage, particularly if they had looked back to the events of pre-Bismarck days. There were lessons of diplomacy emphasizing moderation in both means and ends, compromise, the gains to be had from peaceful economic competition, the wisdom of honoring a treaty or other solemn commitment. Such lessons were unheeded by Hitler and his following.

AIMS AND OBJECTIVES.—Hitler's foreign policy, as announced in *Mein Kampf*, was characterized by certain sharp departures from the policies of Bismarck and Kaiser William II, as well as by the similarities noted above. Where Bismarck would have been satisfied with his "Little Germany," Hitler proposed to add Austria and all the other German-inhabited territories of the Continent so as to bring all the German people of Europe within the boundaries of the *Reich*. In place of the overseas colonization policy of the Kaiser, he advocated German expansion on the European Continent, with the main effort toward the East, in order to gain *Lebensraum* for the eighty million Germans of Europe.[16] Going further in later pronouncements, Hitler proposed the domination by Germany of vassal states in a "New Order." Whether or not he and his Nazi lieutenants consciously pursued a goal of world domination may be an academic question. On the other hand, the dynamic nature of Nazi foreign policy, left unchecked, recognized no limits.

Execution of the first part of Hitler's plan—the incorporation of all Germans into a Greater Germany—involved the acquisition not only of Austria, but also the Saarland, the Sudetenland, Eupen, Malmédy, Memel, Danzig, and the Polish Corridor, at the minimum risk of armed conflict with Germany's traditional enemy, France. Further expansion toward the East was almost certain to result in war with Soviet Russia. Initially, therefore, Hitler pursued the strategy of limited objectives, and made the avoidance of a two-front war a cardinal principle of his policy. He sought friendship with England, Italy, and Japan as a bulwark against France and Soviet Russia.

INTERNATIONAL SITUATION OF THE EARLY 1930's.—Hitler's pronouncements in *Mein Kampf,* if taken seriously, might have aroused the fears of interested nations to the point of immediate and active intervention but for the existence, at the time of the Nazi rise to power, of an interna-

---

[16] When Hitler rose to power in 1933, the population of Germany within her post-Versailles boundaries stood at approximately sixty-five million. By adding to this figure the estimated number of German-speaking peoples outside the *Reich* boundaries (in Austria, the Sudetenland, Alsace-Lorraine, Memel, Eupen, Malmédy, Danzig, etc.), the Nazis arrived at their estimate of "eighty million Germans in Europe."

tional situation which tended to further Hitler's plans. The confusing
world economic crisis had diverted the attention of other nations from foreign affairs to the settlement of their internal questions. Until 1939 Communism, rather than Fascism, was the chief object of fear in the Western
nations; consequently, a large segment of Western opinion, viewing German fascism as a bulwark against Marxism, demanded more liberal treatment for Germany by the victors of World War I. Reaction following that
war had given rise to waves of pacifism. Nations based their security upon
armament-ratio treaties, upon international agreements outlawing war as
an instrument of policy, and, perhaps, upon the power of the League of
Nations to preserve peace. True, in far-off Manchuria the League's failure
to halt Japanese aggression indicated the absence of an international force
capable of preventing military aggression. However, aggression in a quarter outside the areas of major interests of Europe's leading powers was
regarded by many as not meriting decisive action by the League. Furthermore, the democracies were militarily unprepared for war. Against
this international background, Nazi Germany embarked on a step-by-
step fulfillment of Hitler's announced aims.

THE DICTATOR'S WEAPONS AND METHODS.—Granting the favoring international situation in the 1930's, Hitler's string of bloodless victories up
to 1939 was nevertheless a measure of his ability as a strategist in the art
of total war. Like Stalin and Mussolini, he possessed the dictator's advantage of having absolute personal control over the foreign office and
of being able to pursue his policies secretly and with singleness of purpose. Like his fellow dictators, he made full use of economic, political,
and psychological weapons, reserving the use of his military machine as
a last resort. In the course of the Nazi conquest of Germany itself, and in
the first six years of the Nazi regime, he mobilized not only military
strength, but also all of the economic, political, and psychological forces
of the nation until Germany was ready for total war against any country
which stood in her way.

Hitler's methods in the field of international affairs demonstrate
a dictator's combined use of all available weapons. An analysis of his
methods offers many clues to understanding the tactics of the Soviet dictatorship since 1939.

The pattern of bloodless conquest used by Hitler is best illustrated
by two outstanding examples: Austria and Czechoslovakia. Although it
would be an oversimplification from the historical point of view to assume that identical means were used by him in these two countries, in
each case the nation selected as a target was subjected to a well-defined,
systematic, and strikingly similar plan of attack. First lulled by German
overtures of friendship into a false sense of security, the victim was subjected to the undermining influences of a German-directed "fifth column,"
recuited from natives of German descent or of pro-Nazi inclinations.

Such subversive activities were designed to create confusion by terror and by propaganda demanding overthrow of the existing regime and incorporation of the nation, under a new government, into Hitler's "New Order." A minority group noisily demanded representation in the government, through appointment of a few of their members to Cabinet posts. The posts desired invariably were those vital to the nation's security, such as the Ministry of the Interior, the agency in control of the national and local police. Reluctant to acquiesce, the government found itself unable to crush the local Nazis. While denying any link with the local Nazi groups, the Berlin government added harassment at the favorable moment through application of economic and propagandist pressure. "Incidents" created by Germany served to justify ultimate German intervention. By this stage, however, the victim had become so undermined and confused by the terror from within and without that overt German intervention was hardly necessary. The victim merely collapsed into the hands of the local Nazi organization, which immediately set up a Nazi government, voted itself into the "New Order," and extended an invitation to the *Wehrmacht* to occupy all or part of the country. Belated attempts by other powers to intervene in behalf of the victim were brushed aside by Hitler with pious statements about "national self-determination" and with false assurances of Germany's peaceful intentions.

The pattern of conquest differed somewhat in the case of non-German nations, such as the Scandinavian countries, the Low countries, Yugoslavia, and Greece. There the essential tactics included bilateral non-aggression pacts, the familiar undermining from within and without, followed by the sudden launching of undeclared war. Sixty-nine international agreements were violated by Hitler between 1933 and 1941, fair evidence of Nazi unscrupulousness in their diplomacy and the gullibility of the Nazis' victims.

FIVE PHASES OF NAZI AGGRESSION.—The first phase in the development and execution of Nazi plans for expansion (1933-1936) was essentially preparatory. In accordance with Hitler's strategy of limited objectives, Germany first demanded "equality of rights" in the matter of armaments, and then withdrew from the Geneva Disarmament Conference of 1933 when France refused to agree to German insistence on repudiation of the Versailles Treaty restrictions upon Germany's armies and armaments. Hitler subsequently took Germany out of the League of Nations and stopped all further reparations payments, although the Lausanne Conference of 1932 had scaled the total of German reparations down to $700,000,000.

To break France's diplomatic hold on the *cordon sanitaire*[17] to the

---

[17] The term *cordon sanitaire* refers to the ring of Germany's eastern neighbors with whom France had allied herself after World War I. Included in this group were Poland, Czechoslovakia, Yugoslavia, and Rumania.

east of Germany, Hitler negotiated a ten-year nonaggression pact with Poland in 1934, guaranteeing existing Polish-German frontiers. Italy's fears were soothed in the same year when Hitler disavowed attempts of Nazi agitators in Vienna to execute a *Putsch* against the Austrian government. In 1935 the Saarland was returned from international control to Germany by a League of Nations plebiscite, in accordance with provisions of the Versailles Treaty.

Having begun a secret rearmament program in 1933, Hitler had by 1936 instituted universal compulsory military service, had begun openly to rearm, and had remilitarized the Rhineland, all in direct violation of the Treaty of Versailles. By the end of 1936 Hitler had accomplished the essential objective of this preparatory period: the acquisition of military strength and political bargaining power to be used against other nations.

International reaction to Germany's bold moves was even more lethargic than Hitler himself had expected. France hastened to make a defensive alliance with Russia, but this measure was partially offset when Great Britain made concessions, agreeing to repudiate the naval clauses of the Treaty of Versailles in exchange for Hitler's pledge that the strength of the German Navy would not exceed 35 per cent of the British. Friendly overtures to two fellow aggressor nations brought Germany alliances with Italy and Japan.

The second phase of Nazi aggression which ended in March, 1939, was shorter. Having mobilized sufficient internal strength, and having secured her west flank against French interference by reoccupying the Rhineland, Germany was ready to commence expansion eastward. It is worth noting that early during this period Hitler made an important decision. In November, 1937, in a secret conference with the top commanders of the German armed forces, he discussed in detail three possible solutions to Germany's problem of achieving world power status: autarchy, world trade, and military conquest of additional territory. Rejecting the first two as impractical, he announced his choice of the third solution, and his decision to implement it by waging an aggressive war for "living space" on the Continent, not later than the period 1943–1945. Adding that "the question for Germany is where the greatest possible conquest can be made at the lowest cost," he pointed eastward, designating Austria and Czechoslovakia as the first two objectives. Thus, the southern flank would be made secure in preparation for later action on a more ambitious scale.

The Austrian *Anschluss,* accomplished in March, 1938, brought with it not only the achievement of an old national aim but also additional fighting strength, food for a million Germans, and a material improvement in Germany's strategic position vis-à-vis Czechoslovakia. As a glance at the 1938 map of Europe shows, that country was now enclosed by the

German pincers. Italy abandoned Austria; France and England were unable or unwilling to intervene. A few months later, negotiations culminating in the historic Munich Conference of September, 1938, gave Nazi Germany the German-speaking Sudetenland of Czechoslovakia with the consent of France and Great Britain. Since the latter two powers had failed to consult Russian interests during the Munich Conference, the Soviet Union concluded that the Western powers were trying to keep Nazi expansion directed eastward and was, therefore, alienated from her French ally and from Great Britain. Thus the way was paved for Russo-German *rapprochement*. By March, 1939, Germany was ready to complete the absorption of Czechoslovakia.

The third phase of Nazi aggression (March–September, 1939) included the actual seizure of the remainder of Czech territory, the acquisition of Memel from Lithuania, and the preparation for war against Poland. The bloodless solution of the Czechoslovakian problem shortened Germany's frontiers, increased her economic war potential by adding food reserves and armament factories, and improved her strategic position, since Poland was now outflanked from the south. Consequently after a few months of intensive psychological and diplomatic campaign, culminating in the Russo-German nonaggression pact of August 23, 1939, the Nazis were ready to strike at Poland, fully cognizant of the fact that such a step entailed the risk of war with France and England.

The fourth phase (September, 1939–June, 1941) included the actual conquest of Poland, the expansion of the attack into a general European war of aggression by invasions of Scandinavia, the Low Countries, France, and the Balkans, and the preparation for the attack on Soviet Russia.

Hitler had hoped to avoid a two-front war by fighting first "a little war in the West" and then a "big war in the East." After the fall of France in June, 1940, it appeared likely that the sole remaining enemy in the West, Great Britain, could be brought to her knees in short order. Therefore, immediately after the French surrendered, Hitler initiated preliminary plans for the invasion of the USSR. These tentative plans did not crystallize into a final decision to open hostilities, however, until December, 1940, by which time it appeared certain that the uneasy partnership between Nazi Germany and the Soviet Union was scheduled for an early collapse. Based on mutual greed and a cynical determination to divide Europe into Nazi and Soviet spheres of influence, this strange "friendship" gradually deteriorated, principally because of a failure to agree on the disposition of the Balkans. When the air assault on Britain in the autumn of 1940 failed to knock that country out of the war, Hitler became increasingly reluctant to risk invasion of the British Isles while the armies of his Russian "ally" were mobilized on Germany's eastern border. An additional factor which led to his decision to open the "big war in the East" before achieving a final victory in the West was Germany's need for the food supplies of the Ukraine and the petroleum of the Black Sea basin. All preparations completed, including a successful conclusion of the war in the Balkans against Yugoslavia and Greece, the initial offensive against the USSR was launched in June, 1941. Meanwhile Germany's military alliances had been augmented. Italy had come into the war against France in June, 1940; the alliance with Japan had been strengthened; Hungary, Rumania, and Bulgaria had allied themselves with the victorious Nazis; and Germany had overrun a wide area in Europe.

The fifth and final phase of Nazi aggression (June, 1941–December, 1942) saw a continuation of the offensive against Russia, collaboration with Japan to instigate the latter's Pearl Harbor attack on the United States in December, 1941, and expansion of the war to global scale. The story of this phase is too well known to need recounting here.

With the decisive Axis defeats at Stalingrad and El Alamein in late 1942, the tide had turned and Nazi strategy in international politics became primarily defensive. The Western Allies' invasion of the Normandy coast in June, 1944, led to decisive results and sealed the fate of the Nazis.

GERMAN GOVERNMENT OF OCCUPIED EUROPE.—The territories which Germany annexed to the *Reich* after 1938 included Austria, Sudetenland, Memel, Danzig, those provinces of Poland, which, prior to 1918 were German, Eupen, Malmédy, Moresnet, Alsace-Lorraine, Luxemburg, and northern Slovenia. These areas constituted a part of what was characterized as Greater Germany. Bohemia-Moravia in Czechoslovakia was organized into a German protectorate under a German civil administration, and the remainder of the country was organized into an "independent" state of Slovakia. The part of Poland which was not incorporated into the *Reich* was under a special authority called a "government-general," with a German civil administration. In a number of occupied nations, the Germans established Nazi governments called National Commissions (*Reichskommissariat*). Each was headed by a National Commissioner (*Reichskommissar*), responsible for civil administration. This sort of government—with the support of German armies of occupation—was established in Norway, the Baltic nations, and the Netherlands. In Denmark the native government was permitted to function within limitations. The puppet Italian Social Republic in northern Italy, which sprang up after the Italian surrender in 1943, was under the thumb of the German Army, as were the puppet governments of the German-created states of Slovakia, Serbia, and Croatia.

The steps by which these occupied territories were progressively integrated into the German political system were in part the result of

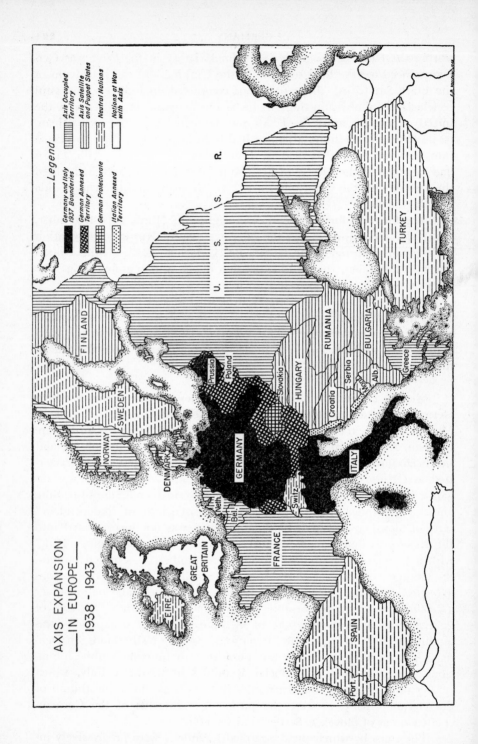

AXIS EXPANSION
— IN EUROPE —
1938 - 1943

Legend

Germany and Italy
1937 Boundaries

German Annexed
Territory

German Protectorate

Italian Annexed
Territory

Axis Occupied
Territory

Axis Satellite
and Puppet States

Neutral Nations

Nations at War
with Axis

wartime necessities as interpreted by Berlin. In greater part they reflected Germany's general objective, the creation of her "New Order" on the European Continent. Thus the purpose to amalgamate the Teutonic racial elements of Europe into a unified whole is clearly shown in the relatively tolerant measures of control pursued—at least at the outset—in Denmark, Luxemburg, and the Low Countries. On the other hand, the policy of ruthless extermination practiced in Poland and in the conquered areas of the USSR was intended to serve the double purpose of checkmating the future dangers anticipated from a high Slavic birth rate, and of creating a territorial vacuum into which would flow the surplus of the Teutonic peoples.

The occupied territories were forced to enrich Germany through the looting of their every resource, not merely capital equipment and priceless art objects, but human beings as well. Under the direction of the Nazi Plenipotentiary for Man Power, Fritz Sauckel, the mass importation and enslavement of conquered peoples served to ease the German labor shortage. In the year ending April 1, 1943, more than 3,600,000 workers were brought to Germany, almost half of whom were assigned to work in the armament industries, where, in addition, 1,600,000 prisoners of war were forced to labor in the *Reich*. In January, 1945, the armament industry was employing almost 5,000,000 foreign workers, no more than 200,000 of whom had come voluntarily. Countless others had been placed as laborers on farms, and hundreds of thousands as domestic servants in German homes. Many others died of the filth and brutality of transports and workers' cells. Extermination of the Jews, plus the incarceration of anti-Nazis in concentration camps, rounded out the ruthless Nazi program.

MILITARY DEFEAT AND SURRENDER.—The first half of the year 1945 saw the complete downfall of Germany and the disintegration of the German government. In January and February, the Russians pushed forward in their great winter offensive. By March, English and American armies crossed the Rhine. Vienna fell in April, and American and Russian armies pouring across Germany met at the Elbe River in the same month. In May, Berlin fell and most of the countries conquered by the Germans saw their invaders surrender to the United Nations. With the announcement of the death of Hitler, the central government of Germany had disappeared. In the absence of a German political administration, the final surrender was made by the armed forces only. General Dwight D. Eisenhower accepted the unconditional surrender of the German military leaders on May 7-8, 1945, first at Rheims and later by formal written instrument at Berlin.

Allied Occupation of Germany: First Three Years

REALITIES INFLUENCING THE PEACE SETTLEMENT.—During and after World War II the Allies devoted much careful study to the problem of building a sound and lasting peace with Germany—a peace that would avoid the mistakes of 1919. The first three years of Allied occupation of Germany brought results which fell far short of the original hopes of the victorious Allies. Several formidable obstacles blocked the road to a wise and just peace. First and foremost among these barriers was the aggressive, expansionist policy adopted by the USSR—a policy which was strengthened and augmented rather than mollified, by early concessions on the part of the Western Allies. A second very real hindrance was the understandable desire of France, twice invaded during a single generation, to prevent the resurgence of a powerful German neighbor. A third impediment, which proved more temporary in nature, was the wave of public opinion generated during the bitter war years in both the United States and Great Britain, in favor of a "hard" peace for Germany. A final obstacle was the listless, uncooperative attitude of the Germans themselves. Stunned by the catastrophe of a second major defeat, they showed little remorse for the criminal record of the Nazis. Indeed, many Germans, after the initial period of shock following the close of hostilities, sought to profit from the failure of the victorious powers to agree on the terms of a peace settlement.

POLITICAL STATUS OF GERMANY AFTER SURRENDER.—The political treatment accorded to conquered Germany by the Allied Nations differed markedly from that meted out to other occupied countries, notably Italy, Austria, and Japan. The reasons for such special treatment are many, beginning with the contrasting basic conditions in those countries at the time of their surrender. Italy, for example, not only surrendered early but gave appreciable aid to the Allied cause during the last two years of the war. Austria, first victim of Nazi aggression, was classified as a "liberated" rather than an "enemy" nation. Enough democratic leaders remained in that country to provide the basis for a new government sympathetic to the Allied aims. And in Japan, the conditions of conquest led to the pre-eminent role of the United States and the utilization of the emperorship as an instrument in the reconstruction of a peaceful Japan.

Different conditions prevailed in Germany. When Nazism collapsed, all government organization vanished. Moreover, Hitler's combination of purge and proselytization had effectively eliminated all except a handful of men capable of providing German leadership in the organization of a democratic form of government. Besides, wartime agreements between

Britain, the USSR, and the United States called for the division of Germany into separate zones of administration during the first stages of reconstruction. Germany, under the Allied Nations' plan, was to remain a political entity, but her sovereignty was to be exercised completely for an indefinite period by the occupying powers in behalf of the United Nations.

ZONES OF ALLIED OCCUPATION.—Military occupation of Germany was established by the United States, the United Kingdom, the Soviet Union, and the provisional government of the French Republic soon after the surrender. At the same time Germany was compelled to revert to its national boundaries of 1937. By joint agreement each nation was assigned the administration of a separate zone of territory, and each zone was placed under the control of the commanding officer of the armed forces occupying it. Occupation and administration of the various zones was undertaken as follows: the Soviet Union—eastern; Britain—northwestern; the United States—southwestern; and France—western. Certain territorial exceptions were made to this general division of areas.

In compensation for certain Polish lands annexed by the USSR, German territory between the Polish boundary and the Oder River was assigned to Poland for administration, permanent fixing of this Polish-German boundary being postponed until the drawing up of the final peace treaty for Germany.[18] The northern part of East Prussia, including the territory around Koenigsberg, was incorporated into the Soviet Union. Bremen and its vicinity, including the port of Bremerhaven, were established as a separate enclave under American control to provide seaport facilities to the American authorities. The city of Berlin became an area of joint occupation by the four powers. An inter-Allied governing authority, consisting of four commandants, appointed by their respective commanders in chief, was established there for the joint administration of the city.

ALLIED CONTROL COUNCIL.—In the summer months following the defeat of Germany, a conference of President Truman, Marshal Stalin, and Prime Minister Attlee produced at Potsdam a statement which crystallized and rounded out the various prior agreements concerning the Allied policy to be pursued with regard to Germany. This statement, called the Potsdam Agreement, covering every important phase of occupation and German activity, became a key document in the administration of post-surrender Germany. The execution of the Potsdam Agree-

---

[18] The principle that final settlement of this border question would be left to the peace conference was announced at the Yalta Conference and reaffirmed by the Potsdam Agreement. Nevertheless, the USSR stand on this matter remained in 1948 as expressed by Marshal Stalin on October 28, 1946, when he stated "Yes it does," in answer to a United Press question, "Does Russia consider the western frontiers of Poland permanent?"

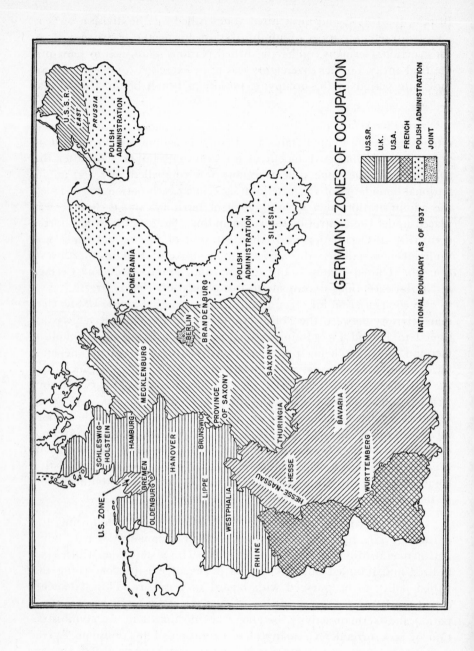

GERMANY: ZONES OF OCCUPATION

U.S.S.R.
U.K.
U.S.A.
FRENCH
POLISH ADMINISTRATION
JOINT

NATIONAL BOUNDARY AS OF 1937

U.S.S.R.
EAST
PRUSSIA
POLISH
ADMINISTRATION

POMERANIA

POLISH
ADMINISTRATION
SILESIA

MECKLENBURG

BERLIN
BRANDENBURG

SAXONY

PROVINCE
OF SAXONY

SCHLESWIG-
HOLSTEIN

HAMBURG

HANOVER

BRUNSWICK

THURINGIA

BAVARIA

U.S. ZONE

BREMEN
OLDENBURG

LIPPE

WESTPHALIA

HESSE-NASSAU

HESSE

WURTTEMBERG

RHINE

226

ment was entrusted to the Allied Control Council which, set up by previous agreement, was reaffirmed in its powers to exercise authority in all matters affecting Germany as a whole. In this respect, the declaration read: "For the time being, no central German government shall be established. . . . Certain essential German administrative departments, headed by state secretaries, shall be established, particularly in the fields of finance, transport, communications, foreign trade and industry. Such departments will act under the direction of the Allied Control Council." On August 30, 1945, the Control Council formally announced its assumption of supreme authority in Germany.

The four Allied commanders in chief constituted the Control Council. Each commander was assisted by a deputy and a political adviser. The Council could take no action until a unanimous decision on any question under discussion had been reached. This requirement soon proved a serious stumbling block to the execution of the earlier plans made by the Allied Nations for the reorganization of Germany. The chairmanship of the Control Council rotated among its four members on a monthly basis. Each member assumed primary secretarial responsibility in the subordinate organs of the council during the period of his chairmanship.

Subordinate to the Allied Control Council was a Permanent Coordinating Committee, composed of one representative of each of the four commanders in chief, and a Control Staff of subordinate officials. The Control Staff was subdivided into directorates of specialists which were organized to handle problems of the following types: military, naval, air, transport, political, economic, finance, reparation, restitution, internal affairs, communications, legal, prisoners of war, displaced persons, and man power. When the Council was first set up, it was intended that the Control Staff and its directorates would carry out the Council's decisions by transmitting them to appropriate central German administrative departments, and by supervising and directing the day-to-day activities of the latter. As we shall see, this part of the Council's plan of operation failed to materialize, partly because of the French obstructionist policy—later modified—but chiefly because the USSR consistently refused to give more than lip service to the basic Potsdam decision that Germany was to be treated as an economic unit. Nevertheless, the Allied Control Council continued to function as a quadripartite governing body until the arbitrary closing of its meeting by the Soviet chairman on March 20, 1948, brought about its virtual dissolution.

THE POTSDAM AGREEMENT.—Essentially this document called for the demilitarization, denazification, deindustrialization, and re-education of Germany. The "Big Three" at Potsdam had denied any intent to enslave or destroy Germany, and had envisaged the eventual reconstruction of a peaceful and democratic Germany which would rejoin the family of nations. Before Germany could take positive steps toward her reconstruction, however, she was to be impressed with her responsibility for the world disaster she had precipitated, and to undergo a purging of the elements which might enable her again to menace world peace.

The accord among the "Big Three," as evidenced in the Potsdam Agreement, waned considerably in subsequent meetings of the Allied Control Council, where the individual desires and interpretations of the participating powers served to limit directives of the Council to those of a broad, general nature. Individual zone commanders implemented these directives in accordance with instructions from their respective governments, and wide differences resulted in the application of Council policies.

DEMILITARIZATION.—Having provided for the dissolution of the *Wehrmacht,* the Council appointed a commission to check on the destruction of mine fields and fortifications by each zonal commander. Orders were issued for the confiscation of all weapons and war matériel, whether abandoned by the *Wehrmacht* or in private German possession. In order to suppress the militaristic spirit, each zone commander was directed to ensure that disbanded *Wehrmacht* personnel were no longer in uniform after December 1, 1945. The liquidation of all militaristic memorials and museums was likewise ordered. Any construction of a military nature was prohibited. Military training was outlawed, and limits were placed on the conduct of German sport activities. All of these projects were largely carried to completion with little difficulty. Quite another matter was the disposition of German prisoners of war. Initially used by the Allies for such tasks as clearing mine fields and collecting German war matériel, the prisoners were a heavy drain on the limited food resources of the European victors. The food problem, coupled with the urgent demand for labor in Germany, hastened their discharge. Nevertheless, as the year 1947 ended, the British still held 279,505, the French 421,058, and the Russians 754,664 German prisoners.[19] Prior to this time the United States had released all of its 8,000,000 prisoners, having first conducted classes in democracy to prepare selected groups of them for participation in the political life of future Germany.

DENAZIFICATION.—The Allied Control Council, having enacted a law abolishing the Nazi party and all other Nazi institutions, seized the

---

[19] According to 1947 press reports, the USSR had organized a German Free Army made up of more than 100,000 German veterans of Stalingrad under the leadership of Field Marshal Friedrich von Paulus and Major General Walter von Seydlitz. These troops were allegedly indoctrinated in Communism and equipped with small arms. Later press reports in the fall of 1948 indicated that a "German" army, headed by these leaders, was being created in the eastern zone of Germany—apparently a counterpart to the Korean Army created for the "liberation" of Korea.

property and records of the NSDAP and its affiliated organizations. Leaders above certain levels were subject to automatic arrest. The liquidation of Nazi memorials and institutions was accompanied by the destruction of all Nazi literature. German criminal and civil law was purged of the enactments and procedures injected by the Nazi regime. The prohibition of the employment in one zone of a person dismissed in another zone was part of an attempt to ensure that the removal of Nazis from public office and positions of responsibility was uniform throughout Germany. Also, the retention in office of close relatives of Nazis was discouraged.

While agreed on the treatment of leading Nazis, the four powers showed marked differences with respect to the lesser fry. Much hinged on the interpretation of the general terms "Nazi" and "positions of responsibility." The French, for example, appeared inclined to distrust all Germans, whether Nazis or not. Great Britain was thorough in its denazification in political and educational fields, but was accused of laxness in handling top-level industrialists. The Russians appeared stringent with regard to public servants and public officials, but were content to denazify only the highest levels of German personnel in agriculture, commerce, and industry.[20] In the United States zone, on the other hand, a more thorough denazification job in all fields of activity took place, often at the expense of the early re-establishment of economic enterprise, schools, and courts. Beginning in 1946, however, the policies affecting denazification in the American zone became increasingly lenient, as indicated by acts like the Youth Amnesty Decree of July of that year, which automatically cleared all Germans born on or after January 1, 1919, except those guilty of serious offenses. An outstanding step in the American zone was the transfer of the remaining denazification program to the established German government agencies under the "Law for Liberation from National Socialism and Militarism" effective March 5, 1946. To give the Germans a further hand in self-government and to permit them to rid themselves of the Nazis, German denazification tribunals (*Spruchkammern*) were set up on a general basis of one per *Landkreis* or *Stadtkreis*. A defendant accused of Nazism was given the benefits of a democratic trial. If found guilty, he was classified into one of five categories of descending culpability, and was sentenced accordingly. Supervision of the process was maintained by American Military Government (AMG) to ensure justice for all concerned, and especially to prevent the degeneration of the procedure into a whitewashing sham. The United States procedure of transferring denazification to German authorities was eventually followed by all zonal commanders. It was expected that denazification would come to an end in all four zones by 1949.

---

[20] At least 60,000 former Nazis were still employed in the civil service of the Soviet zone in late 1947. Most of them had joined the Soviet-backed Socialist Unity party (SED), apparently to prove their reformation.

WAR CRIMES TRIALS.—The key individuals and groups who held the greatest share of responsibility for the international crimes committed in furtherance of the Nazi movement were brought to trial in special war crimes courts.

The International War Crimes Tribunal and the war crimes courts of the individual Allied nations were established in keeping with the Moscow Declaration, October, 1943, and the London Agreement of August, 1945. The former pronouncement stipulated that German military and Nazi personnel responsible for, or acquiescent to, the commission of atrocities and other crimes would be returned, when captured, for trial in the country where the offense had been committed. The International Military Tribunal (IMT), set up at Nuremberg in accordance with Allied Control Council Law Number 10, was charged with the trial of those individuals whose offenses were not confined to any particular geographic location. The prosecution of the cases before the IMT not only resulted in the punishment of the war criminals, but produced volumes of documentary evidence which revealed to the world the shocking details of Nazi crimes against humanity, war crimes, and crimes against peace. The war crimes trials were brought to completion in late 1948.

DEINDUSTRIALIZATION.—The deindustrialization program envisaged at Potsdam encountered far more serious obstacles to its execution than did the other two negative aspects of Allied policy, demilitarization and denazification, chiefly because of its close relationship with the reparations question and with the problem of the eventual creation of a self-supporting German economy. The dismantling of major war plants, begun soon after the Allied Control Council assumed power, was largely carried to completion. However, Allied disagreements and frequent revisions in Allied policy regarding the permissible level of German industry led to repeated delays, and in some cases complete stoppages in the dismantling process as applied to some plants. The plants affected were those which, although not strictly classified as "war plants," had been initially tagged as surplus to Germany's future peacetime economy and, therefore, available for reparations. We shall discuss this matter further in a subsequent section on economic policy.

The huge German industrial combines were stripped of their power through legal action and by seizure of their patents. Cartels were dissolved; trusts were decentralized into independent units; and, as in the case of the I. G. Farben and the Krupp works, former heads were indicted before the war crimes tribunals for their part in planning and waging aggressive warfare for Hitler. Decentralization was especially difficult in the Ruhr and Saar coal regions, where trusts were found within trusts, and where the breakdown of the former highly integrated directorial centers led directly to a reduction in the coal output essential to the general recovery of Europe. Nevertheless, the British attempted to decentralize the industry of their zone, at the same time gradually shifting industrial control to their embryonic German government under a socialization program. The French proceeded slowly, especially in the Saar, toward decentralization.

The most flagrant violation of announced Allied policy was the erection in the Soviet zone of a huge German trust enterprise, embracing at least a dozen industries. Since the controlling stock of the new combine was acquired by the Soviet Union, this German trust was merely a front organization for Russian economic control and exploitation of German enterprise. This action, combined with Soviet refusal to cooperate in implementing the Potsdam decision to treat Germany as an economic unit, caused serious dissension among the Allies.

RE-EDUCATION AND DEMOCRATIZATION.—A people conditioned over several generations to political, social, and economic concepts which are antithetical to the fundamentals of democracy will not be converted overnight to the "Western way of life." The Allies briefly entertained the hope that two major military disasters within a generation would induce the Germans to find merit in the philosophies of their conquerors. But it was soon evident that to the Germans defeat spelled only another lesson in the necessity of better strategy and tactics at the next opportunity for conquest. It was equally evident that nothing short of thoroughgoing reeducation, including a revolution in the Germans' weighing of human values, could prepare them for understanding, much less accepting, the Western democratic concept as a method of living. Moreover, the hope of such a revolution must limit its target to the younger elements of the population, the youth and the children not yet hardened by Nazism and its ideological trappings. The task is no short-range project; education, supplemented by the practical example of the benefits accruing both to the individual and to the state from democratic practices over a prolonged period, may ultimately reverse the trend which led logically to the acceptance of *Mein Kampf* as a Bible.

In the field of education the Allies were at first thwarted by the dearth of non-Nazi teachers. However, schools at all levels were put into operation, ranging from rural elementary institutions to such universities as Bonn, Mainz, Heidelberg, and Marburg. Obstacles to education included the underclad and underfed condition of the students, unheated classrooms, and shortages of suitable texts and ordinary school supplies. The French were outstanding in their contribution toward removing such obstacles; questioning the possibility of changing the older Germans, they bent their efforts toward educating the youth. The United States zone also paid particular attention to the younger German, and the

American troops instituted a program to promote German youth activities. The Russians endeavored to achieve complete ideological control over the schools in their zone by placing members of the Soviet-sponsored political party (Socialist Unity party) in all the important Ministry of Education positions.

The main effort to re-educate the Germans outside the school systems was made through information mediums such as the press, radio, and theater. Here, too, the USSR used German agencies as tools for the spreading of Communist propaganda. Moreover, in violation of a Control Council order forbidding defamation or criticism of the occupying powers, the German newspapers of the Russian zone echoed the propaganda campaign of Moscow against the other three occupation powers. The United States authorities steered the Germans toward publication of nonpartisan papers. Through its Information Control division, the American Military Government licensed and registered the various German agencies, which, once registered, were not subjected to prepublication censorship.

One of the missions assigned the Allied Control Council was "to prepare for the eventual reconstruction of German political life on a democratic basis and for eventual peaceful cooperation in international life." The licensing of political parties was permitted, and as a result four major parties have appeared in Germany. The Liberal Democratic party (LDP) is supported chiefly by the industrialists, business leaders, professional groups, and the propertied class because of its rightist platform of free but nonmonopolistic enterprise, antisocialization, and antipathy toward church-sponsored schools. Another right-wing party is the Christian Democratic Union (CDU), a predominantly Catholic party which has enlisted a strong following among the Catholic population in the labor, agricultural, professional, and industrial classes, and also from a section of the conservative Protestant element. The Catholic influence is reflected in the CDU's strong sentiment against communism and in its demand for church-sponsored schools. Although favoring a future goal of free economy, the CDU is tolerant of moderate socialization and planned economy which it accepts as necessary under present conditions.

The most active party has been the leftist Social Democratic party (SPD), which adheres to Marxism, although violently opposed to the Soviet brand of that ideology. The SPD's platform includes socialization, land reform, social insurance, and religious toleration, coupled with a demand for the abstention of the church from interference in politics. SPD has attracted labor, civil service employees, white-collar workers, and tradesmen. An outstanding feature of the party was its championing of the cause of the unwanted German refugees and expellees from other countries and occupation zones.

On the extreme left of the political scene is the Communist party (KPD) whose platform is stereotyped on the Russian model. Its major appeal, backed by ample funds and effort, has been made to small wage earners, industrial workers, and the extreme radical fringe of the intellectuals. Besides favoring complete socialization, radical land reform, and a proletarian dictatorship, it supports a unified Germany under a strong central, as opposed to a federal, government. Unable to obtain a majority unaided, the KPD engineered a merger with the SPD in the Soviet zone to form a new party, the Socialist Unity party (SED). Strongly upheld by Soviet authorities in the Russian zone, SED captured 47 per cent of the vote in the October, 1946, state assembly elections. Elsewhere in Germany, including the sectors of Berlin occupied by the Western Allies, SED failed to gain recognition as a political party because of overwhelming SPD opposition to a merger with the Communist party.

The CDU and the SPD have been the leading parties in the American, French, and British zones. In the latter zone the Center (*Zentrum*) party, similar but in addition to the CDU party, has been organized. The LDP and KPD are minor parties in those areas. In the Soviet zone, the combined vote of the CDU and LDP matched that of the SED in the October, 1946, elections already noted. Some strength in the LDP in the Soviet zone exists and is attributed by certain observers to the swelling of its ranks by former Social Democrats. Political parties did not come into existence in the Soviet zone in response to popular demand; their establishment was decreed from above by the Soviet Military Government. Soviet manipulation of German politics is well illustrated by the fact that in 1945 when the CDU appeared too strong in relation to the leftist parties, the Soviet authorities as an afterthought decreed the establishment of the LDP—to split the bourgeois vote.

Another step toward democratization of German life was made in the field of labor relations. During the initial period of economic chaos following the surrender the Allied Control Council promulgated laws regulating wages, hours, female and child labor, and insurance. As the situation permitted, the right of collective bargaining was resumed. With Weimar Republic labor legislation as a basis, new laws were promulgated by the Allied Control Council allowing workers' councils and labor courts. The former are committees freely and voluntarily elected by the workers of a shop to represent them in their grievances against their employers. The labor courts, a Weimar experiment in judicial bodies, were reinstated to adjudicate civil disputes arising from collective bargaining and individual labor agreements. These courts, independent of the Ministry of Justice and under the Ministry of Labor for administration only, are located at local level for original and at regional level for appellate jurisdiction. The bench consists of lay members, representing employer, employee, and neutrals, not necessarily possessing professional legal qualifications.

In fulfillment of the Potsdam Agreement, trade-unions were per-

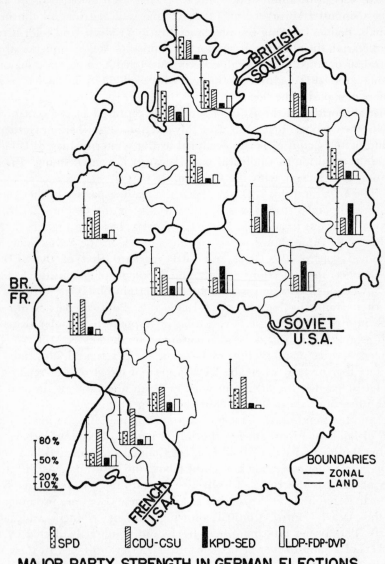

MAJOR PARTY STRENGTH IN GERMAN ELECTIONS
Based on elections of the Fall of 1946

mitted. The traditional desire for a federation of trade-unions again became apparent and was realized at least up to the zonal level in all four zones and also up to the bizonal level in the United States and British zones. Cognizant of deficiencies in the Weimar era, the trade-unions have sought to remain nonpolitical. In this effort they were reasonably successful except in Berlin and in the Soviet zone where the federated union, the *Freies Deutsche Gewerkschaft Bund* (FDGB) came under the control of the SED whose members acquired a majority of seats in the executive committees of both the member unions and the central body. The results of this action became apparent when the FDGB echoed the Soviet and SED condemnation of the European Recovery Program.

GOVERNMENTAL STRUCTURE IN THE FOUR ZONES.—Although democratic processes had not yet taken firm root in German society after three years of Allied occupation and perhaps would not do so for many years to come, the forms, at least, of democratic government were established in all four of the zones of occupation. The respective military governments, initially faced with the complete disintegration of all German political institutions, had to rebuild the governmental structure from the bottom level upward. Within two years after the close of hostilities, considerable progress in this reconstruction process had been made. Democratically elected self-governing bodies in rural communities (*Gemeinde*), counties (*Kreise*), and municipalities (*Stadtkreise*) were in existence in all four zones. State (*Land*) governments were all composed of officials chosen by popularly elected legislatures. Zonal agencies of varying character existed to take care of those functions properly belonging to a central government. Constitutions had been adopted in all states except those in the British zone. The ministries in all states were responsible to the popularly elected state legislatures. Courts were made independent of the executive and legislative branches, although there were variations in the provisions for judicial review of legislation.

In spite of outward similarities in governmental structure, considerable differences existed in the actual operation of the German governments of the four zones. The amount of jurisdiction reserved to military government varied considerably in the different zones, but it was undoubtedly the smallest in the United States zone, where practically all administrative and governmental functions were turned over to the Germans. In the British zone less latitude was given the Germans, as British Military Government still reserved to itself legislative powers over all of the most important matters. In the French zone, legislative powers of the German states were even more strictly limited. In the Soviet zone, at least to all outward appearances, the only restriction on German legislation was that it must not conflict with the laws and decrees of the Soviet Military Government.

Probing still deeper into the actual administration of the German governments of the four zones, we find some startling differences, particularly between the Eastern and Western zones. Any plan for the eventual unification of Germany must take into consideration the political and administrative problems arising out of these differences. In the Western zones there has been a gradual reconstruction of democratic government in accordance with the Western pattern. Variations among the systems of three Western zones were minor, and could reasonably be expected to disappear with the establishment of a central government for the three zones. In the Eastern zone, on the other hand, the Soviet Union gradually replaced the disintegrated Nazi regime with another type of one-party state—conforming to the pattern existing in the USSR.

The structure of Soviet Military Government differs little from that of the Western powers, the most important departures being that Soviet troops live off the land (as have the French, to some extent), that fraternization with the German populace is strictly forbidden, and that at least one agent of the Soviet special secret police is assigned to each county (*Kreis*) detachment, with considerable "advisory" power over the local detachment commander. One additional important difference is that each functional division of the Soviet Military Government is more or less controlled by a corresponding office in Moscow, which frequently by-passes the Soviet commanding general.

At the top or zonal level of the German political structure in their zone the Russians early set up a rather elaborate central administration manned by German civilians. The Interior Division of this administration was given complete control over all local and state police. However, aside from the Interior Division, the Central Administration functioned mainly in an advisory capacity, and was allowed to exercise very little real authority over the *Länder* during the first two years of occupation. There was no zonal constitution, and each of the *Land* (State) governments in the Soviet zone was modeled after the pattern of the autonomous Soviet Republics of the USSR. Not until mid-1947 did the Russians begin to transfer any real governmental powers to the German Central Administration in their zone. By that time the United States and Great Britain had merged their zones of occupation and had begun gradually to build a German bizonal government, the structure of which we shall discuss in some detail in a subsequent section of this chapter. Following the lead of the two Western powers, the Russians reorganized their German Central Administration, creating at its top level a German Economic Commission, which they gradually expanded into a zonal governing body with limited powers over the *Länder*. In contrast with the British and American policy of having the Germans themselves elect their own top officials, the Soviet Military Government appointed the members of the German Economic Commission in the Russian zone. Needless to say, all of the

important top posts went to members of the Communist-dominated SED
party. A prime responsibility assigned the newly organized commission
was the supervision of reparations deliveries from the entire Soviet zone.
In the competition for positions in the Central Administration, or indeed
elsewhere in the bureaucracy set up by the Russians, Germans who were
avowed Communists or SED members were given preference. For positions in the highly centralized police, SED party membership was mandatory.

The constitutions of the five states in the Soviet zone are practically
identical. In each case there is no provision for separation of power; all
authority resides in the state legislature (*Landtag*). The principle of judicial review of legislation is specifically rejected. The Bill of Rights, in
each constitution, is hedged in with sufficient restrictions and conditions
to nullify its meaning. In brief, each constitution can be made to serve as
a framework for a one-party state, through that party's control of the
Landtag.

Decentralization of functions in the county (*Kreis*) and community
(*Gemeinde*) governments is complete, presenting the outward form and
appearance of a true democracy, but in actuality weakening the official
state government apparatus in order to strengthen the SED party apparatus. It is intended that the SED eventually hold the real governing
powers, as is the case with the Communist party in the USSR homeland.

The SED early secured a strangle hold on the bureaucracy in the
Soviet zone, especially in the departments of Interior and Education.
Thus the Nazis' undermining of the old traditional German concept of
a nonpolitical civil service was perpetuated in that zone.

The administration of justice in the Soviet zone is characterized by
a gradual packing of the courts with judges who are members of the
SED, and whose consciences are properly insulated by Soviet ideology.
Hence the concept of an independent judiciary as understood by the
Western democracies and even by Germans under the Weimar Republic
is gradually vanishing. The dividing line between the jurisdiction of
German and Soviet Military Government courts is not based on a set of
legal principles, as is the case, for instance, in the United States zone.
Thus SED favorites of the Soviet Military Government, if charged with
criminal or civil offenses, may escape punishment by having their cases
removed to military government jurisdiction when it appears that a German court might convict them. Moreover, German prosecutors who have
shown the temerity to press charges against Soviet favorites have disappeared to places unknown.

There is a close affinity between the German SED and the Soviet
Military Government. The existence of opposition parties is maintained
to present a democratic front, but the Soviet Military Government possesses, and can use against such parties, a network of restrictions which

renders them ineffectual. The belief in one-party supremacy, planted by the Nazis, retains a firm hold on the Germans in the Soviet zone. Thus, even if the Soviet Army should evacuate its zone, the danger of totalitarianism would persist.

ECONOMIC POLICY: THE STUMBLING BLOCK.—The Allied Control Council was blocked from the start in its efforts to implement the economic policies of the Potsdam Agreement. On one hand, devastated countries were clamoring for reparations from Germany. On the other, attempts to re-establish German political life were hindered by the preoccupation of the Germans with eking out a living in an economically paralyzed country. This situation commanded the attention of the Council during the fall of 1945 and the ensuing winter. An agreement on the level of German postwar economy was reached in March, 1946. German industries were listed in four classes, ranging from those completely prohibited through those restricted at certain levels down to those left completely unrestricted. The plan rested on the basic assumption of a German population of 66,500,000, on the acceptability of German products in international markets, and, most important, on the treatment of Germany as an economic unit. This latter assumption was vital inasmuch as the zonal division of Germany had been made without regard for the economic ability of each zone to become self-sustaining or to furnish equal amounts of reparations.

The March, 1946, level of industry agreement was at the time considered an outstanding achievement of the Allied Control Council. Successful operation of this important plan hinged on the establishing of central German economic agencies. Their establishment was originally blocked by France. Not having been invited to the Potsdam Conference and violently opposing the reconstruction of a German neighbor with a strong central government, France used her veto power in the Allied Control Council to block the passage of any act furthering German economic centralization. France feared that such a course of action would in the future prejudice her claims for the separation from Germany of the Saar and the Ruhr regions. She also feared that the refugees from German land granted to Poland would ultimately cause a dangerous population pressure on the French border.

The stalemate was used to advantage by the Soviet Union to adopt in its zone a new policy of taking reparations from current production, in violation of the Potsdam Agreement. Meanwhile the USSR continued to insist on its reparations from the Western zones and consistently maintained its zonal barriers, thus reducing to a trickle trade between eastern and western Germany. Coincidentally the Soviet Union took unilateral action in the political field which, as we have noted, forced the numerous German Social Democrats of the Soviet zone to unite with the Com-

munist minority, forming, under Communist domination, the Socialist
Unity party (SED). Moreover, a Soviet propaganda barrage directed toward the other zones clamored for a similar merger in the rest of Germany.
The dissension in the Council thus caused by the USSR overshadowed
that originally resulting from the French objection to German economic
unity.

The Allied Control Council finding itself unable to effect a compromise among its members, referred the topics of dissension to the
Council of Foreign Ministers, at the time in Paris attempting to draw up
peace treaties for the lesser defeated nations. The discussion of Germany
was finally begun at the Paris conference in April, 1946, and continued
into the summer months. While the first Paris Conference was in session,
the American zone commander, acting upon orders from the United
States government, suspended removal of plants from the United States
zone for reparations to other nations, announcing that deliveries of reparations would be held up so long as the Potsdam Agreement was not
being complied with in other respects. The first conference ended in a
stalemate, and embittered France when her demand for a decision concerning the western boundary of Germany was left completely unsatisfied.
At the second Paris Conference in July, 1946, the French were further
rebuffed and the United States and Britain further disappointed when
Vyacheslav Molotov, the Soviet foreign minister, accused the other three
powers of attempting to destroy German economy and called upon them
to join in establishing immediately a strong central political as well as
economic German administration. This about-face from previous policy
enabled the USSR to pose as the lone Allied champion of the German
people.

On the day after Molotov's speech, United States Secretary of State
James F. Byrnes countered with two proposals: a motion that each of
the Big Four immediately appoint a special deputy to work on the preparation of the German peace treaty; and an invitation to any or all of the
other three powers to effect an economic merger of their zones with the
American zone. The first proposal was vetoed by Russia, and the second
was accepted by Great Britain only.

Further to parry the Molotov thrust, Secretary Byrnes made a clear
statement of American policy in a speech delivered at a meeting of American and German officials of the United States zone at Stuttgart in September, 1946. While defending the principles of the Potsdam Agreement
and recognizing French claims to the Saar, Mr. Byrnes stated the American intention of sponsoring an early return to normal conditions in
Germany through the institution of democratic self-government and economic unification. He also announced that the United States would stay
in Europe until its aims were achieved. This definite announcement of
American policy strengthened the confidence of the Germans in the

American zone and partially counteracted the propagandist wooing of the German people by the USSR.

Allied lack of harmony was again emphasized when France, at the end of 1946, without having consulted the agencies of the Allied Control Council or the Council of Foreign Ministers, divorced the Saar from the rest of the French zone, placing a customs boundary around it.

Thus, a year and a half after its pronouncement, the original accord reached at Potsdam had broken down. The Allied Control Council had become ineffective because of the veto of first one and then another of the four members. Each occupying power interpreted the generalities of Potsdam in accordance with its own national aims and in agreement with its own political philosophy. Germany had disintegrated into four distinct states between which the boundaries, with the exception of that between the British and American zones, were as impassable as those between any other separate nations.

THE EAST-WEST SPLIT.—While France and the USSR continued to pursue their unilateral policies in Germany, during the last quarter of 1946 the representatives of the United States and Great Britain reached an agreement for an economic merger of their zones in occupied Germany, effective January 1, 1947. Before examining the results of this effort to achieve at least a partial unification of Germany, let us review the attempts of the four Allied powers prior to the Spring of 1948 to settle their differences and to lay the foundation for a lasting peace with Germany.

Engaged with the task of writing peace treaties with the satellite states, the Council of Foreign Ministers did not renew discussions of the German problem until their meeting in Moscow in March, 1947. At this meeting all four delegations agreed that any decision on the future political organization of Germany would be conditional upon the prior establishment of German economic unity. The United States and Great Britain, which had been paying some $700,000,000 a year to feed and supply their zones, took the initiative in urging the immediate economic unification of Germany, in accordance with the terms of the Potsdam Agreement. As her price for agreement to this proposal, the USSR demanded $10,000,000,000 in reparations from German plants and production during the next twenty years, plus a voice in the control of the industrial Ruhr. France's demands were more modest: incorporation of the Saar into her economy and the right to reserve her position with respect to the future regime of the Ruhr and the Rhineland. While willing to compromise with France, the United States and Britain refused the Soviet counterproposal on the ground that the Potsdam Agreement had not provided for reparations from current German production, and that the Soviet plan would cripple German economy indefinitely, thereby making

SECRETARY OF STATE JAMES F. BYRNES

SEPTEMBER 6, 1946

Outlining United States Policies in Germany

The American people want peace. They have long since ceased to talk of a hard or a soft peace for Germany. This never has been the real issue. What we want is a lasting peace. We will oppose soft measures which invite the breaking of the peace. . . .

The United States, therefore, is prepared to carry out fully the principles outlined in the Potsdam Agreement on demilitarization and reparations. . . .

In fixing the levels of industry no allowance was made for reparations from current production. Reparations from current production would be wholly incompatible with the levels of industry now established under the Potsdam Agreement. . . .

We favor the economic unification of Germany. If complete unification cannot be secured, we shall do everything in our power to secure the maximum possible unification. . . .

Germany must be given a chance to export goods in order to import enough to make her economy self-sustaining. Germany is a part of Europe, and recovery in Europe, and particularly in the states adjoining Germany, will be slow indeed if Germany with her great resources of iron and coal is turned into a poorhouse. . . .

Security forces will probably have to remain in Germany for a long period. I want no misunderstanding. We will not shirk our duty. We are not withdrawing. We are staying here. As long as there is an occupation army in Germany, American armed forces will be part of that occupation army. . . .

The Soviets and the Poles suffered greatly at the hands of Hitler's invading armies. As a result of the agreement at Yalta, Poland ceded to the Soviet Union territory east of the Curzon Line. Because of this, Poland asked for revision of her northern and western frontiers. The United States will support a revision of these frontiers in Poland's favor. However, the extent of the area to be ceded to Poland must be determined when the final settlement is agreed upon.

The United States does not feel that it can deny to France, which has been invaded three times by Germany in 70 years, its claim to the Saar territory, whose economy has long been closely linked with France. Of course, if the Saar territory is integrated with France she should readjust her reparations claims against Germany. . . .

The United States will favor such control over the whole of Germany, including the Ruhr and the Rhineland, as may be necessary for security purposes. It will help to enforce those controls. But it will not favor any controls that would subject the Ruhr and the Rhineland to political domination or manipulation of outside powers. . . .

The American people want to return the government of Germany to the German people. The American people want to help the German people to win their way back to an honorable place among the free and peace-loving nations of the world.

a general European economic recovery impossible. The Soviet stand in declaring the existing Polish-German boundary a permanent settlement made impossible any agreement on the future frontiers of Germany. An American proposal, made a year earlier by Secretary Byrnes, calling for a four-power, twenty-five-year pact to assure the continued disarmament and demilitarization of Germany was resubmitted for consideration at the Moscow meeting, but discussion of such a treaty was dropped when the Soviet delegate suggested a multitude of amendments which would have totally altered its scope and purpose. Thus the Moscow Conference adjourned without making any substantial progress toward a settlement of the German question. It was agreed that the Council of Foreign Ministers should reconvene in London late in 1947.

During the interim between the Moscow and London conferences, considerable progress was made by the United States and Great Britain in organizing the economy of their newly merged zones. The economic condition of Germany became a matter of even more concern to all the Western Allies after the announcement in June, 1947, of Secretary of State George C. Marshall of an American plan for the economic rehabilitation of Europe (the "Marshall Plan"—later officially designated European Recovery Program—ERP), whereby all of the states of Europe were offered a chance to achieve economic recovery as an integrated economic bloc. The initial impetus toward this goal would be supplied in the form of financial credits and materials from the United States. Although invited to participate, the Soviet Union refused, and further widened the East-West split by violently opposing the plan, and by preventing her satellite states in eastern Europe from participation.[21] Vital to the success of the European Recovery Program is Germany, since the coal deposits of the Ruhr and the Saar are the key to the industrial rehabilitation of western Europe. Germany's position near the center of the sixteen-nation bloc, her valuable transportation facilities, and her large pool of skilled and semiskilled labor are additional essential factors. France, a nation with much to gain from the plan, now had every reason to come to an agreement with the United States and Britain on German matters.

In preparation for the participation of Germany in the economic recovery of western Europe, the United States government on July 15, 1947, sent a new Joint Chiefs of Staff Directive to the American military commander in Berlin, General Lucius D. Clay. Superseding the JCS directive of April, 1945, it differed considerably from the earlier document, upon which the policies of American Military Government had been based. The new directive stated, in part: "An orderly and prosperous Europe requires the economic contributions of a stable and productive

---

[21] Poland and Czechoslovakia initially accepted the invitation to participate in the Marshall Plan, but subsequently withdrew, following the summons of the government heads of those two states to Moscow.

Germany as well as the necessary restraints to insure that Germany is not allowed to revive its destructive militarism." It was anticipated that future German contributions to European recovery would be made through normal international trade rather than through reparations payments alone. Restrictions on the level of German industry were modified to make possible an increase in German exports. In the political field, military government supervision was to be diminished in order to encourage German self-government. The new directive formalized American occupation policy, which had gradually evolved since 1945 under the influence of changing American public opinion.

An additional step was taken toward making their part of occupied Germany self-supporting when in August, 1947, the United States and the British Military Governments announced a joint program to raise the industrial output of bizonal Germany to the level of 1936. In implementing this program the number of plants to be dismantled in the two zones for reparations was cut from 1600 to 682. Since all dismantling operations had been previously halted, this action opened the way for the resumption of normal reparations allocations to the USSR—provided the latter would join in carrying out the decisions of Potsdam as to German economic unity.

The Council of Foreign Ministers met in London at the end of 1947, in a second attempt to form the basis of a peace settlement with Germany. The background for this conference was hardly conducive to a compromise between East and West. The USSR, having resorted to direct action, through the Moscow-controlled Communist parties in France and Italy, to wreck the European Recovery Program, had every reason to delay decisions on Germany's future, in the hope that results achieved by her Communist agents might conceivably strengthen her hand. The United States and Britain, on the other hand, could ill afford to sacrifice the principles for which they had consistently stood; furthermore, the possibility that France might join them in the economic merger of zones, increased their bargaining power. No serious consideration of a peace treaty could be undertaken without an agreement at the start on the boundaries of the future German state. The three Western Allies expressed agreement that the Saar area should be separated from Germany and integrated into the French economy. The USSR declined to commit itself on this point, and refused to accept a Western proposal for the establishment of boundary commissions to make an expert investigation of the whole frontier question, including the disputed Polish-German boundary. Making his usual propaganda appeal to German listeners, the Soviet delegate, Foreign Minister Molotov, demanded agreement on the immediate establishment of a German central government, at the same time refusing all proposals for elimination of the zonal barriers to German economic unity. Adhering, furthermore, to the Soviet claim for reparations from current German production, and to the total figure of $10,000,000,000 in reparations, Mr. Molotov denounced, as efforts to partition Germany, British-American attempts to make their zones self-supporting by an economic merger and by raising their level of industry. In effect, he asked that the two Western powers continue to pour money into Germany to enable the USSR to take it out in the form of reparations. Agreement to the Soviet proposals was obviously impossible. The London Conference, ending in stalemate, revealed a further widening of the gap between East and West in Germany. France began to consider seriously the merger of her zone with those of Britain and the United States.

It appeared clear by the end of 1947 that the USSR would accept no peace settlement except one whose terms would permit Soviet domination of Germany. Russian control of Germany might well lead to a Soviet-dominated western Europe. Profoundly disturbed by such a prospect, the Western powers sought countermeasures. Great Britain took the initiative in January, 1948, when the British Foreign Secretary Ernest Bevin proposed a West European Union, including western Germany—in effect an alliance to limit Soviet expansion. Against the background of the USSR's coup in Czechoslovakia and Soviet diplomatic attempts to extend the iron curtain to include Finland, the representatives of five western European nations, Great Britain, France, and the Benelux countries (Belgium, the Netherlands, and Luxembourg) met in Brussels in late February, 1948, to consider Mr. Bevin's proposal. By the middle of the following month they signed a fifty-year economic, political, and military alliance. Meanwhile the United States Congress completed the enactment of legislation to implement the European Recovery Program. Moreover, the United States announced a reversal of its earlier decision to turn over its military government in Germany to the State Department by mid-1948, and began to take steps toward a general strengthening of its land, air, and sea power.

Concurrently with the Brussels negotiations, the Western powers began a conference in London in February, 1948, on the subject of Germany. Although the details of these proceedings were not immediately made public, there was discussion of measures providing for the complete economic unity of western Germany, and the incorporation of the three western zones into the European Economic Cooperation Administration as full members.

The USSR's reaction to these Western moves was swift. Under the guidance of the Soviet Military Government an All-German People's Congress met in Berlin in March to discuss the unity of Germany. The USSR announced plans for a plebiscite on the unification of Germany, to be held in their zone and in Berlin between May 23 and June 14. The Soviet delegation walked out of the Allied Control Council meeting on

March 20, 1948. The Soviet Military Government began to apply pressure to force the Western Allies out of the city of Berlin.

Thus, as the third year of Allied occupation ended, the formal partition of Germany into an eastern and a western state, and the official end of quadripartite rule appeared imminent. The crisis growing out of the failure of the victorious powers to agree centered in a struggle for Germany's capital city, Berlin.

TOWARD GERMAN UNITY: BIZONAL GERMANY.—In contrast to the Soviet and French zones of occupation, which not only sustained themselves—after a fashion—but also contributed to the respective Soviet and French economies, the annual deficit of the British and American zones, as we have noted, by 1948 cost the latter governments $700,000,000. A major goal aimed at in the creation of bizonal Germany was the development of German trade and industry in the merged area to a point where the deficit of the two zones might be wiped out by 1949. Under the original merger agreement, the United States was to share equally with the British the expenses of the two zones. Later, in return for economic control over the British zone, the United States assumed a 75 per cent share of the expense burden. Both the United States and Great Britain took pains to announce, and to reiterate from time to time, their desire that the other two zones join in the merger. The ultimate goal was the economic union of all Germany, not a division of the occupied territory between East and West.

The structure of bizonal Germany provided that over-all rule continue to be exercised by the military governments of the occupying powers, acting jointly through a bipartite copy of the quadripartite Allied Control Council, known as the Bipartite Board. Subordinate bipartite groups were set up to coordinate and steer the top-level decisions toward appropriate German agencies. Heavy German participation was permitted in advisory and implementative roles. The top German agency, the Bizonal Economic Council of fifty-two members, elected by *Länder* (state) parliaments was designed not only to suggest legislation to the Bipartite Board, but also, through its executive committee, to obtain execution, by the *Länder,* of Board decisions. The Economic Council's powers over the *Länder* governments were not always well defined.

Following the failure of the London Conference of Foreign Ministers, the German Bizonal Economic Council, upon invitation of the military governments, drafted a plan to extend its powers into the political as well as the economic fields. Based to a large extent on this German draft, a bizonal charter reorganizing the economic government of the combined zones was issued and put into operation in February, 1948, by joint proclamation of the British and American military governors.

The new charter, an important step toward the eventual formation of a central government for all Germany, both clarified and added to the scope of the Bizonal Economic Council's powers. The Economic Council was set up, with primary legislative powers, as a lower house, with its membership increased to 104; a new chamber called the Council of States, with powers roughly corresponding to those of the United States Senate, was added as the upper house of the legislature, two of its seats being allocated to each of the component states. The minister-president of a state was allowed to fill one of these seats. A six-member executive committee, including a chairman without portfolio, was set up, to be elected by, and responsible to, the Economic Council. A supreme court was provided for, to be called "The High Court for the Combined Economic Area," with original jurisdiction over suits between the bizonal administration and any state, or between individual states, and appellate jurisdiction over decisions of state courts on points of law involving bizonal ordinances or regulations. Provisions were made for the establishment of a bizonal bank. Aside from its authorizing the creation of bizonal inspectorates to ensure law enforcement within the *Länder,* the new charter was patterned on the general lines of the old German federal system, with the states providing the enforcement machinery for federal laws.

German reaction to the reorganization of the bizonal economic administration was varied. Many German officials and political leaders, some of whom had actively participated behind the scenes in the drafting of the new charter, disclaimed any responsibility for its creation, for fear of being branded by the uninformed public as collaborators with the occupation forces in an attempt to set up a separate government for western Germany. The Christian Democratic party emphasized, however, that the new charter would not prejudice a future central government in all Germany. The Social Democrats, on the other hand, received the new regime coldly, and the Communists denounced it.

Allied Occupation: Current Phase

THE SIX-POWER ACCORD ON WESTERN GERMANY.—While the USSR was tightening its control on Berlin in an effort to force the evacuation of that city by the Western powers, the latter, along with the three Benelux countries came to an agreement with respect to the three western zones of Germany. Signed in early June, 1948, after four months of negotiations, the Six-Power Accord guaranteed the maintenance of the occupation of Germany by United States, British, and French forces until the peace of Europe is secured. It offered the German people "the opportunity to achieve, on the basis of a free and democratic form of government, the eventual re-establishment of German unity," and it recommended the early convening of a German assembly to write a constitution. The Accord specified that the future German constitution should provide for a federal government which would possess adequate central authority, but which at the same time would protect the rights of the *Länder* and guarantee the freedoms of the individual. The western German government was to be given a provisional character in order to leave the door open for eventual participation of the Soviet zone in a united Germany. An Occupation Statute, to be agreed upon by the military governments of the three occupying powers and the German *Länder* was to define the powers of the new government. The economic provisions of the Accord, while not requiring the political separation of the Ruhr from Germany, placed this important industrial area under the control of an international authority composed of representatives of the six Western powers and of Germany.

CURRENCY REFORM.—All four of the occupying powers early recognized the necessity for currency reform in Germany, although no agreement had been reached on this important subject prior to the Spring of 1948, except, of course, for the very general provisions of the Potsdam Agreement. The USSR had hindered the efforts of the Western powers to bring about this much-needed action, by impossible demands, such as requiring that part of the new currency be printed in the Soviet zone, rather than in Berlin under Allied Control Council supervision.

After the Soviet walkout from the Control Council in March, 1948, four-power agreement on currency reform was out of the question. Consequently, to prevent economic chaos in Germany the three Western powers agreed to put their own currency reform plans into effect in the western zones. On June 20, 1948, they began replacing the old *Reichsmarks* and *Rentenmarks* with the new *Deutschemark.*

The Soviet military governor protested the inauguration of currency reform in western Germany and indicated that the new currency would not be welcome in Berlin, which was considered by the Russians to be integrated economically with the Russian zone. In a four-power discussion of this issue on June 22, 1948, the Russians rejected outright all Western proposals and asserted that they alone would write the currency law for all of Berlin. In addition, the Soviet officials refused to recognize any longer the authority of the Four-Power *Kommandatura* to deal with currency matters in the city of Berlin. Their position violated existing Four-Power agreements for the government of the city.

On June 23 the Soviet officials announced their own currency reform for the Russian zone of Berlin. The Western Allies, while rejecting the Soviet claim to supremacy in Berlin, compromised with the Russians by making the latter's new *"Ostmark"* equally acceptable with the *Deutschemark* in the western sectors of the city for the payment of rent, food, taxes, and electric bills. Shopkeepers dealing in other commodities could, at their own discretion, accept the *Ostmark,* but had to honor the *Deutschemark.* The Soviet reply to this move by the Western Allies was to stop all land communications to and from Berlin.

THE BERLIN CRISIS.—Disagreement over currency reform was by no means the sole cause of the Russian blockade of Berlin. The currency matter merely furnished the USSR a plausible excuse for turning their already existent restrictions on western traffic to and from Berlin into an all-out land blockade. Beginning April 1, 1948, it was clear that the Soviet Union was trying to get the Western Allies to move their troops and other personnel out of Berlin. Success in the endeavor would give the Russians a free hand to impose SED control on the city. The resulting gain in their prestige at Western expense would be so great as to undermine the work of reconstruction already accomplished in western Germany. Tens of thousands of Berliners who had been cooperating with the Western Allies would find themselves without protection from sudden transfer to forced labor units within the Soviet Union itself. The political struggle for Berlin was symbolic of the larger struggle for political control of all Germany.

As a result of the new restrictions imposed on June 24, the Western forces in Berlin found themselves practically besieged by the Russians. Only by means of air transport could they move personnel and supplies between western Germany and Berlin. Moreover, only by air could the Western Allies move in sufficient food and fuel to support the civilian population of the western sectors of the city, for which they were responsible. At best such arrangements were costly and annoying; overshadowing the expense and annoyance was the knowledge that an incident such as the collision between a carelessly piloted Russian plane and one of the Western Allies' cargo transports could lead to war.

Performance of the Western Allies' air lift exceeded all predictions. During the first three months of the blockade (July to September, 1948) United States transport planes alone flew more than 200,000 tons of food, fuel, and medicine into Berlin, traveling more than 15,000,000 miles through good weather and bad, along the narrow corridors from the western zones.[22]

Soon after the inauguration of the blockade the Western Allies took the initiative in seeking a peaceful solution to the Berlin crisis by opening negotiations on the ambassador level with Moscow. On September 27, 1948, all attempts at reaching a satisfactory settlement having failed, the

---

[22] Quadripartite rule in Berlin was disrupted when the Soviet element withdrew from the *Kommandatura* on July 1, 1948. German Communists occupied the city hall, located in the Soviet sector on September 3, and attempted to usurp the functions of the regularly elected Berlin city government. Thereupon the City Assembly and the Executive Council withdrew and resumed their sessions in the British sector.

Western Allies, in compliance with their obligations under the Charter of the United Nations, referred the matter to the UN Security Council.

THE FUTURE.—It will take many years to build a new German state, to establish it securely, to give it a genuinely democratic character, and to bring it within the scope of a world security system based upon treaty arrangements or the United Nations.

The boundaries of the new Germany must be fixed and assured by international guarantee. Left unsettled, this problem alone would be a grave threat to the stability of any central German government established by the Allies. Likewise, it is imperative that action be taken by the Allied powers to effect an internal territorial reorganization of Germany into states of sufficient strength and homogeneity to maintain a balanced distribution of powers in a federal system such as that advocated by the Western Allies. The historical obstacles to such a project are too great to be overcome by German initiative alone. It goes without saying that no progress can be made in this direction until existing zonal barriers are removed.

The serious demographic problems to be solved have a special significance to the Western Allies, since Germany will continue to be the second most populous nation in Europe for the next quarter century. After that, Germany's population may well begin a steady decline. The immediate problem, however, is principally one of overpopulation, accentuated by the influx of Germans expelled from the territories now under Polish administration, as well as from countries with German minorities, particularly Czechoslovakia. This problem is aggravated by Germany's devastated condition and war-wrecked economy. The four occupied zones of Germany, inhabited by about sixty million people in 1939, now hold sixty-six million people, a 10 per cent increase, in spite of war losses. As a result of this increase and of the loss of territory in the east, agricultural acreage in Germany per one hundred people has decreased about one third. Left in her present boundaries, Germany can hardly become more than 60 per cent self-sufficient for food. The increased level of industry in the western zones will eventually help reduce the effects of overpopulation to some extent. In time emigration will help to solve the problem. France has already absorbed substantial numbers of Germans and appears willing to accept more. Outlets in the Western Hemisphere will tend to reopen as wartime sentiments die down. German war brides have led the westward movement—a far cry from Nazi spearheads. Improvements in transportation and urban housing will likewise slowly remedy the labor shortage caused by the present abnormal dispersion of population. Less tangible and infinitely more difficult to cope with is the impact of present population conditions on Germany's family life and on her entire social structure.

Family, church, and state—all of Germany's institutions have been seriously undermined by twelve years of Nazi totalitarian rule, six of which were war years, and by the chaotic internal conditions of the post-war years. The resulting political, social, economic, and spiritual vacuum must be filled to assure a lasting peace in Europe. The internal and external threat of another and even more deadly totalitarianism must be contained or repelled. Germany's best hope lies in the European Recovery Program, in the continued efforts of the Western Allies toward the long-range goals of re-education and democratization, in the energies of the German people, and in their full acceptance of the Western way of life. Only through such acceptance can Germany hope to eliminate fully the barriers to trade and other international intercourse raised during twelve years of Nazi direction of German affairs.

THE GOVERNMENT OF THE

USSR

◇◇

Historical Background of the Soviet Union

THE TRADITION OF AUTOCRATIC GOVERNMENT.—The mainsprings of a nation's policy and actions in any given crisis must often be sought in the traditions and developments which make up its background. That observation holds true for Soviet Russia to an unusual degree. If one were called upon to name a single dominant factor in Russian history for the last ten centuries, it would be the theory and practice of the unlimited power of the ruler. The Russian Tsars were autocrats, absolute in a sense not known in any other European country. Not until 1906 was there a national representative assembly to limit the authority of the ruler.

The vast Russian plain, designed by nature to become the basis of a single, unified state, inherited a tradition of despotism. This early Russian state looked to the Byzantine Empire as its model. At Constantinople the Byzantine emperors had maintained themselves as absolute despots of the Oriental type, even though they traced the political inheritance of their state to the ancient Roman Republic. The Greek-Latin schism (1054) accentuated the effects of Russia's conversion to the Greek Church. Byzantine concepts of law and government, the inheritance of the Greek alphabet, the sense of religious exclusiveness, all tended to separate Russia from the West. The Tartars conquered Russia in the thirteenth century, and their particular brand of Asiatic autocracy also served to affect later Russian rulers. Oriental characteristics of exaggerated formalism were strengthened, along with cruelty and arbitrariness in the operation of the political system. Domination of Russia by these Tartars isolated the country from the West.

When the princes of Muscovy broke the Mongol yoke, their conflicts with the steppe nomads drew them eastward at the time when Sweden, Poland, and the Ottoman Empire were resisting any expansion by Russia toward Europe. In consequence the gulf between Russia and European civilization was broadened. Neither the Renaissance nor the Reformation influenced the cultural development of the country. In this connection it must be kept in mind that, though Peter the Great (1689-1725) strove with undeniable energy to lift Russia out of barbarism and to bring her up to western Europe's level of culture and civilization, the means he used to promote his purposes were in many cases cruel and oppressive. Peter was quick to understand and appreciate many Western advances and administrative methods. He was no less energetic in seeking to adapt them to the needs of Russia. Yet he made no attempt to introduce the theory and practice of individual liberty and private initiative which were adding much to the scientific and technological progress of such countries as England and Holland in his day. On the contrary, Peter's reign left Russian autocracy stronger than ever.

THE BACKWARDNESS OF RUSSIA.—It was not until the nineteenth century that articulate groups in Russia became fully alive to the attitudes, achievements, and realities of Western civilization. Not until then did Russia give the world some of its great names in literature, in music, and in other fields of achievement, and only at this late date did the intellectual fathers of the modern Russian Revolution begin to speak and work against autocracy. Russia's persistent backwardness in a day when the political and economic evolution of western Europe was marked by rapid and sweeping changes profoundly affected her subsequent history. Psychologically it may be considered to have created an inferiority complex among Russians, aptly expressed by their oft-heard evaluation of themselves: "We are a dark people." No dynamic people could be expected to accept such a role indefinitely. Autocratic repression, as Soviet leaders have pointed out, merely added to the explosive forces operating below the surface, ensuring a period of violent revolution before Russia could begin the task of overcoming the evolutionary lag which distinguished her institutions from those of her contemporaries.

THE EARLY REVOLUTIONARIES.—The gigantic political and social upheaval which Russia experienced in 1917 was neither sudden nor accidental. In the nineteenth century many individuals and small groups devoted to the idea of overthrowing the autocracy came to the front, the most important of these being followers of Karl Marx's social philosophy. These revolutionaries were prepared to struggle against what seemed at the time hopeless odds, to face prison, exile, and death. But in spite of their efforts, they were seldom able to establish contact with, and to gain support from, the illiterate masses whose liberation was their avowed objective. Their importance lies not in the meager results which they attained by assassinations of government officials and even of a Tsar or by the stimulation of minor uprisings, but in their influence upon the development of a professional revolutionary movement. Although they were small in number, probably never exceeding a few tens of thousands before 1917, this determined, fanatical minority proved to be strong, in a country where most of the people were illiterate and where the existing institutional system rested on authority, tradition, and inertia rather than on any popular enthusiasm.

The first conscious revolutionary act in modern Russian history was not Marxian in origin. It was the abortive conspiracy of a group of liberal army officers who, in December, 1825, attempted to seize the government in the name of Prince Constantine. Service in the campaigns against Napoleon had taken these zealots into western Europe, where their contact with its superior civilization left a profound impression. Their attempt to seize the government for Prince Constantine was just another palace revolution, even though its objective was a liberal constitution for the Russian people. The new Tsar, Nicholas I, gave orders to open artillery fire on the rebellious troops and resistance collapsed immediately.

Two developments toward the end of the century presaged the revolution to come. The first was a great increase in the industrial working population resulting from the flow of foreign funds into the country at an accelerated rate after the conclusion of the Franco-Russian understanding of 1891. The urban proportion of the population increased from 7½ per cent in 1851 to 13 per cent in 1897. The number of industrial workers doubled between 1885 and 1900 and tripled between 1885 and 1914. For this group Marx's materialistic philosophy had a strong appeal. The second factor was a tendency under the last Tsars to compel non-Russian people to accept the Russian language, Russian culture, and Russian government. This attempt to Russianize non-Russian parts of the Empire converted many Jews, Poles, Finns, and Caucasians into ardent revolutionaries.

In 1898 the disciples of Marx organized in the city of Minsk the Russian Social Democratic party and issued a resolution to the effect that the Russian proletariat should cast off the yoke of autocracy in order to defeat capitalism. The delegates were promptly arrested, but the party remained active. A major split developed among the Social Democrats a few years later. One group, called Bolsheviki (Majority), under the leadership of Nikolai Lenin, stood for centralized party discipline and bold revolutionary action. The other group, the Mensheviki (Minority), took a less strict view of party discipline and maintained that Russia was unready for socialism. They preferred to achieve their ends by parliamentary development rather than through direct forceful action. When revolution did come, it was the well-organized, determined Bolsheviks who seized control of these new radical forces and directed them to their own ends.

In 1905, following Russia's defeat in the Russo-Japanese War, revolution swept through Russia, largely under the leadership of the Mensheviks. The most spectacular incident of this revolt was a workers' demonstration in St. Petersburg in which the mob was fired upon by troops guarding the imperial palace. The immediate result was a series of general strikes, demonstrations, riots, and mutinies which compelled the Tsar to proclaim a Constitution and to establish a parliamentary body, known as the Duma. Although Lenin called this outbreak a dress rehearsal for revolution, its immediate visible effects were a few concessions made by the regime, more liberal in appearance than in fact.

MARCH REVOLUTION OF 1917.—When Russia entered World War I, the prospects of success for the revolutionaries seemed small. Many radical leaders were arrested and others were caught up in a wave of patriotism. However, both Lenin and Leon Trotsky denounced the war as a final product of the capitalist system and worked for the overthrow of the government. Both of these revolutionaries were absent from Russia during the war. Trotsky agitated against the war in Paris (1915-1916) before he was expelled. He was active in New York during 1917. Lenin, in Switzerland, participated in the efforts of remnants of the Second International to unite the socialists in their attitude toward the war. After the March Revolution, German authorities, ready to use his defeatist propaganda to serve their cause, granted him passage through Germany en route to St. Petersburg.

What finally undermined the Russian government, however, was not the revolutionary activity of the radicals but the unsuccessful course of the war. As the early mood of enthusiasm evaporated with lengthening casualty lists, as Russian industry bogged down, as suspicion of pro-German influence at the royal court was magnified, and as a dissolute monk, Rasputin, created court scandal, the autocracy was undermined. The government was not overthrown—it collapsed. In March of 1917 a provisional government was established, dominated by a majority of Liberals and Moderates. With this change, however, the Socialists gained increasing influence. They organized councils of workers, called "soviets," [1] all over the country—in the factories, in the rural districts, and in the Army. As the provisional government found itself confronted by problems which it could not solve, the more radical elements capitalized upon its embarrassments. In May, Alexander Kerensky, a Socialist, succeeded Prince Lvov as head of the government.

NOVEMBER REVOLUTION OF 1917.—Under these circumstances Nikolai Lenin organized a program for the overthrow of the provisional government and the establishment of a republic of soviets. The Bolsheviks were swimming with the popular tide. They urged workers to take over the factories, peasants to seize the land, and soldiers to stop fighting. They did not temporize. On November 7, 1917, the Petrograd Soviet and the sailors from Kronstadt led an active revolt. Very little opposition was

---

[1] A soviet in Russia is a governing council, consisting of workmen, soldiers, or peasants. It may be a local or state-wide organization.

encountered. An All-Russian Congress of Soviets with a Bolshevik majority met the same day, and after a little fighting their forces took over the government. In the civil war which followed, the government was reshaped along the lines suggested by Marxian principles. By 1923 a federated government, known as the Union of Soviet Socialist Republics, was fully established.

Marxian Socialism

THEORETICAL BASIS OF THE SOVIET GOVERNMENT.—The Soviet Union is welded into a unified nation principally because the masses accept a common ideology. They acknowledge a philosophy of society founded largely upon doctrines advanced by Karl Marx (1818-83). The "scientific" socialism (so called to distinguish it from earlier forms of socialism which Marx termed "utopian") of Marx was based upon his theories of political and economic processes which have subsequently been interpreted by the well-known socialist scholars Friedrich Engels (1820-95) and Nikolai Lenin (1870-1924). Marx's theories are still undergoing modification by Soviet scholars under the political leadership of Joseph Stalin (b. 1879) to meet the practical needs of modern Soviet statecraft.

This Marxian Socialism or Communism is to be distinguished from gradualist socialism in that it advocated the creation by violence, if necessary, of a socialist society in which the state power will gradually "wither away" as the dictatorship of the proletariat succeeds in liquidating the last bourgeois elements. Socialism in the non-Marxian sense takes many forms but basically stands for the seizure and collective ownership of all the means of production by the state through *constitutional* means.

HISTORICAL MATERIALISM AND CLASS STRUGGLE.—The background of Marxian theory is the economic interpretation of history which teaches that the political, social, religious, and other institutions of any given historical era are determined by economic forces, that is, by the method of producing goods. Starting with this fundamental proposition, Marx reached the conclusion that the history of the human race must be told in terms of a struggle between economic classes. He found that in essence capitalism was a conflict between the capitalist and the worker, or, as he said, the exploiter and the exploited. He pointed out that the emergence of early modern capitalism had brought into existence the middle class, which had struggled with the nobility until it dominated society. Capitalism, according to Marx, divorced the productive forces from the traditional role of supplying known demands. In order to obtain maximum profits, capital flowed into the most promising fields, demanded the maximum output per unit of labor, and led to crises of overproduction and maldistribution, with consequent depressions and dislocation of economic activity. The era of industrial capitalism brought into being the proletariat or urban worker, another new class which in its turn waged war against the capitalist middle class. To Marx this latest war of the exploited against the exploiter was the final phase of capitalist history. The very nature of this struggle foredoomed capitalism to extinction. Control of the means of production would, according to Marx, inevitably be gathered into fewer and fewer hands; the rich would become richer, while the poor would become poorer. This situation would become increasingly intolerable until eventually the workers would rise in revolt and overcome their masters.

A CLASSLESS SOCIETY.—According to Marxian theory, the aim of this proletarian or workers' revolution would be the creation of a classless society in which public functions would lose their political character. The first step after the revolution, therefore, would be the socialization of the means of production, that is, the abolition of private property controlled by a dominating class. Since under capitalism the national state exists to maintain classes and protect class interests in private property, it would no longer be necessary in the new "classless" era and would, consequently, atrophy. During the transition from the national state to the classless, world-wide Communist society, it would be necessary to have a temporary dictatorship of the proletariat. Initially only the means of production would be socialized, and other small private properties could be retained by their owners, since their private possession exploited no one. The state would cease to function as the instrument for the protection of private property. The withering away of the state would in due time occur through the abolition of the state's agencies. First, the standing army would be abolished and replaced by the armed people, a popular militia. Second, the bureaucracy would go, followed by other state institutions. Lenin, who attempted to create a Communist government and society in Russia, refused to commit himself as to the length of time it would take for the state to "wither away." He merely stated that it was a natural and gradual process. With the destruction of capitalism social evils would disappear. Even human nature would be changed under the impact of the new environment which, according to its protagonists, would eventually produce a true communistic order of society in which each member would produce according to his abilities and receive goods according to his needs.

INTERNATIONAL REVOLUTION AGAINST NATIONAL STATES.—Marxian theory clearly denounces the national state, which it regards as the instrument created in the class struggle by the exploiters for the purpose of keeping the exploited in subjection. Even democracies, according to Marx, merely modify the method by which the ruling class exploits the masses for its own selfish ends. Although history is working for the triumph of the workers over the state which is the instrument of their exploitation, and for the substitution of a classless society for a social order in which the state maintains class distinctions, this process can be accelerated by the revolutionary activity of a well-organized and disciplined party. To this program the followers of Lenin added the use of violence in overthrowing the state, employing it with conspicuous success in the November Revolution of 1917.

Briefly, Marxian theory challenges the institutions of the national state and of private property; it insists on a classless society; it opposes organized religion. It is primarily a doctrine of revolution against the economic and social arrangements of most of the world today, and, as such, it advocates world revolution.

Communism in the Soviet Union

FROM LENIN TO STALIN.—Marxian theory was the basis of the Bolshevik Revolution and of the early economic enactments incident to the establishment of the Soviet Union, but in practice that philosophy has been subject to constant revision within the Soviet Union, first by Lenin and later by his successor, Joseph Stalin as leaders of the dictatorship of the proletariat. After 1921 Lenin found it expedient to revise his militant Communist economics and to make concessions in a phase of development known as the New Economic Policy (NEP). Under this revised program peasants were permitted to retain some of their produce. Private trade within Russia was again legalized, and the government professed its willingness to grant concessions to foreign business interests. The idea of the political "dictatorship of the proletariat" was not abandoned, however, and the Soviet government retained operation and ownership of the large industries, railways, mines, banks, and foreign trade.

In the struggle for power which followed Lenin's death in 1924, Stalin, who advocated an emphasis upon national economic development rather than upon international revolutionary conflict, vanquished his immediate opponent and only serious rival for Lenin's mantle, Leon Trotsky, and forced him into exile. Trotsky believed that world revolution was necessary as well as inevitable and that Communism could not be achieved in the Soviet Union alone.[2] Stalin, on the other hand, believed that the proper strategy was to develop Communism initially within the Soviet Union through the collectivization and industrialization of its economy. He reasoned that the achievement of Communism in Russia

---

[2] Because capitalism had become international in character, many Communists felt that state control in Russia was too limited to succeed against international economic power.

would provide a model for other countries and that in any event capitalism was destroying itself everywhere.

With Stalin controlling Soviet policies, many collectivists have felt that he has been leading the Soviet Union away from, rather than toward, Communism. The masses, they claim, have merely exchanged masters. In this view, Stalin and his followers, instead of the Tsarists, now exploit the people. Others further malign the character of the present regime, declaring that its coerciveness is opposed to the Marxian ideal.

JUSTIFICATION OF A STRONG NATIONAL STATE.—Stalin has ready answers for them all. He insists that, of necessity, consistent with Marxian theory, there must be a period of transition in the process of changing from capitalism to Communism, and that this transitory period is one of state socialism. He reasons that Marx could not possibly have foreseen that the Soviet Union would be encircled by capitalistic regimes, since Marx expected a world revolution of the workers. Accordingly, until capitalism is finally displaced by Communism throughout the world, or until Marxian Socialist regimes are established in at least the leading capitalist countries, Stalin declares that the Soviet Union must maintain a strong state apparatus, including army, navy, and police, and must achieve the greatest possible measure of self sufficiency to protect it from its foreign enemies. Furthermore, if the state is to own and operate the means of production, it must dominate not only the political but also the social and economic institutions. Thus, the state's duties and its bureaucracy must be greatly augmented rather than diminished. Especially after 1933, with mounting evidence that Germany and Japan threatened the security of the Soviet Union, the maintenance of a powerful, closely integrated state was indicated as an overriding essential. For these announced reasons, Stalin has for the present discarded the idea of the withering away of the state. In short, he has relegated to the distant future the attainment of the final objectives inherent in Marxian theory.

ECONOMIC DISTINCTIONS.—Not only have the Marxian ideas of world revolution and a stateless society been set aside by the Soviet regime of Joseph Stalin, but some of the principles of Communism in its final stage have been de-emphasized as well. Marx and Lenin asserted that every worker was to be on a basis of social equality with every other, that each was to receive according to his need. This doctrine was widely interpreted to foreshadow a relatively uniform level of incomes for all classes of workers, with perhaps some favoring of men with high technical skills. Early steps taken in that direction so seriously affected Soviet production, both in quality and quantity, that the government was compelled to institute an extreme form of piecework production in order to prevent economic collapse. Today there are in the Soviet Union variations in income to a degree similar to those prevailing under capitalist, free-enterprise economies. Article 118 of the Soviet Constitution replaced the "need" basis of compensation by specifying ". . . payment for their work in accordance with its quantity and quality." Under that provision the range of compensation varies not only according to the rank or position of the individual worker but is further modified by fairly generous bonuses for "above-the-norm" performance and drastic penalties for failures to achieve the norm. The net result is a scale of compensation the range of which at least matches that of capitalist economies.[3]

INDIVIDUAL PROPERTY INTERESTS.—Two general types of property are recognized in the Soviet Union. The first type is socialized property, subclassified as state property and collectivist property. State property includes all natural resources and the means and implements for their production and distribution. Workers on state projects thus become employees of the state. Collectivist property is owned collectively by communities and other groups. It includes collective farms and consumer and producer cooperatives. Workers on such property are its joint owners. Since the workers share in the returns of collectivist projects, they are regarded as self-employed.

The second general type is described as personal property, likewise of two kinds. It includes small individual enterprises, such as stores and workshops, so long as their operation entails no exploitation of the labor of other individuals. In addition it comprises property in consumers' goods and goods for use, such as savings, personal belongings, dwelling houses, and articles used in domestic production.

Every citizen of the Soviet Union may own books, furniture, clothing, and have a savings account and even an automobile for his own personal use if his ability and earning capacity warrant it. Furthermore, he may invest his savings in interest-bearing government bonds, the return from which is exempt from both income and inheritance taxes. What may seem more surprising in view of Communist ideas of property is that the present Constitution guarantees to an individual the right to inherit the personal property of his immediate family. However, under its planned economy the government attempts to control the allocation of all resources, including investments. Therefore, it is not unusual for it to inflate or deflate the currency to suit its purposes. Thus the confiscation of savings which attended the conversion of the Soviet Union's currency in December, 1947, made a profound change in the amount and distribution of savings. All cash holdings were exchanged at the rate of one new ruble for ten old ones. The savings deposits which were under three thousand rubles were unchanged, but on the next seven thousand rubles two new ones were exchanged for three old, and any balance

---

[3] Stalin himself quoted both Marx and Lenin as having agreed that wage differences would exist under Socialism.

above ten thousand rubles was exchanged at the rate of one new for two old. Likewise all state bonds were re-evaluated at one third their former worth.

HISTORICAL NATIONALISM.—The Marxian interpretation of history could admit no contribution to progress in Russian history by Tsarist leaders and institutions, but Stalinism has abandoned this view. For strong Tsars, like Peter the Great and Ivan the Terrible, there is now discriminating praise, not indiscriminate abuse. Soviet official opinion now endorses every war that contributed to the building up of the Russian state, although Lenin denounced Tsarist wars as having been waged on behalf of capitalistic exploitation and imperialism. National patriotism, which Marx and Lenin rejected, has been exalted by the current Soviet rulers in the last decade. In the Soviet Union today Stalin has discarded at least temporarily the early disdain of the national state as expounded in Marxian theory and glorifies the ideal of Soviet national patriotism. In the recent war with Germany and Japan, his appeals to the Russian people were put in terms of straight old-fashioned patriotism. This development is a logical outgrowth of Stalin's belief in the necessity of building up Communism in one country.

REVOLUTIONARY MODERATION.—Since Lenin's day the Bolshevik revolutionary movement, under Stalin, has entered a relatively moderate phase. In this process the movement has modified the Marxian theoretical conception in which it was rooted in order to meet and solve practical problems as they have arisen. No revolution is perpetual; there must always be stabilization, and the stabilization usually blends the old with the new. Some Marxists lament many of Stalin's recent policies as a betrayal of the original ideals of the revolution. However, Stalinists insist that they are Marxists who are keeping faith with Marxian theory.

Origin of the Revolutionary Soviets

Marxist students consider the Paris Commune (1871) as the first testing ground for the proletariat revolution against the bourgeois regime. One of the lessons they extracted from the history of that episode was that it was necessary for the revolutionaries to have ready a new government of revolutionary leaders to be substituted for the overthrown system. This provision was particularly necessary in order to prevent the launching of a counterrevolution based upon the agencies and officials which would otherwise be held over from the preceding government.

In the Russian Revolution of 1905, the Marxists formed soviets to direct the strikes and street fighting which broke out in the urban-industrial regions. These soviets were elected by the workers of the factories in each region. Delegates were sent to a soviet in St. Petersburg. The soviet in Moscow included some soldiers' deputies. After the revolution had been quelled, the Bolsheviks appreciated the importance of including representatives of the revolutionary-minded soldiers in their councils.

Again, in 1917, strikes and rioting created an atmosphere of disorder in which the agitations of the Bolsheviks bore fruit. The Central Committee of the Bolshevik party issued a manifesto, calling for an armed struggle against Tsardom and the formation of a revolutionary government. Soviets of Workers' and Soldiers' Deputies were formed which included dissatisfied elements from nonsocialist as well as socialist groups.

The soviet spokesmen considered the provisional government, which had taken over after the abdication of the Tsar, as typical of the governments which had failed to carry out successful revolutions. They repeated that it was necessary not only to transfer power to a new ruling class, but to create a new form of government in which the distinction between ruler and ruled would be minimized. This was to be accomplished through the destruction of parliamentarianism. The soviets, as working organs combining executive and legislative functions, representing workmen, soldiers, and peasants, were held to be the ideal form. Thus, the government which took over in the November Revolution (1917) represented only the "proletariat," and worked to establish the dictatorship of that element.

Soviet Constitution

EARLY CONSTITUTIONS.—The present Constitution of the Union of Soviet Socialist Republics has had two predecessors. The first, that of 1918, was the fundamental law of what was called the Russian Socialist Federated Soviet Republic (RSFSR), which gave a legal form to the government established after the November Revolution of 1917. The most challenging features of that instrument established a proletarian dictatorship, abolished all rights capable of being used to the detriment of the revolution, destroyed private ownership of land, disestablished the Orthodox Church, secularized education, and placed every phase of economic life under the control of the state. It organized a federated government composed of units created along ethnographic and national lines but centralized with respect to vital governmental functions. The representative elements consisted of councils of workers, called soviets.

In 1923 the name of the state was changed to the Union of Soviet Socialist Republics (USSR), the word "Russian" being deleted in order to appeal to non-Russian elements of the federation. The Union comprised four republics of which the Russian Socialist Federated Soviet Republic (RSFSR) was one. As other republics were organized, they were brought under increasingly centralized control.

The Constitution of 1923 was the fundamental law for the new federated organization of the USSR. The administrative structure under this constitution was a pyramidal system of soviets, the territorial jurisdiction of which ranged from the village to the federation. On the lowest levels were the village soviets, and above them those of the districts (*raioni*), the areas (*okrugi*), the regions (*oblasti*), the territories (*kraia*), and the constituent republics (SSR). The dominant institution of the Soviet Union, at the apex of this organization, was the All-Union Congress of Soviets.

These first two constitutions did not establish a separation of legislative, executive, and judicial powers. All state powers were concentrated in the hands of the All-Union Congress of Soviets and the agencies which it appointed. Of course, the essential fact was that state affairs were directed by officials who were under the control of the Communist party, an agency not even mentioned in the first two constitutions.

THE CONSTITUTION OF 1936.—Numerous changes in both governmental theory and practice of the Soviet Union took place under Stalin's leadership in the dozen years following 1924. A Five-Year Plan (1928-1932) of economic and social reconstruction was undertaken and two later plans were launched. Agriculture was collectivized, industry subjected to social ownership and control and expanded; the government was stabilized, domestic peace enforced. The Soviet leaders desired to have the basic law keep step with these changes; they desired a revised constitution to be, not so much a blueprint of a future state as a recording and consolidation of the practical results which had been achieved. Since the government was under the authority of Joseph Stalin, the new constitution may be considered his handiwork.

A constitutional commission of thirty-one members, with Stalin as chairman, wrote the Constitution in secret session. It was presented to the All-Union Congress and widely published for the purpose of public discussion. The various soviets recommended approximately 154,000 amendments, some of which were discussed in the All-Union Congress. Finally this body made forty-three minor changes in the phraseology of the original draft, and the Constitution of 1936 was approved. It may be amended by a two-thirds vote of both houses of the Supreme Soviet, the national legislative body (see p. 283).

The principles of the Constitution of 1936 form an interesting theoretical background for the present Communist dictatorship. Politically the Soviet Union is an organization of soviets of workers' deputies. The proletariat of the town and the country possess all political power through their representation in the soviets. Economically the Union is organized along socialist lines. Capitalism is abolished through the socialist ownership of the means of production and the prohibition against "exploitation of man by man." "Socialist property" is defined and the recognition of limited private property is given, as we have previously explained. A state plan of national economy is authorized, calculated to increase the public wealth, to improve the living standards of the people, and to strengthen the capacity of the state for defending its independence. Work is made a matter of duty and honor for every able-bodied citizen, in keeping with the principle that "he who does not work shall not eat." Finally, the Constitution sanctions a variable system of wage payment permitting due recognition of such factors as skill, quality, and quantity of performance.

CONSTITUTIONAL RIGHTS AND DUTIES.—The Soviet Constitution's guarantee of basic rights of the citizen is theoretically broad, although in practice many of its provisions have not been made effective. The citizen has a legal right to work, to leisure, and to material security. These rights are put into effect by the socialist organization of the national economy by provisions for a limited working day, and by social security insurance. The right to an education is guaranteed; on the elementary level it is compulsory. All citizens are constitutionally equal irrespective of their sex, race, or nationality. There is provision for freedom of conscience, separation of church and state, and freedom both of religious worship and of antireligious propaganda. The re-opening of theological seminaries was permitted in 1943. The Soviet citizens, according to the Constitution, are granted freedom of speech, press, and assembly; and explicit permission is given the people to organize street demonstrations.[4] Freedom to express opposition to government policy, an essential of democratic government, has not been allowed by Soviet leaders, although at times criticism of the methods of carrying out policy has appeared. In the interest of the regime the government controls all newspapers, printing establishments, and all means of communication. The Constitution grants the right of asylum to foreign citizens. In the main this has been restricted in practice to escaped revolutionaries of Communist persuasion. Citizens have the right to organize trade-unions, cooperative associations, youth organizations, and cultural, technical, and scientific societies. According to the Constitution, the inviolability of the person and the home of the citizen is protected by the establishment of freedom from arrest except upon order of the judicial authorities. Strict adherence to this right of citizenship has not obtained under the Soviet government at any time.

In addition to these rights the Constitution lists the following as

---

[4] . . . provided that the exercise of these freedoms does not jeopardize the socialist system.

Article 118. Citizens of the U.S.S.R. have the right to work, that is the right to receive guaranteed work with payment for their work in accordance with its quantity and quality.

The right to work is ensured by the socialist organization of national economy, the steady growth of the productive forces of Soviet society, the absence of economic crises, and the abolition of unemployment.

Article 119. Citizens of the U.S.S.R. have the right to rest.

The right to rest is ensured by the reduction of the working day to seven hours for the overwhelming majority of the workers, establishment of annual vacations with pay for workers and employees, and provisions for a wide network of sanatoria, rest-homes and clubs for the accommodation of the toilers.

Article 121. Citizens of the U.S.S.R. have the right to education.

This right is ensured by universal compulsory elementary education free of charge, including higher education, by the system of state stipends for the overwhelming majority of students in higher schools, instruction in schools in the native language, and organization of free industrial, technical and agronomic education for the toilers at the factories, state farms, machine-tractor stations and collective farms.

Article 122. Women in the U.S.S.R. are accorded equal rights with men in all fields of economic, state, cultural, social and political life.

The possibility of realizing these rights of women is ensured by affording women equally with men the right to work, payment for work, rest, social insurance and education, state protection of the interests of mother and child, granting pregnancy leave with pay, and the provision for a wide network of maternity homes, nurseries and kindergartens.

Article 123. The equality of the rights of citizens of the U.S.S.R., irrespective of their nationality or race, in all fields of economic, state, cultural, social and political life, is an irrevocable law.

Any direct or indirect restriction of these rights, or conversely, the establishment of direct or indirect privileges for citizens on account of the race or nationality to which they belong, as well as any propagation of racial or national exceptionalism or hatred and contempt, is punishable by law.

Article 124. To ensure to citizens freedom of conscience the church in the U.S.S.R. is separated from the state and the school from the church. Freedom to perform religious rites and freedom of anti-religious propaganda is recognized for all citizens.

Article 125. In accordance with the interests of the toilers and for the purpose of strengthening the socialist system, the citizens of the U.S.S.R. are guaranteed: (a) Freedom of speech; (b) Freedom of the press; (c) Freedom of assembly and meetings; (d) Freedom of street processions and demonstrations.

These rights of the citizens are ensured by placing at the disposal of the toilers and their organizations printing presses, supplies of paper, public buildings, streets, means of communication and other material conditions necessary for their realization.

duties of the citizen: the observance of the law, the maintenance of labor discipline, the honest performance of public obligations, the safeguarding of socialist public property, and military service.

ELIMINATION OF POLITICAL DISSENTERS.—Although one of the missions of the prerevolutionary planners was to erase the distinction between the state and the people, the result of the revolution has been to add the Communist party as an additional institution separate from the people. Since there can be no legal opposition to the party, no democracy can exist in the Soviet state. There are no civil rights, at least in the sense understood in a democracy. Even the right to emigrate has been denied to the dissatisfied elements. Violators of the emigration laws are subject to extreme penalties, as are the members of their families and other close connections.

Police organs equipped with extraordinary powers to curb dissenters have been an integral element of the State organization, beginning with the Cheka (Extraordinary Commission to Combat Counterrevolution, Sabotage, and Speculation). In 1922 the Cheka was replaced by the OGPU (State Political Bureau). That body was given authority to punish, without resort to the state courts, persons apprehended in banditry and armed robbery, as well as political offenders. Moreover, OGPU directed the state prisons and used prison labor to work mines, lumber camps, and engineering projects.

In 1934 the NKVD (Commissariat of the Interior) took over the functions of the OGPU. In theory NKVD had no power to try anyone. All cases of infraction of law were to be sent to the regular courts. However, a special board in the Interior Department had the power to exile and imprison political offenders for five-year terms. Although the 1936 Constitution made no provision for the use of administrative procedure in the treatment of dissenters, the NKVD which was renamed MVD (Ministry of the Interior) in 1946, retained the power to arrest and imprison suspects without recourse by the latter. Lenin set the pattern for these methods when he said, "I would rather imprison thousands of not guilty in order to protect the workers, than let a few guilty survive to injure society."

SOVIET LAW.—The codes of Tsarist law were repudiated by the revolutionaries of 1917, who substituted for them "action of the masses," that is to say, the actions of revolutionary committees who purportedly spoke for the masses. Eventually much Communist legislation was formulated, often hastily. From time to time statutes, decrees, and administrative rulings have been gathered into codes, which, however, as the stream of legislation rolls on and high policy fluctuates, often became obsolete almost as soon as they were drawn. The Soviet codes of law by force of these circumstances have stood perpetually in need of revision. The codes which were based upon the Constitution of 1936 were published and promulgated in 1943 and 1944.

The Federal Structure of the USSR

THE DIVISION OF POWER.—Under the Constitution of 1936 the Soviet Union is nominally a federal state formed by the union of sixteen constituent socialist republics (SSR). The powers of the federal government are so broad, however, that centralization of authority in the USSR is as complete as in any nation in the world. In point of fact, the system is not in any real sense federal since economic planning does not permit real decentralization. The binding force which cuts across the federal features of the constitutional framework is not the All-Union government so much as it is the integration of the Communist party.

In the constitutional division of power, the Union government has the following powers: to conduct foreign relations in collaboration with the constituent republics, including the power to make war and peace; admit new republics into the Union; enforce the Union Constitution and ensure conformity with it of the constitutions of the constituent republics; confirm changes of boundaries between the constituent republics and the formation of new territories, provinces, and autonomous republics within the constituent republics; control the Army; administer the monopoly of foreign trade; establish the economic plan of the Union; apportion taxes and revenues among the federal, republican, and local budgets; administer banks, industries, agricultural and commercial enterprises of Union significance; administer transportation and communication; control money, credit, and insurance; issue state loans; determine the use of land and natural resources; formulate educational and public health plans; determine the principles of labor legislation; organize the judiciary; prepare civil and criminal codes; determine the rights of citizens and the position of foreigners; and exercise the right of pardon. Moreover, the Union government has power to amend the acts of the constituent republics which are contrary to Union laws or administrative regulations. It is obvious that these powers are broad. In effect they give the Union government power to control every important aspect of the country's life and unlimited opportunity to interfere with local organs of government.

Only outside the limits of these broad powers do the constituent republics possess the ability to function independently. In the administration of education, health, and local economy they experience relatively little interference from the central government. They may freely use and encourage the development of local languages. In local cultural activities, such as art or music, they may exercise considerable autonomy.

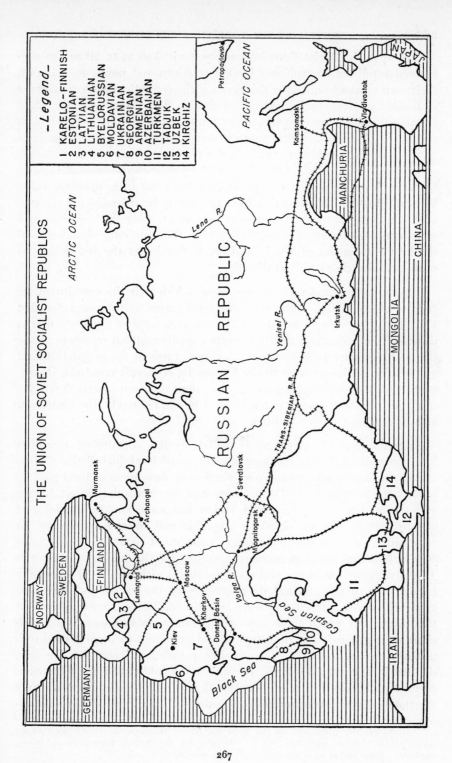

THE UNION OF SOVIET SOCIALIST REPUBLICS

— Legend —
1 KARELO-FINNISH
2 ESTONIAN
3 LATVIAN
4 LITHUANIAN
5 BYELORUSSIAN
6 MOLDAVIAN
7 UKRAINIAN
8 GEORGIAN
9 ARMENIAN
10 AZERBAIJAN
11 TURKMEN
12 TADJIK
13 UZBEK
14 KIRGHIZ

ARCTIC OCEAN

PACIFIC OCEAN

RUSSIAN REPUBLIC

JAPAN

MANCHURIA

CHINA

MONGOLIA

Petropaulovsk

Vladivostok

Komsomolsk

Irkutsk

Lena R.

Yenisei R.

TRANS-SIBERIAN R.R.

Murmansk

Archangel

Sverdlovsk

Magnitogorsk

Moscow

Leningrad

Kharkov

Kiev

Donets Basin

Volga R.

Caspian Sea

Black Sea

IRAN

NORWAY

SWEDEN

FINLAND

GERMANY

267

In 1944 the Soviet Constitution was revised so as to allow the constituent republics control over foreign relations and power to maintain their own armies.[5] Following this revision the republics have participated in limited international diplomatic activities. The Ukrainian and White Russian republics are members of the United Nations and send delegates to the UN Assembly. Actual control of such activities, however, remains in the central government, through the Communist party.

The Constitution of 1936 gives each republic the theoretical right of secession from the Soviet Union. Such a right has little practical value because efforts in this direction have invariably been considered treasonable, counterrevolutionary, and non-Communist. Since the Union government controls the effective military forces, the economic planning, and the heavy industries of the federation, it dominates the individual republics indirectly as well as directly.

PREDOMINANT POSITION OF THE RSFSR.—Although the constituent republics of the Union enjoy the same legal status, the Russian Socialist Federated Soviet Republic (RSFSR) is so large and so populous that it completely overshadows and dominates the other fifteen members of the unequal partnership. It has more than two thirds of the population and 75 per cent of the territory of the Union. Its economic resources, its cultural tradition, and its predominance in the Communist party create for it a position which cannot be challenged by the relatively tiny Caucasian and Asiatic contituent republics.

LOCAL ADMINISTRATIVE AREAS.—The sixteen constituent republics have been divided into governmental areas of local jurisdiction. Time and again the boundaries and organization of these areas of local government have been revised. The primary basis for the subdivisions is race and nationality, since the Soviet Union has some two hundred racial groups with recognized rights to linguistic and cultural autonomy. In recognition of these rights the larger constituent republics (SSR) have been subdivided into autonomous republics (ASSR) and into territories (kraia), regions (oblasti), and areas (okrugi), with degrees of autonomy comparable to the cultural developments of the racial and linguistic groups in whose interest they were established. There is no symmetry in the manner in which these autonomous and semiautonomous subdivisions are organized. The most typical and numerous of them is the intermediate region (oblast). The smaller constituent republics are subdivided in this way. While the autonomous republics and the territories, regions, and areas have a considerable degree of cultural autonomy, they are politically and economically subordinated to the constituent repub-

---

[5] However, the presidium of the Supreme Soviet reorganized the People's Commissariat for Defense into the People's Ministry for the Armed Forces, February 25, 1946. All armed forces were unified under this ministry.

lics of which they are a part in the same way as the constituent republics are subordinated to the government of the USSR.

The small constituent republics and the autonomous republics, and the territories, regions, and areas of the large constituent republics are subdivided into administrative districts (*raioni*) which correspond to an American county. These districts, in turn, are subdivided into towns, villages, or urban wards, which are the primary units of local government.

The All-Union Communist Party of the Bolsheviks

THE POSITION OF THE PARTY IN THE SOVIET UNION.—Since the first day of the November Revolution of 1917, the Soviet Union has been governed by the Communist party, a name which was adopted in 1918 by the Bolshevik or majority wing of the original Russian Social Democratic party. The government of the Soviet Union is totalitarian; that is, the government functions not only in the restricted Western sense, but it likewise has complete power of social and economic regulation, the inspiration of which is the work of a single integrated and relatively restricted political group. This group is the Communist party; it is the only party in the Soviet Union. On paper, the government of the USSR and the party are two distinct and complementary mechanisms. The organization of the two are parallel, from Moscow, the capital, down through the constituent republics, the territories, regions, areas, districts, and into the smaller villages. In each subdivision the party organization has its own headquarters, congress, councils, officers, treasuries, newspapers, and so on. However, there is no pretense of federalism in the party. One hierarchy rules one integrated party. Officially it is the government, not the party, that makes laws, issues decrees, conducts affairs of state, controls the Army and Navy, and gives orders to the police. Actually, however, it is the party which rules by the simple expedient of seeing to it that all of the higher officials and the great majority of lower officials are faithful party members. The government of the Soviet Union is thus completely controlled by the Communist party. The Constitution of 1936 gives this party legal recognition as "the leading nucleus of all of the organizations of the working people." This provision of the Soviet Union makes the Communist party in effect a state within a state.

NATURE OF THE PARTY.—In its organization and its relationship to the government, the Communist party is different from the political parties which function in the traditional democratic state. In the Soviet Union the party has always been a minority in the population; its membership is restricted. In its operation it is authoritarian, although it has claimed to permit intraparty democracy from time to time. It can best be described as a ruling political elite selected from all elements of the population on a basis of interest in and loyalty to Communist party ideals. The Communist party was first controlled by Lenin, and came under the authority of Joseph Stalin only after Lenin's death. Since achieving power over the party, Stalin, presumably with the support and assistance of a small group of high party officials, has formulated party policy, which, although it may be vociferously debated in congresses, committees, and soviets prior to adoption, is invariably and scrupulously followed thereafter. Such policies are known as the "general line" or, more popularly, as the "party line." At any given time this party line is binding upon all party members, and all party activities must conform to it. Over a period of years the line has fluctuated widely in response to the need of the hour, as interpreted by the ruling group (see p. 302). As the line changes, so invariably do the expressions and actions of party members in conformity with the new official statements and slogans.

PARTY DISCIPLINE.—A rigid discipline of all of its members has been insisted upon by the Communist party. Party members are required to persevere in its activities and to work energetically on behalf of its programs. They must accept directions unquestioningly and execute policies with enthusiasm. Their reward for faithfulness is participation in governing the Soviet Union. Should they be remiss in the performance of party duties, they may be expelled or may face even worse consequences.

From time to time the party leadership has required the membership to undergo a rigid examination from the standpoint of ideological purity, loyalty to the Communist cause, integrity of character, and personal behavior. These examinations, or purges, have led to the expulsion of many members and to the demotion of others. Such purges occurred periodically throughout the twenties and especially in the years from 1934 to 1939. When the purges were over, all of the old Bolsheviks who might have disagreed with Stalin's revised Communist policies or challenged his authority had disappeared (see p. 278). Within the party as a whole one fourth, or approximately half a million of the members, had been expelled by 1939, a large percentage of these because of an alleged lack of interest in party activities. In that year it was decided that there should be no more mass purges, although the party retained the right to cut off undeserving members. Rules of admission were relaxed so as to rebuild the size of the party.

Much of the success of the Communist party both in the November Revolution of 1917 and in later years may be attributed to party discipline. It is a united, active organization based upon a dynamic socialist ideology and bound together by an iron discipline. Bases of strength are to be found in party unity and in singleness of will and action, both of which are incompatible with a deviation from its program, a breach of discipline, or the formation of factions inside the party.

PARTY MEMBERSHIP.—Every Soviet citizen is eligible for party membership on the same conditions. According to the relaxed rules of 1939, all applicants must be endorsed by three party members of three years' standing who have known the applicant as their co-worker for at least one year. The applicant must undergo probation for a year and must give satisfactory proof of worthiness during this time. Then the question of admission is decided by vote of the members of the local branch of the party, to whom the application of the aspirant has been addressed. To merit promotion to full membership the probationer must signify his consent to party discipline, his acceptance of the party rules and program, and demonstrate his indoctrination with the principles of Marx and Lenin.

Communist leaders, like the Nazis, have never wished to encourage a rapid and indiscriminate growth of membership. Should the party ever become an extremely large body, its character as an organized, disciplined, governing elite would be diluted or destroyed. Therefore, the aim has been to keep the party large enough to retain an element of mass support and small enough to be manageable. In 1946 its members and probationary candidates for membership numbered 6,000,000 out of an estimated population of 211,000,000. The number of candidates is believed to have been about 1,000,000.

DUTIES AND RIGHTS OF PARTY MEMBERS.—The rigorous system of controls to which party members submit includes a number of specific duties: (1) The party member must pay an initiation fee and afterward support the party by monthly dues ranging up to 3 per cent of his income plus various other contributions. (2) He must accept unhesitatingly the party line of policy and action no matter what his personal views may be. (3) Strict party discipline, party orders, and instruction must be adhered to. (4) The member must participate actively in the political life of the party and of the country by taking part in meetings, demonstrations, drives, and committees. (5) He must study the ideology of Marx and Lenin and explain it to the nonparty masses. (6) Within his community the party member must set an example in the observance of labor and state discipline, master the technique of his work, and continually raise his production and work qualifications. (7) The Soviet Communist must abstain from trade and other lucrative occupations, evince no concern about profits, and turn over whatever he can of his earnings to pension funds and similar public activities. This long list of obligations is calculated to discourage all save those of genuine conviction and enthusiasm, as well as to operate constructively in the party's interests. Although party members must renounce religious affiliations, it is obvious that they must subject themselves to a regimen of discipline, self-denial, and service reminiscent of that enforced by a medieval religious order.

Naturally there are compensations for such sacrifices. Party membership carries with it distinction, a place in the governing group, the assurance of a job, and all sorts of preferential treatment. In addition, party members have certain rights. Although it is the primary duty of the party member to carry out decisions of the party after they have been approved, it is the theoretical right of each member to participate freely in the formulation of these policies. This provision is called intraparty democracy and "conscious discipline." Criticism of party strategy and objectives is usually not permitted, but there seems to be considerable freedom to discuss the best ways of obtaining such objectives. Members of the party have the right to vote in party elections and to hold party office. When their personal conduct is being investigated, they have a right to be heard. Finally, members may ask information of, or make representations to, any party agency.

PARTY ORGANIZATION OF THE LOCALITIES.—The party organization includes an extensive network of agencies. The basic units of the party structure are the "primary party organs," formerly known as Communist "cells." A primary party organ is accredited in every industrial or commercial enterprise, mine, army unit, collective farm, machine-tractor station, university, village, or office where there are at least three party members. The primary party organ agitates for the fulfillment of party slogans, propagandizes for party programs, facilitates the political education of the people in its vicinity, strengthens labor discipline, and cooperates with higher party organs. In state-controlled enterprises, such as collective farms and machine-tractor stations, these party units control the administration of the institution.

Upon the base of the numerous primary party organs is erected the hierarchy of higher party organs with an ever-expanding territorial jurisdiction. Each city and district (raion) has a party conference that meets at least once a year, a committee, a bureau (consisting of five to seven members), and a secretary. The secretary of a city or district organization must have been a party member for three years. Above the city and district organizations are those of the larger subdivisions of the Soviet Union: the national areas (okrugi), the regions (oblasti), the territories (kraia), the autonomous republics (ASSR), and the constituent republics (SSR). Each of these has its party conference, which meets every eighteen months, its committee, and its secretariat. Above these is the party congress of the constituent republics. The primary party organs choose delegates who constitute the party conferences and committees of the cities and districts. These in turn elect the party conferences of the autonomous republics, territories, regions and areas, and they in their turn elect the congresses of the constituent republics. From the party congresses of the constituent republics go the delegates to the All-Union Congress which, with its All-Union Central Committee, caps the party organization. The thread of responsibility and control is unbroken from the top to the bottom of this complex structure. Each organ, though it is elected by those immediately beneath it, has full power over its inferior bodies and officials.

PARTY ORGANIZATION OF THE SOVIET UNION.—Despite the theory that the party organizations of the Soviet Union merely translate into action the will of the rank and file of the party as it is borne to them through converging channels from the primary party organs to the All-Union Congress, the leaders of the top organizations of the party actually make the decisions. In theory supreme authority rests in the All-Union Congress, an assemblage of more than a thousand delegates which meets irregularly. According to party rules this body is supposed to meet at least once every three years, but this provision has not been strictly observed. Its last meeting was held in March, 1939. This body is so large and its sessions are so short that it invariably votes unanimously for the resolutions submitted by party leaders. It hears reports, officially revises and amends the rules of the party, and establishes party programs. It elects an All-Union Central Committee of about seventy members with an equal number of alternates, and a Central Auditing Committee to check on the finances of the party agencies.

Although in theory the work of the party is performed between sessions of the All-Union Congress by the All-Union Central Committee, the latter meets infrequently and the party is largely controlled by four of its agencies: the Secretariat headed by Joseph Stalin as Secretary-General; the Political Bureau (*Politburo*); the Organization Bureau (*Orgburo*); and the Party Control Commission. The members of these bureaus are elected by secret ballot by the All-Union Central Committee.

THE POLITICAL BUREAU AND OTHER CENTRAL AGENCIES.—The nine members and five alternate members of the Political Bureau are probably the fourteen most powerful men in the Soviet Union. They hold the highest positions in both the party and the government. They are the custodians of supreme party authority when the All-Union Central Committee is not sitting; when the latter meets, it ratifies their decisions on political policy without question. Not only is Premier Joseph Stalin the dominant member of the Political Bureau, but he personally selects the members whom the All-Union Central Committee nominally elects to it.

The Organization Bureau has nine members elected by the All-Union Central Committee. Stalin is a member. This body supervises the organization and officials of the party. It has charge of propaganda and conventions. The Secretariat of four members, with Stalin at its head, is

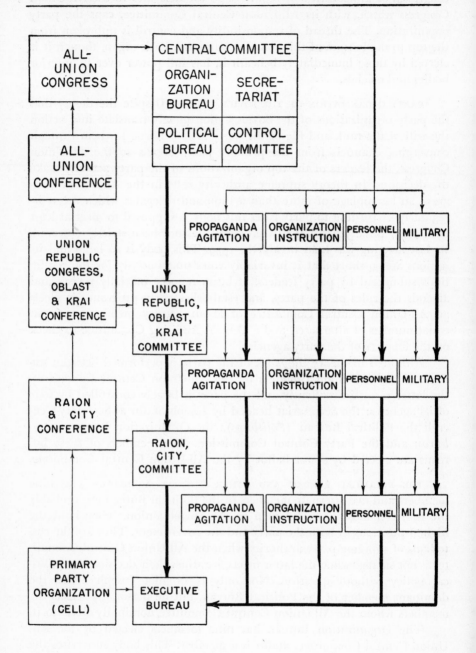

similarly named and exercises executive functions. In this interlocking directorate resides the supreme control of the party, most of it in the capable hands of Joseph Stalin and the Political Bureau which he in reality selects. For years, without holding any important post in the government, Stalin was able through these agencies alone to control for all practical purposes the government of the Soviet Union.

The Party Control Commission of thirty-one members investigates and brings proceedings against members who have violated the program, rules, or discipline of the party.

ALL-UNION CONFERENCE.—In the interval between sessions of the All-Union Congresses, the All-Union Central Committee of the party calls, not less than once a year, an All-Union Conference of party representatives from the local organizations to discuss questions of party policy. Delegates to this assembly are selected by the central committees of the lower units in accordance with the apportionment directives of the All-Union Central Committee. Those members of the All-Union Central Committee not delegated are given a consultative voice in the work of the All-Union Conference. Its decisions, except for those having to do with the All-Union Central Committee itself, must be ratified by the Committee, and thereafter they are binding on all party organizations. The last All-Union Conference was held in 1941.

YOUTH ORGANIZATIONS.—The Communist party sponsors a number of youth organizations and recruits new members from them. The most important of these are the Octobrists, the Pioneers, and the *Komsomol* or League of Communist Youth. The Octobrists are children under ten years of age. They are led and taught by the Pioneers, who are under sixteen years of age. The *Komsomol,* made up of young men and women of from sixteen to twenty-five years of age, directs the work of the Pioneers, and provides the reservoir from which party members are selected. There is some overlapping of ages in these several organizations in order that certain outstanding Pioneers or members of the *Komsomol* may remain as tutors for Pioneers and Octobrist groups.

The youth organizations parallel the organization of the Communist party in every administrative area. They are auxiliary to the adult organizations.

The youth organizations engage in a variety of activities. Improved health is fostered through sports and physical culture. They study and perfect themselves in Communist doctrine. Semimilitary in character, they inculcate the membership with a willingness to defend their homeland. They participate, moreover, to the extent of their capacity in the social, economic, and political life of their communities. Youthfully energetic, and with boundless faith in the ultimate success of Communism, the "graduates" of these youth organizations already predominate in the ranks of the Communist party. The strength of this reservoir of potential party members has been estimated variously at from ten to twenty millions.

Although all applicants for party membership under twenty must be members of the *Komsomol,* selection to the party from the *Komsomol* is by no means assured. They, too, must serve a period of probation and be recommended by party members in good standing. However, it stands to reason that an outstanding youth in the *Komsomol* finds the road to party membership a relatively smooth one.

POWER OF THE PARTY.—Many persons express amazement that a small minority, such as the Communist party, should be able to supply leadership to the Soviet millions. Numerous factors make this control possible however: (1) Since the Communist party is the "official" party of the land, it is the only active political group and would, therefore, be difficult to displace. (2) The membership of the party is highly selective, and is based upon long preliminary training in doctrine. The members possess a fanatical sense of loyalty, duty, and enthusiasm. (3) The party organization is such that it permeates the official organs and agencies of the government. (4) The party exerts complete control over the press, radio, and all other propaganda agencies. It determines educational policies for the Union and is ever watchful that Communist doctrine is not slighted. It fosters Communist youth organizations to ensure party regeneration. (5) The Communist party has earned the gratitude of the majority of the people of the Soviet Union. There is little doubt that the lot of the workers and peasants is better today in a material sense than it was under the Tsarist regime. These workers and peasants, constituting the bulk of the population, form the source of greatest political support for the party. (6) Nonconformity with the new Soviet order has been ruthlessly crushed. Hundreds of thousands of people have been shot or sent to labor concentration camps for political offenses. Political opposition can scarcely be expected to survive in such an atmosphere.[6] (7) Soviet Russia has given to its youth opportunities and responsibilities which they normally could not have achieved. Everywhere one finds in Russia young men and young women in important jobs. This policy has assured the devoted support of the younger generation. (8) Most Russians have known nothing other than dictatorial government. They have no standards of comparison with foreign countries, and they have been taught to consider their own system the best. (9) By flattery and threats the Russian people have been molded into a pattern of national solidarity. The worker who has set the pace in the production line of his factory finds himself a national hero. The saboteur, actual or suspected, mysteriously disappears.

---

[6] In 1947 the number of political prisoners in concentration camps was variously estimated from 11,000,000 to 16,000,000.

For all of these reasons, the majority of Russians today, especially young Russians, may be reckoned as loyal in varying degrees to the Soviet regime.

The stability of the Soviet regime was tested when partial demobilization of the wartime Army in 1946-47 sent back to their homes some millions of soldiers who had discovered in Russian-occupied areas standards of living far higher than anything they had ever known in their homeland. "Re-indoctrination" of these veterans became necessary before they could be released to spread disaffection throughout the land. Russia's acute economic difficulties and the austerity of living conditions produced by the state's emphasis on rehabilitation of the devastated areas and the creation of great new industries made the situation no easier. Nevertheless, no competent observer has even suggested that the resultant unrest of the Russian people created any real hazard to the stability of the state or its ruling class.

THE THIRD INTERNATIONAL.—Officially the All-Union Communist party of the Bolsheviks was a "section" of the world-wide Marxian revolutionary organization called the Third International or the Comintern. Although the latter denied that it was an organic part of the Soviet Union, its headquarters were in Moscow, its chief officials were Soviet leaders, its policies followed the policies of the All-Union Communist party line, and its funds were presumably supplied by the party. The Third International was organized by Lenin and his associates in March, 1919; it was the successor of the First International of 1864 and the Second International of 1889.[7] It was conceived and operated as a world party which accepted as its fundamental purpose the encouragement of world proletarian revolution and the establishment of a classless society in all lands. Most of the larger countries of the world had Communist parties which were "sections" of the Third International and which were controlled and financed by it. A World Congress which met occasionally in Moscow to examine questions of theory, policy, and organization and to coordinate Communist tactics the world over was its supreme organization. It maintained a permanent secretariat in Moscow. In the interest of harmony among the nations with whom Russia was allied in World War II, the Third International was formally "dissolved" in May, 1943. The fact that the "dissolution" of the Comintern was spurious and that it continued in fact to function secretly wherever a Communist cell existed came to light in 1947 when increasing opposition from the Western democracies forced the newly designated Cominform to show its hand.

---

[7] The First International (1864-1876), organized by Marx and Engels, was a revolutionary body which sought to form a world-wide order of Socialist laborers under centralized direction. The Second International (1889) possessed no strong central authority to bind the affiliated national Socialist parties. Its program called for the gradual improvement of the workingman's lot through democratic, parliamentary action.

JOSEPH STALIN.—The present leader of the Soviet Union was born in 1879 in the little town of Gori, in Russian Georgia. His name was Joseph Djugashvili, Stalin being a pseudonym derived from the Russian word meaning "steel" and his choice among a dozen aliases which he used during his revolutionary years. From childhood Stalin's life was grimly poor and hard. His father, a cobbler, managed to produce a bare living for his family; his mother took in sewing and washing to supplement the inadequate family income. She hoped to see Stalin a priest and sent him to a theological seminary for training.

The circumstances of his expulsion from the seminary are obscure, but at about the turn of the century he was a professional revolutionary without any other trade or profession. Five times he was arrested for inciting strikes and circulating forbidden literature. Once he served out a term of punishment, but the other four times he escaped. At the beginning of World War I he was arrested for the sixth time and banished to Siberia. Along with other political prisoners he was released as a result of the March Revolution of 1917 and became a fellow conspirator of the Bolshevik leader Lenin. He was an insider in party councils and was little in the public eye. In the civil war which followed the November Revolution, Stalin was sent to the various fronts as political commissar to the Red Army.

But it was not Stalin's role either in the November Revolution of 1917 or in the civil war which brought him up the ladder to power. It was rather his determined grip on the Communist party machine which he began to acquire in the years before Lenin's death in 1924 and which he later welded into a unified whole. The Communist party was a disciplined, active minority. Stalin knew that control of its organization was a sure means of securing and preserving undisputed personal power, and he pursued this objective relentlessly. After he became Secretary-General of the Communist party and after Lenin's death, he moved swiftly and boldly to eliminate by public disgrace, imprisonment, exile, and death every rival leader of the group of old Bolsheviks, beginning with Trotsky and continuing with the others one by one for a period of fifteen years. When this purge had been completed, Stalin's authority in Russia over the party and the government was completely unchallenged. Of the seven members of the Politburo who had survived Lenin's death in 1924, Stalin alone remained.[8]

Throughout his career Stalin has been an enigma. Normally, he is disposed to retreat from the limelight. In consequence there have grown up about him walls of legend, both eulogistic and hostile. In Russia his followers speak of him as the "steel colossus," the "beloved leader," and the "Greatest of the Great." With this extravagant flattery, which Stalin

---

[8] Zinoviev and Kamenev were shot in 1936, Bukharin and Rykov in 1938; Tomsky was reported to have committed suicide; Trotsky was murdered in exile.

permits, it might seem that he is a vain man. Most observers believe that vanity is not one of his dominant characteristics, for there is abundant evidence to indicate that he is a shrewd, hardheaded realist. It seems quite likely that he permits the cult of personal adulation to grow in the belief that the Russian people need some personal symbol of supreme authority.

Among Stalin's lieutenants, all high in the party councils, are included:

SHVERNIK.—He became the Chairman of the *Presidium* of the Supreme Soviet in March, 1946. A party member since 1902, he was arrested for his political activities under the imperial state. Since the Revolution he has been a trade-union leader, rising to the position of President of the All-Union Central Committee of Trade-Unions (1930-1944). Within the party, he was a member of the Orgburo and is now an alternate member of the Politburo. Shvernik was President of the Supreme Soviet of the RSFSR and was President of the Soviet of Nationalities from 1937 to 1946.

VOROSHILOV.—Marshal of the Soviet Union, a Vice-Chairman of the Council of Ministers, he became Chairman of the Allied Control Commission in Hungary. He started to work in the mines when he was seven years old. Although he received very little formal education, he was politically active. He joined the party in 1903, participated in the Revolution of 1905, and became a War Commissar during the Russian civil war. Between the years 1925 to 1940 he was largely responsible for mechanizing the Red Army. During World War II he was a member of the State Defense Committee. A member of the Politburo since 1926, he has been associated with organizational work in the party, in the government, and in the Army. He was mainly responsible for the removal of factories eastward during the Nazi invasion.

VOZNESENSKY.—A brilliant "new" Bolshevik alternate member of the Politburo, he was appointed Chairman of the State Planning Commission in 1938. A Vice-Chairman of the Council of Ministers, he fathered the Third and Fourth Five-Year Plans.

BULGANIN.—A member of the Orgburo, an alternate member of the Politburo, an Army general, Deputy Minister of the Armed Forces, Mayor of Moscow, and Chairman of the Foreign Relations Committee of the Soviet of Nationalities, his specialty has been in political-economic fields. During the civil war he fought with the Red Army in Turkestan.

MALENKOV.—He is a member of the Party Secretariat, the Orgburo, the Politburo, and is a secretary of the Central Committee of the Communist party He has been a deputy in the Supreme Soviet since 1937. A party member since 1920, he has been an administrative worker. He directs the Orgburo. In order to establish the "party line" abroad, he helped to organize the Cominform in 1947, assisting Zhdanov, who died in 1948.

MIKOYAN.—After he joined the party in 1915 he was imprisoned by the Tsarist government. Subsequently he became a member of the Politburo, Minister of Foreign Trade, a Vice-Chairman of the Council of Ministers, Chairman of the Economic Council, and a deputy in the Supreme Soviet. During World War II he was a Vice-Chairman of the State Defense Committee.

MOLOTOV.—He became a revolutionary agitator while he was a student of the University of Kagan. He joined the Bolsheviks in 1906 and worked on the staff of *Pravda*. During the 1917 revolution he was associated with Lenin and Stalin. In 1921 he became a member of the Central Committee of the Communist party. He entered the Politburo in 1926 and served as premier for eleven years. He is the Minister of Foreign Affairs, a Vice-Chairman of the Council of Ministers, and Chairman of the Economic Council. During the past war he was a Vice-Chairman of the State Defense Committee.

KUZNETSOV.—An alternate on the Orgburo, Chairman of the Soviet of Nationalities, Vice-Chairman of the State Planning Commission, Chairman of the All-Union Central Committee of the Trade-Union of Ferrous Metallurgical Workers, and President of the All-Union Central Committee of Trade-Unions, he has a background in production problems which includes study at Carnegie Institute of Technology. He represented Soviet trade-unions in international labor organizations and the Soviet state in the United Nations.

BERIA.—A deputy chairman of the Council of Ministers, he was appointed Commissar for the Interior in 1938 and later became Commissar for State Security. A member of the Politburo, he is the top man in the Soviet police organization.

Institutional Integration in the Total State

THE TUTELAGE OF THE PARTY.—Although party membership is restricted, the regime rests upon a broad base of mass organizations under the direction of Bolshevik leaders. These organizers constantly stress civic obligations in their efforts to integrate all interests under the stimulus of developing and protecting a new social order. Government and party organs are linked with the various trade-unions, cooperatives, and civic associations in such fashion that all activities are enveloped in citizenship. For example, the Ministry of Education, which is as obedient to the party alignment as is every state office, coordinates the educational features of every organization in conformity with the official propaganda.

LABOR UNIONS AS GOVERNMENT AGENCIES.—The significance of workers' organizations in a "workers' state" can hardly be overestimated. All of Marxian political theory presupposes the existence of a factory-disciplined proletariat. Hence the growth of the place of occupation as the center of extracurricular learning and recreation in addition to being the point of most frequent contact between the state and the workers. The unions are regarded as schools of Communism which educate the workers in the proper attitudes toward labor relations under a planned economy.

During the period of the revolution and the civil war the relationship between the government and the unions was not clarified. Afterward, under the NEP, the unions were considered as nongovernmental organizations which were to strive for the improvement of labor conditions and to serve as a check to the state administration of nationalized industries. With the gradual extension of state management it became necessary to emphasize to the workers that, as a class, they derived more benefits if labor could be persuaded to increase its contribution to society rather than strive for a greater share of the profits of each plant. During the early years of the first Five-Year Plan some friction over the role of trade-unions developed between the union leaders and the state economic administrators. A purge of the union leadership resulted in the clarification of the principle that, when a dispute arises, the manager's orders must be carried out while the arbitration processes advance. Now, although the union representatives discuss on-the-spot problems with the plant managers, disputes are handled by joint labor-management conciliation commissions. If a commission fails to reach a unanimous decision, the disagreement must be settled in court.

The unions participate in over-all management in so far as the top union officials are members of the higher party and government councils. Also, the Central Council of Trade-Unions, which has assumed most of the functions of the former Commissariat of Labor, issues decrees on labor conditions which have the effect of law. In the factories, the unions participate during the discussions which precede the final directives on a plan. They may propose alterations and rationalizations for greater efficiency. The plan fixes the total and average wages. Previous to 1931 the unions assisted the state agencies in the classification of occupations and the setting of wage scales. Since that year the administration has made its decisions without consulting the unions formally. After 1935 the practice of collective bargaining ceased. Since 1933 the unions have administered the social insurance program. This fact is of particular importance because union members enjoy more social welfare benefits than do nonmembers. In general, the unions have become a semiofficial labor army which is organized to fulfill labor's mission on the economic front.

However, it must not be assumed that the unions, or any other institutions in a totalitarian state, are merely passive organs which carry out the directives of the ruling elite. To survive, a dictatorial machine must remain aware of the temper of the masses. Next to the party and the Soviets, the trade-unions are the most important bellwether in the Soviet Union.

STRUCTURE OF THE UNIONS.—Like the organization of the party and the state, the structure of the unions is pyramided, paralleling the party and Soviet levels in each territorial division. The unions are organized by industries which include everyone in each industry from the directors down through the janitors. For example, the union which organizes the judicial workers would include the judges, clerks, police staff, and maintenance workers. Above each union on the all-union level is the All-Union Congress. The All-Union Congress of each union sends delegates to the All-Union Congress of Trade-Unions. The Central Committee of the All-Union Congress of Trade-Unions deals with the Soviet government and participates in international labor movements. The chairman of the presidium of the All-Union Congress of Trade-Unions is usually a member of the All-Union government.

All employees of any industry may join that industry's union. Collective farms do not have unions, nor are collective farmers permitted to join the union in any plant where they may do seasonal work. Unlike the party, the unions are mass organizations which embrace around 25 million members. Membership is voluntary, but a certain amount of pressure is exerted upon eligible workers to join. The advantages of membership include legal assistance, recreational, educational, and social facilities, and special advantages in the national social security program.

The unions appoint the health and safety inspectors in each plant. On each level party representatives from the corresponding party agency direct the administration of the unions. There are no strikes or lockouts in Soviet labor relations, although those actions are not specifically forbidden. Instead, the unions have accepted the mission of influencing the formulation of labor policy through their interconnections with the party and the government. The unions also urge their members to greater productivity, always keeping before them the theory that, in a workers' state, everyone is in effect working for himself.

The Government of the USSR

THE SUPREME SOVIET OF THE USSR.—No very clear line between legislative and executive authority is drawn in the government of the Soviet Union.

Under the Constitution of 1936 the highest organ of all state power is the Supreme Soviet of the USSR. All legislative power is granted to this body. The Supreme Soviet is divided into two separate chambers, which are known as the Council of the Union and the Council of Nationalities.

Normally, elections to both of these bodies are held every four years, but the invasion of the Soviet Union by the German armies in June, 1941 disrupted the elections which should have been held in December of that year, and it was not until December, 1946, that this formality was resumed. The Council of the Union at that meeting consisted of 682 popularly elected deputies chosen from single-member districts on the basis of one for every 300,000 inhabitants. The election districts are redrawn before each national election. The Council of Nationalities, although likewise popularly elected from single-member districts, is chosen on a different basis of representation. Its membership of 657 is fixed according to the principle of national self-determination. It consists of representatives from the separate national groups on the basis of twenty-five from each constituent republic, eleven from each autonomous republic, five from each region (oblast), and one from each area.

The two chambers meet concurrently in separate session twice a year. Each elects its own officers, a president and two vice-presidents, and decides upon the validity of the elections of its members. They meet in joint session for the purpose of (1) selecting the members of the Presidium, an executive and legislative committee which functions in the place of the Supreme Soviet when it is not in session, (2) appointing the members of the Council of People's Ministers, an executive and administrative committee consisting of the heads of government departments, (3) electing members of the Supreme Court of the USSR, and (4) appointing an Attorney-General of the USSR. Special sessions may be called at the discretion of the Presidium or upon the demand of a constituent republic.

The two chambers enjoy equal legislative powers. No distinction is made between financial and other bills. To become a law, a bill must receive a simple majority vote in each house, but a two-thirds vote is necessary to amend the Constitution. In cases of disagreement, the proposed legislation is referred to a conciliation commission, made up of an equal number of deputies from each house. If this commission fails to arrive at a satisfactory compromise, the matter in question is returned to the chambers for reconsideration. If the deadlock still continues, the Presidium may then dissolve the Supreme Soviet and order elections of new deputies for the full four-year term.

Soviet deputies are usually ardent party workers whose election to the Supreme Soviet is considered a recognition of their capabilities. A deputy is granted many special privileges, including freedom from arrest without the consent of the Supreme Soviet, or in the event that body is not in session, of the Presidium.

THE PRESIDIUM.—The *Presidium* is a standing executive committee which has legislative functions in that it exercises the power of the Supreme Soviet when that body is not in session. It consists of a chairman, sixteen vice-chairmen (one for each constituent republic), a secretary, and twenty-four members, all of whom are selected by the Supreme Soviet from its own joint membership. Although the Constitution specifically provides a plural headship of the state in the form of the *Presidium* and makes no provisions for a chief executive, the President of the *Presidium* is usually considered to be the President of the Soviet Union. He performs those ceremonial functions usually performed by the head of state in other countries, such as the reception of foreign envoys.

The *Presidium* has been granted extensive powers, for the execution of which it is responsible to the Supreme Soviet. Included in its duties are the following: (1) convening and dissolving the Supreme Soviet; (2) calling new elections; (3) exercising the right of pardon; (4) awarding decorations; (5) appointing and replacing the high command of the armed forces; (6) carrying out referendums; (7) receiving, appointing, and recalling diplomats; (8) ratifying international treaties; and (9) declaring war in the event of invasion or in fulfillment of international obligations. But perhaps its more potent function is the judicial one of interpreting the existing law. This process consists mainly of examining, annulling, or modifying the orders and decisions of the administrative department heads of the Union and of the constituent republics. Briefly, then, the *Presidium* is a combined plural executive, legislative council, and, in one important respect, a judicial agency.

Since the *Presidium* functions continuously and the Supreme Soviet only periodically, the former is regarded as the most powerful element of the government of the Soviet Union. Joseph Stalin and other prominent Communists are members of the body, and they undoubtedly control its decisions. The influence of the *Presidium* has become so dominant that the Supreme Soviet is reduced to meeting on that body's invitation and ratifying its decrees. The Supreme Soviet has never dissented from any measure which has been submitted to it by the *Presidium*.

THE COUNCIL OF MINISTERS OF THE USSR.—Administrative power is exercised largely by a group of governmental agencies or departments called ministries (known as people's commissariats prior to March, 1946), each of which is headed by a minister. Appointed and removable by the Supreme Soviet, these several ministers are grouped together with certain other high government officials to form an executive council, called the Council of Ministers of the USSR. In addition to the ministers, this council includes a chairman or premier, vice-chairmen, and the chairmen of the following separate agencies: the State Planning Commission, the Commission of State Control, the Committee on Higher Education, the Administration of the State Bank, and the Committee on Arts. In its collective capacity this body is responsible to the Supreme Soviet for (1) directing and coordinating the work of federal departments, (2) administering the monetary and credit system, (3) making effective the Union budget and the Union economic plan, (4) maintaining public order and the defense of the interests of the Union, (5) organizing the armed forces, (6) creating commissions and other administrative organs to deal with economic, cultural, and military matters, and (7) suspending orders of the executive agencies of constituent republics which violate Union laws or decrees. In May, 1941, Stalin emerged from his officially obscure position as Secretary-General of the Communist party to accept the chairmanship of the then called Council of People's Commissars. Since this office is similar to a premiership in western European countries, Stalin may be considered the chief administrative official of the Soviet Union.

Although it might seem that the Council of Ministers bears some ministerial responsibility to the Supreme Soviet, such is not the case. It is true that individual ministers within the Council must answer interpellations addressed to them by members of the Supreme Soviet, yet the controls of the unified Communist party prevent normal ministerial responsibility. Individual members of the Council may be removed for cause, but the regime remains in power.

THE ALL-UNION MINISTRIES AND THE UNION-REPUBLIC MINISTRIES OF THE USSR.—Within the Council of Ministries of the USSR there are two kinds of ministries: (1) the All-Union Ministries, and (2) the Union-Republic Ministries of the USSR.

The All-Union Ministries function in a unitary manner. Directly, or through responsible officials and agencies whom they appoint, they exert control throughout the entire nation over the administration of certain matters of national concern, matters over which the constituent republics possess no individual jurisdiction. To facilitate coordination, each constituent republic sends a representative to Moscow, while each All-Union Ministry in turn maintains a representative in the capital cities of the several republics.

The Union-Republic Ministries of the USSR, on the other hand, operate in certain limited fields definitely local in character and scope. They have counterparts which exist and function entirely within, and as agencies of, the constituent republics. The types of these ministries are listed for each constituent republic and the lists are confirmed by the *Presidium* of the Soviet Union. As we have noted, each constituent republic is permitted a certain degree of independent action in the fields assigned to it. The Supreme Soviet of the constituent republic appoints the ministers and establishes the ministries it needs, to correspond to those of the USSR. The ministries of the constituent republic are to a degree autonomous and are coordinated in each separate field throughout the union by the corresponding Union-Republic Ministries of the USSR, each within its own field.

Since the Soviet government participates not only in the usual political functions of a state, but in every activity of an economic, political, social, and cultural nature, its administrative departments or ministries are numerous. Thus they include such divisions as shipbuilding, coal mining, machine tool industries, building materials, and chemical industries as well as foreign affairs, navy, and agriculture. Also, the divisions are being constantly revised as the Soviet Union becomes more industrialized and smaller industries grow. As a result, it is futile to list the specific ministries, for the list would be no sooner published than out of date.

THE ALL-UNION MINISTRY FOR INTERNAL AFFAIRS.—Since its creation in 1934 as the All-Union People's Commissariat for Internal Affairs, this ministry has had an important part in the preservation of the political power of the Communist regime. It absorbed and has come to direct the secret political police organization—known successively as Cheka, OGPU, NKVD, and MVD—which operates throughout the Soviet Union to extirpate objectors to governmental policy. Although it is an executive agency, this ministry has for years exercised unlimited powers of imprisonment and death over Soviet citizens, without the necessity of complying with judicial procedure calculated to protect individual rights. The principal duties of the ministry are to protect the Communist regime, to repress domestic disturbances, to control the frontiers, and to supervise concentration camps and compulsory labor projects. It has several hundred thousand special troops at its disposal for carrying out these purposes.

THE STATE PLANNING COMMISSION.—The State Planning Commission (*Gosplan*) is the chief economic planning authority of the Soviet Union. It has advisory powers only; the execution of its plans is the function of the Council of Ministers. Since its creation in 1921, however, and since the adoption of the policy of administration on the basis of five-year plans, the Commission has acquired enormous importance. No major step in agriculture, industry, transportation, or finance is taken by the Council of Ministers unless it conforms to the national econmic plan as set forth by the Commission. The balanced economic development of the Soviet Union along socialist lines rests upon the schemes initially formulated by the State Planning Commission. In order to become effective, its plans must be ratified by certain party organs (usually by the All-Union Central Committee, and sometimes by the All-Union Congress); then, as a matter of form only, they are submitted for the approval of the higher institutions of the state. In the formulation of its plans, the State Planning Commission is given authority to investigate the actual performance of the various industrial ministries for the purpose of coordinating separate enterprises and strengthening central administrative responsibility.

The State Planning Commission has seventy members, appointed by the Council of Ministers to head the vast administration established for the collection and correlation of the factual information necessary for the preparation of a feasible national economic plan. Several thousand employees, including a small army of statisticians, assist the Commission. These governmental workers are organized into a complex network of planning institutions.

THE ALL-UNION PEOPLE'S COMMISSION FOR STATE CONTROL.—The Commission for State Control, the governmental counterpart of the Commission of Party Control, was created in 1940. Its purpose is to establish control over the accounting and expenditure of state funds and material values, and over the execution of governmental decisions. The supervision of the nation's economic plans is in its hands.

ELECTIONS AND SUFFRAGE.—The electoral system of the Soviet Union was revised in the Constitution of 1936. The right to vote was given to all citizens over eighteen years of age, irrespective of sex, race, nationality, religion, education, residence, social origin, property status, or past political activity. Only the insane and persons condemned by a court of law were denied the vote. The franchise carries with it the right to hold public office. Both of these rights are expressly granted to members of the armed forces by a special article in the Constitution.

Elections are required to be held by secret ballot. Every citizen casts one vote directly for his choice. The lists of voters are prepared by the local soviets, who also maintain a close check on those who vote and those who do not. On election day ballot boxes are distributed everywhere—even on trains. A voter, absent from his own district, may vote at the nearest polling place by showing the registry slip issued him by his local authorities.

No candidate may stand for election from more than one constituency, although he need not be a resident of the district in which he finally stands for election. To be elected, he must poll a majority of the votes cast. If no candidate receives a clear majority, a runoff election between the two leading candidates is held within two weeks. To date, there is no record of more than one candidate for each position on any ticket. A majority of the voters in any constituency may recall an unsatisfactory representative.

The Communist party controls this electoral system by its initiative and activity on its own behalf. The Communist party as the only official party in the Soviet Union has fortified its position by securing recognition in the Constitution. In addition the party controls the public organizations which are empowered to make nominations: soviets, trade-unions, cooperatives, cultural societies, and Communist party organizations. In recent elections there has been only one list of candidates nominated. That list can be voted for or scratched out by secret ballot. No provision is made for the substitution of names on the ballot.

Governments of Constituent Republics and Local Subdivisions

CONSTITUENT REPUBLICS.—The similarity between the pattern of government for the sixteen constituent republics (SSR) and that of the Soviet Union is striking. The highest organ of state power in a constituent republic is a unicameral Supreme Soviet, popularly elected for a term of four years. Representation in this Soviet is based upon the constitutional provisions of the particular republic. Among the functions of the Soviet of the constituent republic are (1) the adoption of a constitution for the constituent republic, which it may amend in conformity with the provisions of the Constitution of the USSR; (2) the ratification of the constitutions and definition of the territorial boundaries of such autonomous republics as may be appurtenant to it; (3) the approval of a plan of national economy and a budget of the constituent republic; and (4) the election of the constituent republic's Supreme Court. It also elects a *Presidium* for the republic, whose membership and duties are defined in the republic's constitution, and it appoints a Council of Ministers which is the highest executive and administrative organ of state power in the constituent republic.

The Council of Ministers of the constituent republic is responsible and accountable to the Supreme Soviet of the Union. In the intervals between sessions of the Supreme Soviet, this Council is responsible and accountable to the Union's *Presidium*. The Council makes decisions and issues orders on the basis of (1) the laws in operation in the USSR and the constituent republic, and (2) the decisions and orders of the All-Union Council of Ministers. Moreover, it supervises the administration of its directives.

Like the Soviet Union, each constituent republic has two sets of ministries. First, there are those corresponding to the Union-Republic Ministries of the USSR to which they are separately responsible. These agencies are also responsible to their own republic's Council of Ministers. Second, there are ministries of the constituent republic which administer particular fields entrusted to them and are responsible only to their republic's Council of Ministers.

LOCAL SUBDIVISIONS.—Each Autonomous Soviet Socialist Republic (ASSR) within the large constituent republics (SSR) has a constitution.

GOVERNMENT OF THE U.S.S.R.

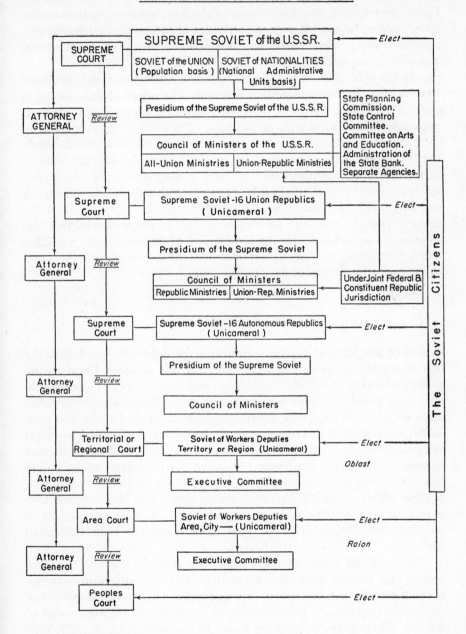

These governments are similar to the governments of the constituent republics, although their spheres of action are more restricted. Like the Union government, the governments of the constituent republics exercise a high degree of control over the activities of the smaller territorial subdivisions under their particular jurisdictions, including those of the autonomous republics (ASSR).

In the territories, regions, areas, districts, cities, and rural communities the organization is somewhat different. The organ of state power in each of these is a Soviet of Workers' Deputies, a committee which is popularly elected for a term of two years. The ratio of representation in these soviets is prescribed in the constitutions of the constituent republics. They direct the activities of the administrative agencies subordinate to them, ensure the observance of laws, protect the rights of citizens, maintain public order, direct local economic and cultural developments, and determine the local budgets. Executive and administrative functions are performed by executive committees elected by the Soviets of Workers' Deputies in accordance with the constitution of the constituent republics. These committees are directly responsible to the soviets electing them and to the executive organs of next higher units.

Judicial Organization

ORIGINS OF THE JUDICIAL SYSTEM.—Following the Bolshevik Revolution, the administration of justice was highly irregular and unstable. Local revolutionary tribunals operated informally in such ways as to be indistinguishable from political groups bent on persecution. Worse, the secret police assumed the power to make arrests, to conduct so-called trials, and summarily to execute their victims without permitting the accused any legal safeguards. Gradually these procedures were regularized and their harsher features ameliorated. Even today, however, justice in the Soviet Union is administered under a revolutionary psychology and under conditions of rigor which would be considered unjust under free governments. Law is not considered to be superior to government. It is an instrument of political rule. Public order is rated more important than individual liberty.

The judicial system operates under the provisions of the Constitution of 1936 and the Judiciary Law of 1938. The administration of justice is conducted by the law courts in cooperation with the legal officers of the state. However, the independence of the judges of the courts and of the law officers exists only in the words of the basic laws. Actually they are subjected to party and administrative pressures to such an extent that the judiciary has only nominal independence. The judiciary's prime function is to protect the regime from its enemies in accordance with

Lenin's declaration that law is politics and jurisprudence the will of the ruling class. As a result, although it normally can be depended upon to adjudicate fairly those cases which arise among citizens, it does not possess the same impartiality with reference to the citizens' claims or interests as opposed to those of the government.

THE SYSTEM OF COURTS.—Constitutionally, the rendering of justice is one of the functions shared by the Union with the constituent republics of the federation, although, as one would expect, all essential control is retained in Moscow. Except for the Supreme Court of the USSR, all courts are organs of the republics or of their subdivisions, and in each jurisdiction there are three levels of courts. The lowest are People's Courts to which minor civil and criminal cases are taken. These courts are usually conducted by a popularly elected judge assisted by two laymen called assessors, who are also elected to a panel from which they serve in rotation. Candidates are nominated by the Communist party, Red Army units, collective farmers, or other groups, and serve for a term of three years. The assessors, however, continue their normal employment, serving on the court for ten days or so a year. All citizens who have had two years' trade-union or other public experience may be selected as judges or assessors. The three members of the court sit on both civil and criminal cases, and each has an equal vote on matters of law and fact. The verdict rendered is the decision of the majority. There are no juries in Soviet courts.

Above the People's Courts are the courts of the territories, regions, areas, and autonomous republics, with the members thereof elected by their respective soviets of working people's deputies for five-year terms. These courts have original jurisdiction for both the more serious offenses of a criminal or civil nature, such as counterrevolutionary activity or theft of socialized property, and actions involving state institutions.

The autonomous and constituent republics have their own Supreme Courts elected by their Supreme Soviets for five-year terms. These courts as well as the inferior courts have assessors and judges.

SUPREME COURT OF THE USSR.—Elected by the Supreme Soviet of the USSR, the Supreme Court of the USSR is the highest court of the land. Its thirty or more judges sit in criminal, civil, and military sections and have five-year terms of office. They handle appeals from the high courts of the republics in cases involving federation law, controversies between republics, and charges against USSR officials. The officers of this court supervise all the courts of the USSR and render advisory opinions on the constitutionality of law without possessing at the same time any power to declare a law or decree unconstitutional.

LEGAL OFFICERS OF THE STATE.—The chief legal officer of the Soviet government is the Attorney-General of the USSR. On his own initiative or following complaint by citizens he investigates and prosecutes for graft, sabotage, or any misuse of public property by administrative departments and individuals alike. In a socialized state, where the livelihood of all depends upon the proper use of public wealth, this office assumes tremendous importance.

The makers of the Soviet Constitution desired that the Attorney-General, as investigator and prosecutor, should be given great independence from all other officials. Thus he is appointed by, and is responsible to, the Supreme Soviet for a term of seven years, which is longer than the term of any other official, elected or appointed. The Attorney-General appoints for a term of five years the state attorneys of the constituent republics. These attorneys in turn appoint, subject to the approval of the Attorney-General, the attorneys of the districts and localities for a term of five years. All attorneys are responsible to the Attorney-General and are independent of any interference or control by any of the lower layers of government. These legal officers of the Union and of the republics work through their respective Ministries of Justice and are limited to the functions of investigation and prosecution. Final judgment is reserved for the court before which the case is tried. The whole state attorney organization, which is more highly centralized than the court system, is entirely independent of any agency save that which appoints it, the Supreme Soviet.

PRINCIPLES OF JUDICIAL PROCEDURE.—Under the law of 1938 certain general principles of judicial practice were stated. They include the equality of all citizens before the law; the uniformity of criminal and civil procedure throughout the union; the independence of judges, who are subject only to the law; the use of local languages in the courts; the right of the defendant (with certain exceptions) to legal defense; the publicity of court records (except in certain cases); and the elective character of the judiciary. In the interests of the independence of the judiciary, judges and assessors may be removed only by being recalled by the bodies which elected them or by decision of a higher court. The Attorney-General is the only official empowered to initiate criminal action against them, and even he must have the sanction of the *Presidium* of the USSR before he can act.

Armed Forces

THE DEVELOPMENT OF THE RED ARMY.—From the standpoint of emphasis, the development of the Red Army may be divided into three main periods. During the first period, 1918-1925, Soviet armed forces were under the control and influence of Leon Trotsky. Major emphasis was placed upon political indoctrination and partisan warfare, to the neglect

RELATIONSHIP OF THE COMMUNIST PARTY to the GOVERNMENT OF THE U.S.S.R.

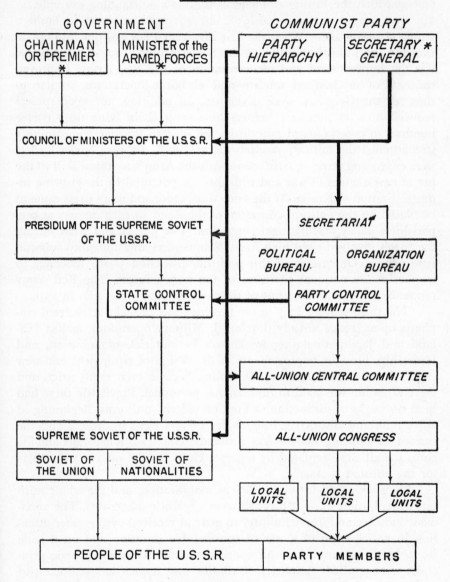

GOVERNMENT

COMMUNIST PARTY

CHAIRMAN OR PREMIER *	MINISTER of the ARMED FORCES *

PARTY HIERARCHY	SECRETARY * GENERAL

COUNCIL OF MINISTERS OF THE U.S.S.R.

PRESIDIUM OF THE SUPREME SOVIET OF THE U.S.S.R.

SECRETARIAT

POLITICAL BUREAU	ORGANIZATION BUREAU

STATE CONTROL COMMITTEE

PARTY CONTROL COMMITTEE

ALL-UNION CENTRAL COMMITTEE

ALL-UNION CONGRESS

SUPREME SOVIET OF THE U.S.S.R.

SOVIET OF THE UNION	SOVIET OF NATIONALITIES

LOCAL UNITS	LOCAL UNITS	LOCAL UNITS

PEOPLE OF THE U.S.S.R.	PARTY MEMBERS

* Indicates positions held by Generalissimo Stalin

of creating strong, standing, professional forces. On the other hand, every effort was made to guarantee the growth of a loyal and politically well-indoctrinated officer corps. Numerous military schools were started, among which the Frunze Academy is the most outstanding example.

The second period, 1926-1936, saw energetic attempts to build a strong standing army. When the first Five-Year Plan was put into operation for the industrialization of the Soviet Union, part of its purpose was the improvement and modernization of the Red Army. Improved concepts of mechanized warfare and air-borne operations, similar to those of the Germans, were developed. In addition, the geographical redistribution of industrial centers in a great chain lying from twelve hundred to two thousand miles from the western frontier immeasurably strengthened the military position of the USSR. By 1934 Soviet leaders were expressing growing satisfaction with the Army's technical skill in the use of new engines of war and with the war potential in the growing industrialization of Russia. At the same time, more and more stress came to be placed on the political education of the Army in such matters as preparedness policy and national patriotism. The purges and trials during the 1930's involved eight high Army commanders and numerous subordinate officers. One result of this political dissension was a tendency to emphasize the national character of the armed forces. The Red Army renounced its role as the army of the international proletariat in 1939.

The third period, 1937 to the present time, brought accelerated emphasis upon trends already developed. Military operations against Finland and Japan, disclosing weaknesses in matériel, organization, and leadership, brought improvements in the design of equipment and new emphasis on tactical training. Discipline became even more strict, and more attention was paid to rank among personnel. Previously there had been no marks of distinction or rank on officers' uniforms. Beginning in 1940, rank and distinctive insignia for officers were instituted, and the custom of saluting officers was restored. The traditional rank-and-file clubs for all were replaced by separate clubs for the officers and others for the enlisted ranks.

Plans were laid for more efficient mobilization, and the whole military organization was put through severe, realistic maneuvers. The armament industry and heavy industry in general received even greater attention in anticipation of a war of considerable duration and on a wide front. In the organization and operation of the Army three basic principles were applied: simplicity, flexibility, and improvisation. Successful application of these principles made the Red Army the effective instrument it became during World War II.

THE HIGH COMMAND.—The supreme direction of the Soviet armed forces is in the hands of Generalissimo Joseph Stalin. He is Commander in Chief of all of the military forces of the USSR. As Chairman of the State Defense Committee, he had over-all control of the country during the war. The Committee had a total of eight members. It was organized when the German invasion of Russia began in 1941, and it exercised full legal authority over all citizens, party organizations, communal institutions, and armed forces. For the duration of World War II this body was the supreme organ of government of the Soviet Union. The Supreme Soviet, the *Presidium,* and the Council of People's Commissars of the USSR delegated to it all of their constitutional powers. Its dual function was to mobilize the people and resources of the Soviet Union and to organize resistance to the invaders. The committee was abolished September 4, 1945.

Under the Constitution, the Supreme Soviet has the power to determine questions of war and peace, a power exercised by the *Presidium* in intervals between sessions. The *Presidium* of the Supreme Soviet is also entrusted with appointments to the high command and dismissals and changes therein, but this power was exercised by the State Defense Committee during the war. The administration of the Ministry of the Armed Forces under Stalin controls all of the military forces of the Union and the General Staff.

The projected Five-Year Plans include plans to improve the defensive power of the USSR and to supply the armed forces with the most modern equipment. Much emphasis has been attached to scientific research (including development of atomic weapons) with respect to national defense.

THE RED ARMY.—The strength of the Red Army and the resources and man-power which support it make the Soviet Union one of the world's leading military powers. The Soviet Union has followed the European practice of conscripting all of its physically fit young men for military service according to age groups. With its population of 211,000,000 people the Union has great man-power reserves for military service. Since 1936 the minimum draft age has been reduced, first to nineteen and then to seventeen. A new peacetime military service law in 1939 established as periods of active service two years for the infantry, three for the air force and border guard, four for coast defense and coast guard, and five for the Navy. After fulfilling his term of service the Soviet citizen passes successively into the first, second, and third reserve, the latter ending at the age of fifty.

A decree published in September, 1941, required all male Soviet citizens between the ages of sixteen and fifty to take military training outside working hours. Before being called up for induction, the Soviet recruit receives preliminary instruction in the elements of soldiering in the Association for Defense through Aviation and Chemical Warfare (*Osoa-*

viakhim). Founded in 1927, it has become one of the largest organizations in the world for instructing civilians in military science. On the eve of the recent war it counted twelve million members of both sexes, and it dealt with almost every aspect of training for war, especially amateur aviation, gliding, parachute jumping, rifle marksmanship, air raid drill and first aid measures, training in the use of gas masks, and physical development. It has been estimated that through such methods as these eleven million Soviet citizens received thorough military training between 1925 and 1940. As a result, Russia entered World War II with vastly more man-power reserves than any other power in the anti-Hitler coalition.

The strength of the Red Army can only be estimated broadly. It was believed that some five million troops were in action on the European front in early 1945, supported by fourteen million reserves in various stages of training. In addition, the Far Eastern armies were supposed to contain at least a million and a half troops. The Soviet government has announced demobilization plans for "millions" of soldiers, but exact figures are not available.[9]

COMMUNISM AND THE ARMED FORCES.—The Communist party plays a unique and vital role in its relationship to the Red Army. The party is officially acknowledged as the organizer, leader, and guiding spirit of the Soviet armed forces, and its influence and control extend to all aspects of military life. Communist party cells are organized in every unit. Political control begins within the governmental agencies of the High Command and extends through the chain of command to a large proportion of the total military and naval personnel. In 1941, just before the German invasion of the Soviet Union, more than 50 per cent of all Soviet armed forces belonged to Communist party organizations.[10]

Beyond Communist control of the higher echelons and its permeation of the rank and file, the party exerts its influence over the armed forces through an extensive and continuing program of political education. The commander of every military unit down to company grade is responsible for the political education of his men, and in every such unit there is an assistant commander for political work. These assistant commanders have had no authority to interfere with the technical command functions of unit commanders since 1942. They have a separate chain of command, however, and in their duties they are directed by the Chief Political Administration of the Red Army and its subdivisions.

Members of the Communist party in the armed forces are expected

---

[9] In June, 1946, a "high Allied military source" estimated that the Soviet Union had six million men under arms, and that the long-range number would be four and a half million.

[10] The *Komsomol*, with a membership of ten and a half million in 1941, in-cluded many members of the armed forces.

to assume special responsibilities. By personal example they are expected to lead all others in military activities. They have an obligation to instill patriotic feeling, loyalty to the regime, and discipline among their fellows in the services.

THE RED AIR FORCE.—The air force of Soviet Russia is designed to cooperate with ground forces and the fleet, to perform long-range bombardment missions, and to defend important strategic areas. The personnel is selected from volunteers among those called up for military service. Before the recent war there were, in addition to the *Osoaviakhim,* more than a thousand flying clubs from which the Red Air Force could draw reserves. Soviet aviation has been pre-eminent in winter and polar flying. It also was an early developer of mass parachute drops.

THE RED FLEET.—In the begining of World War II the Red Fleet had three old battleships, one modern cruiser, six up-to-date cruisers, two old cruisers, an undetermined number of small submarines, and seventy destroyers. Some additions from Britain and the United States included the British battleship "Royal Sovereign," the United States cruiser "Milwaukee," destroyers, submarines, and torpedo boats. Also it has received portions of the German, Italian, and Japanese fleets. The Red naval forces consist of four fleets: the Baltic, the Black Sea, the Pacific, and the Northern; and the flotillas on the Amur, Dnieper, and Caspian Sea. All of the elements of the naval forces are under the administration of the Ministry of the Armed Forces. In 1948, spokesmen for the United States Navy pointed out that the Soviet Union was constructing large numbers of advanced-type submarines.

Foreign Policy

ORIGINS OF SOVIET FOREIGN POLICY.—The objectives of Soviet foreign policy still include many of the objectives of Tsarist foreign policy. The security of Russia's territory from armed aggression remains a prime objective as does the security of the form of government, even though that form of government changed in 1917 from an autocratic monarchy to a totalitarian Marxist state capitalism. The geographic situation inherited by the Soviet government from its predecessor gave it the same interests in areas on the nation's borders and the same ambitions for such objectives as warm water ports and an increased voice in control of the Dardanelles, if not indeed the undisputed control of that waterway. The Pan-Slav movement is another recurring thread in the Russian pattern. Pan-Slavism contributed to the occurrence of the unfortunate incident that precipitated World War I. The threat to the Pan-Slav movement from Nazi moves in the Balkans was a major factor in bringing the USSR into World War II. Indeed, Soviet success in its Pan-Slav movement has far exceeded the fondest dreams of Imperial Russia. The interlocking trade and mutual assistance pacts which today tightly bind the USSR with the Balkan states is a measure of its success. Pan-Slavism coupled with Marxian ideology gives to the USSR foreign policy advantages in the Slavic states with which the Western nations find it hard to compete.

The Bolshevik leaders who came to power in Russia in 1917 had little knowledge of, and no experience in, foreign relations. Their experience and conditioning had been in agitation and in the organization of revolution. Their policy bibles, the writings of Marx and Engels, gave little guidance in diplomacy. Rather, these leaders anticipated that there would be a world-wide revolution of the proletariat and a withering away of states. Hence, there would be no need for foreign relations or a foreign policy. Another grave difficulty, besetting the Soviet state at its birth, was the universal distrust, if not open hostility, with which the remainder of the world viewed the new Soviet regime just come to power in a weakened and disorganized country.

At an early date the Soviet leaders had to make some basic decisions as to their foreign policy. The nature of these decisions must be deduced in great part from the detailed acts of the Soviet government. Presumably these decisions, like most basic policies of nations, were reached by evolution of thought and only after a great deal of conflict among the leaders. The initial trend of thought in foreign policy is apparent in an early decree which declared that the newly formed Soviet government considered it necessary to come to the aid of left-internationalist workers' movements of all countries, and which allocated two million rubles for the needs of the revolutionary Internationalist movement. This initial act indicated that the new Soviet government in its foreign policy was emphasizing the thesis of world revolution.

It appears that the Soviet leaders definitely decided with the expulsion of Trotsky to direct their initial foreign relations primarily to building the USSR as a single socialistic state, rather than devoting their first efforts to permanent world-wide revolution. This decision was not reached all at once, and not without great internal conflict, in which the high light was the struggle between Stalin and the leading advocate of permanent revolution, Trotsky.

In the Communist parties within the other nations of the world, the Soviet leaders had subterranean implements of foreign relations which could be utilized either to advance the cause of Soviet nationalistic foreign relations, or the cause of Communist world revolution—or both. The Third International, or Comintern, organized in 1919, was an implement for directing and controlling these fifth-column spearheads of the Communist movement. When originally organized, the Comintern appears to have been directed primarily toward the promotion of world revolution. As Stalin's control developed, however, the Comintern was soft-pedaled for a period of six years, and when it reappeared in 1935 it seems to have set as its basic objective the support of Soviet national interests, whatever they might be, rather than world revolution.

Put very simply, then, the major objective of Soviet foreign policy between the two World Wars became the increase of the strength and security of the USSR. This end could be achieved in two ways: increasing the absolute strength of the USSR, and decreasing the strength of possible opponents. Action along either of these complementary lines contributed, moreover, to the cause of world communism. If a country can be weakened by internal political dissension, or its government actually taken over by Communists, the relative position of the USSR national state is thereby enhanced. Hence, for reasons of nationalism, as well as world revolution, the Soviet government would obviously support, either officially or unofficially, or both, the interests of Communist, revolutionary, and left-wing parties in other countries of the world.

It is noteworthy (and logical) that the Soviet government conducted its foreign relations with the element of suspicion as a strong basic factor. Suspicion and deceit were major elements in forwarding the Communist revolution in Russia. Suspicion is a major element in the Soviet internal administration system. The Soviet government was launched in a world which, at that time, clearly showed its distrust of the new USSR. The basic ideology of Soviet Communism, throughout its various changes, has preserved as a main tenet the irreconcilable conflict between Soviet Communism and other forms of government and economic orders. In 1924 Stalin specifically stated that, ". . . . as long as there is a capitalist encirclement there will be danger of intervention with all the consequences that flow from that danger. . . ."

Although Stalin's observation was made in connection with his defense of what he called "organs of repression," the Army and the secret police, it indicates the essential consistency which must exist between the domestic and foreign policy of any nation. Apparently, in 1924 the Soviet government felt it necessary to present the specter of capitalist encirclement in order to excuse its internal governmental policy as a drastic contrast to the dearth of government controls and governmental interference outlined in pure Marxian theory. The specter of capitalist encirclement has not been discarded but rather has been paraded more vividly, and more often, in the post-World War II period.

PERIOD OF ISOLATION, 1917-1921.—The national foreign policy of Soviet Russia during its embryonic period 1917-1921 can perhaps best be described as latent. Because of the weakness of the new government it was a policy of isolationism designed to give the Bolsheviks opportunity to consolidate their position and strengthen their control. In order to withdraw from World War I the Bolsheviks were forced to accept from Germany the harsh terms of the Treaty of Brest-Litovsk. From 1917 to 1921 Russia was the scene of bitter civil wars and armed foreign intervention which was in part directed at preventing war materials from falling into German hands, but also tended to support the re-establishment in Russia of a more politically acceptable form of government and one that would continue active participation in the Allied war effort. During this period the Russian people were subjected to the most militant form of Communism. The statements of the Bolshevik leaders indicate clearly that they were imbued with the Marxian doctrine of the creation of a global commonwealth of workers through the revolutionary overthrow of all existing bourgeois governments. In 1919 the Comintern, as we have noted, was formed under the aegis of the Soviet Communist party for the avowed purpose of spreading the Marxian revolution and thus world Communism. Although there was no official connection between the Comintern and the Soviet government, the identity of their policies was strikingly apparent. The year 1921 found the USSR in a state of economic chaos, shorn of many former Tsarist-Russian border regions, and barred diplomatically and economically from Europe by a *cordon sanitaire* (designed by the capitalist states of Europe for that very purpose), but finally emerging in a state of peace under which the Communist experiment might be furthered.

PERIOD OF RAPPROCHEMENT, 1921-1933.—The next twelve years found the USSR directing her foreign policy toward breaching the *cordon sanitaire,* which blocked Soviet contact with the remainder of the world. The USSR sought security by separate pacts of neutrality and nonaggression with individual neighboring nations rather than depending on the League of Nations and its collective action except for disarmament. Her efforts were in part successful, and a number of diplomatic and trade pacts were signed with such states as Great Britain, Germany, China, Turkey, and others. By 1925 the European countries began, though hesitatingly, to acknowledge the Soviet regime. In succeeding years Moscow was successful in signing an even more elaborate network of neutrality, nonintervention and nonaggression pacts. The *cordon sanitaire* had been effectively breached, and Moscow felt that the infant Communism was fairly safe from outside interference. The bogey of capitalistic encirclement and aggression was, however, resurrected by the Soviet rulers when the internal political situation demanded.

With the immediate security of the Soviet state seemingly guaranteed, the USSR turned to another facet of her foreign policy—that of weakening her "enemies." She proposed a number of disarmament conferences and was the first to sign the Kellogg-Briand Pact in 1928. The sixth World Congress of the Comintern (1928) explained the motives of the Soviet's disarmament policy: "The aim of the Soviet proposals was not to spread pacifist illusions, but to destroy them; not to support capitalism . . . but to propagate the fundamental Marxian postulate that disarmament and the abolition of war are possible only with the fall of capitalism. . . . It goes without saying that not a single Communist thought for a minute that the imperialists would accept the Soviet disarmament proposals."

The role that the Marxian world revolution was to play in the Soviet scheme of things had been hotly contested in Soviet councils. This role was superficially determined by the overthrow of the Trotsky faction in the USSR by the Stalin group in 1926. Stalin propounded the thesis of "socialism in a single country" and rejected the Trotsky thesis of the necessity of continued violent and unrelenting action to achieve the revolutionary overthrow of all bourgeois governments. Subsequent actions, too numerous to be ignored, raise a very serious question as to whether Stalin rejects the ultimate Marxian goal of world Communism by world revolution. Perhaps Stalin was, and is, merely following the opportunistic tactics advocated by Lenin at an earlier date.

THE "POPULAR FRONT," 1934-1938.—The emergence of the militarists as the real power in Japan and the establishment of Hitler as the German dictator caused Russian policy to enter upon its third phase. Collective security was accepted in a series of political alliances with capitalist nations. The Soviet Union exhibited a great readiness to cooperate with the liberal forces in capitalistic countries and to enter into arrangements which would be more positive than nonaggression pacts. In a reversal of its former attitude, the Soviet Union joined the League of Nations. Treaties of mutual assistance were entered into with France and Czechoslovakia.

The Comintern, responsive to this shift in the foreign policy of the Union, abandoned its advocacy of violent revolution for advocacy of a "popular front," in opposition to Fascism, a unity of combined socialist, radical, and liberal groups and parties. However, the USSR's interest and support of the policy of collective security waned as British and French appeasement of the Fascists with regard to Ethiopia, Spain, and Czechoslovakia convinced Soviet policy makers that British and French policy was primarily anti-Soviet. The exclusion of the Soviet Union from the Munich Conference in the fall of 1938 was a severe blow to Soviet pride. Germany had succeeded in isolating the Soviets. The British, who in Soviet eyes were attempting to play the Soviet Union off against Germany, by the same interpretation had successfully drawn France away from her Soviet alliance. After this rebuff, the Soviet Union again withdrew from the collective security system and by her agreement with Germany in August, 1939, came to rely once more on her own resources in the international game of power politics.

THE SOVIET-GERMAN PACT, 1939-1941.—The USSR was not invited to the Munich sacrificial table in September, 1938. Eleven months later the Soviet Union concluded a trade and nonaggression pact with Germany whom she had seemingly been opposing violently up to the date of signature. The startled world had again witnessed a tactical maneuver in foreign policy amounting to a diplomatic revolution. The Communist party line, the world around, shifted on the date of signature from a prodemocracies, anti-Fascist talk to emphasis on the "capitalistic, imperialistic" nature of both the Allies and Axis. The mutual division of Poland by the USSR and Germany followed the Nazis' conquest of that nation. With forced equanimity these two strange partners watched each other go into the Baltic States, Finland, Bukovina, and France. The equanimity vanished, however, when both powers began to focus attention on the Balkans, an area apparently envisioned by each as its special sphere of action. Within three months of the German invasion of Yugoslavia the strange partners were at war with each other. At "best" the policy of the USSR had bought her time to prepare, had produced some sapping of resources of Western nations, and had permitted the occupation of certain strategic areas. If she could win in the end, it might prove a fairly good "best." Soviet "short-run" foreign policy, however, had to undergo again a chameleonlike reorientation. No longer could Molotov proclaim, as he had a year previously, that "ideology cannot be destroyed by force. It is, therefore, not only senseless but criminal to wage such a war (against Nazi Germany) camouflaged as a fight for 'democracy.'"

The publication in January, 1948, by the United States State Department of the documents pertaining to Nazi-Soviet relations, 1939-1941, which were in the captured German Foreign Office files, threw definitive light on Soviet foreign policy during this period. The records appeared to confirm that the USSR programed a hardheaded territorial exploitation of the crisis between the Axis and the Western democracies. The Soviet objectives included not only the Baltic States, portions of Poland, and Bessarabia but also control of the Dardanelles, security of the Balkans, and assurance that "the area south of Batum and Baku in the general direction of the Persian Gulf (Iran, Iraq, Afghanistan) is recognized as the center of the aspirations of the Soviet Union." Soviet objectives stated to Hitler were a logical continuation of Tsarist foreign policy and, when Hitler rebelled from acceding to them, the USSR was precipitated into the camp of the ultimate victors in World War II.

USSR IN WORLD WAR II, JUNE 1941–FEBRUARY 1945.—The Communist parties in every country now eagerly and even fanatically supported the

Allied states in their war, a war which a few days before they had derided
as a "capitalistic, imperialistic slaughter of the worker." Communists and
Communist organizations worked fanatically in the undergrounds of the
German-occupied countries. While they contributed to the war effort,
they also established themselves in relatively strong positions for the readjustment which was bound to come in each country with axis defeat, and
unquestionably anticipated and prepared for their postwar course of
action by paving the way for the communization of the liberated countries.

Numerous expressions of mutual good will and singleness of purpose were exchanged between the leaders of the other Allied states and
the Soviet. Stalin officially disbanded the Comintern in 1943 and proclaimed that his act "exposes the lie of the Hitlerites that Moscow in-
tends to intervene in the life of other nations." [11]

Victory swung to the so-called United Nations, slowly at first in late
1942 and early 1943, then with ever-increasing acceleration. It was apparent that, for the first time since the peace of Vienna in 1815, the Russian
role in general world readjustment would be important. It was logical
that the USSR, as well as every other potential victor, should be far-
sighted and forehanded in guarding postwar interests. Wars are not
fought with military victory as the sole end objective. Rather, military
victory is the means to achieve certain nationalistic aims. From a standpoint of practical world politics, therefore, it was sound for the Soviet
Union to direct her military force and military arrangements, at the time
of axis capitulation, so that national objectives would be "in hand"
rather than "in the bush" of peace treaty negotiations.

The other major members of the United Nations had made known
their war objectives in statements which were often broad generalities.
The USSR had subscribed to these—the Atlantic Charter (1941), the
United Nations Declaration (1942), the Teheran Declaration (1943),
the Yalta Declaration (1945), and the Potsdam Declaration (1945). Only
the declarations pertaining to the Pacific indicated any precise nature of
specific implementation. The USSR cooperated in the steps to set up the
United Nations as a postwar world organization. At the same time the
USSR pressed the immediate opportunity to advance specific national
interests which was given by her increasingly favorable military position.
Her military strategy carried her armies over the Balkan countries, enabling her to achieve objectives beyond the fondest hopes of the Tsarist
Pan-Slav movement.

The Soviet military advance into Poland enabled her to settle, *de*

---

[11] The Comintern, if it ever was buried, may have been exhumed from its shallow
grave in 1947 clumsily disguised as the Communist Information Bureau (Cominform),
an organization of the Communist parties of the USSR and its satellite states, and of
Italy and France, with the avowed objective of fighting the European Recovery Program.

facto, the long controversy over the Polish-Russian boundary. Since Allied arrangements as to occupation of Germany had to be made long in advance of surrender, at a time when United States-British policy on the disposition of Germany was still a matter of internal controversy in the United States and also at a time when it seemed likely Soviet troops would overrun most of Germany, the occupation arrangements likewise are in retrospect favorable to Soviet national interests. The isolated position of Finland from the rest of Europe, together with the world-wide numerous complications overshadowing in the American mind the Finnish situation, indicated that the USSR would have considerable freedom of action in dealing with that country. Incidentally, the United States never declared war on Finland which for a short period in the early part of the war when the United States was a neutral, had been viewed by the American people as a heroic small country fighting for its rights against the aggression of the Soviet Union. Unfortunately for the Finns, their territory had extended to within heavy artillery range of Leningrad, an item of strategic vulnerability which the Soviets remedied by the terms of the peace treaty. The Soviets put pressure on Norway for Spitzbergen for analogous reasons.

In eastern Asia the Soviet and Japanese foreign policy interests were oddly compatible in the short run. Neither wanted a two-front war. Hence both were anxious for an armed truce. The Soviet Union was meticulously careful in its public actions to avoid associating itself with any actions or statements pertaining to the Japanese war. After the USSR entered the Asiatic war it immediately subscribed to the Cairo Declaration, which defined many territorial objectives of the Allies, and to the Potsdam Declaration, which was specific enough to constitute the outline of a peace treaty with Japan. As part of the Allied arrangements at Yalta (1945) for the entrance of the USSR into the Japanese war Stalin received assurances of possession of the Japanese southern half of Sakhalin (which had been Russian prior to 1905), the Kuril Islands, rights in the Manchurian railroad to Dairen, and a naval base at Port Arthur. These were all national objectives consistent with long-term Tsarist and Soviet foreign policy. In fact, from a practical standpoint, there seems in retrospect no way in which the Soviets could have failed to gain *de facto* possession of these objectives (except perhaps the Kuriles) in the breakup of the Japanese Empire bound to occur in the final days or weeks of Japanese military defeat—whether that defeat came in the summer of 1945 or at a later date. Also the USSR had the capability of gaining *de facto* possession of Manchuria. She relinquished this chance, however, by her subscription to the Cairo Declaration which provided for return of Manchuria to China. This pledge was implemented in part by withdrawal of Soviet armed forces leaving the area both in chaos and in great part in the hands of Chinese Communists. Soviet arrangements incident to entrance into the Japanese war included reaching an agreement with China (with American help), recognizing the independence of the Outer Mongolian People's Republic. Thus the Soviet Union had achieved a step in the program of "satellization" of border areas which was to become much more obvious two years later.

It remains to be determined whether "satellization" is merely an intermediate foreign policy step prior to possible incorporation as a member of the Union of Soviet Socialist Republics. Latvia, Lithuania, and Estonia were incorporated directly without any intermediate step. Certain Balkan countries, Poland, Hungary, and Czechoslovakia, are now in the intermediate status. The federal nature of the Soviet Union with its superficial partial autonomy of the individual republics, combined with the effective centralized Communist party, provides a ready mechanism for an expansion which would conceivably become a Eurasian or possibly a world federation.

As to Korea, it appears that no very clear mutual understanding was reached between the USSR and the other Allies prior to the Japanese surrender. It was clear that Soviet forces could overrun part or all of Korea before other Allied forces arrived to engage in combat with the Japanese or take Japanese surrenders. However, the Soviets scrupulously respected the line of demarcation (the 38-degree parallel just north of the capital city Seoul) suggested by the United States as a dividing line for taking surrender of Japanese forces. The foreign policy intent of the USSR in Korea may be presumed to be to assure a "friendly," i.e., Communist government as in Outer Mongolia, or incorporation in the USSR similar to the Baltic countries and Tannu Tuva.

THE PERIOD SINCE V-J DAY, SEPTEMBER 2, 1945.—The situation in foreign affairs confronting the USSR during the period after V-J Day stood in sharp contrast to the circumstances existing after World War I or, for that matter, the situation existing in 1939. Instead of being a weak, internally disorganized nation, distrusted by the remainder of the world, the USSR had just completed a demonstration of its great military power and exceptional stamina. It was a member of the victorious Allies. Instead of having Germany in Europe and Japan in Asia as probable foes, the USSR found herself the leading military power in Europe and Asia. Consequently, the USSR possessed a freedom of action in foreign affairs which had not been possible during the period of caution which Stalin's government had previously been forced to follow. Not only was Soviet Communism in the USSR firmly established, but for the first time since its inception the Soviet Union found its borders unqualifiedly secure.

Another striking contrast between 1939 and the period after 1945 developed in the disappearance of the multiple great-power system in the world and the substitution therefor of only two great world powers—

the United States and the USSR. Germany, Japan, and Italy were pros-
trate. France and Great Britain, though victorious, were gravely weakened by the war. The specter of capitalistic encirclement which Stalin
had used as early as 1924 as Russia's justification for maintenance of the
"organs of repression" could no longer logically be paraded as an excuse
for continuance of these organs unless some new power or coalition were
presented as a threat to Soviet security. The states of the Western world,
particularly the United States, were, therefore, presented to the Russian
public as such a threat.

The non-Soviet world, on the other hand, had developed a new respect and enhanced trust for the USSR by the end of World War II.
The Western world stood ready to cooperate and work amicably with the
USSR. It awaited, however, detailed actions of the Soviet Union to indicate the true direction of Soviet foreign policy.

The USSR had already greatly strengthened her territorial position
by outright acquisition of extensive areas on the Baltic, Bessarabia, and
Sakhalin and the Kuriles in the Pacific. It quickly developed that the
seemingly reasonable stand of the USSR that the defeated Balkan countries and Poland should have "friendly governments," meant in reality
that these governments should be Communist governments on the Soviet
model.

Soviet action in Poland illustrates the means used to accomplish this
seemingly reasonable objective of the USSR, and reveals a pattern used
many times subsequently to transform an independent nation into a
satellite state of the Soviet Union. Normally the first step was infiltration
into the existing non-Communist government, that is, winning acceptance into a coalition government of members of the indigenous Communist party. The existence of the Soviet-sponsored Lublin government
made this procedure unnecessary in the case of Poland; however, the step
was necessary in other countries upon whom the pattern has been imposed. As the London Polish government in exile was the government
recognized nationally by the Poles and internationally by the majority
of the world, it was necessary first to depose the London government
and then secure recognition of the Lublin government. This objective
was facilitated by the military situation, since Poland was liberated by
the Soviet army which was thus able to install the government recognized by the USSR in the liberated areas. The eventual acceptance of
the Soviet-sponsored Lublin regime in place of the London government
was aided by the war-born warmth of feeling felt toward a powerful ally
and toward the liberating power.[12] Nevertheless, in order to secure the

---

[12] In this connection the failure of the Polish underground revolt in Warsaw
(August, 1944) led by General Bor and sponsored by the London Polish government
discredited that government. It is significant to note that the Soviet army refrained
from giving any aid to this revolt.

measure of national support of the Lublin government necessary to satisfy the democratic qualms of the Western Allies, Moscow considered it necessary to broaden its base. Consequently, a coalition government was formed by including some of the popular leaders of the now defunct London Polish government. For obvious political reasons the greatest publicity was given to the appointment of Mikolajczyk, leader of the Polish Peasant party and former premier of the London Poles, as Deputy Premier of the Lublin government.

However, in forming the coalition government in Poland, as in all other countries where the pattern has been applied, regardless of how the coalition has been achieved the all-important departments of Interior (state police), Army, Justice, and Education or Communication (propaganda) were headed and largely staffed by Communist members. Having gained control of these agencies, it was a relatively easy task to destroy the capability of the opposition parties to resist, or of individuals to oppose the Communist elements of the coalition government. Opposition parties were denied free use of press and radio, and were themselves subjected to an intense propaganda campaign designed to decrease their following; non-Communist political rallies were broken up by the police and individual members of opposition parties were faced with arrest by state police and trial by Communist-dominated courts. Often important or popular non-Communist leaders were imprisoned and some were executed. Even Deputy Premier Mikolajczyk of Poland was charged with treason and escaped execution only by fleeing the country. The blunt methods used in the elimination of the Polish non-Communist leaders were possible, in large part, because of the presence of Soviet armed forces and secret police agents in the country. In short, when minority (Communist) power was established, when the popular ability to resist was destroyed, the popular leaders were purged and Poland became a Communist police state. By such strategy the USSR promoted both her nationalist interests and the cause of world Communism—a cause which had not been supported in official Soviet pronouncements during the more cautious years of USSR foreign policy.

In Germany, USSR policy seemed to be directed initially toward maintaining unsettled conditions unless the formula for a peace treaty included provisions as to reparations and a form of government which would serve to strengthen the USSR with German production, while at the same time giving an excellent opportunity for a Communist government to come to power in the new Germany. Thus, although the Potsdam Agreement called for the treatment of Germany as an economic unit, expressly enunciated the principle that no reparations would be exacted from current production, and reaffirmed the earlier Yalta agreement specifying that the German-Polish boundary question would be held in abeyance until the German peace treaty was written, the Allied

Control Council (see p. 227) early encountered insurmountable difficulties in implementing these provisions. In spite of the announced Soviet concurrence in the operating principles as enunciated at Potsdam, the USSR violated them consistently. Attempts by the ACC to persuade the USSR to lift the zonal trade barrier which effectively blocked the normal trade between the Soviet and the western occupation zones, and to cease taking reparations from current production, not only failed but resulted in the USSR's adopting a recriminatory and unfriendly attitude. The matter was, therefore, referred to the Council of Foreign Ministers. This latter body discussed the problems of policy arising over the occupation of Germany in meetings at Paris in August, 1946, at Moscow in March, 1947, and at London in November-December, 1947. Attempts by the Western powers to gain the official assurance of the Kremlin that the USSR would carry out the agreements they had made at Potsdam met with complete failure. Refusing to commit itself to future compliance with the Potsdam Agreement, the USSR made virulent charges that the Western powers were violating the Potsdam Agreement themselves by organizing Nazi armed forces, which were to be used against Communist elements in Germany. At the same time the Soviet Union demanded that the USSR be granted ten billion dollars of reparations from both plant and the current production of the next twenty years as a price for their adherence to the Potsdam policy of treating Germany as an economic unit. Furthermore, at the foreign ministers' meetings, USSR Minister Molotov made it clear that Moscow considered the existing Polish-German boundary along the Oder permanent and not subject to review.

Attempts to solve these fundamental and basic issues having failed at both the ACC and foreign minister levels, any prospect of the return of normal political and economic conditions in Germany was stalemated. The ACC struggled along, solving the day-to-day minor issues necessary for a semblance of administration to continue, but the essential divergence between the eastern and the western zones broadened. As we have noted in the chapter dealing with the government of Germany, the German government in the Soviet zone took the form of Eastern (Communist) "democracy." In spite of an ACC edict forbidding public expression of criticism of the occupying powers, the German press in the Soviet zone pursued a campaign of defamation of the actions and motives of the Western powers in occupation. This propaganda barrage matched the vituperation of the United States which poured out of the government-controlled press of the USSR.

With the announcement of the European Recovery Program (ERP), later named Economic Cooperation Administration (ECA), the question of the resumption of normal trade between eastern and western Germany became more vital and pressing, since the success of ERP as originally conceived depended upon the resumption of normal trade between

industrial western Europe and agrarian eastern Europe. Equally essential
to the recovery of Europe was the restoration of a German industrial
economy. The Soviet zonal barrier in Germany and its geographical extension (the iron curtain) which blocked the normal and natural flow
of trade were obviously being used by the USSR to implement its anti-
ERP policy. Thus it was plain that Soviet policy in Germany was tailored
to fit the Soviet policy in postwar Europe. The Soviet boycott of the
ACC which was instituted in March, 1948, merely formalized the already
existing breach.

By the summer of 1948 it had become apparent that Soviet policy
toward Germany had changed. The June, 1948, Warsaw Conference, attended by representatives of the Soviet Union and her eastern European
satellite states, clearly enunciated the new Soviet policy. No longer was
Germany to be pastoralized. The traditional Soviet fear of an aggressive
German state on her western frontier had been accommodated to the
rebirth of an industrial Germany. However, the conditions under which
Germany would be permitted to renew her independent life were such
that only a Germany dominated by Soviet power, and thus a subservient
tool of that power, could emerge. The Berlin blockade which began
June 23 and continued despite Western attempts via conferences in Moscow itself to terminate it; the attempted "spontaneous" seizure by open
violence of the Berlin city government by the German Communist party;
the innumerable petty but seriously irritating pinpricks at Western officials; the arrest and not infrequent kidnaping of native German officials
in Western employ all made it clear that the USSR was determined to
force the withdrawal of the Western powers from Berlin. (See p. 248.)
Berlin, the historic capital of the German nation, was to emerge as the
Soviet capital of Germany in competition with Frankfort, which had
become the "capital" of western Germany. This changed Soviet policy
toward Germany is consistent with long-term Soviet policy. Soviet security could be quite as safe as if Germany were broken as an industrial
power; the spread of Communism into Germany could be just as readily
achieved by pressure as by the economic chaos engendered by the forced
and unnatural switch to an agrarian economy. In addition, the USSR
would gain by a German industry which would be responsive to Soviet
control. The effect upon western European economy would be the same if
German industry were either destroyed by the pastoralization policy, or
if the distribution of German production were subject to Soviet control.
However, the specter of reborn German power and the further solidifica-
tion of the East-West split resulting from the Warsaw Conference was a
bitter prospect for the hapless satellite states, who, with good cause, also
have a traditional fear of Germany, and who can see themselves only as
expendable pawns in the event of an open war resulting from the East-
West split.

In the Far East, the USSR refused to proceed with any solution on Korea which would permit that country, still struggling to be born as an independent nation, to be other than a Communist state. In fields simpler of comprehension, because of the lack of a major ideological element, the USSR put pressure on Iran, on Turkey for increased control over the Dardanelles, and on Norway for greater control over Spitzbergen.

The general tenor of developing Soviet foreign policy appears consistent with the internal policy in the USSR. Internally the Soviet government brooks no criticism and no opposition. Externally their policy seems to permit no genuine compromise or consideration of any views other than their own in areas or situations of Soviet interest. The insistence on total control by Communist minorities in the Balkan states clearly exemplifies the Soviet frame of mind.

This Soviet insistence on total control by Communist minorities in the satellite states has encountered difficulties which perhaps disclose an internal fracture within the monolith of Soviet Communism. The aforementioned Cominform appears to have become, under the leadership of the late Colonel General Zhdanov, the foreign policy agency of the Politburo. That is, it has increasingly fallen into the Comintern role of Foreign Office of the "international" Communist party. Acting in this role, the Cominform startled the world on June 28, 1948, with a virulent denunciation of Marshal Tito, the Communist leader of satellite Yugoslavia. According to the Cominform denunciation, Marshal Tito had strayed from true Marxism-Leninism. He had unduly delayed the total collectivization of Yugoslav agriculture; and, worse, instead of turning over political leadership in Yugoslavia to the simon-pure Communist party, he had permitted the coalition Popular Front to retain leadership. Thus, according to the Cominform, bourgeoisie, kulaks, and other dissenters were permitted to form policy and Yugoslavia was being kept from the path of "true" democracy.

An analysis of the situation existing not only in Yugoslavia but in all the European satellite states leads one to conclude that the traditional nationalism of these states is restless under the dictation of Politburo "internationalism." The native Communist leaders are unquestionably Communist in ideology; however, they are also Czech, Yugoslav, Rumanian, Polish, Bulgarian, and Hungarian nationalists. For example, Yugoslavia has chafed under the forced acceptance of the Trieste decision concurred in by the USSR. The lack of Soviet support of and occasional opposition to various nationalist demands for bordering territories, as Yugoslav insistence upon parts of Austria and Italy, has embarrassed native Communist leadership, as has Soviet coolness to the Balkan federation which was proposed especially vigorously by both Bulgarian and Yugoslav Communist officials. Soviet exactions of heavy reparations in the form of industrial plants, money, and goods from present satellite but former enemy states, such as Rumania, Hungary, and Bulgaria, and Soviet infiltration into native industry by demanding and securing controlling stock in various heavy industry, transportation and communications enterprises, have bred discontent among articulate elements of the peoples. Indications of popular opposition to such affronts to the nationalistic sentiments of native satellite peoples consist of the growing frequency of purges of high-ranking Communist officials in all the dominated countries. The party-line denunciations of these liquidated officials has increasingly tainted them with the sin of advancing nationalistic causes rather than pure Communist internationalism.

The various national Communist parties the world over undertook rapid positive action paralleling the various steps in Soviet foreign policy. It seemed obvious that these parties were, and always had been, instruments of Soviet foreign policy—and much cheaper instruments than the expensive contributions of food and goods the United States was making to war-impoverished peoples in the interests of world stability and rehabilitation. It is worth while noting the statement of Igor Gouzenko, a former Soviet Embassy official who testified that "It is clear that the Communist party in democratic countries has changed long ago from a political party into an agency net of the Soviet Government, into a fifth column in these countries to meet a war."

This evaluation of the native Communist parties is not invalidated by the afore-mentioned strains imposed by nationalist sentiments. It is important to note that, even in the extreme case of Yugoslavia, Marshal Tito and his government vehemently proclaim undying loyalty to the Soviet Union and to Communism. There has been no fracture at the government level; the apparent or possible fracture in the Communist monolithic structure exists at the party level, and represents a difference of opinion in the manner of implication of the Communist ideology, not in the ideology itself. The USSR has continued to accept the Tito government of Yugoslavia despite Cominform denunciation. At the Danube Conference in late July and early August, 1948, Yugoslavia attended with apparently full Soviet support.

This conference was of great economic significance and contained many political ramifications. Its purpose was to re-establish the prewar international controls over the use of the Danube as an international inland waterway, thus eliminating prohibitive barriers to Danubian commerce which uncontrolled forces of economic nationalism might erect. Prior to the war this control was not restricted to Danube countries but also represented other powers, such as Great Britain, France, and Germany. Inasmuch as the controlling agency included Axis powers, the re-establishment of such an agency properly fell within the sphere of a general postwar settlement. The United States, Great Britain, and France sent representatives to the Danube Conference, as did all the Danube countries and the USSR. From the outset it was apparent that the Danube countries and the USSR were acting as a solid bloc and, of course, had the overwhelming majority vote. This bloc of votes became an effective steam roller, voting down every proposal, no matter how inconsequential, of any of the Western powers. On August 18 the conference closed. The net result was the proposal that future international control would be exercised exclusively by the Danube countries, of which the USSR was considered to be one. In short, the Conference moved the Danube and all Danube trade and commerce behind the iron curtain, thus creating one more chain binding the satellite Danube nations to Soviet domination. Of course the Western powers refused to sign the agreement and do not recognize its legality as an instrument of international law; however, it remains effectively a *fait accompli.*

The war years briefly interrupted one phase of Soviet foreign policy, namely, the support of left-wing revolutionary movements in non-Soviet states. In the furtherance of that policy the Soviet Union has always represented itself as the champion of depressed and dependent peoples, an extremely practical posture for obtaining sympathy for the USSR in world leftist public opinion. Regardless of the justice or injustice of the issue at stake in any such political crisis, Soviet intervention or support usually results in the weakening of some other power or coalition of powers, thereby enhancing the power position of the USSR, and perhaps also advancing the cause of world Communism. Soviet support in the UN of the cause of the guerrillas in Greece is an excellent example of the application of this policy. At the minimum it weakens a capitalistic state. At the maximum it might give the USSR a bridgehead Communist state beyond and dominating that century-old Tsarist objective—the Dardanelles.

USSR tactics in the various UN agencies has indicated clearly a realization of the new strength and position of the Soviet Union in foreign affairs. It has also indicated the realization that the disorganization and national weaknesses incident to the end of World War II provided exceptional opportunities for the advancement of both Soviet national interests and of world Communism. In fact, the USSR seems to have contributed little if anything to the restoration of a stable world order. Instead, she has used the veto and other methods to retard or prevent progress toward an organized world order and world security. In doing so, however, the USSR has shown some respect for world public opinion and has attempted to present its obstructionism in the best light possible —principally, by interjecting complicated and confused issues into every problem on which the Soviets find themselves arrayed against the remainder of the world, thus beclouding the real issues at stake.

In their new post-World War II position, which involves them in a great proportion of the international issues in the world, the USSR has found it necessary to take stands which frequently embarrassed the national Communist parties. Examples are the issue between Italy and Yugoslavia over Trieste; the issue of the eastern border of Germany; and the issue of the annexation of the Saar by France. When the USSR, as the recognized fountainhead of Communism, took a stand contrary to the objectives of a particular country, the Communist party in that country lost, at least temporarily, some of its appeal to the people. When the issue was between two states having strong Communist parties, the USSR was in a particularly difficult position when forced to get off the fence on one side or the other, since Communism was bound to receive a setback in one of the countries. The USSR seemed to solve such problems on the hardheaded opportunistic basis of picking the side which offered most promise of furthering her own national interests.

The basic problem of world rehabilitation was bound to become a major item in international relations after World War II. This problem crystallized around the ECA program. The USSR not only failed to cooperate in the draft and execution of any such plan, but flatly refused to enter into the program and took drastic measures to prevent cooperation by any of her satellite states. The result was the exclusion of some of the war-ravaged states from any benefits of ECA and an active campaign waged by the Soviet Union and her satellites against the project. Secretary Marshall described the actions of the Communists as "everywhere . . . waging with increased venom a calculated campaign of vilification and distortion of American motives. . . . These opponents of recovery charge the United States with imperialist design, aggressive purposes, and finally with a desire to provoke a third world war."

A stable, healthy Europe as envisioned by ECA would prove a desert for the spread of the seeds of Communism. The Soviet proposals seemed designed to keep European nations weak, divided, and helpless in line with Lenin's oft-quoted aphorism, "Bolshevism feeds on broken peoples." The announcement by the Cominform of their united efforts to sabotage the European Recovery Program marked a new advance in Soviet foreign policy. Zhdanov, member of the Politburo, outlined the program for the Cominform and the USSR when he said, "The Communists must be the leading force in coopting all anti-Fascist freedom-loving elements in the struggle against the new American expansionist plans for the enslaving of Europe." That announcement indicated the readiness of the Soviet leaders to (1) oppose more boldly the opinions, plans, and programs of the non-Soviet people of the world, (2) widen the rift separating the Soviet Union from the non-Soviet world.

Whatever doubts remained as to the Soviet attitude seemed dispelled by the fruitless efforts of the Council of Foreign Ministers, sitting in London during the closing week of 1947, to arrive at a final settlement of the German and Austrian treaty issues. Russia's only contributions to the discussions consisted of an uninterrupted, historically unparalleled campaign of noncooperation and obstruction. Also, according to United States Secretary of State Marshall, "the continuous accusations against the good faith, the integrity, and the purposes of the governments of the Western powers, particularly the United States, necessarily added greatly to the confusion . . . there was no apparent will to reach a settlement but only an interest in making more and more speeches intended for another audience." It was in this manner that Secretary Marshall expressed himself concerning the meeting in London. The meeting broke up having accomplished nothing other than even more clearly delineating the cleavages between the USSR and the United States.

In summary it appears that Soviet foreign policy is now based on four cardinal principles:

1. Continuation of the traditional Russian drive for the territorial expansion, increased power, and influence of the Russian state. Coupled with this expansionist urge is a policy which seeks maximum security through national means rather than on the collective, international basis contemplated in the creation of the UN.
2. Allegiance to a militant, proselyting ideology closely tied to the thesis that an irreconcilable conflict exists between Soviet Communism and the political, economic, and social doctrines of non-Soviet nations.
3. Confidence in the inevitable and universal triumph of Communism as the way of life of all nations. It expresses itself in the willingness of the Soviet Union to bide its time where opposition is strong, while pressing all possible advantages where resistance is weak.
4. Constant characterization of the Soviet Union as the outstanding opponent of imperialism and as champion of dependent peoples, along with direct or indirect support of left-wing revolutionary movements wherever they occur.

Any foreign policy actuated by the four principles just enumerated must necessarily be highly dynamic. It will likely be directed toward the mutually supporting objectives of strengthening the Soviet Union and spreading world Communism. In cases where the two major objectives seem to conflict one may expect the abandonment of the cause of international Communism, temporarily, in behalf of the nationalistic Soviet goals. The whole trend of Soviet foreign policy is disturbing when viewed against the great need of world stability and a system of world security in which the people of the world place their trust. The world must be prepared for a period of tension, a battle of nerves, and a series of hard bargains which may involve the risk of war; for only in that way can the non-Communist world preserve peace and simultaneously protect its interests.

THE GOVERNMENT OF

JAPAN

◇◇◇

Japan in Transition

INTERIM CHARACTER OF CURRENT POLITICAL INSTITUTIONS.—At this moment Japan lives and functions as a political organism under the direction of the twelve Allied Nations represented in the Far Eastern Commission. Immediate executive control is exercised by General Douglas MacArthur, Supreme Commander for the Allied Powers (SCAP). Many of the traditional Japanese institutions were swept away by the terms of the surrender instrument signed August 14, 1945. Many others have since been abolished either by direction of the Supreme Commander or upon the initiative of the Japanese people themselves. Those which remain have been modified to assist in carrying out the task of the Army of Occupation or to conform to the Japanese Constitution of 1947. Even where their voice is Japanese, the will behind these changes and modifications is the will of the conqueror.

Out of this interim situation a new Japanese government is beginning to emerge. The surrender document of September 2, 1945, calls on the Emperor, the Japanese government, and their successors to carry out the provisions of the Potsdam Declaration, which, in turn, requires that the Japanese government shall "remove all obstacles to the revival and strengthening of democratic tendencies among the Japanese people." Already many Japanese political institutions have been reshaped to fit this pattern so that the present administration is both representative and democratic. Will the new Japanese government conceived under their new fundamental law, the Japanese Constitution of 1947, remain representative and democratic after the treaty of peace has been signed and Allied occupation troops withdrawn? Has Japanese acceptance of Western democratic institutions, which were neither originated by them nor evolved by them through the slow and often painful processes of political experience, been more superficial than real? Or, on the contrary, will this new government soon revert to the old system under the guise of the new law? The answer to these questions is of course not immediately apparent, but must await the test of time. A concept of the magnitude of these problems, and a basis upon which to evaluate current efforts toward their solution, can best be attained by an examination of earlier Japanese governmental experience.

Background of Japanese Government

WESTERN POLITICAL INFLUENCES IN JAPAN.—Many students look on Japan's presurrender political organization and procedures as a product of wholesale borrowing from the Western nations. In large part that view is correct. In politics as in industry, commerce, and finance, she imitated and borrowed the tools and techniques of a modern world whose imperialist ambitions threatened to run over the backward nations. In no other way could Japan have risen in ninety years from the half-light of her feudal status to dominate, even temporarily, all of east Asia and the western Pacific.

Before adopting for their own use any part of the constitutions, legal systems, and governing procedures of the great Western powers, however, the Japanese skillfully modified them to suit their own needs and national customs. The result was a scheme of government in which the basic law or constitution was essentially Prussian in origin, the structure of the lawmaking bodies was patterned on those of Britain, and the system of local government was similar to that of France's Third Republic. Manhood suffrage, a privy council, political parties, a bicameral parliament with an aristocratic upper house, the secret ballot, prefects and mayors, national law codes, a constitution, trial by jury, and administrative courts—all of these were features of modern Japanese government; yet none was indigenous to the country.

It must be repeated that Japan's political borrowings underwent extensive adaptation in every instance, not only when they were first introduced on a trial-and-error basis, but at frequent intervals thereafter. Only those elements which were in harmony with basic Japanese concepts of organized group life—the family, the social group, the religious pattern, and above all the sacred institution of the Emperor—retained a firm foothold. Thus a swift reaction after 1930 swept away nearly all the democratic gains, replacing them with stark authoritarianism as extreme as that of Japan's medieval days. From the standpoint of the source and possession of authority, little difference was evident between the political conditions of 1850 and 1944, except that at the latter date Japan's authority spoke on an imperial scale, whereas in the earlier days the Shogun's authority stopped at the coast line. Regression from liberalism to military authoritarianism is but part of the story. Each backward step resulted in closer conformity to the deep-seated Oriental complexes which the Japanese had never shed for a moment even while they overlaid their political organization with a Western veneer.

Such a transmutation of institutions is understandable enough; for institutions, like plants, grow best in the native environment in which they originally existed. It would be more remarkable if a Japanese statesman took, say, the British parliamentary system, which is the product of centuries of experimentation and adaptation to the needs of an individualistic society, and imposed it wholly and successfully upon the authoritarian society of late nineteenth-century Japan. The Japanese people had shared none of that experience of testing, their society was of an entirely different pattern from that of Great Britain, and they had ended their feudal system only a score of years earlier. The superficial similarities between the Japanese government and those of the Western nations must therefore be tested in terms of the changes which occurred in the process of borrowing. To repeat, the Japanese utilized only those elements which could best be adapted to their needs and purposes, and then usually made changes which seemed to them to be desirable.

EARLY TRIBAL GOVERNMENT.—Traditionally, the Japanese Empire stemmed from ancient origins. The Japanese insist that it went back to 660 B.C. Foreign opinion, after careful research, holds that the first Emperor, actually a tribal chief, may have ruled from about 30 B.C. The Japanese declare also that their present Emperor is a direct descendant of their first ruler in an unbroken line. However, outside Japan that claim is classed with mythology.

In its early history Japan was ruled by tribal chiefs. The mountainous topography of the country lent itself to the development of small, independent tribal states—each with a hereditary chieftain who ruled over his clan and who claimed to have descended from some deity of heaven or earth. Among the chieftain's duties was the principal one of supervising the sacrifices to this deity from whom all the members of the clan were likewise supposed to have descended. Beneath the clansmen there were groups of farmers, artisans, and slaves who were socially inferior because they lacked such ties of kinship.

When the clan chieftain who ruled the strategic neck of the island of Honshu, where the present-day cities of Kyoto and Osaka are located, extended his authority over the surrounding tribes, he fitted their chiefs into subordinate capacities within his government. He bolstered his own political position by arranging a hierarchy of deities to correspond to his governing hierarchy. He arranged his own ancestress, the great Sun Goddess, in the central position as the supreme Deity of Heaven and the ancestral gods of the chieftains whom he had conquered in the ranks of a lower order. Thus did the gods and men correspond, one to the other, in neatly serrated rows. In time the earthly ranks were broken. Jealous leaders of other powerful clans made the heir of the supreme deity a puppet in the course of the bitter political struggles which followed. The legendary basis of power, too, was challenged as the more sophisticated ethical teachings of Confucius and the religious doctrine of Buddha began to undermine the more primitive Shinto worship of ancestors upon which the loyalties of the clansmen rested.

CHINESE INSTITUTIONS.—Feeling that their old political institutions had at last outgrown their best usefulness, the clan chieftains looked abroad to China, with whom in the seventh century they were beginning to have some trade and communication, for devices which would bolster their faltering ones. There the powerful and prosperous T'ang Emperors governed a well-ordered state. The clan chieftain, who claimed descent from the highest deity but who had not succeeded in maintaining so stellar a dignity in Japan, now transplanted the Chinese institution of the emperorship to his island, and created an imperial court and an imperial family system. This new arrangement no longer relied principally on sacerdotal influences but, in the Chinese manner, upon bureaucratic and economic power as well. All of the land became the Emperor's land, all of the people his direct subjects. The other clan chieftains were made important officials of the new Empire. Primitive tribal institutions were discarded for a highly centralized bureaucracy based, like the Chinese, upon a merit system.

Although the Japanese adopted the Chinese governmental forms, they did not imitate blindly their neighbors across the sea. In fitting Chinese institutions to the peculiar political, social, and economic conditions of Japan they changed them so significantly as to make impossible the functioning of these institutions in their original manner. In Japan the merit system of Chinese bureaucracy, which had made public office open to all who chose to take examinations on the Confucian classics, was stripped of value by permitting only those members of a certain social status to take the examinations. After a time the Japanese bureaucracy reverted to hereditary inefficiency once more. In the process ambitious members of lesser families were forced to seek their fortunes as military men in the provinces, thereby contributing to the breakdown of the central government and the rise of feudalism.

The form of the new administration persisted, however, from the seventh to the twelfth centuries. The civil bureaucracy came largely to consist of adherents of the Fujiwara clan, who, by inheritance, intrigue, intermarriage with the imperial house, and intimidation of the emperors, became civil dictators of Japan. They permitted the Emperors to retain the exercise of their duties as high priests of their people, at the same time divesting them of all governing power. This authority they delegated to their own clansmen, who became a powerful civil aristocracy.

The net result deprived the theocratic emperor of his sovereign power, which was taken over by the Fujiwara oligarchy.

FEUDALISM IN JAPAN.—The Fujiwara clan became content to possess control of the civil government of Japan, leaving military matters to subordinate clans. They were remarkably successful as rulers until the time when families which had been satisfied with a mere monopoly of military offices also became ambitious for civil political power. These military clans had secured for themselves and their tenants the fighting experience which the civilian Fujiwara lacked. They were, therefore, easily able to use force to supplant the Fujiwara in the position of highest power in the twelfth century when they determined to do so.

In their effort to secure political power the military clans were assisted by conditions prevailing in the country. Since imperial salaries were ordinarily paid in land, large tax-exempted estates had been built up among the aristocracy. As a result the central government's sources of revenue were reduced to such an extent that its governing machinery collapsed. Ultimately it became impossible for the Fujiwara to maintain order in the provinces. This responsibility devolved upon the local landlords, who established semi-independent feudal baronies and organized a soldiery, the samurai, for their own protection. In time the samurai, like their knightly counterparts in Europe, became a distinct and privileged military class. They were used by the landlords to maintain the decentralized, feudal government which had been brought into existence.

There were some changes of emphasis in their system as a result of the political disorders and private wars which characterized it. Many of the members of the civil and military aristocracy were wiped out and an influx of new blood from the lower social classes infiltrated to the top stratum of society. The status of the farming class was elevated somewhat as a result of the dependence of the feudal barons on the peasants for supplies and fighting men. Both domestic and foreign trade grew with the concessions which were granted to merchant guilds and new cities. In the sixteenth century Portuguese and Spanish traders and missionaries accentuated these trends by bringing firearms and general merchandise, as well as Christianity, into Japan. They were followed in the early seventeenth century by Dutch and English traders. These developments marked the beginnings of the influence of a wealthy class in Japan which was to grow in strength in succeeding centuries.

THE SHOGUNATE.—More immediately, however, a few feudal lords and warriors maintained and consolidated their power. The strongest of them restored the power of the central government when he forced the Emperor to create for him the office of Shogun (barbarian-quelling generalissimo), with supreme military power. As a result the government of Japan took on a militaristic character with the Shogun as its most powerful official. The imperial office was retained, as was the semblance of civil authority which had been exercised by the Fujiwara. Military and civil affairs were separated—the one controlled by the Shogun and the other by the Fujiwara clan. A civil bureaucracy composed of nobles of the Fujiwara family exercised sovereignty in the name of the Emperor in civil matters limited to education, custom, and etiquette. All military affairs and the maintenance of law and order were entrusted to the military dictator, the Shogun. This kind of dual arrangement was similar in major respects to the system which prevailed following the restoration of the emperor in 1868 to the end of World War II. The basis of sovereignty remained theocratic, as it had been earlier. The emperor still officiated as the high priest of his people, though he had little other power.

The whole governing pattern resulted in the creation of two aristocracies, one civil and the other military, with the latter irregularly but steadily limiting the power of the former until it virtually controlled all state activities. Here was a fitting preview of the post-1930 period of political reaction. The military feudal hierarchy gained its final form and established its supremacy in the early seventeenth century when the Tokugawa clan secured control of the Shogunate—a control which they retained for more than two hundred and fifty years.

THE TOKUGAWA SHOGUNATE (1603-1868).—The foundations of the power of the Tokugawa clan were laid by Ieyasu Tokugawa when he seized control of the Shogunate in 1603. From its accession to power this remarkable family retained control of the Japanese government until 1868. During this long period the feudal instrument of Tokugawa power —the Shogunate—registered its most mature organization, its greatest stability, and its ultimate decline.

The political system of the Tokugawa Shogunate was organized and controlled on strict lines of social classes and overlordships, for it was a feudal arrangement. Theoretically the emperor stood at the head of the state as the spiritual and temporal ruler. Actually he reigned ceremonially without governing, just as he had done for centuries. His position was still high and sacred, but it remained so only because its limited powers offered no real attraction to a successful military leader. The Emperor was relegated to the obscurity of his capital city of Kyoto where he was surrounded by a decadent and similarly powerless court nobility. It is noteworthy that this very impotence, this harmlessness which aroused no rivalries, accounts for the continuance of the family which provided the line of emperors for Japan.

Actual power was in the hands of the Shogun, or rather in the institution which he headed, the Shogunate. Yet, with meticulous attention to the propriety of preserving the dignity of the emperor, this mighty military lord and ruler regularly sought and as invariably received his investiture from the emperor and preserved the fiction of ruling in the Emperor's name. When the Tokugawa clan came into power it already possessed and largely ruled about one fourth of the country's territory, including its important cities and seaports. When the clan head became Shogun, he established his capital at Yedo, the old name for Tokyo. In keeping with the Japanese pattern of family control, he established a Council of Elders as the central agency of government. The Council became so powerful in time that no Shogun dared deny or abuse its orders. The councilors were members of the family, who usually served for life and appointed their successors. They were assisted by a junior council from whom their successors were usually chosen. Thus, although the emperor was a mere ornament in the government, the Shogun came to have a position of not much greater personal authority. This situation is an instance of what for want of a better name may be termed the figurehead system of government which is noticeable throughout the whole course of Japanese history and which is an outgrowth of Japanese social and political ideas. It is the kind of dualism which permeates Japanese institutional life.

Several steps were taken by the Tokugawas to ensure the loyalty or control of the great feudal lords (daimyo). A feudal bureaucracy under the Shogun and his family councils was organized within the territories under direct Tokugawa clan control. Posts in this government were open only to lords and warriors who were the hereditary vassals of the Shogun. The remaining three fourths of Japan was divided among feudal lords who were willing to acknowledge the Tokugawa overlordship and other feudal lords who were related to the Tokugawas or their vassals. The estates of the more powerful members of the former were separated territorially by the interposition of the estates and domains of the latter and more loyal group, in order to help secure the Shogun against rebellion. Among the group whose rebellious tendencies had to be curbed, the powerful western clans of Satsuma, Choshu, Hizen, and Tosa were looked upon with more than usual suspicion by the Tokugawas. Consequently, to keep them and their warriors under control, the Tokugawa Shogunate not only excluded them from all posts in the administration but compelled the lords of these and outlying clans to live a part of each year in Tokyo, the seat of the government, and to leave their immediate families there throughout the entire year as hostages for their good behavior and continuing loyalty. Furthermore, these lords were forbidden to make any agreements among themselves or to go near the Emperor and his court at Kyoto. They could engage in relations with foreign countries only with the permission of the central government. In return for submission to these conditions, the Shogun, having exerted his authority to an extreme limit, refrained from meddling in the internal affairs of the various feudal states unless their peace was disturbed.

In theory all of the feudal lords (daimyo) were next to the Shogun in importance. They ruled the territorial subdivisions of Japan, supported in their power and position by the central government and by their warriors, the samurai. Yet again, the figurehead pattern was to be found in their fiefs, which with a few exceptions were ruled not by the lords personally but by groups of trusted retainers who held office hereditarily in their respective clans. By the time of the arrival of Commodore Perry in Japan the actual administration of practically all local affairs had passed into the hands of the business samurai of the various clans.

Since the power of this governmental arrangement had rested from the beginning upon its military arm, the warrior class or samurai enjoyed a position of unusual privilege. The samurai were the defenders of the *status quo*. Other than being subject to call to defend the country itself as well as the interests of their chiefs, the samurai lived in idleness, supported by the farmers and townspeople who, in a society of rigidly drawn class lines, ranked at the bottom of the scale. After the Shogunate had consolidated its power and position to the point where its dependence on a fighting class was more nominal than real, the samurai became a highly favored but largely ornamental and parasitic social class.

DECLINE OF THE SHOGUNATE.—With the passage of time the social, political, and economic system of this well-ordered state deteriorated. Although the Tokugawas did what they could to maintain intact the arrangement from which they had benefited so handsomely, they were unable to do so. Shortly after the beginning of their Shogunate they went so far as to close off the country from virtually all foreign intercourse, isolating Japan from contact with the outside world lest foreign contacts might induce rebellion. Even this strong measure failed. The seclusion of Japan was accompanied by an internal and external peace which caused the Tokugawa Shoguns to relax their erstwhile firm military control of the country. The clans could not singly dispute the Tokugawa power so long as the possibility of their acting in concert against the government had been reduced to a minimum, and the time when Europeans would insist on their right to trade in Japan was slow in approaching.

Thus the unchallenged Shoguns turned to the pleasures of the palace. They neglected their military efficiency, while the strength of the rival clans tended to increase. The Shoguns intentionally diverted the interests of the restless samurai to literary and cultural pursuits. The results of this policy were far different from what the Shoguns originally intended that they should have been. A revival of the old Shinto worship of ancestral deities occurred. The study of history was intensified, with a resulting consciousness of the fact that the emperor was the spiritual head of the nation whose temporal powers had been usurped by the Shogun. Two unexpected consequences of the revival of learning were the development of a new loyalty to the emperor and the stimulation of the sentiment of nationality.

A noticeable break came in Japanese economy under the Shogunate when metallic money, first brought surreptitiously from China and later minted in Japan, began to replace the system of barter and the use of rice as a standard commodity of exchange. With that change, groups of rice merchants and money-changers, all recruited from the despised townspeople, achieved in time a new prominence and a financial strangle-hold on the majority of the feudal lords and the warrior class. By 1850 it is estimated that the change had become so effective that about fifteen sixteenths of all the property of the feudal lords and their retainers was mortgaged to the newly prominent townspeople. At that date, also, the Tokugawa Shogunate was virtually bankrupt.

Class lines became blurred also as increased wealth placed the merchant class in a position to demand power and recognition. Merchant families advanced their social status by such devices as having their sons adopted into samurai families and by marriage with the nobility. This interpenetration of the merchant and privileged classes and the consequent supplanting of one by the other had great importance in creating the slow revolution which culminated in the breakdown of the feudal Shogunate and the resumption of intercourse with foreign countries after two centuries of seclusion. Thus, internal change as well as external pressure led to the reopening of Japan.

WESTERN PENETRATION OF JAPAN AND THE RESTORATION OF THE EMPEROR.—The Tokugawa Shogunate had permitted only the Dutch and Chinese to trade continuously with the Japanese, and then in a most restricted manner. Both Russia and the United States made several attempts to open Japan in the nineteenth century, but the United States was the first country to succeed in entering into formal relations with Japan. The desire to develop on the Japanese Islands coal stations for American vessels in the China trade, the determination to obtain better treatment for shipwrecked sailors on the coast of those islands, and the desire to trade with the Japanese prompted the United States to send several missions, the third of which was, under Commodore Perry, successful in obtaining these concessions in 1853. The success of that move led the European states to present similar demands. Despite the popularity of the policy of seclusion in Japan, the Shogunate had to permit peaceful foreign intercourse as an alternative to threatening forceful intrusion which it was unprepared to withstand. The weakness which this policy revealed within the dual system of government contributed to the already growing demands within Japan for a restoration of legitimate authority under the emperor.

A second influence for the restoration of imperial authority came from the alliance of the dissident western clans of Satsuma, Choshu, Hizen, and Tosa (the so-called Satcho-Hito combination). At first they had opposed the reopening of Japan, hoping to make the position of the Shogun more difficult. Then, after Western fleets attacked Choshu in 1864 and Satsuma in 1865, the antiforeign attitude of the clans was reversed. So impressed were they by the strength of these attacks, that they decided to seek knowledge of the Western military powers. The uncertainties resulting from the vacillation of the western clans on this issue helped to undermine the position of the Shogun.

Finally, at an opportune moment in 1867 the lords of Satsuma, Choshu, Hizen, and Tosa allied themselves with the court nobles (kuge) of Kyoto and the great mercantile families to demand the abdication of the Shogun and the restoration of the emperor's powers. Discontent with the existing government was so apparent that their demands were accepted by the Tokugawa ruler. Within a year the young emperor Mutsuhito was installed in the former Shogun's palace at Tokyo, taking as the title of his reign Meiji ("Enlightened Government"). However, the Tokugawa clan soon discovered that the real intention of those behind the restoration of the Emperor Mutsuhito was not to set up a personal rule by the emperor in the place of the rule of the Shogun, but to replace the Tokugawa as advisers to the emperor. The followers of the former Shogun then took up arms in defense of their interests. The uprising was speedily overcome, the Tokugawa lands were confiscated, and the way was cleared for a reorganization of the government.

Japanese Political Philosophy

A BASIS OF COMPARISON.—Just as it is necessary to comprehend the evolution of early Japanese government if the modern developments which derive from it are to be understood, so it is important at this point to consider briefly the principles underlying the Japanese conceptions of politics if any basis for the comparison of Western and Japanese institutions is to be achieved. Except for certain aberrations, it may be said that Western political thought tended to emphasize individualism, the equality of men before the law, and the separation of church and state. On the other hand, Japanese political thinking has been derived largely from the influence of two religions—Shintoism and Buddhism—and the ethical teachings of Confucianism. In consequence, it held the community as of greater importance than the individual. It stressed the idea of the inequality of human beings and the interdependence of religion and politics.

REGIMENTATION OF THE INDIVIDUAL.—Through these political, religious, and ethical precepts, society as a whole became more important to the Japanese than the individual. European civilization, since the Renaissance and Reformation, has laid emphasis upon the development of individualism in the fields of knowledge, the arts, religion, economics, and politics, and has placed high value upon the resulting differentiations. Japanese culture, on the other hand, has adhered to an integrated development in which individualism is subordinated. This integration is observable in family life where the individual is primarily a member of a group and only secondarily a person in his own right. In the economic life of Japan businesses were likely to be group or family enterprises in which the individual shared but did not possess control. In politics this concept carried the idea that political parties were distasteful for the reason that they stood for ideological division and disunity in the national family. In short, the tendency of Japanese psychology was to subordinate the individual and to exalt the group.

INEQUALITY AMONG MEN.—Japanese political thought, as we have already stated, begins with the postulate of human inequality—the antithesis of the Western democratic concept of human equality. Inequality, the product of inheritance, is a basic tenet of the Shinto faith. With the emperor reposing in solitary glory as the most direct descendant of the Sun Goddess, all others find their particular niche in the social group according to the nobility of their individual blood streams. Even those on the lowest rung of the ladder are rated as descendants of some one of the ancient gods. Confucianism, likewise espousing the theory of human inequality, rearranges the brackets according to the inherent virtues of the individual. Buddhism in turn insists that the inequalities represent rewards or punishments for behavior in some previous incarnation. In their net effect these variations in religious and ethical dogma are unimportant since there was complete agreement on the concept which emphasized inequality among the various ranks and degrees of Japanese yet stressed its common membership in a family descended from the Sun Goddess. With this basic idea of human inequality in common, therefore, it is not surprising that both Confucianism and Buddhism found acceptance in Japan and were readily adapted to Japanese philosophical thought, thus becoming a vital factor in the inculcation of a feeling of superiority over all other peoples. Moreover, the idea played no small part in the fanaticism of the Japanese soldier, trained to die but never to surrender.

ALLIANCE OF GOVERNMENT AND RELIGION.—The state and religion were interdependent in Japan; they had never been separated prior to the surrender in 1945. From its origin as a primitive nature worship, Shinto had become an integral part of contemporary Japanese nationalism, and was, in fact, the central element of the national spirit. It began with the worship of the Sun Goddess, the supreme deity from whom the Emperors were supposed to have descended, and included a great diversity of lesser gods and venerated ancestors. The Emperor was the high priest of the faith, and his administrative assistants supervised its observance. As early as the restoration of the Meiji emperor and with increasing emphasis after 1937, Shintoism was used by the leaders of Japan to promote the obvious objective of national unity. Toward this end new shrines were erected on the Asiatic mainland and in other recently conquered territories in honor of the Sun Goddess and the spirit of the Meiji emperor, and all Japanese, regardless of their religious faith, were required to go through the formal observances of worship at the Shinto shrines.[1] The functional value of Shinto was to symbolize an eternal state with an original politico-religious national unity. It was the chief ground for the belief in the one-tribe origin of the nation, all of whose members descended from a common ancestor. It was the basis of a spiritual mobilization program that was carried in a thousand ways to the length and breadth of the Empire, a basis of unity and authority in human affairs. It was the deification of the political might of the pre-1945 military state.

To Shinto was added Confucianism with its belief that the affairs of men are a part of the universal order of things and must be regulated in harmony with the "will of heaven." The governors of the people were held to be of superior virtue and hence were accorded authority. Buddhism also contributed to the union of church and state and was consistently looked upon as an instrument of government in Japan. The emperor in ancient times was regarded as the manifestation of the universal Buddha spirit in that he was above all mundane concerns. Official sanction was given to the building of temples and the conduct of ceremonies in honor of the various Buddhas in order that their spiritual powers would defend Japan and her people from all natural calamities, such as famine, earthquake, and war. Thus while Shintoism was deliberately manipulated to promote national unity, Confucianism and Buddhism were adapted to the same purpose.

SUPERIORITY OF RULERS TO LAW.—The Western concept that in "a government of laws and not of men" lies the protection of the rights of

---

[1] Because of the grant of religious freedom in the Constitution of 1889, the government took steps to establish a distinction between sectarian and state Shinto. As a result, when sectarian Shintoists attended a shrine, they performed an act of worship. But when those of other faiths paid periodically required visits to the shrines, they performed an act of patriotism.

the people was controverted by Japanese philosophy. In Japan a government of men was considered superior to a government of laws. In this aristocratic view, an individual who insisted on his own rights under law tended thereby to destroy the unity of the society which should be regarded and regulated as a whole. Laws establishing the rights of persons were believed to destroy the unity of society. On the other hand, the superior virtue of rulers and officials placed them above the law. The law was regarded simply as an expression of the opinion of certain rulers at a given time concerning a specific subject. It was rigid and inflexible. However, the official, being a man of superior virtue, was supposed to have a conscience which was a far better guide than the written law, because his conscience was not bound by time and place as is the law. Therefore, justice was considered to be best served by an official's interpretation of the law, even if he disobeyed it. In the direction of the state, the governing class was more important than the law, the men more than the theory. It was the officials, the ruling group, who really made the state.

PATRIARCHY IN GOVERNMENT.—Finally, the Japanese held that the patriarchal family pattern is the ideal form of state. In such an arrangement their whole philosophy could be summed up: the individual of the family subordinated his life to the good of the whole; the members of the family were of unequal status according to sex, age, prestige, and degree of kinship to the head of the clan; the family was of ancient, divine origin; and, finally, the elders of the family would exercise their wisdom and virtue for the benefit of all in correct proportions. Time and again in Japanese political writings the state was described simply as a gigantic patriarchal family with the emperor at its head.

The emperor was the Shinto high priest and father, the head of the family of which all Japanese were blood members, each with a place derived from his ancient ancestry. That the Japanese people be the obedient and loving children of their fathers and ultimately of the Emperor was the fundamental doctrine of the "Imperial Way" (Kodo). The "Imperial Way" both focused and summed up Japanese political philosophy.

INFLUENCE OF JAPANESE POLITICAL IDEAS.—Japanese political beliefs inevitably had unfortunate, and even disastrous repercussions. The Shinto emphasis on ancestry in particular repeatedly contributed to a concentration of privileges in the hands of a closed aristocracy which grew progressively corrupt until, time and again, it destroyed itself. Insistence on unity led to a long history of regimentation of the Japanese people. Perhaps the most baleful results came from the idea of government by men rather than by law, for this concept robbed the common man of any protection from tyranny.

WESTERN POLITICAL IDEAS IN JAPAN.—After Japan was opened to Western commerce, Western political ideas came to be taken up by many Japanese. Soon many of the liberal intellectuals who traveled in the West were talking glibly about liberty, equality, and fraternity; the social contract theory, the separation of powers, and *laissez faire*. The demands for some form of representative, constitutional government became so vehement that the ruling clique considered it wise to have the emperor issue an imperial decree in 1881, promising the establishment of a parliamentary system in accordance with the Charter Oath of 1868. The promise was fulfilled in a peculiarly Japanese way, as will presently be described. Later other Western political ideas had a vogue in Japan, even socialism and communism, but they were countered by strong popular reaction. After 1931 Japan moved rapidly in the direction of a native type of fascism and economic nationalism which found expression in the dictatorship of a military oligarchy.

Transition to Constitutional Government, 1868–1889

EARLY GOVERNMENT OF THE RESTORED EMPEROR.—Since no single clan of the coalition which had terminated the Tokugawa Shogunate was sufficiently powerful to create a new and stable government, the mantle of authority was draped about the emperor once more. Having no inherent right of their own to demand the support of the people, the new leaders who controlled the Emperor took advantage of the emotional reverence for him, and turned it into a revived cult of Emperor worship. In order to allay the suspicions of agitators for governmental reform, the leaders of the restoration movement persuaded the emperor to issue a Charter Oath in June, 1868, pledging the establishment of a national deliberative assembly. The full fruition of that promise, however, was not to appear for another generation. During the first years of the Meiji regime one temporary administration followed another with bewildering rapidity. All were characterized by the normal leadership of imperial princes, court nobles, and great feudal lords. But the real leadership, which was largely concentrated in the hands of samurai from the four powerful western clans, operated behind this façade of great names in the offices of advisers and councilors. Also, a pretense of consulting public opinion was maintained by the establishment of a sort of national assembly to which delegates were sent from the various feudal fiefs, and later, when these were abolished, from local governmental units. None of these assemblies had any actual power.

ABOLITION OF JAPANESE FEUDALISM, 1871.—The entire feudal system was abolished in 1871 by an imperial rescript which transferred the ownership of land from the feudal lords to the emperor. A uniform system of taxation was established, based on the value, not on the produce of the land. Class privileges were also abolished and the warrior class which had formerly disdained engaging in business began to do so. For the first time all Japanese were made equal before the law. This step, however, did not imply the erasing of class distinctions. In return for the promise of posts of authority in the new government, most of the feudal lords had assented to the transfer of the land to the sovereign before it was officially decreed. Further support of the government was assured from the feudal lords when it promised to compensate them handsomely for their land. Also, the feudal lords and the court nobility were given a superior position and hereditary titles in the European fashion, such as marquis, count, and baron.

ORIGIN OF CONSTITUTIONAL GOVERNMENT.—Objection to the corruption of the restoration officials and the special position given to the aristocracy created a good deal of criticism and a demand for the introduction of a parliamentary system. To meet the demand, the emperor promised in 1881 that a constitution would be granted and an elective parliament established as soon as a thorough study of the country's political needs and capacities could be completed. Meantime, the councils in the districts, cities, and villages were placed on an elective basis. In the following year a national political party was established, while Hirobumi Ito (later Prince Ito and one of the outstanding statesmen of the period) went to America and Europe to study Western constitutions and administrative practices.

Prince Ito returned to Japan deeply impressed with the Prussian Constitution and convinced that some such form of autocratic government was desirable for Japan. In 1885 a Cabinet was established with Ito as premier, and its ministers were declared to be directly responsible to the emperor alone. The premier's powers were modeled after those of the German chancellorship. A civil service was inaugurated, and in 1887 a Supreme War Council was established to advise the Emperor on matters affecting the fighting forces.

In the meantime, Prince Ito was assigned the task of drafting a modern constitution for Japan. This he did with the aid of only two secretaries. However, to assure the acceptance of this Japanese Constitution as drafted, all newspaper criticism of the government was forbidden, and secret societies and assemblies were suppressed. A Privy Council was created by the emperor in 1888 to consider the document. Prince Ito was appointed President of the Privy Council. After the Council had considered and approved the Constitution in secret session, it was promulgated by imperial decree on February 11, 1889, along with the five supplementary imperial ordinances: the Imperial House Law, the Ordinance concerning the House of Peers, the Law of the Houses of the Diet, the Law of the Election, and the Law of Finances. Taken together, these instruments comprised the fundamental law of Japan until the new Constitution of 1947 became effective.

No opportunity for public discussion was given to the people before the Constitution was issued to them, nor was any popular ratification sought. Premier Ito, in a twisted imitation of the work of the authors of *The Federalist,* which explained to the American public the ideas of their Constitution before they voted upon it, did issue with his Japanese Constitution an elaborate, authoritative commentary explaining its various provisions. The Constitution, however, was promulgated as a gift of the emperor to his people and was so interpreted during its life. The contrast between its birth and that of the British and American Constitutions, both of which owe their origin and subsequent development to the people's will, is significant.

The Constitution of 1889

BASIS OF JAPANESE CONSTITUTIONAL GOVERNMENT.—The creation of a new fundamental law in Japan in 1889 was a natural development, largely attributable to the acceptance of the idea that a backward Japan, forced into intercourse with modern nations, must modernize in turn to assure her survival in an imperialistic world. The Constitution of 1889, therefore, represented a compromise between the many conflicts of conditions and opinions which Japan faced after the abrupt termination of her long isolation from the outside world. On the one hand, the majority of Japan's leaders, the men charged with the responsibility of creating a viable and durable pattern of government, had been brought up under the feudal conditions of the Shogunate. On the other hand, a minority of broad-visioned statesmen saw the need of winning the active and intelligent support of the masses of the people through their active participation in governmental affairs, if the rival ambitions of the former feudal lords were to be prevented from effecting Japan's disintegration. Both groups united in the determination to convince the Western world that the Japanese were a modern, enlightened people—strong enough to prevent economic and military penetration of their islands and entitled to equality of treatment.

THE NATURE OF THE CONSTITUTION.—Despite its Western origins, the Japanese Constitution of 1889 became something different from its original models. It functioned in an Oriental atmosphere and was accepted as an organic development in the tradition of an Oriental people. Its principal author and his advisers were men who thought in terms of

Japanese political philosophy, who chose the phrases of Western statutes which suited their purposes, and who interpreted the words they wrote in keeping with their beliefs. The Japanese Constitution thus became a document embodying older Japanese political principles under a cloak of representative institutions, largely disregarded in themselves.

The Constitution of 1889 itself was concisely worded and brief. In addition to a preamble it contained only seventy-six articles, arranged in seven chapters. Five integral imperial ordinances, as we have noted, implemented the framework so as to create a fairly elaborate basis of government. The resultant pattern was a highly centralized monarchy with a hereditary emperor and numerous official advisers. The national administration was managed by a premier and his Cabinet of ministers, whose responsibility to the sovereign was confirmed. A national legislature, or Imperial Diet, of two houses was provided—the one an elected House of Representatives and the other an aristocratic House of Peers. A national system of courts rounded out the tripartite distribution of general powers—executive, legislative, and judicial—each set off distinctly from the other, with functions and authority assigned to each. Under the Constitution each separate branch of the government functioned only in the name of the Emperor, whose office was the constitutional repository of all sovereign power.

CONSTITUTIONAL AMENDMENT.—Since the Constitution of 1889 was the declared gift of the emperor to his people, he alone could initiate an amendment. That instrument provided that an imperial proposal, to become effective, must receive a vote of approval of two thirds of the members of both legislative houses. As a matter of fact, not a single amendment was ever added to the Japanese Constitution.

However, the Constitution of 1889 was altered and developed by interpretation, by statute, and by usage. Often it was enlarged by the simple process of disregarding it in the enactment of new laws which went beyond the words and presumptive intent of the Constitution. This was a perfectly safe procedure since no court in Japan could declare any law unconstitutional if it had been enacted by the national legislature and had received the emperor's assent. The Japanese therefore seldom debated constitutionality in projecting changes but moved blithely along on the principle that since the throne was the source of the Constitution, any law to which the emperor gave his assent must be within the bounds of constitutionality. And in any event the Japanese Constitution was couched in such general terms that within very broad limits its development and modification by statute was infrequent.

Evolution of Constitutional Government

EARLY TRENDS IN JAPANESE CONSTITUTIONAL GOVERNMENT.—Japan's political history under the Constitution of 1889 may be divided into four distinct phases, each of which was characterized by a particular pattern of national leadership. Over the period of years since the adoption of Western forms of government, the Japanese nation has been dominated in succession by her elder statesmen, political party leaders, militarists, and, since 1945, her conquerors. Although the Constitution itself remained untouched until 1947, the functional characteristics of the government varied widely in each period of different leadership.

From 1889 to 1918 Japan's elder statesmen, the leaders of the early Meiji period, held the principal seats of power. These were the relatively progressive leaders of the late feudal period who had the vision to insist on Japanese adoption of Western ideas of government, Western social and economic patterns. These were the men who directed Japan's policies during her transition from a medieval monarchy to a modern state. They had seen to it that Japan adopted Western democratic forms, and they had retained control of the nation under the new Constitution. Never really liberal or democratic in their feeling, the elder statesmen maintained a preponderantly reactionary and aristocratic point of view as advisers to the Emperor.

POLITICAL PARTIES IN POWER.—The victory of Japan and her Allies in World War I gave such impetus to the process of democratization in the world that the dominant elder statesmen could not wholly withstand its force. Japanese veneration for age and ancestry did not permit the exclusion of the former leaders from all influence. At the same time the new enthusiasm for democratic expression gave the political parties their chief influence during the decade of the twenties. Naturally the new leadership expressed itself most clearly by increasing the power and prestige of the House of Representatives during the period of its importance. During their period of ascendancy the measure of the party leaders' strength was found in the degree to which they exercised control of the Cabinet.

Unfortunately party government in Japan, very like that in France and Italy, never fully matured. Japanese parties were built around the personality and influence of individual leaders, rather than around meaningful principles and party platforms. Their dependence on big business corporations for financial support and their corrupt election practices undermined public confidence in them. The two most prominent political parties prior to their dissolution were probably successful largely because each was backed by the economic interests of a powerful Japanese family corporation: the *Seiyukai* party by the financially powerful Mitsui family and the *Minseito* party by the Mitsubishi interests. Together these two families controlled a major portion of the business life of Japan. With such powerful financial backing and with the election expenditures of a candidate for the House of Representatives reaching fifty times the amount of the annual salary for the office, the public could no longer be misled as to the real issues at stake. Corruption in and out of office became so closely identified with party politics in Japanese life that as a premise for all their claims it became easy for the military opposition to use the viciousness of Japanese politicians as a class.

The prestige of the political parties was further weakened by the fact that just at a time when a constructive program was most urgently needed, they failed to present any real solutions of the critical national problems facing Japan. On the contrary, the military leaders insisted that a policy of expansion on the Asiatic continent would solve Japan's most vital problems, and their proposals fired the imagination of the Japanese people.

THE RISE OF THE MILITARISTS.—By the beginning of the decade of the nineteen thirties the weakness, quarreling, and corruption of the party politicians had largely discredited party control of the government. At the same time radical young elements in the Japanese Army, supported in varying degrees by like-minded Navy men and fascist-minded civilian groups, launched in 1930 a campaign of pamphleteering and oratory, assassination and violence which sealed the fate of any political leader who opposed their militaristic program. As the parties lost strength, liberal Japanese made desperate efforts to rehabilitate and maintain them as vehicles of popular expression. They organized a Social Mass party which was wholly disassociated from the corruptive influences of the older parties. Their effort came too late. That party suffered from the militarists' charge that its views represented "dangerous thought"— anathema to the Japanese.

In reality, the militarists began to control the national government when they launched the attack on Manchuria in 1931. From that event forward, their influence was preponderant, and even though it may have fluctuated slightly from time to time, it remained so to the end. The high tides of military victory and the moments of international crisis which marked much of the subsequent period were utilized by the dominant military clique to promote the national unity needed to further ambitious programs—aimed at undisputed rule over the western Pacific area and eastern Asia. Setbacks and periods of quiescence in the development of that program afforded only occasional opportunities for opposition elements to resist the militaristic leaders of the nation.

GOVERNMENT OF JAPAN UNDER THE CONSTITUTION of 1889

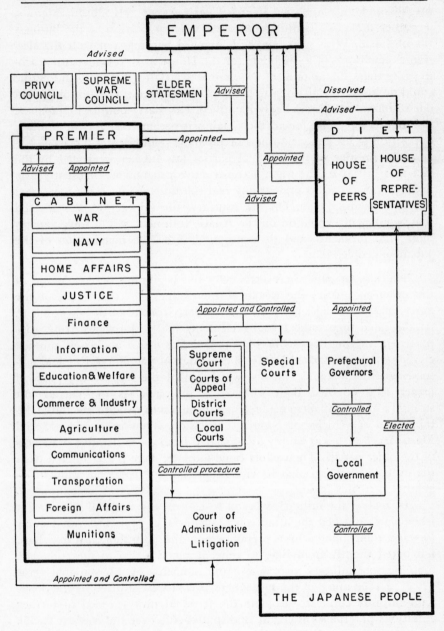

Executive Organization

THE IMPERIAL DYNASTY.—Emperor Hirohito, Imperial Son of Heaven of Great Japan, succeeded to the imperial throne upon the death of his father, the Emperor Yoshihito, December 25, 1926. According to the Japanese claim, he is the 124th emperor and a lineal descendant of the founder of the imperial dynasty, Jimmu Tenno. No other royal family can boast anything comparable in continuity. Succession is limited to male descendants of the line by the rule of primogeniture. Since no female can inherit the throne, emperors who have had no sons by their consorts have kept the male succession "unbroken" by adopting sons or by obtaining male heirs through the recognized concubinage system. The tradition of an ancient line explains in part the high degree of veneration in which the Emperor is held by all his subjects. With the roots of the imperial family tree not only permeating the soil of all feudal Japan but penetrating deeply into the underlying ancient stratum of social organization, the Japanese people inevitably bowed before an august concept.

THE DIVINE EMPEROR.—The Emperor, in both his person and his office, enjoyed a religious significance already mentioned. The Shinto faith proclaimed him to be the descendant and representative on earth of the greatest deities of heaven, the high priest of his people, their intercessor before the gods, and the head of the family of which all Japanese were considered members. Thus the result of emperor worship in Japan was in the past a positive impetus to national unity since it permitted all Japanese to participate in Shinto rites honoring the emperors. (See footnote, page 326.)

As we have noted, in ancient times Buddhists considered the emperor a descendant of the supreme Buddha, who manifested himself in Japan as the Great Sun Goddess. He was, therefore, an incarnation of the eternal and universal Buddha spirit. Confucianism taught that the emperor was the repository of benevolence, righteousness, and justice. He had supreme virtue, was the moral guardian and guide of his people. In his religious and ethical personality, therefore, the emperor personified the most revered qualities in Japanese life.

The military leaders of modern Japan carefully encouraged the ideas of the sacredness and inviolability of the emperor. By so doing they strengthened their own position in the eyes of the Japanese people and won support for whatever policy they advocated, for they always maintained that such a policy was carried out in the name of and for the benefit of the emperor.

POLITICAL POWERS OF THE EMPEROR.—The Japanese, somewhat like the British, made a distinction between the powers of the ruler and the powers of his office which were exercised by his titular subordinates. According to the Constitution of 1889 the emperor of Japan was the head of the Empire, possessing in himself the rights of sovereignty outlined in the Constitution. As we have previously pointed out, all executive, legislative, and judicial powers were exercised by the emperor in a general constitutional sense. In addition he enjoyed specifically enumerated constitutional prerogatives, among them the power to convoke, open, close, and prorogue the Imperial Diet, and to dissolve its House of Representatives. He issued imperial ordinances having the effect of law and only in certain instances requiring the approval of the Imperial Diet and the Privy Council. He had an absolute veto on all laws. The organization of the branches of the administration of the government, the salaries, appointments, and dismissal of almost all civil and military officials were within his powers. He was Commander in Chief of the Army and Navy. He could declare war, make peace, conclude treaties, or decree a state of martial law. The granting of titles of nobility and other honors, the proclamation of amnesties and commutations of sentences were likewise among his specific prerogatives. He had unlimited power to appoint and remove judges.

The important fact is not that these sovereign attributes belonged constitutionally to the Emperor, but that he never acted on any of them except upon the recommendation of the oligarchy which "advised" him. The Emperor was not expected to manifest a will of his own, except in so far as he might persuade his advisers to alter whatever advice they had originally contemplated. According to the Japanese theory of government, the emperor delegated his authority to his ministers and they and their subordinates carried out their administrative duties on his behalf. Hence the responsibility for every executive act rested not on the emperor but on the person appointed to perform it.

Such power as the Emperor actually exercised was derived from two sources. In the first place, he normally received advice from so many sources that his resultant perspective qualified him to influence to some degree the formulation of policy. Whereas the British king is advised by a single Cabinet, the emperor of Japan took advice from the Cabinet, the Privy Council, the Imperial Diet, the supreme military command, elder statesmen, and the Imperial Household Ministry. He was free to accept only the advice agreed to by the dominant element in the government, but by occasionally playing one group against another he might influence policy to an important degree. A striking exception to that rule was the initiative taken by the emperor in the successive moves to effect Japan's final surrender to the Allied Nations. To attain that end, he had to override the military extremists, who insisted on resistance to the finish. Since there had to be some measure of agreement between advising groups before imperial policy could be formulated, the emperorship made for stability in government. In the second place, he derived some power from his influence with the people, their reverence for and their worship of him.

With the capitulation of Japan, the emperor was required to accept and act upon the advice of the Supreme Allied Commander in Japan. In effect, therefore, the emperor was given the task of implementing the orders of General MacArthur through the utilization of domestic institutions surrounding the throne and of domestic political forces which are becoming articulate.

THE IMPERIAL FAMILY COUNCIL.—In presurrender Japan all members of the imperial family were subject to the control of the emperor, acting through the Imperial Family Council. This body was composed of all of the princes of the imperial family who had reached maturity, and was presided over by the emperor. The Council dealt with the imperial court and with family business interests. In addition to receiving the equivalent of a million and a half dollars annually from the government, it formerly controlled a huge income from family investments.[2]

THE IMPERIAL HOUSEHOLD MINISTRY.—The Lord Keeper of the Privy Seal and the Minister of the Imperial Household were two of the emperor's closest advisers. The former authenticated imperial ordinances and laws with the imperial and state seals. The latter had charge of the administration of family affairs. Both were appointed by the Emperor on the nomination of the premier for an indefinite, usually permanent, term of office.

THE GENRO OR COUNCIL OF ELDER STATESMEN.—This group of elder statesmen disappeared with the death in 1940 of Prince Saionji, its last surviving member. Although the *Genro* was not mentioned in the Constitution of 1889 or any law, its experienced and trusted members met privately for years and quietly decided momentous affairs of state. Working behind the whole legal framework of Japanese government, they ruled Japan. For the most part they upheld autocratic government against the advance of democratic, representative institutions. In spite of the disappearance of the old *Genro*, the theory persisted that the advice of venerable statesmen should be sought on important matters of state, and subsequent Japanese governments continued to consult a body of elder statesmen, including former premiers and Army and Navy officers of high rank.

---

[2] By direction of the Supreme Allied Commander the private wealth of the imperial family was impounded for disposition under the terms of the treaty to be imposed on Japan.

THE PRIVY COUNCIL.—Originally established to approve the Constitution of 1889, the Privy Council was a consultative body designed to deliberate on important matters of state and to give advice to the Emperor. It consisted of twenty-six members appointed by the Emperor for life on the advice of the premier and the Council's president, plus Cabinet members ex officio. A reactionary body of veteran bureaucrats opposing and retarding the growth of parliamentary principles, for many years it was able to impose its will in the selection of important officials. All important legislation touching constitutional and administrative law, as well as treaties, was referred to the Council for consideration. Moreover, its interpretations of the Constitution in disputes between different government agencies were final.

THE IMPERIAL CONFERENCE.—Meeting infrequently in normal times, this body of advisers to the Emperor was made up of elder statesmen, the premier, the chief of military advisers, the Lord Keeper of the Privy Seal, and other influential officials. It was a policy-making body, convened only at times of crisis.

THE PREMIER.—On the basis of the power which he exercised, the Japanese premier became in time the most important person in the national government. He was appointed by the Emperor after consultation with the Minister of the Imperial Household, the Lord Keeper of the Privy Seal, the President of the Privy Council, and the elder statesmen. In turn, the premier selected the members of his Cabinet, and they were then appointed by the emperor.

The premier's principal duties were the supervision of the Cabinet's activities and advice to the sovereign on all matters of interest to the Cabinet. He represented the Cabinet to the emperor. The premier could order the suspension of any administrative function pending a decision by the Emperor. Appointments of officials of the second highest rank were made by the premier. In addition, he directed the Tokyo police and important local officials.

With Japan's participation in World War II, the premier strengthened his power over the Cabinet and the national administration. The wartime premiers generally held several of the most important portfolios personally. The national legislature accepted an Extraordinary Wartime Authority to Act measure after its introduction in January, 1943. This legislation gave the premier direction, whenever he deemed it necessary, over the expansion of production of key war materials, and authority to execute the duties of any state minister on matters concerning labor, material, motive power, and capital. A Cabinet Advisory Council and a Wartime Economic Council were established to assist the premier in the effective implementation of this new legislation. These overriding powers placed the premier in a position to dominate the government.

THE CABINET.—The Japanese Constitution of 1889, like the American, made no provision for a cabinet. It did, however, state that the respective ministers of state should give their advice to the emperor and be responsible to him for it. This provision, and the fact that the organization of Japan's first Cabinet antedated the Constitution by four years, resulted in the continuation of the executive branch of the government. Moreover, the functions of the Cabinet were defined by an imperial ordinance a few months after the Constitution was promulgated.

An exceptional procedure entered into the selection of the Ministers of War and Navy. Although they were selected by the premier, only active or retired generals or lieutenant-generals, admirals or vice-admirals were eligible for these posts. Moreover, no officer in either of the services would accept appointment unless he felt that he had the confidence of his service colleagues. Since no Cabinet could exist without ministers for the armed forces, the dominant officers in the services could, and, at times did, control the formation of Cabinets and their continuance in office by the simple procedure of withholding support from a Cabinet. In addition, the Ministers of War and Navy, as well as other top-ranking military officials, enjoyed the privilege of direct access to the Emperor on the most important military matters, ignoring the Cabinet and premier when it was to their advantage to do so. Other Cabinet ministers could advise the Emperor only as a group through the premier. This special position of the service ministers and their consequent independence of action often nullified the decisions of other ministries and embarrassed the Cabinet as a whole.

Despite this important limitation, the Cabinet remained the central administrative and policy-determining body. Its advice to the emperor was therefore decisive in normal times. In consequence, control of the Cabinet signalized control of the government. As a result, aristocrats, businessmen, bureaucrats, and militarists fought for the domination of that body.

The Cabinet was relatively free from popular controls since its members were primarily responsible to the emperor and only secondarily to the elective branch of the national legislature, the House of Representatives. In theory each minister was responsible to the emperor, but usually the Cabinet assumed a united responsibility under the leadership of the premier. If the legislative branch was critical of national policy, the premier could request its dissolution by the emperor without harm to the standing of the Cabinet. Cabinets rarely fell for lack of legislative confidence. More often they were overthrown because of such reasons as the resignation of the military or naval ministers, criticism in the House of Peers or by the Privy Council, public criticism or violence, or on occasion because of the assassination of premiers or ministers. In the last years of the Constitution of 1889, military defeat became an added cause of mortality for Japanese ministries.

The limitations of the Cabinet were important for several types of policy making remained outside its purview. Military and naval affairs were separately controlled; most laws and the annual budget required the assent of the Imperial Diet; treaties and various types of ordinances had to be approved by the Privy Council; major decisions of long-term national policy were formulated by special Imperial Conferences; and finally, the advice of elder statesmen might be decisive in case of a change of Cabinet or disagreement within it. Because of these exceptions to Cabinet control, the Japanese Cabinet was weaker than its British counterpart. To be successful it had to retain to some degree the confidence of the military leaders, the career civil service, the Privy Council, the elder statesmen, and the Imperial Diet.

MINISTRY OF GREATER EAST ASIA AFFAIRS.—The war in the Pacific necessitated numerous changes in the administrative structure of the Japanese Cabinet and its subordinate agencies. Prominent among these was the creation of the Ministry of Greater East Asia Affairs in October, 1942, and the extensive reorganization which it entailed. The two factors which contributed most to the establishment of the new ministry were the administrative problems which were a result of Japan's rapid advance to the south Pacific and the desire of the Army and Navy leaders to control the economic exploitation of the newly conquered areas. Army leaders had such a firm control of the ministry that it was considered practically a division of the War Ministry.

The new ministry had full administrative jurisdiction over all business affairs in the Japanese Empire, except in Japan, Korea, Formosa, and Karafuto. The functions of the ministry included Manchurian, Chinese, and south Pacific affairs, a general supervisory bureau and a bureau for Asiatic trade. The Ministry of Foreign Affairs, which formerly had opposed the proposal of the military politicians, was practically excluded from participating in Greater East Asia affairs. Its only remaining function in the area was the supervision of diplomats and consuls.

MINISTRY OF MUNITIONS.—As the fortunes of war became less favorable for Japan, and as a lack of integration between the government and Japanese big business developed to serious proportions, further governmental reorganization became necessary. A Cabinet Planning Board had been established in 1937 to assume responsibility for the expansion and mobilization of Japan's national strength in the war with China. It drafted plans for Japan's mobilization and presented them to the Cabinet for its consideration. To coordinate the Cabinet Planning Board's plans with the various governmental ministries, control associations were established by the end of 1941 for each important industry. These associations were under the supervision of the Ministry of Commerce and Industry and were directed by the former heads of the leading cartels of big business houses. The program schedules of production in Japan proper, in colonial territories, and in occupied territories were first drawn up by the Cabinet Planning Board and after their approval by the Cabinet were transmitted to the control associations. However, the demands of the war for increased production resulted in competition among the various control associations for raw materials and other supplies. Consequently, far more complete and drastic control measures had to be inaugurated by the government at the insistence of Army leaders. The result was that the complete and direct military control of all phases of Japanese government and business activity was finally achieved in the autumn of 1943 through the establishment of a Ministry of Munitions and the inauguration of widespread administrative changes within the government.

The Munitions Ministry was established as the chief organ of administration for the production of essential war materials. The Cabinet Planning Board was abolished and the General Mobilization Bureau of the Munitions Ministry took over its functions. The new ministry likewise was responsible for the functions formerly carried out by the control associations. In short, the purpose of the Munitions Ministry was to give the military leaders of the government direct control over all activities of industry to increase production of war materials.

With the inauguration of the Munitions Ministry, the militarists in the government were able to enforce a policy of total mobilization and to eliminate the dissension which was present during the period of the Cabinet planning board and control associations. In the waning months of the war, the attempt was made to decentralize control of the Munitions Ministry through its regional offices.

OTHER CABINET AGENCIES.—Several important organizations functioned in liaison with, or under the direction of, the Cabinet. The Cabinet Secretariat administered archives, correspondence, and clerical services for the Cabinet under the direction of the premier. A Cabinet board of information collected and disseminated information on national policies which related to publications, broadcasting, motion pictures, and theaters. A Cabinet Supreme Council for the Direction of the War was created in August, 1944, to formulate policy and to harmonize political strategy with the war effort. As such it was the main coordinating body between the political and military branches of the government. In February, 1945, a wartime Commodity Price Investigation Council was formed within the Cabinet to reorganize the existing price administration machinery and to act as a supervisory organ for local price control offices. Minor Cabinet agencies attended to patents, statistics, pensions, and the drafting of legislation.

THE CIVIL SERVICE.—Japan's civil servants were grouped into four ranks. Those of the highest rank were appointed in person by the Emperor for such offices as premier, minister in the Cabinet, privy councilor, important judicial posts, or ambassadorships. Those of the second rank served as judges, vice ministers, or directors of bureaus. They were appointed by the emperor on the advice of the premier. The third and fourth ranks, the most numerous group, were appointed after having passed an examination and having secured the approval of the Emperor. In 1937 there were approximately 160,000 civil service officials and about 330,000 national employees, not on civil service status.

Practically all branches of government service were open to those who passed the examinations. As a result the best material in the universities was attracted to the civil service. The bureaucrats boasted high morale, efficient standards, and a large measure of public confidence.

Naturally, efforts were made to influence the civil service politically. At the same time the bureaucrats often penetrated political life. Civil servants have led political parties, and high-ranking officials have been chosen from the bureaucracy. As a result a bureaucratic clique was created, so characterized by exclusiveness and homogeneity that on various occasions it aroused the hostility of party politicians, private businessmen, and military leaders.

Legislative Organization

THE IMPERIAL DIET.—The Japanese Diet under the Constitution of 1889 was a bicameral legislature consisting of an upper house, the House of Peers, and a lower house, the House of Representatives. The Diet was convoked annually by the emperor for a session of three months. The session could be extended only by imperial decree. Extraordinary sessions were called by the emperor as the necessity arose. The emperor could prorogue the Diet as often as he wished but not for more than fifteen days at any single time. He could dissolve the House of Representatives at will, but his authority in this respect was limited by the necessity of calling a general election in time to permit the newly elected body to meet within five months after the dissolution of the old.

Except for the right of the Diet to enact new legislation, its powers were distinctly limited. It had no voice in foreign affairs or military and naval matters other than the right to question Cabinet ministers. Furthermore, it had only limited financial power, for if the Diet refused to accept the budget submitted by the Cabinet, the budget of the preceding year automatically became effective unless the Cabinet in turn was unwilling to accept that previous budget. Immune from purse-string control, and equally oblivious to such moves as a vote of no confidence in the Diet, the Cabinet might, at first glance, be considered powerful enough to flout the public will with impunity. In a period of crisis, like that of the decade from 1935 to 1945, such was actually the case. In a more normal period, however, neither the electorate nor its voice, the Diet, could be ignored so easily, a fact clearly demonstrated in the collapse of several ministries which insisted on pursuing a course independent of, or opposed to, the public will. Moreover, the former practice of selecting the premier and the majority of his colleagues from among the leaders of party representation in the Diet helped to keep the Cabinet both representative of the national will and responsive to the national voice during the twenties.

THE HOUSE OF PEERS.—The aristocratic tradition of old Japan had a stronghold in the composition of the House of Peers. Six classes of members, divided into two general categories, made up the membership of the upper house of the Diet. The first category, holding life membership, included princes of the blood, princes and marquises, and imperial nominees selected for their services to the state or for their erudition. Members of the second category, nominated for seven-year terms, included counts, viscounts, and barons; representatives of the highest taxpayers; and representatives of the Imperial Academy of Sciences.

Organization along political lines never went so far in the House of Peers as in the House of Representatives. However, the House of Peers was at one time divided into recognized groups sometimes referred to as parties. These vanished with the dissolution of all political parties in 1940.

The House of Peers enjoyed certain important immunities. It could not be dissolved and its organization could be changed only by imperial ordinance, to which it must consent.

THE HOUSE OF REPRESENTATIVES.—The electoral law of 1925 set the membership of the House of Representatives at 466. Members were elected by adult male suffrage for a four-year term. The annual salary of ordinary members, as in the case of the House of Peers, was so low that only men of independent means or those who were subsidized by vested interests could afford to hold a seat. The latter group became the center of long-lived public scandal in the twenties, providing the militarists with one of their most powerful arguments for wiping out what remained of the democratic process. The minimum age for membership was set at thirty years.

From its very beginning the lower house attempted to make itself an effective instrument of popular government, well beyond anything anticipated by the framers of the Constitution. There, at last, the agitators for representative government found a proper outlet for their energies and ideas. For more than ten years preceding the opening of the first Diet in 1890, these reformers had banded together in a score of political societies. Their objective attained, they re-emerged as political parties, but parties with little power for almost three decades. Notwithstanding the resistance of court circles and conservatives in general, the party movement grew until in the late 1920's it became clear that no Cabinet could survive unless the leader of the majority party in the lower house was designated as premier. Technically the Cabinet remained independent, but for a few years its leadership coincided with that of the majority political parties. However, the weaknesses of the political groups and the nationalist reaction which the militarists led against them after 1930 reversed this picture. Liberal government along democratic lines won its last victory in 1930 when popular pressure, expressing itself through the House of Representatives, finally compelled the reactionary bureaucrats and military extremists to accept and sign the London Naval Agreement. This bill carried reduced naval appropriations as a corollary; the Army group feared a like treatment and instituted terrorism to prevent such action. The signing of the London Naval Agreement meant the death knell of party government in Japan. The premier was assassinated. Open political war raged—a struggle which in less than a decade reduced the Imperial Diet to political impotence. The war with China was used as an acceptable excuse to do away with the last vestige of party influence. In 1940 all political parties were dissolved in Japan. Thus, the House of Representatives, which was formerly the nation's most powerful agency of popular expression, became ineffective.

THE LAWMAKING PROCESS.—Both houses of the Diet were equal in legislative power, but in practice the lower house was more active in government affairs. The routine of legislation followed Western precedents. Bills might be introduced in either house, except that the budget must first be presented to the House of Representatives. Neither body had any control over certain financial items, such as treaty obligations, imperial household expenses, or legal governmental obligations. Budgetary control over several types of government revenue was likewise lacking, among them the income from the post office, government railways, and passports. Moreover, as we have mentioned, the Diet's control over the annual budget was very weak—a decided contrast to the situation normally prevailing in countries like the United States or Great Britain.

All statutes required a majority vote of each house for passage. Nevertheless, in the name of the Emperor the Cabinet had the power between sessions of the Diet to issue imperial ordinances which had the effect of law, subject to the Diet's approval at its next session. Should approval be withheld, however, there was no way of preventing their reissuance as soon as the Diet was adjourned. In theory legislation was submitted by a private member of the parliamentary establishment after political parties were eliminated. It became customary for the Diet to legalize all measures presented to it by the Cabinet and then to retire.

SUFFRAGE.—In 1925 all property qualifications for voting were abolished so that all male inhabitants above the age of twenty-five who had lived in a locality for two years were eligible to vote and hold office. This step brought the total number of voters to about thirteen million out of a total population of nearly sixty million in Japan proper. Members of the armed forces engaged in active service were not permitted to vote.

Judicial Organization

WESTERN INFLUENCE ON THE JUDICIARY.—In the articles of the Constitution of 1889 which gave Japan its modern judicial system, Western theory and practices were of greater influence than they were in the clauses which related to the executive and legislative systems. The leaders of the nation realized that extraterritoriality, with its humiliating bar against Japanese court action in cases involving citizens of the great foreign powers, could be eliminated only if Japan could convince the Western powers that their nationals would receive just treatment, judged by Occidental standards, in the Japanese courts. To accomplish that end it was necessary to give the courts a degree of freedom from control which had been previously unknown in Japan. As a result, the governing constitutional clause declared that judicature is "exercised by the courts of law according to law in the name of the Emperor." The corresponding clauses establishing the executive and legislative agencies announced that "the Emperor exercises" the stated powers.

ORDINARY COURTS.—The regular or ordinary courts, dealing with civil and criminal cases between individuals, were of four gradations. At the first level were found the local courts which dealt with minor offenses and with civil controversies in which the amount at issue was small. Above these were the district courts with a more extended jurisdiction. Seven courts of appeal from these district courts were located in various parts of the country; and finally, a court of cassation or supreme court which sat in Tokyo in nine sections of five judges each. Provision for jury trial was made in the district courts only, and was not widely used there.

ADMINISTRATIVE COURTS.—Following the European pattern, the Japanese distinguished between ordinary and administrative law; that is, on the one hand, law affecting private individuals only and, on the other hand, law applying to claims against the government or involving official action. Japan had but one administrative court, the Court of Administrative Litigation. Its judges were appointed for life on the recommendation of the premier. This court was competent to handle such cases as controversies between individuals and government authorities concerning such matters as taxes, licenses, and abuse of public power. It had no jurisdiction over criminal accusations against public officials, for these were tried in ordinary courts.

A considerable number of special courts had been established, among them juvenile, police, prize, and consular courts; a court of accounts; and courts within the jurisdiction of Japan's outlying possessions.

CODES OF LAW AND JUDICIAL INTERPRETATION.—Japanese codes of commercial and civil law were modeled on those of Germany, and the criminal code was patterned after that of France. Very early in the constitutional period certain modifications were made to align the laws and courts more closely with Japanese precedents and customs. The codes of law were promulgated in 1908.

Although laws having imperial sanction could not be invalidated by court decisions, they were subject to judicial interpretation. Questions of interpretation arising between private individuals were handled by the ordinary courts. Generally cases involving an individual and a governmental agency were referred to the administrative courts. In rare instances in which two governmental agencies were at odds over constitutional interpretation of their powers, the case was referred to the Privy Council.

These restrictions limiting the power of the courts to interpretation did not apply to the ordinances and decrees which were issued by the ministers or by their subordinates to carry out provisions of imperial laws. An ordinance or decree at variance with either the Constitution or the laws might be held invalid by the courts.

LEGAL PROFESSIONS.—All judges were appointive and enjoyed life tenure unless removed for cause. Selected by examination and highly trained for their profession, they represented an outstanding, though small, group in Japanese life. Appointments were made on the recommendation of the Minister of Justice. Prosecuting attorneys or procurators were attached to all courts, and in cases of necessity police officers might act as procurators in local courts. These procurators formed a separate professional group, distinct from lawyers, and were appointed from among those who had passed a severe examination. They were subject to the control of the Minister of Justice and, like the judges, enjoyed life tenure. As might be expected, both these groups were subject to a variety of official and unofficial pressures which not infrequently made a mockery of justice. Most notable in recent years were the instances of the mob clamor evoked in the interest of confessed criminals and assassins who insisted that their crimes were motivated solely by patriotism. It mattered not at all that such brigandage struck at the highest figures in the government and society, nor that the ultranationalist militarists were employing such means in their drive for complete control of the state. The combination of official and mob pressure almost invariably resulted in a nominal sentence for the accused.

JUDICIAL PROCEDURE.—Japanese procedure differed from that of the democratic nations chiefly in its lack of safeguards for the rights of the accused. Preliminary examinations were conducted in secret, and by a single judge. The writ of habeas corpus was unknown, as was the grand jury. Procurators played a predominant role in the prosecution of criminal cases. They conducted preliminary investigations, prosecuted criminal cases for the state, and supervised the execution of criminal judgments. In civil cases of public concern they represented the public interest, but had no functions in ordinary civil cases. Under Japanese procedure, the accused, denied counsel until an indictment had been reached, often found himself undergoing weeks of "third degree" treatment. Many persons were incarcerated for an indefinite period by the simple device of not issuing an indictment against them. Until the accused was brought to public trial he was not allowed counsel, but when he did have his day in court, he faced not only a procurator but a judge bent on wringing from him all the evidence prejudicial to his cause. In criminal cases the accused was presumed guilty until proved innocent.

Cases of treason and serious offenses against members of the imperial family were reserved for action by the Supreme Court. That body also conducted the preliminary examination in cases where it exercised original jurisdiction. Much of its work was concerned with cases appealed from the lower courts. It should be noted again that the Supreme Court, unlike its counterpart in the United States, had no power of interpreting the Constitution; that function was vested in the Privy Council.

Civil Rights

CONTROL OF PUBLIC EXPRESSION.—Modern newspapers made their appearance in Japan in 1871, but freedom of the press did not exist until it was ordered by the Allied Supreme Commander in Japan in 1945. Formerly all newspapers had to be sent to the police for censorship before being distributed; whole editions were suppressed. All newspapers or magazines publishing political information had to deposit with the government specified amounts of money to cover the payment of anticipated fines. In times of particularly severe press control newspapers were known to employ "jail editors" whose sole duty was to serve out imposed sentences. Frequently the government flatly banned the printing of information which it wished to suppress.

Mail, wire, and radio communications were not only owned by the government but were subject to government censorship. All code messages were required to be accompanied by true renderings. All telephone conversations had to be in the Japanese language.

Armed Forces

ALLIED CONTROL OF JAPANESE ARMED FORCES.—It must be clearly understood by the student of contemporary Japanese government that all of the instrumentalities of that government are subject to the control of the Allied powers. This point has more emphatic meaning in connection with Japanese armed forces than with any other national instrumentality, for it was the stated purpose of the conquering powers to insist on the complete disarmament of Japan. The process was quickly consummated. It is the hope of the United States government that militarism can be eliminated from the political, economic, and social life of a reconstructed Japan. The following discussion of military and naval institutions therefore is included in this chapter in order to show the historical relationships of former Japanese military institutions to the government of that country.

THE EMPEROR.—The powers of commanding the Japanese Army and Navy, determining their organization, making war, and concluding peace belonged to the emperor under the Constitution of 1889. Actually he delegated his authority to ranking officials in both services, the Ministers of War and Navy, and to numerous councils. From these he took advice on all military councils: the Board of Marshals and Admirals and the Supreme War Council. In wartime these two bodies continued to exist, but with purely nominal functions, and an Imperial Headquarters exercised the supreme command.

THE BOARD OF FIELD MARSHALS AND FLEET ADMIRALS.—This group consisted of those officers of the Army and Navy who held the rank of Field Marshal or Fleet Admiral. It was largely an honorary body and, except in war, membership was limited to imperial princes.

SUPREME WAR COUNCIL.—From the day of its establishment in 1887 the Supreme War Council was a stronghold of militarism. It consisted of the Board of Field Marshals and Fleet Admirals, the Ministers of War and Navy, the chiefs of the Army and Navy General Staffs, and other generals and admirals nominated by the emperor. Its function was to advise the Emperor on all matters pertaining to war and the administration of the two services. Inasmuch as the Army and Navy ministers and the Chiefs of Staff gave independent advice to the Emperor, any Cabinet was compelled to act in complete cooperation with the body in which these officers sat. Thus the Supreme War Council was independent of civilian control. It had tremendous influence and prestige, including the ability to make or break a Cabinet.

IMPERIAL GENERAL HEADQUARTERS.—This organization assisted the Emperor in the exercise of supreme command in wartime. When the "China Incident" unexpectedly developed into a major and continuing war, the Emperor, in November, 1937, re-established this wartime institution, first created in 1902 and unused since the Russo-Japanese War of 1904-1905. Headed by the emperor, as Commander in Chief, its membership included the Chiefs of the Army and Navy General Staffs, the Ministers of War and Navy, the Inspector General of Military Training, and the Inspector General of (Army) Aviation. Its principal functions were the coordination of military and naval activities and liaison between these agencies and other leading organs of the state.

In March, 1945, the emperor sanctioned the presence of the premier at Imperial Headquarters, a departure from tradition, probably made because of the failure of the Supreme Council for the Direction of the War to integrate military operation and production.

ARMY AND NAVY ADMINISTRATION.—Subordinate to the Emperor and Imperial General Headquarters, the direction of the Army was in the hands of four principal agencies. These were the General Staff, the Ministry of War, the Inspectorate General of Military Training, and the Inspectorate General of Aviation. Until 1938, the Chief of the General Staff, the Minister of War, and the Inspector General of Military Training were the most powerful figures in the Army and were known as the "Big Three." The Inspectorate General of Aviation was created in 1938 to supervise air corps training. The head of this department had to be a general or a lieutenant general, appointed by and responsible to the Emperor for aviation training. In other respects the Inspector General of Aviation was subordinate to the "Big Three," ranking with, but after, them. The establishment of this inspectorate represented a decided step in the trend toward increased prestige and greater independence of the Air Corps. The Minister of the Navy and the Chief of Naval Staff were the corresponding "Big Two" of the Navy.

THE FIGHTING SERVICES AND THE SECRET SOCIETIES.—Soldiers and sailors of Japan were rated superior to ordinary subjects of the emperor. With the Son of Heaven as his commander and the inherited prestige of the samurai feudal tradition, the Japanese in uniform looked down on his civilian fellows as an inferior breed.

Renewed emphasis by the military leaders on the traditional superiority of the soldier played a part in the organization of numerous secret propaganda and militarist groups. Of chief importance were the Imperial Reservists' Association, with a membership of three million; the Black Dragon Society, promoter of Japanese imperialism; and the Black Ocean Society, whose program called for maritime and Asiatic expansion. The peak of such activities was reached in the years culminating in the Pearl Harbor attack, without any perceptible abatement thereafter.

CONSCRIPTION.—The Japanese Army had used some form of universal conscription since 1873. Under the system that prevailed in peacetime, all males between seventeen and forty except the physically disabled and certain criminals were liable to military service. In practice they were examined and classified on reaching the age of 20, and a certain number of those classed as fit for active service were given two years' training in units. Increasingly large numbers of men classed as fit for replacements were in recent years given up to six months of training. In this way Japan was able to build up large reserves of trained and partly trained men. With the increasing demands of World War II, however, Japan found it necessary to extend the age limits for conscription. In December, 1943, the limit was raised to forty-five and lowered to nineteen, and in October, 1944, it was lowered still further to seventeen years of age. Physical standards for induction were likewise lowered.

MILITARY TRAINING.—The process of military indoctrination in Japan began at an early age, followed by formal regimentation and training at about the age of eight years. This training continued until the individual was old enough to serve his required two years in the active service. After active training had been completed, the Japanese passed into the Conscript Reserve and First Reserve until the age of thirty-eight when he became a member of the First National Army. The liability for service continued until the age of forty. Such was the peacetime program. Wartime needs, as indicated above, brought into the ranks of the armed forces every male capable of bearing arms.

CIVILIAN VOLUNTEER CORPS.—In April, 1945, the Koiso Cabinet approved the establishment of the Civilian Volunteer Corps to carry out work necessary for the war effort, such as increased production of munitions and food. In June, because of increased losses, the Volunteer Military Service Act, which provided a legal basis for changing local organizations of the Civilian Volunteer Corps into a combat force when need arose, was announced by the Emperor. Japan's surrender prevented its implementation.

Local Government

PREFECTURES AND MUNICIPALITIES.—The centralization of authority in the Japanese national government naturally resulted in the formation of local government with only limited powers. Japan became a unitary state wherein most of the administrative policies of the localities were created and executed on a national scale. Local officials were usually responsible to the central government.

The country was subdivided for local government into prefectures. For administrative purposes, Japan in 1944 included not only the main islands but also Korea, Karafuto, and Formosa. Each of these former colonial territories was considered a separate prefecture except Korea which was divided into several; the main islands, including the special administrative unit of Hokkaido and the Kuril Islands, were divided into forty-seven prefectures. Since Hokkaido and the Kuriles are sparsely populated, they had a special administration for exploitation, colonization, and the supervision of national forests. Except for this distinction these islands were administered in the normal prefectural pattern. The cities of Osaka and Kyoto (and formerly Tokyo, which later had a special government) were organized into city prefectures.

The whole operation of the prefectural governments was under the control of the Ministry of Home Affairs. The prefectures in turn were composed of municipalities, towns, and villages, which constituted the basis of local government. Each prefecture had a governor, appointed by the Minister of Home Affairs, a council which was partially appointed and partially elected, and a popularly elected assembly. Governors had authority for the final ratification or refusal of any measure passed by the assembly.

Similar to the prefectural government, though on a smaller scale, was that of its subdivisions. Thus, each municipality had a mayor, council, and assembly. Towns and villages had no council, administration being in the hands of a chief magistrate and an assembly.

The lack of local authority on the part of the prefectures cannot be overemphasized. While each prefectural government was composed of at least the three bureaus of General Affairs, Police, and Economics, these bureaus had no policy-making functions and acted only as the administrative agent of the central government. For example, in the administration of education within the prefecture, the prefectural governor and the Division of Education in the General Affairs Bureau of the prefectural government were responsible for the implementation of national educational policies. Likewise, all police in the localities were national police, and the police bureau in each prefecture was responsible to the prefectural governor and thus indirectly to the Minister of Home Affairs in Tokyo for the operation of all police activities in the prefecture.

REGIONAL ADMINISTRATIVE DISTRICTS.—Japan's highly centralized political system obviated any serious conflict of jurisdiction between the national and local authorities. The local authorities were considered the agents of the national government without policy-making powers. In reality, however, certain inefficiencies existed in the implementation of national policies in different localities. The necessity of having various prefectural governors and mayors effectuate the recent wartime measures and policies of the national government in each of their localities created some conflicts over national and local jurisdiction. Questions arose as to whether the new policies were primarily the responsibility of the national government or local prefectural governments. To eliminate duplication, to force the prefectural government to comply with national policies, and to create geographical units which would be as economically self-sufficient as possible, eight Regional Administrative Districts were formed, each created by the amalgamation of several prefectures. A Regional Administrative Council was set up for each region.

This reform became effective in July, 1943. It was intended not only to eliminate the difficulties mentioned but also to increase the production of armaments and ordnance. A president for each of the Councils, appointed by the Emperor for each district, acted as liaison officer between the central and local governments and as the governor of the most important prefecture in each district. He was assisted by a nationally appointed regional councilor and by the heads of the eleven bureaus in each administrative district. These bureaus are responsible for problems of communication and transportation, resources, labor, and finance. Through periodic meetings with representatives from the various national ministries, the president of each administrative district was able to carry out national policies in his region.

Even before the regional districts were established, the city prefecture of Tokyo was abolished and the Tokyo prefectural and municipal administrations were combined into Tokyo Metropolis. The governor of this new administrative unit was appointed directly by the Emperor. Eight bureaus, covering the fields of education, economics, public affairs, planning, defense, transportation, flood defense, and harbors functioned under the governor's direction. In June, 1945, the Regional Administrative Councils were replaced by a system of Offices of Superintendents, with the purpose of bolstering the production of munitions and strengthening home defense by making each of the eight regional administrative districts self-sufficient. By that means it was hoped to avoid the complete disruption of internal communications which invasion would have brought to an integrated nation-wide system of administration. The main difference between this system and the former was the separation of the post of Superintendent General from that of Prefectural Governor.

Government of Japanese-Occupied Territories

JAPANESE AGENCIES OF CONTROL.—When the Ministry of Greater East Asia Affairs was created in 1942 it absorbed the bureaus of the former Overseas Ministry which had originally administered the territories of the mandated islands (the Carolines, Marshalls, and Marianas), the Kwantung leased territory, and occupied areas in China and the south Pacific. The ministry worked with the Japanese Army in maintaining complete control of all the areas conquered by the Japanese. In actual theaters of operation control was vested wholly in the hands of the armed forces.

MANCHUKUO.—After the outbreak of hostilities at Mukden in September, 1931, the Japanese government maintained the fiction that the native Manchurians were supported by Japan merely in their fight for independence against China. On February 25, 1932, a Japanese-inspired State Founding Conference met at Mukden to proclaim formally the existence of the state of Manchukuo. The coronation of Henry Pu Yi[3] as the Emperor Kang Te occurred the next month, followed by official recognition of the state by Japan, Germany, Italy, and El Salvador. Although the Manchukuoan government purported to be an independent organization, it was in practice entirely dominated by the Japanese occupying forces. Its constitution and governmental organization resembled that of Japan in almost every respect. Its legislative council did not meet once in the decade of its supposed existence; all legislation was enacted by a State Council, headed by the premier, who was appointed by the emperor. The actual ruler of Manchukuo was the Commander in Chief of the Japanese Kwantung Army, who also served as Japanese Ambassador to Manchukuo.

OCCUPIED CHINA.—The Japanese formally organized into three jurisdictions the portions of China which they occupied: the National Government of China at Nanking, the Mongolian government, and special administrative areas along the south coast of China.

---

[3] Since his flight from Peiping during the Chinese Revolution of 1911, the "Boy Emperor," now grown up, had been living at the Japanese concession in Tientsin under the name of Mr. Henry Pu Yi. Although he suddenly left for Dairen by Japanese steamer one day in November, 1931, the Japanese denied any knowledge of his departure. His next appearance was at his coronation as the Emperor Kang Te of Manchukuo on March 1, 1932.

The National Government of China at Nanking was a puppet state headed by Chen Kung-po, former President of the Legislative Council of the Nanking government, who succeeded Wang Ching-wei upon the latter's death in November, 1944. This government claimed control over all of China. Actually it existed only with the sufferance and support of the Japanese occupying armies. Structurally the government was complete, having assemblies, ministries, provincial districts, governors, and magistrates. All civil government was carried on under the close supervision of Japanese advisers, who in fact dictated policy. Japanese bureaucrats of all types came to China to "assist" and "advise."

Opposed to the Nanking regime was the government of Republican China, led by Generalissimo Chiang Kai-shek from his capital at Chungking. He was supported by the United States and Great Britain in his efforts to restore the control of his government over the areas of China which were occupied by the Japanese. In the Northwest the Chinese "Communists," while steadfast in their opposition to the expansion of the Japanese, never worked in harmony with the Chungking regime.

Before the outbreak of the Sino-Japanese War in 1937 groups of Mongols in Inner Mongolia under the leadership of a Mongol chief, Prince Teh, had attempted to gain autonomy from Chinese control. They were unsuccessful until the Japanese invasion of north China, when these groups created the present Federated Mongolian Autonomous Government. This government, theoretically controlled by Prince Teh, was actually under the control of the Japanese Kwantung Army.[4]

On the south China coast, the Amoy region and several other districts constituted separate administrative areas under local puppets. Here, for strategic reasons, the Japanese refused to allow any control by the Nanking regime.

In the occupied areas of southeast Asia, Japan attempted to pose as the liberator of Asiatic peoples from Western domination by granting "independence" to the Philippines and Burma in 1943, by signing a pact of "equality" with Thailand, and by experimenting with various forms of "autonomy" in Java. Despite the subsequent disillusionment with the sham independence granted by the Japanese, native aspirations toward freedom were definitely stimulated thereby.[5]

---

[4] In a treaty negotiated between the Chinese Nationalist Government and Soviet Russia, signed August 14, 1945, Chungking relinquished sovereignty over Outer Mongolia. The following month a plebiscite of its inhabitants voted for the independence of that Sovietized area.

[5] Added impetus was given by the careful training in Japan of hundreds of selected natives of the areas occupied by Japan's armed forces between 1942 and 1945. Graduates of the system played an important part in the independence movements which broke out on the Asiatic mainland and the Netherlands Indies in the fall of 1945. The situation was aggravated by the extreme economic exploitation which accompanied Japan's military control in all of those areas, to the point where starvation of the natives, even in relatively rich agricultural regions, was not uncommon.

The "New Structure" of Government

DISSOLUTION OF POLITICAL PARTIES.—The discrediting of the political parties and the rise of the Japanese militarists to power in the early 1930's created undercurrents of popular dissatisfaction with representative institutions. At the same time the stability of the government demanded a retention of the major national institutions. The result was a compromise. The House of Representatives was retained by the military clique which ruled Japan, but political parties were abolished.

The latter step was taken in 1940 when Prince Fumimaro Konoye became premier with the support of the militarists. As a condition of his acceptance of office he demanded in the name of national unity the voluntary dissolution of all political parties. Behind his demand stood the insistence of the dominant military clique that a New Structure of Government supersede the older party system. By 1940 the militarists had been impressed with the apparent successes of the European Fascist and Nazi elements in controlling the economic, political, and cultural activities of their states and in building up strong military power. In conscious imitation of these policies the Japanese government proposed the creation of a new structure of government under which all of the influences in the nation would be brought into harmony with national policy. As a result, not only the political parties, but various other associations and pressure groups, ranging from Rotary Clubs to labor unions, were blotted out. At the same time a Preparatory Commission was appointed to set up a New Structure which would absorb and represent all of the old organizations.

THE IMPERIAL RULE ASSISTANCE ASSOCIATION (IRAA).—This national political agency was organized by Japanese Army and government leaders in October, 1940, as the agency for creating the New Structure of Government. It was a governmentally controlled propaganda agency which replaced or absorbed all political parties and mass organizations and assumed their functions. It had branches for both adults and youths; it acted in economic as well as political matters; and it functioned on both the national and local levels. Despite this wide extent of its activities, the Imperial Rule Assistance Association (IRAA) did not become an all-powerful, single political party in the Fascist pattern. It was rather a somewhat top-heavy and decidedly heterogeneous organization improvised to create the means for popularizing governmental policies. Its chief purpose seems to have been to provide for the Japanese people the illusion that they were actually participating in the governing process and to avoid the danger of opposition which independent organizations might create.

Because of its limited success in achieving national harmony in political, economic, and cultural life, the IRAA was subject to several reorganizations. In March, 1944, when the lengthening shadows of military defeats could no longer be ignored, a further attempt to arouse popular support for the government's policies was made with the inauguration of the "People Rise to Action" drive. This movement attempted to coordinate the activities of the IRAA and the Cabinet.

The ramifications of the IRAA spread throughout the nation and included a vast hierarchy of councils, extending from the Central Cooperative Council, through the prefectural and city councils, down to local neighborhood councils. Each council of the IRAA corresponded to a political subdivision of the government. Although these councils had no legal authority, they advised the government officials in the subdivision to which they corresponded and received instructions from them. Thus a pyramidal structure was created through which the government could issue orders to the people and, in theory, the people could transmit their wishes to the government.

In its political sphere the IRAA functioned as a single political "party," or a united pressure group. In April, 1942, in the only elections held since the old parties were dissolved, the IRAA won only 81 per cent of the seats in the House of Representatives. This evidence of dissenting opinion resulted in the organization of the Imperial Rule Assistance Political Society (IRAPS) in order to exercise more complete political control over elections thereafter. Apparently Japan had not yet reached the degree of deceptive "national unity" which the European totalitarian nations managed to demonstrate in national elections or plebiscites. It was probably unnecessary to accord great powers to the IRAA because of the absence of any large opposition inimical to the general national unity.

Though the IRAA and the IRAPS attempted to "examine" all legislation to be submitted to the Imperial Diet, their most prominent activity was in the field of home propaganda, conducting spiritual movements, patriotic contests, war-bond rallies, drives to promote production, and programs to encourage rationing.

Since both the IRAA and the IRAPS were public associations and supported by the government, the difficulty in defining the jurisdictional limits of the two was recognized. In September, 1944, it was announced that the IRAA would be concerned chiefly "with measures to stabilize the people's livelihood and further the war effort through measures dealing with production," and the IRAPS would "effect closer relationship between the Army and the people, advise the government, and weigh the practicability of government-proposed measures to be applied throughout the Empire."

Dissatisfaction with this overlapping and complicated system reached a crisis in the spring of 1945, when it was proposed to organize a new political party to replace the IRAPS. Meanwhile there was a tendency in the House of Representatives to form several political parties instead of one unified party. But on March 30, 1945, a single political organization, the Dai Nippon Political Association, was inaugurated; this party was to be "purely an executive organization of the Defense of the Fatherland Movement, in contrast to the IRAPS whose activities were in connection with the functions of both houses of the Diet." The IRAA, with its young men's and women's organizations, was disbanded, and its functions were assumed by the Civilian Volunteer Corps.

No further detail is necessary to show the confusion, overlapping of political functions, and conflicts present in the Japanese political system during the war. This was no novelty in a nation long plagued by the feuds of bureaucrats, militarists, and liberals of an earlier day. The uncertainties and amateur fumblings which characterized Japan's attempts to evoke public support for national wartime policies were in sharp contrast with the hard, clear lines of Nazi Germany's organization and procedures.

Foreign Policy

TERRITORIAL EXPANSION.—It was inevitable that a people who in Commodore Perry's day were living at a bare subsistence level would soon look to territorial expansion as an escape from their poverty. The fact that the same territory which in 1853 provided a poor living for thirty millions of people was able to support seventy millions in 1937 on a somewhat higher standard did not alter the basic motive for expansion. Nor was it changed by the Japanese government's actively pursued policy of the present century which aimed always at a larger population. The paradox between basic conditions and the program of population increase had by that time been resolved by Japan's fixed purpose to make herself supreme master of east Asia and the western Pacific area. Only a high birth rate could meet the needs of her growing armies.

From her original base in the homeland (the islands of Hokkaido, Honshu, Shikoku, and Kyushu) Japan began late in the nineteenth century to acquire nearby islands, chiefly at the expense of China. Partially rebuffed by the Western powers when her ambitions sent her armies of invasion into the Asiatic mainland, she took the great gamble of challenging Russia's might in 1904. By that time her sea approaches were doubly guarded by a small but efficient fleet and the firm treaty with Great Britain, signed in 1902. The benevolent neutrality of the United

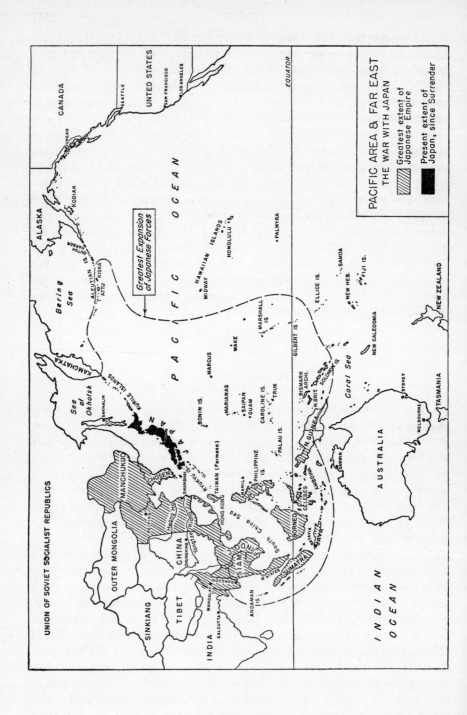

PACIFIC AREA & FAR EAST
THE WAR WITH JAPAN

Greatest extent of
Japanese Empire

Present extent of
Japan, since Surrender

Greatest Expansion
of Japanese Forces

UNION OF SOVIET SOCIALIST REPUBLICS

CANADA

UNITED STATES

SEATTLE

SAN FRANCISCO

LOS ANGELES

EQUATOR

ALASKA

JUNEAU

KODIAK

DUTCH HARBOR

ALEUTIAN IS.

KISKA

ATTU

Bering
Sea

PACIFIC OCEAN

HAWAIIAN ISLANDS

HONOLULU

PALMYRA

KAMCHATKA

Sea
of
Okhotsk

KURILE ISLANDS

SAKHALIN

MIDWAY

MARCUS

WAKE

MARSHALL
IS.

GILBERT IS.

ELLICE IS.

NEW HEB.

SAMOA

FIJI IS.

NEW CALEDONIA

JAPAN

CHOSEN

SHANGHAI

RYUKYU IS.

TAIWAN (Formosa)

HONG KONG

BONIN IS.

MARIANAS

SAIPAN

GUAM

CAROLINE IS.

TRUK

PALAU IS.

BISMARK
ARCHI.

N. BRIT.

SOLOMON IS.

Coral Sea

SYDNEY

TASMANIA

NEW ZEALAND

OUTER MONGOLIA

MANCHUKUO

PEIPING

Hwang Ho

Yellow
Sea

CHINA

CHUNGKING

Yangtze

SINKIANG

TIBET

INDIA

CALCUTTA

MANDALAY

RANGOON

ANDAMAN
IIS.

SIAM

INDO CHINA

M. STATES

SUMATRA

BATAVIA

BORNEO

CELEBES

AMBOINA

N. GUINEA

DARWIN

AUSTRALIA

MELBOURNE

South China Sea

MANILA

PHILIPPINE
IS.

INDIAN
OCEAN

358

States in the Russo-Japanese War likewise buttressed her in this first major test of her military prowess. The war's end saw Japan firmly established as one of the great powers.

Japan's foothold on the mainland was regarded by her leaders as only a steppingstone to a vastly greater prize, the complete domination of China and her four hundred million useful workers. However, division of opinion had occurred between the Army and Navy planners as to priorities in the projected scheme of conquest.[6] The navalists insisted on "southward expansion," the acquisition of the island groups which stretched down into the southwestern Pacific. The Army, on the contrary, wished to establish itself firmly in Asia proper. The compromise policy which followed during and immediately after World War I gave Japan an increasingly firm grip on China while at the same time it brought into the Japanese net four groups of mandated islands (Marianas, Carolines, Marshalls, Palaus). The latter, in open violation of the League Covenant, were immediately transformed into Japanese defense areas from which all outsiders were debarred. Meanwhile, the Army-Navy quarrel continued down to the day of Pearl Harbor.

In her final drive for Pacific mastery, Japan craftily used the opportunity created by the world-wide obsession over peace without force which conditioned Western policy in the early thirties. Her seizure of Mukden in 1931 touched off the train of events which put willful military aggression to its greatest modern test. Prior to the Battle of Midway in May, 1942, Japan committed few errors in the execution of her plans. But those were serious enough in their consequences to ensure her final defeat. Japan was at her best in capitalizing to the full on the Western powers' will to peace, a will so strong that nothing except a succession of humiliating military defeats could replace it with the will to fight to the finish. She erred in her estimate of the power which her opponents could generate and the time needed for their development. She erred no less seriously in her estimate of China's capacity for resistance. Finally she was wholly wrong in her belief that her projected "Co-Prosperity Sphere of Greater East Asia," promulgated by the Konoye Ministry on August 1, 1940, would bring into the Japanese fold Asiatics and Pacific islanders to a total of more than half the world's population, all eager for exploitation by their Japanese masters. With few and relatively unimportant exceptions, the presence of Japan's armed forces brought with it everywhere a blight of resistance, sabotage, and greatly reduced production.

A long period of consolidation and development might conceivably have altered such conditions, always provided that Japan had learned

---

[6] Prince Ito in the first decade of the twentieth century had outlined before the Japanese Diet a program of expansion envisioning initially the acquisition of all island territories from Sakhalin and the Kamchatka peninsula down to and including the Netherlands East Indies.

to give real meaning to her slogan of "Asia for the Asiatics." The opportunity for such growth was denied Japan by the combination of the swiftly rising military might of the United Nations, in particular the United States, and the slower rise of internal resistance in the conquered areas. Three years before Japan's unconditional surrender ended the fighting, she had shown beyond any last doubt her inability to deal with a conquered native population except on a basis of master and slave. True, her earlier experiences in Formosa, Korea, and Manchuria had already established that fact. But, on paper at least, Japan had forecast a reversal of the older system when she projected her "Co-Prosperity Sphere." Japan's habits and traditions of centuries were obviously too strong to permit the introduction of any suggestion of equality and democracy in her dealings with non-Japanese.

RELATIONS WITH FOREIGN POWERS.—In carrying out her policy of national self-interest, Japan consistently showed herself unable to establish any bonds which savored of real and lasting friendship or cooperation with other nations. She enjoyed support from time to time as she pursued her various ventures. But, with the single exception of the flurry of enthusiasm in the United States when Japan challenged Russia in 1904, the supporting power has invariably been one which could discover some immediate gain to be had from her arrangements with Tokyo. Absent from such dealings was the atmosphere of trust and confidence which alone can beget true understanding between two nations. Japan never was able to dismiss or conceal the deep-seated hostility to an outside world which had first led her into more than two centuries of national hermitage, had then blasted her out of such isolation, and thereafter put her through several decades of apprenticeship before she was asked to sit at the international table as an equal. Moreover, the equality never seemed real. In fact, when the recognition of her equal status was brought to a vote at Japan's instance at the Versailles Conference in 1919, it failed of the unanimous support necessary to give it full validity. That incident served to strengthen the inferiority complex of a proud people. Self-vindication then had to be found in military supremacy and conquest. In that process, Japan subordinated the means to the end.

It was but natural that craft and force should thus have become Japan's major tools of international relations. When difficulties with her rivals pointed to war, that war was invariably launched without warning and in full disregard of any existing agreements. Whatever the damage suffered by Japan's reputation as a result, her leaders were willing to balance it against the concrete advantages which a surprise attack assured her. In the intervals between wars, treaties and pacts were sought which would serve the double purpose of protecting the nation's security and simplifying the problem of her future campaigns of aggression. Thus, the

Anglo-Japanese Treaty of 1902 blocked the road to any renewal of the European power concert (Russia, Germany, and France) which had deprived Japan of most of the territorial gains scored in her war with China, 1894-1895. Moreover, it secured for Japan the protection of her sea lanes by Britain's powerful fleet in a day when Japan's rating as a naval power was still negligible. The combination likewise assured the two partners some degree of cooperation in the exploitation of a sick China. And when Japan sought to make capital of Britain's involvement in World War I by making her Twenty-One Demands of 1915 on China, the British were left in no position to protest, even though China's acceptance would have left Japan virtually sovereign over all Chinese territory. It was left to the United States to save China at that juncture.

Japan was equally alert to align herself with the Western Allies in World War I, an act which permitted her to fall temporary heir to Germany's holdings in China and subsequently to secure the strategically important mandated islands in the central Pacific. In her next—and last —major move in such diplomacy she joined her fortunes in 1936 with those of the Rome-Berlin Axis.

Such high-powered politics did not always provide smooth sailing for the Japanese ship of state. The tendency to overreach herself was curbed repeatedly by outside intervention too strong to be withstood. Such, for example, were the setbacks experienced at the Washington Conference of 1921-1922, where Japan acquiesced in the scrapping of the Anglo-Japanese Treaty, agreed to the withdrawal of her troops from the Shantung peninsula, and became a signatory to the Nine-Power Treaty guaranteeing the independence and territorial integrity of China. In return, as already mentioned, Japan was accorded in the Five-Power Naval Treaty a level of maritime strength sufficient to ensure her dominance of Far Eastern waters. The over-all result of these various setbacks was deemed so unfavorable by Japan's militarists that her subsequent diplomatic moves were aimed at securing freedom from her treaty commitments. Successively she broke away from the League of Nations (1933), denounced the London Naval Treaty of 1930 (1934), and after 1937 repeatedly refused to be bound by earlier obligations respecting China's sovereignty. From that stage it was but a short step to linking her interests with those of the Rome-Berlin Axis in 1939, followed by her agreement to become a full-fledged partner of the Axis in 1940. At the same time Japan held fast to her Non-Aggression Treaty with Soviet Russia, a fact clearly reflecting her fears of Soviet bombers over Japan's tinder cities. That treaty came to an abrupt end when Soviet Russia declared war on Japan August 8, 1945.

How close were the ties which bound Japan to her European wartime partners in World War II is a matter of doubt. There could be little warmth in an atmosphere charged with the contempt which Hitler and other Nazi writers had frequently expressed for Japan. In turn, the Japanese had been at no pains to spare the Germans and Italians in their program to rid Asia of Occidentals. Unity was further impeded by the distance separating the Eastern and Western partners, with the Allied fleets barring the way to effective communications. The real unity thus became essentially one of joint opposition against a common rival, with each partner seeking to make the utmost for itself out of the arrangement. Even the vision of Axis victory must have raised for Japan the specter of a final settlement with Germany. Italy's fate pointed clearly to the difficulties which might be anticipated in such an eventuality.

All such doubts were resolved after 1942. From that point on it was a question not of whether but of how long Japan could retain any part of an empire which in the half century after 1894 had expanded through military conquest from a community of forty millions living in an area about the size of Montana to one of 4,415,000 square miles, with a population of two hundred millions. By 1945, an unbroken succession of military disasters led Japan to offer the Allies the bait of several "peace feelers." The story of surrender, occupation of the islands by Allied forces, and the measures and policies imposed upon a defeated Japan are the subject of the remainder of this chapter.

Japan, the Conqueror's Ward

BACKGROUND OF THE OCCUPATION.—Since her formal surrender to the Allied forces on September 2, 1945, the Japanese have witnessed revolutionary changes to their political, economic, and social systems. The Japan which will finally emerge from this dynamic period cannot be foretold. In large measure the outcome depends on whether the deep-rooted indigenous traits which made the Japanese people ideal clay for molding by Japan's dominant clique of military reactionaries can be exercised by her enforced experience with the patterns of democratic government. The abortive efforts of Japan's native liberals to set their nation in the Western mold has already been noted. The extent and depth of her re-education by occupation forces harbors a definite handicap from the very fact that force lies behind the democratic pattern, a handicap which may be reduced in some degree if the nation's material well-being makes substantial advances before Japan is released from external control. The test will come only after those controls have been removed.

Obviously Japan's surrender loosed new forces and generated new issues fully as portentous as those which had been resolved by eight years of warfare. The victors' responsibility clearly extended beyond Japan proper into Manchuria, Korea, and north China since they too figured in the collapse of the Japanese Empire. It is not surprising, therefore, that with the cessation of hostilities between the United Nations and Japan, the Far East became one of the vital areas in which the struggle between Democracy and Totalitarianism has been waged. This circumstance and the fact that the chief burdens of the occupation of Japan have fallen to the United States demand our careful study of Japan's development since her surrender in 1945.

CAIRO DECLARATION, DECEMBER 1, 1943.—The policy which, in an external sense, is molding Japan today, derives directly from the war aims of Japan's conquerors. Even before the Allied offensive in the Pacific was fairly under way, President Roosevelt, Prime Minister Churchill, and Generalissimo Chiang Kai-shek met in Cairo and declared the joint resolve of the United Nations at war with Japan to continue operations until the unconditional surrender of their common enemy. The Cairo Declaration further provided that Japan would be stripped of all islands or possessions occupied since the beginning of World War I and that all the territories she had taken from China, such as Manchuria, Formosa, and the Pescadores, would be restored to the Republic of China. Moreover, Japan was to be expelled from all other territories taken by violence and aggression, and enslaved Korea was, in due course, to become free and independent. Finally, the three Allies proclaimed that they harbored no thought of gain or territorial expansion for themselves.[7]

THE YALTA CONFERENCE, FEBRUARY 11, 1945.—The next important step in the formulation of international policy toward Japan and the Far East was taken by President Roosevelt, Prime Minister Churchill, and Marshal Stalin at Yalta in the Crimea. The Allies, assured of victory both in Europe and Asia, agreed to the entry of the USSR in the war against Japan two or three months after the surrender of Germany under the following conditions:

1. The preservation of the *status quo* in Outer Mongolia, i.e., Mongolian Peoples Republic.
2. The restoration of Russian rights violated by Japan's attack in 1904.
3. The handing over of the Kuril Islands to the Soviet Union.[8]

In addition, Marshal Stalin declared the readiness of the Soviet Union to conclude a pact of friendship and alliance with the Nationalist Government of China in order to liberate China from the Japanese yoke.

---

[7] The USSR, while not a party to the Cairo Conference or Declaration, agreed by her later acceptance of the Potsdam Declaration (1945) that "the terms of the Cairo Declaration shall be carried out. . . ."

[8] These provisions of the Yalta Agreement were made binding on the condition of Chiang Kai-shek's later concurrence.

AGREEMENT REGARDING JAPAN

Between the Leaders of the Three Great Powers—

THE UNITED STATES OF AMERICA
THE UNION OF SOVIET SOCIALIST REPUBLICS
THE UNITED KINGDOM OF GREAT BRITAIN
AND NORTHERN IRELAND

Signed at Yalta February 11, 1945

The leaders of the three Great Powers—the Soviet Union, the United States of America and Great Britain—have agreed that in two or three months after Germany has surrendered and the war in Europe has terminated the Soviet Union shall enter into the war against Japan on the side of the Allies on condition that:

1. The status quo in Outer-Mongolia (The Mongolian People's Republic) shall be preserved;

2. The former rights of Russia violated by the treacherous attack of Japan in 1904 shall be restored, viz:

(a) the southern part of Sakhalin as well as all the islands adjacent to it shall be returned to the Soviet Union,

(b) the commercial port of Dairen shall be internationalized, the preeminent interests of the Soviet Union in this port being safeguarded and the lease of Port Arthur as a naval base of the USSR restored,

(c) the Chinese-Eastern Railroad and the South-Manchurian Railroad which provides an outlet to Dairen shall be jointly operated by the establishment of a joint Soviet-Chinese Company it being understood that the preeminent interests of the Soviet Union shall be safeguarded and that China shall retain full sovereignty in Manchuria;

3. The Kuril islands shall be handed over to the Soviet Union.

It is understood, that the agreement concerning Outer-Mongolia and the ports and railroads referred to above will require concurrence of Generalissimo Chiang Kai-Shek. The President will take measures in order to obtain this concurrence on advice from Marshal Stalin.

The Heads of the three Great Powers have agreed that these claims of the Soviet Union shall be unquestionably fulfilled after Japan has been defeated.

For its part the Soviet Union expresses its readiness to conclude with the National Government of China a pact of friendship and alliance between the USSR and China in order to render assistance to China with its armed forces for the purpose of liberating China from the Japanese yoke.

February 11, 1945

J. STALIN
FRANKLIN D. ROOSEVELT
WINSTON S. CHURCHILL

THE POTSDAM DECLARATION, JULY 26, 1945.—While conferring at Potsdam on measures for defeated Germany's disposition, the United States, Great Britain, and China issued a proclamation which in effect outlined measures to be accepted by Japan as a prerequisite to her surrender. The Potsdam Declaration defined Japan's future in the following terms:

1. Elimination of irresponsible Japanese militarism.
2. Occupation of Japan until the achievement of Allied objectives.
3. Execution of the terms of the Cairo Declaration and the confinement of Japan to her main islands.
4. Disarmament and repatriation of Japanese forces.
5. Punishment of war criminals and the revival and strengthening of democratic tendencies but not the enslavement or destruction of the Japanese people.
6. Stabilization of Japanese economy on a peacetime basis with provision for payment of reparations.
7. Withdrawal of occupation forces upon the accomplishment of the above objectives and the establishment of a peacefully inclined, responsible government chosen by the freely expressed will of the Japanese people.
8. Immediate and unconditional surrender of Japan's armed forces and assurance of good faith, or the alternative of prompt and utter destruction.

THE SURRENDER DOCUMENT.—Fifteen days after the Potsdam Declaration, one day following the entrance of the USSR in the Far Eastern war, and one day after the second atomic bomb had been delivered, Japan acting through neutral Switzerland agreed to the Allied terms "with the understanding that the said declaration does not comprise any demand which prejudices the prerogatives of His Majesty as a Sovereign Ruler." United States Secretary of State Byrnes, at the direction of the President and acting on behalf of the Governments of the United States, Britain, the USSR, and China, replied to the Japanese: "From the moment of surrender the authority of the Emperor and the Japanese Government to rule the state shall be subject to the Supreme Commander of the Allied Powers who will take such steps as he deems proper to effectuate the surrender terms." Three days later the Japanese made their second offer of surrender following which on August 14 President Truman issued a statement of acceptance in which he noted Japan's agreement to "a full acceptance of the Potsdam Declaration which specifies the unconditional surrender of Japan." General Douglas MacArthur and representatives of the United Nations whose armed forces had fought in the Pacific received Japan's formal surrender aboard the United States battleship "Missouri" in Tokyo Harbor on September 2, 1945. On September 6, President Truman designated General MacArthur as the Supreme

THE POTSDAM DECLARATION

AUGUST 14, 1945

To our good and loyal subjects:

After pondering deeply the general trends of the world and the actual conditions obtaining in our Empire today, we have decided to effect a settlement of the present situation by resorting to an extraordinary measure. We have ordered our Government to communicate to the Allied Governments . . . that our Empire accepts the provisions of their joint declaration.

To strive for the common prosperity and happiness of all nations as well as the security and well-being of our subjects is the solemn obligation which has been handed down by our Imperial ancestors, and which we lay close to the heart.

Indeed, we declared war on America and Britain out of our sincere desire to ensure Japan's self-preservation and the stabilization of East Asia, it being far from our thought either to infringe upon the sovereignty of other nations or to embark upon territorial aggrandizement.

But now the war has lasted for nearly four years. Despite the best that has been done by every one . . . the war situation has developed not necessarily to Japan's advantage, while the general trends of the world have all turned against her interest.

Moreover, the enemy has begun to employ a new and most cruel bomb, the power of which to do damage is indeed incalculable, taking the toll of many innocent lives. Should we continue to fight, it would not only result in an ultimate collapse and obliteration of the Japanese Nation, but also it would lead to the total extinction of human civilization. Such being the case, how are we to save the millions of our subjects, or to atone ourselves before the hallowed spirits of our Imperial ancestors. This is the reason why we have ordered the acceptance of the provisions of the joint declaration of the powers. . . .

The thought of those officers and men as well as others who have fallen . . . pains our heart night and day.

. . . The hardships and sufferings to which our Nation is to be subjected hereafter will be certainly great.

We are keenly aware of the inmost feelings of all you, our subjects. However, it is according to the dictates of time and fate that we have resolved to pave the way for a grand peace for all the generations to come by enduring the unendurable and suffering what is insufferable. . . .

Beware most strictly of any outbursts of emotion which may engender needless complications, of any fraternal contention and strife which may create confusion, lead you astray, and cause you to lose the confidence of the world.

Let the entire Nation continue as one family from generation to generation, ever firm in its faith of the imperishableness of its divine land, and mindful of its heavy burden of responsibilities, and the long road before it. . . . Cultivate the ways of rectitude, foster nobility of spirit, and work with resolution so as you may enhance the innate glory of the Imperial state and keep pace with the progress of the world.

Commander for the Allied Powers (SCAP) for the occupation of Japan and forwarded to him a statement of policy which defined the powers of SCAP:

1. The authority of the Emperor and the Japanese Government to rule the state is subordinate to you as Supreme Commander of the Allied Powers.
2. Control of Japan shall be exercised through the Japanese Government to the extent that such an arrangement produces satisfactory results.
3. The statement of intentions contained in the Potsdam Declaration will be given full effect. The Potsdam Declaration forms a part of our policy stated in good faith with relation to peace and security in the Far East.
4. You will exercise your authority as you deem proper to carry out your mission. Our relations with Japan do not rest on a contractual basis, but on an unconditional surrender. Since your authority is supreme, you will not entertain any question on the part of the Japanese as to its scope.

OBJECTIVES OF THE OCCUPATION OF JAPAN.—Military considerations were the essence of the occupation force's immediate mission. Accordingly, steps were taken to establish control promptly over designated key areas, to effect the disarmament and demobilization of the Japanese armed forces, to repatriate Japanese military and civilian personnel, and to establish safeguards against the outbreak of disease, public disorder, and starvation. These immediate missions of the occupation were quickly and efficiently executed in order to clear the way for the long-range objective: the creation amid the ruins of an ignominious past of a stable, friendly, and democratic Japan.

Originally American when it moved into Japan in September, 1945, the occupation force was soon augmented by troops from the other powers directly concerned with the future of Japan. Australia, for example, acting for Great Britain, New Zealand, India, and herself, provided balanced forces drawn from those four members of the British Commonwealth to a total of 45,000 troops.

Having established the general terms for the occupation, the United States proceeded to conduct the occupation of Japan in conformity with two basic principles, namely, the preservation of the predominant position of the United States in the war in the Pacific and the protection of the legitimate rights and interests of the Allies. Thus, the United States first proposed the establishment of a Far Eastern Advisory Commission (FEAC) through which the governments of Australia, Great Britain, Canada, China, France, India, the Netherlands, New Zealand, the Philippine Commonwealth, and the USSR were invited to express their interest in the execution of occupation policy. The Soviet Union, however, boycotted this "advisory" agency and demanded nothing less than a "control" commission. A compromise was reached at the Foreign Ministers' conference at Moscow in December, 1945, in view of the American conviction that the absence of the Soviet Union from Japan's occupation might create a hazardous condition in the Far East, possibly to the extent of undermining the cooperative principle on which the United Nations rested. Consequently, two bodies were created: a Far Eastern Commission (FEC), which replaced the abandoned FEAC, and an Allied Council for Japan (ACJ).

THE FAR EASTERN COMMISSION.—The broad base of membership established for membership in the Far Eastern Commission initially was accepted by all eleven nations originally invited to join the FEAC. In addition, provision was made for the later inclusion of other interested governments. The functions of the FEC were succinctly stated in the instrument which gave it legal status:

1. To formulate the policies and standards in conformity with which the fulfillment by Japan of its obligations under the Terms of Surrender may be accomplished.
2. To review, on the request of any member, any directive issued to the Supreme Commander for the Allied Powers or any action taken by the Supreme Commander involving policy decisions within the jurisdiction of the Commission.
3. The Commission shall not make recommendations with regard to the conduct of military operations nor with regard to territorial adjustments.

By conducting its negotiations in secret and thus avoiding immediate pressures of public opinion, the FEC has achieved a remarkable record of policy formulation.

The headquarters of the FEC was established in Washington, although special meetings were held at other places whenever a specific situation made such action advisable. In its procedures, the Commission respected the chain of command from the United States Government to the Supreme Commander and the latter's command of the occupation forces. On the other hand, the United States was required to prepare directives in accordance with policy decisions of the FEC and to transmit them to SCAP. However, two further provisions in FEC's charter gave the United States considerable latitude in the conduct of the occupation. The United States was authorized to issue interim directives to SCAP pending action by the Commission whenever urgent matters arose which were not covered by policies already formulated by FEC. It was also decided that any directives dealing with fundamental changes in the Japanese constitutional structure or in the regime of control, or concerning

ORGANIZATION OF FAR EASTERN COMMISSION

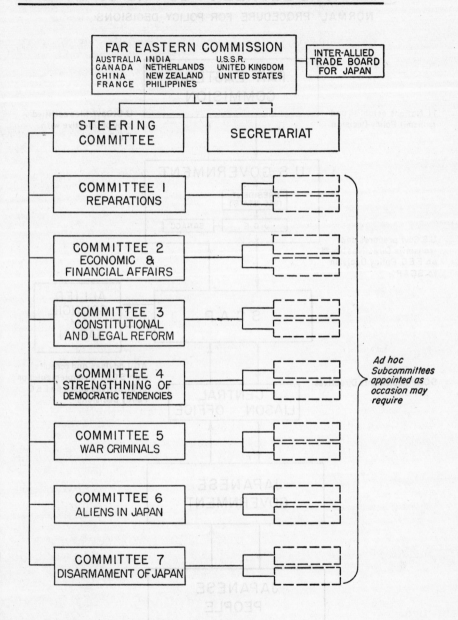

RELATIONS BETWEEN FEC AND SCAP

NORMAL PROCEDURE FOR POLICY DECISIONS

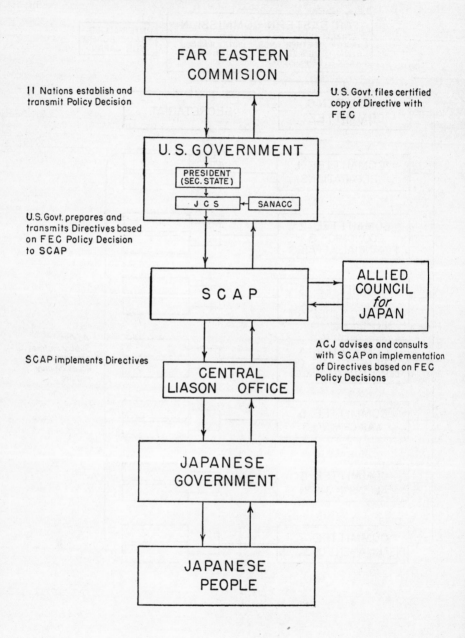

11 Nations establish and transmit Policy Decision

U.S. Govt. files certified copy of Directive with FEC

FAR EASTERN COMMISION

U.S. GOVERNMENT

PRESIDENT (SEC. STATE)

JCS — SANACC

U.S. Govt. prepares and transmits Directives based on FEC Policy Decision to SCAP

SCAP

ALLIED COUNCIL *for* JAPAN

ACJ advises and consults with SCAP on implementation of Directives based on FEC Policy Decisions

SCAP implements Directives

CENTRAL LIASON OFFICE

JAPANESE GOVERNMENT

JAPANESE PEOPLE

370

a change in the Japanese government as a whole would be issued only following consultation and the attainment of agreement in the FEC. Since directives of the latter type required the unanimous approval of the USSR, China, Great Britain, and the United States, they were seldom issued. Consequently, the United States was able to prescribe "interim directives" for execution by SCAP.

THE ALLIED COUNCIL FOR JAPAN.—The second agency created by the Foreign Ministers at Moscow, ACJ, was composed of the Supreme Commander or his deputy as chairman and United States member, one representative from the USSR, one from China, and one representing jointly Great Britain, Australia, New Zealand, and India. Established in Tokyo, ACJ's chief functions were to consult with and advise SCAP in regard to the implementation of the terms of surrender, the occupation and control of Japan, and of directives supplementary thereto. The ACJ was also given certain authority to put into effect the policy decisions of the FEC concerned with major changes in the form of the Japanese government. The ACJ could disagree with SCAP either as a unit or by a single member and thereby require SCAP to withhold action on the question at issue until agreement thereon should be reached by FEC. In practice individual members of the ACJ also performed the function of liaison agents between their respective governments and the activities of SCAP.

What we have said thus far about the early formulation of basic policy toward Japan and the agencies created by the Allied powers to give effect to their decisions leads to three conclusions of major importance. First, much of the basic policy toward Japan was formulated before the occupation actually began. Second, the leadership of the United States in the Far East as demonstrated by its war effort was sustained after cessation of hostilities. Third, the problem of the occupation of Japan was facilitated by the possibility of dealing with the nation as a unit; no artificial, airtight compartmentation in defiance of developed political, economic, or social ties was instituted. The net result of these three factors was to permit the vesting of immediate occupational control in the hands of one authority—SCAP, thus allowing the exercise of personal prestige and initiative and in turn promoting a high sense of mission among occupation forces.

Revolution in Japan

THE OCCUPATION'S REFORM OBJECTIVES.—The conqueror set a high goal for himself and for the Japanese in imposing a broad reform destined to touch almost every aspect of Japanese life. The proposed reforms directly reflected Great Power agreements in the FEC and previous decisions such as the Potsdam Declaration. Specific reforms contemplated the destruction of the stranglehold which ultranationalism and monopoly capitalism had exercised over the Japanese people and sought the elevation of the Japanese citizen to a position of responsibility. In short, the proposed reforms assumed the proportions of a revolution, a distinct break with most of Japan's past.

POLITICAL REFORM.—To accomplish its immediate security missions with a minimum of delay and a maximum of economy, SCAP utilized much of the existing Japanese governmental structure both at national and local levels. Undesirable elements, particularly those that had been intimately associated with Japan's military Fascist structure, were eliminated from government posts and acceptable agencies of the indigenous bureaucracy were modified to give a more liberal foundation to the whole structure of the Japanese nation. Political purges, preventive rather than punitive in purpose, were instituted as early as October, 1945, in order to ensure the elimination of influence or exercise of power by persons responsible for Japan's program of aggression. By this procedure some 183,000 career officers of the Army and Navy, members of the *gendarmerie*, and former intelligence agents were categorically denied influential positions in the political, economic, and social life of the country. In the absence of evidence to the contrary, SCAP was directed to assume that persons who had held key positions of high responsibility since 1937 in the Imperial Rule Assistance Association, who were active exponents of militant nationalism and aggression, or who were influential members of any Japanese ultranationalistic, terroristic, or secret patriotic society were disqualified from any participation in government. To prevent the infiltration of undesirables into the fields of education, police, or government, SCAP assigned responsibility to the Japanese government for screening persons occupying or seeking to enter those fields.

Between January and July, 1947, the Japanese government screened more than half a million individuals, most of whom were candidates at the national or local elections in April, 1947. Since only 1,681 persons were purged, it is assumed that few culpable persons risked probable exposure and proscription by running for office. When the purge directive was issued in January, 1946 some twenty thousand Japanese officials resigned to avoid its penalties.

More drastic steps were taken against the criminally liable leadership of Japan's aggressions. The International Prosecution section of SCAP promptly began investigating, arraigning, and bringing to trial those persons who as Class-A war criminals could be charged with crimes against peace; that is, the planning, initiating, or waging of aggressive war contrary to international law or treaties, agreements, and assurances, or participating in a conspiracy to perform any such acts. The Investigation and Prosecution division of SCAP's legal section also undertook the investigation and preparation of charges and specifications, and the trial of Class-B and Class-C Japanese war criminals. Included in the two latter categories were persons charged with atrocities committed in prisoner-of-war camps, aboard transports conducting prisoners of war to Japan, and against airmen forced down in Japanese territory.

PROMOTION OF DEMOCRATIC FORCES.—Destruction of ancient and barbarous practices and ideas of the Japanese was only the first phase of reform. A reconstruction policy was initiated and designed with the hope that it would in time grow roots as deep and strong as those which previously supported the nation. Thus, the Japanese people have been encouraged and given an opportunity to become familiar with the history, institutions, culture, and accomplishments of the United States and the other democracies. The practices of free assembly and public discussion, subject to the security requirements of the occupation, were permitted and encouraged. Laws, decrees, and regulations which established discrimination on grounds of race, nationality, creed, or political opinion under the Empire were abrogated. Furthermore, personal liberties such as those of religion, press, and speech were guaranteed by the adoption of a Japanese "Bill of Rights." As laws which had submitted the many to the will of the few fell on every side, so too did the myths and legends which had blinded men's eyes to the dignity of all citizens. On January 1, 1946, the Emperor Hirohito issued an imperial rescript which renounced the divinity of the Emperor and the previous claim that the Japanese people are superior to other races and fated to rule the world. At the same time Hirohito reasserted the Charter Oath, which—fashioned in the early Meiji period but forgotten in Japan's struggle for expansion and world conquest—had provided that:

1. Deliberative assemblies shall be established and all measures of government decided in accordance with public opinion.
2. All classes high and low shall unite in vigorously carrying on the affairs of State.
3. All common people, no less than the civil and military officials, shall be allowed to fulfill their just desires so that there may not be any discontent among them.
4. All the absurd usages of old shall be broken through and equity and justice to be found in the workings of nature shall serve as the basis of action.
5. Wisdom and knowledge shall be sought throughout the world for the purpose of promoting the welfare of the Empire.

JAPANESE POLITICAL PARTIES.—One immediate result of the opportunity given the Japanese people to establish democratic processes was the emergence of some sixty political parties, their platforms ranging all the way from the extreme left to an equally extreme right. No similar pattern had ever appeared in Japan's previous history. Within two years, however, the political outlines of the country became more distinct as five major parties corralled the bulk of the popular vote. Extremism lost out partly because the Japanese decided to follow a "middle of the road" program. Extremist groups also suffered from SCAP directives which forbade the existence of political parties, associations, societies, and other organizations whose purpose or the effect of whose activity was resistance or opposition to the occupation force, support or justification of aggressive Japanese militarism, or the assumption of Japanese leadership over other Asiatic peoples. All five major parties professed to favor democratic government, anti-bureaucracy, social insurance, stabilization of the people's livelihood, better rationing methods, abolition of the black market, entry of Japan into the United Nations, a speedy peace treaty, and justice in international relationships. Differences as to the ways and means by which these results might be accomplished separate the parties.

The Social Democratic party, a center party, won a plurality in national elections in 1947. It won major support in the cities because of its large labor-unionist membership and its stand for the creation of a peaceful democratic revolution, the progressive nationalization of essential key industries beginning with coal and iron, the taxation of incomes derived from war profits, and the suspension of interest on war bonds.

The Democratic party, the successor of the former Progressive party, draws its strength from the more conservative elements of the population both in the urban and rural sections. It is reputed to contain many remnants of the prewar Menseito party and is oriented slightly right of center in that it favors strict economic supervision by the government in contrast to the more socialistic base of the Social Democratic party, in whose platform governmental ownership rather than mere economic supervision is stressed.

The Liberal party, drawing its strength from businessmen and financial interests, and headed by former Prime Minister Yoshida, emphasizes anti-Communism as its strongest platform plank. A champion of individual enterprise, the party argues that it would achieve its liberal ends gradually and through evolution rather than by immediate drastic action.

The People's Cooperative party, founded originally as an agrarian party based upon existing semiofficial producing and distributing monopolies, stands for the cooperative principle in national production and distribution, the promotion of education, and the stabilization of Japan upon a generally conservative basis. Friction between city and farm members reduced the power of this party.

The Communist party, locally called the Social Science Club, claims to be the party of the masses, although it has won the support of less than 2 per cent of the voters. The Communists seek the elimination of capitalism and the Imperial system. The party is led by Sanzo Nosaka and Ryuichi Tokuda; the former is well known for his propaganda work among Japanese troops captured by Yennan Chinese Communists. Tokuda, after eighteen years in prison, was released under the terms of SCAP's civil liberties directive.

A sixth political organization, the Independent party, achieved widespread success in local elections by its tactic of supporting individuals who were popular in one region but entirely unknown elsewhere in Japan. Thus, in the April, 1947, election the municipal candidates of the Independents received more than twenty-three million of the thirty million votes cast. In the national election, however, the party candidates received few votes.

Japanese politics have not yet stabilized but remain a tangled maze of personalities, crosscurrents, compromises, and uncertainties. Elections have been marked by the disregard of electors for party lines and the selection of candidates whom they consider personally well qualified by character and experience. Not the least important consideration in the political scene is the fact that after full, fair, and free discussion the Japanese have repudiated extremist leadership.

GENESIS OF THE CONSTITUTION OF 1947.—The liberal aims of the United States in Japan were epitomized in the new, fundamental law of the land, the Constitution of 1947, which replaced the Meiji Constitution of 1889. The draft document of the new constitution, sponsored by the Japanese government and endorsed by General MacArthur, appeared early in March, 1946. The Far Eastern Commission thereupon established criteria for the adoption of the new constitution to ensure that (1) the Constitution was a free expression of the will of the Japanese people, (2) adequate time and opportunity would be allowed for its discussion, (3) legal continuity for the Constitution of 1889 obtained, and (4) the *manner* of adoption would conclusively demonstrate that the new Constitution affirmatively expressed the will of the Japanese. Two months later, May, 1946, decision was reached in the FEC on the following basic principles for inclusion in the constitution itself:

1. An executive deriving its authority from the electorate or from a representative legislative body, and responsible to the source of its authority.
2. A legislature enjoying full financial responsibility.
3. An independent judiciary.
4. A ministry collectively responsible to the legislature.
5. In the event of retention of the Emperor as a political institution, that office should enjoy no absolute executive powers, but in all matters should act in accordance with the advice of the Cabinet.

than three per cent of the votes. The Communists seek the elimination of

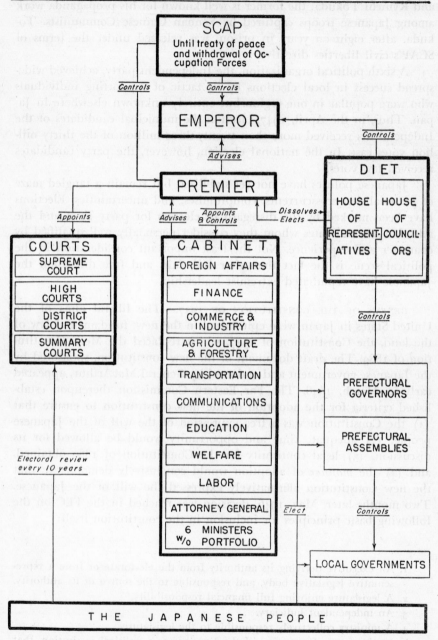

GOVERNMENT OF JAPAN UNDER THE CONSTITUTION of 1947

SCAP
Until treaty of peace
and withdrawal of Oc-
cupation Forces

Controls — *Controls*

EMPEROR

Controls

Advises

PREMIER

Appoints — *Advises* — *Appoints & Controls* — *Dissolves Elects*

DIET

HOUSE OF REPRESENT-ATIVES | HOUSE OF COUNCIL-ORS

COURTS

SUPREME COURT

HIGH COURTS

DISTRICT COURTS

SUMMARY COURTS

CABINET

FOREIGN AFFAIRS

FINANCE

COMMERCE & INDUSTRY

AGRICULTURE & FORESTRY

TRANSPORTATION

COMMUNICATIONS

EDUCATION

WELFARE

LABOR

ATTORNEY GENERAL

6 MINISTERS W/o PORTFOLIO

Controls

PREFECTURAL GOVERNORS

PREFECTURAL ASSEMBLIES

Electoral review every 10 years

Elect — *Controls*

LOCAL GOVERNMENTS

THE JAPANESE PEOPLE

The new constitution became effective in May, 1947, seven months after promulgation by the Emperor the preceding November. Such features of the old form of government as could readily and usefully be adapted to the new democratic frame of law were retained in the new instrument. A more detailed examination of the Constitution of 1947 in comparison with the Meiji Constitution will reveal major features in which both old and new have been artfully blended.

POPULAR SOVEREIGNTY AND THE EMPEROR.—In the new constitution popular sovereignty has replaced divine, imperial sovereignty. Whatever prerogatives accrued to the Japanese people under the Meiji Constitution were understood to have been *gifts* of the Emperor Mutsuhito.[9] The new sentiments and beliefs were advanced in Article I of the 1947 Constitution which breaks the feudalistic hold of the Emperor on the country and sets the stage for a democratic process by which the Emperor becomes "the symbol of the state and of the unity of the people, deriving his position from the will of the people, with whom resides sovereign power." Hardly was the constitution promulgated when two distinct interpretations of the source of sovereignty achieved currency among certain elements of the population. The first idea, the more dangerous since it lent support to the views of reactionary groups, was that the new fundamental law did not essentially alter the characteristics of the state. This concept held that even though the Emperor had been shorn of legal sovereignty, he retained his moral leadership, which is essentially the index of national policy. The more liberal interpretation agreed that the Emperor maintained his moral leadership but argued that sovereignty is a legal, not a moral, concept, and that the Emperor's surrender of his legal sovereignty had fundamentally altered the character of the state. That the present Emperor will ever seek actually to govern is regarded as unlikely since he was only the symbol of rule under the Meiji Constitution, and in the new Constitution is specifically forbidden to "exercise powers related to government." And yet the danger will long continue that a misdirected bureaucracy—a real enemy of democracy— might again seek to advance its aims under the cloak and guise of exercising the Emperor's moral leadership.

THE CABINET AND THE LEGISLATURE.—The status of the Cabinet under the Meiji Constitution and the political techniques through which it was able to infringe upon the power of the Diet were indicated earlier in the present chapter. The 1947 Constitution inaugurated a fully demo-

---

[9] Quoting from the Preface of the 1889 Constitution: "Having, by virtue of the glories of our ancestors, ascended the throne of a lineal succession unbroken for ages eternal . . . we hereby promulgate . . . a fundamental law of state, to exhibit the principles by which we are to be guided in our conduct. . . . *The rights of sovereignty of the State we have inherited from our ancestors and we shall bequeath them to our descendants. . . .*"

cratic pattern for the legislature by providing for the election of the premier by the Diet and making him responsible to the Diet. Furthermore, a majority of the members of the Cabinet must now be members of the Diet, and resignation of the Cabinet or an appeal to the country through election must follow a vote of want of confidence in the House of Representatives. Not only does the new Constitution definitely subordinate the Cabinet to the Diet, but it also weakens the executive branch as a whole by scrapping those provisions and conventions of the old Constitution which often prevented a relatively liberal Cabinet from exhibiting responsibility to the Diet. Thus, the Cabinet can no longer be hamstrung by a Privy Council, Imperial Household Ministry, or a politically entrenched oligarchy of militarists. Instead, the Cabinet must secure from the Diet the mandates which shape its policies as well as the funds to implement them.

The previous dualism in the Japanese government, most notably instanced in the unique control exercised by the Cabinet representatives of the armed services, is eliminated. The prime minister and other ministers of state must be civilians. The constitutional prohibition against the maintenance of military forces of any kind and the absence of war and navy ministries from the Cabinet, while perhaps premature and idealistic in an insecure world, does ensure that future conspirators against civilian government will have difficulty regaining control.

The status of the legislative branch under the new Constitution is made clear by the provision that the Diet is "the highest organ of state power . . . and the sole lawmaking organ of the state." Real legislative power, however, resides in the lower house, the House of Representatives —a replica in that respect of the British system. The upper house, the House of Councilors, has been shorn of its previous prestige by the abolition of the peerage, the provision that it too must be popularly elected, and its subordination to the House of Representatives. It appears that the House of Councilors may serve the nation by becoming a consultative body combining the valuable attributes of the old Privy Council and the House of Peers but, at the same time, deprived of their crippling control of the government.

THE JUDICIARY.—The Meiji Constitution invested the Emperor with final judicial power and prevented the creation of an independent judiciary. The new Constitution and subsequent legislation strengthen the position of the courts by creating an independent judiciary headed by a supreme court and supported by high courts, district courts, and summary courts. Moreover, the supreme court now has the power of judicial review of legislation and the authority to nominate judges of the inferior courts.

The Chief Justice of the Supreme Court is appointed by the emperor upon his designation by the Cabinet, and fourteen associate justices are appointed directly by the Cabinet. Ten of the justices must be recruited on the basis of strict professional requirements such as long experience as judge, lawyer, or professor of legal science. The remaining five may be persons with backgrounds of other than normal legal experience. A popular check upon the power of the judiciary is provided by making the appointed judges of the Supreme Court subject to recall by popular referendum. Judges in inferior courts may be impeached by legislative action.

While the court system was being overhauled, it was essential to give the new system a firm basis in revised national and local legal codes. Thus new laws were enacted dealing with the changed position of the imperial family, the organization of the new Cabinet, the Diet, administrative offices, the finance services, and the civil service. The newly gained rights of the individual were codified and their administration was provided for by bills relating to civil liberties. Even the judicial administration itself was provided for by the new legislation.

LOCAL GOVERNMENT.—Perhaps the clearest example of the elimination of totalitarian tendencies and the fuller opportunity for free expression of the public will in contemporary Japan is found in the revised system of local government provided for under the Constitution of 1947. The Ministry of Home Affairs, probably the oldest formal branch of the government in Japan—since it dates as far as the year A.D. 549—became, under the Meiji Restoration, the most powerful of all ministries. Under the Constitution of 1947 the Home Ministry no longer reaches directly into the domestic affairs of the people by compelling them to conform to ritualistic state Shinto, holding their spirit in subjection and infusing them with ultranationalistic and militaristic doctrines. Nor does its Local Affairs Bureau any longer exercise control over even the minutest details of local government. The home minister has been shorn of his authority to appoint all prefectural governors, subject them to his discipline, and to remove or transfer them at pleasure. The old chain of command has been further broken: no longer may the governors refuse to follow actions and recommendations of the prefectural assemblies. Instead, these elective bodies today exercise freedom of thought and action in response to democratic impulses. Similarly, the mayors and governments of Japan's cities have gained local autonomy to such a degree that the home minister does not remain the virtual monarch of internal Japanese administration that he formerly was. The freeing of election procedures is also a blow at the total control once exercised to coerce the electorate, to intimidate opposition candidates by a strong-armed police, or to swing elections as the home minister saw fit. Also abolished were the extreme regimentation of the Japanese people by the police force, imprisonment of dissident elements without lodging specific charges or presenting the accused for trial, restriction of free movement within the country and abroad, and strict censorship of books, magazines, and newspapers. So efficient had Japanese totalitarianism become under such agencies as the Home Ministry that it is little wonder Hitler and Mussolini used them as models for their own controls.[10] Generous grants of local autonomy, the elimination of the Tonari Gumi system by which communities were broken down into units of ten families to facilitate control of their activities, the decentralization of the police force, and draft legislation to abolish the Home Ministry are the cornerstones of current reform in local government.

ECONOMIC REFORM.—History records no time when Japan could provide more than a bare living for the great mass of her population. The situation grew worse during the two decades preceding World War II which saw Japan's leaders campaigning for an increased birth rate. Long before Pearl Harbor, her population could be sustained only by an economic system under which her low-cost, labor-sweating production transformed imported raw materials for processing and export at a figure which could not be met by Western industry. When military catastrophe destroyed that system, nothing except large-scale relief, backed by stern military authority, prevented serious economic troubles involving unemployment, strikes, and starvation. Such temporary restraints, however, had to be eliminated, while at the same time Japan was provided with lasting means for attaining real self-sufficiency before economic and political health could be restored.

SCAP's first and greatest problem in the economic field was to provide the bare necessities of life for seventy-three million people, living on approximately 148 thousand square miles of land, the residue of territory left Japan in her four main islands and adjacent islets. Rationing was supplemented by the importation of items in short supply. Improved scientific methods were introduced in agriculture, better food distribution facilities were established, black market activities incurred severe punishment. The fishing industry was revived and pushed to provide in full measure an important item of the Japanese diet.[11] As a result of such activities, the average Japanese was living better in 1948 than

---

[10] The budding Fascists of Germany and Italy, after noting the ease and efficiency with which Japan launched her program of military aggression and expansion in 1931, carefully analyzed the political factors in Japan's success. The part played by the Home Ministry in the regimentation of the Japanese was duly noted and promptly copied. Italy, to be sure, had already gone a long way in that direction; Japan's example showed Mussolini where his controls could be tightened.

[11] Whale meat was expected to furnish upward of 30 per cent, possibly 40 per cent, of Japan's meat supply in 1948—the direct result of SCAP action in pushing Japan's exploitation of Antarctic whaling regions.

nearly all other Orientals, better, in fact, than the citizens of postwar Germany and Austria.

Simultaneously with the project to provide the Japanese with necessary sustenance was begun a guided democratizing program in each of the specific fields of labor, industry and industrial reparations, foreign trade, finance, price control and rationing, science and technology, antitrust and cartels. Basic economic research necessary for an understanding of the several fields was undertaken. The purpose of this far-reaching program was threefold: to ensure that Japan will not again wage aggressive war; to reform and democratize the Japanese economic structure; and to restore to the Japanese people their right to a peaceful and fruitful existence.

By the end of 1948 the picture in the industrial field was not without hope. Thus, the decisions to liquidate the great cartels and to restore production to a level approximating the 1930-1934 average level were followed by a definite revival of industrial activity. At the outset major emphasis was placed on the production of coal, building materials, transportation equipment, fertilizer, and replacements for worn-out machinery.

SOCIAL REFORM—ELEVATION OF THE INDIVIDUAL.—A most significant gain in the direction of democracy in Japan from the standpoint of social reforms occurred in the inauguration of measures seeking the elevation of the individual Japanese from his previous position of a worshiping, obedient son of a divine Emperor to that of a respected citizen whose person and property have the protection of the laws—laws to which even the emperor himself is subordinate. A good illustration of this trend in Japan is the emancipation of woman. Today she stands as man's equal before the law, in the factory, on the farm, and in the Diet. Present encouraging indications are that the women of Japan are freely and enthusiastically embracing their new-found freedom, as evidenced by their participation in politics and industry. Furthermore, the rigid discipline of a home dominated by the tribal autocracy of the oldest living male is steadily breaking down under the impact of these new forces.

RELIGIOUS REFORMS.—Reform in the field of religion included the grant of religious freedom. State sponsorship of Shinto was eliminated and prohibited, as also were militaristic or ultranationalistic societies operating under the guise of religion. The influence of Christianity has been greatly enhanced by the principles of justice, tolerance, and understanding which have characterized the Occupation, with a resultant increase of foreign Christian missionaries to a total of 1250 by the end of 1947.

DECONTROL OF INFORMATION MEDIUMS.—Hand in hand with the social reforms already discussed were the efforts of SCAP to free information mediums in Japan from bureaucratic restriction and control. Realizing that the simple grant of free speech and press to a people who have never before enjoyed such liberties would hardly begin to set in motion the dissemination of honest and accurate information, SCAP has systematically worked toward educating the Japanese in the use of their new liberty. Editors and publishers have been thoroughly informed as to their right to publish news and editorial comment free from domination of any kind. The Japanese have become alert to the increased importance of public opinion as shown by the action of private agencies created since the surrender to test the people's views on matters of importance. SCAP itself has maintained an active mediums analysis section to scan newspapers, magazines, and the works of representative Japanese writers in order to keep in touch with the trends of public opinion.

EDUCATION.—Implementing the provisions of the Potsdam Declaration and the Constitution of 1947 and following closely the recommendations of the United States Mission for Education, efforts were directed toward rooting out the traditional authoritative teaching methods and replacing them with democratic methods of instruction. The Fundamental Law of Education passed by the Diet in March, 1947, is the principal Japanese effort in their own behalf. Noteworthy among these educational reforms are the elimination of objectionable teachers and texts, military schools and militarism, the protection of schools from political influence, compulsory education extended through the seventh year, and the unrestricted availability of higher education. New textbooks have been prepared for all grades of students. In the treatment of the social sciences the net effect is revolutionary. Mythology and synthetic thought patterns have given way to truth and objectivity. At the same time the educational process has been decentralized by according the local and prefectural governments greater control over the schools within their respective areas.

AGRARIAN REFORM.—The feudal economic structure of the country has long brought exceptional hardships to the Japanese farmer. Whether as landowner or servile tenant of an exacting landlord, he has suffered from heavy taxation, political domination, the impersonal disasters of flood and drought, and a farming technique calling for much higher output of hard work per unit product than is required of the farmers of any Western nation. Postwar agrarian reform in Japan has taken the form of land redistrubution, education in improved farming techniques, and the general easing of the farmer's tax burden. Furthermore, by encouraging and assisting the Japanese government to establish a national health and welfare program SCAP has alleviated the plight of thousands of Japanese families who suffered casualties during the war. The price of defeat, as measured in terms of casualties, has been most heavily felt among Japan's impoverished farmers, since their ranks furnished the bulk of the military conscripts. For that reason alone, the special welfare programs have met an acute need in agrarian Japan.

JAPAN AS A FUTURE FORCE IN WORLD POLITICS.—The action of the United States in proposing an early peace settlement with Japan raises a number of questions. For better or for worse, her geography and her human and material resources will continue to make her an important political and strategic factor in the Far East. If the hopes and plans of the Western powers are fulfilled, Japan's potential will be released along democratic lines, a healthy and stabilizing element in the general ferment now stirring the east Asiatic region. That area is inhabited by almost two thirds of the world's population. Japan as a workshop supplying a large amount of the low-price consumers' goods needed by the hundreds of millions of the Far East could help materially in raising living standards in that area. At the same time, Japan might resume her role as political leader of eastern Asia, exercising her leadership in the direction of co-operation, rather than conflict, with the Western world.

Such a role would clearly be the reverse of that planned by Japan's military Fascists of the twentieth century, with their slogans of "Asia for the Asiatics" as bait for the organization of the "Greater East Asia Co-Prosperity Sphere." Indeed, it is entirely conceivable that an independent, unregenerate Japan might revert to her earliest ambitions and dreams of mastery over the world's most populous area, particularly if the growing tension between the Western powers and the Soviet Union give her once again the chance to fish in troubled waters. Any discussion of Japan's future as a nation must, therefore, take into account the position, potential, and aims of the USSR in the Far East. If Moscow's moves in Korea, Manchuria, and China reflect expansive ambitions as far-reaching as her aims in eastern and central Europe, it follows that an early peace between the Soviet Union and Japan will not further Japan's interests. The history of Russo-Japanese relations is a record of war and truce. Of real peace there has been none. In Japan's eyes, a Soviet Russia dominating the land area from Kamchatka to north China, whether directly or through satellites, would have a series of batteries aimed at Japan's heart, the lanyards of their guns to be pulled at a convenient moment. In short, Japan's existence as an independent nation in these circumstances would depend on Soviet sufferance unless United States assistance, at least in terms of air and sea power, was readily available either through a Pacific regional arrangement or through a strengthened UN.

Japan is not a completely helpless pawn on the chessboard of international affairs. Seventy-five million people of proved energy and industrial aptitude are in a position to win some concessions from the victors, particularly when a difference exists within the ranks of the victors such as the current difficulties between the Soviet Union and the Western democracies. Furthermore, Japan, although critically deficient in food and many minerals, has already been promised freedom and "access to raw materials" in the Potsdam Declaration. The details of the peace settlement are greatly obscured, however, by the interests and fears of neighboring countries who have felt the impact of Japanese aggression. Hence China, the Philippines, Australia, and Indonesia will have appreciable influences on the future of Japan. Japan may soon emerge again as a "great" power in an orderly world, may become through economic and military dependence a powerful "Janissary" on one side or the other in a world split by ideological conflict, or may remain for a long while in an obscure, unstable situation in world affairs. The determination turns in great part on two related factors: (a) the outcome of the struggle going forward in Korea, Manchuria, and China; and (b) the policies of the Western democracies both as to Japan herself and in the ideological East-West struggle of which those of the United States are overriding in their importance.

NATIONAL SECURITY AND INTERNATIONAL ORGANIZATION

◇◇◇

The Problem of Security

INTRODUCTION.—Discussion of the problem of international organization in today's system of nation-states must include reference to earlier efforts at the solution of the problem. In our consideration of these attempts we shall see that they had the common goal of promoting the security of their adherents. One of the major functions of government of each of the nation-states that make up our world is also (and always has been) the preservation of national security. It is appropriate, therefore, that we preface our survey of historic efforts toward such a world order with an examination of the problem of security and the general characteristics of systems intended to preserve it.

THE MEANING OF SECURITY.—For a long time national security was considered as being merely the preservation of the nation from attack or threat of attack, and from partial or complete destruction by the armed forces of any enemy state or coalition of enemy states. As the nations and areas of the world became more interdependent economically, however, a broader interpretation came to be given to the words "national security." The objectives sought were expanded to include preservation of the form of government and the way of life of the people from catastrophic change due to forces generated beyond the nation's boundaries. These forces might be economic, ideological, or psychological in nature, and more often than not combined with military power. In international relations the meaning of the word "security" must therefore be interpreted in the light of the situation to which it is applied and the significance given it by the governments concerned.

THE EXPANDING SECURITY PROBLEM.—When nations were relatively independent of each other economically, when military aggression was definitely limited by inability to support effective armed forces far from the homeland, and when wars were fought by relatively few armed participants, the problem of security was definitely areal rather than global

DECLARATION BY UNITED NATIONS

JANUARY 1, 1942

A Joint Declaration by the United States of America, the United Kingdom of Great Britain and Northern Ireland, the Union of Soviet Socialist Republics, China, Australia, Belgium, Canada, Costa Rica, Cuba, Czechoslovakia, Dominican Republic, El Salvador, Greece, Guatemala, Haiti, Honduras, India, Luxemburg, Netherlands, New Zealand, Nicaragua, Norway, Panama, Poland, South Africa, Yugoslavia.

The Governments signatory hereto,

Having subscribed to a common program of purposes and principles embodied in the Joint Declaration of the President of the United States of America and the Prime Minister of the United Kingdom of Great Britain and Northern Ireland dated August 14, 1941, known as the Atlantic Charter,

Being convinced that complete victory over their enemies is essential to defend life, liberty, independence and religious freedom, and to preserve human rights and justice in their own lands as well as in other lands, and that they are now engaged in a common struggle against savage and brutal forces seeking to subjugate the world,

Declare:

(1) Each Government pledges itself to employ its full resources, military or economic, against those members of the Tripartite Pact and its adherents with which such government is at war.

(2) Each Government pledges itself to cooperate with the Governments signatory hereto and not to make a separate armistice or peace with the enemies.

The foregoing declaration may be adhered to by other nations which are, or which may be, rendering material assistance and contributions in the struggle for victory over Hitlerism.

Done at Washington, January First, 1942

Notes:

This Declaration was signed by representatives of the governments above listed on January 1, 1942. Subsequently the following nations communicated their adherence to the Declaration on the dates given below:

Mexico	June 5, 1942	Ecuador	Feb. 7, 1945
Philippines	June 10, 1942	Peru	Feb. 11, 1945
Ethiopia	July 28, 1942	Chile	Feb. 12, 1945
Iraq	Jan. 16, 1943	Paraguay	Feb. 12, 1945
Brazil	Feb. 8, 1943	Venezuela	Feb. 16, 1945
Bolivia	Apr. 27, 1943	Uruguay	Feb. 23, 1945
Iran	Sept. 10, 1943	Turkey	Feb. 24, 1945
Colombia	Dec. 22, 1943	Egypt	Feb. 27, 1945
Liberia	Feb. 26, 1944	Saudi Arabia	Mar. 1, 1945
France (GPRF)	Dec. 26, 1944		

in nature and scope. This compartmentalization of security problems first began to break down in the eighteenth century when wars between France and England brought disruption and destruction in such widely separated areas as India, Africa, and North America. For purposes of destruction, the globe was then already shrinking. But it was not until the full import of the first and second World Wars, separated by the short armistice of 1918-1939, had been driven home to statesmen that anything like common agreement could be reached on concepts like the following:

1. A nation's security can be threatened or destroyed by means short of war—economic, psychological, ideological—with armies acting only as mop-up forces following the application of these more sophisticated techniques of "cold war."
2. The means of war have become so destructively efficient that another armed conflict may well destroy civilization.
3. Peace and security for any one nation can be guaranteed only by assuring peace and security for the entire world.[1]

By 1947 it had become clear that national security was identical with, and inseparable from, world security. General acceptance of this principle unfortunately does not achieve world security. Realization can come only after the means and mechanisms for the implementation of the principle have been set up on a foundation of support broad enough to ensure their effective functioning in a crisis.

Nations are slow to give up their traditional systems of security, but any practical system of world security must evolve from the old systems of national security. It is well, therefore, to comment briefly on the experience of the past in the field. All systems and schemes have been predicated on the independent sovereignty of each nation-state to maintain its own security against attack or threat of attack.

The Search for Security

SECURITY BY INDIVIDUAL NATION-STATES.—The first system of security might be described as each nation for itself. Centuries ago national security could be achieved by the maintenance of armed forces and the manning of adequate natural barriers. Even these simple requirements created the first dilemma in the search for security by nations, a dilemma that still plagues the world and that has been intensified by the new and more terrible ways of war, as well as by such factors as the economic interdependence of nations. A particular nation-state such, for example,

---

[1] "When peace has been broken anywhere, the peace of all countries everywhere is in danger."—Franklin D. Roosevelt, Fireside Chat on the European War, Washington, D. C., September 3, 1939.

as Belgium might not be large or rich enough to maintain the armed forces needed to provide security against its neighbors. Adequate natural barriers might not exist on the boundaries, and their acquisition might involve war and the impairment of the security of a neighboring state as the history of the French eastern and northern borders illustrates. Finally, when a nation attained the level of military power and geographical security which eliminated national uneasiness, neighboring states, fearing aggression, might feel that their security was threatened. In other words, the quest for absolute security by a particular nation generally has spelled insecurity for its neighbors.

SECURITY BY ALLIANCE.—A direct result of the difficulties confronting states acting individually has been the ever-changing galaxy of alliances, coalitions, and leagues which march through the pages of modern history. By these measures nations sought security through agreements with other nations having common security interests. The deficiencies in the alliance system were and are substantially the same as those arising from the unilateral search for security by nations. Alliances tend to engender opposing alliances. Moreover, a situation which one alliance considers as providing adequate security for itself leaves neighboring states and alliances with a feeling of insecurity whether or not that feeling is justified. Distrust is fostered because the elements which constitute security for one nation or coalition of nations are often the very elements necessary for successful aggression. And their application, whether for security or for aggression, rests at length with the national leaders involved.

Furthermore, any alliance is at best a cooperative effort, formalized by a written agreement, usually couched in the most general terms, for the furtherance of certain common security interests which frequently are hard to define. Since the problem of security is continually changing, little chance of permanence exists. Nations in alliance do not constitute a superstate capable of compelling the continued adherence of the partners to the original agreement. Hence, the history of alliances is a history of broken or only partially implemented contracts, and of individual nations going from one alliance or coalition to another and opposing coalition. Italy, for instance, was the ally of Germany and Austria-Hungary, prior to World War I, but nevertheless switched sides and fought against them in that war. Japan was Britain's ally of long standing prior to 1920, only to become an aggressive rival soon after, and Britain's bitter enemy in World War II.

The stumbling block of national sovereignty, combined with the continual shifts in national interests and objectives, has served to prevent the assured stability and permanence of any system of security based on the alliance principle.

SECURITY THROUGH THE "BALANCE OF POWER."—Like the word "security," the concept of the "balance of power" often has meant different things to different nations. Basically the latter method represents a special case of the search for security through alliances. Thus the nations on the continent of Europe tended to consider the quest for security through the balance of power as being the attempt to attain and maintain a situation under which no nation or coalition of nations felt strong enough to attack another nation or another coalition. The application of this principle obviously required some very delicate estimates as to when to change sides and also called for continual adjustment as the power of nations changed with time and as national interests became world-wide in scope.

On the other hand, Great Britain tended to interpret the balance-of-power principle as one under which she could attain security through a balance of forces between nations and coalitions on the continent of Europe (and later in the world), which would be tipped in whatever direction Great Britain threw her influence and her military power. So long as the nation holding the increment of power capable of tipping the scales was a nonaggressive, peacefully inclined nation, the British version of the balance-of-power system was probably the best thus far devised for area and world security. It worked well during the nineteenth century after the fall of Napoleon; then its inherent weaknesses contributed heavily to the outbreak of two devastating world wars in the twentieth century.

With the passage of time one nation or coalition may readily develop the belief that it is stronger than any other possible coalition. Unequal growths of population in different nations, changes in industrial and military technology, varying rates of economic development, and the differing portions of national income devoted to security and armaments, all contribute to the imbalance between rival alliances. At that point the stronger is apt to stretch its muscles and look for a fight. Germany and her allies in 1914 fairly represent such a historical progression.

Two important requirements for the success of the British balance-of-power system are the necessity for maintaining in readiness sufficient means to tip the balance at the proper moment, and the willingness of the nation or coalition concerned to use those means. Great Britain's balance-of-power principle broke down prior to World War II probably because of her failure to maintain adequate means and her unwillingness, demonstrated in 1938 at Munich, to throw her full weight into the scales against the Axis forces which were destroying European and world security.

We should note that the balance-of-power principle was essentially negative. It did not in itself provide any positive mechanism for settling those problems between and within nations which often evolve toward a violent solution. Nevertheless the system could theoretically be used to promote the readjustment of territories, distribution of economic resources, compromises and peaceful settlement of differences—providing that some machinery existed to handle such problems.[2]

SECURITY THROUGH COOPERATION OF THE GREAT POWERS.—It is obvious that if all the Great Powers can at all times be induced to cooperate in the maintenance of peace, there will be world security, at least in the narrow sense of that word. History has shown that the integrity of territory and governments can be maintained. Thus the system of Great Power cooperation combined with the balance-of-power principle, prevented any great war from 1815 to 1914. At best, however, Great Power cooperation is subject to quick disintegration in a crisis. It does not provide easily for settlement of issues and problems on a basis of justice to the many less powerful nations (of which there are at present over sixty, as compared to two or three truly great powers). The loose affinities between some of the Great Powers, their individual sympathies and aims in relation to the lesser nations, and the lack of any element of force superior to the sovereignty of the Great Powers—all combine to make a system of world security through this kind of cooperation an unstable arrangement. Yet it is still unhappily apparent that there can be no lasting system of world security today, either in the narrow or broad sense of the term, without the cooperation or at least acquiescence of all the Great Powers.

SECURITY THROUGH CONFERENCE, PACT, AND LAW.—The thesis that world security could be attained through the growth of a respect for international laws and through agreements resulting in peaceful settlements and adjustments between nations is not new. The development of principles and mechanisms in these fields has, however, been greatly accelerated during the last century, as will be seen later in the chapter. Certain of these principles and schools of thought are discussed briefly in the following paragraphs in order to complete the summary of the problems and proposals in the ever-accelerating search for security in the world.

I. SECURITY THROUGH INTERNATIONAL LAW.—The individual citizens of a nation are subject to its laws, and in general respect and obey them. Behind the law there exists a national police power ready and able to punish the individual lawbreaker. Nations, however, are not individuals; consequently they recognize no power superior to them and, to date, have

---

[2] Such promotion of settlements was undoubtedly undertaken by Disraeli at the Congress of Berlin in 1878. Whether that particular promotion was chiefly motivated by desire for justice and world peace, or largely influenced by Britain's special interests (which did happen to include world peace), is an interesting question for historians.

been unwilling to set up a superpower strong enough to enforce international law and to punish the lawbreakers. Furthermore, respect for the rule of law is a major factor in causing individuals to conform to laws. Nations conditioned through centuries of international anarchy lack this fundamental respect for the rule of international law, although such lack varies in degree among the nations. As a result, the development of an effective working system of international law becomes an exceedingly slow process. Nations thus far have adopted the attitude that they would be bound by the interpretations of so-called international laws, such as the laws of war, only when, of their own free will, they have previously agreed to accept such interpretations. Even within that restricted sphere of conformance, violations of written agreements have been so common and so flagrant whenever the violator felt that such action would secure for it some military advantage, that faith in international law suffered a tremendous setback. Germany's initiation of unrestricted submarine warfare in World War I is a classic example of such violations. Nevertheless, there are many problems disturbing to world security which can be settled temporarily at least by agreements between nations. Implementation of these agreements and failures to carry them out are susceptible of review on a legal basis, thereby contributing in some degree to the preservation of world order and peace.

II. SECURITY THROUGH PACT, ARBITRATION, COMPROMISE, AND CONFERENCE.—The basic problems of security are more susceptible of initial solution through compromise, arbitration, mediation, or conference between interested nations, perhaps with the assistance of other powers. A solution, if achieved, may often provide a satisfactory basis for solving succeeding aspects of the problem through the mechanism of an international court which, as we have seen, can pass on the legality of acts executed under an international agreement. If, however, there is no such international agreement, and furthermore, no agreement to accept the decision of an international court, there will be no international law to interpret and no power to compel adherence to the interpretations.

Logically the solutions achieved through arbitration, mediation, and conference can rarely be based entirely on principles of dispassionate abstract justice. The relative power and resolution of the parties interested are, therefore, major items in achieving a practical solution. Consequently, the end result may be one of equal dissatisfaction to all concerned, or great dissatisfaction to only one of the parties. Particularly under the latter circumstance the seed of insecurity and unrest remain firmly planted. The Arab dissatisfaction over the UN Assembly decision in 1948 to partition Palestine is an excellent example of such a situation.

From time to time considerable faith has been voiced that security can be evolved by the conference method and thus preserved on a basis short of world dominance by a single police state. Such conferences might have prevented or postponed World War I. But World War II was preceded by almost continuous meetings of the League of Nations marked by abundant debate. Then followed the final critical meetings at Munich between representatives of the Great Powers concerned (except the United States and the USSR). All such oratory, conversations, and conferences failed to keep world peace. In fact, by displaying the lack of realization, readiness, and resolution of some of the nations involved, they probably helped instead to destroy the peace.

SECURITY THROUGH DISARMAMENT.—A nation or coalition cannot physically violate the security of another nation or coalition unless it has military means adequate and ready for the undertaking. Hence, it has been urged that security can be achieved through the regulated reduction and eventual elimination of armaments. When we recall the broad objectives implicit in the term "security," however, it is apparent that disarmament measures can achieve at most security only in the narrowest sense of the term. Disarmament does not deal with the wider and more intangible aspects of the problem, which are no less dangerous to security, such as the economic, political, and ideological forces which may impair or even destroy a nation's integrity without the active employment of armed force.

Some nations, because of their industrial power, political regimentation, or both, have tremendous capacities for quick rearmament in case the security system breaks down. Others do not. In order to provide any guarantee of permanency, disarmament must be accompanied (or preceded) by the establishment of some system which prevents such rearmament as a resolute nation can undertake in a few years, as did Nazi Germany. Disarmament also has major technical and political obstacles because of diverse natures and missions of armed forces of different nations. It is difficult, if not impossible, for example, to find a common denominator of the power inherent in ground, sea, and air weapons.

Armaments are merely the final instruments used in carrying destruction to an opponent in open war. However much arms may tempt a congenitally, belligerent people possessing them to put the weapons to active use, the mainspring of aggression is still to be found in the minds and hearts of the aggressors, not in their material tools. For that reason all causes of world insecurity must be controlled at least concurrently with reduction of armaments. Otherwise, from a practical standpoint, no wise nation will consent to reduce its armaments, thereby giving up its power to defend itself. Yet the existence of large armaments gravely complicates any system of world security. In certain countries, e.g., Germany and Japan, they helped to foster a war psychosis in the people, at the same time stimulating in the national leaders gross overconfidence in the nation's capacity for all-out war. A second difficulty in the maintenance of adequate armaments is that the financial strain may leave the nation gravely weakened, economically, politically, or both, thereby perhaps contributing to world unrest and insecurity. Nevertheless, world security must first be assured before those nations best able to afford armaments will consent to relinquish them.

SECURITY THROUGH "COLLECTIVE SECURITY."—After World War I it was proposed that mutual guarantees of the military security of nations be given by nations on a wide basis—perhaps world-wide. This proposal might be called a variation of the principle of security through alliances. It is certainly related to the alliance principle but is much broader in its concept. France was particularly interested in promoting this method of attaining world security because of her continuing fear of Germany. The proponents of collective security argued that if all the nations banded together in a compact to jump hard and promptly on any aggressor attacking one of their number, breaches of the peace would be discouraged. This thesis is attractive and plausible in principle. Nations such as the United States, however, were unwilling to commit themselves to an agreement which in effect committed them to war, long in advance of a crisis and without further review of the situation. The plan provided no superpower to hold a nation to its agreement when and if the time came to discipline an aggressor. Definition of an "aggressor" and proof of "aggression" or its intent were difficult. Inherent in an agreement to promote collective security might be the guarantee of the *status quo* of territory and national influences for a long period, thereby bottling up forces which might eventually blow the stopper through even a strong system. For such a system to work, a willingness to surrender some elements of national sovereignty must exist and there must be provision for peaceful evolutionary change in the world order and for adjustment to the very real, if intangible, factors which have a continuing impact on security.

SECURITY THROUGH AREA AND WORLD GOVERNMENT.—All of the various principles bearing on national and world security which have been discussed thus far have been built on the premise of unimpaired national sovereignty—the obstacle over which every program has stumbled sooner or later. Various proposals have been advanced, usually by associations of individuals rather than by nations, that this stumbling block should be leveled or surmounted through the medium of a superstate possessing final authority over nations and individuals in matters pertaining to security. Some of these proposals have projected a superstate starting in one area, such as Europe or the nations bordering the north Atlantic. Such an area superstate launched initially by a federation of nations having a large common denominator of mutual characteristics and interests would gradually expand by federation, according to its advocates, until it included other states, and perhaps the entire world. Other proponents of the superstate concept propose that a world-wide superstate be set up at once. It is generally agreed that the world of nation-states may be proceeding through greater integration toward what could in time be a world state. Differences of opinion develop over the timing—some think it may be a thousand years—and on its practicability. Certain of the difficulties are obvious. Most of them are either those which beset the other principles for world security already discussed, or are related to them.

A strong federation established on an area basis, such as Europe or the Atlantic community, might be interpreted by the rest of the world as being tantamount to an alliance unbalancing the relations of nations in and adjacent to the area. The reaction to be expected in such circumstances, unless history is reversed, is not further federation but rather a counteralliance and war.

The basic difficulties facing an area or world federation can be divided into two categories: first, how to form it; secondly, how to make it effective. There are only two ways to create any international organization: (1) by force; (2) by common consent. The first method is inconsistent with the objectives of such an organization and, if attempted, would doubtless precipitate a major war. The second method is feasible only to the extent to which the most recalcitrant member is willing to relinquish portions of its sovereignty. The nations of the world drew the present UN charter under the sobering impact of World War II, then still in progress. Far from being the constitution of a world superstate, the UN Charter sets forth a formal mechanism for world cooperation for peace and security. This accomplishment is apparently the present limit of national self-abnegation attainable from those nations whose inclusion in any system seeking world security through joint action is necessary.

The problem of making an area or world government effective presents perhaps even more difficulties than its formation. If the government proves in fact too weak to achieve its basic objective of security in the broad sense of the term, the resultant failure may precipitate on an even greater scale that Armageddon which the world fears today. Initially there is the basic practical difficulty of protecting from unsound practices of the superstate individuals and national groups of widely varying racial, political, and economic systems, widely varying standards of living and productivity, and different comprehensions and principles. At the same time the superstate must enjoy a wide range of authority over and above the police power of orthodox military forces if it is to operate positively in the elimination of causes of internal friction rather than negatively to suppress the human reaction to such causes. The economic field alone could be expected to create frictions warranted to test the genius of any superman chosen to guide the destinies of the superstate. Finally, it is interesting to speculate on the procurement of the individuals who would constitute the administration and exercise the police power of the superstate. The world today is made up in considerable part of individuals conditioned to place loyalty to their country, and even its aggrandizement, above all other allegiances. Certain individuals and groups, notably on religious and ideological grounds (as the Communists, who in practice hold that their allegiance to Communism overrides loyalty to any national government except the USSR) insist that they have transcended national loyalties.[3]

The problem of exercising police power has been partially or wholly solved at times by some states through the use of foreign individuals called "mercenaries"—generally considered an opprobrious term. It is not impossible that the highest level of loyalty will someday be that of the superstate "mercenary" who serves and dies with an incentive transcending normal national loyalties. Needless to say, the merit of that accolade would depend on how and with what objective the hypothetical superstate came into being and how it lived thereafter.

APPLICATION OF THESE PRINCIPLES.—The world has tried in some form at least seven of the eight different formulas for security which have just been discussed, and perhaps is now seriously considering certain aspects of the eighth—area and world government. All seven others have been tried in various combinations. All attained some success in dealing with specific types of world security problems, at certain times and in certain places. All have failed in many cases and the dread sum of their failures in the twentieth century has been reaped in the histories of World Wars I and II, as well as in the fears which beset the world today.

It is essential that the countries of the world go forward in the search for world security. The search seems now to be one for world preservation and there may be little time to complete it. Even in the failures of the past, however, there are lessons which give hope. The weak points of one system are often covered by combining it with others and operating them together. It would appear that from a realistic standpoint the best of all practical systems of world security for today is one which combines aspects of all those which have been discussed. We shall see that such a combination was attempted in the ill-fated League of Nations and presently in the United Nations.

Early Ideas of International Cooperation

FIRST STEPS: THE ANCIENTS.—The antecedents of modern efforts to establish an international organization for the preservation of peace are deeply

---

[3] It need hardly be pointed out that this flight to a "higher loyalty" boils down in this instance to the substitution of loyalty to a foreign state for one's native allegiance. In time of war such transference has always been identified—and punished—as treason.

rooted in the past. Four centuries before the Christian era the ancient Greeks, after sensing the dangers inherent in particularism, made definite though belated attempts at federation as a means of preserving the peace among their city-states. From that time forward the problems of inter-state, regional, and even larger scale organization have challenged the imagination and constructive thought of intellectual leaders the world over. The growth of the concept was by no means continuous. The time gaps which separated the successive efforts to attain security often extended over centuries. Rome, herself, sought and achieved security through world conquest. So complete was her control over the Western world—the Pax Romana—that her fall brought on the anarchy of the "Dark Ages"; for no nation had arisen capable of succeeding her.

MEDIEVAL AND EARLY MODERN EFFORTS.—The medieval period, with its almost continuous warfare on a petty, though ruinous scale, records the church's efforts to alleviate the situation of the victims of this state of affairs by imposing the Peace of God and the Truce of God.[4] In the early seventeenth century, the Duke of Sully persuaded his monarch, Henry IV of France, to propose his "Grand Design" General Council of Europe as a means for the preservation of peace. Patterned on the ideas of the ancient Greeks, it aimed at the maintenance of peace through international collaboration on the removal of the causes of war. National ambitions proved too strong to permit the "Grand Design" to get beyond the talking stage. The proposal is said, however, to have inspired in large measure one of the first great texts in international law, Grotius' *On the Laws of War and Peace*. Grotius, whose work was published in 1625, proposed conferences of the powers in which international difficulties could be adjusted. He endorsed the principles of compromise and arbitration, but, being more interested in humanizing warfare, suggested no complete plan for international organization. Sully's plan also inspired the *Project for Perpetual Peace* published by the Abbé de St. Pierre in 1713, and through him the Russian Tsar Alexander I's idea of a universal Holy Alliance. In spite of the scorn with which St. Pierre's ideas were greeted by the critics of that period, his plan nevertheless contained persuasive arguments for international organization. The Abbé saw that the private wars of medieval times had been abolished only to be supplanted by greater and more terrible conflagrations between national states. An armed league, ever ready to resist or destroy aggressors against the system of balance of power, was prescribed by him as the antidote to perpetual conflict. However, this idealistic proposal encountered more criticism than support.

---

[4] A series of clerical decrees in the tenth and eleventh centuries designed to impose feudal self-regulation in the conduct of war.

PENN'S STATE OF EUROPE.—William Penn embodied his conclusions on peace between nations in his *Essay toward the Present Future Peace of Europe,* drawn up in 1693. Its chief importance lies in its embodiment of the substantive ideas on international organization, arbitration, and peace which later were used as bases for the plans of other seekers of world security. Penn was convinced of the futility of war and declared that "by the same rule of justice and prudence by which parents and masters govern their families, and magistrates their city, and estates their republics and princes and kings their principalities and kingdoms, Europe may obtain and preserve peace among her sovereignties." Penn proposed a sovereign parliament or state of Europe, admitting that the use of force would sometimes be necessary to combat the recalcitrance of states.

KANT'S FEDERAL REPUBLIC.—At the close of the eighteenth century, the great German philosopher, Immanuel Kant, produced an essay, *On Perpetual Peace,* in which he outlined an international system constructed on a philosophical basis. Kant believed that the enlightened self-interest of people provided a philosophical basis for peace, the abolition of war being ultimately guaranteed by nature itself through the forces inherent in human desires. The two principal political ingredients of his thesis are found in the prescription that the civil constitution of every state must be republican, and that the law of nations must be established and enforced by a federation of free states embracing all the world's peoples.

THE HOLY ALLIANCE.—After Waterloo, the depredations of Napoleon's France gave rise to the birth of the Holy Alliance, proposed by Tsar Alexander of Russia. Whatever else may be said about its successes and failures, it can be argued that the Alliance, initially directed primarily against France, was an exclusive league of Great Powers. The Tsar, in a letter to his ambassador in London, declared: "The sole and exclusive object of the Alliance can only be the maintenance of peace and the union of all moral interests of the people which Divine Providence has been pleased to unite under the Banner of the Cross." The Alliance in fact proposed to guarantee to each power such territories as had been allotted it by the Congress of Vienna. The Concert of Europe, springing from the Holy Alliance, was itself a search for security through balance of power. For a time the Concert functioned successfully, but in the latter nineteenth century it fell into discard with the beginning of the era of alliances and counteralliances which led to World War I.

THE HAGUE CONFERENCES.—The latter part of the nineteenth century also witnessed the initiation of movements looking toward political unions designed specifically to preserve the peace. Some of these projects were world-wide in scope, others resulted in the regional groupings of nations. One of the most significant of such proposals, as measured by tangible results, was that which led to the Hague Conferences.

In 1898 Tsar Nicholas II of Russia invited a number of nations to send representatives to The Hague to consult on the best means of promoting international understanding and peace. The two Hague Conferences of 1899 and 1907 were of particular importance in that they revived the concept of continuous handling of international problems through successive conferences of states. Moreover, it is significant that the participants met to consider such problems, not after a great war, but in the effort to avert one. The conferences resulted in the adoption of several international conventions governing the laws of war in their application to prisoners, noncombatants, and neutrals. However, security through international law was proved to be premature by the subsequent violation of the Hague conventions in World War I.

Regional Collaboration: The Pan American Union

EARLY EFFORTS TO ORGANIZE.—The most important development in regional collaboration occurred in the Western Hemisphere with the establishment of the Pan-American movement which dates back to the Congress of Panama in 1826. The American hemispheric conferences fall into two well-defined groups: those held before 1889 and those which occurred subsequently. In the earlier period neither the United States nor Brazil was represented. Despite the repeated efforts of the young Spanish-American republics to create an international organization, sponsorship and direction of the conferences lacked sufficient support to produce a firm basis for such an institution.

PAN-AMERICAN CONFERENCES.—The first International Conference of American States, which met in Washington in 1889, marks the beginning of an effective Pan-American system. The result of that conference was the inauguration in 1890 of the Pan American Union and the establishment of its permanent secretariat at Washington, D. C. Under the Pan-American system some fifty-odd organizations have been created for the performance of specific tasks. To date, more than 160 conferences have been held. The vast majority of them have been called for the handling of technical problems common to the states of the Western Hemisphere. The most important meetings, however, have been the regular International Conferences of American States.[5]

---

[5] These were held in the following places: Washington, 1889; Mexico City, 1901; Rio de Janeiro, 1906; Buenos Aires, 1910; Santiago, 1923; Havana, 1928; Montevideo, 1933; Lima, 1938; and Bogota, 1948.

A number of additional important political conferences have been held, such as the Buenos Aires Conference for the Maintenance of Peace in 1936. Under the treaty arrangements agreed to at that time and during the Eighth Conference at Lima, 1938, a number of major political decisions affecting the maintenance of peace was reached. Special meetings of the American ministers of foreign affairs conducted during such gatherings played a vital part in the final results. Today the Pan-American system includes a vast network of treaties under which the American nations have undertaken to solve technical problems, perform administrative tasks, and preserve the peace. In 1939, when the shadow of Axis ambitions fell across the Western Hemisphere, these earlier efforts to secure Pan-American collaboration made it relatively easy to erect a common front against the Old World menace. Only the Argentine Republic, dominated by a hard-bitten minority sympathetic to the Axis cause, failed to participate in the execution of joint defense measures. Argentine support of hemispheric solidarity was finally won early in 1945 when the hopelessness of the Axis situation became indisputable.

Pan-American solidarity was demonstrated in the Inter-American Conference on Problems of War and Peace, held in Mexico City (Chapultepec), February-March, 1945. The delegates present were fully conscious of the fact that Nazi and Fascist strategy had counted on fifth-column uprisings in the states south of the Rio Grande to establish puppet states subservient to Axis direction, thus converting Latin America into one of the major bases for the final drive against the United States after the Axis had completed its conquest of the Old World. Chapultepec's major objective, in consequence, became an agreement of reciprocal assistance and solidarity to ward off aggressive action by either a non-American state or by one within the Hemisphere system. In addition, a wide range of political, social, and economic problems was considered, resulting in agreements which in the long run cannot fail to promote the well-being of the member states.

Problems of regional security received special emphasis in the Treaty of Rio de Janeiro drafted by the Inter-American Conference for the Maintenance of Continental Peace and Security, which concluded its sessions in September, 1947. This treaty clearly defined a regional security zone in the Western Hemisphere of paramount interest to the Pan-American nations. Extending from the North Pole to the South Pole, the zone includes the continents of North and South America, certain islands lying off their coasts (including Greenland but not Iceland), and several hundred miles of the sea adjacent to the continents.

The treaty provided for inter-American action against armed attack from without this zone and against member nations who resort to arms in the settlement of internal disputes. Provision was also made to meet acts of aggression not involving the use of armed force which threaten the territorial integrity or political independence of any American state. The terms of this treaty served to solidify the previous efforts to attain regional security in this hemisphere.

THE BOGOTA CONFERENCE.—The Pan American Union was finally cemented and given definite form and legality with the creation of the Organization of American States at the Ninth Conference in Bogota, Colombia. The Charter was signed by the representatives of all twenty-one nations in May, 1948, and will give the Organization definitive status as a regional agency within the United Nations.

Part I of the Charter is devoted to an exposition of the principles on which the Organization is founded; the rights and duties of states; the pacific settlement of disputes; and the economic, social, and cultural standards to be attained. On the question of collective security the Charter is unequivocal. Every act of aggression which threatens the territorial integrity, sovereignty, or political independence of an American state "shall be considered an act of aggression against the other American states." Furthermore, an act of aggression is not confined to an armed attack but includes any act which threatens the political independence of an American state. The problem of outside political interference was brought into clearer focus by the attempted revolution precipitated by the assassination of Jorge Gaitan, a prominent Colombian political leader, shortly after the Bogota Conference convened. The United States Secretary of State, Mr. Marshall, charged that the disorders were inspired by the Communists.

The organs authorized by the Charter are six in number: the Inter-American Conference; the Meeting of Consultation of Ministers of Foreign Affairs; the Council; the Pan American Union; the Specialized Conferences; and the Specialized Organizations. The names applied indicate the broad functions of each body.

The supreme body of the Organization of American States is the Inter-American Conference, convened at least once every five years, or sooner if a two-thirds majority so directs. Each nation is entitled to one vote and the Conference is empowered to consider "any matter relating to friendly relations among the American states." The Meeting of Consultation of Ministers of Foreign Affairs is to be convened only to consider matters of an urgent nature; its convention may be requested by any member. It is provided with an Advisory Defense Committee and serves primarily as an organ for the exchange of views.

The Council is the real executive body and is composed of one representative from each member state. Normally the diplomatic representative accredited to the country in which the Council has its seat will hold this appointment. The Council considers all matters referred to it by the Conference or Foreign Ministers, supervises the functioning of the

Pan American Union, concludes agreements with specialized agencies and, in general, coordinates all activities of the Organization. It carries out many of these responsibilities through three subsidiary organs: the Economic and Social Council; the Cultural Council; and the Council of Jurists. Probably only the last requires some elaboration, for it is in no sense a court of arbitration. It is simply a committee of eminent jurists selected by the Council to act in an advisory capacity and "to promote the development and codification of public and private international law." The practicability of developing limited uniformity in the laws of the various American countries is also to be studied.

The Pan American Union is designated as the secretariat headed by a Secretary-General elected by the Council for a ten-year term. The Secretariat is charged with the usual administrative tasks as well as the maintenance of technical and informational services.

Specialized Conferences are called to deal with such special technical problems as may arise from time to time and which do not come within the scope of the existing Specialized Agencies. The latter are such autonomous intergovernmental organizations as have been established by previous agreements and have been brought into relationship with the Organization through negotiation with the Council, which may also create new specialized agencies as required.

The Charter may be denounced by any member state and such denunciation will go into effect two years after written notification is received by the Pan American Union.

At this early date it is obviously impossible to evaluate the merits of such an organization. It appears, however, to provide an excellent framework within which the multitudinous agreements and activities of the American nations can be coordinated and administered. At the same time it presents a solid regional grouping of individual nation-states and represents another step forward in the field of international agreement.

Allied Cooperation, 1914–1918

ATTENTION TO INTERNATIONAL PROBLEMS.—The train of events which led to the outbreak of World War I clearly disclosed the inadequacy of the machinery then available for the maintenance of world security. The real weakness, of course, lay in the inability of the institutions striving to preserve peace to cope with national ambitions which could be satisfied only through the application of armed force. At the same time the material and human losses suffered by both the belligerents and the more vulnerable neutrals in that war re-emphasized the importance of creating a powerful world organization for the prevention of future wars. Consequently, Woodrow Wilson's proposal of a League Covenant fell on ground which included not a few fertile areas. Moreover, by 1918 the exigencies of the war had compelled the Allies to discover and develop the ways and means for effective cooperation in the prosecution of the war. Supporters of the Wilson thesis argued that the machinery employed to make wartime cooperation effective could, with little modification, be applied to the problems of preserving world peace.

ECONOMIC AND MILITARY COOPERATION.—The number and geographical distribution of the nations eventually allied in military opposition to the Central powers in World War I gave rise to many difficult problems of coordination. In part, they were met by the creation of various types of Inter-Allied organizations. Economic problems were handled by such bodies as the Allied Maritime Transport Council, the Inter-Allied Food Council, and the Inter-Allied Munitions Council. After the defeats suffered by the Allies in France in the spring of 1918 and Italy's disaster at Caporetto, a unified command was agreed upon, whereupon France's Marshal Ferdinand Foch was given supreme command of the Allied forces. In the latter period of the war various proposals were offered looking to the maintenance of the Inter-Allied war machinery during the stage of reconstruction and peace, as a rudimentary international organization to handle administrative problems of an international character. The Inter-Allied economic organizations were superseded by the Inter-Allied Council of Supply and Relief, and this body in turn gave way to the Supreme Economic Council. Despite efforts to continue collaboration after the war, the states soon fell back into the old groove of nationalistic policies, pursued with ever-lessening regard for the common good of all. One asset saved from the wreck of the original hopes was the war experience in collective action which was embodied in the machinery of the League of Nation's secretariat for the handling of international administrative problems. Moreover, the wartime agencies furnished much of the personnel which manned the agencies of the League.

The League of Nations

BIRTH OF THE LEAGUE.—The magnitude of the destruction and loss of life brought about by World War I determined the peoples of all nations to seek a secure system of world order in order to ensure that such a catastrophe would never be repeated. The Phillimore Commission of the British Government in 1918 had explored and drafted a plan of world organization which had not been accepted nor published by that government. President Wilson of the United States, who had been perfecting his ideas over several years, seized the initiative as well as the public

ORGANS OF THE LEAGUE OF NATIONS

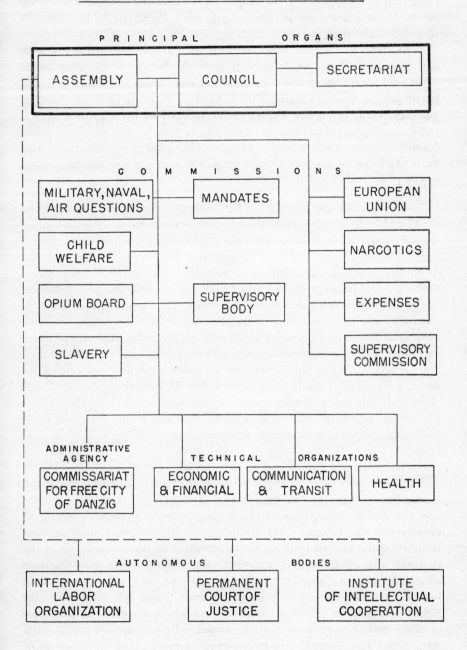

PRINCIPAL ORGANS

- ASSEMBLY
- COUNCIL
- SECRETARIAT

COMMISSIONS

- MILITARY, NAVAL, AIR QUESTIONS
- MANDATES
- EUROPEAN UNION
- CHILD WELFARE
- NARCOTICS
- OPIUM BOARD
- SUPERVISORY BODY
- EXPENSES
- SLAVERY
- SUPERVISORY COMMISSION

ADMINISTRATIVE AGENCY — **TECHNICAL ORGANIZATIONS**

- COMMISSARIAT FOR FREE CITY OF DANZIG
- ECONOMIC & FINANCIAL
- COMMUNICATION & TRANSIT
- HEALTH

AUTONOMOUS BODIES

- INTERNATIONAL LABOR ORGANIZATION
- PERMANENT COURT OF JUSTICE
- INSTITUTE OF INTELLECTUAL COOPERATION

fancy of the world by strongly advocating a League of Nations based on collective security and disarmament. Hence the formulation of a Covenant of a League of Nations quickly became one of the major efforts of the Paris Peace Conference of 1919, with President Wilson himself serving on the drafting committee.

Needless to say, the other nations of Europe, particularly France and Britain, had proposals of their own. At last, however, after much effort and compromise, the Covenant was completed and made part and parcel of the Peace of Paris. The League of Nations thus was born in January, 1920, when the Treaty of Versailles had been ratified by the requisite number of nations. Like the Concert of Europe which stemmed from the Congress of Vienna in 1815, another plan of world security had been produced by the victors in a great war and was inextricably bound to the peace settlement of the conflict.

STRUCTURE OF THE LEAGUE.—The Covenant of the League established an Assembly, in which each of the member nations was given equal representation and a single vote. Secondly, a Council was provided, consisting of five permanent and four (later nine) nonpermanent members. As originally planned, the permanent members were to be France, Great Britain, Italy, Japan, and the United States. The nonpermanent members of the Council were chosen by the Assembly. The Assembly and Council, together with a Permanent Secretariat to administer the League's affairs, were established at Geneva. The Treaty of Versailles also provided for two other international institutions: a Permanent Court of International Justice (Article 14 of the Covenant) to settle legal disputes arising between nations; and an International Labor Organization to coordinate efforts to improve and make uniform working conditions throughout the world. The former of these organizations was made independent of the League while the latter was designated an auxiliary activity of that body.

The signers of the several treaties which terminated World War I and the members of the League pledged themselves to support the following principles: (1) "to respect and preserve against external aggression the territorial integrity and existing political independence of all members of the League"; (2) to recognize "the friendly right of each member of the League to bring to the attention of the Assembly or of the Council any circumstances whatever affecting international relations which threaten to disturb international peace or the good understanding between nations upon which peace depends"; and (3) to impose economic penalties, or sanctions, upon nations which wage war in disregard of their promises to submit their disputes for arbitration or judicial settlement. The Council was empowered to recommend to members of the League the adoption of military measures against aggressor nations.

THE UNITED STATES AND THE LEAGUE.—It is important to remember that although the United States Senate in November, 1919, rejected the Treaty of Versailles, together with the Covenant of the League of Nations, which action the result of the Presidential election of 1920 apparently endorsed, nonmembership of the United States in the League of Nations did not prevent her from collaborating repeatedly with the League after 1923 in the handling of international problems. Despite the fact that a substantial percentage of American voters regarded the question of the League and European security as none of the nation's concern, certain questions with international implications could not be ignored. As a consequence, the United States in 1923 began to send unofficial observers to those meetings of League committees which were concerned with nonpolitical questions. In addition, delegates were sent to League conferences in 1924. By the end of the decade American representatives had participated in more than forty League gatherings of one kind or another. Far from remaining completely isolated from the world during the early postwar period, the United States signed nine draft conventions concerned with traffic in narcotics, slavery, and forced labor. In fact, as the atmosphere of World War I retreated into the background, the United States threw increasing weight on the side of cooperative efforts to prevent another great war whenever crises arose to threaten the general peace. Self-imposed restrictions on her scope of action, however, greatly reduced the effect of United States diplomacy.

The substance of the formal opposition in the United States to full-scale collaboration with other powers for the preservation of world security was fairly disclosed in the original reservations to acceptance of the League Covenant introduced by the Senate opposition: (1) the United States should not accept the obligations inherent in Article X, whereby the nation would have been obliged to assist in preserving against external aggression the territorial integrity and political independence of all members of the League; (2) the United States should specifically reserve the right of withdrawal from the League; (3) the United States should specifically reserve the power to decide what questions came within its domestic jurisdiction, hence those lying outside League jurisdiction; and (4) the United States would refuse to admit League competence in questions arising out of the Monroe Doctrine.[6] Despite unwillingness to give wholehearted and formal acceptance to the League, the platforms of both major parties and the actions of subsequent administrations refute the oft-expressed view that the United States, by its postwar stand on the League, had isolated itself from world affairs.

---

[6] The final vote in the Senate recorded 57 votes for the Treaty with reservations (34 Republicans, 23 Democrats), to 39 against it (15 Republicans, 24 Democrats). It was thus defeated by operation of the two-thirds rule.

FUNCTIONING OF THE LEAGUE.—When the League convened in 1920, the Assembly was composed of representatives of forty-two member states, and by 1931 had increased in size to sixty-two members. The Assembly's functions are best described as deliberative, advisory, and consultative. It could not legislate nor had it the power, other than moral suasion, to enforce its decisions. Specifically, it admitted applicant states to membership, established the budget, elected nonpermanent members of the Council, and could reconsider treaties registered with the League which were approaching expiration date, were inconsistent with the Covenant, or, due to the course of events, required revision. Its meetings were held annually at Geneva, Switzerland.

Despite its rather limited functions, the Assembly's most important contribution to world security was that it provided a forum where world affairs could be discussed. Here a constructive and instructive approach could be made to the solution of vexing international questions. If for no other reason, the free discussion of problems among members, supplemented by research of the world's experts, was a step toward agreement. Slowly but surely, this body by wielding the majority opinion of its members moved to a position on a par with the Council. In the closing years of the League, the Assembly was able to influence the work of the Council to a considerable degree.

The Council was empowered to draw plans for disarmament, indicate methods to be employed in protecting member states from aggression, mediate cases involving nations, and receive reports from mandatory powers. To become effective a decision of the Council in important cases required the unanimity of its members.

It should be stressed that the Council constituted the executive power of the League. Yet the Council, in order to enforce disarmament, decisions in mediation, and the protection of its members from aggression, was dependent solely upon the cooperation of the League membership of sovereign states. The Council could, of course, invoke economic sanctions and thereby call upon the League members to cease trade, financial, commercial, and individual relations with an offender. But the effectiveness of these measures was likewise dependent upon the cooperative will of the nations, particularly the Great Powers. Thus it came to pass that when national interests conflicted with the League, enforcement became impossible.

The use of military force by the League was discussed by that body and a Permanent Committee to consider the question was instituted. The Committee's conclusions, however, were never implemented. Proposals that armed forces be made available to the League by the members in strengths proportionate to the supposed relative power of the members were rejected when questions were raised concerning the composition, numbers, equipment, and command of such forces.

THE INTERNATIONAL LABOR ORGANIZATION (ILO).—Separate from the League, but a part of its system, the International Labor Organization (ILO) was established for the purpose of solving through international action the problems of labor. Membership in the League carried with it membership in the ILO but states could become members of the ILO without becoming members of the League, as did the United States in 1934. Despite the collapse of most of the League's machinery with the approach of World War II, ILO survived and was incorporated in the machinery of the UN.

Distinctive features of the International Labor Organization included a general Conference, held at least once a year, and the International Labor Office (administrative organization). Control of the latter activity was vested in the Governing Body which, like the Conference, comprised representatives of governments, employers, and workers. In the Conference each state was accorded representation by four persons (two, government; one, employer; one, labor). The Governing Body with a membership of thirty-two apportioned in the same ratio was chosen by the Conference. Eight of the government members of the Governing Body were required to be representatives of states of chief industrial importance.

The International Labor Office, primarily a fact-finding, research, and publication agency, assembles data for the use of the Governing Body and the Conference and issues reports on labor conditions. Both directly and indirectly ILO's operations have helped to eliminate friction arising from industrial and labor relations, thus performing an important function in the promotion of international harmony in that field.

THE PERMANENT COURT OF INTERNATIONAL JUSTICE.—Pursuant to Article 14 of the Covenant of the League, the Permanent Court of International Justice was established with the election of the judges in September, 1921, conducting its first session in January, 1922. The tribunal consisted of fifteen judges appointed for a nine-year term by joint action of the League Council and Assembly. The Court was charged with the interpretation of treaties and obligations under international law, and with the settlement of "any dispute of an international character which the parties thereto submit to it." It was also required to give advisory opinions when requested by the Council or the Assembly. Compliance with opinions rendered was not mandatory unless the nations in dispute had so agreed in adhering to the statute setting up the Court. Prior to World War II, the Court held forty-six sessions, delivered thirty-one judgments and twenty-seven advisory opinions.

Despite the bitter opposition in 1920 to the entry of the United States into the League of Nations, both major American political parties in 1925 advocated affiliation with the "World Court," as the tribunal was called; and the House of Representatives went on record that year favoring American membership. In 1927 the Senate adopted a resolution in support of United States participation in the Court, although with five reservations. Of these reservations the more important specifically disavowed our direct association with the League and placed limitations on the power of the Court to issue so-called advisory opinions. The fifty-one countries, parties to the protocol establishing the Court, were willing to accept most of these reservations except the one relating to advisory opinions. It was necessary, therefore, to arrive at new compromises. Both President Hoover (in 1930) and President Roosevelt (in 1935) requested Senate ratification. Although a majority of the Senate was favorable in 1935, the vote taken in January of that year lacked seven of the required two-thirds majority.

War and Peace in the Thirties

THE KELLOGG-BRIAND PACT.—Notwithstanding its abstention from membership in the League, the United States displayed an interest in that body's efforts to maintain peace. In 1928, following an exchange of views between the American Secretary of State Frank Kellogg and Premier Aristide Briand of France, the governments of the two nations proposed a pact aimed at outlawing war. The Franco-American proposal was incorporated in a treaty which was signed at Paris in August of the same year by the principal nations of the world. Renouncing war as an instrument of national policy, the pact pledged the signatories to settle all disputes, whatever their nature, by pacific means. In effect, it constituted a statement of high principle and an innovation in the concept of basic law between nations. Lacking provisions for either military or economic measures to be taken against an aggressor, however, it became in due time no more than an unenforceable mandate governing international behavior.

HIGH TIDE OF THE WORLD PEACE MOVEMENT.—Hopes for world peace reached their zenith in the early thirties. The League had scored a number of minor successes in the settlement of issues between small states which might have led to war. A world-wide drive for universal disarmament was scheduled to open in Geneva. The leading naval powers had found a way to scale down their fleets through agreements which likewise put a check on new construction. Nevertheless, the fundamental conflicts of national desires, heightened by the world economic crisis and depression precipitated in 1929, were pushing the world toward a new global war. In the light of later events, the cooperative measures described below appear now as no more than short-range palliatives.

INTERNATIONAL FINANCIAL RELIEF.—President Hoover, as head of the principal creditor state involved in the multilateral problem of war debts and reparations, took the initiative in 1931 toward declaring a one-year moratorium of "all payments on intergovernmental debts . . . both principal and interest." This stopgap proved to be inadequate to stem the flood of international default and bankruptcy. Payments on intergovernmental debts did indeed cease, not to be resumed except in isolated instances. The lasting importance of the Hoover proposal lies in its sincere effort to solve a problem of the highest international importance through global approach and procedure.

LIMITATION OF NAVAL ARMAMENTS.—Similarly, during this period the United States took the initiative in the general endeavor to find a solution to the over-all problem of limitation of armaments. The American government was host to the first great postwar conference on limitation of armaments—the Washington Naval Conference of 1921-1922, marking the first serious effort in modern times to reduce the armaments of leading sea powers in the interests of world peace. The agreements reached included the scrapping of a number of capital ships either afloat or building, a holiday in their construction till 1931, and the establishment of capital-ship ratios for the five leading naval powers in the following ratios: United States—5, Great Britain—5, Japan—3, France—1.67, Italy —1.67. This ratio was based on the idea of giving these powers security in their respective areas only. Most of the effect of that move was lost when the United States alone among those powers embarked on a true naval construction holiday. Keeping to the letter of the agreement, the other powers steadily expanded the "non-treaty" elements of their fleets. When the Geneva Naval Conference, held in 1927 at Washington's insistence, failed of restrictions on the construction of cruisers and smaller types of vessels, the United States countered with a construction program of her own. This action produced partial results in agreements reached in the London Naval Conference of 1930 by Britain and the United States on the matter of cruiser construction. By that time, however, Japan was demanding parity in fleet strength with her two leading rivals. She was no longer content with security in her own area. As for Italy and France, their growing rivalry led them to abstain from the agreement. And Japan, denouncing the treaty a few years later, embarked after 1936 on an all-out naval building program.

LIMITATION OF ALL ARMAMENTS.—Beginning in 1926, in accordance with the provisions of the League Covenant that the Council was to formulate plans for general reduction of armaments, an international commission worked on the larger aspects of this problem. The Council had, however, found it difficult to make serious headway, since neither Russia nor the United States was a member of the League. The cooperation of these two nations was indispensable but not easy to secure. Nevertheless, during the innumerable discussions concerning qualitative and quantitative methods of naval reduction the views of the American government were made clear, and the subcommittee which in due course recommended the establishment of a fact-finding commission at Geneva included an American member.

The report drafted in 1930 by the Special Commission of the League of Nations on the limitation of armaments, after five years of study of the problem, was little more than an expression of pious hopes. Nevertheless, the political forces in the League's membership supporting the drive for world peace through disarmament were successful in securing League action to provide for a general conference on the problem. To Geneva in 1932 came the delegations of the League's member nations; with them were the delegations of Soviet Russia and the United States, both nonmembers. Like the efforts of the earlier Special Commission, those of the Disarmament Conference ended in failure, principally because the delegates concerned themselves only with the instrumentalities of war, rather than with its fundamental causes. Even in that relatively limited sphere, it became impossible to agree on just what constituted arms, that is, military power. It is strikingly significant that, as shown by subsequent events, each of the five major disarmament programs considered, submitted by as many powers, would have operated to the definite military advantage of the sponsoring power. To the American citizen, the active participation of the United States in the conference is no less significant, foreshadowing its more intensive interest in international cooperation during and after World War II.

EFFORTS TO CURB JAPANESE AGGRESSION.—In September, 1931, when Japanese aggression in Manchuria challenged the whole concept of collective security, the United States led the way in the attempt to block this clear violation of the League Covenant, the Kellogg-Briand Pact, and the Washington Treaties of 1922. Shortly after the Japanese had launched their attack, the United States Minister to China reported to Secretary of State Henry L. Stimson that there was every evidence that it had been accomplished with cynical disregard of Japan's obligations under the Kellogg-Briand Pact. The League of Nations immediately undertook consideration of the Manchurian problem, and Secretary Stimson instructed the United States Consulate at Geneva to inform the Secretary General of the League that it was most desirable that the League in no way relax its vigilance and in no way fail to assert all its pressure and authority toward regulating the action of China and Japan. The American Secretary of State further stated that the United States, acting independently, would "endeavor to reinforce what the League does" and would make clear its keen interest in the matter and its awareness of the obligations of the disputants under the Kellogg-Briand Pact and the Nine-Power Treaty, "should a time arise when it would seem advisable to bring forward these obligations." In identical notes to China and Japan, the United States in October, 1931, called attention to their obligations under the Kellogg-Briand Pact, and expressed the hope that they would refrain from measures which might lead to war and that they would agree to a peaceful method for resolving their dispute.

Although the Japanese government stated that it desired to continue friendly relations with China and that it had no territorial designs on Manchuria, it nevertheless continued military operations, and by the end of the year had destroyed the remaining administrative authority of the Chinese Republic in south Manchuria. As a consequence, the United States in January, 1932, notified both the Chinese and Japanese governments that it would not admit the legality of any *de facto* situation nor would it recognize any treaty or agreement entered into between the two governments which might impair the treaty rights of the United States or of its citizens in China. It further stated that it would not recognize "any situation, treaty, or agreement" which might be brought about by means contrary to the obligations of the Kellogg-Briand Pact. In accordance with this "nonrecognition" policy, this country refused to recognize the Japanese puppet government which had been established by the Japanese in Manchuria.

By early 1932 the conflict between China and Japan had spread to the Shanghai area. At this point the Japanese government requested the United States to use its good offices in stopping hostilities. In response, this country made the following proposals in February, 1932: (1) All acts of violence on both sides should cease; (2) No further preparation for hostilities should be made; (3) The combatants of both parties should withdraw from the Shanghai area; (4) Neutral zones should be established for the protection of the International Settlement at Shanghai; and (5) Upon acceptance of the foregoing, immediate negotiations should be undertaken to settle all outstanding controversies between Japan and China with the aid of neutral observers or participants. This same proposal was made to the two governments by Great Britain, France, and Italy. Although promptly accepted by the Chinese government, the proposal came to nothing because of Japanese refusal to accept the second and fifth points. The Secretary of State then proposed to the British government that the United States and Great Britain issue a joint statement invoking the Nine-Power Treaty and the Kellogg-Briand Pact, making clear that the two governments considered these treaties fully binding, and stating that they would not recognize the validity of any situation created in violation of them.

The government of Great Britain did not accept the American suggestion. It did, however, introduce a resolution into the League Assembly in March, 1932, which was unanimously adopted and bore a strong resemblance to this government's proposal. In part, the resolution stated that "it is incumbent upon the members of the League of Nations not to recognize any situation, treaty or agreement which may be brought about by means contrary to the Covenant of the League of Nations or to the Pact of Paris." This resolution, in effect, echoed the Stimson doctrine of "nonrecognition."

THE LYTTON REPORT.—Concurrently, the League had formally adopted a resolution creating a special commission to investigate on the spot the whole conflict between China and Japan. The Lytton Commission, in which France, Germany, Italy, and the United States were also represented, took its name from its British chairman, Lord Lytton. After a thorough investigation, during which time Japan was extending and consolidating her conquests and had formally recognized her puppet state of Manchukuo (Manchuria and Jehol), the Commission brought in a report which was adopted by the League Assembly in February, 1933. It declared that Japanese military operations in Manchuria could not be regarded as legitimate measures of self-defense, that the regime which the Japanese had instituted there was not in accord with the wishes of the people of Manchuria, and was inconsistent with the fundamental principles of existing international obligations. Secretary Stimson immediately informed the Secretary General of the League that the United States was in substantial agreement with the findings and conclusions of the League. Censured by an overwhelming vote in the League Assembly, Japan gave notice in March, 1933, of its intention to withdraw from the League. In the final denouement of Japan's fourteen-year drive for undisputed control of the Pacific and east Asia, which included her Pearl Harbor attack, the United States assumed and maintained the military leadership in the counter action, just as it had earlier taken the diplomatic lead.

ITALIAN AGGRESSION IN ETHIOPIA.—Japanese aggression was not, however, the only threat to the world's peace at this time. Two major European states were also actively engaged in preparations for conquest. It became only too clear that the failure of the League and associated powers to restrain Japan had emboldened both Italy and Germany to embark upon adventures which led immediately to World War II. As early as September, 1934, the United States Ambassador at Rome, Breckinridge Long, reported to the Department of State on the apparently extensive preparations for war against Ethiopia then being made in Italy. As the aggressive intent of the Italian state became clear, both Secretary of State Hull and President Roosevelt expressed the attitude of this country toward the impending hostilities. They particularly stressed, in direct conversations with the Italian Ambassador and in a personal appeal to

Premier Mussolini, that a war between Italy and Ethiopia would be a world calamity adversely affecting the interests of all nations.

A United States embargo on the export of arms to the belligerents, instituted immediately after the outbreak of war, October 3, 1935, in accordance with the provisions of the Neutrality Act of the same year, not only failed to halt Italy but actually operated to her advantage. As pointed out by the political opposition to the bill in the Congress, the defender in such a situation—always the weaker nation—is almost certain to stand in greater need of such imports than the aggressor. Diplomatic efforts to secure combined action by the League against Italy were equally unavailing, and in 1936 Ethiopia was added to the Italian Empire. At the crucial hour, Britain and France were unwilling to impose the drastic, unlimited economic sanctions which alone would have compelled Italy to abandon her scheme of aggression. Like the Manchurian incident of a few years earlier, Italy's conquest of Ethiopia threw the spotlight on the fatal weakness of any peace preservation plan which stops short of the use of force in a crisis. The statesmen who sat in the League of Nations could not commit their countries to any line of action which would seriously restrict an aggressor on the warpath. The United States in the meanwhile had withdrawn into deeper isolation with the passage of the Neutrality Act. Like our refusal to recognize the Italian conquest, the effect of our seclusion was, for the time being at least, purely negative. Behind the statesmen who won universal condemnation for their failure to stay the new school of aggressors there stood in each case an electorate overwhelmingly in favor of any policy which would avoid the use of force.

THE SPANISH CIVIL WAR.—A bare two months separated Italy's conquest of Ethiopia from an even more serious test of the little stability remaining in Europe. What began as an internal struggle between Spain's Fascists and their opponents in August, 1936, soon developed into the thinly concealed alignment of the European forces which were to fight it out for supremacy in 1939-1945. The United States remained relatively aloof, a consequence of the joint resolution passed by Congress prohibiting the export of arms and munitions to the belligerents.

GERMANY COMES TO THE FORE.—Germany's intervention in the Spanish Civil War gave notice that henceforth she was a military power to be reckoned with in any move on Europe's political chessboard. The three years that had passed since Adolf Hitler had established himself as dictator of the Reich witnessed her withdrawal from the League, the Nazis' vigorous denunciation of its policies and actions and repeated declarations of the Nazi determination to achieve for Germany a status in world affairs in keeping with their estimate of her importance. In October, 1936, the League found itself definitely confronted by a rival, the Rome-Berlin Axis, a union which was committed, among other things, to the drastic revision of the treaties which terminated World War I. The successive steps which engulfed Europe and eventually most of the world's nations in a global war have been reviewed in previous chapters. Certain inescapable implications of these events, however, demand repetition. To begin with, the rise of the Axis marked the rejection of the thesis of world peace through the joint agreement of equals. In its place, Hitler and his partners threatened to impose by force of arms a peace of slavery, no less extreme in its implementation than that which had characterized ancient Assyria's rule nearly three thousand years earlier. Secondly, the temporizing, truth-dodging mood of Geneva led to repeated efforts at appeasement of the Axis long after it should have been clear that nothing except armed force could curb the aggressor. The early victims of the Axis were, in fact, beaten before Hitler sent his armies into Poland.

DISASTER AS A BASIS FOR COLLABORATION.—The shameless general abandonment of Czechoslovakia by the Great Power members of the League in her mortal crisis stirred long dormant moral chords the world over. To millions of ardent supporters of peace it brought the realization that peace could not be kept in the long run by default of action. Practically speaking, this event marked the death of the League; for, although it continued to function, it had become completely ineffective. Last-hour pleas by President Roosevelt to the heads of the governments represented in the Munich Conference proved unavailing. The holocaust which followed is no part of this account except as disaster led the statesmen of the United Nations to seek a more realistic approach to the joint problems of world security and peace. That development, however, became possible only after the years from 1939 to 1942 had seen the democratic peoples more than once on the brink of final collapse. These years witnessed, moreover, the fall of the United States to the nadir of its influence in world affairs since the time of her emergence as a Great Power.

EVALUATION OF THE LEAGUE.—The League of Nations, a unique type of world security system, embodied in whole or in part elements of the several systems described earlier in this chapter. The League was not a superstate, for national sovereignties were not infringed; for the same reason it was not a world federation; nor was it a state of any type.

It was not an alliance, since not all its members were allies; therefore, the exclusive relationships of an alliance could not be present. Moreover, drawn up by the victorious Allies of World War I, the League was open to all the neutral states and eventually to the defeated powers as well.

Certain parts of the Covenant were characteristic of a multilateral treaty in that the members were bound to obligations and to common action for stated purposes. Yet this classification is not accurate since the very purpose of the League and many parts of its Covenant were so vague and so inclusive in a moral sense that the obligations assumed by its members exceeded those imposed by any treaty.

The League was, in fact, a voluntary association of nations; its strength was proportionate to the degree of cooperation its member nations were willing to lend to achieve its purposes, particularly the Great Powers. To quote a French statesman of the League, "It is akin rather to an association or trade-union or cooperative society of States."

With this thought in mind, it should be remembered that the League was supposed to carry out certain parts of the Paris peace treaties which gave it birth. As a cooperative society of nations, it had neither the means nor the powers necessary to accomplish this objective without the cooperation and determination of at least the major powers. No less important is the fact that the United States which fostered the League was not a member; that Soviet Russia was ignored until 1934; and that the defeated Central Powers were not invited to join until several years after the League was established. The principle of collective security endorsed by the Covenant could neither be collective nor secure with Great Powers lying outside the League.

Although its Covenant committed it to the principle of disarmament, the League had no means to ensure the reduction of arms. It is not surprising, therefore, that the major disarmament conferences were conducted outside the League.

Apart from the defection of the United States in rejecting the Covenant, perhaps the greatest obstacle to the successful functioning of the League was the necessity of securing the unanimous consent of the members of its Council to a course of action. Each of the small-nation members of that body could, by its veto, effectively thwart action by the Great Powers. Such a contingency was inconceivable under the Concert of Europe, which had preserved the peace reasonably well for about a century. Although the older system rested largely on the balance-of-power principle, it was also a cooperative organization; it sought the cooperation of only the Great Powers, however. Japan and Italy soon exploited the weakness of the League in this respect with results that proved fatal to the organization.

The League had a fair measure of success in solving disputes which involved small powers. Notably the League adjudicated the Aaland Islands dispute between Finland and Sweden in 1920, and the Graeco-Bulgarian border conflict in 1925. Nevertheless, when Italy, a major power, seized the Greek island of Corfu in 1923 to enforce her demands for indemnity payments, the League could only weakly order Greece to comply. Several years later Turkey and Iraq (a British mandate) disputed ownership of the rich Mosul oil fields. Owing largely to British pressure, the League decided in favor of Iraq.

Outside the political field, the League initiated and performed signal humanitarian services to the world. These included, among other things, repatriation of prisoners of war, uniform regulations with regard to the international traffic in narcotics, and supervision of the exchange of populations in 1923 following the Graeco-Turkish war. The agreements reached in these fields have had lasting effects and were carried forward to the United Nations.

World War II

UNITED NATIONS COLLABORATION.—The common peril of the nations in conflict with the Axis led promptly to collaborative efforts in the prosecution of the war. The neutrality of the United States initially prevented her substantial participation in those efforts, although such neutrality became increasingly benevolent to the nations at war with Germany and Italy with each advance of the Axis toward its goal. Pearl Harbor finally ended the remaining self-imposed restraints on United States collaboration. Thereafter joint action of the Allies became truly joint in a sense and to a degree never achieved in World War I. Initially the common effort was directed almost entirely toward the destruction of the Axis military power. But even at the outset of combined action and increasingly thereafter, attention was given to the long-range problem of creating through joint agreement a global political organization fully empowered to maintain world peace. The first step in that direction, in fact, preceded the entry of the United States into the war by several months, when President Roosevelt and Prime Minister Churchill announced in August, 1941, the Atlantic Charter of "certain common principles in the national policies" of their countries "on which they base their hopes for a better future for the world." The base of that pronouncement was broadened in January, 1942, when twenty-six governments pledged their total resources to the struggle against the Axis, thus bringing the United Nations into being.

THE COORDINATION OF THE UNITED NATIONS STRATEGY.—The major drive of the United Nations fell of necessity on three leading military powers—the United States, the Soviet Union, and Great Britain. Together with China and France, they achieved increasingly efficient military coordination. The most concerted and continuous effort to develop a combined strategy was accomplished by the Combined (Anglo-American) Chiefs of Staff, established in February, 1942. At the highest level, the leaders of the Allied Nations met from time to time to settle major problems in the field of grand strategy, with all its ramifications of politics, war production and distribution, and finance. Out of those meetings came such decisions as the pooling of all the resources available to the United Nations[7] for the common effort; likewise the agreement to give priority to the destruction of the European Axis, leaving for the Pacific campaigns only enough military force to contain Japan—and a bit more. By January, 1943, the United Nations military prospects had reached a stage where the heads of the United States and British governments, in conference at Casablanca, could announce unconditional surrender of the Axis powers as their objective, and proceed to the draft of plans for the accomplishment of that end. In August of the same year China's representatives met in Quebec with the government heads of Britain and the United States to agree on further plans, including an increase of military support for China. Three other conferences in 1943 (Moscow, October; Cairo, November; Teheran, November-December) helped to provide the blueprints of military victory. Plans for the final drives which knocked Germany and Japan out of the war in quick succession were similarly previewed at Quebec, in September, 1944; at Yalta, in February, 1945; and at Potsdam, in July, 1945.

The above summary outlines only in the rough the most ambitious and widely ramified measures ever attempted for the achievement of a common end. Their implementation called for combined representation and coordination in all spheres of war activity and in all fronts, not excluding the home fronts. They led to such gatherings as the International Food Conference at Hot Springs, Virginia, in 1943, where critical studies of actual and potential production the world over resulted in plans and action affecting the world's total food supply for some years after the end of hostilities. Combined planning brought into being Anglo-American boards empowered to maintain direct control over such items and fields as raw materials, munitions, shipping, food, production, and distribution of the United States and the British Commonwealth of Nations. Indirect control, at least, was likewise established over the United Nations as a whole.

THE DRIVE FOR A STABILIZED WORLD.—As we have indicated above, the problem of lasting peace and security early injected itself into the the councils primarily concerned with the prosecution of the Allied Nations' grand strategy. The Moscow Conference of Foreign Ministers in 1943 both broadened the base enunciated in the Atlantic Charter and laid down the details of a plan for restoring democratic principles of

---

[7] The success of the United States-Canadian Permanent Joint Board for the defense of North America, created in 1940 and followed by the pooling of the two nations' economic resources for military purposes, pointed the way for the later, larger-scale combinations. A United States-Mexican Joint Defense Commission, established in 1942, was a further step in the same direction.

THE TEHERAN DECLARATION

We, the President of the United States of America, the Prime Minister of Great Britain, and the Premier of the Soviet Union, have met these four days past, in this, the Capital of our Ally, Iran, and have shaped and confirmed our common policy.

We express our determination that our nations shall work together in war and in the peace that will follow.

As to war, our military staffs have joined in our round-table discussions, and we have concerted our plans for the destruction of the German forces. We have reached complete agreement as to the scope and timing of the operations to be undertaken from the east, west and south.

The common understanding which we have here reached guarantees that victory will be ours.

And as to peace, we are sure that our concord will win an enduring peace. We recognize fully the supreme responsibility resting upon us and all the United Nations to make a peace which will command the good will of the overwhelming mass of the peoples of the world and banish the scourge and terror of war for many generations.

With our diplomatic advisers we have surveyed the problems of the future. We shall seek the cooperation and active participation of all nations, large and small, whose peoples in heart and in mind are dedicated, as are our own peoples, to the elimination of tyranny and slavery, oppression and intolerance. We will welcome them, as they may choose to come, into a world family of democratic nations.

No power on earth can prevent our destroying the German armies by land, their U-boats by sea, and their war plants from the air.

Our attack will be relentless and increasing.

Emerging from these cordial conferences we look with confidence to the day when all peoples of the world may live free lives, untouched by tyranny, and according to their varying desires and their own consciences.

We came here with hope and determination. We leave here, friends in fact, in spirit and in purpose.

Signed at Teheran, Dec. 1, 1943.

ROOSEVELT, STALIN, CHURCHILL

government in Italy and Austria, once they had been freed of the Axis yoke. The Declaration of Four Nations[8] on General Security produced by the conference guaranteed, among other things, "international peace and security with the least diversion of the world's human and economic resources for armaments." In addition it promised to establish as soon as possible "a general international organization, based on the principle of the sovereign equality of all peace-loving states, large and small, for the maintenance of international peace and security." In the Fulbright Resolution, passed by the United States House of Representatives in September, 1943, and the Connally Resolution, adopted by the Senate in November, 1943, this country strongly endorsed the principles and objectives laid down at the Moscow Conference.

The Cairo Conference in 1943, with the Soviet Union absent since she was not at war with Japan, gave effect to such principles when it announced peace terms for the Far East. Specifically, China was assured that all of the lands which she had lost to Japan's aggression since 1894 would be restored to her. Korea, the pronouncement declared, would "in due course become free and independent." And Japan was to "be stripped of all the islands in the Pacific which she has seized or occupied since the beginning of the first World War, in 1914." In substance those declarations forecast Japan's return to her territorial status as of the time of her emergence from isolation in the middle of the nineteenth century.

Each of the subsequent conferences of Allied Nations heads contributed something to the evolution of the broad plans previously laid down for world stabilization. Of chief importance in this connection were certain decisions reached at the Crimea (Yalta) Conference, as announced in February, 1945. Assurance was given the people of Europe's liberated states and former Axis satellite states that necessary emergency relief would be provided by the United Nations, to be followed by aid in establishing independent governments broadly representative of all democratic elements in the populace. Looking further ahead, the conferees recognized the foundations laid down at the Dumbarton Oaks Conference, held in Washington in the fall of 1944, for an international organization to maintain peace and security, noting at the same time its summons to a United Nations Conference beginning April 25, 1945, at San Francisco. A harsh note broke the harmony when the conferees departed from the principles of the Atlantic Charter in the settlement of the Polish issue. Poland's eastern boundary was set approximately on the "Curzon Line" of 1919.[9] Compensation for her loss of territory to Russia was promised Poland in the form of accessions in the North and West, the details to be decided in the German peace settlement.

---

[8] The United States, Great Britain, the Soviet Union, and China.

[9] A boundary between the USSR and Poland proposed by the Supreme Council of Western Allied Powers at Versailles. It was rejected by Poland, who then proceeded to make good her claim for considerable territory east of the line by defeating Soviet Russia in the Russo-Polish War (1919-1920).

The United Nations

FORMATION OF THE UNITED NATIONS.—The Charter of the United Nations (UN) was drawn up at San Francisco in June, 1945, and ratified by the requisite twenty-nine nations by October 24 of the same year. Thus there was created a new organization for the preservation of international peace and security. The UN Charter provided the organization with six principal organs and a number of subsidiary activities for the accomplishment of its task. The chief agencies are the General Assembly, the Security Council, the Trusteeship Council, the International Court of Justice, the Secretariat, and the Economic and Social Council.

THE GENERAL ASSEMBLY.—Composed of representatives of all the nations holding membership in the UN, the General Assembly is empowered to discuss any question which falls within the scope of the Charter, or which relates to the powers or functions of the organs of the institution. The General Assembly may make recommendations on all such questions except those concerning a dispute which is under consideration by the Security Council. In the latter event the General Assembly may submit its recommendation when so requested by the Security Council.

Each member nation is accorded one vote in the General Assembly. Two thirds of the members present and voting are required to approve decisions on important questions which the Charter defines as relating to the maintenance of international peace and security, election of nonpermanent members of the Security Council, election of members of the Economic and Social Council and of the Trusteeship Council, admission of new members, suspension of rights and privileges of new members, expulsion of members, operation of trusteeships, and budgetary matters.

THE SECURITY COUNCIL.—Eleven members comprise the Security Council. Five hold permanent seats: China, France, Soviet Russia, the United Kingdom, and the United States. The remaining six seats are occupied by nonpermanent members who normally are elected for periods of two years, provision having been made in the first election for three nations to serve one-year terms and three to serve terms of two years. Thus three nonpermanent members are replaced each year.

The Security Council has the primary responsibility for maintaining international peace and security. To enable it to discharge this responsibility all members of the United Nations are committed to making available armed forces and facilities to the Security Council upon the latter's request, subject to special agreement concerning details of strength, composition, location, and command of such forces and installations.

ORGANS OF THE UNITED NATIONS

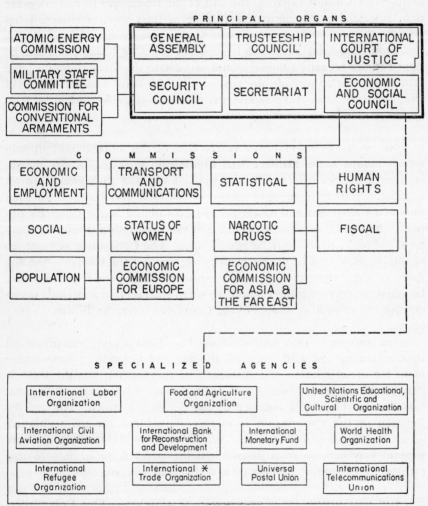

PRINCIPAL ORGANS

ATOMIC ENERGY COMMISSION	GENERAL ASSEMBLY	TRUSTEESHIP COUNCIL	INTERNATIONAL COURT OF JUSTICE
MILITARY STAFF COMMITTEE			
COMMISSION FOR CONVENTIONAL ARMAMENTS	SECURITY COUNCIL	SECRETARIAT	ECONOMIC AND SOCIAL COUNCIL

COMMISSIONS

ECONOMIC AND EMPLOYMENT	TRANSPORT AND COMMUNICATIONS	STATISTICAL	HUMAN RIGHTS
SOCIAL	STATUS OF WOMEN	NARCOTIC DRUGS	FISCAL
POPULATION	ECONOMIC COMMISSION FOR EUROPE	ECONOMIC COMMISSION FOR ASIA & THE FAR EAST	

SPECIALIZED AGENCIES

International Labor Organization

Food and Agriculture Organization

United Nations Educational, Scientific and Cultural Organization

International Civil Aviation Organization

International Bank for Reconstruction and Development

International Monetary Fund

World Health Organization

International Refugee Organization

International ✱ Trade Organization

Universal Postal Union

International Telecommunications Union

✱ Not yet brought into relationship with the United Nations.

421

Since in the last analysis the UN depends for its success on the co-operation and support of the five Great Powers, their unanimous vote is required for the approval of any substantive measure. Obviously this veto power in the hands of any one of the Big Five is open to abuse. Abstention from voting by any member on an issue ordinarily indicates disapproval without negating the will of the majority. On matters other than substantive the affirmative vote of at least seven members is required.

From this brief outline it is apparent that the broad functions assigned to the Security Council would necessitate the formation of a large staff of experts to provide the requisite technical information and control. To accomplish this purpose, the Charter authorizes such subsidiary organs as may be required.

THE MILITARY STAFF COMMITTEE.—One of the more important subsidiary organs is the Military Staff Committee, operating under the direction of the Security Council to advise and assist the Council on all questions relating to military requirements. It is also charged with the duty of employment and command of forces placed at the Council's disposal, the regulation of armaments, and the supervision of any disarmament measures which may be agreed upon. The Committee is made up of the chiefs of staff of the permanent members of the Council—the Big Five—or their representatives. Any member of the United Nations may be asked to serve with the Committee when such service is deemed necessary for the efficient discharge of the Committee's responsibilities.

THE ATOMIC ENERGY COMMISSION.—This Commission was organized by the General Assembly to assist the Security Council in formulating plans for the regulation of armaments. Its composition was the same as that of the Security Council with the addition in January of Canada. Canada also became a member of the Security Council. The specific function of the Commission is to formulate plans for the regulation of all mass-destruction weapons. While under certain conditions any weapon may achieve mass destruction, the trend is to include in this category only atomic, biological, and chemical weapons.

THE COMMISSION ON CONVENTIONAL ARMAMENTS.—This Commission was organized in February, 1947, by the Security Council in accordance with a recommendation of the General Assembly. As its title suggests, it is concerned with plans for the general regulation and reduction of armaments and armed forces other than weapons of mass destruction, as well as effective safeguards therefor. It is, therefore, a parallel organization to the Atomic Energy Commission. Its membership is composed of representatives of the nations in the Security Council. Some idea of the magnitude of the difficulties facing any such commission when it attempts to devise a system of regulating and reducing national armed forces has already been indicated.

THE TRUSTEESHIP COUNCIL.—Membership in this body is equally divided between members of the organization which administer trust territories and those which do not, each member having one vote. Decisions are made by a majority of those present and voting. Acting under the General Assembly, the Trusteeship Council is charged with the responsibility for supervising the administration of dependent peoples and of helping them toward self-government or independence. The Charter defines trust territories as those inhabited by dependent peoples which may be placed under the authority of the United Nations by subsequent trustee agreements, that is, areas not integral parts of sovereign nations or peoples not yet ready for self-government. The trusteeship system is intended to apply to the territories under the League of Nations mandate system; to territories which may be detached from enemy states by peace treaties and placed under the Trusteeship Council; and to territories voluntarily placed under the system by nations responsible for their administration.

THE INTERNATIONAL COURT OF JUSTICE.—As a judicial organ of the United Nations for the settlement of legal controversies, the Charter provides for the creation of an International Court of Justice. All nations that are members of the United Nations are, by virtue of that fact, parties to the statute of the Court. A state that is not a member of the organization may become a party to the statute and have access to the Court on conditions to be determined in each case by the General Assembly upon recommendation of the Security Council. The Court consists of fifteen members, elected for nine-year terms by the majority vote of the Assembly and the Security Council acting separately.

The International Court is subject to limitations in jurisdiction. It is not the final arbiter of the meaning of the Charter; its jurisdiction is confined to cases involving states and only to those member nations that have agreed to present their legal disputes to the Court. Furthermore, in the event of any specific dispute all parties thereto must agree to refer the case to the Court. Individuals may not be parties in any case. By agreement, however, states may accept compulsory jurisdiction of the Court in all legal disputes involving treaty interpretation, questions of international law, breaches of international obligations, and reparations resulting from breaches of obligations. Once having accepted the compulsory jurisdiction of the Court in such matters, the nation must abide by the decision. If such a nation does not accept or abide by the decision, the Security Council is required to enforce the decision.

The Court will also render advisory opinions, when so required, to the Assembly, Security Council, and such other UN bodies as the General Assembly authorizes.

THE SECRETARIAT.—The Secretariat, including a Secretary General and such other personnel as the United Nations may require, is provided as the operating staff of the organization for the performance of day-to-day administrative tasks. Personnel is chosen from among the members of the organization. The Secretary General is appointed by the General Assembly, on the recommendation of the Security Council. In addition to his purely administrative duties, he has authority to bring to the Security Council's attention any questions which in his opinion involve international peace and security.

THE ECONOMIC AND SOCIAL COUNCIL.—Although the political and military aspects of security were the predominant considerations underlying the establishment of the UN, it was realized that wholesome economic and social conditions are prerequisite to the preservation of peace. Accordingly, the UN Charter provided for an Economic and Social Council of eighteen members and charged this body with the task of promoting general economic and social progress, including higher standards of living, full employment, health, education, and related problems. The Council was authorized to conduct studies, make recommendations, and draft conventions for consideration by the General Assembly. The Economic and Social Council is further empowered to call international conferences to deal with matters which lie within its jurisdiction.

ECONOMIC AND SOCIAL COLLABORATION: THE SPECIALIZED AGENCIES.—In practice the Economic and Social Council functions as a coordinating body for a number of organizations known as specialized agencies, which are established by international agreement and are autonomous and independent of the UN. The Council conducts negotiations and prepares agreements by which the specialized agencies are "brought into relationship with the UN." This relationship signifies that the mission and methods of the specialized agency concerned are consistent with the principles of the Charter of the UN.

The specialized agencies are groups of experts in their several social and economic fields rather than political organs. Agencies which by mid-1948 had been brought into relationship with the UN included:

International Monetary Fund
International Bank for Reconstruction and Development
International Civil Aviation Organization
World Health Organization
International Labor Organization
Food and Agriculture Organization

United Nations Educational Scientific and Cultural Organization
International Refugee Organization
Universal Postal Union
International Telecommunications Union.

The first four of the bodies listed and the International Trade Organization (proposed), not yet a specialized agency, will be discussed briefly in the following paragraphs.

THE INTERNATIONAL MONETARY FUND (IMF).—The proposals of the Bretton Woods Conference of July, 1944, culminated in the establishment of two intergovernmental agencies: the International Monetary Fund and the International Bank for Reconstruction and Development. The objectives of the International Monetary Fund are threefold: (1) to stabilize the value of currencies in terms of each other; par values of currencies are announced by the Fund and may not be changed more than 10 per cent without its approval, (2) to hasten removal of exchange controls and other barriers to international payments, (3) to provide an additional source of foreign exchange to which a member may apply for temporary assistance. In short, the Fund is an instrument which members use to cooperate in bringing about stable currency, freedom in exchange transactions, and elimination of discriminatory currency practices.

The capital quota was established at $8.8 billions but is subject to variation depending on the number of subscribers. The United States' quota was set at $2.75 billions, or 31¼ per cent. The Fund is a great pool of all currencies, but each nation must contribute one fourth of its quota in gold or dollar balances. The remaining three fourths is to be paid in the nation's own currency.

The Fund will advance foreign currency to tide a member country over during a period of imbalance in its international payments. At the same time this member must pay into the Fund an amount of his own currency having the same gold value as the foreign currency tendered by the Fund. After a period the process is reversed and the member must repurchase his currency with foreign exchange or gold equal to his own currency. Thus the Fund's assets always have the same gold value, though continually paid out and returned.

The Fund's operations are kept secret between its quarterly reports to safeguard against speculation. The first quarterly report in September, 1947, established par value of the currencies of all but nine of the Fund's member nations. These nations were given an extension of time in which to arrive at the exchange value of their currencies.

THE INTERNATIONAL BANK FOR RECONSTRUCTION AND DEVELOPMENT (WORLD BANK).—As implied by its title, the purpose of the International Bank is to facilitate the flow of capital to war-devastated countries and to those countries requiring assistance in developing their industries and improving their living standards. Although the IMF is a revolving fund for settling current trade balances and by such action may extend short-term credit, the Bank is designed primarily to extend long-term credit and to supplement normal investment and banking institutions.

The Bank accomplishes its function by guaranteeing loans made by private investors, thus encouraging a healthy volume of private international investment. A member nation may request the Bank's help in securing capital that cannot be raised by normal methods, or a country may request the Bank to assist it in finding new investments. As an example of this procedure, assume that a private investment corporation requests a loan guarantee. First, the Bank assures itself that the project seeking the loan is sound. Second, it requires evidence that the funds needed cannot be raised from private capital sources at reasonable interest rates. Third, it determines whether the borrower and the country will be able to repay the loan; and finally, it secures the guarantee of the government of the country where the project is to be located. Satisfied as to this assurance, the Bank adds its guarantee, thereby placing the loan risk on all its member countries.

Authorized capital for the International Bank was established at $10 billion of which over 90 per cent was subscribed to by its members by the end of 1948. The United States, largest single stockholder, was allotted a subscription quota of $3.175 billion. The Bank initially called for 20 per cent of the members' quotas, which was paid by May, 1947. As prescribed, the first two per cent of the subscription was paid in gold, the remainder in the respective currencies of the various members. This 20 per cent is the portion of the Bank's assets from which it may make direct loans. Members will not be called upon to advance the remaining 80 per cent of their subscriptions unless this action becomes necessary to meet losses. No member is required to pay in more than 20 per cent of its quota unless a borrower defaults and the Bank cannot cover the loss from its accumulated reserves. By the end of 1948 the Bank had sold a $250 million issue of bonds in the United States. By October, 1948, loans had been extended as follows: $250 million to France, $195 million to the Netherlands, $40 million to Denmark, $12 million to Luxemburg, and two loans to Chile totaling $16 million. After Poland refused to participate in the then projected European Recovery Program, her prior loan application was rejected in December, 1947.[10]

THE INTERNATIONAL CIVIL AVIATION ORGANIZATION (ICAO).—The tremendous technical stimulus given to aviation by the war, during which international discussion and agreements were largely confined to purely strategic matters, resulted in the accumulation of a huge volume of unfinished business for the diplomats in the aerial field. Two items alone, namely, the opening of scores of new air routes to parts of the world hitherto closed to modern traffic, and the amazing evolution in planes

---

[10] It is interesting that, after criticism of the Bank for her refusal to lend to the Soviet satellites in the Balkans, a loan was advanced to Czechoslovakia in the fall of 1948.

suitable for air transport, left it clear that the prewar impediments to free use of the air must be revised if the world was to reap the dividends of wartime technical advances. Aside from these considerations, it is obvious that some standard procedure applicable to all nations must be formulated if a UN air force is to have quick and unhampered access to those areas it has been directed to police. As a first step toward international cooperation for the common good the United States called an international conference, which convened in Chicago in the late fall of 1944. Except for the Soviet Union, the Argentine Republic, Saudi Arabia, and the enemy states, all the world—fifty-four states—participated. The most signal accomplishment of the conference was the transit agreement, popularly described as the "two-freedoms agreement." It proposed to give accepting states the unlimited right of passage for planes of each state through the airspace of every other, and the general right to interrupt the plane's passage for refueling or mechanical attention. General acceptance would ensure the universal use of air as a medium of communication to an extent which has never been possible for the other two mediums, land and sea.

The second major achievement of the conference was its approved plan for an international aeronautical organization on far broader lines than those of its predecessors. Two phases for the effectuation of the plan were provided. An interim agreement was arrived at to pave the way for a Provisional International Civil Aviation Organization, the latter to become active as soon as twenty-six states accepted the compact and the Interim Agreement. By June, 1945, representatives of fifty-one states had signed the Interim Agreement and thirty had formally ratified both Agreement and compact. Consequently the Provisional Organization came into existence. By April, 1947, agreement between the UN and the Organization had been reached, and the ICAO came into permanent operation. In accordance with the UN's directive, Spain was expelled from membership. In May, 1947, Italy was admitted.

Since that time the ICAO has been perfecting its organization, and has initiated a program of regional conferences to discuss route services and related matters. Regions covered by these conferences include the north Atlantic, European and Mediterranean, Middle East, Caribbean, south Pacific, South America, south Atlantic, southeast Asia, north Pacific and African-Indian Ocean.

The ICAO has fairly broad advisory powers over air traffic rules, air safety regulations, pilots' licenses, and similar problems. Its powers over the essentially economic aspects of air transport, such as international air routes and commercial air-line operations, are also advisory but considerably more limited. The principal duties of the organization are the study of problems of international civil aviation, the collection, analysis, and reporting of information relating to air transport and navigation, and advice to the member states. Actually it has no power to enforce its technical regulations or to give effect to its recommendations on air transport. On the other hand, the operation of its machinery makes it possible to disclose the identity and nature of nationalistic obstructionism which may arise to interfere with the proper development and use of modern aviation, thus indirectly exercising a lever on the obstructionist. The absence of the USSR from the organization has impeded its progress in view of the size and extent of that country.

THE WORLD HEALTH ORGANIZATION (WHO).—An example of the humanitarian services included among the specialized agencies is the WHO. This organization had its articles of relationship with the UN approved by the General Assembly in late 1947, and in April, 1948, became a permanent organization when its constitution was ratified by the necessary twenty-six nations.

Its purposes, wholly advisory, are to foster and coordinate international health work; to assist governments, upon request, in strengthening health services; to furnish technical services and emergency aid to countries upon their request; to standardize certain medical procedures, to promote and conduct medical and sanitary research; and, in general, to attempt to raise standards of health and well-being.

Its organization consists of (1) an Assembly of members meeting annually and formulating policy; (2) an executive board of eighteen members elected for three years, meeting twice each year, and executing policies of the Assembly; (3) an appointive director-general to operate the staff and administer, and responsible to the executive board.

Although in its infancy, the WHO was eminently successful in the prompt checking of a severe cholera epidemic in Egypt in late 1947. Moving trained medical teams into the area, procuring emergency supplies of cholera vaccine, and, in effect, "quarantining" Egypt, the WHO succeeded within two months in checking the epidemic which had spread at a rate in excess of one thousand cases a day. Similarly, the field services of the WHO working in Greece have reduced materially the incidence of malaria in many areas of that country.

These direct attacks on disease are in addition to long-term projects such as education of doctors and nurses by means of fellowship awards, and compilation of internationally recognized compendiums of medical terms and procedures.

THE INTERNATIONAL TRADE ORGANIZATION (ITO) (PROPOSED).—This organization was proposed by a resolution of the Economic and Social Council, but by the end of 1948 had not yet become a specialized agency in relationship with the UN. Its proposed organization is expected to be similar to that of the other specialized agencies with an assembly of members, executive board of limited size, and a chief administrative officer. Its objectives as proposed in the Charter are:

1. To set up a universally recognized code of rules for international trade relations.
2. To foster negotiations between members to reduce tariffs, other import and export charges, and to eliminate trade preferences.
3. To cooperate and act in those fields which affect trade such as employment, development of backward countries, production, and consumption.
4. To establish an organization and permanent administration with authority to settle disputes which might arise in the international economic fields.

The Preparatory Committee of the United Nations Conference on Trade and Employment drew up the draft charter at meetings held in London and New York in 1946 and at another meeting at Geneva in 1947. As a result of proposals by the United States, a number of trading countries were invited to consider tariff reductions and removal of trade restrictions while at the conferences and these discussions were duly held as another funtcion of the Preparatory Committee. They were completed at the Geneva Conference in October, 1947, when the Conference ended. As a result, twenty-three countries controlling about 70 per cent of the world's trade completed over one hundred bilateral tariff agreements. It is estimated that the agreements cover trade valued at about ten billion dollars. This accomplishment is one of the greatest single contributions ever made to the removal of trade discrimination. It is significant that this action was taken in advance of the formation of an ITO and augurs well for the success of such a body.

The draft charter of the ITO, completed at Geneva, was presented to the United Nations Conference on Trade and Employment at Havana, Cuba, which convened in November, 1947. The final act, authenticating the text of the charter, was signed by fifty-three nations in March, 1948. At the same time an interim commission was established to function until the organization actually comes into being.

COMPARISON OF THE LEAGUE AND THE UN.—Certain similarities in the structural organization of the League of Nations and the United Nations are apparent. Thus, both institutions were provided with assemblies in which all members were given equal status. Both bodies were equipped with councils in which permanent membership was reserved to the Great Powers. Both institutions were furnished permanent secretariats. More significant than these superficial similarities, however, are the contrasts in the authority and methods of functioning of the various organs of the two societies. In the first place, both the League Assembly and its Council were authorized to deal with matters affecting international peace. This overlap of authority is absent in the UN wherein the General Assembly is limited to submitting to the Security Council its recommendations dealing with such matters, and then only if the question is not already under study by the Council. A second significant difference lies in the respective veto powers of the memberships of the League Council and the UN Security Council. In the former body the rule of unanimity was applied. In the latter organ, as we have seen, effective veto power is restricted to the "Big Five."

A third contrast between the two institutions is seen in the greater decentralization achieved in the UN by the establishment of the Trusteeship Council and the Economic and Social Council. Comparable agencies existed in the League but were relegated to a status subordinate to both the Assembly and the League Council, an arrangement which served to increase the volume of work of the higher organs.

Yet both the League and the UN were dedicated to the promotion of international security, and both institutions were established as cooperative associations dependent, in the final analysis, upon the willingness of their respective memberships to support a given program of action. Under the UN Charter, as under the Covenant of the League, the principle of national sovereignty remains relatively unimpaired.

THE UNITED NATIONS IN ACTION.—Action which may be taken within the framework of the UN is exceedingly complex and diverse; complex because of the parliamentary procedures involved and diverse because of the latitude allowed by the Charter. The following is a brief discussion of some of the issues which have confronted the organization and the methods utilized by it to deal with them.

The first security question to face the Council at its initial meeting in January, 1946, was the complaint registered by the Iranian government to the effect that the USSR through its officials and armed forces still remaining in Iran was interfering in the internal affairs of that nation. The Anglo-Russian-Iranian Treaty, concluded in 1942 after the occupation of Iran by the Allies, had provided for the withdrawal of all foreign troops six months after "the end of the war." This agreement was reaffirmed in the Teheran Declaration in December, 1943. The United States and Great Britain promptly announced plans for withdrawal to implement this agreement. The USSR, on the other hand, proceeded to consolidate its position in Azerbaijan and supported the autonomous regime set up by the Communist-inspired Tudeh party.

The Soviet Union answered this charge before the Security Council by raising the question of the presence of British troops in Greece. The Iranian matter was resolved for the time being by resort to Article 33 of

the Charter, providing for bilateral negotiations to settle disputes between neighboring states. The Council decided to keep the matter on its
agenda, however, and requested a report as to the progress of negotiations. On April 2, 1946, the Iranian government informed the Security
Council that the negotiations had failed to achieve satisfactory results.
The Soviet representative requested that discussion of the question be
postponed until April 10 and, when this resolution was rejected, dra-
matically withdrew.

The negotiations appeared to hinge upon the grant of an oil concession by Iran to the Soviet Union as well as recognition of an autonomous
government in Azerbaijan. These differences were finally adjusted and
on April 15 Iran notified the Security Council that in view of the Soviet
pledge to remove all troops by May 6 her complaint was being withdrawn.
While the USSR complied with this agreement, the case still remains
one of the matters with which the Security Council is seized.

Another method of handling disputes is illustrated by the Greek
question. In December, 1946, the Greek government charged that her
Balkan neighbors were supporting the guerrilla warfare raging in northern Greece, and the matter was referred to the Security Council. A
virtual deadlock ensued when the USSR supported her satellites on
each issue that arose. Agreement was finally reached to send a commission of investigation composed of eleven members, one to be designated
by each of the Council members.

This commission proceeded to gather evidence by personal investigation in the areas concerned and, in June, 1947, submitted a voluminous
report. The majority report generally supported the contentions of the
Greek government and made several proposals designed to solve the
border problems. One of these proposals envisaged the formation of a
permanent impartial commission, with free access to the territories and
governments involved, empowered to investigate and report on all incidents. When action to implement this proposal was consistently vetoed
by the USSR, the United States introduced a similar resolution in the
General Assembly where it was approved in October, 1947. The Slav
bloc immediately announced a boycott of the commission, thus restrict-
ing its activities to Greek territory. The commission's presence has no
doubt served to retard Greece's northern neighbors; definite action by
the UN to settle the issue, however, is still lacking.

One of the most difficult problems facing the United Nations is the
Palestine conflict. While the claims and counterclaims of the chief protagonists, Great Britain, the Arabs, and the Jews, are too numerous and
too confusing to set forth in this brief space, some of the major aspects of
the issue may be considered.

Great Britain has long held political and economic dominance of
the strategically located Near East which is a vital crossroads of the

world's land, water, and air routes. Furthermore, the probable oil reserves of the region are 40 per cent of the earth's total and its local commerce is substantial. Within this area British influence, as we have noted, is waning, and the Palestine conflict contributes to this decline. A solution to the conflict acceptable to the British is a necessary concomitant to British hegemony in the Near East as well as to the retention of the Mediterranean life line. Until May 15, 1948, Great Britain was the League of Nations' appointee (and, therefore, legal governor) to implement the Mandate of Palestine which was created upon the demise of the Ottoman Empire in 1920.

The majority of the inhabitants of Palestine are Arab ethnically and adhere to the Moslem faith. From the seventh century until 1920 Palestine was politically a small part of a larger Arabic or Turkish state. Consequently, the Arabs consider Palestine an integral part of the world's Arabic and Moslem community and are violently opposed to partition. To bolster their stand, they stress the commitments contained in the British promise in the famous McMahon letters of 1914-1916 of Arab independence in an area including Palestine.[11]

The claims of the Zionist Jews[12] to Palestine stem from the existence of an independent Palestine with a distinctive culture under the Davidic Kings of Israel. There appears little doubt that the greatest contribution to modernizing the Palestinian economy has been made by the Jews. Homeless, unwelcome, and persecuted, Jews have long sought to return to their Promised Land. This urge was immensely heightened by the genocidal Nazi policies toward the Jews in Europe. The Zionists, like the Arabs, stress the British promise of a national home for the Jews in Palestine in the Balfour declaration of 1917.[13]

The period between the two World Wars was marked by violent conflicts between Jews and Arabs with Britain striving futilely to pacify the region. Unable to arrive at an acceptable solution to the counterclaims, in the spring of 1947, Britain announced the surrender of her mandate over Palestine to the UN, effective May 15, 1948. After several months of study, the General Assembly of the UN adopted the plan of the majority of its Special Committee to partition Palestine into a Jewish and an Arab state and recommended this course of action to the Security Council. At the same time a UN Commission on Palestine was created to effect partition. Open hostilities between Arabs and Jews ensued and

---

[11] A series of official letters between Sir Henry McMahon, British High Commissioner for Egypt and Sudan, and Sharif Hussein of the Hejaz concerning the attitude of the British government toward Arab independence.

[12] The Zionists are members of a militant Jewish organization whose purpose is to re-establish an independent Jewish state in Palestine.

[13] An official letter from Lord Balfour, British Secretary for Foreign Affairs, to Lord Rothschild, Zionist leader, concerning the attitude of the British government toward Zionist claims to Palestine.

the Commission reported its inability to accomplish its task. In March, 1948, the Security Council declined to act on the General Assembly's partition plan and instead asked the Big Five to consult and then recommend appropriate action. The Big Five recommended (1) to suspend partition indefinitely; (2) to take steps to stop hostilities in Palestine; and (3) to call a special session of the General Assembly and advise it to place the Holy Land under a temporary trusteeship. The Security Council adopted this recommendation and a special session of the Assembly was called for April 1.

When the Assembly convened various plans to resolve the dilemma were offered, but the only achievement was a truce between Arabs and Jews in Jerusalem. Meanwhile the Zionists announced the formation of the new state of Israel within the boundaries of the proposed partition. Only two days remained prior to British surrender of her mandate when the US proposed that (1) a UN mediator in Palestine be chosen by the Big Five to work with a Truce Commission previously appointed by the Council in seeking an acceptable solution to the strife; and (2) that a temporary trusteeship be set up for Jerusalem. The following day, within a few hours of the dead line, the trusteeship plan for Jerusalem was defeated. The seeming impasse was broken when announcement was made of the United States' recognition of the new state of Israel; the mediation proposal was quickly adopted 31-7, with 16 abstentions.

With the UN Mediator, Count Folke Bernadotte, at work in Palestine with the Truce Commission, a truce was accepted by both Arabs and Jews. Bernadotte was assassinated September 19 by Israeli terrorist elements. Nevertheless, his plan for settlement of the problem, in essence a new plan of partition, was submitted to the Security Council a few days later. Arab and Jewish objections to the plan, coupled with the reluctance of the United States to support it, served to delay action by the UN to replace the uneasy truce with a more permanent settlement.[14]

The veto power of the Big Five in the Security Council was intended to apply only to matters of grave international concern. The abuse of this original concept is well illustrated by the action of the USSR in the relatively minor Corfu Channel dispute. Two British destroyers had been sunk by floating mines in Corfu Channel with considerable loss of life. Albania, accused by Britain of perpetrating the incident, refused to accept responsibility and compensate for the damage. In January, 1947, therefore, the United Kingdom presented its case against Albania to the Security Council. Albania, although not a member of the UN, consented to accept the Council's decision. A subcommittee was appointed to gather evidence which was presented to the Council in March.

[14] In December, 1948, however, the Bernadotte plan was rejected by the UN General Assembly, and a Conciliation Commission was appointed to seek once again a peaceful solution to the problem.

A United Kingdom proposal to fix responsibility on the Albanian government was defeated by the veto of the Soviet Union, whose action was supported only by Poland. Blocked by this maneuver, Great Britain moved to have the case referred to the International Court of Justice which was approved by a vote of 8-0, Poland, the USSR, and Great Britain abstaining. Briefs were presented to the Court late in 1947 and oral arguments were heard early in 1948. After lengthy hearings over Albania's objections to the jurisdiction of the Court in the case, agreement was reached. It was decided to seek a decision as to whether (1) Albania was responsible under international law for the loss of life and (2) whether the United Kingdom had violated the sovereignty of Albania through acts of its Navy in Albanian waters.

The conflict between East and West has also served to hamper the subsidiary organs of the Security Council. The Military Staff Committee reached an impasse with regard to the UN security forces as a result of the USSR's consistent advocacy of "equal" contributions of land, sea, and air forces by the Great Powers. Since one or more of the Big Five lack battleships, carriers, and long-range strategic bombers, none of these weapons could be included in the security forces. The more practicable principle of "comparable" contributions, depending on the composition of a nation's existing forces, as advanced by the other powers, has been effectively blocked by the Soviet Union.

The Atomic Energy Commission, after an auspicious start, encountered the same difficulty. The majority viewpoint that effective control and inspection of atomic energy installations is essential before vital information is released and available bombs are destroyed is directly counter to the formula advanced by the Soviet Union. The latter plan requires the destruction of all atomic weapons before measures to control their production are seriously considered. In the light of these irreconcilable views, the Atomic Energy Commission in May, 1948, suspended further discussion of the vital question of atomic controls.

Similarly, unalterable and opposing viewpoints caused the Commission on Conventional Armaments to suspend work.

The Trusteeship Council has not been subjected to the same stress, since the USSR did not appoint a representative to that body until April, 1948, in order to participate in the Palestine decision. Trusteeship agreements have been executed and approved by the General Assembly for nine of the League mandates. The Union of South Africa's proposal for annexation of her League mandate, South West Africa, was disapproved by the Assembly. An invitation was extended to that government to submit a Trusteeship Agreement instead. The Central Pacific Islands, a League mandate to Japan, were made a "strategic" trusteeship of the United States under the supervision of the Security Council.

The problem of Korea, of vital interest to the Soviet government, was not so susceptible to solution. In 1947 the Assembly, upon the recommendation of the Great Powers, invited the Korean people to elect representatives to form a government in preparation for ultimate independence. A commission of nine UN members was also appointed to supervise the elections to be held originally not later than March, 1948. As this commission was denied permission to enter the USSR zone of occupation, the scheduled elections were canceled. Elections were finally held only in the southern, or American zone of occupation, in May, 1948, and a government headed by Dr. Syngman Rhee took office in the late summer of 1948, being recognized by the UN in December of that year.

In concluding this brief survey of the UN in action, the Interim Committee of the Assembly, or so-called "Little Assembly," deserves special attention. Since the General Assembly is in session only several months of each year, an Interim Committee was established in 1947 to function until the regular 1948 meeting at which time it was to report on the advisability of a permanent "Little Assembly." The Committee was empowered to consider (1) matters referred to it by the Assembly or Security Council; (2) any dispute or situation brought before the Assembly requiring study and considered important by two-thirds vote; (3) methods to implement Charter provisions on general principles of cooperation in maintenance of peace; (4) whether a special Assembly session is required in connection with any matter before it. In addition the Committee was authorized to conduct investigations and appoint commissions of inquiry with the consent of the states in which the inquiry is to take place. It is significant that the question of use of the "veto" by the Great Powers was given to the Interim Committee for study and report. The "Little Assembly" was also boycotted by the Soviet Union and its satellites.

EVALUATION OF THE UNITED NATIONS.—Any determination of the efficacy of the United Nations based upon its record of performance since its creation in 1945 must take into consideration the chaotic conditions prevailing in the world following the end of hostilities in that year. Thus, a period in which the Council of Foreign Ministers failed to agree upon a peace treaty for Austria, in which Germany was divided into two regions, and in which an increasing tendency toward the bipolarization of the world developed, could scarcely be expected to facilitate the tasks of the new organization for the maintenance of world security. Our examination of the UN's structure has revealed that its founders sought to incorporate in the institution the best features of previously known security systems. Especially did they attempt to eliminate the proved weaknesses in the League of Nations' organization. While the UN Assembly is not possessed of actual executive authority over the actions of its members, it is nevertheless a great international forum in which the nations of the world, great and small, may express their views. The impact of the discussions and decisions on world public opinion, especially in those nations in which public opinion is freely expressed and taken into consideration, is tremendous. Even the governments of those nations in which information and public opinion are suppressed are often sensitive to the majority views of the other nations of the world. No single nation will risk being branded an international outcast through consistent failure to conform to the will of the majority of the Assembly if it can avoid that stigma. The debates and discussions which fill the atmosphere of the Assembly's meetings serve two purposes: They afford each proponent an opportunity to establish his nation's position with respect to a problem as the most logical and most beneficial; and they permit the rephrasing of proposals and recommendations into terms which are more acceptable to all interests concerned.

The Security Council is potentially capable of discharging the important task with which it is charged. If it is not now actually so capable, it is because of the inability of its members to practice a common code of international ethics. This divergence is mirrored by the failure to agree upon the organization of the international force to be placed at the Council's disposal. This failure is not necessarily permanent. It may be merely the interim result of lengthy and seemingly fruitless discussions. But the opportunity for discussion continues and human experience does not reveal the accomplishment of any project so vast and so important as the creation of an international police force without elaborate and seemingly endless debate.

In the economic and social field much has been accomplished; a great deal more remains to be done. The League, although poorly organized for the purpose, was particularly beneficial in this line of endeavor. It is reasonable to assume that the more efficiently organized UN will show greater progress in a more complicated world order.

Regional Security

INTRODUCTION.—In addition to the security system inherent in the Pan American Union previously described, two other regional security systems have come into being since the formation of the United Nations. They mark other milestones in the world's search for security and may have especially significant long-term effects.

EUROPEAN RECOVERY PROGRAM (ERP).—By the middle of 1947 it was apparent that neither piecemeal aid from the United States nor the economic and financial agencies of the UN would suffice to lift Europe from the depths of economic chaos resulting from the war. It was also obvious

SECRETARY OF STATE GEORGE MARSHALL

JUNE 5, 1947

Proposing a Plan for European Recovery

"The truth of the matter is that Europe's requirements for the next three or four years of foreign food and other essential products—principally from America—are so much greater than her present ability to pay that she must have substantial additional help, or face economic, social and political deterioration of a very grave character.

"The remedy lies in breaking the vicious circle and restoring the confidence of the European people in the economic future of their own countries and of Europe, as a whole. . . .

. . . "It is logical that the United States should do whatever it is able to do to assist in the return of normal economic health in the world, without which there can be no political stability and no assured peace.

"Outside policy is directed not against any country or doctrine but against hunger, poverty, desperation and chaos. Its purpose should be the revival of a working economy in the world so as to permit the emergence of political and social conditions in which free institutions can exist. Such assistance, I am convinced, must not be on a piecemeal basis as various crises develop. Any assistance that this Government may render in the future should provide a cure rather than a mere palliative.

"Any government that is willing to assist in the task of recovery will find full cooperation, I am sure, on the part of the United States Government. Any government which maneuvers to block the recovery of other countries cannot expect help from us. Furthermore, governments, political parties or groups which seek to perpetuate human misery in order to profit therefrom politically or otherwise will encounter the opposition of the United States.

"It is already evident that, before the United States Government can proceed much further in its efforts to alleviate the situation and help start the European world on its way to recovery, there must be some agreement among the countries of Europe as to the requirements of the situation and the part those countries themselves will take in order to give proper effect to whatever action might be undertaken by this Government.

"It would be neither fitting nor efficacious for this Government to undertake to draw up unilaterally a program designed to place Europe on its feet economically. This is the business of the Europeans. The initiative, I think, must come from Europe. The role of this country should consist of friendly aid in the drafting of a European program and of later support of such a program so far as it may be practical for us to do so. The program should be a joint one, agreed to by a number, if not all European nations."

that the western European nations would be unable to withstand the ideological attacks of Communism then rapidly gaining in strength.

To meet this emergency, Secretary of State Marshall in an address at Harvard University in June, 1947, called upon all the European nations to take the initiative and make a supreme effort to help themselves. He further indicated that any plan which promised lasting recovery would probably be supported by the United States with additional financial aid.

The effect of this brief statement was electrifying. The British foreign minister, Mr. Bevin, announced that Great Britain would immediately undertake to bring the European nations together to begin work. France joined with Great Britain in issuing an invitation to Mr. Molotov, the Soviet foreign minister, to come to Paris for a preliminary conference. After several short meetings Mr. Molotov announced that any program dependent upon the economic support of the United States would be unacceptable and thereupon withdrew. Poland and Czechoslovakia had indicated great interest in the project and an intention to send representatives to the proposed general conference. Shortly after Mr. Molotov's pronouncement, however, both nations announced that they would not participate in the ERP, or Marshall Plan, as it was more commonly designated.

An invitation was issued by Great Britain and France to all European countries for a general conference to be held in Paris to discuss ways and means of implementing this program. Sixteen nations accepted and sent representatives to Paris early in July. Within several months they had drafted and transmitted to the Department of State an over-all economic program for the period 1948-1951. The plan provided for production scales considerably above 1938 levels; pledged the nations to exert the greatest efforts to establish domestic stability; and also required the elimination of unreasonable trade restrictions at the earliest possible date. The cost to the United States was estimated at sixteen to twenty billion dollars spread over a four-year period. Legislation as finally enacted by Congress in April 1948 provided 5.3 billion dollars for the first year and established a comprehensive organization to supervise the execution of ERP.

Besides its economic significance and the fact that it seems to offer the one hope of recovery from the devastation of war, the Marshall Plan represents probably the greatest cooperative effort ever undertaken by European countries to integrate and coordinate their economies. Of still greater import is the possibility that it may lead eventually to some form of union which alone can solve the many problems confronting the nations concerned. While the Soviet bloc has taken no part in the plan, and in fact has made every effort to oppose and disrupt it, the door is left open for her participation at any time. An expanded membership and the restoration of economic stability cannot but facilitate the establishment of a sound basis for peace.

FIVE-POWER PACT FOR MUTUAL AID.—The first major step toward possible future union was taken when the British foreign minister suggested consultation among a number of western European nations toward this end as a security measure. In response to his call representatives of Great Britain, France, Belgium, the Netherlands, and Luxembourg met in Brussels and, on March 17, 1948, signed the first military alliance of Europe's democracies. The need for haste was emphasized by the Communist coup in Czechoslovakia, which occurred midway in the negotiations.

The Five-Power Pact in clear, unmistakable language binds the parties to afford all military aid and other assistance to any one of them subjected to armed attack in Europe. In addition there is provided a Consultative Council organized to function continuously and "to consult with regard to any situation which may constitute a threat to peace" or "a danger to economic stability." The treaty is to remain in force for fifty years and provision is also made for the adherence of other states to the pact on conditions to be agreed upon by all parties.

While presumably directed against any future attack or pressure from the East, the fact that western Europe has found a basis for a agreement in the economic and military spheres promises well for the future. The emphasis placed on close collaboration in almost all fields of human endeavor under this regional organization as well as in the UN indicates an overwhelming desire to eliminate the causes of international friction that threaten world security.

BIBLIOGRAPHY

The Government of Great Britain

GENERAL REFERENCES.—Adams, George B. *Constitutional History of England*. Revised by Robert L. Schuyler. New York, Holt, 1934. 600 p.; Barker, Ernest. *Britain and the British People*. New York, Oxford University Press, 1942. 141 p. (*The World Today*); ———— *British Constitutional Monarchy*. New York, Oxford, 1944. 27 p.; British Information Services. *Labor and Industry in Britain, A Quarterly Review;* ———— I.D. Reference Material; ———— *Great Britain, Parliamentary Papers, Command*. London, His Majesty's Stationery Office; Clarke, J. J. *Outlines of Central Government, Including the Political System of England*. 10th ed. London, Sir Isaac Pitman, 1945. 324 p.; *Current History; The Economist; Foreign Affairs;* Gooch, Robert K. *The Government of England*. New York, Van Nostrand, 1937. 326 p.; ———— *Source Book on the Government of England*. New York, Van Nostrand, 1939. 494 p.; Greaves, Harold R. *The British Constitution*. London, G. Allen, 1938. 296 p.; Jennings, W. Ior. *The British Constitution*. New York, Macmillan, 1941. 232 p.; Knappen, Marshall M. *Constitutional and Legal History of England*. New York, Harcourt Brace, 1942. 607 p.; Marriott, Sir John A. R. *English Political Institutions; An Introductory Study*. 4th ed., with introductory chapters on the constitution, 1910-1938. Oxford, Clarendon Press, 1938. 348 p.; Muir, Ramsay. *How Britain Is Governed; A Critical Analysis of Modern Developments in the British System of Government*. 4th ed. with a new preface. London, Constable, 1940. 335 p.; *New York Herald Tribune; The New York Times;* Parry, Hugh L. *English Central Government*. London, King, 1939. 226 p.; Ogg, Frederic A. *English Government and Politics*. 2d ed., thoroughly rev. New York, Macmillan, 1936. 786 p.; Simm, E. *Rebuilding Britain—A Twenty Year Plan*. London, Gollancz, 1945. 256 p.; Stephenson, Carl and Marcham, Frederick G., ed. and tr. *Sources of English Constitutional History; A Selection of Documents from A.D. 600 to the Present*. New York, Harper, 1937. 906 p.

GENERAL PRINCIPLES OF BRITISH DEMOCRACY.—Burns, Cecil DeLisle. *Democracy*. London, Butterworth, 1935. 255 p.; Edwards, William. *Crown,*

People and Parliament, 1760-1935. Bristol, Arrowsmith, 1937. 256 p.; Gaus, J. M. *Great Britain, A Study of Civic Loyalty.* Chicago, University of Chicago Press, 1929. 329 p.; Marriott, Sir John A. R. *This Realm of England: Monarchy, Aristocracy, Democracy.* London, Blackie, 1938. 402 p.; Thomson, David. *The Democratic Ideal in France and England.* Cambridge (Eng.) University Press, 1940. 136 p.

THE BRITISH CONSTITUTION.—Amory, L. S. *Thoughts on the Constitution.* London, Oxford University Press, 1947, 166 p.; Bagehot, Walter. *The English Constitution.* New ed. London, K. Paul, Trench, Trubner, 1929. 300 p.; Dicey, Albert Venn. *Introduction to the Study of the Law of the Constitution.* 9th ed., with introduction and appendix by E. C. S. Wade. London, Macmillan & Co., Ltd., 1939, 681 p.; Jennings, W. Ior. *The Law and the Constitution.* 3d ed. rev. and enl. Bickley, Kent, England, University of London Press, 1943. 322 p.; Keith, Arthur B. *An Introduction to British Constitutional Law.* Oxford, Clarendon Press, 1931. 243 p.; Ridges, Edward W. *Constitutional Law; Being the Seventh Edition of Ridge's Constitutional Law of England.* Rev. and largely rewritten by A. Berriedale Keith. London, Stevens, 1939. 726 p.

EXECUTIVE ORGANIZATION.—Jennings, W. Ior. *Cabinet Government.* New York, Macmillan, 1936. 484 p.; Keith, Arthur B. *The British Cabinet System, 1830-1938.* London, Stevens, 1939. 648 p.; —— *The King and the Imperial Crown; The Powers and Duties of His Majesty.* London, New York, Longmans, 1936. 491 p.; Kingsley, J. Donald. *Representative Bureaucracy.* Yellow Springs, Ohio, Antioch Press, 1944. 324 p.; Robson, Wm. A., ed. *The British Civil Servant,* by Wm. A. Robson, Prof. Ernest Barker, the Hon. Harold Nicolson (and others) London, G. Allen, 1937. 254 p.; Stout, Hiram M. *Public Service in Great Britain.* Chapel Hill, University of N. C. Press, 1938. 189 p.; Willis, John. *The Parliamentary Powers of English Government Departments.* Cambridge, Harvard University Press, 1933. 214 p.

LEGISLATIVE ORGANIZATION.—Jennings, W. Ior. *Parliament.* New York, Macmillan, 1940. 548 p.; Laski, Harold J. *Parliamentary Government in England; A Commentary.* New York, Viking, 1938. 383 p.; Ross, James F. S. *Parliamentary Representation.* New Haven, Yale University Press, 1944. 245 p.

POLITICAL PARTIES.—Attlee, Clement R. *The Labour Party in Perspective.* London, Gollancz, 1937. 387 p.; Brand, Carl F. *British Labour's Rise to Power.* Stanford University, Calif., Stanford University Press, 1941. 305 p.; Hearnshaw, F. J. C. *Conservatism in England; An Analytical, Historical and Political Survey.* London, Macmillan & Co., Ltd., 1933. 322 p.; Slesser, Sir Henry Herman. *A History of the Liberal Party.* London, New York, Hutchinson, 1944. 172 p.; Smellie, Kingsley B. *A Hun-*

dred Years of English Government. London, Duckworth, 1937. 468 p.;
Young, M. *Labour's Plan for Plenty.* London, Gollancz, 1947. 169 p.

NATIONALIZATION OF INDUSTRY.—Davies, E. *National Enterprise: The Development of the Public Corporation.* London, Gollancz, 1946. 173 p.; O'Brien, T. H. *British Experiments in Public Ownership and Control.* New York, Norton, 1938. 304 p.

JUDICIAL ORGANIZATION.—Amos, Sir Maurice Sheldon. *British Justice, An Outline of the Administration of Criminal Justice in England and Wales.* Published for the British Council by Longmans, Green & Co., Inc., New York, 1940. 52 p.; Carr, Sir Cecil Thomas. *Concerning English Administrative Law.* New York, Columbia University Press, 1941. 189 p.; Cohen, H. *The Spirit of Our Laws: British Justice at Work.* 3rd ed. London, Methuen, 1932. 293 p.; Howard, Pendleton. *Criminal Justice in England; A Study in Law Administration.* New York, Macmillan, 1931; Jackson, Richard M. *The Machinery of Justice in England.* Cambridge (Eng.) University Press, 1940. 342 p.; Patterson, Caleb P. *The Administration of Justice in Great Britain.* Austin, Tex., University of Texas, 1936. 326 p.

LOCAL GOVERNMENT.—Gooch, Robert K. "England." (In: Anderson, William, ed. *Local Government in Europe.* New York, Appleton-Century, 1939, chap. 2); Finer, Herman. *English Local Government.* New York, Columbia University Press, 1934. 533 p.; Harris, George Montagu. *Municipal Self-Government in Britain.* London, King, 1939. 342 p.; Hasluck, Eugene L. *Local Government in England.* Cambridge (Eng.) University Press, 1936. 363 p.; Robson, William A. *The Development of Local Government.* London, G. Allen, 1931. 362 p.; Smellie, K. B. *A History of Local Government.* London, G. Allen, 1946. 192 p.

CIVIL RIGHTS.—Barker, Ernest. *Reflections on Government.* London, Oxford University Press, 1942. 424 p.; Laski, Harold J. *Liberty in the Modern State.* New York, Harper, 1930. 288 p.; Rhys, Ernest, ed. *The Growth of Political Liberty; A Source Book of English History.* New York, Dutton, 1921. 331 p.

THE BRITISH EMPIRE-COMMONWEALTH.—*The British Empire. A Report on Its Structure and Problems by a Study Group of Members of the Royal Institute of International Affairs.* 2d ed. New York, Oxford University Press, 1938. 342 p.; Keith, Arthur B. *The Governments of the British Empire.* London, Macmillan & Co., Ltd., 1935. 646 p.; ———— *The Dominions as Sovereign States; Their Constitutions and Governments.* London, Macmillan & Co., Ltd., 1938. 769 p.; Wheare, Kenneth C. *The Statute of Westminster and Dominion Status.* 2d ed. New York, Oxford University Press, 1942. 328 p.; Zimmern, Sir Alfred E. *From the British Empire to the British Commonwealth.* New York, Longmans, 1941. 52 p.

FOREIGN POLICY.—Brinton, Crane. *The United States and Britain.* Cambridge, Harvard University Press, 1945. 305 p.; Corbett, P. E. *Britain: Partner for Peace.* New York, Harcourt Brace, 1946. 177 p.; Langford, R. V. *British Foreign Policy: Its Formulation in Recent Years.* Washington, the American Council on Public Affairs, 1942. 226 p.; Seton-Watson, Robert W. *Britain in Europe, 1789-1914; A Survey of Foreign Policy.* New York, Macmillan, 1937. 716 p.; —— *Britain and the Dictators; A Survey of Post-War British Policy.* New York, Macmillan, 1938. 460 p.; Stimson, Henry L. and Bundy, McGeorge. *On Active Service in Peace and War.* New York, Harper, 1947. 698 p.; Wolfers, Arnold. *Britain and France between Two Wars; Conflicting Strategies of Peace since Versailles.* New York, Harcourt Brace, 1940. 467 p.

The Government of France

GENERAL REFERENCES.—Barthélemy, Joseph. *The Government of France.* Authorized translation by J. Bayard Morris. London, G. Allen, 1924. 222 p. (latest French edition, 1939); *Cahiers français d'information* and other publications of the French Embassy, Information Division, New York; Catlin, George. *The Story of the Political Philosophers.* New York, McGraw-Hill, 1939. 783 p.; Marriott, J. A. R. *A Short History of France.* New York, Oxford University Press, 1944. 291 p.; Middleton, Wilfrid L. *The French Political System.* New York, Dutton, 1933. 296 p.; Pickles, Dorothy M. *The French Political Scene.* New York, Nelson, 1939. 180 p.; Sharp, Walter R. *The Government of the French Republic.* New York, Van Nostrand, 1938. 373 p.; Shotwell *et al. Governments of Continental Europe.* New York, Macmillan, 1942. 1104 p.; *The New York Times; New York Herald Tribune.*

L'ANCIEN RÉGIME AND THE FRENCH REVOLUTION.—Bainville, J. *History of France.* Translated by A. and C. Gauss. New York, Appleton, 1926. 483 p.; Brinton, Clarence C. *A Decade of Revolution, 1789-1799.* New York, Harper, 1934. 330 p.; Carlyle, Thomas. *The French Revolution.* London, G. Bell, 1904. 3v.; Ergang, Robert. *Europe from the Renaissance to Waterloo.* New York, Heath, 1939. 752 p.; Grant, Arthur J. *French Monarchy, 1483-1789.* 2v. 4th ed. New York, Macmillan, 1920; Lowell, Edward J. *Eve of the French Revolution.* Boston, Houghton, 1893. 408 p.; Perkins, James B. *Economic and Social Conditions in France during the Eighteenth Century.* Translated by E. H. Zeydel. New York, Knopf, 1927. 245 p.; Seignobos, C. *The Evolution of the French People.* Translated by C. A. Phillips. New York, Knopf, 1932. 382 p.

FRANCE 1815-1939.—Bainville, Jacques. *The French Republic, 1870-1935.* Translated by H. Miles. London, J. Cape, 1936. 253 p.; Bourgeois, Emile. *History of Modern France, 1815-1913.* 2v. New York, Macmillan,

1919. 394 p.; Brogan, Denis W. *France under the Republic; the Development of Modern France* (1870-1939). New York, Harper, 1940. 744 p.

GOVERNMENT OF THE THIRD REPUBLIC.—Gooch, Robert K. *The French Parliamentary Committee System.* New York, Appleton-Century, 1935. 259 p.; Heinberg, J. G. "Personnel Structure of French Cabinets." *American Political Science Review,* April, 1939, v.33:267-279; Morrison, Henry. *The French Constitution.* London, G. Allen, 1930. 96 p.; Rogers, Lindsay. "Personal Power and Popular Government." *Southern Review,* 1937, v.3, no.2. 225-242 (A study of the French presidency); Sharp, Walter R. *The French Civil Service: Bureaucracy in Transition.* New York, Macmillan, 1931. 588 p.; Soltau, Roger H. *French Parties and Politics, 1871-1921* (With a new supplementary chapter dealing with 1922-1930). New York, Oxford University Press, 1930. 88 p.

DOWNFALL OF FRANCE.—Armstrong, Hamilton F. *Chronology of Failure: The Last Days of the Third Republic.* New York, Macmillan, 1940. 202 p.; Cameron, Elizabeth R. *Prologue to Appeasement; A Study in French Foreign Policy.* Washington, D. C. American Council on Public Affairs. 1942. 228 p.; France. Ministry of Foreign Affairs. *The French Yellow Book.* London, Hutchinson, 1940. 368 p. (Diplomatic documents, 1938-39); *France Talks with Hitler.* London, Hutchinson, 1940. (Based on *French Yellow Book;* foreword by Harold Nicolson); Géraud, André. *Gravediggers of France.* New York, Doubleday, 1944. 612 p. by Pertinax (pseud.); Lorraine, Jacques. *Behind the Battle of France.* Translated by Gerard Hopkins. New York, Oxford University Press, 1943. 136 p.; Ogg, Frederic A. *The Rise of Dictatorship in France.* (Supplement to: *European Governments and Politics.* 2d ed. New York, Macmillan, 1941. 28 p.); Rice, Howard C. (comp.) *France, 1940-1942; A Collection of Documents and Bibliography.* Cambridge, Mass., Harvard Co-operative Society, 1942. 224 p.; Simon, Yves. *The Road to Vichy, 1918-1938.* Translated by James A. Corbett and George J. McMorrow. New York, Sheed, 1942. 207 p.; Werth, Alexander, *The Twilight of France, 1933-1940.* Edited with an introduction by D. W. Brogan. New York, Harper, 1942. 368 p.; Weyer, Mary E. *The Decline of French Democracy; The Beginning of National Disintegration.* Washington, American Council on Public Affairs, 1940. 73 p.

THE VICHY REGIME.—Clough, Shepard B. "House that Pétain Built; Corporatism." *Political Science Quarterly,* March, 1944, v.59:30-39; Heinberg, J. G. "French Government under Pétain." (In Zink, Harold, and Taylor, Cole, eds. *Government in Wartime Europe and Japan.* Boston, Houghton, 1942:180-205); Kammerer, Gladys M. "Political Theory of Vichy." *Journal of Politics,* November, 1943, v.5: 407-434; Langer, William L. *Our Vichy Gamble.* New York, Knopf, 1947. 412 p.; Lapie, P. O.

"Government of France." *Fortnightly Review* (London) January, 1944, v.161:26-33; Lemkin, Raphael. *Axis Rule in Occupied Europe.* (Carnegie Endowment for International Peace) Concord, N. H., Rumford Press, 1944. 674 p.; Lowenstein, Karl. "The Demise of the French Constitution of 1875." *American Political Science Review,* October, 1940, v.34:867-895; Tissier, Pierre. *The Nazification of Vichy France.* New York, Oxford University Press, 1942. 40 p.; ———— *The Government of Vichy.* London, Harrap, 1942. 347 p.

THE RESISTANCE.—Aghion, Raoul. *The Fighting French.* New York, Holt, 1943. 315 p.; Barrès, Philippe. *Charles de Gaulle.* New York, Brentano's, 1941. 316 p.; de Gaulle, Charles. *The Speeches of General de Gaulle.* New York, Oxford University Press, 1942. 115 p.; ———— *The Speeches of General de Gaulle.* London, Oxford University Press, 1944. 189 p.; Price, George W. *Giraud and the African Scene.* New York, Macmillan, 1944. 282 p.

THE FOURTH FRENCH REPUBLIC.—*A Constitution for the Fourth Republic.* Foundation for Foreign Affairs Pamphlet No. 2. Washington (n.p.), 1947. 125 p.; *Current History:* February, 1947, v.12 no.66:123-127; Knapton, Ernest J. "The Fourth French Republic." *Foreign Affairs:* July, 1945, v.23 no.4:556-566; Siegfried, André. "The Rebirth of the French Spirit." ———— April, 1947, v.25 no.3:433-450; Géraud, André. "The New French Constitution." ———— 451-464; Rist, Charles. "The French Financial Dilemma." ———— 465-475; Ehrman, Henry W. "French Labor Goes Left." ————. Wright, Gordon. *The Reshaping of French Democracy.* New York, Reynal and Hitchcock, Inc., 1948. 277 p.

ARMED FORCES.—Dennery, Étienne. "Democracy and the French Army." *Military Affairs,* 1941, v.5:233-240; de Gaulle, Charles. *The Army of the Future.* Philadelphia, Lippincott, 1941. 179 p.; Davis, Shelby C. *The French War Machine.* London, G. Allen, 1937. 221 p.; Weygand, Maurice. "How France Is Defended." *International Affairs,* July, 1939, v.18:459-477.

FOREIGN POLICY OF THE FOURTH REPUBLIC.—*Current History:* December, 1946, v.11 no.64:475-480; Knapton, Ernest J. "France and the Latins: Protection." May, 1947, v.12 no.69:477-482; Knapton, Ernest J. "French Plans for Peace." July, 1947, v.13 no.71:22-26; Garbuny, Siegfried. "The Ruhr—Valley of Decision." September, 1947, v.13 no.73:144-148; Knapton, Ernest J. "France and the Reconstruction of Europe." *Foreign Affairs:* October, 1947, v.26 no.1:24-35; Géraud, André, "Can France Be a Great Power?" ———— January, 1948, v.26 no.2:325-334; Philip, André. "France and the Economic Recovery of Europe." ———— April, 1948, v.26 no.3:497-504.

JUDICIAL ORGANIZATION.—Alibert, Ralph. "French *Conseil d'état.*" *Modern Law Review* (London), April, 1940, v.3:257-271; Amos, Sir Maurice Sheldon and Walton, Frederick P. *Introduction to French Law.* Oxford, Clarendon Press, 1935. 393 p.; Deak, Francis. "Development of French Law." *Georgetown Law Journal,* March, 1936, v.24:551-567; Riesenfeld, Stefan. "French System of Administrative Justice; A Model for American Law?" *Boston University Law Review,* January-November, 1938, v.18:48-82, 400-432, 715-748; Siegfried, André. "The French Democratic Tradition." *Foreign Affairs,* July, 1939, v.17:649-662; Thomson, David. *The Democratic Ideal in France and England.* Cambridge (Eng.) University Press, 1940, 136 p.

LOCAL GOVERNMENT.—Sharp, Walter R. "France." (In: Anderson, William, ed. *Local Government in Europe.* New York, Appleton-Century, 1939, ch.2, p.107-222.); Gooch, Robert K. *Regionalism in France.* New York, Century, 1931. 129 p.

THE FRENCH COLONIAL EMPIRE AND THE FRENCH UNION.—Priestley, Herbert I. *France Overseas; A Study of Modern Imperialism.* New York, Appleton-Century, 1938. 463 p. maps; Royal Institute of International Affairs. *The French Colonial Empire.* London, 1940. 52 p.; Southworth, Constant. *The French Colonial Venture.* London, King, 1931. 204 p.; Stern, Jacques. *The French Colonies, Past and Future.* New York, Didier, 1944. 331 p.

The Government of Italy

GENERAL REFERENCES.—Borgese, Giuseppe A. *Goliath; The March of Fascism.* New York, Viking, 1937. 483 p.; Ebenstein, William. *Fascist Italy.* New York, American Book, 1939. 310 p.; Finer, Herman. *Mussolini's Italy.* London, Gollancz, 1935. 564 p.; Gibson, Hugh. ed. *The Ciano Diaries, 1939-43.* New York, Doubleday, 1946. 584 p.; Megaro, Gaudens. *Mussolini in the Making.* New York, Houghton, 1938. 347 p.; Neumann, Sigmund. *Permanent Revolution.* New York, Harper, 1942. 397 p.; Salvemini, Gaetano. *Under the Axe of Fascism.* New York, Viking, 1936. 402 p.; Schmidt, Carl T. *The Corporate State in Action; Italy under Fascism.* New York, Oxford University Press, 1939. 173 p.; —— *The Plough and the Sword; Labor, Land, and Property in Fascist Italy.* New York, Columbia University Press, 1938. 197 p.; Schneider, Herbert W. *The Fascist Government of Italy.* New York, Van Nostrand, 1936. 173 p.

BACKGROUND OF THE ITALIAN GOVERNMENT.—Croce, Benedetto. *A History of Italy.* Translated by Cecilia M. Ady. Oxford, Clarendon Press, 1929. 333 p.; Hentze, Margot. *Pre-Fascist Italy; The Rise and Fall of the Parliamentary Regime.* London, G. Allen, 1939. 400 p.; King, Bolton. *History of Italian Unity.* 2 Vols., London, James Nisbet & Co., 1912. 866

p.; King, Bolton, and Okey, Thomas. *Italy Today*. New York, Scribner, 1909. 397 p.; Salomone, A. William. *Italian Democracy in the Making*. Philadelphia, University of Pennsylvania Press, 1945. 114 p.; Sforza, Count Carlo. *Contemporary Italy; Its Intellectual and Moral Origins*. Translated by Drake and Denise De Kay. New York, Dutton, 1944. 430 p.; Sprigge, Cecil J. S. *The Development of Modern Italy*. New Haven, Yale University Press, 1943. 216 p.

THE FASCIST GOVERNMENT, 1922-1943.—Ebenstein, William. "The Impact of the Second World War on Italian Fascism." (In: Zink, Harold and Cole, Taylor eds. *Government in Wartime Europe and Japan*. Boston, Houghton, 1942, p.154-179.); Steiner, H. Arthur. *Government in Fascist Italy*. New York, McGraw-Hill, 1938. 158 p.

THE EARLY FASCIST PARTY.—Mussolini, Benito. *My Autobiography*. London, Hutchinson, 1939. 354 p.; Rossi, Angelo. *The Rise of Italian Fascism, 1918-1922*. Translated by Peter and Dorothy Wait. London, Methuen, 1938. 376 p.; Salvemini, Gaetano. *The Fascist Dictatorship in Italy*. New York, Holt, 1927. 319 p.

FASCIST DOCTRINE.—Ascoli, Max, and Arthur Feiler. *Fascism for Whom?* New York, Norton, 1938. 341 p.; Florinsky, Michael T. *Fascism and National Socialism; A Study of the Economic and Social Policies of the Totalitarian State*. New York, Macmillan, 1936. 292 p.; Mussolini, Benito. *The Political and Social Doctrine of Fascism, and Aims and Policies of the Fascist Regime in Italy*. New York, Carnegie Endowment for International Peace, 1935. (*International Conciliation*. January, 1935, no.306.)

THE CONSTITUTIONAL BASIS OF THE GOVERNMENT.—Steiner, H. Arthur. "Constitutional Position of the *Partito nazionale fascista*." *American Political Science Review*, April, 1937, v.31: 227-242; U. S. War Department. Provost Marshal General's Office. Military Government Division. *Civil Affairs Handbooks. Italy: The Italian Civil Code*. Washington, 1944. 5 volumes.

EXECUTIVE, LEGISLATIVE, AND FASCIST PARTY ORGANIZATIONS.—Cole, Taylor. "Italy's Fascist Bureaucracy." *American Political Science Review*, December, 1938, v.32: 1143-1157; Lasswell, Harold D. and Renzo, Sereno. "Governmental and Party Leaders in Fascist Italy." *American Political Science Review*, October, 1937, v.31: 914-929.

ARMED FORCES.—Poole, Ernest. "Sons of the Wolf." *Harper's Magazine*, October, 1937, v.175: 460-469; Schneider, Herbert W. and Clough, Shepard B. *Making Fascists*. Chicago, University of Chicago Press, 1929. 205 p.

LOCAL GOVERNMENT.—Rossi, Carlo. "Local Government in Italy under Fascism." *American Political Science Review,* August, 1935, v.29: 658-663; Steiner, H. Arthur. "Italian Law on Communal and Provincial Government." *National Municipal Review,* September, 1936, v.25: 520-527; —— "Local Government in Italy." (In: Anderson, William, ed. *Local Government in Europe.* New York, Appleton-Century, 1939, ch.4, p.305.)

COLONIAL ADMINISTRATION.—Quaranta di San Severino, Baron Ferdinando. *Ethiopia, an Empire in the Making.* London, King, 1939. 120 p. (Condensed ed. New York, Italian Library of Information, 1939. 101 p.); Royal Institute of International Affairs. *The Italian Colonial Empire, with Chapters on the Dodecanese and Albania.* London, 1940. 72 p.; Steiner, H. Arthur. "Government of Italian East Africa." *American Political Science Review,* October, 1936, v.30: 884-902.

FOREIGN POLICY.—Tittoni, Tommaso. *Italy's Foreign and Colonial Policy.* Translated by Bernardo Quaranta di San Severino, London, Smith, Eder and Co., 1914. 114 p.; Ward, Barbara. *Italian Foreign Policy.* London, Oxford University Press, 1941. 32 p.

THE BADOGLIO REGIME.—Luzzatto, Riccardo. *Unknown War in Italy,* ——, New Europe Publishing Company, 1946. 135 p.; Sturzo, Luigi. "Italy after Mussolini." *Foreign Affairs,* April, 1943. v.21: 412-426; Tregaskis, Richard W. *Invasion Diary.* New York, Random House, 1944. 245 p.

ALLIED MILITARY GOVERNMENT IN ITALY.—Ascoli, Max. "Italy, An Experiment in Reconstruction (A.M.G.)" American Academy of Political and Social Science, Philadelphia. *Annals,* July, 1944, v.234: 36-41.

THE ITALIAN REPUBLIC.—Brockwell, Ronald. "Party Struggle in Italy." *Central European Observer,* 24:118, 2 May, 1947; Einaudi, Mario. "Economic and Political Reconstruction of Italy." American Academy of Political and Social Science, Philadelphia. *Annals,* July, 1944, v.234: 42-46; Gindrod, Muriel. *The New Italy.* Royal Institute of International Affairs, London, 1947. 118 p.; Public Relations Branch, Allied Commission, "Review of Allied Military Government and of the Allied Commission in Italy," APO No. 394. U. S. Army; Sturzo, Luigi. *Italy and the Coming World,* New York, Roy Publications, 1945. 303 p.; Wall, Bernard. "Italy and Europe," *Free Europe,* v.13: 74-77, April, 1946.

The Government of Germany

GENERAL REFERENCES.—Cobban, Alfred. *Dictatorship, Its History and Theory,* New York, Scribner, 1939. 352 p.; Friedrich, Carl J. *Constitutional Government and Politics,* New York, Harper, 1937, 591 p.; Hitler, Adolf. *Mein Kampf,* New York, Reynal & Hitchcock, 1940. 1003 p.; Hitler,

Adolf. *My New Order,* Edited with commentary by Raoul de Roussy de Sales, New York, Reynal & Hitchcock, Inc., 1941. 1008 p.; ——— *The Speeches of Adolf Hitler, April, 1922–August, 1939.* Translated and edited by Norman H. Baynes. New York, Oxford University Press, 1942. 2 v.; Lowenstein, Karl. *Hitler's Germany; the Nazi Background to War.* New ed., New York, Macmillan, 1940. 230 p.; Neumann, Sigmund. *Permanent Revolution,* New York, Harper, 1942. 388 p.; ——— *The Future in Perspective,* Putnam, 1946, 393 p.; Neumann, Franz S. *Behemoth: The Structure and Practice of National Socialism.* New York, Oxford University Press, 1942. 532 p.; Valentin, Veit. *The German People,* New York, Knopf, 1946. 730 p.

BACKGROUND OF GERMAN GOVERNMENT.—Gooch, George Peabody. *Germany.* London, Benn, 1929. 360 p.; Shotwell, James T. *What Germany Forgot.* New York, Macmillan, 1940. 152 p.; Shuster, George N., and Bergstrasser, Arnold. *Germany: A Short History.* New York, Norton, 1944. 238 p.

DEVELOPMENTS UNDER THE WEIMAR REPUBLIC.—Brecht, Arnold. *Prelude to Silence,* New York, Oxford University Press, 1944, 156 p.; ——— *Regionalism and Federalism in Germany,* New York, Oxford University Press, 1945, 202 p.; Kraus, Herbert. *The Crisis of German Democracy; A Study of the Spirit of the Constitution of Weimar.* Edited with an introduction by William Starr Myers and with an English translation of the German constitution by Marguerite Wolff. Princeton, N. J., Princeton University Press, 1932. 223 p.; Quigley, Hugh, and R. T. Clark. *Republican Germany; A Political and Economic Study.* New York, Dodd, Mead, 1928. 318 p.; Villard, Oswald G. *The German Phoenix; The Story of the Republic.* New York, H. Smith & R. Haas, 1933. 358 p.; Watkins, Frederick M. *The Failure of Constitutional Emergency Powers under the German Republic.* Cambridge, Mass., Harvard University Press, 1939. 148 p.

THE RISE OF NATIONAL SOCIALISM.—Heiden, Konrad. *A History of National Socialism.* Translated from the German. New York, Knopf, 1935. 430 p.; ——— *Der Fuehrer; Hitler's Rise to Power.* Translated by Ralph Manheim. Boston, Houghton, 1944. 788 p.; Hoover, Calvin B. *Germany Enters the Third Reich.* New York, Macmillan, 1933. 243 p.; Pollock, James K., and Heneman, Harlow J., comps. *The Hitler Decrees.* 2d ed. Ann Arbor, Mich., G. Wahr, 1934. 86 p.

NATIONAL SOCIALIST DOCTRINE.—Butler, Rohan d'O. *The Roots of National Socialism.* New York, Dutton, 1942. 304 p.; U. S. Dept. of State. *National Socialism; Basic Principles, Their Application by the Nazi Party's Foreign Organization, and the Use of Germans Abroad for Nazi Aims.* (Prepared by Raymond E. Murphy, Francis B. Stevens, Howard

Trivers, and Joseph M. Roland.) Washington, U. S. Govt. Printing Office, 1943. 510 p.

THE GOVERNMENT OF THE THIRD REICH.—Duncan-Jones, Arthur S. *The Struggle for Religious Freedom in Germany*. London, Gollancz, 1938. 319 p.; Hamburger, Ludwig. *How Nazi Germany Has Mobilized and Controlled Labor*. Washington, D. C., Brookings, 1940. 63 p.; Institute of Jewish Affairs. *Hitler's Ten-Year War on the Jews*. New York, World Jewish Congress, 1943. 311 p.; Jones, John W. *The Nazi Conception of Law*. Oxford, Clarendon Press, 1939. 32 p.; Micklem, Nathaniel. *National Socialism and the Roman Catholic Church; Being an Account of the Conflict between the National Socialist Government of Germany and the Roman Catholic Church, 1933-1938*. New York, Oxford University Press, 1939. 243 p.; Morstein Marx, Fritz. *Government in the Third Reich*. 2d ed. New York, McGraw-Hill, 1937. 199 p.; Munk, Frank. *The Legacy of Nazism; The Economic and Social Consequences of Totalitarianism*. New York, Macmillan, 1943. 288 p.; Pollock, James K. *The Government of Greater Germany*. New York, Van Nostrand, 1938. 213 p.; Roper, Edith, and Leiser, Clara. *Skeleton of Justice*. New York, Dutton, 1941. 346 p.

LOCAL GOVERNMENT.—Boerner, A. V. "Toward *Reichsreform—the Reichsgaue*." *American Political Science Review*, October, 1939, v.33: 853-859; Morstein Marx, Fritz. "Local Government in Germany" (In: Anderson, William, ed. *Local Government in Europe*. New York, Appleton-Century, 1939, p. 225-303); Wells, Roger H. *German Cities; A Study of Contemporary Municipal Politics and Administration*. Princeton, N. J., Princeton University Press, 1932. 283 p.; ——— "Municipal Government in National Socialist Germany." *American Political Science Review*, August, 1935, v.29: 652-658.

THE NATIONAL SOCIALIST PARTY (NSDAP).—Brennecke, Fritz. *The Nazi Primer; Official Handbook for Schooling the Hitler Youth*. Translated from the original German with a preface by Harwood L. Childs. New York, Harper, 1938. 280 p.; *Germany Speaks*, by 21 Leading Members of Party and State, with a Preface by Joachim von Ribbentrop. London, Butterworth, 1938. 406 p.

ARMED FORCES.—Benoist-Mechin, J. G. *History of the German Army since the Armistice*. Paris, A. Michel, 1936. 2 v.; Fried, Hans E. *The Guilt of the German Army*. New York, Macmillan, 1942. 426 p.; Hermann, Hauptmann (pseud.). *The Luftwaffe, Its Rise and Fall*. New York, Putnam, 1943. 300 p.; Rosinski, Herbert. *The German Army*. New rev. ed. Washington, Infantry Journal, 1944. 220 p.

FOREIGN POLICY.—Borkenau, Franz. *The New German Empire*. New York, Viking, 1939. 167 p.; Lemkin, Rafael. *Axis Rule in Occupied Eu-

rope. Washington, Carnegie Endowment for International Peace, 1944. 674 p.; Office of United States Chief Counsel for Prosecution of Axis Criminality. *Nazi Conspiracy and Aggression.* Washington, U. S. Government Printing Office, 1946. 8 v. 1 sup.; Royal Institute of International Affairs. *Occupied Europe; German Exploitation and Its Post-War Consequences.* London, 1944. 75 p.; Strauzz-Hupé, Robert. *Axis America: Hitler Plans Our Future.* New York, Putnam, 1941. 274 p.; Whittlesey, Derwent S., Colby, Charles C., and Hartshorne, Richard. *German Strategy of World Conquest.* New York, Rinehart, 1942. 293 p.

ALLIED OCCUPATION OF GERMANY.—*American Political Science Review;* Bach, Julius, Jr. *America's Germany: an Account of the Occupation.* New York, Random House, 1946. 310 p.; Council of Foreign Ministers Secretariat, Civil Affairs Division, OMGUS. *Summary of Agreements and Disagreements on Germany.* (1947 and 1948 editions.); *Current History;* Dulles, A. W. *Germany's Underground.* New York, Macmillan, 1947. 207 p.; *Economist,* April 24–May 8, 1948. *Report from Germany,* pp. 674-676, 716-717, 767-768; *Foreign Affairs;* Holborn, Hajo. *American Military Government.* Washington, Infantry Journal Press, 1947. 243 p.; *International Conciliation;* Meisel, J. H. and Pollock J. K. *Germany under Occupation.* Ann Arbor, Michigan, Wahr, 1947. 306 p.; *New York Herald Tribune; The New York Times;* Office of Military Government, U. S. Zone, Germany, Official Reports; U. S. Department of State. *Occupation of Germany, Policy and Progress.* (Publication 2783). Also Bulletins for 1947-1948; *Vital Speeches of the Day;* Warburg, James P. *Germany, Bridge or Battleground.* New York, Harcourt Brace, 1947. 386 p.; *The Yale Review.*

The Government of the USSR

GENERAL REFERENCES.—SOVIET RUSSIA, a selected list of recent references, Library of Congress, Division of Bibliography, Washington, 1943; Fischer, John. *Why They Behave Like Russians,* New York, Harper, 1947. 262 p.; Chamberlin, William H. *The Russian Enigma, An Interpretation,* New York, Scribner, 1943, 321 p.; Florinsky, Michael T. *Toward an Understanding of the USSR; A Study in Government, Politics and Economic Planning.* New York, Macmillan, 1939, 245 p.; Williams, Albert R. *The Russians; The Land, The People, and Why They Fight.* New York, Harcourt Brace, 1943, 248 p.; ——— *The Soviets.* New York, Harcourt Brace, 1937, 554 p.

BACKGROUND OF THE SOVIET UNION.—Pares, Bernard. *A History of Russia,* New York, Knopf, 1948, 565 p.; Chamberlin, William H. *The Russian Revolution, 1917-1921.* New York, Macmillan, 1935, 2v.; *History of the Communist Party of the Soviet Union (Bolshevik).* Edited by a committee of the Central Committee of the C.P.S.U. (B). New York, International

Publishers, 1939, 364 p.; Sumner, Benedict H. *A Short History of Russia*. New York, Reynal & Hitchcock, Inc., 1943, 469 p.

RUSSIAN COMMUNISM.—*Communism in Action*. 79th Congress, 2d session. House Document No. 754. 1946; Stalin, Joseph. *Leninism; Selected Writings*. New York, International Publishers, 1942, 479 p.; Maynard, John. *Russia in Flux*, New York, Macmillan, 1948. 564 p.

SOVIET CONSTITUTION.—*Russia (USSR) Constitution of the Union of Soviet Socialist Republics*. New York, The National Council of American-Soviet Friendship, 1941. 39 p.; Schuman, Frederick L. *Soviet Politics at Home and Abroad*. New York, Knopf, 1946, 663 p.

THE FEDERAL STRUCTURE OF THE USSR.—Hazard, John N. "Federal Organization of the USSR." Russian Review, Spring, 1944, v.3:21-29; Kohn, Hans. "Nationality Policy of the Soviet Union" (In: Harper, Samuel N., ed. *Soviet Union and World Problems*. Chicago, University of Chicago Press, 1935, part 4); Stalin, Joseph. *Marxism and the National and Colonial Question, Selected Speeches*. New York, International Publishers, 1942, 222 p.

THE ALL-UNION COMMUNIST PARTY (BOLSHEVIK).—Communist Party of the Soviet Union, 18th Congress, Moscow, 1939. *Land of Socialism Today and Tomorrow; Reports and Speeches*. Moscow, Foreign Languages Publishing House, 1939, 487 p.; Harper, Samuel N. *Civic Training in Soviet Russia*. Chicago, University of Chicago Press, 1929, 401 p.

THE GOVERNMENT OF THE USSR.—Harper, Samuel N., *The Government of the Soviet Union*. New York, Van Nostrand, 1938, 204 p.; Hazard, John N. "The Impact of the War on Soviet Political and Economic Institutions." (In: Zink, Harold, and Taylor Cole, eds. *Government in Wartime Europe and Japan*. Boston, Houghton, 1942, p. 129-153).

GOVERNMENTS OF CONSTITUENT REPUBLICS AND LOCAL SUBDIVISIONS.—Maxwell, Bertram W. "The Soviet Union" (In: Anderson, William, ed. *Local Government in Europe*. New York, Appleton-Century, 1939, Chap. 6); Mikhailov, Nickolai N. *Land of the Soviets: A Handbook of the USSR*. Translated from the Russian by Nathalie Rothstein, New York, Furman, 1939, 351 p.

FOREIGN POLICY.—*Trends in Russian Foreign Policy Since World War I*. 80th Congress, 1st Session. Committee Print. 1947; Carr, Edward H. *The Soviet Impact on the Western World*. New York, Macmillan, 1947, 113 p.; Dallin, David J. *Soviet Russia's Foreign Policy, 1939-1942*. Translated by Leon Dennen. New Haven, Yale University Press, 1942, 452 p.; Dulles, Foster R. *The Road to Teheran; The Story of Russia and America, 1781-1943*. Princeton, N. J., Princeton University Press, 1944, 279 p.; Laserson, Max M. *The Development of Soviet Foreign Policy in Europe,*

1917-1942, A Selection of Documents. New York, Carnegie Endowment for International Peace, 1943, 95 p. *(International Conciliation . . .* January, 1943, no. 386).

The Government of Japan

GENERAL REFERENCES.—Benedict, Ruth. *The Chrysanthemum and the Sword: Patterns of Japanese Culture.* Boston, Houghton, 1946. 324 p.; Borton, Hugh. *Japan Since 1931, Its Political and Social Developments.* New York, Institute of Pacific Relations, 1940. 149 p.; Kitazawa, Naokichi. *The Government of Japan.* Edited with an introduction by William Starr Myers. Princeton, N. J., Princeton University Press, 1929. 130 p.; Latourette, Kenneth S. *The History of Japan.* New York, Macmillan, 1947. 290 p.; Nitobe, Inazo. *Japan; Some Phases of Her Problems and Development.* New York, Scribner, 1936. 398 p.; Reischauer, E. O. *Japan, Past and Present.* New York, Knopf, 1946. 192 p.

BACKGROUND OF JAPANESE GOVERNMENT.—Harris, Townsend. *The Complete Journal of Townsend Harris, First American Consul General and Minister to Japan.* Introduction and notes by Mario E. Cosanza. New York, Doubleday, 1930. 616 p.; Sansom, Sir George B. *Japan, A Short Cultural History.* Rev. ed., New York, Appleton-Century, 1943. 554 p.

JAPANESE POLITICAL PHILOSOPHY.—Fujisawa, Rikitaro. *The Recent Aims and Political Development of Japan.* New Haven, Pub. for the Institute of Politics by Yale University Press, 1923. 222 p.; Holtom, Daniel C. *Modern Japan and Shinto Nationalism.* Chicago, University of Chicago Press, 1947. 226 p.

THE TRANSITION ERA, 1867-1889.—Griffis, William E. *The Mikado: Institution and Person; A Study of the Internal Political Forces of Japan.* Princeton, N. J., Princeton University Press, 1915. 336 p.; Norman, E. Herbert. *Japan's Emergence as a Modern State; Political and Economic Problems of the Meiji Period.* New York, Institute of Pacific Relations, 1940. 254 p.; Treat, Payson J. *Japan and the United States, 1853-1921.* Revised and continued to 1928. Stanford University, Calif., Stanford University Press, 1928. 307 p.

THE CONSTITUTION OF 1889.—Colgrove, Kenneth. "The Japanese Constitution." *American Political Science Review,* December, 1937, v.31: 1027-1049. Fujii, Shinichi. *The Essentials of Japanese Constitutional Law.* Tokyo, Yuhikaku, 1940. 463 p.; Ito, Hirobumi, Prince. *Commentaries on the Constitution of the Empire of Japan.* Translated by Miyoji Ito, Tokyo, 1889. 259 p.

EXECUTIVE ORGANIZATION.—Borton, Hugh. *The Administration and Structure of Japanese Government.* Washington, Dept. of State, 1944. 17

p.; Colgrove, Kenneth. "The Japanese Cabinet." *American Political Science Review,* October, 1936, v.30: 903-923.—"The Japanese Emperor." *American Political Science Review,* August-October, 1932, v.26: 642-659, 828-845. ———— "Japanese Privy Council." *American Political Science Review,* August-November, 1931, v.25: 589-614, 881-905.

MILITARY ORGANIZATION.—Lory, Hillis. *Japan's Military Masters; The Army in Japanese Life.* New York, Viking, 1943. 256 p.; Norman, E. Herbert. *Soldier and Peasant in Japan: The Origins of Conscription.* New York, Institute of Pacific Relations, 1943. 76 p.

LEGISLATIVE ORGANIZATION.—Colgrove, Kenneth. "Powers and Functions of the Japanese Diet." *American Political Science Review,* December, 1933, v.27: 885-898; also see: February, 1934, v.28: 23-39.

THE JAPANESE TOTALITARIAN STATE.—Fahs, Charles B. *Government in Japan; Recent Trends in Its Scope and Operation.* New York, Institute of Pacific Relations, 1940, 114 p.; Byas, Hugh. *Government by Assassination.* New York, Knopf, 1942. 369 p.; Colgrove, Kenneth. "Totalitarian Government in Japan." (In: Zink, Harold, and Taylor, Cole, eds. *Government in Wartime Europe and Japan.* Boston, Houghton, 1942. p. 220-263).

JUDICIAL ORGANIZATION.—De Becker, Joseph E. *The Principles and Practice of the Civil Code of Japan.* Yokohama, Kelly and Walsh, 1921. 853 p.; Miyake, Masataro. *An Outline of the Japanese Judiciary.* 2nd ed. Tokyo, The Japan Times and Mail, 1935. 78 p.

LOCAL GOVERNMENT.—Asami, Noboru. *Japanese Colonial Government.* New York, Columbia University Press, 1924. 82 p.; Heneman, H. J. "Administration of Japan's Pacific Mandate." *American Political Science Review,* November, 1931, v.25: 1029-1044.

GOVERNMENT OF OCCUPIED TERRITORIES.—Bisson, Thomas A. *Japan in China.* New York, Macmillan, 1938. 417 p.; Colgrove, Kenneth W. "The New Order in East Asia." *Far Eastern Quarterly,* November, 1941, v.1: 5-24; Kanai, Kiyoshi. *Economic Development in Manchukuo.* Tokyo, Japanese Council, Institute of Pacific Relations, 1936. 69 p.

FOREIGN POLICY.—Bisson, Thomas A. *Shadow over Asia; The Rise of Militant Japan.* New York, Foreign Policy Association, 1941. 96 p.; Kuno, Yoshi S. *Japanese Expansion of the Asiatic Continent; A Study in the History of Japan with Special Reference to Her International Relations with China, Korea, and Russia.* Berkeley, University of California Press, 1937-1940. 2 v.; *Papers Relating to the Foreign Relations of the United States—Japan: 1931-1941.* Washington, Dept. of State, 1943. 2 vols.; Quigley,

Harold S. *Far Eastern War, 1937-1941.* Boston, World Peace Foundation, 1942. 369 p.; Yangga, Chitoshi. "The Military and the Government in Japan." *American Political Science Review,* June, 1941, v.35: 528-539.

JAPAN SINCE SURRENDER.—*Occupation of Japan, Policy and Progress.* Dept. of State, U. S. Government Printing Office, Washington, 1946. 173 p.; *Two Years of Occupation, Political, Economic, Social.* Washington, Public Information Office, Dept. of the Army, Civil Affairs Division. Reproduced from typewritten copies. August, 1947. 86 p.; *Activities of the Far Eastern Commission, Report by the Secretary General,* Washington, U. S. Government Printing Office, 1947. 100 p.; Quigley, Harold S. "Japan's Constitutions: 1890 and 1947." *American Political Science Review,* October, 1947, v.XLI No. 5: 865-874; Borton, Hugh. "United States Occupation Policies in Japan since Surrender." *Political Science Quarterly,* June, 1947, v.LXII No. 2: 250-257; Hulse, Frederick S. "Some Effects of the War on Japanese Society." *The Far Eastern Quarterly,* November, 1947, v.VII No. 1: 22-42; Haring, Douglas G., ed. *Japan's Prospect.* Cambridge, Mass., Harvard University Press, 1946. 474 p.

National Security and International Organization

GENERAL REFERENCES.—Eagleton, Clyde. *International Government.* New York, Ronald, 1948. 554 p.; Mower, E. C. *International Government.* New York, Heath, 1931. 736 p.; Vinacke, H. M. *International Organization.* New York, Roy Publications, 1934. 483 p.; Potter, P. B. *An Introduction to the Study of International Organization.* New York, Appleton-Century, Crofts, 1948. 479 p.; Walker, T. A. *A History of the Law of Nations.* London, Cambridge University Press, 1899. 42 p.; U. S. Department of State. *The Department of State Bulletin.* Washington, D. C., U. S. Government Printing Office; Schevill, F. *A History of Europe.* New York, Harcourt Brace, 1947. 937 p.; Hayes, C. J. H. *A Political and Cultural History of Modern Europe.* Vol. I and II, New York, Macmillan, 1939. 1725 p.; Fisher, H. A. L. *A History of Europe.* Cambridge, Mass., Riverside Press, 1939. 1304 p.; Simonds, F. H. and Emeny, B. *The Great Powers in World Politics.* New York, American Book, 1939. 731 p.; Council on Foreign Relations. *Foreign Affairs Reader.* New York, Harper, 1947. 492 p.; Hedges, R. Y. *International Organization.* New York, Pitman, 1935. 212 p.; Benns, F. L. *Europe since 1914.* New York, Crofts, 1948. 672 p.; Langsam, W. C. *The World since 1914.* New York, Macmillan, 1948. 837 p.; World Peace Foundation. *International Organization.* Boston, Mass. (quarterly); Current History, Inc. *Current History.* New York (monthly); New York Herald Tribune, Inc. *New York Herald Tribune.* New York (newspaper); New York Times Company. *The New York Times.* New York (newspaper); Carnegie Endowment for International Peace. *International Conciliation.* New York (monthly); Foreign Policy

Association. *Pamphlets and Reports*. New York; Council on Foreign Relations. *Foreign Affairs*. New York (quarterly).

SECURITY.—Bowman, I. *The New World*. Yonkers, New York, World, 1928. 803 p.; Whittlesey, D. *The Earth and the State*. New York, Holt, 1939. 618 p.; McIver, R. M. *The Modern State*. New York, Oxford, 1926. 504 p.; Baker, P. J. N. *Disarmament*. New York, Harcourt, 1926. 366 p.; Barnes, H. E. *World Politics in Modern Civilization*. New York, Knopf, 1930. 608 p.; Brierly, J. L. *The Law of Nations*. New York, Oxford University Press, 1936. 271 p.; Cambon, J. M. *The Diplomatist*. London, Allen & Son, 1931. 152 p.; von Clausewitz, Karl. *On War*. New York, Dutton, 1914. 3 vols.; Cresson, W. P. *The Holy Alliance, The European Background of the Monroe Doctrine*. New York, Oxford University Press, 1922. 147 p.; Cruttwell, C. R. M. F. *A History of the Great War, 1914-1918*. London, Oxford University Press, 1936. 655 p.; Dutt, R. P. *World Politics, 1918-1936*. New York, Random House, 1936. 389 p.; Friedrich, C. J. *Foreign Policy in the Making*. New York, Norton, 1938. 296 p.; Gooch, G. P. *Nationalism*. New York, Harcourt Brace, 1920. 127 p.; Jessup, P. C. *International Security*. New York, Council on Foreign Relations, 1935. 157 p.; Langer, W. L. *European Alliances and Alignments, 1871-1890*. New York, Knopf, 1931. 509 p.; Manhart, G. B. *Alliance and Entente, 1871-1914*. New York, Crofts, 1932. 90 p.; Mattern, J. *Concepts of State Sovereignty and International Law*. Baltimore, Johns Hopkins Press, 1928. 200 p.; Moon, P. T. *Imperialism and World Politics*. New York, Macmillan, 1926. 583 p.; Mowat, R. B. *The European States System, A Study of International Relations*. London, Oxford University Press, 1929. 108 p.; Myers, D. P. *World Disarmament*. Boston, World Peace Foundation, 1932. 370 p.; Phillmore, Sir W. G. F. *Three Centuries of Peace Treaties*. Boston, Little, Brown, 1918. 227 p. London, 1919; Salter, Sir A. *Security, Can We Retrieve It?* New York, Reynal & Hitchcock, Inc., 1939. 391 p.; Schuman, F. L. *International Politics*. New York, McGraw-Hill, 1948. 922 p.; Sontag, R. J. *European Diplomatic History, 1871-1932*. New York, Century, 1933. 425 p.; Streit, C. K. *Union Now*. New York, Harper. 315 p.; Wright, P. Q. *Neutrality and Collective Security*. Chicago, University of Chicago Press, 1936. 277 p.; Hoover, H. and Gibson, H. *The Problems of Lasting Peace*. Garden City, New York, Garden City Publishing Company, Inc., 1942. 295 p.; Sharp, W. R. and Kirk, G. *Contemporary International Politics*. New York, Rinehart, 1940. 876 p.; Mowat, R. B. *The Concert of Europe*. New York, Macmillan, 1931. 368 p.; Coudenhove-Kalergi, R. N. *Crusade for Pan-Europe*. New York, New York, 1943. 318 p.; The Royal Institute of International Affairs. *International Affairs*. (quarterly), London, Chatham House; Report of the President's Air Policy Commission. *Survival in the Air Age*. Washington, D. C., U. S. Government Printing Office, January, 1948. 166 p.; Report of the President's Advisory Commission on Universal Training. *A Program for National Security.* Washington, D. C., U. S. Government Printing Office, May, 1947. 449 p.

PAN AMERICAN UNION.—Bailey, T. A. *A Diplomatic History of the American People.* New York, Crofts, 1941. 864 p.; Duggan, S. *The Two Americas.* New York, Scribner, 1934. 277 p.; Hughes, C. E. *Our Relations to the Nations of the Western Hemisphere.* Princeton, N. J., Princeton University Press, 1928. 130 p.; Munro, D. G. *The United States and the Caribbean Area.* Boston, World Peace Foundation, 1934. 322 p.; Stuart, G. H. *Latin America and the United States.* New York, Appleton, 1938. 510 p.; *Reports.* Washington, D. C., The Pan American Union.

THE LEAGUE OF NATIONS.—Zimmern, Sir A. E. *The League of Nations and the Rule of Law.* New York, Macmillan, 1936. 527 p.; Rappard, W. E. *The Quest for Peace.* Cambridge, Mass., Harvard University Press, 1940. 516 p.; Wright, Q. *Mandates Under the League of Nations.* Chicago, University of Chicago Press, 1930. 634 p.; Pollard, A. F. *The League of Nations in History.* New York, Oxford University Press, 1918. 14 p.; Miller, D. H. *My Diary at the Peace Conference.* New York, Appeal Printing Co., 1924; and *Drafting of the Covenant.* New York, Putnam, 1928. 2 vols. 555 p., 857 p.; Morley, F. *The Society of Nations.* Washington, D. C., Brookings, 1932. 678 p.; League of Nations. *Ten Years of World Cooperation.* Geneva, Switzerland, 1928. 467 p.; Fleming, D. F. *The United States and International Organization.* New York, Columbia University Press, 1938. 569 p.; Rappard, W. E. *The Geneva Experiment.* London, Oxford University Press, 1931. 115 p.

THE UNITED NATIONS.—Goodrich, L. and Hambro, E. *The Charter of the United Nations, Documents and Commentary.* Boston, World Peace Foundation, 1946. 413 p.; Holborn, H. *War and Peace Aims of the United Nations.* Boston, World Peace Foundation, 1943. 730 p.; Arne, S. *United Nations Primer.* New York, Rinehart, 1945. 156 p.; Dolivet, L. *The United Nations: A Handbook on the New World Organization.* New York, Farrar, Straus, 1946. 152 p.; Dulles, A. W. and Lamb, B. P. *The United Nations.* New York, Foreign Policy Association, 1946. 96 p.; United Nations Dept. of Information *Yearbook of the United Nations, 1946-1947.* New York, Columbia University Press, 1947. 991 p.; and *United Nations Bulletin.* (biweekly), Lake Success, New York; Woodrow Wilson Foundation. *United Nations News.* (monthly), Boston; United Nations. *Documents* and *Official Records.* Lake Success, New York, U. N. Dept. of Information.

INDEX